Relocating Postcolonialism

Relocating Postcolonialism

Edited by

David Theo Goldberg

and

Ato Quayson

Blackwell
Publishers

© 2002 by Blackwell Publishers Ltd
a Blackwell Publishing company

Editorial Offices:
108 Cowley Road, Oxford OX4 1JF, UK
   Tel: +44 (0)1865 791100
Osney Mead, Oxford OX2 0EL, UK
   Tel: +44 (0)1865 206206
Blackwell Publishing USA 350 Main Street, Malden, MA 02148-5018, USA
   Tel: +1 781 388 8250
Iowa State Press, a Blackwell Publishing company, 2121 State Avenue, Ames, Iowa 50014-8300, USA
   Tel: +1 515 292 0140
Blackwell Munksgaard, Nørre Søgade 35, PO Box 2148, Copenhagen, DK-1016, Denmark
   Tel: +45 77 33 33 33
Blackwell Publishing Asia, 54 University Street, Carlton, Victoria 3053, Australia
   Tel: +61 (0)3 9347 0300
Blackwell Verlag, Kurfürstendamm 57, 10707 Berlin, Germany
   Tel: +49 (0)30 32 79 060
Blackwell Publishing, 10, rue Casimir Delavigne, 75006 Paris, France
   Tel: +331 5310 3310

First published 2002 by Blackwell Publishers Ltd

Library of Congress Cataloging-in-Publication Data

Relocating postcolonialism / edited by David Theo Goldberg and Ato Quayson.
      p.   cm.
   Includes bibliographical references and index.
   ISBN 0-631-20804-6 (alk. paper) – ISBN 0-631-20805-4 (pb. : alk. paper)
   1. Postcolonialism.   I. Goldberg, David Theo.   II. Quayson, Ato.
   JV51 .R44 2002
   325'.3 – dc21

                                                              2001043231

A catalogue record for this title is available from the British Library.

Set in 10 on 13 pt Meridian
by Best-set Typesetter Ltd., Hong Kong
Printed and bound in the United Kingdom by MPG Books, Bodmin, Cornwall

For further information on
Blackwell Publishers, visit our website:
www.blackwellpublishers.co.uk

Contents

Contributors

Pal Ahluwalia is Senior Lecturer, Department of Politics, University of Adelaide.

Anne Bailey is Assistant Professor of History at Rutgers University.

Homi Bhabha is Professor of English, Harvard University.

John L. Comaroff is Harold H. Swift Distinguished Service Professor of Anthropology and Sociology at the University of Chicago and Senior Research Fellow of the American Bar Foundation.

Eve Darian-Smith is Director of the Program in Law and Society and Associate Professor of Anthropology, University of California, Santa Barbara.

Dawn Duncan is Associate Professor of English, Concordia College.

David Theo Goldberg is Director of the University of California Humanities Research Institute and Professor of African American Studies and Criminology, Law and Society, University of California, Irvine.

Barnor Hesse is Senior Lecturer in Sociology, University of East London.

Jonathan Hope is Reader in Literary Linguistics at the Department of English Studies, University of Strathclyde.

Wendy Ann Lee is a freelance journalist and editor in New York.

Zane Ma-Rhea is Lecturer and Consultant at the National Centre for Gender and Cultural Diversity, Swinburne University of Technology, Melbourne.

John K. Noyes is Professor of German Literature, University of Toronto.

Olu Oguibe is an artist, poet, and art historian, and Senior Fellow, Vera List Center for Art and Politics, New School University.

Benita Parry is Honorary Professor of English and Comparative Literary Studies, University of Warwick.

Ato Quayson is Director of the African Studies Centre, Lecturer in English, and Fellow of Pembroke College, University of Cambridge.

Edward Said is University Professor of English and Comparative Literature, Columbia University.

Gayatri Chakravorty Spivak is Avalon Foundation Professor in the Humanities, Columbia University.

Ann Laura Stoler is Professor of History and Anthropology, University of Michigan.

Rosemarie Garland Thomson is Professor of English at Howard University.

Françoise Vergès is Lecturer in the Centre for Cultural Studies, Goldsmith's College, University of London.

Laura Wright is Lecturer in English, University of Cambridge.

Preface

Relocating Postcolonialism is designed to rethink many of the assumptions and discursive maneuvers of postcolonialism and to assess its relationship to other academic disciplines and fields of inquiry. Composed substantially of newly commissioned essays, the collection brings together many of the key and well-established contributors to postcolonialism as well as the voices of emergent scholars. Several of the essays are in dialogue with each other. The conversational quality of the volume provides a compelling portrait of postcolonialism's development that will be valuable to scholars, students, and teachers. Probing well-known ideas as well as unexplored areas of concern – the Internet, the relation between disability studies, urban studies, and postcolonialism – *Relocating Postcolonialism* locates the current state of postcolonial studies by examining its critical apparatus and its central lines of inquiry.

Transatlantic collaborations face their own late modern challenges, and ours has been no exception: long silences, failed faxes and email attachments, little face to face conversation, overlooked or buried deadlines due to multiple schedules. Many people accordingly have made this volume possible. The contributors' patience and commitment in the face of numerous requests, reasonable and unreasonable, has been exemplary. Kim Furomoto at Arizona State University and Doug Feremenga at the University of California, Irvine, provided assistance far exceeding any ordinary expectations. Our editors at Blackwell, Andrew McNeillie in Oxford and Jayne Fargnoli in Cambridge, Massachusetts, always knew when to push and when to leave us alone, when to feed us and when to insist on finality. We appreciate also the terrific work of their staff, most notably Annie Lenth in Cambridge, as well as David's fabulous colleagues and staff at the University of California Humanities Research Institute whose collective efforts freed up the time for completion of the volume.

David Theo Goldberg
Irvine, California

Ato Quayson
Cambridge, England

Acknowledgments

The author and publishers gratefully acknowledge permission to reproduce copyright material as follows:

"Edward Said in Conversation with Neeladri Bhattacharya, Suvir Kaul, and Ania Loomba," New Delhi, December 16, 1997, *Interventions* 1: 1 (1998) http://www.tandf.co.uk; Olu Oguibe, "Connectivity and the Fate of the Unconnected," *Social Identities* 5: 3 (1999), Taylor and Francis Ltd, http://www.tandf.co.uk/journals; Pal Ahluwalia, "Towards (Re)Conciliation: The Postcolonial Economy of Giving," *Social Identities* 6:1 (2000), Taylor and Francis Ltd, http://www.tandf.co.uk/journals; Rosemarie Garland Thompson, "Theorizing Disability," in *Extraordinary Bodies: Figuring Disability in American Culture and Literature*, Columbia University Press, reprinted with the permission of the publisher.

The publishers apologize for any errors or omissions in the above list and would be grateful to be notified of any corrections that should be incorporated in the next edition or reprint of this book.

Introduction:
Scale and Sensibility

Ato Quayson and
David Theo Goldberg

There are now many recognizable genealogies for postcolonial studies. They are regularly rehearsed in books and articles undertaking to map the field. Starting with comments on the significance of Said's *Orientalism* (1978), they veer through Ashcroft, Griffiths, and Tiffin's *The Empire Writes Back* (1989), and then expand into examinations of the relevance of postcolonialism for discussions of image culture and representation, studies of imperial and colonial history, anthropology, cultural studies, multiculturalism, and diaspora, among assorted other areas. In developing this cartographical scale, these genealogies almost always also develop a set of arguments about the supposed usefulness or otherwise of the term. Is it merely a temporal marker suggesting that the effects of colonialism and empire have somehow been superseded? How does it relate to other "posts" such as postmodernism and poststructuralism? And what are the family resemblances between it and other standpoint and anti-hegemonic theories such as feminism, gay/lesbian and ethnic studies, and to theories of colonialism, decolonization, and resistance?[1]

There is no doubt that such genealogies have proved stimulating in extending to the landscape a particular form of cartographical coherence. Operating on the assumption that such rehearsals are now standard fare in the field and are therefore easily accessible and recognizable, we open our remarks to *Relocating Postcolonialism* by suggesting that these genealogies represent particular thematizations of the field, which, though obvious, nevertheless conceal important contradictions. Every intellectual history is a form of conceptual and methodological investment aimed at converting a set of perspectives into an ever-expanding realm of knowledge. The success with which such a conversion takes place depends as much on the degree of disagreements as to what exactly constitutes a field as it does on the specific methodologies and assumptions that inform the debates.

Postcolonial Studies as it has been constituted in the past twenty or so years has at least three significant clusters of attitudes and ideas. These, in turn, might be taken as constitutive of generative ambiguities in the field. The first cluster clearly concerns the desire to speak to the Western paradigm of knowledge in the voice of otherness. Thus there have been many attempts to show how, for instance, empire was the laboratory of modernity; how the very constitution of Western subjectivity from the period of empire and colonialism depended on interactions with subjected others; and how, currently, the processes of transnational migration and globalization ensure that these dialogic encounters destabilize centers and peripheries (Stoler 1995; Bhabha 1994; Ong 1999; and Parry chapter 4, this volume, among others). What is invoked conceptually, epistemologically, and politically in this cluster is a general idea about the radical interdependency of forms. The interdependency is primarily explored, however, by identifying binary oppositions (self/other, center/periphery, whiteness/blackness etc.). This binaristic premise then is destabilized and shown to have been false or designed to subserve a larger if concealed project of power and hegemony. This rhetorical strategy is itself a recuperation of a major insight of poststructuralist theory; namely, that all binary oppositions are value-laden, with the first term often implicitly assumed to have an ethical or conceptual, normative or indeed logical priority over the second.

Postcolonial critics have demonstrated great nuance in questioning and destabilizing such binaries, ranging from straightforward unmaskings of their continuing hegemonic role in both Western thought and postcolonial self-conceptualizations (Mudimbe 1988; Talpade Mohanty 1992; Chatterjee 1993), through strategic inversions (Ashcroft, Griffiths, and Tiffin 1989), to more nuanced and sometimes confusing relays of such inversions and counter-inversions (Spivak and Bhabha). However, always embedded in the destabilization of binaries is a particular assumption that provides the enabling pre-text of the destabilizing procedures in the first place. This pre-text is the idea that postcolonial criticism is itself an ethical enterprise, pressing its claims in ways that other theories such as those of postmodernism and poststructuralism do not. This ethical pre-text is hardly ever expressed directly but is inherent in the very object relations referenced by the binary oppositions. The destabilizations of the binaries are often proffered as attempts at rectifying disorders in the extra-textual world of social relations, and in so doing define a peculiar paradox. On the one hand, they are of a necessity anti-foundationalist, being that they are suspicious of any given metanarratives, whether these be centered on assumptions about subjectivity, history, or the value of Western canonical literature. And yet, contradictorily, these essentially anti-foundationalist procedures are aligned to the assertion of an ethical standpoint implicitly conveyed in the attempt to critique structures of power as a means of placing it on a different and unstable footing. It is this particular contradiction that perhaps has generated the most bitter criticisms of postcolonial theory. These criticisms center mainly on the degree to which textual analysis seems to take the place of engagement with real-life struggles (Ahmad 1992; Dirlik 1994; Kennedy 1996; San Juan, Jr. 1998). Since the social referents of postcolonial studies, ranging from the peculiar political incoherencies of the postcolony to the problematic conditions of adult education for migrants in the Western metropolis (Moshenberg 1999), it is difficult if not impossible to separate post-colonial discourse completely from an ethical project, even though the means by which its ethical ends are to be achieved remains a highly contentious issue.

In the case of the second cluster, Postcolonial Studies is afflicted by the fact that it has to claim an object for academic study which it is obliged simultaneously to disavow. The claim and disavowal are constitutive of its very object of study. If underpinning Postcolonial Studies are social referents marked by violence and anguish, and if the ultimate purpose of postcolonialism is to dismantle the conditions that produce such violence and anguish, then it must follow that Postcolonial Studies inherently focuses on an object that it is committed to dismantling even while necessarily analytically fixated with it. This particular paradox is similar to the one discernible in Feminist Studies. Feminist Studies names woman only to show how this naming is a constraint imposed by the voice of patriarchal power. Ideally, "woman" should be completely freed from that constraint, but once freed, would it not entail the demise of that academic field? Academic fields such as Postcolonial Studies accordingly – and distressingly – benefit from the constitutive injustices within which the object of study is articulated and brought into view.

One possible disposition in the face of this dilemma is offered by Theodor Adorno's related insight concerning philosophy. Adorno writes at the end of *Minima Moralia* that "the only philosophy which can be responsibly practised in the face of despair is the attempt to contemplate all things as they would present themselves from the standpoint of redemption." It follows that a crucial question for Postcolonial Studies concerns how to shape itself from the standpoint of its imagined future irrelevance. This is not to imagine utopias, though in certain circumstances that would be desirable, but to consider what forces in the real world the *informing* ethical impulse of Postcolonial Studies is designed to strengthen. This entails in effect the definition through both theory and practice of an ethics of becoming. An ethics of becoming would require a rigorous attention to the details of the object under scrutiny to discern the aspects within it that speak to an imagined freer future. It requires a careful grounding of the specificities of the local, not to impose a regime or tyranny of the local and specific but to show how such an ethics might disclose a transfigurative relationship to the world. It also requires what might be described as a full-spectrum approach to phenomena, embedding these in a variety of social, cultural, historical, and political contexts that would disclose the layered significances through which a transfigured and better future might be brought into view.

Consider, in this regard, the possibilities for such an approach provided by Olu Oguibe's essay in this collection (chapter 9) on the implications of the Internet for those without connectivity. Essentially, Oguibe's point is that with the potential that the Internet has for circulating representations, peoples without connectivity run the real danger of being misrepresented. His interest is particularly on the images of indigenous art on the Internet, where there is

every danger of unscrupulous people not only circulating such art without permission but, more disturbingly, of misrepresenting the indigenous peoples who
might not have the same connectivity to the Internet to rectify the misrepresentations. In setting the argument, Oguibe focuses mainly on its function as
a portal of information. Though this suffices for the main thrust of his discussion, it is also arguable that the Internet is much more than just an information portal. It is, as well, as much a portal of attitudes and attitudinal shifts as
it is an entryway, an opening, to development infrastructure. And all three
portals are interlinked in varying forms that are significant for a postcolonial
analysis.

As is evident from the amount of projected online business in the next few
years, the Internet is going to be a major channel for determining the direction of business investment. One thinks for instance of the fact that though
much is bought and sold virtually, a whole range of secondary infrastructure
is necessary to deliver and receive the goods purchased on the Net. Materiality is still the end of the virtual highway. Postal systems have to be stream-
lined, roads and airports have to be highly efficient, vans and related
equipment have to be purchased and maintained, administrative personnel,
drivers and packers have to be employed and their conditions of labor reproduced. In this light the Net is generating a whole range of secondary infrastructure closely related to it for its expansion. The problem for those societies
not connected to the Net, then, is not merely that they are outside the circuits
of representation (something which might be more easily rectified than not)
but that they are also outside the circuits of capital and development flows. In
other words, not being connected is to miss out on a whole range of secondary
infrastructural resources which connectivity and Internet business render
imperative. The virtual domain of the Net thus easily converts itself into and
reproduces – indeed, intensifies – acute material effects linked to economic
and financial flows of vast orders. As Oguibe notes, it is important to augment
Appadurai's (1996) famous explications of the interconnected "scapes" of
transnationalism – ethnoscape, technoscape, financescape, mediascape, and
ideoscape – with a sixth one, "netscape". Its full implications ramify at all the
levels suggested by Appadurai's other conceptual scapes.

The Internet is also a portal of attitudes. Consider the anxiety and frustration that descend on people when faced with the failure of their computer
technology. But we should not think of these attitudinal responses simply in
terms of the individual's perennial struggles with technology, something given
a humorous and wry twist in the varied discomfitures to which Disney's Goofy
is exposed in his epic struggles with household appliances. Consider them on
a larger scale, rather, as the production of particular forms of aspirations and
nostalgias. Every technological "advance" brings with it not just the fruits of
the technology but certain structures of feeling, to cite Raymond Williams's
felicitous phrase. The railway line established a transformation in the idea of
the frontier. But for some it also promoted paradigms that shaped a series of
material relations having to do with rural–urban mobility, attitudes to home,

landscape and nature, and general responses to space and time. These in turn helped undergird the national longing for form which was gradually articulated as a relation between civil society and the state during the height of European nation-state formation in the nineteenth century (Anderson 1994). Not for nothing did the train accrue to itself all kinds of anthropomorphizing imagery, culminating in its cannonization in the image of Thomas the Tank Engine, of the "little engine that could," which in the face of enormous adversity and environmental threat, of timetables and schedules, could still satisfy people and have commodities delivered in time. Obligations are met, discipline circulated, cultural habits universalized in the pleasure of a text offered by adult to child. From a postcolonial perspective, by contrast, Sembene Ousmane offers a wonderful description of the emotional impact of the Dakar–Niger line on the lives of the workers and their families in *God's Bits of Wood* (1960). Here the railway line affected not just labor relations between the French and the local people, but also had a subtle impact on gender relations. These effects coalesced into a process of nationalist agitation in which ethnicities, gender and intergenerational relations are challenged and reshaped when the railway workers decide to strike in support of their demands for better conditions and pay.

The Internet represents an entirely different technological epoch. Some commentators have suggested, altogether optimistically, that the rate of development of computer technology in the last 15 years is equivalent to 25 million years in humankind's evolution. But implicit in the outwardly celebrated optimisim appear to be the dominant – and related – emotions of extreme power and of abject anxiety, both sometimes successively inhabited in nanoseconds, in the time, for instance, between pressing a command and the crashing of a computer. This anxiety gained a peculiar inter/national resonance with the fears about the millennium bug towards the end of 1999. It is estimated that $400 billion was spent on addressing this large-scale (and largely fabricated) anxiety. Yet this massive nervousness about what might have happened to computers was not unrelated to security concerns and the general question of (the conditions for) the circulation of commerce. The point to note is that the anxiety seemed far from rational considering that most Third World countries had none of the resources to combat the bug and would have had to go ahead with the pressing management of their fragile economies notwithstanding. $400 billion would satisfy the total debt suffocating the world's developing countries *five times over* and ten times the total global public expenditures on cancer research.[2]

But the differential in the ability to maintain a smooth connectivity does not assuage the anxiety. The brutal fact is that the Net is actually leading to a new epoch of the economic marginalization of those who may not be able to benefit from the secondary infrastructural development that connectivity brings with it. The connections to be drawn out here have to be between the Net as expressive of a political economy of anxiety and how this anxiety feeds into class differentiations both within and between countries in a postcolonial world. The Net, then, is the site through which socioeconomic disparities on a global scale will be reproduced and mediated in the years to come.

The third set of themes in Postcolonial Studies is prompted by the fact that postcolonial theory thus seems to locate itself everywhere and nowhere. This offers a mixed blessing. On the one hand, literary and cultural fields not considered to be postcolonial or the obvious objects of its focus have been illuminated by a postcolonial analysis. Works such as Loomba and Orkin's *Postcolonial Shakespeare* (1999) and Jeffrey Cohen's *The Postcolonial Middle Ages* (2000) exemplify this tendency. And yet, on the other hand, a number of ambiguities is also generated from this theoretical expansiveness. Postcolonial Studies is *appropriatively* interdisciplinary. In other words, it is not just that it is interdisciplinary, but that anything that serves its purposes, whether originally thought of as postcolonial or not, is pressed into the service of a postcolonial analysis. The classic example of such appropriations has been the extension in a postcolonial way of the work of Foucault, Lacan, Derrida, Deleuze, and Guattari and, more recently, of the work of Adorno and the Frankfurt School, among others.[3]

But this suggests as well the threshold of an enigma. Is postcolonial theory the content of particular social referents, or the form of the discursive application of theories? Or is it the oscillatory interaction of the theoretical form and experienced content of postcolonial verities? It is of course possible to disturb the shapes and contours of appropriated discourses by reading back into their form the position of their appropriation. One can think here of the many ways in which, for example, Nietzsche might be read after Soyinka (1975), or Lacan after Fanon (1952), Deleuze and Guattari after Benitez-Rojo (1992). This goes beyond what Ashcroft, Griffiths, and Tiffin describe in *The Empire Writes Back* about the degree to which postcolonial writers have sought to rewrite the Western canon. It conjures the particularly resonant pairings postcolonially referenced, like Lamming/Shakespeare, Coetzee/Defoe, Rhys/Brontë, Achebe/Conrad, Borges/Kafka, among many others.

Posed in this way, however, the form/content oscillation seems fairly banal, if not altogether irrelevant. The thing to be noted here, however, is the degree to which various theories, seemingly with no interest in postcolonial issues, have been corraled into service, thus generating a new discourse of postcolonialism that simultaneously resonates with concerns elsewhere and yet seem only discursively coincident with them. This produces a conceptual alliance between postcolonialist and feminist, gay/lesbian, ethnic, and disability studies, all of which draw on similar theories to address issues of representation, hegemony, and othering. The discursive and theoretical cross-references established between these various discourses have made for stimulating analyses of cultural and other phenomena. But it is not always clear that this has issued forth in specific and unified political agendas both within universities and outside.

A case in point concerns Postcolonial Studies' relationship to the expanding field of Disability Studies. Discussions of disability have traditionally been the concern of either the medical or the social sciences, and of education. It is only in the last decade that a strong effort has been made by disability scholars to draw attention to its implications for the humanities (Linton 1998). In pointing this out, Disability Studies scholars have marshalled some of the arguments about the material efficacy of representations that have been the staple diet of Postcolonial Studies. They have also sought to show how the idea of the "normate" depends on a series of exclusions, one of the most important of which is that of the disabled (Thomson 1998). Even though the potential theoretical overlaps between the two fields is quite immense, it is not at all clear that Postcolonial Studies has paid any serious attention so far to the implications of the "normate" for social hierarchies when viewed from the perspective of disablity and race, rather than solely from the latter. As Thomson points out, it is now imperative to add to race, class, and gender the category of disability to make for a more sensitive understanding of the cultural constructions that shape attitudes and ultimately impact upon social relations. It is necessary to pursue joint projects of agitation for justice that would embrace the disabled equally with the racially ordered, gendered, and postcolonial subject. It is in recognition of this gap that that we include a chapter from Rosemarie Garland Thomson's work on representations of disabled women in Toni Morrison's writing and place it in dialogue with Ato Quayson's piece on the tropes of disability in postcolonial writing. The dialogue might be considered a diasporic conversation which seeks to illuminate how the intersections between race, class, and disability attempt to shape docile subjects, both in the postcolony and among African Americans. They also hint at the possibility of thinking of disability as not self-evident and demonstrable, but the interaction between physiognomic factors and social environments that thrive on conceptualizations of difference as the means by which to imagine the normative and to render it unquestioned and invisible.

Many of the most important theoretical concepts in Postcolonial Studies (subalternity, hybridity, mimicry) have been developed in essays rather than in monographs and this in its own way has had an impact on how concepts have been circulated and maintained as governing assumptions. It is also arguable, however, that the essay, as a form, generates a particular kind of knowledge. It is often polemical for the sake of impact, necessarily concentrated and intent on demonstrating its key assertions over a limited range of examples. In this regard, the essay form makes for generalizations rather than sustained demonstrations, for the felicitious and stimulating turn of phrase rather than the steady exploration of sources and materials. This is by no means to say that some essays are incapable of transcending the limits of their formal contraints, but that precisely because of their constraints they generate knowledge in stimulating but fragmented ways. It is this perhaps that has triggered what might be termed the tyranny of quotationality and citation in Postcolonial Studies. Thus phrases from Spivak and Bhabha (in particular, but not exclusively) are endlessly quoted with minimal evocation of the contexts in which they were originally produced.

Underpinning this regime of quotationality is also the acceptance of a strenuously evocative mode of rhetorical grounding, which in itself is also a particularly fragmented structure of thought. Research remains to be done on whether this mode of rhetorical grounding is due to the influence of French theory on postcolonial critics or whether its energy comes from the practices of oratorical exuberance which many indigenous cultures prize as a sign of high cultural attainment.[4] For anyone who has heard Spivak, Bhabha, Soyinka, Wilson Harris, Mbembe, and Mudimbe speak, there is a strong if inchoate sense that they are drawing on oratorical resources that are not merely Western. It is then noteworthy, even if regrettable, that Gayatri Spivak seized a recent opportunity provided by an invitation to write a foreword to the *Blackwell Companion to Postcolonial Studies* (2000) to correct what she thought were misreadings of her much-cited essay "Can the Subaltern Speak". It is not the particular effacements of the subject of her essay which she points out that is of relevance here, but the fact that she has to defend herself against perceived misunderstandings generated from the infinite quotationality of her own essayistic style. Yet one is bound also to note a more felicitous side to this process: that in fact it is precisely the processes of rhetorical dislocation that both attend the essayistic form in which key ideas are circulated and the manner in which these are then appropriated that gives the field its peculiar dynamic of restless questioning. The thing, though, is to decide on what the configuration of dislocations is meant to serve, whether these merely shore-up a sense of textual instability or school us into a greater sensitivity to the supple forms in which injustice and inequality often articulate themselves.

If the essays in this collection are offered as examples of "relocating" postcolonialism, we take them as thresholds for exploring the ramifications of different vectors of disciplinary and local conditions for thinking about the field. Some of the essays attempt a direct rethinking, such as those of Parry on the directions and dead-ends of Postcolonial Studies. But there is no common agenda of revision among them. However, we have attempted to set up minidialogues between different essays, with the expectation at the same time that wider connections may be drawn from between apparently dissimilar contexts and theoretical articulations. Thus Edward Said's interview with Neeladri Bhattacharya, Suvir Kaul, and Ania Loomba opens the collection on a wide-ranging set of issues to set the tone for what is to follow. As has been remarked variously in the field, Said's relentless pursuit of justice shows itself everywhere in his life and work. The interview draws him out on some of his beliefs and observations concerning the condition of Palestine, the impact of Orientalism, his relationship to other anti-hegemonic theories, and his views on the field of Postcolonial Studies. As always, his answers are candid and incisive and the interview conveys the impression of a man of enormous intellectual and personal energy. The conversation between Homi Bhabha and John Comaroff (chapter 2) is a fascinating dialogue between two key thinkers marked in different ways by postcolonial theorizing. Their conversation reveals shared cognitions about the place of their education in postcolonial 1960s Britain, the role of different forms of Marxism in shaping both their theoretical allegiances and dissatisfactions, and the implications that India and South Africa have for thinking about the postcolonial. Spivak's essay on the Resident Alien (chapter 3) introduces the idea of the migrant intellectual, but opens up this idea by looking at it from various, seemingly contradictory, perspectives. A rigorous requirement of historical grounding is then made essential to the very business of problematizing an ungrounding of the concept in the first place. These three pieces are followed by Benita Parry's overview of the directions and dead-ends in Postcolonial Studies (chapter 4).

The next cluster is tentatively on race theory and diaspora. Goldberg's essay (chapter 6) historicizes two dominant attitudes in racial theorizing – the naturalist and the historicist – and demonstrates the implications that each paradigm has for the processes of nation-state formation and colonial arrangements. His conclusion that race is constitutive of nation-state formation in Europe and elsewhere finds echoes in Stoler's piece (chapter 7), which attempts to evaluate the cultural politics of the French Right and how these disclose a new and disturbing raciology reflective of transformed structural conditions in contemporary France. Both Anne Bailey (chapter 5) and Barnor Hesse (chapter 8) share a concern with slave narratives and oral histories from Africa, but from different methodological standpoints. Bailey focuses on a fundamental methodological question that confronts the historian of slavery on the West African coast: how are the contemporary residual oral narratives and rituals from this area that have slavery as their central theme to deliver their insights about the historical processes of slavery that took place several centuries ago? With a keen eye for detail and a rigorous attention to the subtle relations between orality and the historical archive, Bailey produces startling insights about the place of collective memory in the constitution of history. Quayson's and Thomson's essays (chapters 12 and 13) on disability might be seen as extensions of the central debates about the constitution of identity discussed in the previous essays on diaspora and race theory. Olu Oguibe's essay (chapter 9), the shortest in the collection, stands on its own and divides the text. Ahluwalia (chapter 10) and Ma-Rhea (chapter 11) both revisit the concept of the gift, but this time to situate it within concerns with the formation of the Commonwealth university and with issues of reconciliation for minorities in Australia, Rwanda, and Palestine in the face of the traumas of their various histories. Noyes (chapter 14) picks up this thread on reconciliation, but the focus this time centers on the social and political processes taking place in post-apartheid South Africa with unsettling questions posed and open-ended and provisional answers provided. Noyes's discussion is prompted by Achille Mbembe's now-classic essay in *African Studies*, "Provisional Notes on the African Postcolony." Originally published in 1992,[5] Mbembe's intervention draws on Bakhtinian notions of the grotesque and the carnivalesque to situate a discussion about the place of ordinary people's negotiations of the nightmare of the African postcolony through various forms of complicity and subversion, often articulated in the same gesture of song, dance, or insult.

Wendy Lee (chapter 15) offers a humorous but astute account of the psychological stresses of performing identity as Korean American. This is complemented by Eve Darian-Smith's analysis (chapter 16) of the conflictual bases of international property law for Hong Kong, as the territory finds itself between seemingly mutually exclusive conceptions of property that have been produced by different histories, the Western and the Chinese.

Dawn Duncan's essay (chapter 17) joins the growing scholarship linking Ireland to the postcolonial world by pressing for a dialogic and flexible model of discussing the postcolonial condition in which race, even though significant, would not be allowed to obscure the different trajectories by which peoples, whether white or other, *become* postcolonial. Wright and Hope's essay (chapter 18) offers an example of a situated practice of postcolonial pedagogy centring on linguistic details and their embeddedness in cultural and social forms. Françoise Vergès's "Post-Scriptum" (chapter 19) provides a fitting close to the collection. Vergès interrogates the intersecting contradictions of postcolonial conditions, claims to citizenship, and criticism. She thus calls into question the tensions of post-imperial themes and theorizing, at once reflecting the prevailing disposition of the volume in particular and as a whole to relocate the terms of postcolonial studies. In each instance, the detail is also the perspective, the scale the sensiblity.

Notes

1   For wide-ranging introductions to the field, see Young (1992), Childs and Williams (1998); Moore-Gilbert (1998); Ghandhi (1998); Loomba (1999); Quayson (2000).
2   Anatol Kaletsky, *The Times of London*, January 6, 2000.
3   The borrowings from Lacan, Derrida, and Foucault are everywhere evident. On the growing interest in Delueze and Guattari, see chapter 7 of Robert Young (1995) and Antonio Benitez-Rojo (1992). On Adorno, see Varadharajan (1995).
4   For African examples, see Kwesi Yankah's (1995) superb account of the uses of rhetoric among the Akan and Karin Barber's (1991) account of praise-naming.
5   See Achille Mbembe, *On the Postcolony* (Berkeley: University of California Press, 2001).

References

Adorno, Theodor 1996 *Minima Moralia: Reflections from Damaged Life*. London: Verso.
Ahmad, Aijaz 1992 *In Theory: Classes, Nations, Literatures*. London: Verso.
Anderson, 1994 "Exodus," *Critical Enquiry*, 20:324–35.
Appadurai, Arjun 1996 *Modernity at Large: Cultural Dimensions of Globalization*. Minneapolis: University of Minnesota Press.
Ashcroft, Bill, Griffiths, Gareth, and Tiffin, Helen (eds.) 1989 *The Empire Writes Back: Theory and Practice in Postcolonial Literature*. London: Routledge.

Barber, Karin 1991 *I Could Speak until Tomorrow: Oriki, Women, and the Past in a Yoruba Town*. Edinburgh: Edinburgh University Press.

Benitez-Rojo, Antonio 1992 *The Repeating Island: The Caribbean and the Postmodern Perspective*. Durham, NC: Duke University Press.

Bhabha, Homi 1994 *The Location of Culture*. New York: Routledge.

Chatterjee, Partha 1993 *The Nation and its Fragments*. Princeton, NJ: Princeton University Press.

Childs, Peter and Williams, Patrick 1998 *An Introductory Guide to Postcolonial Theory*. New York: Prentice-Hall.

Cohen, Jeffrey (ed.) 2000 *The Postcolonial Middle Ages*. London: Palgrave.

Dirlik, Arif 1994 *Asia/Pacific as Space of Cultural Production*. Durham, NC: Duke University Press.

Fanon, Frantz 1952 *Black Skin, White Masks*, trans. Charles Lam Markham. New York: Grove Press.

Gandhi, Leela 1998 *Postcolonial Theory: A Critical Introduction*. Edinburgh: Edinburgh University Press.

Jameson, Frederic and Miyoshi, Masao (eds.) 1993 *Cultures of Globalization*. Durham, NC: Duke University Press.

Kennedy, Dane 1996 "Imperial History and Postcolonial Theory," *Journal of Imperial and Commonwealth History* 24.3:345–63.

Linton, Simi 1998 *Claiming Disability: Knowledge and Identity*. New York: New York University Press.

Loomba, Ania 1999 *Colonialism/Postcolonialism*. London: Routledge.

Loomba, Ania and Orkin, Martin (eds.) 1999 *Postcolonial Shakespeares*. New York: Routledge.

Mbembe, Achille 1992 "Provisional Notes on the African Postcolony," *Africa*, 62:3–37.

Moore-Gilbert, Bart 1998 *Postcolonial Theory: Contexts, Practices, Politics*. London: Verso.

Moshenberg 1999 "'*No nos Pasaran*': The Politics of Literacy and Adult Education for Salvadorean Women in the US," *Interventions*, 1.2:291–304.

Mudimbe, V. Y. 1988 *The Invention of Africa: Gnosis, Philosophy and the Order of Knowledge*. Bloomington: Indiana University Press.

Ong, Aihwa 1999 *Flexible Citizenship: The Cultural Logics of Transnationality*. Durham, NC: Duke University Press.

Quayson, Ato 2000 Postcolonialism: *Theory, Practice or Process*. Cambridge: Polity Press.

Said, Edward 1978 *Orientalism*. New York: Pantheon.

San Juan, Jr., E. 1998 *Beyond Postcolonial Theory*. London: Palgrave.

Schwarz, Henry and Ray, Sangeeta 2000 *Blackwell Companion to Postcolonial Studies*. Oxford: Blackwell Publishers.

Sembene Ousmane 1960 *God's Bits of Wood*. London: Heinemann.

Soyinka, Wole 1975 "The Fourth Stage" in *Myth, Literature and the African World*. Cambridge: Cambridge University Press.

Stoler, Ann 1995 *Race and the Education of Desire: Foucault's History of Sexuality and the Colonial Order of Things*. Durham, NC: Duke University Press.

Talpade Mohanty, Chandra 1992 "Under Western Eyes: Feminist Scholarship and Colonial Discourse" in *Colonial Discourse and Postcolonial Theory*, ed. Patrick Williams and Laura Chrisman. London: Harvester Wheatsheaf.

Thomson, Rosemarie Garland 1998 *Extraordinary Bodies: Figuring Physical Disability in American Culture and Literature*. New York: Columbia University Press.

Varadharajan, Asha 1995 *Exotic Parodies: Subjectivity in Adorno, Said and Spivak*. Minneapolis: University of Minnesota Press.

Yankah, Kwesi 1995 *Speaking for the Chief: Okyeame and the Politics of Akan Royal Oratory*. Bloomington: Indiana University Press.

Young, Robert 1992 *White Mythologies*. London: Routledge.

——1995 *Colonial Desire: Hybridity in Theory, Culture and Race*. London: Routledge.

Chapter 1

In Conversation with Neeladri Bhattacharya, Suvir Kaul, and Ania Loomba

Edward Said

Ania Loomba: We have decided to structure this conversation around three or four major issues, and then we will keep homing in. What we thought we'd tell you by way of introduction is that some of these issues may seem either reductive or repetitive. But they tap into critiques of your work current in India. So instead of quoting names and mentioning people and particularities, we have actually consolidated a set of issues, which are recurrent.

Edward Said: So, who beginneth?

Suvir Kaul: All right, this is our 'beginnings'. This is a quotation from *Orientalism*, which I am sure you will recognize: 'My contention is that without examining Orientalism as a discourse one cannot possibly understand the enormously systematic discipline by which European culture was able to manage – and even produce – the Orient politically, sociologically, militarily, ideologically, scientifically and imaginatively during the post-Enlightenment period.' Have you revised or rethought the conceptual frameworks suggested here?

Said: Perhaps I may have overdone the notion of how systematically – I mean to what extent, to what level of detail – the system operated. Maybe I overstated it. But that there was, to use Foucault's language, a kind of discursive regularity, I have no doubt. Second, I think, maybe what you are getting at is the common misunderstanding and misreading of that passage, which claims that I was saying at the same time that there was no answering voice. That is not implied here at all. In fact, I say very often that the question of the Other in this sense was irrelevant, and the example I love to give is the case

of Gérard de Nerval who goes to visit Syria for his *Voyage en Orient* and immediately when you read the book – and if you know Syria – you realize that he
is talking about some other place. You look a little further and you notice that
what he is doing is simply repeating what Edward Lane says about Egypt. That
is what I am talking about. There is a kind of occlusion, which by virtue of its
authority, and by virtue of its successes, academic and artistic, gave Orientalism this kind of – persistence, you could call it.

AL: It is amazing how that misreading, as you call it, has persisted. But
I want to shift the discussion slightly because it has been suggested by various
recent critics that in postcolonial studies the emphasis is routinely on the analysis of colonial discourses instead of more material institutions, and often your
own work, especially *Orientalism* (and this is ironic because everyone concedes
that you are politically engaged and one of the few people who will talk
about the material legacy of imperialism and colonial structures of authority)
is seen as the source to which all these askew notions of discourse travel
back.

Said: No, but I make very clear in *Orientalism* – to the best of my ability to
discuss it in a manageable frame – that none of this could have happened
without institutions, for example. For instance, the influence and the importance of the French school of Orientalism founded by Silvestre de Sacy in
France in the late teens: you know that most of the great German Orientalists
studied with him and went back to Germany and established colleges of Oriental studies and so on and so forth. That is a persistent theme throughout the
book. I also talk about the institutionalization of knowledge about the Orient
as epitomized by the *Description de l'Egypte*. And of course in the last part of the
book (I am just jumping around now) I talk about the importance of this kind
of knowledge to the State Department, to the Defence establishment, to the
Intelligence establishment, and the connection between those and Anthropology, Political Science, 'field work' and the construction of paradigms – it is all
in there. Later, of course, and in other essays, I developed this more and quite
specifically.

AL: So do you think the field of postcolonial studies is subject to some of
the same problems?

Said: I would rather not myself talk about it because I do not think I belong
to that. First of all, I don't think colonialism is over, really. I don't know what
they are really talking about. I mean colonialism in the formal sense is over,
but I am very interested in neocolonialism, I am very interested in the workings of the International Monetary Fund and the World Bank and I have
written about them. I care very much about the structures of dependency and
impoverishment that exist, well certainly in this part of the world and my part
of the world and in all parts in what is now referred to as the global South.
So I think to use the word postcolonialism is really a misnomer and I think I
referred to the problems of that term in the Afterword to *Orientalism*.

AL: I just wanted to finish this by saying that there is a whole debate about
the literary emphasis of postcolonial studies or the genesis, the disciplinary

home, from which it began. One of the unfortunate spillovers is that precisely those material details – you know what Arif Dirlik says . . .

Said: [intervenes] are left out. Yes, I agree. I have quoted Arif Dirlik precisely for that reason.

AL: So would you think it is slightly unfair if everyone cites *Orientalism* as a poststructuralist text?

Said: Now, listen, that is not even half as unfair as the way *Orientalism* is cited as a kind of sacred text of [religious and cultural] fundamentalism. I mean that is the most difficult burden for me to shake. You know I publicly insult these people [fundamentalists] – I mean, in my part of the world. I will be very happy to do it here, but nobody gave me the chance. . . . *Culture and Imperialism* has just been banned in the entire Gulf.

AL: Really?

Said: Yes, absolutely. I mean the Arabic translation. I suppose the English version is allowed, but the Arabic translation has been banned from all the countries of the Gulf. I am very opposed to that. The idea of banning books is so primitive and so inimical to everything I believe; and to think that in some way my book licenses these characters [fundamentalists] to fulminate against something called the West, which is a position I abjure. I say even the notions of the Occident and the Orient are ideological fictions and we should try to get away from them as much as possible. And then people say, 'well, your "identity"'. I remember . . . (I am getting excited now) I remember this past summer in Beirut there was a conference held to honour me in the Arab world, and one of the big discussions was my attack in *Culture and Imperialism* on 'identity'. 'Identity' bores me, I am simply not interested in defending 'identity'. I mean Palestinian identity, or in the case of something about to be exterminated or where there is political oppression, then of course I will defend against that. But the idea of defending the notion of identity as a kind of – how shall I put it . . .

AL: essential?

Said: . . . essential, as a kind of necessary thing, and that we – this may not at all be true in India – but that we as Arabs need to defend our identity against the onslaughts of the West, I believe this is complete nonsense.

SK: No. There are versions of that claim offered here on almost exactly those terms.

Said: Yes, of course. I have great difficulty with those kinds of reductions.

Neeladri Bhattacharya: To continue with the question of Orientalism: in *Orientalism* you suggested two alternative structures of Orientalism. One, which seeks to appropriate and represent the Orient in scientific ways, codifying and recording the Orient objectively and from a distance; and the other which seeks to commune with the Orient, voyage to the Orient, and in some way exoticize the Orient. Yet, we find that in most criticisms of your book there is a recurrent claim that you have seen only the consolidation of a homogeneous Orient, the crystallization of an Orientalist vision, which is homogeneous and has a unitary essence. Would you agree with the criticism and if not, if you were rewriting the book today, would you look at the fractures within Orientalist ideology in other ways?

Said: Yes – though not to the extent that is done by some postcolonialist theorists, that is to say, you look at the structures of anxiety and suspicion and narcissism and all these other things that suggest a kind of deep fracture within the Orientalist gaze during the period of high imperialism. I mean, both in *Orientalism* and *Culture and Imperialism*, these facts are to me unassailable: you know if you are a white man in the South or in the Tropics or in the East, that is a very powerful thing. There is no way of saying that you are overcome by fear or suspicion and all the rest of it or that you are anxious – you know, Homi Bhabha's elaborations of that just don't speak to me. I don't think they are that important because the other is much more important. Now – as to the business of homogeneity: I am not sure which one you mean, the homogeneity of the Orient or the homogeneity of the Orientalist?

NB: The homogeneity of the imperial conception of the Orient.

Said: Well if it was homogeneous, I wouldn't have spent so many pages talking about it and giving, adducing, so many examples. The point is that it is not homogeneous, but it is possible that, as Chomsky has shown in his work on syntactic structures, you can devise a fantastically complicated structure, endlessly variant, out of a very small number of elements. I think this is the case with Orientalism. I think there is a kind of deep structure of Orientalism, which is able to multiply and proliferate in all kinds of ways. Orientalist writers all depart from the same premise, that there is a line separating 'us' from 'them'. And it keeps recurring. I mean look at that Huntington's *The Clash of Civilizations*: it has re-emerged and it's been there all along, I mean, for hundreds of years. That doesn't mean it's the same, you understand, but it can be reappropriated. I come back to a model I referred to in *Culture and Imperialism*, namely counterpoint, where you have one line, a *canto fermo*, a sort of base line, and in the case of a composer like Bach he can devise the most complex contrapuntal structures. But that doesn't diminish the fact that the Goldberg variations are based on a very simple descending motif in the bass.

AL: There is a related question to all of this: there are different models of colonial relations which are now circulating, and it is curious that both the people who have criticized you from within colonial discourse studies – you have mentioned Bhabha, who says that the relationship between the colonizers and the colonized is far more interactive . . .

Said: [interrupts] I say that too, actually.

AL: Well, I think you do. But what I am going to come to . . .

Said: . . . excuse me, I say that explicitly in *Culture and Imperialism*, which is why I wrote it.

SK: But *Culture and Imperialism* is taken to be the text in which you rewrite some conceptual problems from your earlier work.

Said: Well, I don't know about conceptual problems, but I expand the notion. In other words, what I said specifically in the Introduction to *Culture and Imperialism* – although I didn't say that I should have done it in *Oriental-*

ism – is that I didn't pay enough attention to other regions of the world. And because of the time – look, I mean, I wrote *Orientalism* in 1975. I was attempting something for the first time, on a relatively open field as it were. Second, I thought that the notion of interaction precisely played an important role, which in *Culture and Imperialism* I wanted to look at, which didn't mean I needed to look at it in *Orientalism* because I was talking of something quite different.

AL: I am going to push this a little bit. People have argued that even in *Culture and Imperialism* you look at domination and then you look at resistance, whereas someone like Megan Vaughan working out of African materials, and a lot of people working out of Indian materials, say that the problem is not a question of simply domination and then resistance, but that, as Vaughan puts it, customs and traditions were created out of face-to-face encounters of colonizer and colonized. She specifically says that this is something you don't do and she then goes on to say that older models of writing social history were actually far better in a way for understanding the nature of colonial power than a kind of Foucauldian emphasis, which again she sees – though I must say, she is quite fair to you in some ways because she says that you are interested in the question of resistance – as a contradiction in your work, because the method you imply is not that of the actual interaction. So it is not domination versus resistance, but how do you understand their imbrication. I would like you to spell this out.

Said: Well I don't disagree with that. I suppose what the problem is, is how do you stylistically get around the problem of representing an interaction, which has to be represented as – I mean, in your own prose – as basically sequential. I mean it is a going back and forth, but that is still a sequence – it's not getting away from the sequence. There wouldn't have been resistance had there not been colonial incursion, right? So to say that domination and resistance continue is to say what I think is a commonplace. Obviously they continue and they are implied in each other. There has been far more work developed along these lines. Terence Ranger has done a huge amount of work on primary and secondary anti-colonial resistance. But the question is: how is it best described? I think we probably would agree on the fact that it takes place from the moment the white man sets foot somewhere – that he is immediately resisted, I mean, I don't think we have any doubt about that. The question is what is the best way to represent that in a posthumous prose, if you see what I am trying to say. There are different ways of doing it and I find that analytically, the way I did it in *Culture and Imperialism* is, how should I put it, more convincing, more analytically clear and in the end probably more certain of what it is doing. I find most of the other things that have been written in this style unreadable – let's put it that way.

NB: I am continuing the same question. There are two related issues: one is how do you bring in resistance in *Culture and Imperialism* and the other is, how is the question of resistance best incorporated in an argument. When I read *Culture and Imperialism* I felt that you have a temporal argument there –

in the way you present it – that first there is a phase of consolidation of empire, consolidation of an Orientalist vision through the writing of novels and other discursive processes, etc., and then there is a process of anti-colonial struggle when this vision is contested and questioned. Most of your evidence of contestation shows a twentieth-century questioning of the colonizer. Now I felt that creates a problem.

Said: No that is not entirely correct. I talk very specifically for instance about the response to Napoleon's invasion by Abd-al-Rahman al-jabarti that is simultaneous, that is contemporary with Napoleon. So there are examples like that, but I don't think it is always necessary to give [other] examples from the same time because then it becomes very cumbersome.

NB: No, I am not talking about that kind of resistance. There obviously has been resistance. What we are bothered about in History is to see how specific forms of contestation lead to the restructuring and refiguration of ideology, of colonial ideology. There I felt that your evidence has problems. For instance, you cite Guha's *A Rule of Property for Bengal* approvingly as an instance of empire writing back. But Guha's conception of ideology in that book conforms to your earlier model for the study of Orientalism. Guha argues that Western ideas, physiocratic and mercantilist, shaped policies in India, whereas subsequent historical work suggests that is not the case, and that ideas were refigured through contestation and questioning and the local situation – and that is really the question. If that is occurring then what is the power of ideology to structure colonial society? Does it not also get refigured in the act of domination?

Said: Yes, in a chapter on the consolidation of the imperial vision, I tried to describe changes that take place, and – to go to the question of the novel – to ask what is the difference between, say, reading a few pages of Jane Austen and then reading a few pages of Kipling or of Conrad? The imperial vision is much more explicit, there is much more ready and available 'content' in that respect. This is extremely striking, as is the contrast between one period and another. But what you are talking about is something that has to do with I think a more, how shall I put it, a more minute or more detailed interaction between ideology and resistance. Is that right?

AL: Actually, could I rephrase that because it need not even be resistance. I think if you think of it as just 'power' and 'resistance' then possibly what you are saying is correct, that actually it is impossible to represent either unless you keep them separate. I think that some social historians suggest that colonial authority consolidates itself, indeed articulates itself, by resonating dynamically with what it encounters, whether that is resistance, or earlier structures of power. Or it might be indeed what Terence Ranger talks about, that the creation of the idea of the 'tribe' is with local participation, so it is that element of dynamism . . .

NB: . . . and dialogue. There is continuous dialogue, where people are not necessarily resisting, but for instance you depend on local informants for knowledge and their information is actually structured through traditional categories and notions of local people, so their ideas get inscribed in . . .

Said: Yes, that's extremely interesting, but that wasn't my subject. I can see how extremely important that is for social historians, but I was talking in particular about a domain I call culture, where culture is, according to my definition of it, a realm that is – let us say like Orientalism – relatively impervious to *that* kind of dialogue, or *that* kind of interaction. Now there is of course a subcultural tradition, for example, as Guha and others have shown, a whole range of colonial writing which is not artistic but is administrative, is investigative, is reportorial, has to do with conditions on the ground, has to do with interactions depending on the native informant. All that exists, there's no question about that. I was trying to adumbrate, perhaps a less important, but to my way of thinking, a larger picture of a certain kind of stability, which, because of my education, because of my training, has impressed me. Why is it so stable, why does it shake off the kinds of things you are talking about or why does it seem to succeed? Maybe I am wrong, maybe it doesn't, but I think I am not wrong. And why does it seem to hand itself on as 'the culture' quite without regard for all kinds of experiences, from horror to interaction, which are somehow excluded from it? Camus is a perfect example. For there's a long history, which he incorporates in some of his prose writings, I mean non-fictional prose, which he deliberately leaves out of *L'Etranger* – you know, the life of a lower-middle-class colon in Algeria who is outraged at the treatment of Algerians like himself and Arabs and Muslims by the French colonial system. But that is left out entirely in this particular vision, and I am really talking about vision in the end, more than I am about policies and working methods of the kind that you're talking about.

SK: Part of the problem with your concern with what you just described as the, and I like that word, 'vision' of imperialism is that it's opened you up to the kind of critique that says that in *Culture and Imperialism* you lavish a great deal of hermeneutical attention on the explication of metropolitan artists like Conrad, Kipling, Austen, or indeed when you do an allegoric reading of Magwitch in *Great Expectations*, as opposed to the moments in the text when you consider Ngugi, Césaire and Achebe, who come across – in Michael Sprinker's terms – in a 'comparatively straightforward analysis'. Sprinker suggests that in doing so, you valorize that kind of metropolitan culture and its aesthetic achievements, as opposed to a flattened understanding of what exists at the other end. How does your sense of your emphasis on imperial vision work with your reading of these different texts?

Said: Well look, there is also the fact that you're writing, or at least one is writing, a book, something one wants to be read; one isn't writing a didactic manual, one isn't writing a workbook for future students who want everything spelt out! And of course I was writing for a largely metropolitan audience, I was not being published by a local Arab press. I was writing for a commercial press in the United States where one wants to get the largest number of readers. Now, your question of the 'valorization' of one or the other: first of all, I never use a word like valorization! But I mean, to think that one is better than the other is inimical to my argument. I never said that. But I am not trying to describe the same thing in both texts, you see, and they try to do different things. And the nature of my subject – perhaps it's a mistake on my part to have made that assumption – is that I was trying to show a wide range of quite dramatically different, impressive responses from Césaire to C. L. R. James to George Antonios to Guha to Ngugi to Naipaul – a lot of writers – and to go through each of them painstakingly in a book that was already far too long – actually the book was cut – so it was an exigency of sorts.

SK: If we can shift tack a little to slightly more theoretical questions: various forms of poststructuralist inquiry have argued for the political necessity of giving up the 'grand narratives' of historical explanation in favour of a more nuanced understanding of local hierarchies of power, etc. Such scepticism asks us to decouple our analysis of, for instance, capitalism and colonialism, which have often been understood and interlinked (that is, one couldn't have taken the form that it did without the other), or indeed to give up a 'world systems' approach. Do you have a . . .

Said: [interrupts] I have a very strong critique of the world systems approach, in an essay I wrote about fifteen years ago. It will be published in a collection of my essays which is going to appear in a year or so when I have the time to put it together and write a preface for it. There I spoke about the problems of a world systems approach, which is that most of the work they have done, and I am speaking of Perry Anderson here, or even Samir Amin, depend very heavily on what I consider to be Orientalist sources. I mean, who is the major authority that they cite for example on the emergence of the Ottomans – it is Bernard Lewis. I give a lot of such examples. So, in that sense, I find it flawed. It doesn't take enough account of local scholarship or what you might call new knowledge of that kind – not that I have it. I mean what are we talking about if I have to depend upon this kind of thing ['Orientalist sources'] to understand. There is therefore, a kind of lack of understanding. I remember having used the example of Alatas's book, *The Myth of the Lazy Native*. It is an extremely important book because there he looks very carefully at pre-cisely the kinds of figures, estimates, trends cited by colonial economists, which they [world systems theorists] rely on, and over which there's a lot of dispu-tation. Also, for instance, it was taken to be the case that capitalism was entirely a Western, European invention, and that in Islam capitalism really never had a local base. There has now been some very interesting work by economic historians of a younger sort, anti-Orientalist historians like Peter Graham, who shows that in Egypt, seventeenth- and eighteenth-century Egypt, there was the emergence of a local capitalism which was quite powerful and which has really never been studied as such.

SK: Versions of that argument have been made about India.

Said: I'm sure. So the 'world system' approach, yes, but with a kind of scep-ticism about the data that one is using – some of it of the kind that you have expressed and some of it expressed by the critique I get. Such data is always challengeable and one has to be careful about what one is using and what one is not using. But in the end, if one is attempting a global perspective, one then falls into the trap, but at least one is aware of it.

AL: I was going to say that this has been a big debate around Subaltern Studies as well: they are doing all these local things, they are writing post-foundational history rather than thinking about capitalism, etc. But I was going to ask you about a slightly different version of this debate, which is that in *The World, the Text and the Critic* you have said that you find the Foucauldian understanding of power not sufficient for a politically engaged criticism and now . . .

Said: I wrote something beyond that. What I say is basically that Foucault writes always from the point of view of power, there's never any doubt in your mind when you pick up one of his books that power is going to win out in the end. So that the whole idea of resistance is really essentially defeated from the start. Poulantzas says the same thing, that the sites of resistance in Foucault are very difficult to follow.

AL: And Stuart Hall says that Foucault doesn't have any understanding of a system. That's the problem. But this idea that this Foucauldian notion of the dispersal of power is incompatible with Gramsci's notions of hegemony and power: you rightly said that you believe you can combine critical methods and that there is no necessary contradiction. Now some people have offered a critique of Subaltern Studies saying that if you try and combine Foucault and Gramsci, it's like trying to ride two horses at the same time. And Gyan Prakash answers by saying then we all need to become stunt riders!

Said: I was just thinking of Charlton Heston!

AL: I wanted to ask you to comment in a little more detail on what you think is the potential of such combinations. Is this a productive tension at all between Foucault and Gramsci?

Said: Extremely productive. Well look, one of the problems with Gramsci (having been a very, very assiduous student of Gramsci for many years – I was the first to lecture on Gramsci at Columbia about twenty years ago) is the state of the texts. When you talk about Gramsci, you are talking about something that is extremely slippery. When I gave a series of lectures on Gramsci (which I recall very vividly) and I think this is still the case, I felt that it was necessary to do a kind of philological analysis of the different ways in which he uses the word 'hegemony', for instance, or the different ways in which he uses the word 'intellectual'. All the key words – 'war of position', 'war of manoeuvre' and others – are constantly shifting and constantly changing because of the way in which he wrote and because of the condition of his notebooks.

Most of the readers of Gramsci have read him only in that one-volume compendium, which is full of mistakes, by the way. I have corrected some, I don't know whether you know this, but there are passages in it which I quote in *Orientalism*, in a footnote I believe. The four volumes of *The Prison Notebooks* had just come out in the middle seventies, and I noticed that what the translators [Quentin Hoare and Geoffrey Nowell Smith] had the tendency to do was to lop off bits of Gramsci. For instance in that passage that I quote: 'history is deposited as an infinity of traces in you without leaving an inventory'. That's what you get in the book. But Gramsci goes on to say (and I put it in there) that therefore it is necessary to make an inventory, which is quite a different thing than to say that it leaves us with an infinity of traces without an inventory. And therefore, of course, you have to start by making an inventory. So that problem is very strong.

Once you've begun to circulate a bit in Gramsci, you realize that he is talking about very different situations at very different times, and that there is a danger of abstracting from the situation to a general theoretical term – which is almost impossible, I mean the danger is almost too great. Nevertheless, Gramsci, unlike Foucault, is working with an evolving political situation in which certain extremely important and radical experiments were taking place in the Turin factories in which he was involved, and from them he generalized periodically, I mean in periodical form. You don't get that sense in Foucault; what you get instead is a sense of teleology where everything is tending toward the same end, and so the attempt to bring the two together involves in a certain sense breaking up the Foucauldian narrative into a series of smaller situations where Gramsci's terminology can become useful and illuminating for analytical purposes. In other words if you are talking about, let us say, the state of the clinic or the prison at a certain moment, [you need to ask] what else do you need to know about the situation besides what those people have written about it? What is the condition of factory workers at the time or what was the condition of convicts at that time, what class do they come from, what type – that's never been referred to in that book on the prison – what type of people are put into prison? In that sense, the introduction of historical, what I would call a historical context, to Foucault is extremely important and worth doing.

AL: And then it becomes possible to negotiate some of the larger tensions of ideological orientation?

Said: Yes. But what is ideological? There is a big difference with Gramsci you see, who is always trying to change the political situation.

AL: That's what I meant.

Said: Foucault isn't. Foucault is really not interested in that. I mean there was a little period in the sixties to the middle seventies when he was very interested in the condition of prisoners and so forth, but by the time he came to America – I think it was in the late sixties for the first time, but he came consistently during the seventies – he had changed and he was really not interested in the social movements at all and I think that is clear in his work. I am much more interested in that aspect of Gramsci; in other words how do you modify a political situation by organization and so on, all of which begin – since I am writing at a very restricted level – as Gramsci says, with trying to take stock of the situation. You sit down and work it out, the way he did on the Southern question, which is the only systematic analysis he ever did. So I find myself in that position, which is not the position Foucault found himself in. And from that, because of my political writing, which is enormous in volume, I am always trying to gear my writing not towards the theoretical constituency but towards a political constituency.

SK: This may be the time to switch to our last rubric: I had said that some forms of poststructuralist inquiry have asked us to give up on – as a political necessity – grand narratives.

Said: You mean Chantal Mouffe and Laclau?

SK: Yes, exactly. That is the model.

Said: I have no time for that. That's the answer to that question. What does it mean? And Baudrillard! It's just nauseating, it's just gobbledegook. No, Laclau is a serious man, I don't mean that. Both Baudrillard, and what's the name of that other guy – Lyotard, it's a kind of provincial atavism of a very very unappealing sort, and I feel the same way about postmodernism. I think it's the bane of Third World intellectuals, if you will pardon the expression. I'm not accusing you, of course; present company excluded!

NS: Again, carrying on from the earlier question about productive tensions and opposite frames: I felt, when reading your books as well as hearing you lecture, that there is a strong tension or opposition between two kinds of frames in your writing. One is what is often identified as a constructionist frame, in which you see nation as a narration, you see the Orient as a narrative, and the imperial idea as a discursive product, etc.; on the other hand there is also the recurring objectivist emphasis which you have in all your work on fact, on reality, on objective events, etc. I was wondering: it is not that these two cannot be reconciled, but how do you reconcile these two conceptual frames?

Said: I don't think they can be reconciled. I think the relationship is frequently, in my experience, and I am coming increasingly to that view – there's a sense in which the relationship between one and the other is a relation of distortion, and manipulation. Now we are perfectly ready to accept that when Harold Bloom talks about a poet misreading another poet. We are perfectly willing to accept it in the case of a novelist misrepresenting or misreading or misinterpreting reality in order to produce a fiction. But we tend sometimes to find it just as acceptable (and this is one of the great problems with postmodernism) to say 'well, the media always lies, we know that', and to say that we know that representations are always just representations. My interest is in the more pernicious forms of these relationships, where actual lives, actual identities, actual political destinies are distorted and destroyed by a process of this sort. That's why I think the relationship between the 'constructionist' and the other one ['objectivist'] increasingly is in my view irreconcilable. It is reconcilable in a way, but for my purposes it's always been something to be profoundly suspicious of – the relationship between the two. Perhaps I am not answering your question?

NB: No, I had a feeling that in your own writing you are drawing from both.

Said: Of course, I am drawing from both.

NB: And you want to retain that opposition between them?

Said: Yes, I do.

SK: These last two sets of questions have to do with the other important part of your life, which is your role as a public intellectual, your ideas and your performance. You have argued for, and your own career has demonstrated, the need for the public intellectual to work alongside larger collectivities and causes (and this is the Gramscian notion of the organic intellectual). But in recent years, and this too has been paralleled in your own life, you have talked at great length about independence and of the importance for intellectuals to resist the seduction of office and power. Is this a shift in your understanding of the role of a public intellectual or is this to be explained with reference to the peculiar circumstances of the Oslo agreement and the Palestinian–Israeli accord?

Said: No, I think it's a development, because I was always close to political power in one way or another, by virtue of my education, by virtue of my class, by virtue of my political involvement. I am not going to waste your time by trying to explain that, except to tell you that's the case.

SK: We understand that in India.

Said: Exactly. But what I found increasingly important to me was independence. And of course this caused a tremendous debate when the Arabic version of *Representation of the Intellectual* came out, because a word which means 'not committed' in Arabic was substituted for the phrase 'independent intellectual', and I don't mean it that way. In other words, what I find is that if one is close to power, it takes an increasingly greater effort as one grows older to maintain that distance, and the cost is greater because you have to weigh the consequences, which are that if you did get involved maybe you could make things better, to put it bluntly.

I made a choice which is not to do that, and to remain distant from it, and this was well before Oslo. It was all during my period of very close association with the PLO when I was on very close terms with them and *with* them. And not only with them – it's an interesting part of now-forgotten history – but during the seventies the PLO in Beirut was the lodestone for every liberation movement in the world. When I went to South Africa in 1991, for example, when Mandela had just been released, I remember seeing him then, apartheid was still on, but the ANC was acknowledged and had their headquarters in the Shell building in downtown Johannesburg. One of the things that astonished me was how many faces were familiar to me. It was my first trip to South Africa, but many of them I had seen in Beirut or PLO embassies elsewhere: Nicaraguans, Irish, various European liberation groups, but mostly Third World liberation groups that I had come to know. So in that respect I was very close to all that and I knew what was happening in many instances, not *everything* that was happening, but a lot.

The thing that impressed me the most was a paradox: on the one hand, in the case of a people who had suffered a great deal, like prisoners, or the spouses of prisoners who disappeared, I saw the importance of the party, of the organization, how it gave hope, how it sustained one, but it exacted a price from one, a price of submission, which was that you gave up a critical distance. And of course on the other side were those who were in power, who used that power in a certain sense to insulate themselves from their mistakes, and from the fact that there were things, particularly in the Palestinian case, that involved tremendous destruction. You couldn't have lived through the various Israeli invasions, or the bombings, or the siege of Beirut in 1982 – I was in Amman during the Black September of 1970 – you can't have lived through that without realizing that you are to some extent responsible for that kind of damage, which produced nothing, only more suffering. So I always had the sneaking suspicion that if you were too close, and you accepted too much, the prerogatives of power, and the insulations of power, and what my sister used to call quite brilliantly, a seat in the front row, you don't see what is going on behind you. Then, of course, it came to the fore, but my break with Arafat really occurred in 1988 or 1989. I did a public denunciation of him in the Arab press. Then there is the whole question of where you do it; in America where they are already attacked, it doesn't help me to attack him more, so I tried to confine myself mostly to writing in Arabic, which I still do. But then after Oslo, I felt that it was so disastrous, and the Gulf War, and the alliances and the whole tremendous . . . [his voice trails off].

Now – to conclude – I have become in my late years, I suppose, partly because of my illness and partly because of other things, I have become very involved in a different view which is – you know, Adorno is very important to me now – the idea of trying to maintain a certain kind of tension without resolving it dialectically, as a sort of witness, a testimonial to what is happening. That seems to me to be something worth trying. You know, our situation as Palestinians, and, generally speaking, in the Arab world is so parlous, so desperate, that, *I feel*, perhaps hubristically, that it is important to maintain that distance and the voice. It gives me hope, when they ban my books and I am not allowed to go there and all that sort of thing, to see people reading me in faxes and emails and that's a possibility which I exploit. That means a lot to me. Logically, the next step would be to enter politics, because I could, and I am sure that I could spearhead a very serious political opposition to Arafat, but I am too ill to do it, I am too weak physically.

SK: And bearing witness is a powerful historical practice.

Said: Yes, it's something, but let's not exaggerate it. But it *is* worth doing, I think; anyway that is all I can do. I don't now have much activity unfortunately, but I place great hopes in my political activities which I now try to confine to the young. I try to see students, Arab students, throughout the world and I always speak to them, and that's important.

SK: Last question. This has to do with the whole notion of tradition and its weight that you talked about in your lecture at Jamia Millia Islamia, which is of great consequence not simply within the confines of Jamia but in India generally. Now what you have been saying is that tradition has proved to be one of the biggest stumbling blocks in the achievement of democracy and human rights in many nations across the world. You have also talked about – you referred to Terence Ranger, for instance – the fact that tradition is always a motivated reinvention of the past to serve the interests of present-day power. Yet tradition is not only invoked by cultural and religious fundamentalists, but also by more secular communities concerned that they must resist the effects of modernization in so far as they understand modernization to be synonymous with American globalization, or consumer culture, or the media culture of the West. What is your sense of – how do you negotiate these?

Said: I don't take any comfort in tradition. I think it's exaggerated and I think we know too much about its misuse. I very much admire analysts of tradition like Nasr Hamed Abu Zeid, who had to leave Egypt because he did a discursive reading of the Qu'ran and showed to what extent Islamic fundamentalist discourse was a discourse of power and not of vision or ethics as it pretends to be. For which they tried to make him divorce his wife, and he had to leave the country because he lives under a death threat. I think that kind of 'us analysing our traditions' is of the utmost importance. It's the most urgent thing we can do, and understand how traditions are live and not passive things stuck in a closet but they are – and I go back to Vico – made by human beings and that they are recollections, they are customary practices, collective memory, they are all kinds of things, but they are certainly not the simple pure thing to which people return and get comfort in. Maybe because I am so rootless myself and deracinated in that sense, I firmly believe that it is a tremendous mistake to give up to tradition as much as is being given up to it, certainly in the Arab world. You know better about it in India.

AL: Here too, and quite dangerously.

Said: Is it the same? Yes, the BJP and so on . . .

Acknowledgments

This is an edited version of the original interview conducted in New Delhi on 16 December 1997 and published in *The Book Review XXII* (1–2) (January–February 1998). The interview itself is exclusive to *The Book Review*, and this version is published with the permission of the Book Review Literary Trust, New Delhi.

Chapter 2

Speaking of Postcoloniality, in the Continuous Present: A Conversation

Homi Bhabha and John Comaroff

Political Prefigurations

JC: Let me begin with a statement at once in the indicative and the interrogative voice. An assumption we share, I know, is that, whatever might be said about it, "postcoloniality" does not refer to one thing. Apart from all else, the term is now conventionally said to describe both a state of being, defined by its place in the passage of epochal history, and a critical orientation toward the reading of the past, not least of its textual traces. Patently, many different things are invoked under its sign. And it has its own historicity, a diachrony still unfolding. In this respect, and here comes the interrogative, does it make any sense to parse its past into two broad phases? Is it plausible or useful to separate the first – which began with the "decolonization" of India in 1947, brought forth most of the "independent" nations of the "Third World," and ushered in the age of high neocolonialism – from a second, imagined to have had its genesis in 1989, with the end of the Cold War, the "triumph" of neoliberal capitalism, democratization movements, and the rise of a new wave of postrevolutionary societies in Central Europe, South Africa, and elsewhere?

HB: Well, I think it is very useful to place the term "postcolonial" in these two time-frames. The post-1947 (or mid-century) decolonization movements took sharp aim at the long history of imperialism and the somewhat shorter history of postwar capitalism in its reconstructive phase. The Second World War had a widespread effect on the moral and political fiber of Third World peoples who had, in the main, supported the Allies – not without exceptions – and expected to be given their freedom in return. So the anti-colonial movements in Asia and Africa were movements fired by a moral purpose, seeking a new ethico-political order – a new humanism, as Frantz Fanon put it – that had its most visible manifestation in the Bandung Conference and the movement of non-aligned nations. What followed were problematic experiments in socialism, planned economies, new articulations of agriculture and industry in national governance. But the twin forces of economic deprivation and cultural and technological dependence created indigenous national elites of a neo-colonial cast that became the willing or unwilling operatives of the IMF, the World Bank, and other international cartels. Despite their rhetorics of insurgency and autonomy it was hard to resist the power of the hegemonic interests of "West-oriented" international capitalism. Much, of course, is lost in such an abridged and accelerated narrative but I indulge in it to emphasize, at once, the tragic and prefigurative configuration of this mid-century moment. Tragic, because the desire to construct a genuinely "postcolonial" moral and social order was thwarted by "internal" forces of nepotism and corruption, and by hegemonic external agencies of "modernization" or "rationalization". But this tragic tension prefigures the historic moment of the late 1980s in an uncanny way. The democracy movements that emerged in opposition to the oppressive regimes of state socialism were acting in a just and necessary cause. However, the neoliberal triumphalist "aura" that accompanies the boom-and-bust of economic globalization (especially in Asia) while celebrating "free markets" creates its own historical melancholias and political amnesias. It is as if the advance of science, technology, and dot.com consumerism will somehow transform the unequal world into a level playing field – but the favelas, ghettos, townships, and shantytowns have not turned into silicon valleys fifty years after independence, Indian literacy and poverty rates have hardly budged, the poverty line in the US has barely shifted in this half-century, while we delight in the accelerated connectivity between California and Bangalore –

JC: If it does make sense to distinguish between those two broad periods as a history of materialities, are we – in tracing out the move from industrial capitalism, in its postwar apotheosis, to some (as yet underspecified) form of global capitalism – also tracing out the processes which are said to be transforming the nation-state?

HB: Well, in the postcolony, the postwar period represented a phase of nation-building, while the current "global" moment seems to be concerned with the construction of the "transnation" or the international [EU, Mercosur, others]. But what interests me particularly is the shift we observe in the self-representation of national peoples. Would you agree with me that today there exists, on a global scale, a growing awareness of the "imagined community" of national belonging as a process and practice of minoritization? By this, I want to suggest a whole set of circumstances. First, the growing migrant, diasporic, and refugee populations of our times; then, the way in which emergent nation-states, such as Palestine, inaugurate a sense of national peoplehood that is nonetheless afflicted with a persistent sense of being a minority population; then, of course, there is the way in which emergent groups and collectivities experience their cultural citizenship as minorities and claim recognition on the grounds of alterity or difference – race, ethnicity, gender, sexuality, historical trauma. By minoritarian identification, I want somehow to get beyond the polarized geographies of majority vs. minority, where it is assumed that the political desire of the minority is to achieve the hegemonic, majoritarian position. I also want to suggest something distinct from a multiculturalist pluralism that dreams of a federation of "minority" or ethnic groups stitched together in a multi-culti quilt. The articulatory logic of such a pluralist perspective, despite its dicing with difference, aspires towards the assimilative and the consensual: it neglects the problems of power differentials, conflicts of interest, and cultural dissonance. The kind of minoritization that impresses me is the sort of thing W. E. B. Du Bois was hinting at when he said that there are minorities who do not want to become majorities; their sense of minorities who seek a kind of public articulation or affiliation that does not depend on associating social authority with cultural sovereignty; a "metonymic" minoritization (if I may) in which the "agency" of any specific recognition of difference – gender, race, generation, location – is not grounded on a primordial identity, but in a lateral ethical movement (*à la* Levinas). It is in the process of negotiating or translating differences that "agency" becomes recognizable; agency becomes individuated and instantiated in and through the process of deciphering a collective project whose "identity" is not identitarian – it does not try and conserve the totality or continuity of race or gender or culture; an agency that is genuinely "projective" in the sense that its identifications are open to historical contingency and its affiliations are genuinely open to the agonistic and antagonistic process unleashed in the search for solidarity. When I think of these forms of minoritarian political identification and then try and articulate them with the modes of protest we saw in Seattle during the International Summit, I somehow think we need to insert the history of the sixties somewhere between the fifties and the nineties.

JC: As a graduate student in those days, I recall well the contradictions of the late sixties. How, as they turned their face towards neo-Marxism, campus radicals were more acute in exposing the contradictions of the New Left than they were in dealing with the Right – and tended to look more to Europe, especially to the European labor movement, than outside of it for inspiration. Anti-colonial struggles worried and animated those of us who came from the former British and French empires more than it did our metropolitan colleagues. Or the Americans abroad, who were fired by the Vietnam War.

HB: Right, absolutely.

JC: But there is one sense in which the late 1960s were significant for the epistemic history of Western thought as we see it unfolding today. In retrospect, though we did not know it then, it was the moment at which structural Marxism began to founder; at which, too, many of the paradigmatic certainties of the classical social sciences ran aground. Recall the angst in academia at the time. It spoke to a truly Kuhnian conjuncture. Very much like in the late nineties, it evoked a great deal of talk about the crisis of theory, the triumph of method, the ascendance of empirical description over grand explanatory schemata. . . . This was the moment of failure – or perhaps, of the recognition of an impending failure – of totalizing rhetorics.

HB: Do you think that this failure of the "totalizing" rhetorics of knowledge and society had something to do with the fact that the sovereignty of "class" as the primary "cause" of social transformation and the master discourse of political struggle was being surpassed by other "subaltern" narratives and practices of political movement – women, youth, Black power, civil rights, curricular reform, etc.? Were these the early energies of those events and engagements that, in the eighties and nineties, came to be known as the politics of difference, the culture wars or new social movements?

JB: Yes, almost certainly. In retrospect, it seems clear that the displacement of class – "*an und fur sich*" displacement into the four-dimensional material and cultural geographies of the "new" world order that were to sediment at *fin de siècle* – was occurring, largely unnoticed, at a moment when its sign was being most vociferously invoked as a call to arms. At least in Europe. At that historical moment, however, the renunciation of theory was not accompanied, explicitly, by the kind of neoliberalism on the ascendant today: a neoliberalism which bears within it a unified theory of being-in-the-world, of polity and economy and sociality, yet presents itself as atheoretical, hiding its praxis in quotidian, commonsensical practice. The political movements of the period, unencumbered by the terrifying triumphalism and the brute excesses of global capitalism, still retained a great measure of optimism in modernist knowledge and its production; in the idea that, while old totalizing rhetorics might have failed, something liberatory might be found to take their place. Remember how sanguine, at the time, were apologists for various forms of methodological individualism.

HB: But there was also an emphasis on radical anarchism and a certain faith in violent protest as part of the possibility of breaking open undemocratic disciplinary orders – intellectual, epistemological, and social. New forms of political organization and agency were in the air – community activism, communes, neighborhood politics rather than national parties, an emphasis on the municipal and "local" state rather than the centralized, "national" state. There was also an emphasis on "lifestyle" politics – the personal is the political, and such redefinitions of privacy and publicity.

JC: I think that is true, but that it emerged out of the failures of the sixties. Recall, for example, that there was not a feminist movement to move the politics of gender in the same way as would be the case in the seventies. Its roots were there, of course, but its full articulation as social movement was yet to come. Similarly Cultural Studies, another indirect progeny as yet unborn, which also was to grow out of the failure of 1968. In May 1968 no one knew what was going to happen, of course. Nobody anticipated the purge of the centers of radicalism, the LSE, where we were students, notably among them. But that quiet purge in the early seventies came to symbolize a sense of the evacuation of politics, of the neutralization of the academy, of the emascula-

tion of labor, that gave rise to the conditions out of which an ever more articulate feminism, an ever more vocal, more polymorphous identity politics, an
ever more nuanced Cultural Studies, a range of post-Marxisms and post-
modernisms were to arise. Also postcoloniality, in its various revealed and
reviled guises.

HB: But what about the sixties sense of living anxiously in a moment of
transition? Or was it a much more upbeat utopian feeling?

JC: Well, for one thing, it was a deeply contested moment. I remember
sitting at innumerable meetings while the LSE was closed arguing about the
nature of the times. Many American draft dodgers believed that a revolution
was imminent – although it was very difficult to get them to specify the steps
from an antiwar politics to a social revolution. Of course, for those whose point
of reference was Paris, the hope for insurrection and radical change was
invested in an alliance – which they took actually to be emerging – between
"the" student movement and workers. In England, of course, proxies for
government, the universities notably among them, did much of the work of
repression. The LSE, to be sure, succeeded in producing a very docile student
body and a very docile faculty. For those of us who had come from the colonies
and for whom revolutionary struggles were very much an object of concern,
the whole thing quickly looked like a fantastic carnival of liberal desire.

HB: Or misrecognition?

JC: Yes, precisely. Having seen the South African state in ghastly operation,
we well knew that noise in the streets does not produce revolution. Marching
on Grosvenor Square was not going to put an end to US imperialism. But it
was not only former South Africans who were painfully aware of this. At the
time, the LSE was like a lightning rod against which the empire was striking
back; it was well populated with students from "the colonies." For many of
them, 1968 might have been fun. But, as one put it to me in retrospect, there
was always another voice in their ear, a voice telling them that this was a non-
momentous moment, so to speak – precisely because it was not founded on
any kind of revolutionary praxis. It was merely a struggle against something,
something quite inchoate, not for anything. At the time, there were people
who likened 1968 to 1956 in Central Europe. But that was fanciful even then.
Woodstock was a better icon of that false millennium than was Hungary.

HB: But did it not raise the question of the possibility of cultural rights, the
politics of representation, and symbolic forms of protest, as having a powerful
hold on the political imagination, and creating the conditions for solidarity and
resistance?

JC: That is a fascinating question. The evocation of emerging popular cultural forms certainly did feature in the notion of a new politics. After all, it
was out of this maelstrom that Dick Hebdige's *Subcultures*, and related work,
was going to come. But in the foreflash of the late sixties, that politics was still
embryonic, ill-defined, untheorized. On the Left, in fact, there was a tendency
to dismiss talk of culture as a "soft," overly humanist, concern with ideology.
Again, I think that the null terrain of the early seventies was a more fertile

ground for revisioning culture and politics, cultural politics, the politics of culture; recall the battle of the British "cultural" Marxists, famously Thompson and Williams, to be heard at all in "radical" circles at the time. There are some ironies here too. When Cultural Studies emerged in Britain, many of those in the British academy whose specialist interest actually lay in the study of representation, textualization, mediation, and symbolic practice – on both the Right and the Left, in both the humanities and the social sciences – did not merely ignore the Birmingham School. They were actively hostile towards it. To the day we left England, in 1978, almost no anthropologists read Cultural Studies. It simply felt outside their discursive frame of reference; even worse, it was actively vilified by many. I think that Jean Comaroff was the first anthropologist in Britain seriously to engage with anybody in that field at all. As you know, the Left was very uneasy with the Birmingham School, like everyone else. Certainly, history bore no traces at all of its influence. In short, on one hand, 1968 might have occurred amidst the signs and ciphers of "swinging" London, of a new moment in the archeology of popular culture. But I don't think that anybody foresaw then the kinds of arguments that were later to surface about the politics of culture – or about popular culture as politics.

HB: As you were just talking about the deep skepticism and apprehension felt by the British Left about the importance of cultural struggles as crucial to political transformation, I was reminded of Perry Anderson's *New Left Review* essay, "Components of the National Culture," which suggests why this might be so. He makes a strong (post-Althusserian point) about the lack of a theoretically reflective Marxist or socialist tradition as the "determinate absence" in the construction of British culture. This vacuum sucked in those rather conservative migrant European thinkers who took refuge in British academia and shaped its postwar intellectual history. How strange to be reminiscing about Britain in the sixties as if we were native informants. You had barely arrived to do graduate work at the LSE and in 1968 I was in my first year as an undergraduate at Elphinstone College, Bombay. I experienced the "events of May" quite indirectly, from "overseas," as the colonial phrase had it . . .

JC: [Laughing] I was going to say that these reminiscences force one to think about lacunae in the ways we were reading the history of the moment at the moment. These were times of great optimism. Why had we not yet begun to ask deeper questions about the relationship between postcoloniality and neocolonialism, for example? Why didn't we see the obvious for so long?

HB: I think that we didn't ask those questions because the materialist critical paradigms that were dominant at the time had very restricted, stereotypical "readings" of the cultural histories of the colonial and postcolonial conditions. Despite all the interesting rethinkings of Hegelian causality, Lukácsian "totality" or Althusserian "Ideological State Apparatuses" (remember the keywords?) there was only limited intellectual and ideological space for evaluating or validating cultural translation, metissage, creolization, hybridization. The history and politics of empire was thought of as a thoroughly economic or

sociological reality; and despite our theoretical obeisances to "relative autonomy," if you suggested that there were specifically "cultural," symbolic, or linguistic strategies for the retrieval of subaltern power or subversive political
agencies you were treated as a boss-eyed idealist riddled with *mauvaise foie*.
One of the most enduring lessons of recent postcolonial thinking, don't you
think, has been the proper suspicion of the Western hermeneutics of "progress"
and "rationality" in both imperialist and nationalist discourses which, though
profoundly opposed to each other ideologically, are often cut from the same
philosophical cloth. They counter each other's political account which is very
important, but nationalist and imperialist thought are often committed to
similar forms of historicism and individualism.

I had some rather early, unformed thoughts or questions along these
lines when I was a graduate student at Oxford, soaking up all the
structuralist–Marxist theory I could get from Terry Eagleton, and trying, at the
same time, to write about the novels of V. S. Naipaul that had no academic
presence in Oxford at that time. In the seminar room I learnt that the "inter-
pellative" function of ideology was to produce a subject in a posture of coherence, straddling the fissures, the cracks, and constitutive contradictions of
bourgeois capitalist society. To become conscious of oneself as an agent or an
"individual" one had to experience oneself in this illusion of a self-fulfilling,
plenitudinous personhood. Working on Naipaul reminded me of the fact that,
in literature at least, no colonized subject had the illusion of speaking from a
place of plenitude or fullness. The colonial subject was a kind of split-subject
and "knew" it both phenomenologically and historically. Whereas I was being
taught that such a splitting of the subject was the general condition of the
psyche (Lacan), or the act of enunciation itself (Benveniste), there was a much
more specific or "local" historical and affective apprehension of this which was
part of the personhood of the postcolonial subject. The "decentering of the self"
was the very condition of agency and imagination in these colonial or postcolonial conditions, and it becomes more than a theoretical axiom; it becomes
a protean, everyday practice, a way of living with oneself and others while
acknowledging the "partiality" of social identification; it becomes part of one's
ethical being in the sense that such a "decentering" also informs the agency
through which one executes a care of the self and a concern for the "other,"
in the late Foucauldian sense.

JC: A quick interpolation here: To what extent is "the colonized subject"
being portrayed here as an undifferentiated figure? Are there refractions of
that subject? How does one figure into its being the dimensions of gender, of
generation, of class, of race, of positionality? Or was that not important? Was
there something transcendent about the colonized subject that occluded other
forms of differentiation? What differences made a difference?

HB: No, not transcendent at all; I'm so glad that you brought that up. This
is a difficult thing to talk about. There is always the danger of sounding transcendent or formulaic when you make a claim about a structuring principle
that is iterative or repetitive rather than teleological or dialectical. An iterative

structure might be something like notions of "splitting" in the construction of subjectivity or in the process of enunciation (enonce/enonciation); a governmental problem of iteration might be the way in which a modal form like the "nation" is iteratively revised or reinvented in various societal histories, both maintaining a kind of genealogy with the "history of the nation" but each time revising the form and rearticulating the causality and the cultural value of that designation – a problem central to many anti-colonial nationalisms. An iterative structure is not strictly meaningful "in itself," but can only be recognized or represented as it repeats differentially across discourses, emerges out of varied historical circumstances, or becomes meaningful as it is specified or instantiated in a practice or across practices. It relates to the general principle but the case is not causally tied to it. It is somehow much easier to talk about the relationship of the general to the particular if you are thinking in terms of a dialectical schema or a teleological one: in the dialectical process the instance of differentiation is part of a destiny of sublation (it will become part of the Geist; in terms of teleological progress the moment of difference is a step towards a larger truth, a higher or wider view). But we know that the very structure of gender, generation, or race resists such logics of representation. But it is difficult to prevent such iterative structures from not seeming immanent and invariant; they look "universal" but the point is that their repetition does not secure their similitude. Each iteration of "splitting" sutures the "subject" into differential dimensions of gender, generation, class, race, or positionality. But what has to be "worked on" by the colonial subject experientially or phenomenologically, and "worked out" by the postcolonial critic theoretically, is the way in which such "suturings" are never synchronous or equivalent: they require the subject to be "marked" iteratively so that each "differentiation" is a skein of identifications and can no longer be "read off," or relegated to, an ontological or originary ground of difference or identity.

JC: This, in turn, raises two important questions of theory. One has to do with the old Manichean opposition between colonizer and colonized, those "iteratively marked," positionally conflated points of reference around which the human geography of empire is so widely imagined. How, other than purely by descriptive insistence, does one displace the crushing logic of binarism in terms of which colonial worlds are apprehended and narrated? The other has to do with culture and agency. Interestingly, one of the reasons that there was resistance in some Leftist academic quarters to Althusserian readings of history – history, that is, without a subject – was precisely because they wrote the "native" entirely in the passive voice. Or worse, rendered that "native" mute and inert, a *tabula rasa* onto which "Europe," equally reified, inscribed its desires, demands, determinations. In purely empirical terms, leaving aside principled political and theoretical concerns, structural Marxist accounts of colonial processes had almost nothing to say about the agency of culturally endowed colonized peoples. Which left unanswered one of the most fundamental conundrums of all: Why was it that, when the same inexorable forces of colonial capital alighted on terrains across Africa or South Asia or Latin America, the dialectics of their encounter with autochthonous peoples produced such a wide variety of social and economic formations not to mention political struggles? Human agency, cultural difference, it seems, had a highly palpable impact.

A Postcolonial Optic

JC: Let us circle back to where we began – by parsing postcoloniality, that is – and head off in another direction. What does it mean to you to be a postcolonial scholar at this millennial moment? Many people are writing at present about the nature of neoliberal capitalism, of globalization, of the world post-1989. What does a postcolonial optic bring to the discourse that is different?

HB: Before approaching the scholarly side, let me say something about postcoloniality and practical life – something quite subjective and impressionistic, but nonetheless inspiring. I grew up in a city where, despite recurrent communalist Hindu–Muslim riots, there was a deep sense of the need to be hospitable to "differences" and to produce a negotiated sense of cultural coexistence. This makes the most recent events all the more tragic. Western liberals and neoliberals ponder the problems of multiculturalism while riding the crests of economic booms and technological advances, making fine distinctions between communitarianism and cosmopolitanism, but in the practice of law and politics they often find it difficult to imagine a form of ethical neighborliness amongst peoples of different cultures or races or religions. Colonial and postcolonial societies were given no such options, nor comparable privileges of economic development or academic reflection. Colonized societies had "multiculturalism" imposed upon them from above, and they evolved an ethic of survival that encompassed the presence of "otherness" as a practice of everyday life and language. Of course, you can fault me for being too general, even sentimental, but this feeling I have is grounded in a very real sense of "coexistence" that inhabits societies that are often too quickly described as lacking the liberal virtues of toleration and individualism. Even as I say this, I need to acknowledge the presence of Hindutva nationalists, the profound discrimination against women, untouchables, gays. I deny none of this, but I still want to assert the peculiar kind of negotiated accommodationism that is part of the neighborliness and hospitality of many postcolonial societies.

Related to this is another concept that I am trying to work through at the moment – vernacular cosmopolitanism as a mark of the postcolonial experience. W. E. B. Du Bois, Gandhi, Ambedkar, Fanon, Toni Morrison – these are writers, thinkers, and politicians who did not inherit a "great tradition" of worldly knowledge as a cultural inheritance. The enslaved, the colonized, the untouchable dalits earn and learn their way through a world culture as a way of understanding not simply its glories but its horrors, not simply its major events but its small, forgotten voices. The postcolonial endorses a vernacular cosmopolitanism that has to translate between cultures and across them in order to survive, not in order to assert the sovereignty of a civilized class, or the spiritual autonomy of a revered ideal. Vernacular cosmopolitans are the heirs of Walter Benjamin's view of modernity, that every act of civilization is also an act of barbarism. Vernacular cosmopolitans find their ethical and creative direction in learning that hard lesson of ambivalence and forbearance. My postcolonial provenance includes a middle-class cosmopolitan intellectual experience – Bombay, Oxford, London, and the US – and it would not have been possible for me to think postcoloniality without thinking through Marxism or semiotics or psychoanalysis, or feminism or socialism, or post-structuralism. The work of feminist scholars and activists was particularly important to me in finding my feet, because they took seriously the place of the body – psyche, affect, skin-ego, fantasy – in deciphering the discriminatory structures of the body politic. This is a simple point about the life world of the word "postcolonialism" that, in my own experience, is somewhat eclectic, ex-centric and translational in its perspectival and pedagogical formation. Is there an overarching, overwhelming thematic that comes out of this bricolage? Well, I think there is. It is the conviction that being colonial or postcolonial is a way of "becoming modern," of surviving modernity, without the myth of individual or cultural "sovereignty" that is so central a tenet of liberal individualism and its sense of serial progress or cultural evolution. The disciplinary and temporal orders of Progress, Rule, Rationality, and the State become corrupted in the colonial and postcolonial conditions where they play a double, aporetic role: as norms of value they make emancipatory claims, crucial to the definition of modern citizenship; however, as part of the power practices of the colonial state they create inequality, injustice, and indignity. It is from the interstices of this paradoxical situation that the postcolonial perspective emerges. It unsettles the ubiquity, the ordinariness of those orders of common sense, those polarities of perception, that modernization has bequeathed on the rest of the world. So, for instance, postcoloniality is open to the contingent and hybrid articulations of the sacred-in-the-secular, psychic fantasy as part of social rationality, the archaic within the contemporaneous.

The Satanic Verses provides a prototypical postcolonial problematic: a radical stylist unsettles some of the most cherished conventions of the realist traditions of the liberal novel in order to establish a form of migrant mimesis, which he repeatedly acknowledges as a mediatory act of "translation." The risks and trials of translation – which always include accusations of mistranslation and treachery – result in a dramatic denouement. Although Rushdie's tragic history was frequently represented as symbolic of the fate of Western liberalism imperiled by the growth of Islamic fundamentalism, *Rushdie vs. the Bradford Mosque* was only one, quick reading of the event. What time and distance teach us is that both Rushdie and his opponents in England (I am not talking of Iran) shared a common postcolonial predicament. Both parties represented a growing, global gulf between political citizenship, still largely negotiated in "national" and statist terms, and cultural citizenship which is often community-centered, transnational, diasporic, hybrid. Rushdie's book, at its best, was an attempt to evolve a new language of affiliation and creation that emerged from this "split" citizenship. He sought to explore an image of vernacular cosmopolitical life through the translational worlds of migration – Sufiyan, the owner of the Kandahar Cafe in Southall reads Ovid on the problematic transformation of cultural selves – in order to oppose both Mrs. Torture's (Thatcher) authoritarianism and Islamic fundamentalism. This is of course my reading of the book; it may not have been Mr. Rushdie's intention; nor can I argue for its success in terms of *realpolitik*. But it does seem to me to be textually plausible and politically hopeful as a postcolonial proposal – not a resolution. It suggests a way out of the ideological polarity, liberalism/ fundamentalism, which is far too simplistic, far too symmetrical, and, ironically, mutually sustaining – what would the one do without the other. My reading returns the "conflict" to the contemporary grounds of its emergence, a postcolonial Britain; and it gets away from an Orientalist scenario with the dogma-bound Ayatollah slugging at the free-spirited liberal Artist. The real challenge may be to work out the historic and cultural modalities of this double and disjunctive inscription of the political and the cultural citizen, a citizen who is part of the same geographical territory, but belongs to different temporalities of cultural and customary tradition or vice versa. The history of liberalism needs to be rewritten from the perspective of what happened in the colonial and postcolonial world post the modernist project of civilizing mission and its hybridized genealogies developed over a century and a half. It doesn't surprise me at all that some of the most distinguished, revisionary perspectives on liberalism and critiques of neoliberalism should be coming out of places like India, South Africa, Latin America, and the Middle East. The devil is less in the dogma and more in the enlivening detail.

JC: I agree entirely that, once one finds an angle of vision from which to decenter Eurocentric narratives of late modernity – narratives now mired in exquisitely irrelevant arguments about the death, survival, or rigor mortis of the nation-state – it is possible to read world history in interesting new ways. Take, for instance, the current obsession with civil society. Much contemporary discussion, scholarly and populist alike, treats the "struggle" for this utopian idea as a symptom of the triumph of democracy and the free market; as the completion of a civilizing progress which had been interrupted, rudely, by the perverse history of the rise and fall of the Soviet Union. But the pursuit of civil society ca.1986–99, in Africa and Central Europe, parallels a similar process in Britain and Western Europe toward the end of the eighteenth century. Why in these specific periods and places? Both were epochs during which the world was undergoing a palpable compression of space and time; both were moments of great transformation, ontological and geographical alike, in which the very construction of social order, of human being-in-the-world, of citizenship and subjectivity, were in question. The first Age of

Revolution, 1789–1848, gave us not merely the ideological scaffolding of modernity, but also the conceptual lexicon of the orthodox social sciences. What is interesting about the current Age of Revolution, the age symbolically associated with 1989, is the failure of that modernist vision, of its social sciences and humanities, to make adequate sense of the metamorphosis of the world in which we live, especially when viewed from its postcolonial peripheries.

HB: Can I ask a question? Do you think that the emergence of the emphasis on civil society, human rights, and the new emergent disciplines may be tied together? How important do you think are the issues of migration, diaspora, refugees, and other forms of minoritization for the redefinition of modernity in the global age? Does minoritization evoke some anthropological anxieties?

JC: The issue of migration and movement is crucial. For a start, the immigrant has become a living metonym for the global age, for a world imagined as a four-dimensional series of flows, for a world no longer reducible to an international order of territorial polities existing in perpetuity. The immigrant both reinforces and ruptures boundaries. She/he is ambiguity, contradiction, doubling incarnate: a cipher of new signs and practices, of novel imaginings, of possibility, of danger and pollution, illness and contagion. The postmodern witch. Interestingly, Mary Douglas, by associating dirt and defilement with matter out of place, anticipated the polluting attributes ascribed to the immigrant. But there is more to the matter of migration and movement than mere symbolic transgression. With the ascendance of neoliberalism, as we hear *ad nauseam*, the present and future of the nation-state is itself called into question. Until recently, it was fashionable in many circles to proclaim its imminent demise; thank goodness, that particular mode of trivialization is *passé*. One of the more interesting corollaries of the question – there are many, of course – has to do with the nature of boundaries that are no longer barriers. The sovereign domain of the nation-state is no longer effectively signified by closure and confinement: for example, the capacity to control the flow of information, so fundamental to the semiotic politics of imagining community, barely exists anymore, largely because of the open nature of cyberspace and electronic media. The regulation of the flow and velocity of money – again, an old Weberian diacritic of the modern state – is seriously undermined. Compromised, too, is exclusive control over the legitimate means of violence, which, these days, may also be bought and sold on the market. (Worldkill, I call it. Buy yourself a coup, or a counter-coup, from Executive Action!) Add to this the hugely heightened flow of populations in recent years, especially in search of work under post-Fordist conditions, and the dimensions along which the nation-state constitutes itself are going to alter palpably. Of course, given the political economy of the global order, the degree to which states have been eroded, and have found themselves transformed, is highly variable. (In some parts of the world, "the state" barely exists at all. In others, like the USA and Germany, it remains very powerful; which may be why the US and Germany are the two coordinates on the academic map at which there remains most cynicism about the very existence of "globalism" and where the tendency is strongest to see "it" as no different from earlier forms of internationalism.) In this ever more refractory universe, the problem of what constitutes a society, of what constitutes a culture, becomes especially acute. As Ferguson and Gupta have said, there are significant methodological implications to the fact that, with the transnational flow of humans, it is no longer possible to equate culture with place. Where does, say, "Senegalese culture" situate itself? In Dakar? In the Senegalese countryside? In Paris or New York? In the world music section of Tower Records? On the net? Clearly, in all of these places and virtual spaces.

HB: You are quite right: what it means to be Senegalese or what Senegalese culture signifies is a more disseminatory and iterative experience – each "sign" of Senegal has to be reread and revalued in the practice and context of its enunciation. It is difficult to synchronize "culture" and "place" within the containments of the contemporary nation-space. Aren't current forms of nationalism less about the coherent origins of a national culture and its belonging, and more about making a restorative (often rebarbative) claim in the name of an "authentic" culture that is thought to be in danger of being lost, obscured, or appropriated? It seems to me that current "origins" of nationalism and fundamentalism have everything to do with an anxiety provoked by the complex processes of cultural hybridization that challenge atavistic identifications. Such hybridization is as much part of the national scene as it is a global phenomenon – it does not have to be exclusively associated with the various diasporas of our times. But there are political forces that are so threatened by the kind of hybridization that you describe, and by the fact that political citizenship and cultural citizenship can stand at cross-purposes, that there is also the pressure to create a kind of coercive, lethal closure, and all the technologies that allow the dissemination of cultural signs can also cause them to congeal with unspeakable violence. Virtual reality, the Internet – such an apparently immediate, open and accessible cultural form – has also become the trysting place of some of the most violent and vociferous voices of fundamentalism in America, India, and other parts of the world.

JC: Sadly, that is true. . . . Appearances, of course, are both revealing and misleading. Unspeakable violence in the name of nationalism and identity politics is certainly not new. But there are features of that violence in the here-and-now that do speak to a perception of crisis at the core of the modernist world order. Why did the fatwah on Salman Rushdie evoke such horror in Europe? I don't think it had a great deal to do with the fate of the man himself, although that did carry its own fascination. It had much more to do with the frightening notion that a religious leader in Iran could pass a capital sentence against an Indian living in Britain and have a realistic chance of it being executed by someone unknown. This act, at a stroke, called into question the international legal system: its notions of jurisdiction, sovereignty, and the legitimate exercise of violence. What is more, it made the "international terrorist"

– that shadowy figure who slips across borders, who is invisible and anonymous, who eludes all legal jurisdictions – into an instrument of a justice at once divine and secular. Like the immigrant, the international terrorist erases boundaries and opens up new ruptures in which the uncontrollable, the unmentionable, might take place. Similar ruptures are opened up by the development of cyberspace, of course. Its capacity to cross dimensions and coordinates, to bring into shared discursive spaces things previously kept apart, to force conversations among those whose voices might never have resonated together, has its dark underside. Which is why it, too, has elicited so many calls for regulation in an age of deregulation. Its impact on conventional politics, as we have seen lately, can be quite disconcerting, at once decried and despised and yet decisive. The specter of unregulated flow and its impact on local sovereignty seems everywhere to be a matter of concern, even moral panic – and violence. I was fascinated in 1995–6 by the British obsession with the Euro: the sovereign coin and sovereignty, it seems, became elided in the English imagination. Remove one and you negate the other. This iconic apparition of an infiltrating Europe, of boundaries violated, loomed very large indeed. (Much like that other, more persistent apparition: formerly colonized peoples of color who "return" to the UK.) All of which expressed itself both in the brutal treatment of refugees and asylum seekers by British immigration authorities and in skinhead nationalist violence in the streets and soccer stadiums of various elsewheres. The two species of savagery are, of course, much more similar than polite British society might like to admit.

The paradox of so-called postmodern subjectivity is this: the more multiple and dispersed it becomes, the more it appears to breed its own will to totalization. Nationality, ethnicity, gender, generation, race, position: each element of a fragmented subjectivity makes its own claim to a potent form of closure. Which, dialectically speaking, sounds like an impossibility.

HB: What seems to be genuinely complex about what you were saying (I want to return for a moment to the Rushdie event) is the attempt to understand and describe a situation in which one site of jurisdiction is not simply replaced by another jurisdictional territory, but the condition in which there is a more general jurisdictional unsettlement and a jurisdictional doubting and doubling produced by the dissemination of cultural forms and contents. For instance, the Westernized liberal response to the fatwah was that it was an archaic practice, a violation of all that was liberal, modern, civilized, and, in any case, its jurisdiction could not exceed the territory of the Ayatollah's Iran. However, the belief of those members of the Islamic diaspora who supported the fatwah was quite different. They considered Khomeini's jurisdictional domain in virtual, not strictly territorial, terms. Khomeini's authority was not restricted by the boundaries of the nation-state; the power of the fatwah was invested in the bodily presence of believers wherever they happened to live communally and transnationally. Some British Muslims were quite explicit about this. So once again, you see, the postcolonial condition is one where, within nations and across them, there is a split imperative between the associations of political citizenship and the affiliative and affective conditions of cultural citizenship.

JC: At the same time, though, it effected social death for Rushdie. In this sense, it was a classical performative, *sensu stricto*: the enunciation of the fatwah was its own effect.

HB: Yes, it was. The enunciation of the fatwah did have its own effect. It threatened the death of an individual, but it brought with it a great historic fear of the death of individualism, the death of a certain notion of the liberal artist, the death of the possibility of "authorship," to the autonomy of the subject and the freedom of cultural expression. The fatwah, for all its "savagery," pushed the neoliberal discourse to engage with its own limit-texts: what are the governmental and cultural constraints on the universal value of "autonomy"? How "liberal" are the foundationalist assumptions of secular democracy? What are the limits of tolerance?

JC: . . . which, I suppose, is why "fundamentalism," as a standardized nightmare, is so readily equated with savagery in both the liberal and the conservative imagination.

The Culture of Psychoanalysis

JC: Let me push you a little bit on your interest in psychoanalysis. We are sitting in the Department of Anthropology at the University of Chicago, a place in which devil's advocacy is on home turf. From the perspective of the anthropology of late modernity, psychoanalysis appears to be a profoundly Western cultural practice. It apotheosizes the radically individuated subject, a peculiarly Eurocentric idea, making it the prime site of therapy which, in turn, depends on the construction, synoptically, of a normative life course, of a coherent notion of identity, as its point of reference.

HB: The ventriloquism of the bourgeoisie?

JC: Precisely. From the perspective of a critical anthropology, to make a therapeutic subject of the neoliberal self – with its own autonomous being-in-the-world, its own authorial voice, even its own "private" pathology – is to refract culture-in-practice into applied science, to turn an ideological trope into a positivist sense of personhood. As a critic of neoliberalism, but one who values psychoanalysis as a fertile source of social analysis, how do you react to this anthropological challenge?

HB: Psychoanalysis is not easily recuperable within the liberal paradigm, nor is it easily framed by the neoliberal agenda. Neoliberal pragmatism, with its faith in the rationalization of social processes, is hardly compatible with the psychoanalytic interest in the place of projection, introjection, and other facets of identification and social fantasy as they play out in the interstices between private and public life. Secondly, the distinctive mark of the neoliberal self is an autonomy founded on the advantages of the free market, while the psychoanalytic subject is a split, decentered entity that only becomes "it-self" as an after-effect of the intersubjective experience. Finally, we live in a technophilic age in which there is a boundless, unreal sense of epochal optimism about scientific progress, the overcoming of nature, the achievement of individual freedoms. Psychoanalytic temporality is markedly different from such historicisms and teleologies. The epistemological assumptions and ethical commitments of psychoanalysis emerge from its commitment to "deferred action" which is the temporality that introduces the unconscious into the procedures of everyday life and rationality. It requires one to continually "work through" the past-in-the-present, to negotiate the relation of memory to history, to relocate the psychic in the construction of the social, or the other way around. Psychoanalysis turns its clinical and philosophical attention to melancholia, failure, the restlessness and hesitation of the mind, the gap between our desires and needs, aspirations and achievements, by striking against the vain culture of narcissism and self-satisfied consumption that is celebrated today under the sign of Generation X.

What seems to me particularly interesting for our own times, and for the kinds of questions we have been asking, is the nature of psychoanalytic temporality. The fact that the moment of an event may not be the moment of the meaningfulness of the event. That the "agency" of an action may have to be deciphered, in a time-lag, at some distance from its performance. A childhood trauma may present itself as a symptom much later in life, but the "meaning" of the sign of distress must not be simply traced back to the "original event" because that moment of origin is not a cause or a source "in-itself"; it has been translated, transformed, revised and rearticulated so that the symptom must be dealt with as a contingent and conjunctural sign, a constellation of (what we may call) an "archaic contemporaneity" or a "foreshortened futurity," or some such complex articulation of past, present, future in disjunct synchrony that has to be staged and interpreted. Sorry this is all so conversationally cumbersome but it is the best I can do.

The very structure of our conversation today may have illustrated this kind of reconstruction of historic events. In trying to frame postcoloniality, we telescoped the fifties into the nineties and then set that articulation in the context of a third term – the sixties – at an oblique angle to the other two moments. Postcoloniality, our defining term, became less a name or a topic, and more a way of making connections or articulations across a range of topics and themes, a locus for theoretical and political reflection rather than a label. Such a constellated conjunction is precisely the kind of event, psychic or social, that psychoanalysis helps you to work with or work through. For psychoanalysis never just attends to the past-in-the-present, but catches up with a proleptic past, a past literally dying to be born in the present so that we may survive the future. I think psychoanalysis takes "survival" seriously. Oppression and emancipation are seen as agential conditions, but to survive is often considered a form of passivity, the denial of agency. This is deeply neglectful of a very significant area of phenomenological and political life. Survival is the agency of the everyday, the strategic actions and activities of the group or the individual in the interstices of major events or grand narratives. The material practices of every-day life require continual ethical attention. In the wear and tear of history the self needs to be darned as tears open up. Loose threads have to be knotted knowing that they will come apart tomorrow and will have to be knotted again. There is an ethics of survival, and an agency of survival, that psycho-analysis attends to with patience and purpose, learning and revealing the rules of living from the ongoing flux of desires, identities, and instincts – these informing intimations of human life that can so easily be lost when we read our histories in the light of uplifting, tall stories of normative principle that institute normalizing procedures.

JC: That is persuasive, Homi, but it raises a question. To what extent is your characterization of psychoanalysis founded on a very specific genus of human subject? A bourgeois Western subject, not to put too fine a point on it? What about non-Western forms of selfhood, in which the construction of the person lies less in iteration than in irreducibly social practices of collaboration, inter-connection, interpellation? In a mode of being, that is, in which it is all but impossible to decide where one "person" ends and another begins?

HB: To the extent to which the psychoanalytic subject, as I have suggested, is constituted in and through the intersubjective realm of symbolic, linguistic, and performative practices, I cannot imagine it to be anything other than socially and communally constructed. The "talking cure," when productively executed, is precisely a social practice of collaboration and interaction and interconnection. The analyst and the analysand are in a dynamic, even dialec-tical relation of transference and counter-transference, of projection and introjection. What is at stake is not simply the exploration of fantasy and the unconscious, but a painful lesson in setting the bounds of reality and acknowl-edging it as being a negotiated realm of meaning and social existence. The objectifying discourse of language and experience mediates the psychoanalytic relationship, and never lets it become simply dyadic, because language is the third term that makes both parties confront the contingent and interruptive reality of a historically shared world outside of any binary relationship of Self and Other.

JC: Where, then, experientially and epistemically, does that subject begin and end? It is one thing to say that psychoanalysis always demands a rela-tional subject . . .

HB: . . . or a processual one.

JC: . . . or a processual one, yes. But a relational subject, in the Western imaginary, is also an autonomous person with clear biological and legal margins without which it is impossible to conceive of intersubjectivity. What happens in cultural and historical contexts in which the boundary of the subject is not necessarily coterminous with the biolegal individual?

HB: What psychoanalysis allows us to think through is indeed the contin-gency of boundaries, the fact that within a particular social relation the bound-ary may demarcate "you" as a "person" at point A, and in another relational moment, you may have to reconstruct "personhood" at point B in a different identificatory mode. What psychoanalysis allows you to think through is the possibility that those boundaries may fall in different places at different times and yet be connected without being congruent. There is no way of transcending your splitting, your anxiety or ambivalence; but there are ways in which you can relate and reflect upon these conditions and follow a mode of conduct based on a deeper understanding of these affects and their psychic and somatic consequences for your personality. And the relation between A and B may neither be synchronic nor continuous. Which is why there is, in the Oedipal myth of psychoanalysis, this unending struggle between demand and desire. The subject is always in excess of itself, supplementary to its selfhood and it is this "excess" or liminality that becomes the basis of the intersubjective relation. As a practical example of this "relationality/sociality-through-excess," I think of your earlier Senegalese example with "subject" substituted for "culture." "Where does, say, the Senegalese subject situate itself? In Dakar? In the Senegalese countryside? In Paris or New York? In the world music section of Tower Records? On the Net? Clearly, in all of these places and virtual spaces."

There is a circulatory network of signs that is "Senegalese," undeniably so, but it is constructed through a metonymic and iterative process, in excess of any singular or punctual location of being Senegalese. Such a process of identification produces an intersubjective and intertextual relation that we would still recognize, in its differential and disseminatory aspect, as a kind of Senegalese "being-in-time."

The Birth of a Nation

HB: I want to ask you, John, about the painful birth of a "new" nation in South Africa. All the elements of postcoloniality, cultural translation, and hybridity that we have associated with the neoliberal, historical moment surely apply to South Africa too. And yet, in the midst of it all, Mandela steps out, and the rest of the world, East and West, sees it as an exemplary, grace-giving moment, a redemptive act, an exemplary site. What's going on?

JC: As I have said to you before, Homi, the reason that South Africa grabbed so much world attention in the mid-1990s is because it represented a heroic, hopeful effort to build a modernist nation-state under postmodern postmortem conditions; at just the time, that is, when the contradictions of modernity were becoming inescapable. As Eric Hobsbawm said then, the African National Congress was perhaps the last great Euronationalist movement. He was not altogether wrong.

HB: Was he wrong at all?

JC: Probably not. The fetishism of constitutionality in configuring the nation, the obsession with equality before the law in imagining a "new" South Africa, the faith in a future of "rational" development, human rights, and social justice; all these things were narrated in the language of modernist sovereign statehood. And neoliberal capitalism. (This despite the fact that the country had one of the few powerful communist parties left in the world.) In 1956 the African National Congress and other organizations in the anti-apartheid Congress Alliance signed the Freedom Charter, a call to struggle with a distinctly socialist mandate. Once in office, however, the ANC let that commitment go. In part, it had little alternative. For one thing, global economic realities had shifted. For another, the ANC found itself faced with a political paradox, at least in the early years. Because of the peculiar nature of the negotiated transition, it inherited government but not the state whose old apartheid personnel, especially in the civil service, had been given tenure.

HB: How much of the state has remained?

JC: . . . in the control of former ruling whites? Well, for one thing, the military has a disproportion of old cadres. So does the financial sector . . .

HB: You mean the governance of banks?

JC: Yes, although, since 1994, there has been a sustained effort on the part of the ANC to seize the state. But the more fundamental point I wanted to make is that South Africa is perhaps the most dramatic instance of a contemporary polity living in the netherworld between two antithetical images of nation-statehood. On one hand, it speaks the familiar language of late nineteenth and early twentieth-century Euronationalism, the Andersonian (or, more accurately, Durkheimean) language of an imagined community-in-the-making under the material trusteeship of a democratically elected government. On the other, it has become radically neoliberal. In a recent essay, Steve Robins, an anthropologist at the University of the Western Cape, makes a cogent observation: while racial capitalism was excoriated by the ANC in the late apartheid years, he says, something that looks awfully like it is now in the ascendant. What is more, the Mandela regime brooked no criticism of it; nor does Mbeki. Constitutively and constitutionally, race has given way to class. But, demographically speaking, emergent class lines still bear a very tight correlation with old patterns of racial division. In the upshot, while more blacks have a stake in aspects of the economy, the emergence of the so-called "liberation aristocracy" is quite striking – the vast majority of unemployed, unwaged, and homeless remain people of color; this notwithstanding repeated calls for their "empowerment" and for whites to repudiate their undiminished sense of privilege. The post-apartheid regime has left most of the wealth of the country in the hands of the same citizens who monopolized it before, and has not tried to fashion a welfare state. Like everywhere else, a great deal has been ceded to multinational corporations; like everywhere else, the public sector has been severely cut back. This is well captured in a television documentary made a few years ago by John Pilger, "Apartheid is Not Dead." The title says it all; although, if anything, the film underplayed the degree to which the effects of global capital, not to mention neoliberal ideology, had worsened the predicament of all but a few blacks. Liberation and (neo)liberalization, coming together, have added up to less, not more. Not surprisingly, the government was blisteringly condemnatory of Pilger and elicited the counter-reproach of

being in heavy denial. In fact, some South Africans claim that white criticism
is being systematically stifled, if not by censorship, then by more subtle techniques. I have also heard disillusioned former anti-apartheid activists argue
that anything said in censure of the ANC or, more generally, of postcolonial
culture and society is likely to be deemed "racist."

HB: Why then, John, has South Africa emerged as this great moral corr-
ective to the rest of the world? Is this redemptive imaginary sustained by
Mandela?

JC: Mandela is iconic of the route by which South Africa has entered into
the consciousness of a watching world. He is not its cause. Indeed, to attribute
cause to his charisma alone would be to ascribe to a *simpliste* Big Man theory
of history. As I said, I think that South Africa has come to represent the last
great hope for the modernist nation-state and the telos upon which it is
erected. In the wake of 1989 – marked especially by the genocidal fracturing
of Yugoslavia, by the Chechen and Rwandan catastrophes, by the demise (or
near demise) of the state in Somalia and elsewhere in Africa, by uncontained
ethnonationalist violence in the fissures opened up between nation and state
in so many places – South Africa was the one success story. Or so it seemed.
Here was an instance of liberation through liberalism, liberation apparently
facilitated by the rational forces of the market, by a democratic social movement, by the good offices of international institutions. Here was a nation that
won its freedom without a bloody revolution and did not celebrate its emancipation by an orgy of repressive violence. All of which reassured many people
the world over that the liberal dream of history-making was still thinkable,
even in the most austere and impossible of conditions. That everybody's fright
nightmare did not come to be, that a Judeo-Christian sense of morality prevailed, that a "peaceful" transition actually occurred . . . these things surprised
even the most sanguine. This, of course, does simplify the story a great deal.
Hidden, sometimes not so hidden, in the process was a great degree of brutality, a civil war in fact, fomented by the apartheid state; a reign of terror now
fading into the recesses of memory, except among those who suffered its bombs
and bullets and beatings. That narrative of peaceful transition also occludes the
forms of economic violence still being suffered by many black South Africans.
More are now out of work than before: South Africa has an unofficial,
acknowledged unemployment rate of 38 percent, which is probably a gross
underestimate. For those between 15 and 40, in particular, things look very
bleak indeed.

HB: And South Africa is predominantly a young nation.

JC: It is a young nation and it is predominantly young black males who have
no real prospects of work, of the wherewithal to marry, of social reproduction.
The florescence throughout the 1990s of occult-related violence and witch
burnings in the countryside relates closely to this. It also dramatizes the two
sides of the story of South Africa, the two sides, *sui generis*, of the neoliberal
nation-state at the end of the twentieth century. On one side is South Africa,
the newest first-world nation, realizing its millennial dreams. On the other is

a postcolony with all the problems endemic to those who live, in the slipstream of late capitalism, under the dominion of the masters of the "free market": large numbers of unwaged citizens, crime as an increasingly banalized mode of production and income redistribution, terrifying violence of various kinds, the demonization of immigrants, and the attachment of blame for social disorder to young black males; as if none of this had anything to do with the legacy of apartheid. Such are the wages of a tragic dialectic working itself out at great human expense.

HB: But what is the alternative?

JC: I wish I knew the answer. Part of me is deeply pessimistic because I see all of these things as an outworking of this new Age of Revolution, of the rise of millennial capitalism and its forms of production. I mean here not merely material production; also symbolic production, cultural production, the production of identities. Ours are times in which it is difficult to determine where and how history is being made. As a result, for many people at least, we seem to be living in an Age of Impossibilities. Or, more accurately, an Age of Simultaneous Possibility and Impossibility. For young black South Africans, everything appears both possible and impossible right now. There is no regular employment, no steady income, no security, no basis on which to create a family or an adult life, no tomorrow. Yet, at the same time, they do not have to look far to see "new" business people making fortunes very quickly. Images of easy wealth come at them through cyberspace and through the media, images in which capitalism expresses itself through rampant consumption. Capitalism, to go back to Marx and Weber, has always had a mystery, a specter, at its core. In its neoliberal form, that mystery inheres in space-time compression: in the capacity to move people, objects, information, and currency across the planet without any visible effort but with value added. All of which makes it seem possible to produce wealth without working; a possibility underscored by the much-narrated centrality to the economy of both legal forms of gambling, notably the stockmarket, and their illegal spin-offs, like pyramid schemes, which are as epidemic in Africa as they were in Central Europe a few years back. No wonder capitalism is perceived by postcolonial peoples primarily as a mode of consumption. And as a millennial cult which, if one could only discover its alchemic charms, might yield up untold treasures. This is why there is so much experimental practice, so much dabbling in the occult, in postcolonies. Here is cargo capitalism with a neoliberal twist. Cargo cults in the colonial period were largely communal movements; they were cults of the repressed calling for a return. If only it were possible to appropriate the secret techniques of the white man – their hidden Bible, their means of bringing planes to land – collective riches would follow. Now, by contrast, it is individual supplicants at the altar of capital who seek salvation and stores of wealth albeit, to complicate matters a bit, often along with a measure of moral regeneration. No longer is it The Trumpet Shall Sound. It is The Cash Register Will Ring.

HB: Has this occult evasion replaced utopianism?

JC: It is a form of utopianism. Its means and ends are different, as are its referents. But it has not, as I hinted, erased talk about communal regeneration. There is a lot of that around, especially in the countryside. In part, this has taken the form of efforts to "cleanse" communities of malign forces – witches, corrupt leaders, and the like – and to restore moral order. But it has increasingly become embroiled in struggles over rights. The language of the law, right and entitlement, takes on magnified importance in postcolonies built on difference and radical heterogeneity; those which suffer a lack of hyphen-nation, wherein nation-and-state do not fuse imaginatively into a body politic with internal coherence. In these postcolonies, law appears to provide the only lexicon in terms of which the incommensurable may be negotiated. South Africa, like India, is composed of a multiplicity of identities, many of them emergent and hybrid, all competing on a distinctly inchoate terrain for self-expression, for cultural recognition, for political and material entitlement, for their very being-in-the-world. Under these conditions, "the" law and its ultimate point of reference, the constitution, becomes a standard of value in terms of which social value can be produced, defended, capitalized, traded, consumed. Indeed, it stands to the creation and transaction of social value as does money to material life: as an apparently universal, neutral standard and medium of exchange. (I stress "apparent," since we all know how deceiving is the claim of anything to being a neutral, universal medium of transaction.) The resort to law takes on exaggerated salience once people make demands on each other, or on the nation-state, in the name of a right to cultural difference, ethnicity, race, gender, generation. But there is another complexity, I think. In the "new" South Africa, and perhaps other postcolonies, the struggle for rights has four modalities: universal human rights, the great fetish of the neoliberal age, which transcend the nation-state; the rights of citizenship, which attach to right-bearing individuals, but exclude immigrants; cultural rights which are guaranteed to people by virtue of ethnic identities; and communal rights, which are claimed by the populations of villages, towns, provinces, and the like. (Notable, here, has been the assertion of a right to be protected by the state against the release of convicted criminals; much like, in the USA, the demand that a community be informed of the arrival in their midst of a pedophile). Claims in the name of these different species of rights, which sometimes flatly contradict one another, often potentiate conflict.

HB: What are the limits of each of them?

JC: That is deeply contested, and cannot be answered in the abstract. Which, interestingly, is why witch killing has become a subject of debate in South Africa. The constitution guarantees cultural rights and, hence, protects belief in the occult as long as they do not interfere with other kinds of rights.

HB: But that is an impossibility.

JC: Of course it is. If the various species of rights could coexist seamlessly, occult-related violence would not have become such a contested issue. Or as an intriguing one. Take the following instance. A group of villagers in the

Northern Province put to death a person whom they accuse of witchcraft. The police arrive on the scene and immediately treat the incident as first degree murder. At trial, the defense argues that the accused believe in witchcraft, which is their constitutional right; that, furthermore, this is not just a cultural right, but also an individual right to freedom of religion. Their clients, they continue, hold that they had sufficient forensic evidence, obtained by proper customary means, to prove that the deceased had, in fact, killed her victims by means of medicines; that they had, therefore, not committed a common crime, but had engaged in cultural policing, which is tacitly recognized under section 12 of the constitution. What is the court to do? Judges have reacted in various ways up to now: some have taken traditional beliefs and practices to constitute cause for mitigation, others have refused to do so. (Among the former, especially white magistrates, a few have treated witch beliefs as something akin to alcoholic inebriation or mental disturbance, thereby equating culture with diminished responsibility and treating it as a pathology.) A local Tswana judge once told me that, in his view, there is no principled basis on which to deny that cultural policing, *per se*, is sanctioned by the constitution; that, consequently, witch killing ought perhaps to have the same status in mitigating a "murder" as does killing in self-defense under European law. It is clear, in sum, why the potential for conflict between cultural rights and other kinds of rights should be so problematic for the postcolonial state. What about the right to life under American law of somebody who enters a house and threatens its owner with a gun? If the property owner can demonstrate that they believed in all good faith . . .

HB: That they were going to kill you . . .

JC: Exactly. The fixation in the USA on the right to carry arms, and to use deadly force, is a piece of local culture that is regarded as irrational even, dare I say it, pathological in many parts of the world.

HB: So would the legal claim then be: "Had this witch existed, I would have been dead."

JC: Not necessarily me, more likely my children. What is more, it is seldom that a witch is accused without forensic evidence, sometimes even in the form of a cadaver that had allegedly been used in the preparation of medicines. As I said, the courts have begun to take beliefs in mystical evil much more seriously than before. While none have, to my knowledge, ever treated witch killings as cultural policing or as a culturally appropriate form of communal self-defense, some judges have declared that the judicial system ought to regard witchcraft as a real and present phenomenon. The problem remains, of course, that, while talk of cultural rights abounds, culture is criminalized whenever "traditional" practices, especially "traditional" modes of legal remedy, are deemed dangerous by the state. Which, in turn, raises the very complicated question of what precisely is a "dangerous cultural practice"? Zulus were allowed to carry around clubs in apartheid South Africa – so-called knobkerries, cudgels with a capacity to inflict grievous bodily harm – because they were deemed, explicitly, to be "cultural weapons". Yet, during the 1960s

and 1970s, Sikhs working on London Transport were not allowed to wear
turbans; they were said, among other things, to be a health hazard. Now which
of these is the "dangerous cultural practice"? Which is likely to endanger
others? The threat of the turban, as we all know well, lay in its symbolic power,
its power to signal that the empire was striking back. (Also that the empire
might just go on strike, and thereby cripple metropolitan London!) The Punjabi
headdress served as a visible, ever circulating reminder of imperial contraflow:
of the stream of immigrants who were crossing the hermetic edges of British
nationhood, thus to pollute and dilute its sovereign exclusivity. Note the crashing irony, in the case of the turban. Here lay the danger in this dangerous cultural practice.

HB: What you have so cogently shown, John, is a profound contradiction
or undecidability that inhabits the governmentality of the nation-state today.
The constitutional right to a belief in witchcraft is, I take it, an attempt to
democratize the "culture" of legitimation on the grounds of which the state
addresses its newly enfranchised, "nationalized" peoples. But the sphere of
legality is in conflict with this expanded understanding of rights. This is,
perhaps, an illustration of one of my pet theories, that what we actually mean
when we talk of the attenuated sovereignty of the nation is not that nations
have suddenly become subordinated to a new transnational polity, but that
the national people have a split or double affiliation that is often conflictual.
As political citizens they are law-abiding, tax-paying members of society who
provide the "imagined community" with what Benedict Anderson described
as a sense of synchronicity and sociological solidarity. But as cultural citizens
they may have affective and identity-bearing affiliations centered around
sexual preference, cultural or group differences, "orthodox" practices, religious
beliefs or customs that may not fit the agenda of modernity or modernization,
and so on. Spatially, this leads often to the charge against minorities that they
"ghettoize" themselves, and create their own minor *gemeinschaft* life worlds. At
the level of cultural temporality, minorities are often accused of having "tra-
ditionalist" or orthodox affiliations, or that they are insistently experimental,
unsettled, and avant-garde. Both may be true; but what interests me is the
way in which the articulation of "difference" often comes to be recognized and
represented as a kind of temporal undecidability neither modern nor non-
modern that is troubling in its hybrid juxtaposition of values. As if some transcendent teleology of national–cultural being has been violated. What this
often means is that the sense of contemporaneity, or the "now-time" of modernity, is being disturbed and questioned.

JC: I think that is right, Homi. But, speaking of undecidability, what seems
to me to be undecidable right now is the character of the twenty-first-century
nation-state. My guess is that there are going to arise new forms of federalism, forms that are not necessarily grounded in territorial contiguity. There are
many ways to think about this. But it may well be for reasons having to do
with the growth of the global economy that, in the future, states are going to
have to devolve a great deal away from themselves in order to survive. What

constitute jurisdictions, in both form and content, are likely to change. As I intimated earlier, it is difficult to see the nation-state of the coming century constituting itself on the basis of anything like the modernist sense of a common weal. Apart from all else, few states control their own tax bases, their currencies, their labor markets, their productive sectors, or the distribution of commodities any more. Their regulatory functions have changed fundamentally under the impact of the worldwide electronic commons, a virtual terrain whose complexity is only now being comprehended and then largely by the corporate sector.

HB: But will we need to name territories in particular ways?

JC: I think there may well be major struggles over the definition and the naming of territories in the future; even, probably, over what it is that constitutes jurisdictional space. On one hand, states are sure to expend great effort to sustain a notion of political community, however federally distended it might be, by appealing to the functional necessity of exclusive sovereignty. And perhaps, to the unthinkability of anything else. On the other, I would anticipate increasing efforts to assert alternative kinds of jurisdiction. Recall, again, the Rushdie fatwah, a claim to jurisdiction that moved through space and time by invoking a spiritually based legality – an authority which is not localized, but which flows along the ontological planes of numinous connection.

HB: Would there be intersectional jurisdictions?

JC: I think there would have to be intersectional jurisdictions. But the principles of intersection are likely to be multidimensional and highly complex.

HB: But if these jurisdictions are intersectional, will our decisions always fall on the intersective axes? I mean, where do we stand when we decide, or choose, or judge?

JC: A difficult question, which might be answered from a number of different epistemic and political perspectives. To take just one: What sorts of legal system, given the fetishism of the law in the Age of Millennial Capitalism, is likely to prevail? In the spirit of neoliberalism, we may well see a move away from a legal order dominated by the state – by national policing, by an elaborate judicial system, and by the primacy of the courts toward one that stresses mediation and arbitration, based increasingly on private regulation and policing. This, in effect, would involve a shift away from criminal to civil law. (It is a shift that would not favor the poor and powerless, nor underwrite equity; also, it might have any number of unforeseen legal consequences. But that is another story. . . .) Any move away from criminal toward civil law, broadly conceived, would actually be a move toward "traditional" Africa and its cultures of legality. In most of those cultures, no distinction was made between the two domains of judicial process; all proceedings required a complainant and a defendant. The notion that the neoliberal West is likely to "progress" in a similar direction, however slowly, accords with my perverse theory that, at least in some respects, Europe is evolving toward Africa; this in spite of the fact that many of the basic tenets of neoliberalism – the notion of an amoral autonomous sphere of "the market" or "the economy," for example – run counter to long-standing Afrocentric values. Our family law, for example, is becoming more and more like African family law, emphasizing process over contract, the substance of relations over their formal status. Likewise notions of personhood, which, in Africa, has always been regarded as a state of becoming rather than being. This, again, is a topic for another time. But I think that we may witness a tangible move toward an arbitration based jurisprudence, located in corporately established jurisdictions: neoliberal worldviews conduce to private mediation, negotiated dispute resolution and financial remedies, especially under the "neutral" supervision of technocratic, professional managers. Corporations already purchase private means of enforcement and have long preferred mediated solutions to conflict; citizen associations are likely to follow suit. In sum, I think that we are likely to see the gradual privatization of justice everywhere. Already victims' rights are a major issue. It is a short step from recognizing these rights to the treatment of crime as a civil matter; indeed, we have had plenty of foreshadowings. Recall the Stephen Lawrence murder in the UK: in the face of sustained racism and incompetence on the part of police and prosecuting authorities, only the civilian efforts of the victim's parents kept the case alive. What, in theory, is to prevent a crime victim from paying a security firm to gather evidence, to "induce" the perpetrator into private arbitration, and to enforce the payment of compensation? Of course, the implicit threat here is that, if the defendant refuses to comply, the case might be handed over to the state; but the police, and criminal proceedings, would be circumvented, except as last resort. True, at the moment this seems farfetched, at least in respect of serious felonies, which most states would not allow to go unpoliced; but such may not be true forever. Witness the vast expansion in commercial arbitration and divorce mediation, neither of which were anticipated twenty years ago. Or another notorious foreshadowing, the O. J. Simpson case. For most whites in the USA, the "real" trial was the civil suit; to be sure, the criminal proceeding seriously set back the credibility of the US jury system in many quarters. The growing tendency to make the criminal into the civil is motivated and mediated by the discourse of rights, by the assertion of the private over the public and the individual over the state – all, again, in consonance with a neoliberal notion of the law-in-practice.

HB: Will we even recognize democracy as we used to talk about it?

JC: In the postcolonial epoch, democracy exists in inverse proportion to politics: wherever politics become irrelevant – or so diffuse as to be nowhere in particular – democracy becomes important. Wherever politics become important, democracy becomes irrelevant. At worst, abased, displaced, appropriated, erased. At best, rendered purely procedural; a matter merely of casting ballots, of exercising so-called freedom of choice, not of empowerment.

HB: Are we in a cul-de-sac, or at a cross-roads? There was a time, not so long ago, when the slogan "the personal is the political" was at the forefront of radical demands to recognize the inequities of the private sphere which for women generally, but migrant women in particular, constituted a site of unacknowledged labor, invisible oppression, transparent exploitation under the sanitized and sanctified sign of "family life." But what you are arguing now suggests that the "private" is no longer in tension with the public; it is now colonized by the "corporate" state and becomes incorporated into a retreat from the whole notion of the "social" as a shared, democratic project. An echo of Mrs. Thatcher's dictum, "Society does not exist, there are only individuals"?

JC: This returns us to the argument I was making about the law. It is the law – conventionally the domain of the public *par excellence* – that is likely to serve as the superconductor for privatization: for blurring the line between the public and the private in such a way as to reproportion the realms of, and relations between, the market and the state. The old, taken-for-granted distinction, itself fundamental to the rise of industrial capitalism and bourgeois modernity, is likely to be revalorized; perhaps even rendered meaningless. I suspect that, along with new forms of federalism, we are also likely to see the emergence of new forms of voluntarism, new forms of contextualism, new forms of consociation. Just as the ideological and social construction of the public and the private spheres were the product of a specific historical conjuncture, so the postcolonial conjuncture will deconstruct and recast them. Arguably, they are being recast already. Hence the epochal changes, however glacial they may turn out to be, in the practical workings of our legal culture. Hence also certain recent events in American political history, like the so-called "crisis" of the presidency. I refer, of course, not to Ms. Lewinsky, but to the burlesque played out in the Starr Chamber and the US Congress: a burlesque in which an intimate, "private" affair was transformed, through the conduit of spurious legalism, into public spectacle, thus making sexuality into a site in which to conduct partisan warfare under the sign of moral discourse. The whole process would have been inconceivable ten, fifteen, twenty years ago, when a much sharper ideological division marked the private from the public. The haste of some American academics to read the scandal purely as a moral saga is misguided. It is a saga with deep roots in political sociology: in the transformation, over the long run, of modernist governance and the public sphere. Politics have been diffused, their contents revisioned.

HB: In this context, though, is sexuality something that is normalized or will it create a properly transgressive space in the public domain?

JC: I think that sexuality both in its discursive register and in the implications of its practice has always been a potential vehicle of the revisionary. For example, the so-called current crisis of masculinity is not merely about changing experiences of maleness. Nor is it simply about the situation of sexuality within the prevailing gender system. It is equally about the reconstruction of the nature of labor, of work and worth, of the interpenetration of the material and the social, of the alignment of production and reproduction. To be sure, in the US at least, the obsession with family values, which extends far beyond the Christian Right, is an obsession with the social division of labor, its gendering and its sexual implosion. Sexuality, it seems to me, is literally the seamy side of the semiotic, the side that escapes containment and always has within it the capacity to reconstruct sociality in its name.

HB: I think that is a splendid description of both the intersectional and the interstitial. But do you think the fact that Clinton's popularity ratings remained so strong was a vote for trying to preserve this realm, to preserve the privilege of privacy? Or was it a vote for the view that once that kind of sexual enigma is out, we accept its public presence and want to get on with life as more or less normal or perverse?

JC: There are several possibilities. But, in the end, it is probably undecidable. On one hand, the public reaction has much to do with the growing irrelevance of normal politics. For many Americans, what happens in the Beltway – whether or not it is way below the belt – has nothing to do with the pursuits of everyday life. The triumphalism of the market, of the notion that ultimately everything that counts is determined outside Washington, registers the public recognition of that irrelevance, of the displacement of the political. This reflects itself in the fact that, except under extraordinary conditions of the kind that prevailed, interestingly, in the US presidential election of 2000, most people do not bother to cast ballots any more. Among the younger generation, even the most politicized of college students often do not vote because they sustain a principled belief that the politics that matter occur beyond the institutionalized domains of governance.

HB: Is this a principled displacement of the political into other spheres so as to extend the nature of democratic politics, to take it beyond the "party" or to dilute it and weaken it? Is this the good side of the federalism you were talking about?

JC: Well, potentially perhaps; although I would hate to see what was formerly thought of as political become a reflex of the market. Or of its spectral claims.

HB: Right.

JC: The danger of the displacement of the political is the forfeiture of social policy to the ostensibly technical imperatives of economy. This, like many other corollaries of neoliberalism, I find terrifying. On the other hand, if the displacement of the political facilitates the localization of agency – if it allows space for radical initiatives to remake community and to rethink the social as a site of collective responsibility, equity, liberty – it would certainly be a positive thing.

HB: But that is different.

JC: Very different. It demands that we embark on the pursuit of an altogether new epistemic frame, a praxis that makes sense of the sociology of the millennial moment and transforms it into an emancipatory vision. It is not enough, in the circumstances, to look for a panacea in the vacuously utopic idea of Civil Society or, for that matter, in communitarianism which has produced some truly incoherent political "thought" in recent years. It merely replays the neoliberal refrain in another key.

HB: Yes, because civil society and communitarianism assume a particular kind of cultural homogeneity . . .

JC: But this does not fully answer your question about the receding line between the public and the private. There is, in that respect, a circumstantial irony in the Lewinsky spectacle. The Right, both old and new, has long been most vociferous in sustaining that line and yet it is conservative congressmen who indulged in the publication of the most lurid intimacies in order to serve their political fortunes.

HB: Absolutely. It is those who have censored pornography most avidly, who want pornography published as part of the freedom of the market . . .

JC: . . . who made pornography into politics and politics into pornography. But there is another thing here too. It is possible that this moment signals the public, explicit recognition of an unspoken cultural "fact" of American political life: that sex and charisma exist in a perfectly permissible relationship, each validating the other, as long as that relationship remains invisible. Promiscuity may be presumed, even discussed *sotto voce*, but it cannot enter the public gaze. In the unfolding biography of William Jefferson Clinton, ostensibly disgraced but effectively empowered, we saw this paradox being played out. It had everything, this story: gothic horror, Christian morality play, Southern family epic, sexy sitcom . . .

HB: . . . very sexy. With a touch, almost, of Cecil B. de Mille.

JC: Yes. Another possibility is that, for many Americans, the Lewinsky affair actually did reaffirm the need to sustain the public–private distinction – mainly because it demonstrated the dangers that attend its erasure. Without this distinction, the great secret of modern American family life, its very moral economy, would be at risk. The sorry saga of Bill Clinton – for these purposes not William Jefferson, just plain Bill – evoked the uneasy sense that, if you scratch at any US household, exactly the same things are probably going on. The First Family is every family in prospect: a husband screwing around, unhappy, and in therapy; his wife, in an heroic supportive role, perhaps also having an affair occasioned by her neglect, unhappy, and in therapy; the children as inevitable victims, suitable cases for therapy when the faeces hit the air conditioner. A nightmare because it is so ordinary, so mundane.

HB: Did you see Toni Morrison's line in her piece in the *New Yorker* where she says that this was really not about sex – even though they wanted it to be about sex – but about the destruction of the first "black" president. Did you read that?

JC: I agree with her in part, but I do think that the sexual dimension was culturally significant; perhaps the two things are inseparable. Why, after all, was it necessary for the Right to destroy Clinton? Morrison is correct that, for them, he represented a radical threat, a successful Democratic president with a stated commitment to social welfare – which is ironic given his contribution to its demise – and a penchant for the causes of blacks and women. It is not so much that Clinton is a black president; although I can see why, imaginatively, this claim has a brilliant plausibility. It is, I think, that he came to stand for the reversal of Reagan Republicanism. It is as if time had been rewound to 1981, and the American-presidency-as-movie started all over again in the opposite direction, moving back through the Carter years towards the great society. This, to even centrist Republicans, is pure nightmare. The more fanciful, the greater the horror.

HB: Do you think that Clinton stands for a certain measured success of the feminist movement?

JC: . . . in the eyes of the Right, definitely. Less so in my own, although he did expand the presence of women in government and foster an increasing awareness of gender discrimination in the workplace. More generally, however, I found it difficult in 1996 to vote for a man who had just, in effect, dismantled the welfare system. Still, a very different story is told among neo-conservatives. Nor is it entirely groundless; not, at least, if we pay heed to Clinton's public utterances. Recall his State of the Union address after the Lewinsky scandal broke. It might have been his most eloquent moment. In it he said a great deal that could, from the Right, have been read as a promise to reconstruct the welfare state.

HB: But what is it that bears the mark of his great charisma? I mean, apart from the person, what does he bring to the personal as political icon or totem?

JC: The answer to that question, I am sure, will become the subject of a long public conversation once he leaves office.

Transition or Transformation?

HB: Are we in a peculiar situation of transformation, of transition? Is there something about the transitionality of our times that creates a sense that we are somehow suspended in the performance of the present without a horizon of transformation in sight? So many of the epochal events of our times seem to have turned into anxious and undecidable conditions: the ongoing struggle of the Palestinians after the Palestinian State; the perils of the South African situation after Independence; the ongoing problems of German unification after the destruction of the Wall. Is this preoccupation with our continuous present a modernist rather than postmodernist predicament? Are we living in especially transitional times or is such a view more to do with the kind of conversation we are having?

JC: That is an impossibly difficult question. Radical change, as a reading of the history of the present, is always in the eye of the beholder. It depends on epistemic orientation, on a politics, on sheer intuition. But, if we are to theorize the moment, indeed, if we are to theorize history at all, it demands an answer, however provisional. One might have asked the same question at the time of the Scottish Enlightenment. Hence my earlier observation. The parallel between then and now, between the Time of the Adams – Ferguson and Smith – and the Millennium, is very obvious. If I may be so crass as to repeat myself, that parallel is represented metonymically in a return of the populist obsession with civil society – itself a discourse of creative regeneration in the face of radical transformation. It is no surprise to me that Ferguson has been resuscitated as our *philosophe du jour*. It may be a hugely speculative association, but he seems to have come to stand as an icon of the struggle to make sense of what was to unfold during that inchoate, messy Age of Revolution at the dawn of modernity; an age which, in retrospect, we render coherent by means of a signifier of periodicity, 1789–1848. A similar sense of living at the edge of a period of rapid space-time compression, of social and material metamorphoses, is widely evident both in popular culture and in acadamies across the globe.

HB: And you think a new or alternative teleology will arise?

JC: My worm's-eye view of history says no, my bird's-eye view says yes. [Laughter] For obvious reasons, it is hard to divine what its content might be. At the same time, with apologies to Francis Fukuyama, it is equally difficult to imagine the end of history. It is true that the problem in talking about an Age of Revolution is that so much in the world of the everyday seems unchanged. And yet it may not be. To me, the true terror of theory at the end of the century lies in the fact that between sameness and difference lies indifference. It is indifference – political indifference, social indifference, indifference about the need to estrange the familiar, indifference in confronting the exorbitant human costs of neoliberal capitalism – that really challenges us. We tell our students that they ought to be thinking about politics. But we have no satisfactory description of "the political" any more, save to know it by what it is not, to make it an alibi for pure interest, or to reduce it to metaphors, signs, styles. The cosmic irony in all this is that, in retrospect, the great outrages of the twentieth century – the Holocaust, apartheid, colonialism, racism, the excesses of industrial capitalism – were morally transparent, politically stark. The adversaries were obvious. It was easy enough to weave a substantive social vision out of the struggle against them. If nothing else, socialisms of various kinds promised alternatives. The Age of Modernity, in that respect at least, was relatively simple. Its "posts-" are much less so. I have heard it said in black South Africa that the problem these days is that nobody any longer knows who or what the enemy is. Your neighbor might as well be a witch as a friend, the state as much of a problem as a solution. Indifference is all too easy . . .

HB: Indifference is a real problem in the post Cold War world. There is no question that the levels of collusion and caricature between the superpowers had become mutually corrupting and deeply exploitative of the rest of the world, particularly the Third World, which, not entirely innocently, became the site for some of the most hideous projections of superpower conflict and collaborationism. That said, it was still possible to create a historical argument that was about different systems, alternative ideologies, conflicting values, diverse worldviews. That tension was too easily polarized and simplified, but it was a historic and structural political tension and it raised the issue of commitment and action. Today's "indifference" is partly caused by the myth that we are all living in more or less the same "globalized" world, scions of the new technologies, free participants in the fungible, free markets, members of dot.com communities. But there is a more serious kind of phenomenological and political issue of "living-in-difference," if I may put it that way. It has arisen out of the growing sense of minoritization that seems to have replaced more hegemonic and horizontal forms of national peoplehood. We are committed to the ethical and political necessity of living in the midst of "differences" that are processual, changeable, and yet no less invested in the interests and the passions of social life. The national "body" is gripped in an ontological unde-cidability (to use your word) that then creates what I have called the growing fault-lines between political citizenship and cultural citizenship. Perhaps we are, in our own times, subject to that process of "occult instability" that Fanon described as the principle of an emergent peoples entering that transitional movement that might lead them to a difficult, yet necessary, freedom.

JC: Perhaps that is why we are having such difficulty finishing this conver-sation. It is because we are living in a continuous present whose bearings seem irreducibly inchoate. We simply do not know where it is going, let alone where it is going to end. Except in hopes of new beginnings.

Note

The conversation reproduced above took place in Chicago in November 1998. It was recorded by Maureen Anderson and transcribed by S. Lily Mendoza.

Chapter 3

Resident Alien

Gayatri Chakravorty Spivak

Large-scale movements of people – renamed "diaspora" – are what defines our time. As a result, the premodern principle of demographic frontiers is encroaching upon imperial territorial frontiers. The new African, Asian, and other "diasporas" connect globally in unprecedented ways. Some philosophers suggest that it is an ethics of hospitality that we must ponder now. But the contemporary metropolitan philosopher cannot conceive this demographic redrawing of frontiers between place of departure and place of arrival. When they think hospitality or recognition, philosophers as different as Etienne Balibar and Charles Taylor begin and indeed end with the migrant in metropolitan space, although Balibar does offer an astounding redefinition of mass movements as movements of people. Even the global concept of "multitude" in *Empire* takes on a migratory cast: "the kinds of movement of individuals, groups, and populations that we find today in Empire, however, cannot be completely subjugated to the laws of capitalist accumulation."[1] Derrida has opened hospitality into teleopoiesis – a structure of touching the distant other that interrupts the past in the name of the future rupture that is already inscribed in it. But his specific figurations remain named *arrivant* or *revenant*, arriving or returning.

The figure of the Resident Alien is excentric to this dynamic.

Reda Bensmaïa has called the immigrant intellectual in the metropolis a "phantom mediator."[2] Being Algerian by birth, he generalizes from the Algerian case. The way back is barred him, let us hope not for long. In the Indian case, there is not much ghostliness in the coming-and-going of the New Immigrant intellectual and her counterpart on the mainland. It is a shuttling, not a mediation. There is, by contrast, a sheltered ghostliness in the figure of the long-term Resident Alien, a curious residual – in Raymond Williams's powerful phrase – that seems to run counter to the contemporary tendency toward the emergence of virtual frontiers that are demographically defined. The figure of the long-term Resident Alien belongs to a tenaciously held territoriality that is, also, of course, abstract; as all territoriality must be; yet it robs the figure of the more salient abstractions of an everyday civility, a willing suspension of civil rights. The virtuality of the new demographic frontiers is accretive rather than privative, it enlarges rather than shrinks. It creates the kind of para-state collectivities that were part of the predication of the shifting multicultural empires that had written the spatialized temporizing of the planet before monopoly capitalist colonialism – colonialism in the narrow sense. The figure of the Resident Alien seems to belong, by contrast, to postcoloniality in the narrow sense.

I have used the following words to situate a stereotype of myself on two other widely disparate occasions.[3] I feel that such a stereotype is most appropriate to my rereading of Rabindranath Tagore's *Gora*.[4]

I was born during World War II. In the estimation of my generation in India, the war was, to use an obsolete German adjective that Marx often uses, *zwieschlächtig*, the site of two contradictory pulls. The horror of the Holocaust was what made it European. It was a *world* war because for us – with our quarter of a million dead fighting for the Allies and the highest number of military honors won by any national group – and subsequently for a number of colonies – the war was a remote instrument for the end of specifically territorial imperialism. Negotiated Independences redefined themselves as neocolonialism from the West. Failure of decolonization at home and large-scale Eurocentric economic migration began to fix the new world's demographic outlines. With the fall of the Berlin Wall and the subsequent events in Eastern and Central Europe, these outlines have become altogether unstable.

I belong to the very first waves of postcolonial migration. I came to the United States forty years ago, when the virtualized demographic frontiers of the modern world had not yet begun to destabilize the territorial frontiers over which so much blood had been shed. A bit of anachronistic nationalism clings to me still. I retain an Indian passport and remain no more than a permanent resident in the US. However common this may be among European nationals, Asians and Africans emigrate to gain metropolitan citizenship. My small group, however, is in both worlds, deeply, without being quite of them. I believe that slight anomaly gives us a certain distance, which may perhaps be valuable. You will judge. Whatever your judgment, this Resident Alien is a vestigial postcolonial figure.

Rabindranath Tagore's *Gora* was first published in serial form between 1907 and 1909. The story is well known. An Irish foundling of the Sepoy Mutiny grows up believing he is a Brahman's son and observes strict doctrinal Hindu orthodoxy as an expression of nationalism. At the seeming approach of death, his adoptive father reveals his alien birth to him, for he has not the right to perform the funeral rites of a Brahman. The father recovers, but Gora, relinquishing orthodox Hindu doctrine, emerges a true nationalist Indian. Gora's last utterances in the novel – after he knows his biological birth and national origin – will give us a sense of the use of women in the staging of this Resident Alien:

Gora said, "Ma, you are my only mother. The mother whom I'd sought wandering – had herself entered my room, attending. You have no caste, no caste-judgment, no contempt – you are nothing but the image of our good! You are my Bharatvarsha [ancient Sanskrit name of India], indeed." . . . A few moments later, he said, "Ma, will you call Lachhmiya and tell her to get me a glass of water now?" (477)

Two clarifications. In a polytheist culture, "image" is a divine image, without the weight of the monotheist metaphor. Lachhmiya is the Christian outcaste servant, from whose hands the earlier Gora, orthodox Brahman, could not accept drinking water, although there was no lack of affection. This sort of internalized caste-judgment is of course infinitely more powerful and dangerous than overt oppression.

Gora is set at a conjunctural moment of consolidation of a peculiarly "Indian" territoriality: the end of the 1857 Mutiny. With such a consolidating moment as external focalization, Tagore imagines the unwilling imperialist as a sort of "Resident Alien." It is a curious act of hospitality where the host–guest relationship is reversed. This textual–figural analogy cannot be a narrative parallel to the situation of the "real" metropolitan Resident Alien today. And yet much of the mysterious fun of literary reading, half-constructing relationships between singular and unverifiable figures, rises from such differences. Much of the tedium of a sociological use of literary examples arises from its occlusion. Paradoxically, the literature of cultural difference is peculiarly susceptible to such tedium, in the name of identity. *Gora* is a singular novel, an unusual novel, a peculiar riff on mere nationalism, and a major experiment in Bengali fictional prose. I want to see my own civil status replicated in it. Can anything be gained from such a reckless and sinister disregard of speculative sobriety?

Meenakshi Mukherjee has recently discouraged us from drawing parallels between Tagore's *Gora* and Kipling's *Kim*.[5] I accept this admonition as part of the general warning about narrative parallels. Yet the central similarity has been so often pointed out that not to mention it seems odd. *Kim*'s hero is Irish; in spite of an effort at British-style schooling, throughout the book he is more "Indian" than any of the natives, who remain irretrievably local. *Kim* is also a Resident Alien figure, though his depiction is startlingly different. In *Kim* the Resident Alien's alien status is given in denial. In *Gora* that status is the achievement of the entire narrative energy. There are other differences. *Kim* is picaresque, *Gora* a *Bildungsroman*. Kim does not grow, neither his residency nor his alienness is existential. The plot of apprenticeship states a cultural commonplace of access to wisdom, of course. But *Gora*'s nationalism is subjectivized, not just narrated, in rather an Aristotelian way: peripety and anagnoresis, reversal followed by removal of non-knowledge.[6] Further, the delicate affective efficiency of women that is part of gentrifying nineteenth-century Bengal is the condition and effect of *Gora*. Kipling is derisive of the colonial subject. The women in *Kim* are stock types of ethnic magico-erotic instrumentality in a predominantly male world.

So much said, let us honor Professor Mukherjee in the breach. Away with narrative parallels. Let us concatenate the figural dynamics – the making-into-figure – of the two figures. The first move is to notice that they are nicknames – not proper names – that entitle, that provide the title of these two considerable books. Entitling nicknames may be imagined to have a structural relationship with the permanent Resident Alien's relationship to two communities. The full patronymic, with citizen's rights, belongs elsewhere. It sutures genealogy to nation. (This is a male argument, of course, but our heroes are male.) The proper name is more unilateral, it can claim locationist identity with assurance.

If the times produced the two nicknames, Gora and Kim – the characters as well as the books – they produced the times as well. These are what Michel Foucault would call "watershed texts."[7] As a reader, I carry the history of that condition-and-effect relationship between literary text and social text. I can say "yes" to these texts – without which there is no reading – in two different ways. I am tied in with the comic hybrid in *Kim*, an MA from Calcutta University (K 210). By contrast, I am something like the implied reader of *Gora*, the emancipated secularist Bengali middle-class woman in the future anterior of the book. In both cases my Mother Sivani Chakravorty is closer to the mark. I escaped before my MA. She received hers, from Calcutta University, in 1937. She was born and brought up on Cornwallis Street, the area where most of *Gora's* action takes place. And, since her degree was in Bengali Literature, or – as it used to be called then – "Indian Vernaculars," a phrase embarrassingly replicated in a recent *New Yorker* by Salman Rushdie – her generation read *Gora* as its first appropriate readers.[8] I am here as my Mother's proxy, as perhaps in life. But she has been a US citizen, a New Immigrant, for the last twenty-nine years. As a Resident Alien, tenaciously retentive of lost territorialities, I seem to "belong" more to the United States as well – Professor Spivak to the "Indian" Gayatri Chakravorty. "Figures in the carpet" is the lovely phrase of Henry James, the American novelist, long-term Resident Alien in Europe.[9] "Assigned subject-positions," to quote Foucault again.[10]

I cannot resist the temptation here to recount a teaching tale. As part of my History of Literary Criticism Part 1, I was hesitantly teaching some Bhartrhari to my undergraduates. Typically, in a premodern History of Criticism course, English Literature students start with Greek antiquity: Aristotle, Longinus, Plotinus. But since there are many kinds of English-speaking Americans today, it seemed appropriate that my class should read pre-Columbian, Arbi-Farsi, ancient East Asian, African; hence Bhartrhari, the seventh-century philosopher of grammar. (There is some hostility to this in my department. I don't get to teach this course often.)

In the famous Book 3, Verse 3.3 of the *Vakyapadåœßya* – meaning simply "Of Sentences and Words" – Bhartrhari suggests that the connection between word and meaning, signifier and signified, *v~caka* and *v~cya*, is simply dependent upon a genitive suffix – what in English would be the "'s," but, more commonly, the auxiliary construction with "of": as in citizen *of*, resident *of*.

Thus, Bhartrhari goes on, the identity of word and meaning is, in the felicitous translation of Bimal Krishna Matilal, "designated." Identity is in the
domain of signs. To explain this to my diverse national-origin students, I used
that Foucauldian sentence: "Subject-position is *assigned*."

I am rather dubious about explaining modern "culturally different" writers
simply in terms of "traditional" models. Please remember that I am not drawing
parallels here. I am speaking of Bhartrhari and Foucault. They had not read
each other as far as I know. They were merely inspired by a similar intuition:
of the semioticity – sign-character – of identity. The word is resident in the
meaning by virtue of a case: the genitive. In that spirit I would say that Tagore's
Gora and Kipling's *Kim* are both attempting to animate that indeterminate
space of identity as sign, dependent upon a case – the locative as the genitive
– ~dh~r~mdhikarana as *samvandha* – space as copula, rather differently.

The difference is felt in their being in language. Both Kipling and Tagore are
writing experimental prose. Kipling places a variety of "Indian English" that
gets its punch from its distance from the standard English that is the primary
medium of narration; rather like an expanded version of Mark Twain's Black
dialect. This tradition has been appropriated by writers such as Rushdie and
Farouk Dhondy; though not I think by Amitabh Ghosh, Hanif Kureishi, Arund-
hati Roy, Vikram Seth. Tagore bends the bones of Bangla. Hard to catch in
translation.

The difference is also in their being-in-space. "India" does not name the
same space for them. In the passage I have quoted above, is Sujit Mukherjee
right in keeping the Bengali word *Bharatbarsho* spelled in the Sanskrit way? I
think I see his reasons. The Hindu-nationalist Gora would certainly fill that
word with aggressively confected and prior religio-philosophico-cultural
meaning. He entertains all his scandalized class-equals with such soliloquies.
But that meaning – underlying talk of "Indian values" today – is abreactive to
imperialism, formed by back-formation from it – quite as the signifier "indigenous knowledge" is abreactive to biopiracy.

Kipling cannot enter that space, marvelously flowering from the furrow
of a violated episteme, with a peculiar species of class-consent that Tagore's
hospitality would recode – like Jawaharlal Nehru's invitation to Le Corbusier
to build Chandigarh half a century later.[11]

No. Kipling could not enter that space. He had a vague idea of its worlding,
and he treated the idea with contempt as a merely "imagined community"
would deserve. Writing only six years earlier – he locates his Kim in the para-
colonial space where the project was to control shifting demographic frontiers
by strict territorial lines, a control that has come and gone today. "India" (the
Greek name), "Hindostan" (the central Asian name), is the name of a prize in
a game. And Kim's picaresque apprenticeship is as a player in that "Great
Game" for the control of South and Central Asia by Russia or France/Britain.
No doubt this is also an effort, on Kipling's part, to exculpate colonialism as
feudalism – the feud as game, rather like two football teams, winner take all.
It is Kipling's genius to stage the imperialist as child, a child who, in his sym-

bolic apprenticeship at once to the Game (British with collaborating Muslims) and to the ethical system (or Way) of Buddhism, concentrated in the lama alone, is never the vehicle of internal focalization, and is treated with affectionate derision by the Muslim players.[12] This entire problematic is laid out in the final reunion – no anagnoresis here – between Master and disciple, hosted by Mahbub.

> "I was dragged from no river," said the lama simply . . . I found it by Knowledge." "Oh, ay. True," stammered Mahbub, divided between high indignation and enormous mirth. . . . "It seems that I stand by [he says a bit later] while a young Sahib is hoisted into Allah knows what of an idolater's Heaven [he is wrong about associating the Buddhist "Nibban," put in the lama's mouth by Kipling, with idolatry, but that may be part of the staging] by means of old Red Hat. And I am reckoned something of a player of the Game myself! But the madman is fond of the boy; and I must be very reasonably mad too." "What is the prayer?" said the lama, as the rough Pushtu rumbled into the red beard. (K 333–4)

The "Great Game" was apparently a phrase invented by "Lieutenant Arthur Conolly of the 6th Bengal Native Light Cavalry . . . [who], aged 16, . . . [had] joined his regiment as a cadet."[13] To follow the trajectory of the Great Game as played in the Northwestern frontier area called "India" by Kipling as by Alexander the Great in 324 BC, we must flash forward to the *New York Times* of October 6, 1996.[14] There we will find an item called "Afghanistan Reels Back into View."[15] A picture of "the bodies of Najibullah, left, and his brother hang[ing] from a Kabul traffic post." A crowd of peering men from behind, looking as much at the cameramen as at the backs of the bloody bodies, as far as one can tell. What is the lesson of this public spectacle? I quote the *Times*:

> In the months before Afghanistan's new rulers marched him from a United Nations compound in Kabul and summarily beat, shot and hanged him, Afghanistan's last Communist President, Najibullah, spent much of his time preparing a translation into Pashto, his native language, of a 1990 book about Afghanistan, "The Great Game," by the English writer Peter Hopkirk. Mr. Najibullah told United Nations officials that he wanted Afghans to read the Hopkirk text because of what they would learn from it of the 19th-century struggle between imperial Britain and imperial Russia for influence in Afghanistan. "They can see how our history has represented itself," he said. "Only if we understand our history can we take steps to break the cycle."

What characterized the para-colonial theater loosely called Afghanistan, was that upon that stage, the masters masqueraded as the native. As in *Kim*, the Great Game was almost invariably played in disguise. Hopkirk's pages are strewn with pictures of British and Russian soldiers in Afghan, Persian, Armenian dress. This planned indeterminacy, like the indeterminacy of the demographic rather than territorial frontiers in this theater, is much closer to the postcolonial hybridized world of today than nationalist colonialisms, which were as much a historically contained phenomenon as Bolshevism. Today the

Taliban, brought into being by the United States in reaction to Afghanistan's entry into the Soviet sphere of influence, allegedly masquerades as Americans in order to escape the hegemony of the United States, latest entrant into the Game.

If in Foucault's story, as told in *Discipline and Punish*, the transformation of the soldier into a docile body "could become determinant only with a technical transformation: the invention of the rifle," the rifle clinched no great narrative in Najibullah's.[16] Plate 35 in *The Great Game* shows a British officer in native dress surrounded by Afghans. "Many minor players," the caption runs, "were involved in the Great Game. An anonymous political officer (rifleless), hardly distinguishable from his companions, is seen here with friendly Afghan tribesmen," who all carry rifles, but are not called "soldiers." This picture is outside of Foucault's beautifully organized system, so beloved by the disciplines, but also "inside," for this is the wild counter-narrative, rifle-toting tribesmen and rifleless white soldier, that keeps the story of efficiency and leniency going in the metropolis.

Although the Afghan subalterns, "the people" according to Najibullah, were perhaps not sufficiently aware of the "Great Game," the principal players were, of course. I offer a reflection of the Kim–Gora relationship in a cracked mirror.

In 1886 Muhammad Mahfuz Ali, an Indian Muslim, translated his own book *The Truth About Russia and England: From A Native's Point of View* from Urdu into English. A move that Najibullah was obliged to reverse, as it were. It is interesting that even Mahfuz Ali, inimical to the Amir of Afghanistan, himself on the one hand a loyal subject of the Crown, and, on the other, a Muslim, spoke of "the national spirit of the Afghan people." The bibliographer at the India Office Library advises that the Urdu text is unavailable. What interests me is that Mahfuz Ali, very much the colonial subject – at one point he writes of "the oriental mind" (what had that phrase been in Urdu?) – had thought that the appropriate translation of the Urdu word was "nation." Yet it is also quite clear that he was aware that Amir Abd-ur Rahman was not an initiate of colonial knowledge. For in the same passage he calls the Afghans "a savage and united race" – that last word too is interesting – and Afghanistan a "wretched country." What had he meant by the word applied to someone who did not share his own epistemic enclave?[17]

With respect, the problem with the brilliant body of speculation undertaken by Benedict Anderson and Etienne Balibar is that it cannot acknowledge that such questions, inhabiting the cusp where the rupture of colonialism is also a repetition, although finally unanswerable, are worth pondering. The word that is translated "nation" names a hardy "residual," not an "emergent" which would allow us to claim that "citizenship" – the model of which is much more directly linked to the development of civil societies in Northwestern Europe – "and nationality have a single, indissociable institutional base."[18]

By transcribing the loyal colonial subject into the reverse-imperialist Resident Alien, by splitting the colonizer (Gora's biological mother and her son) and rendering the product indeterminate, by renaming him "Gora" – of course the diminutive of Gourmohan – but also "Whitey," metonymically the colloquial nomenclature of the British soldier, Tagore rewrites Mahfuz Ali, and in the process messes with hospitality, in an impossible impracticable model. That is its strength.

About when I was writing the first version of this essay, I read Derrida's *Of Hospitality*. I wanted to add a different kind of foreigner to the ones that Derrida had listed: "exiles, the deported, the expelled, the rootless, the stateless, lawless nomads, absolute foreigners" (H 87–8), the colonizer as guest.[19] *Gora* attempts to look at the *xenos* – the foreigner – from below. The Indian looks at the British as guest.[20] The foreigner is welcomed in Tagore's book by the colonized host by (forgetting) the death of the father (Gora's biological father had been killed by Indians). The scene of that forgetting is finally obliterated in the novel by the banal failed death of the querulous and unwilling adoptive father, the colonized host. It is not that the foreigner as guest has no right to burial but that he has no right to bury (in this case cremate): "it is first of all the law of burial that becomes – let us say the word – determining. The question of the foreigner concerns what happens at death and when the traveler is laid to rest in a foreign land" (H 87). Access to the law without law (H 83) is, perhaps, the embrace of the mother who is foreign to the foreigner – which puts the murder of the father under erasure, only for the space of the book, so to speak. This impossible Irish/Indian foreigner *is* the Law that he questions. The encounter between the Law and the Laws, which is also the encounter between the Law and the foreigner (H 31–2, 73), is in that brave scene on the boat where Gora is disgusted by a Mahfuz-style colonial subject, that bold scene with the white Magistrate whom Gora (the Whitey) scorns, and the furtive silence at the foster father's bedside, when he knows he is Irish, and is in the presence of a white doctor. I will deal with these scenes in detail later. I want to add these to the encounters imagined by Sophocles or the Platonic Socrates, or yet the Bible. Here *hostis* is indeed both enemy and guest – enemy turned guest, and, finally, enemy turned host.

Derrida looks at the Platonic Socrates in *Crito*, who makes the Laws interrogate him thus: "Did we not give you life in the first place? Was it not through us that your father married your mother and became your parent?" (H 33). I remember Aristotle, who described himself as precisely *xenos*, as opposed to Plato – a *polites*, to whom the Laws of the City of Athens could not have posed these questions.[21] Diogenes Laertes claims that he had an exchange of letters with Antipater, where he implied that, since he never became a citizen of Athens, he had no burial rights there. There is also a reference to a passage on Xenocrates: "Such was his character, and yet, when he was unable to pay the tax levied on resident aliens, the Athenians put him up for sale." In *Politics* Aristotle writes about the difference in civil status between the citizen and the *metis*, closing thus: "a citizen in the fullest sense means the man who shares in the honours of the state, as is implied in the verse of Homer [']Like to some alien settler without honour['] – since a native not admitted to a share in the public honours is like an alien domiciled in the land."[22] It is possible to imagine that Aristotle, writing in the aftermath of the Periclean Enlightenment, himself a Resident Alien, devised a theory of drama as social therapy that is in both worlds, of the *ethnos* and the *ethnikos* deeply, without being quite *of* them. I believe that slight anomaly might have given him a certain distance, which might perhaps have been valuable. Tragedy purges by calling up all the positive and negative elements that the other as other – hero or villain, but precisely not me – can call up: *elios* (inadequately translated as "pity"), all the positive feelings toward the other alien-ated by the tragic aura; and *phobos* (inadequately translated as "fear"), all the rejecting/repelling affects toward a similarly alienated figure.[23] I should like to think that *Gora* runs through the *phobos/elios* scale for both the British and the Indian as other(self) and (self)other.

We must, however, stop short of expanding the notion of the Resident Alien into the epistemico-affective. If we do so, we open the door to a vast taxonomy, involving anyone who welcomes the grafting of the "alien" onto the heritage. Indeed, since breaking the same is the rule rather than the exception in history, at the limit one could suggest that we are nothing but resident aliens on earth. This would be particularly applicable, then, to such Afghan figures as I will invoke below.

No. I wish to confine "Resident Alien" to abstract juridico-legal structures, as does Aristotle. It would indeed involve a movement, from home to elsewhere, but full citizenship of that elsewhere would not be forthcoming, withheld, or unsought.

Gora as fiction rings changes on these structures, of course. It invites the singular imperialist to achieve the intimacy of the Resident Alien – the permanent visitor. I will come back to this point.

In the para-colonial space – the space of the "Great Game" – for which Kipling's "India" is no more than a screen-identifier, there were repeated efforts at producing a colonial subject without the validating agency of colonialism. Abd-ur Rahman, the last nineteenth-century Amir of Afghanistan (fl. 1880–1901), had struggled to establish something resembling a "constitutional government" in Afghanistan, a peculiar failed Resident Alien program. He had imported Euro-US men and women to train Afghans, rather than encourage the production of the pharmakontic (medicine as well as poison) enabling violation of the full-fledged colonial subject.[24]

The Afghan "national identity" is a provisional moment in the alternative internationality of Islam. It is fascinating to read the Amir's awareness of the diversity of Islam and yet its provision for thinking a collectivity, pervasive in the text. For "the struggle between imperial Britain and imperial Russia for influence in Afghanistan" was not unknown to him. But the production of the colonial subject in order to administer a settled colonial possession could not appear on the agenda of this region, perceived always as an in-between, a buffer. Between 1919 and 1929 Abd-ur Rahman's grandson Amanullah, by upbringing separated from his grandfather's tribal base, attempted to introduce a fantasmic "constitutionality," and was obliged to retire to Italy, where he died peacefully in 1960. I think of E. M. Forster's Fielding in *A Passage to India*, retiring to Italy in the end, thinking, again and again, that he had been mistaken in locating beauty in India.[25] Remember Forster too was speaking not of British "India," but a slightly para-colonial space, a native state. The generation that came of age in the 1960s, my generation, produced Najibullah, a man radicalized at university. He attempted once again to establish a "constitutional" state, this time with the validating agency of communism. Gorbachev sold him out in the end.

There is no hope that anyone will question the identity of the monster painted by John E. Burns, the *New York Times* correspondent: "Mr. Najibullah, who in life served the KGB's efforts to eliminate opposition to Marxism, died a death as miserable as any his secret police meted out." Under pressure from both the USSR and the US, possibly because he was a capable and convinced man, he had resigned on the promise of a government of unanimity. When that was not forthcoming, he had sensed his vulnerability and made arrangements to leave his country. He was stopped at the airport and turned himself in to the UN. Commenting on his demeanor on the eve of his resignation, Diego Cordovez, the former Undersecretary General of the United Nations who negotiated the Soviet withdrawal from Afghanistan, remarked in 1995: "He was not a scared or a nervous man; quite the contrary, he seemed serene, fully in control, and ready to face all the ominous eventualities that could follow the Soviet withdrawal."[26] In less than a year the *Times* had written his epitaph: a flunky of Stalinism.

Najibullah's translation remained unfinished. As we move back into "India" or "Bharatvarsha," we are obliged to leave him hanging, like the dead of the Sepoy Mutiny in Farhad Mazhar's poem "Jimmed~r Bidroher L~sh" (The Corpse-Keeper of Revolt):

> Lord, Dhaka's mosque is world-renowned
> Much varied work on pillar and cloister. In British days
> the Whites, right or wrong, put in place
> th' Asiatic Society and researched it all
> Here. In the white eyes
> of whites the new Bengalis dig now
> and look for things we see.
> I wish them good luck. But doctor's degrees,
> make them twice
> as wily as their White forebears.
>
> Lord, I'm an unlettered fool,
> can't grasp the art of architecture, paint,
> yet my heart aches empty
> as I stand by the old Ganga.
> The Sepoys seem to hang still on hangman's ropes
> waiting for last rites, the ropes uncut,
> their bodies still aloft, none to mourn,
> to perform *zannat*.
> Don't you mock me with minaret and arcade,
> me, the corpse-keeper of revolt.[27]

Colonial and postcolonial discourse measure their distance in Tagore's and Mazhar's different figuration of the Sepoy Mutiny – as a site of hope and of despair.

I said earlier that Tagore reinscribed and revised, turned around, and displaced Mahfuz Ali, the loyal Indian subject of the Crown, as Gora. That is actually not quite correct. It is Binoy, the major actor of *Gora*, Engels to Gora's Marx, who is Mahfuz Ali transmogrified. In order to appreciate this, let us see how Kipling pre-wrote him. There is the offensive and familiar passage, speaking to my worst fears, the resident made alien:

> He became thickly treasonous, and spoke in terms of sweeping indecency of a Government which had forced upon him a white man's education and neglected to supply him with a white man's salary. He babbled tales of oppression and wrong till the tears ran down his cheeks for the miseries of his land. Then he staggered off, singing love-songs of Lower Bengal, and collapsed upon a wet tree-trunk. Never was so unfortunate a product of English rule in India more unhappily thrust upon aliens. (K 286)

It is possible to say that Tagore himself, poet and love-song-writer from Lower Bengal, appropriates this subject-position in his magnanimous novel. But not quite. Kipling's Hurree Babu sang something like his songs. In conceiving Binoy, Tagore gives narrative flesh to Hurree Babu. The novel takes place between Binoy's "white man's education" and his job, that would not "supply him with a white man's salary." Here is the initial description of Binoy's situation: "College studies done with long ago, yet no entry into the real world as yet, Binoy's situation is such" (1). I have already made the point that these are upper-middle-class Indians, the above of the below, the space of Frantz Fanon, perhaps. Ranajit Guha has recently made the point that *Hutum Penchar Naksha*, a Bengali riff on *Sketches by Boz*, takes place in the borrowed interval of carnival time, denoted in the text by the period between two cannon-shots from Fort William.[28] In the introductory chapter, before we have encountered Gora, such is the extended space of Binoy's nationalism, college studies done, but no entry into the real world. "He'd devoted himself to running committee meetings and writing for the newspapers," the sentence continues, "but his spirit was not fulfilled by this." It is as if *Gora* the novel, via Binoy, the educated Bengali, undoes Hurreebabu (a "love-song from lower Bengal," sung in the next paragraph by a robed minstrel, may be a meta-narrative sign) and illuminates a liminal space of narrative time pulled out of *Kim*, in the sense that Keats's "Ode to a Grecian Urn" pulls out a space on a Grecian urn remembered only by way of Keats's poem. It is what classical rhetoric might call an ekphrastic displacement. The phrase or articulation from within a text is taken outside of the original. Tagore's novel operates an ekphrastic displacement of a moment of the colonial subject – between education and job – in *Kim*.

I am of course not suggesting that Tagore writes *Gora* in this way. I am reading *Gora* in this way. You can take it or leave it. My friend Meenakshi Mukherjee would probably leave it.

Indeed, the text marks its distance not only from the *xenos* from above who dis-locates hospitality, declaring himself host by force of his law. At its very threshold, the text also distances itself from the located and local space of the *oikotes* below from which Tagore took so much. The song that inaugurates the book's action and the minstrel who moves out of the book on its first page – creating a matrix within which the story begins to happen – belongs to the older radical culture of Bengal:

> In front of a nearby shop, a baul in a long robe broke into song: How does the unknown bird fly in and out of the cage. If I caught it, I'd put mind-cuffs on its feet. Binoy felt like calling the baul home and writing down this song about the unknown bird. But he did not . . . [T]he baul remained uncalled, the song unwritten, but the tune telling of the unknown bird played in his mind. (1–2; translation modified)

It is the *Baul* tradition of folk minstrelsy.[29] The poet is Lalan Shah Fakir (1774–1890), a poet who enhanced the humanist *Baul* tradition with devotional counter-theology and many poems of peace, of which I quote a verse: "When will such a human society be built. That there will be no caste, no lineage, no Hindu Muslim, no Buddhist, no Christian."[30]

Within this space Gora makes his mistakes. When I read his story I think of the famous repetitive epithetic tabulation of Visnu Maya or Visnu's fiction in *Candi*.[31] In this Hindu text the gods are devising a killer for the great Buffalo-demon who cannot be killed by a god. Their solution is a fictive female – a goddess fictively produced. She can destroy evil because she is not-quite-not a god. She is not legitimate. At the beginning of *Gora* Tagore had laid the old order to rest, perhaps, in the figure of the singing minstrel. Here it is as if Gora himself can usher in an Indian modernity because he is not legitimate – a fictively produced foster-child. For me this fiction makes visible what was historically impossible for Amir Abd-ur-Rahman: the achievement of a regional modernity.

It is as if Gora celebrates the trajectory of the goddess who is resident in all existents (in the *Seiend*, *à la* Heidegger) as error: *ya devi sarvabh, tes, bhr~ntirupena samsthit*. I am not explaining a modern Indian text of secularism like a cultural Hindu conservative. The scriptural line is in praise of error, errancy.[32] And I have earlier described Gora's anagnoresis (the dispelling of his error) by way of Aristotle. For me, *Candi* and Aristotle are both instruments to theorize with, as are Foucault and Bhartrhari.

I am emboldened in this by Tagore's introduction of Gora in the third person, citing the Sanskrit Pandit of his college, by way of a well-known epithet of Siva – *rajatagirinibha* or Silver Mountain(-like). I am happy that Sujit Mukherjee has now corrected the earlier anonymous translator who translated this as "Snow Mountain." No, Rajatgiri is an epithet of Siva uttered by little Hindu girls before daybreak hoping for a good husband: *Dhy~yennityam mah~sam rajatagirinibham c~rucandr~vatamsam*. That this connection was not far from the narrative and indeed from the *mythos* or plot of the narrative is confirmed in the opening conversation between Mother and Son: "My love, your mother did indeed follow ritual once. . . . Daily I molded a Shiva lingam and sat down to worship, and your Dad threw it away. . . . When I took you in my lap I let ritual wash away, do you know that?" (14–15).

These introductory motifs and exchanges, full of dramatic irony, give us a sense of the role of woman in this novel, radical yet willingly subordinate. More about that at the end. Now two words about Gora's errancy.

As substance of Gora's error there are some persuasive speeches by him on the appropriateness of an ennobled Hindu India. This is the superb risk of playing the *viv~di* in a performance, the note in a raga that can break the raga, but can be used by a master artist. There is no reasonable refutation of Gora's espousal of orthodox Hinduism in the novel, only a narrative one: he discovers he is not a Brahman. It is only if we read the novel as novel, that we say "yes" with affective sympathy to the end: that this is the best India: "What I wanted to be day and night but couldn't be, I am today. I am Indian today. In me today there is no conflict among Hindu, Muslim, and Christian society" (475). This is in the affective declarative. If you read the text as a tract for the times, without entering its textual protocol, you cannot garner its strengths to undermine religious violence today. Gora as a Hindu is most persuasive.

Reading him as a figure in a textuality that includes the social and the verbal, I point also at another line of anagronesis. Gora listens with distaste to a Bengali Babu and a British functionary mocking underclass pilgrims on a steamer. He leaves the First Class deck with the impassioned statement: "My place is not with the two of you together – my place is with those travelers. But, let me ask you not to oblige me to come to this class again" (48).

In Tagore's hospitable representation of this imaginary incident, the Englishman acknowledges a bond with this noble position: "He walks quickly to Gora before alighting, lifts his hat slightly and says, 'I am so ashamed of my behavior – I hope you will forgive me'."[33] In between, when Gora confronts Magistrate Brownlow to say: "Since you have decided not to redress these wrongs, and since your ideas about the villagers are inflexible, I have no other choice, I will encourage the villagers to stand in resistance against the police by their own efforts," it is again a Bengali Babu who says: "Most people have not earned the right to absorb the best part of an English education" (180). The colonizer and the colonized are both split and split again. I draw this textual line to a bit of interior monologue toward the very end of the book. The European doctor enters with the Bengali family physician. Gora is still dressed in ritual clothes, with the marks of ritual upon his face and body. The doctor looks at him and thinks: "'Who is this person?' Before this Gora would have felt a resentment," Tagore continues, "at the very sight of an English doctor. Today he kept looking at him with a special eagerness [*bishesh ekta out-shukyer shohit*] as he examined the patient. He kept asking himself the same question again and again, 'is this man my closest kin here?'" (472). No direct resolution to this is offered. The question of biological identity is left unanswered. But to the doctor's question, the reader can now construct a two-step answer: do not be deceived by the inscription of the body; and then, this is you, transformed. This second answer touches the book's aporia. Gora's case, if generalized, would undo the line between imperialism and independence. Perhaps it is the textual task of those persuasive defenses of orthodoxy, uttered by an impassioned Gora, not to let the book cross over to that conclusion.[34]

In a few pages we get the final series of declarations from which I have already quoted. It is the grandeur of the text that identity is thus left dependent on case. If we wish to use this as a socially useful document, we must admit that the new demographic virtual frontiers are not located in such territorialities. Today we must attempt to displace Gora himself: today's NRI [non-resident Indian] is no Resident Alien. He is on the Internet, conjuring up Hindu nationalism. He is a DIPSO – dollar-income-private-sector-operator – sitting in Bangalore but part of what Robert Reich has called the secessionist community of electronic capitalism.[35] He is in the metropolis, recoding upward class-mobility (mimicry and masquerade) as resistance, destabilization, intervention.

I left Najibullah hanging, as he must hang suspended when we celebrate our postcoloniality. Let us look at a displacement of his translation project, upon this terrain where the reverse hospitality of the colonized misfired.

A Swiss anthropologist had apparently noticed "primary school students changing out of their traditional clothes into their Western-style school uniforms while on the way to [the] school[s established by Abd-ur Rahman's grandson]."[36] In my fancy, that quick-change is grotesquely reversed in the difference between the smiling and plump Najibullah, dressed in suit and tie, shaking Gorbachev's hand – as depicted in a famous photograph – and the emaciated man, dressed in Afghan costume, hanging from the traffic post in Kabul. If we are to credit the second volume of the *Life*, Abd-ur Rahman had attempted to substitute trim European clothing for the voluminous attire of the male Afghan.[37] No translation from English to Pashto must ignore the translations from Pashto to English – in an earlier dispensation. And the woman is elsewhere, even on this terrain, as the US may conceivably strike a deal with the anti-Taliban Northern Alliance. Who cares for the subjective constitution of subaltern women here?[38] After the destruction of the World Trade Center, the *New York Times* reports:

> After a crucial moment in 1996, days after the Taliban overran Kabul in a display of brutality, the Clinton administration decided to seek friendly ties with the Islamic movement. The plan was abandoned after the Taliban began oppressing women, but American diplomats continued to say until the bin Laden terror attacks became a focus of American policy that the Taliban might be the best government Afghanistan could hope for after a generation of conflict.[39]

In my fancy, Najibullah was trying to provide a means to educate the people of Afghanistan to want a civil society, to imagine a public sphere, and to mourn a violent past. We supplement it by reminding his ghost of subalterns, of women, *if* we deserve that haunting. It is hard; for the languages are Farsi

(Abd-ur Rahman), Urdu (Mahfuz Ali), Pashto (Najib)! This is where British colonialism is an enabling violation; it provides a connection, as does something called "communism," with Najib. This is why I translate, and, in closing I turn to my translation of Mahasweta Devi, and ask you to look at Mary Oraon, the central character of "The Hunt."[40]

Derrida ends *Of Hospitality* with the biblical story of the gang rape of a woman, authorized by a host for male guests, and ends with a question: "Are we the heirs to this tradition of the laws of hospitality?" (H 155; translation modified). Gora ends with a call to Lachhmiya, the Christianized outcaste domestic worker, permitting her to be hospitable at last. Mahasweta takes the hybrid and puts a machete in her hand. Daughter of the rape of a Christian tribal domestic worker by a white imperialist displaced at Independence, she corrects the failure of decolonization by the solitary exercise of a wild justice, a reinscription of aboriginality. As impossible a model as Gora, as all conceptual art must be. In her impossibility, she remains my favorite Resident Alien, a quick-as-a-flash reinscription of the majestic and longwinded Gora. A bit of the history of Bengali literature is caught in that move. But between Aristotle the Resident Alien and Abd-ur Rahman the untimely modernist, between Foucault and Najibullah, there is no connecting line.

Notes

1 Michael Hardt and Antonio Negri, *Empire* (Cambridge, MA: Harvard University Press, 2000), p. 397; Etienne Balibar, *Masses, Classes, Ideas: Studies on Politics and Philosophy Before and After Marx*, trans. James Swenson (New York: Routledge, 1994); Charles Taylor, *Multiculturalism and the Politics of Recognition: An Essay* (Princeton, NJ: Princeton University Press, 1992).

2 Reda Bensmaïa, "The Phantom Mediators: Reflections on the Nature of the Violence in Algeria." *Diacritics* 27.2 (1997), pp. 85–97.

3 G. C. Spivak, *Imperatives to Re-imagine the Planet* (Vienna: Passagen, 1999), pp. 34–6; and "Our Asias," forthcoming from Hong Kong University Press in a volume edited by Angelina Yee.

4 Rabindranath Tagore, *Gora*, trans. Sujit Mukherjee (New Delhi: Sahitya Akademi, 1997). Page references will be hereafter cited in the text; translation modified whenever necessary. For a study of *Gora* placing the novel within the Indian sociohistorical context, and within Tagore's own psychosocial biography, see Ashis Nandy, *The Illegitimacy of Nationalism: Rabindranath Tagore and the Politics of Self* (Delhi: Oxford University Press, 1994). I am grateful to Partha Chatterjee for bringing this book to my attention and for a rigorous first reading of my essay at short notice. In my effort to reconstellate Tagore's novel within the current obsession with migration, I have chosen to ignore one specific and important strand within the novel: "an ideological debate which makes no sense to the non-Bengali reader . . . [the] debate between orthodox Hinduism and the Brahmo reform movement" (Nandy, *Illegitimacy*, p. 35). Insofar as it represents the debate between orthodoxy and secularism, it forms part of my analysis. For a comparative study of *Kim* and *Gora* see Kalyan Kumar Chatterjee, "Incognitos and Secret Sharers: Patterns of Identity, Tagore, Kipling and Forster," *Indian Literature* 32.3, pp. 111–30. Chatter-

jee's remark that "Indian society regarded Anglicization especially in education as welcome" (ibid, p. 111) gives us a clue to the power of the image of Gora as Resident Alien. "There had been already an English educated elite in India even before Macaulay appeared on the scene, but the literature-based education with its liberal Victorian ethos ran parallel to the phenomenon called Indian Renaissance with its images of change and adoption, of rebirth and renewal, in an atmosphere of millennial hopes" (ibid, pp. 111–12). This is, of course, a class-based phenomenon. Elsewhere I have called it an "enabling violation."

5   Meenakshi Mukherjee, "Introduction," *Gora*, pp. ix–xxiv. Rudyard Kipling, *Kim* (New York: Viking, 1987). Hereafter cited in the text as K, with page reference following.

6   Nandy's remarks are worth quoting here: "Gora is seen not as an Indian who is finally shown to have alien roots but as an outsider who has come to stay as an insider. . . . In *Kim*, there is no re-birth" (Nandy, *Illegitimacy*, pp. 43, 46).

7   Michel Foucault, "What is an Author?" in Paul Rabinow (ed.), *The Foucault Reader* (London: Penguin, 1984), p. 114.

8   Salman Rushdie, "Damme, This is the Oriental Scene for You," *The New Yorker* (June 23, 1997), pp. 50–61. The root meaning of "vernacular" is "of or belonging to home-born slaves," although the secondary meaning – "indigenous" – developed in late Latin.

9   Henry James, "The Figure in the Carpet" in *Complete Stories 1892–1898* (New York: Library of America, 1996), pp. 572–608.

10   Michel Foucault, *The Archaeology of Knowledge*, trans. Alan M. Sheridan Smith (New York: Pantheon, 1972), p. 95.

11   Freud wrote that the uncanny could appear in fiction as it could not in the psyche. Tagore's fiction creates a full-fledged program – an affective apprenticeship using women – of alien residency. Neither Abd-ur Rahman – the Afghan Amir (about whom more below) – nor Nehru could swing that outside of colonialism, para- (about which more later) or post. No historical access to modernity. Chandigarh is an alien outgrowth, not resident as it would be upon a landscape recognizably fictive, site for upscale architectural conferences, where aging architects nostalgically recall "Corbu" as guru for enthralled to uncomfortable international audiences.

12   In this new episode of the Great Game, we see the same lineaments appearing. George W. Bush as boy-hero, speaking the language of hunting down his prey, Osama bin Laden as the named enemy, belongs to the semiotic field of the Wild West: "we'll get him dead or alive," or, as he said to the Congress on September 22, 2001: "If you are not with us, you are with the terrorist." The boy-hero can redefine democracy – predicated on the possibility of responsible opposition – as feudalism. Fareed Zakaria, the conservative ex-editor of *Foreign Affairs*, can mistake this for "moral seriousness" (Channel 13, 9/22/01). The morally serious attempts to understand or imagine the other side. It is the adolescent who reduces everything to black or white, himself an object in a world of similar objects, before the entry into the register of the Law as we understand it. In the useful language of Hardt and Negri's *Empire*, this is the Empire misperceiving the multitude – attempting to control the global by a recourse to a feudal gesture that can only lead to destruction and civil war. If Kipling's text wins assent by figuring the imperialist as child, Bush's position wins mass approval by figuring the Empire as the Wild West.

13 Peter Hopkirk, *The Great Game: The Struggle for Empire in Central Asia* (New York: Kodansha, 1994), pp. 123–4.

14 This portion is taken from Spivak, "Foucault and Najibullah," in *Other Asias* (forthcoming from Blackwell Publishers).

15 Afghans are the largest group of migrants to Switzerland. I cannot here elaborate the suggestions I had made to Stiftung Dialogik about a more just asylum ethics, in Switzerland. Transnational literacy attempts to make the global writable of capital-as-impossible-abstraction readable, again and again, as permanent parabasis, locating paratactically in fragmented narratives. This agenda despairs over metropolitan identity politics, which has, of course, its own situational justifications.

16 Michel Foucault, *Discipline and Punish: The Birth of the Prison*, trans. Alan Sheridan (New York: Pantheon, 1977), p. 163.

17 Muhammad Mahfuz Ali, *The Truth About Russia and England: From A Native's Point of View* (Lucknow: London Press, 1886), p. 51. "Besides, the oriental mind" – we read in the next paragraph – "does not much appreciate a friendship which is based on high principles and noble intentions – a friendship which is always insisting on dealing in a straightforward and honest way with all questions, political or otherwise. For instance, the Ameer could never perhaps understand how it would be consistent with real friendship on the part of the British Government to help him *only on condition* that he never entertained any aggressive aims towards his neighbours". Perhaps the Urdu text would have provided the solace of irony.

18 Etienne Balibar, "Globalization/Civilization" in Catherine David and Jean François Chevrier (eds.), *Politics/Poetics: Documenta X – The Book* (Ostfildern-Ruit: Cantz Verlag, 1997), p. 786.

19 Jacques Derrida, *Of Hospitality*, trans. Rachel Bowlby (Stanford, NJ: Stanford University Press, 2000). Hereafter cited in the text as H, with page reference following.

20 Assia Djebar's impulse toward placing Delacroix, or the French Captain who occupied Algiers, into teleopoesis, shares something of this impulse from the above of the below, but she foregrounds that subject-position as a woman. See "Forbidden Gaze, Severed Sound," in *Women of Algiers in their Apartment*, trans. Marjolin de Jaeger (Charlottesville: University of Virginia Press, 1992), pp. 136–40; and *Fantasia: An Algerian Cavalcade*, trans. Dorothy Blair (London: Quartet, 1985), pp. 6–8.

21 David Whitehead, "Aristotle the Metic," *Proceedings of the Cambridge Philological Society* 21 (new series, 1975), p. 97.

22 For the actual passage, see Jonathan Barnes (ed.), *The Complete Works of Aristotle, Vol. 2* (Princeton, NJ: Princeton University Press, 1984), p. 2461. The passage on Xenocrates is to be found in Diogenes Laertius, *Lives of Eminent Philosophers*, trans. R. D. Hicks (Cambridge, MA: Harvard University Press, 1925), Bk IV: 14, p. 391. The final quotation is *Politics* III.III. 4–6, to be found in Aristotle, *Politics*, trans. H. Rackham (London: Heinemann, 1932), pp. 197–9.

23 In the interest of making the metapsychological visible as the lesson of psychoanalytic ethics, Jacques Lacan takes Aristotle beyond the phenomenal affects of *elios* and *phobos* and showcases the tragic hero as beyond *Atè*, by which he means "an irreplaceable word [which] designates the limit that human life can only briefly cross. . . . Beyond this Atè, one can only spend a brief period of time." See Lacan, "The Splendor of Antigone," in *The Ethics of Psychoanalysis*, trans. Dennis Porter (London: Routledge, 1992), p. 263.

24 Sultan Mahomed Khan (ed.), *The Life of Abdur Rahman: Amir of Afghanistan G.C.B., G.C.S.I* (Karachi: Oxford University Press, 1980), vol. 2, pp. 17–19, 24–7, 58–60.

25 E. M. Forster, *A Passage to India* (New York: Harcourt Brace, 1952), p. 282.

26 Diego Cordovez, *Out of Afghanistan: The Inside Story of the Soviet Withdrawal* (New York: Oxford University Press, 1995), p. 374.

27 Farhad Mazhar, "The Corpse-Keeper of Revolt," in *Eb-datn-m-I* (Dhaka: Prabartana, 1989), p. 36. Translation mine.

28 Ranajit Guha, lecture delivered in the Anthropology Department, Columbia University, 1997; Charles Dickens, *Sketches by Boz and Other Early Papers, 1833–39*, ed. Michael Slater (Columbus: Ohio State University Press, 1994).

29 For information on the relationship between Lalan Shah and Tagore, see *Baula-Lalana-Rabindranatha* (Kolkata: Paribeshaka, 1995).

30 Lalan Shah Fakir, *Lalan Sangeet* (no publication information), v. 2, p. 71. When Sancho Panza walks out of the frame of *Don Quixote* at the very end, his departure indicates that which lies beyond the text, an invocation of modernity, perhaps. When Christophine walks out of the middle of Jean Rhys's *Wide Sargasso Sea* it is a comment on the limits of the Creole upper-class episteme. See Spivak, *A Critique of Postcolonial Reason: Toward the History of the Vanishing Present* (Cambridge, MA: Harvard University Press, 1999), pp. 129–31. The departure of the wandering minstrel is given no such structural task in *Gora*. At best it remains a trace that is interrupted.

31 Thomas B. Coburn, "Encountering the Goddess: A Translation of the 'Devi-Mahatmya' and a Study of its Interpretation" (Albany: State University of New York Press, 1991), pp. 53–4.

32 Revising, I notice that Derrida frames Kant's famous injunction to tell the truth even if it endangers a guest – thus breaking the law of hospitality – in Kant's thinking of the right to lie (H 63ff.). The general teleopoietic hospitality of *Gora* allows the stranger to err before he can acquire permanent residence.

33 Page 48. I have elsewhere commented on the conjunctural connections between Tagore and W. E. B. Du Bois. See Spivak, "Deconstruction and Cultural Studies," in Nicholas Royle (ed.), *Deconstructions* (Oxford: Blackwell Publishers, 2000), pp. 14–43. This nod to the good British spirit reminds me of Du Bois's "the South is not 'solid'" (*Souls of Black Folk*).

34 Lukács, unable to read Bengali, caught the point but read Tagore's peculiar aporetic hospitality, to this reader politically preferable to today's Eurocentric liberal multiculturalism, as the mark of a bourgeois writer without national liberationist progressivism and without talent. In 1922 Lukács wrote as follows about Tagore's *Home and the World* (1919): "The English bourgeoisie has reasons of its own for rewarding Mr. Tagore with fame and riches (the Nobel Prize): it is repaying its intellectual agent in the struggle against the Indian freedom movement. . . . For a pamphlet – and one resorting to the lowest tools of libel – is what Tagore's novel is, in spite of its tediousness and want of spirit. These libels seem all the more repugnant to the unprejudiced reader the more they are steeped in unctuous 'wisdom' and the more slyly Mr. Tagore attempts to conceal his impotent hatred of the Indian freedom fighters in a 'profound' philosophy of the 'universally human'" (Georg Lukács, "Tagore's Gandhi Novel," in Peter Palmer (ed.), *Reviews and Articles* (London: Merlin, 1983), pp. 8–9. My essay thus belongs to a more general struggle to decolonize socialism from within.

35 See G. C. Spivak, "Megacity," *Grey Room* I (fall, 2000), pp. 8–25. Nandy points out the difference between Tagore's vision and that of the modern Indian in India (Nandy, *Illegitimacy*, pp. 3, 83, 86, 89 and *passim*.

36 Barnett R. Rubin, *The Fragmentation of Afghanistan: State Formation and Collapse in the International System* (New Haven, CT: Yale University Press, 1995), p. 76.

37 Khan, *Life*, vol. 2, pp. 43–5.

38 I asked such questions in "Can the Subaltern Speak?" in Cary Nelson and Larry Grossberg (eds.), *Marxism and the Interpretation of Culture* (Urbana: University of Illinois Press, 1988), pp. 271–313; and in "Righting Wrongs," forthcoming in *boundary 2*.

39 John F. Burns, "Pakistan Antiterror Support Avoids Vow of Military Aid," *New York Times* (September 16, 2001), p. 5.

40 Mahasweta Devi, "The Hunt," *Imaginary Maps*, trans. Gayatri Chakravorty Spivak (New York: Routledge, 1995), pp. 1–17.

Chapter 4

Directions and Dead Ends in Postcolonial Studies

Benita Parry

The active participation of materialists and Marxists in postcolonial studies has not deterred perceptions of the field as inextricably associated with post-mortem theory. A similar reputation attended colonial discourse analysis during the 1980s, but perhaps because a textual idealism was not yet as insistent, interactions between diverse intellectual spheres generated a cross-disciplinary and theoretically eclectic demystification of the colonial archive (Hulme 1989). Such powerful and still influential work disclosed how Western writings and disciplines had constructed versions of non-European worlds directed at normalizing the imperial project. These representations included the pathologizing in biomedical texts of the perceived difference of the "normal" African (Vaughan 1991); European inventions of the African continent and its peoples where alterity featured as a negative category (Mudimbe 1988), and the spatial and temporal distance devised by Europe to remove the colonized from simultaneity (Fabian 1983). Meanwhile, concurrent investigations recuperated the many symbolic, cultural, and physical styles of colonial insubordination and insurgency, thus overturning the view of subjugated populations as passive or willing recipients of imperial domination (Brennan 1997; Lazarus 1993; Parry 1994; Said 1993; San Juan 1998).

In retrospect colonial discourse analysis can be seen as the precursor to the more extensive postcolonial discussion, under whose sign a considerable body of work has since been produced in anthropology, history, and geography; literary, film, gender, cultural, psychoanalytic, spatial, and queer studies; political science and art history. With the proliferation of enquiries favouring a textualist stance, the work of materialists was outnumbered, and the specificity of a word initially pertaining to historical processes, came to be eclipsed by an indiscriminate and often celebratory usage. Said, who at the time *Orientalism* appeared (1978) was identified as a Foucauldian, has since dissociated himself from "theoretical cults" where the pull and primacy of historical conditions is relegated (Said 1993, pp. 366–7). Procedures fitting this description, and elsewhere censured as "facile textualist thought" that contrives to block "the appeal to any kind of real-world knowledge and experience" (Norris 1993, p. 182), are abundantly manifest in those modes of postcolonial criticism where the politics of the symbolic order displaces the theory and practice of politics. I will be considering the explanatory consequences of a revisionist narrative lacking in conceptual credibility and amenable to neither intertextual confirmation nor empirical validation. But for the moment I am concerned with the new dimensions which the postcolonial discussion has brought to understanding colonialism's global reach.

Previous critical enquiries into empire and its consequences – as distinct from the learned apologies masquerading as disinterested scholarship – had focused on colonialism and imperialism as projects of an expansionist Western capitalism, and therefore integral to an economic and political *system*. Amongst the objects of discussion were the violent territorial advancement of Western capitalism on non-capitalist worlds, the extraction of raw materials and the exploitation of labor, authoritarian rule and institutional coercion, protection of investments in agriculture, mining, industries, and public works, the uneven and combined development within peripheral capitalist structures and the class formations consequent on the introduction or acceleration of new modes of production, shifts within traditional hierarchies, the redistribution of power in favor of emergent elites, and the dilemma of developing productive forces without installing commodity relations (see the extensive work of Samir Amin and Immanuel Wallerstein).

Many of these matters had already been addressed by theorists of anticolonial movements, who had also recognized culture as both a means of exerting power and a resource in the struggle against imperial rule. But it was in the wake of *Orientalism* that academic studies came to examine the range of cultural resistance together with colonialism's elaborate and hitherto overlooked deployment of knowledge in the exercise of political subjugation, and the extent of empire's dissemination in the culture and consciousness of the imperial homeland.

It had for long been recognized by students of British history that the making of the domestic economy and state was inseparable from overseas empire, whether in the form of mercantile and plantation colonialism, territorial rule, or the installation of financial and political power through trade and, from the later nineteenth century onwards, the export of capital. One of the achievements of postcolonial studies has been to extend this understanding to the tangible and imaginary presence of empire within the quotidian existence of the imperial homeland. By uncovering its immanence in both high and popular culture, as well as the everyday practices of the domestic society, these enquiries have countermanded chronicles of the imperial relationship which addressed only Europe's instrumentality in shaping the economies, social forms, and cultures of the colonized territories, and where consequently the imperial centers featured as catalysts.

By the last decades of the nineteenth century, visible and symbolic signs of empire were pervasive within the increasingly commodity-saturated and con-sumer-directed metropolis. These included imported luxury products, such as carpets, shawls, and jewels, household goods (foodstuffs, fabrics, and soaps) containing raw materials from the West Indies, Asia, and Africa, and tex-tiles and ceramics, both hand-crafted art works and factory-produced items, inspired by Eastern designs and motifs. At this time, too, there appeared a stag-gering quantity of ideologically saturated printed and visual matter promising to verify the many rumors about distant places and peoples. Produced by state institutions, civil agencies, and the purveyors of a growing mass culture, these widely circulated representations included popular and juvenile fiction, il-lustrated newspapers and magazines, paintings, drawings, prints, and pho-tographs, school textbooks, religious tracts, displays in ethnographical museums, *tableau vivants* staged as freak-shows, exhibitions in art galleries, magic lantern entertainments, music hall turns, theatrical spectacles, and logos with imperial themes on the packaging of biscuits, teas, coffee essences, and soaps (Coombes 1994; MacKenzie 1984, 1995; Pieterse 1992; McClintock 1985; Richards 1990).

Within the literary culture, countless books on the imperial project were written by politicians, historians, political scientists, social commentators, and "men of letters." Newspapers and journals were awash with opinion on em-pire, innumerable memoirs of travelers and those in the employ of colonial administrations were published, as well as a prodigious quantity of light but phantasmagoric fiction fabricated by "service" wives celebrating the exemplary lives of exiled British communities, and excoriating the wicked ways of the colonized. With some notable exceptions – E. D. Morel, Roger Casement, R. Cunninghame Graham, J. A. Hobson – whose reputations as unequivo-cal anti-imperialists all the same require qualification, this heterogeneous body of writing commended colonial ambitions and policies and reiterated British claims to a civilizing mission. Together they contributed to the making of colonialist ideology, and abetted the construction of a British *imperial* identity.

Until recently, discussion on the imperial project in British literary consciousness was confined to the literature of colonialism or the colonial novel, and the received criticism was in large part concerned with measuring "authenticity" and assessing empathy, rather than understanding the fictions as belonging in a larger discursive field. When these same texts are reread as originary or rehearsed enunciations of colonial discourse, what emerges is the confidence or insecurity in the exercise of representational power, and the ide-ological construction or ironic reinscription of the tropes, *topoi*, and rhetorics that came to form domestic perceptions of empire. Furthermore, because the presence of empire, whether overt or coded, has now been recognized in both canonical and popular metropolitan writings (Bivona 1990), "the colo-nial novel" appears as a category of convenience covering a range of genres and qualities, and one which does not exhaust the extent to which empire circulates or inheres in the English novel. Readings attentive to the colonial registers of canonical and mainstream Anglophone literature (these include *The Tempest*, *Robinson Crusoe*, *Mansfield Park*, *Castle Rackrent*, *The Rime of the Ancient Mariner*, *Daniel Deronda*, *Jane Eyre*, *Wuthering Heights*, *The Moonstone*, *Dorian Grey*, the Sherlock Holmes stories, *Tono-Bungay* and *The Waves*) uncover colonial locations, figures, and artefacts as sources or signifiers of mystery, danger, and exoticism, of dismay, disturbance, anxiety, fear, infection, and corruption. These glosses have enlarged the established interpretative frame, bringing a further dimension to the lethal Indian serpent in Conan Doyle's "The Speckled Band" (Hennessy and Mohan 1989) and the ill-gotten and malevolent Indian jewel in his novel The *Sign of Four*; and the unlucky gem stolen from an Indian holy place in *The Moonstone*. The commentaries have also substantiated the association of opium with the East, racial contagion and decadence (Marez 1997), and offered new insights into *fin de siècle* novels such as *She*, *The War of the Worlds* and *Dracula*, where anxieties about colonial contamination are displaced into minatory visitations from other distant, unknown and unknowable places (on *Dracula*, see Halberstam 1995).

Nevertheless there are problems attendant on identifying the signs of the imperial project in domestic fictions, one of which is a neglect of the distinction between the ornamental and the determinant function of empire within the texts. In Spivak's pioneering reading of *Jane Eyre*, a narrative of proto-feminist liberation is placed within imperialism's discursive field which produces ideological correlatives for the text's *narrative structuring* (Spivak 1985). The preferred procedure of critics, however, is to demonstrate how novelists brought colonial figures and colonialist rhetorics to their dramatizations of domestic oppressions. Thus the sources of the Bertram wealth in *Mansfield Park* (1814), the slave trade and plantation economy, are read as metaphors for class and gender wrongs at home, where the conditions of an Antiguan estate are reenacted in the blighted social relationships of an English country-house (Ferguson 1991; Fraiman 1995; cf. Said's (1993) gloss, which is concerned with the ways a colonial relationship is embedded in the novel's *form*, or Wood's (forthcoming) contention that the book produces an extended critique of the effects of slavery on English society). In similar vein, it has been suggested that the authors of *The Moonstone* and *Daniel Deronda* consciously associate the repressive politics of empire with the hierarchies of gender and class undergridding British society (Heller 1992; Lineham Bailey 1992).

Some time ago Peter Hulme, who remarked that the Brontës' close knowledge of slavery and the abolitionists' campaigns was on record (Heywood 1987), had faulted "the vast critical enterprise, which produced [their] novels as works of genius unconnected with the conditions of their production and sheered from the materials which went into the making of them, materials already shot through with colonial colours" (Hulme 1994, p. 85). This vacuum has since been abundantly filled, though not in the directions indicated by Hulme, and as well as recognizing the previously disregarded or unnoticed colonial traces in *Jane Eyre*, critics have decoded a rhetoric of slavery in *Wuther-*

ing Heights, interpreting Heathcliff as "a racial other" whose deportment sum-
mons the specter of slave rebellion (Von Sneidern 1995; Heywood had previously perceived Heathcliff as a slave-figure who protests his condition in the
idiom of the anti-slavery movement). But the novel which has attracted the
greatest number of studies alert to its colonial registers is *Jane Eyre*, about which
it has been observed that "a vocabulary and imagery of oppressed oriental
womanhood" is deployed to present metropolitan feminist interests (Perera
1991, p. 81); and that "Jane's struggle to overcome the class and gender
restrictions placed on her is articulated through colonial tropes of bondage and
liberation" (Sharpe 1993, p. 28).

Whereas these readings situate the importation of colonial *topoi* to configure metropolitan dominations as paratactic, that is without narrative coordinates, other accounts rearticulate the *unsecured linkages* in this and other texts
as constituting a critique of "the systematic operation of sexism and imperialism" (Lineham Bailey 1992, p. 332 on *Daniel Deronda*); or as critically inscribing gender, race, and class as intertwined or mutually reinforcing subsets
(Ferguson on *Mansfield Park* and Heller on *The Moonstone*); and as demonstrating an historical alliance between the ideology of male domination and the
ideology of colonial domination (Meyer on *Jane Eyre*).

Intent on establishing equivalencies between the different modalities of subjection and exploitation at home and abroad, critics introduce category errors
that cannot be attributed to the texts, since it is they, the critics, who claim
that historical knowledge about the interchangeability of the sites and temporalities of different dominations can be derived from figurative transferences
and metonymic transpositions; and moreover it is they who read the fictions'
ambiguous articulations and representations as orchestrating a coherent
impeachment of bourgeois social order simultaneously sustaining patriarchy,
class divisions, and colonialism. Nancy Stepan has cautioned that because
interactive metaphors shape our perceptions and actions, while at the same
time neglecting or suppressing information that does not fit the similarity,
"they tend to lose their metaphoric nature and be taken literally" (Stepan 1990,
p. 52). The risk associated with the use of analogical strategies is echoed by
those who find that the use of "metaphorics of slavery" to represent domestic
subjection in *Jane Eyre* obscures the literality and historicity of slavery (Plasa
1994).

In a larger context a related argument has been made about metropolitan
women writers who use the idiom of abolitionism or anti-colonialism to articulate their own struggles for equality: for while identifying themselves rhetor-
ically as black slaves or subjugated populations, they do not necessarily identify
politically with black slaves or the colonized. Rather than allotting an immanent critique to this novelistic stratagem, critics observe that it registers the
tension between solidarity with the condition of oppression, and disengagement from the conditions of the oppressed (Chrisman 1995; Sharpe 1993;
Ledger 1995; Kaplan 1996). Because tropological connotation is necessarily
casual about historical specificities, the incommensurate colonial metropolitan

conditions brought into proximity by its usage in fiction do not in themselves produce critical perceptions of empire, and may serve to underwrite authorized versions. However, compelling testimony to the extent and depth of an imperial imaginary does emerge where the transcoding between historical moment and literary practice is located in form and sylistics – as when Jameson (1981, 1988) and Said (1993) associate narrative authority in the nineteenth-century novel with confidence in the bourgeois management of overseas empire, and connect the emergence of modernist uncertainty with disconcerting shifts in metropolitan apprehensions of the imperial project (see Chrisman 1998 on the differences in the paradigms of these theorists).

The work that has been and is being done, in disfiguring colonialist configurations and uncovering traces of empire in the domestic imagination, is matched in importance by studies on the cultural production, past and present, of peoples formed by what the Caribbean novelist and critic Edouard Glissant cryptically calls The Relation, the process of disclocation and detour, and of self-constitution and return. Here, critics have devised new ways of reading past and contemporary fictions of once-colonized worlds, as well as the literatures written in the post-independence diasporas. Older commentaries on "commonwealth," "new" or "world literatures in English" had attempted to incorporate such texts into a common Anglophone tradition, and the writings were judged by conformity to standard English and approximation to the standards of the mainstream English novel (Bhabha 1984). What a postcolonial criticism has shown is that far from being imitations of Western modes, fictions written within other cultural contexts or from the margins of metropolitan centers are complex transformations and transgressions of existing conventions, whether realist or avant-garde. Such writing elaborates the broken Englishes invented by users fluent in other tongues, and disrupts/invigorates prior modes by integrating the narrative forms, such as performed storytelling and public recitation, the aesthetic languages and the perceptual resources from non-Western literary heritages and cognitive traditions (Boehmer 1995; Brennan 1997; Quayson 1997; Lazarus 1990). The best-known instance of intriguing received form is the deeply political "marvelous or magic realism" of Latin American, Caribbean, African and Asian fiction, where the mixing of styles, idioms, and voices animates the surrealism of violently disrupted histories, and manifests the alchemy of transmuting both autochthonous and cosmopolitan cultural forms into new genres (Dash 1973).

Whereas the postcolonial novel covers heterogeneous narrative styles from the former British, French, Portuguese, and Dutch empires in Africa, Asia, and the Americas, critics display an excessive interest in the fiction of migrants, and within this subgenre, in extravagant innovation. Hence partisan and resistance literature, as if considered devoid of aesthetic qualities, remains a minority interest (Harlow 1987; San Juan 1988), "realist" diasporic writing is marginalized, while popular fictions from the post-independence nation-states written in local languages and deemed uncongenial to metropolitan taste are untranslated and largely undiscussed within the academies. There is, for example, a whole corpus of testimonial literature from Central and South America, the Philippines, Asia, and Africa which is known by specialists who recognize its multivalencies, but is not easily available to English readers who are familiar with Marquez, Fuentes, Soyinka, Rushdie, and Coetzee. (The exception is the transcribed testament *I, Rigoberta Menchu: An Indian Woman in Guatemala* which was a best seller in the West). These variations suggest that, instead of attempting to compile a canon of Postcolonial Literature, we need to think about postcolonial literatures as a web of different strands, not all of which are woven out of "postmodern" materials.

The preference within the postcolonial discussion for hybrid, mestizo, or creolized formations privileges a fissured postcolonial identity, and scants the intelligibility, mutability, and inventions of the indigenous (Brennan 1997). Indeed it is argued that the rapt interest of Western academics in migration or exile entails a neglect of situations in post-independence nation-states, since "diaspora" has swelled "to demarcate the entire experience of post-coloniality" and "the subject-position of the 'hybrid' is routinely expanded as the only political–conceptual space for revisionist enunciation" (Loomba and Kaul 1994, pp. 4, 13, 14). Furthermore the use of "diaspora" as a synonym for a new kind of cosmopolitanism that is certainly relevant to writers, artists, academics, intellectuals, and professionals can entail forgetfulness about that other, economically enforced dispersal of the poor from Africa, Asia, Latin America, the Caribbean, and the Philippines. Perhaps the time has come for postcolonial studies to promote empirical investigations of these unsettled diasporas, and undertake the dissemination of the experiences spoken by scattered, impoverished, and despised populations stranded in temporary and exploited employment as contract workers, casual laborers, or domestic servants in Europe, North America, and the Gulf States.

Having suggested some significant initiatives, I want now to consider what I see as impediments to the development of postcolonial criticism, and in specifying these begin with semantics, for despite many instances of its arbitrary and ill-considered use, it is apparent that the "postcolonial" is, for the present at least, here to stay within and beyond the academic vocabulary. Some critics value the term because it is fluid, polysemic, and ambiguous. The consequence to this plentitude of signification is that the word has come to indicate a historical transition, an achieved epoch, a cultural location, a theoretical stance, and indeed in the spirit of mastery and impenetrability favored by Humpty-Dumpty in his dealings with language, whatever an author chooses it to mean. Amongst the more capricious definitions is one offered in the editorial introduction to the first issue of the journal *Postcolonial Studies*:

> Postcolonialism is what we employ to excavate the marginal, the magical, the erotic and the everyday . . . 'our' postcolonialism offers a new promiscuity which not only heads 'downmarket', but . . . breaks through the cordon that separates the anthropological-based cultural studies practised in relation to non-Western

societies from the popular culture schools that focus on the popular in the West. (Seth, Gandhi, and Dutton 1998, p. 10)

Where with greater gravitas the postcolonial denotes "a critical dimension" that goes beyond a previous body of theory, it infers a contentious discursive stance occupied by critics in relationship to the state of knowledge they necessarily inhabit. For Gayatri Spivak, whose inspiration is Derrida, post-coloniality is a case of a deconstructive philosophical position towards the logocentrism and identitarian metaphysics underpinning Western knowledge, a position from which the truth-claims of Eurocentric discourses and categories are dismantled and displaced (Spivak 1988, 1990). In a different register and with different implications, Neil Lazarus, who is uneasy about the category of "Eurocentrism" and is concerned to recuperate an ethical "humanism" and "universality" for a reconstructed social sphere beyond the capitalist world-system, rejects the Western provenance and habitation of modernity, argues for understanding it as a global phenomenon, and uncovers its articulations in non-metropolitan spaces. By appropriating Adorno's phrase "hating tradition properly," Lazarus enjoins a postcolonial practice which is simultaneously committed to "'the philosophical discourse of modernity' and to its urgent critique" (Lazarus 1999).

As a temporal designation where the "post" is understood as past and decolonization marks the definitive end of North/South inequalities, its usage is manifestly unsustainable. Because an international stratification of resources and labor persists under global capitalism, some critics consider that the very term mystifies, both politically and methodologically, a contemporary situation more appropriately described as late imperialism (Miyoshi 1993; Dirlik 1997; Parker 1995). Others make a case for understanding "the postcolonial domain" in terms of a society's "continued subjection to or disengagement from metropolitan forces" (Coronil 1992, p. 101) – a provocative designation of the situation but one whose scope must be qualified by the constraints on legally sovereign decolonized states to disengage from a global system still dominated by Western powers.

Aijaz Ahmad has recalled that "the first major debate on the idea of the postcolonial took place . . . not in cultural studies but in political theory where the object of inquiry was 'the postcolonial state'," discussions were conducted in Marxist terms, and the categories of colonialism and decolonization designated "identifiable structural shifts in state and society" (Ahmad 1995, p. 5). It is noticeable that where the postcolonial state was amongst the subjects of a recent debate in a journal of cultural studies, the interest in symbols of power exceeded consideration of its political, economic, and institutional implementation, with few participants referring to the conflicting class interests within post-independence political formations, or the international alliances forged by the new indigenous ruling classes (*Public Culture*, 5: 1, 1992).

Practices which privilege the signifier over the signified conform with a trend in cultural studies where, according to one commentator, there has been a move "to an essentially textualist account of culture," despite its "material-ist inspiration" (Sparks 1996, pp. 97, 98). Within the postcolonial discussion there are manifold consequences to a theoretical project which construes colo-nialism as a cultural process and is committed to reconstructing its histories and aftermaths from a theoreticist and selective reading of textual and sym-bolic significations. The dismissal of political economy in analysis means that the imperial project is detached from its beginnings in and inseparability from capitalism's trajectory. What follows is that globalization is divorced from capitalism, married to postmodernism, and despite an egregious inequality between and within center and periphery, the promotion of transnational cultural flows is applauded (Sivanandan 1998; Lazarus 1998). A related con-sequence is that the anti-capitalist momentum of past liberation movements is ignored, as is the continuing struggle against corrupt, repressive, and com-prador post-independence regimes who are the beneficiaries of an incomplete anti-colonialist project.

The paradox is that those who resist the foundational and determinist think-ing which they attribute to historical materialism are themselves militant in privileging language as foundational and deterministic in the making of society and culture. A recognition of texts as multivalent and subject to the play of signification, and of discourse as constitutive of consciousness, does not sanc-tion claims "about the inherent susceptibility of all social practices, conceived as signifying systems, to structural linguistic analysis" – a procedure which involves transposing a methodology devised to examine arbitrary and con-ventional signs operating within a self-enclosed domain without referents, in order to explain *over-determined* processes in the material and social worlds (Lazarus 1991, pp. 122, 126). Where the linguistic turn in its strong form is brought to a postcolonial criticism, the world is interpreted according to the principle of indeterminacy derived from shifts and disruptions in language. This move enables the occlusion of the contradictory, volatile but all the same *struc-tural* positions occupied by the heterogeneous categories of colonizer and col-onized, and it dissolves the antagonistic interests and aspirations immanent to colonial situations into a consensus.

It has been noted by a skeptical critic that "reconciliatory postcolonial thought fuse[s] postcolonialism with postmodernism in [its] rejection of re-sistance along with any form of binarism, hierarchy or telos" (During 1998, pp. 31, 2). A paradigm fulfilling these specifications is all too evident in work seeking a middle-ground between the terms "domination" and "subordina-tion," and where axiomatically governed readings of the imperial archive are projected as evidence that colonial relationships were ambivalent and colonial locations the site of negotiation. For one initiator of this fashion, a revision of the old story serves to disrupt "the customary epistemological divisions between colonized and colonizer, revealing colonialism as 'a mode of author-ity that is agonistic (rather than antagonistic)" (Bhabha 1994, p. 108) – which I take to imply a contest between voluntary contenders (Parry 1994). For another, the rhetoric of English India performs a *dialogue* across cultural boundaries, thus demonstrating the *complicity* linking the imperial power with the disempowered culture (Suleri 1992; pp. 3, 32; my emphases). Where does history figure in the story of colonialism now told by those who in obedience to the dictates of a theory opposed to binaries (and also perhaps in an effort to restore agency to the colonized, albeit a negative agency as collaborators with a system of subjugation), render their textual deconstructions of the colonial/colonized opposition in discourse, as identical with its displacement in the social world? To translate instabilities in colonialist utterances as secreting "the dynamic of powerlessness at the heart of the imperial configuration" implies more than an observation of textual anxieties, since the author goes on to assert that the psychic disempowerment which she detects in British writing, underlay "the colonial system *of control*" (Suleri 1992, pp. 15, 4; my emphasis) – that is, *colonialist practices*. There is a similar equation of textual readings with event when a critic, on detecting the inner contradictions in the *categories* of colonialism and the vicissitudes in its *discourses*, offers these observations as testimony to the insecurities in the *exercise* of colonial power, and evidence that its *"functioning"* was "heterogeneous with its founding oppositions" (Prakash 1996, p. 188; 1993, pp. 16, 17; my emphases).

If history is perceived as one narrative fiction amongst many, then validation becomes irrelevant and proclamations concerning the weakness of colonial authority deduced from instabilities in *selected* utterances require no corroboration, either intertextually or in other disciplinary investigations. Any skeptical and vigilant reading of written and oral records will confirm that colonial power was never total, since subordinated populations devised multiple ways to thwart the implementation of policies, and colonialism's agents, despite boasts of their excellence as firm rulers, were vulnerable. At the same time, empirical investigation will confute the bridging of binary divisions, demonstrating instead that resistance from the colonized was met with punitive responses from colonial regimes.

The representation of the colonial context as a hegemony is strenuously contested by eminent scholars associated with the postcolonial project for whom an emphasis on the collusion of the colonized with the British empire obscures the Raj as a project of capitalism and, with it, the irreconcilable differences between the peasants and workers and their colonial rulers. Thus "a sweet and sanitized image" of consent cannot "illuminate and explain the harsh realities of politics" or the enforcement of order through the coercive state apparatus of the Raj (Guha 1989, pp. 228, 234). Nor, as an anthropologist has observed, can the centrality of routine exchange in everyday practice be construed as a sign of concordance, since such practices do not encompass "the larger field of power relations that constitutes the circumstances of colonized populations" (Thomas 1991, pp. xi, 9).

It is an irony that the story of mutuality now being composed by some postcolonial critics makes an inadvertent return to the benign narrative of colonialism once disseminated by British imperial historiography, and one which in the metropolis continues to have a purchase on the official and popular memory of empire, especially the Indian empire. The blurring of conflict in colonial situations by those preoccupied with uncovering a middle-ground of negotiation has little to do with acknowledging the necessary and often coerced "intimacies" between ruler and ruled, or understanding the discrepant experiences of the parties as constituting one history. The case for refusing the domination versus resistance model in the interest of revealing the imbrication of "face-to-face encounters between colonizer and colonized" (Loomba and Kaul 1998, pp. 85–6) is probably directed at the putative epistemological error and empirical misrecognition of a Marxist Manichaeanism unable to relinquish conflict as immanent to colonialism. It does not, however, dispose of the obstinate material, social, and cultural conditions of empire.

To derive knowledge about the disablement of power in the social world from intimations of perplexity and equivocation in discourse is an example of what has been called the failure "to acknowledge any difference . . . between historical fact and literary or fictive representation" (Norris 1994, p. 12). Transcoding is a disjunctive process and it is unsafe and unsound to extrapolate the making and operation of social practices from the enunciative act. As well as mediating or estranging historical circumstances by ostentatiously displaying the source, or disseminating this matter indirectly through tropes or inflections, writing can repress existing conditions by fabricating an alternative scenario. Thus the texts of the Raj are saturated in declarations about a mission to rule and elevate a degraded but grateful people, while any traces of base interests – India as a source of raw materials, cheap labor, secure markets, and protected investment, or India as the linchpin of Britain's wider imperial ambitions – are erased.

What literature does do is tell us "what a period thinks about itself" (Machery 1990, p. 134) and because fiction works on ideology and can reinvent, defamiliarize, or undermine authorized versions, the traces of uncertainty which are discernible in some colonial writing should be read as a troubled response to the colonial condition, but not as attesting to the fragility of imperial rule. When Conrad wrote his anguished and dystopian representations of empire, colonial regimes were energetically pursuing aggressively expansionist policies in Africa; when Kipling cryptically contemplated the insecurity of the Raj, British rule was extending its bureaucratic apparatus in India and flexing its military muscle to deal with organized opposition; when Graham Greene perceived a loss of imperial will, the British regime was fighting colonial wars in Malaya and forcibly repressing independence movements in Africa.

The larger intellectual context which postcolonial studies must inhabit and negotiate is intimated in the embattled announcement from a group of postmodern theorists who, on detecting "an attempt at consensus-building among Left Conservatives . . . founded on notions of the real," declare: "A specter is haunting US intellectual life: the specter of Left Conservatism" ("A Workshop on 'Left Conservatism'"). Rather than rally other self-proclaimed Left radicals to the barricades, the legend on their banner may instead promote the case for restoring "the real" to critical theory, and with this, to postcolonial criticism. Its absence in the discussion has many and often bizarre repercussions: one critic who appears to have no knowledge of anti-colonialist theory and practice, has declared that "the strategy of blur" or "blur politics" is "a virtual program for resistance theory," and especially for decolonizing discourse:

> Effective anti-colonial struggle does not reside in those categories derived from the oppositional logic of imperialism, but in those exchanges and practices wherein the reality of the colonial is refused and the stereotypical discourses through which the colonial formation reproduces itself are disrupted. (Smyth 1997, p. 157)

Where the politics of the symbolic order displaces politics, and the theoretical assault on the retention of oppositional categories writes out conflict, there is no space for anti-colonialist theories inscribing irreconcilable contest, or anti-colonialist practices that were/are manifestly confrontational (critics attentive to anti-colonialism on its own terms include Brennan, Chrisman, Lazarus, Parry, Said, and San Juan). For Stuart Hall, however, the surmounting of binary forms of representation evoked in anti-colonial struggles is

> a move from one conception of difference to another . . . from difference to différance, and this shift is precisely what the serialized or staggered transition to the "postcolonial" is marking. But it is not only marking it in a "then" and "now" way. It is obliging us to reread the very binary form in which the colonial encounter has for so long itself been represented. It obliges us to reread the binaries as forms of transculturation, of cultural translation, destined to trouble the here/there cultural binaries forever. (Hall 1996, p. 247)

But surely a necessary condition of "transculturation," as distinct from contiguities, interactions, influences, and effects, is reciprocity, a situation where each party recognizes the other as an architect of cognitive and intellectual traditions; and because any such acknowledgment was ostentatiously withheld by the colonizers, the term appears singularly inappropriate to a colonial context.

A turn from a rhetoric disparaging the master narratives of revolution and liberation, and a return to a politics grounded in the material, social, and existential, now appears urgent. When the testimony of history is derived from its modes of writing, this renders redundant explanations of events which call on empirical enquiry and invoke texts which do not yield to the *a priori* theoretical requirements of the critic. Where agency is conceived as enacted and recoverable at the level of enunciation (Bhabba 1984, pp. 24, 110–11, 172), then resistance as the experiential reality and social practice of human subjects is dismissed as repeating the error of a discredited humanism. The theoretical aversions and/or ignorance of eminent critics, together with the dedicated followers of their fashion, has led to reiterated misconstructions of anti-colonialism as always nativist, wedded to premodern ideologies or parasitic on colonialist categories. Their work has elided the distinctive decolonizing transitions which have overdetermined contemporary conditions in post-independence states, and removed from the agenda the continuing resistance to comprador regimes and new oligarchies. Their failure to study the struggles against imperial domination has preempted informed discussion on the differences between moderate nationalist movements for independence within the global status quo, and revolutionary programs animated by the aspiration to an internationalism beyond an imperialist globalism.

Predictably those committed to postmodern analytic paradigms are hostile to the movement of sublation, or preservation/cancellation/transcendence in liberation theory, where the anticipation of egalitarian postcolonial conditions subsumes the retention and supersession of the technical advances inadvertently effected by capitalism-as-colonialism. In scorning liberatory expectations as naive, the purpose of critics has been to render nugatory the joining of intelligible and still viable indigenous resources and age-old traditions of colonial resistance with the ethical horizons and utopian reach of socialism. The sanctioned occlusions in postcolonial criticism are a debilitating loss to thinking about colonialism and late imperialism. The dismissal of politics and economics which these omissions reflect is a scandal.

References

"A workshop on 'Left Conservatism'" (1998) Center for Cultural Studies, University of California at Santa Cruz.

Ahmad, Aijaz (1995) "The politics of literary postcoloniality," *Race and Class*, 36: 3, pp. 1–20.

Bailey, Katherine Lineham (1992) "Imperialism in *Daniel Deronda*," *Texas Studies in Literature and Language* 34: 3, pp. 325–46.

Bhabha, Homi (1984) "Representation and the colonial text," in *The Theory of Reading*, ed. Frank Gloversmith, Brighton: Harvester Press.

——(1994) *The Location of Culture*, London: Routledge.

Bivona, Daniel (1990) *Desire and Contradiction: Imperial Visions and Domestic Debates in Victorian Literature*, Manchester: Manchester University Press.

Boehmer, Elleke (1995) *Colonial and Postcolonial Literature*, Oxford: Oxford University Press.

Brennan, Timothy (1988) *Salman Rushdie and the Third World*, New York: St Martin's Press.

——(1997) *At Home in the World: Cosmopolitanism Now*, Cambridge, MA: Harvard University Press.

Chrisman, Laura (1995) "Empire, race and feminism at the *fin de siècle*: the work of George Egerton and Olive Schreiner," in *Cultural Politics at the Fin de Siècle*, Cambridge: Cambridge University Press.

——(1998) "Imperial space, imperial place: theories of empire and culture in Fredric Jameson, Edward Said and Gayatri Spivak," *New Formations* 34, pp. 53–69.

Coombes, Annie (1994) *Reinventing Africa: Museums, Material Culture and Popular Imagination in Late Victorian and Edwardian England*, New Haven, CT: Yale University Press.

Coronil, Fernando (1992) "Can postcoloniality be decolonized? Imperial banality and postcolonial power," *Public Culture*, 5: 1, pp. 89–108.

Dash, J. Michael (1973) "Marvellous realism – the way out of Nègritude," *Caribbean Studies*, 13: 4, pp. 57–70.

Dirlik, Arif (1997) *The Postcolonial Aura: Third World Criticism in the Age of Global Capitalism*, Boulder, CO: Westview Press.

During, Simon (1998) "Postcolonialism and globalization: a dialectical relation after all?" *Postcolonial Studies* 1: 1, pp. 31–47.

Fabian, Johannes (1983) *Time and the Other*, New York: Columbia University Press.

Ferguson, Moira (1991) "*Mansfield Park*: slavery, colonialism and gender," *Oxford Literary Review*, 13: 1–2, pp. 118–39.

Fraiman, Susan (1995) "Jane Austen and Edward Said: gender, culture and imperialism," *Critical Inquiry*, 21, pp. 805–21.

Glissant, Edouard (1989) *Caribbean Discourse: Selected Essays*, trans. Michael Dash, Charlottesville: University of Virginia Press.

Guha, Ranajit (1989) "Dominance without hegemony and its historiography", *Subaltern Studies* 6, Oxford: Oxford University Press, pp. 210–309.

Halberstam, Judith (1995) "Technologies of monstrosities: Bram Stoker's *Dracula*", in *Cultural Politics at the Fin de Siècle*, ed. Sally Ledger and Scott McCracken, Cambridge: Cambridge University Press.

Hall, Stuart (1996) "When was 'The Post-Colonial?' Thinking at the limits," in *The Postcolonial Question: Common Skies, Divided Horizons*, ed. Iain Chambers and Lidia Curti, London: Routledge.

Harlow, Barbara (1987) *Resistance Literature*, London: Methuen.

Heller, Tamara (1992) *Dead Secrets: Wilkie Collins and the Female Gothic*, New Haven, CT: Yale University Press.

Hennessy, Rosemary and Mohan, Rajeswari (1989) "The construction of woman in three popular texts of empire: towards a critique of materialist feminism," *Textual Practice*, 3: 3, pp. 323–59.

Heywood, Christopher (1987) "Yorkshire slavery in Emily Brontë's *Wuthering Heights*," in *Review of English Studies*, 38: 150, pp. 184–98.

Hulme, Peter (1989) "Subversive archipelagos: colonial discourse and the break-up of continental theory," *Dispositio*, 14, pp. 1–23.

—— (1994) "The locked heart: *Wide Sargasso Sea*," in *Colonial Discourse/Postcolonial Theory*, ed. Francis Barker, Peter Hulme, and Margaret Iversen, Manchester: Manchester University Press.

Jameson, Fredric (1981) *The Political Unconscious*, London: Methuen.

—— (1988) *Modernism and Imperialism*, Derry: Field Day.

Kaplan, Cora (1996) "'A Heterogeneous Thing': female childhood and the rise of racial thinking in Victorian Britain," in *Human All Too Human*, ed. Diana Fuss, London: Routledge.

Lazarus, Neil (1990) *Resistance in Postcolonial African Fiction*, New Haven, CT: Yale University Press.

—— (1991) "Doubting the new world order: Marxism, realism, and the claims of postmodernist social theory," *Differences: A Journal of Feminist Cultural Studies*, 3: 3, pp. 94–113.

—— (1993) "Disavowing decolonization: Fanon, nationalism, and the problematic of representation in current theories of colonial discourse," *Research in African Literatures*, 24: 3, pp. 69–98.

——(1998) "Charting globalization," *Race and Class*, 40: 2/3, pp. 91–109.

——(1999) *Nationalism and Cultural Practice in the Postcolonial World*, Cambridge: Cambridge University Press.

Ledger, Sally (1995) "The New Woman and the crisis of Victorianism," in *Cultural Politics at the Fin de Siècle*, Cambridge: Cambridge University Press.

Lee, Debbie (1998) "Yellow fever and the slave trade: Coleridge's The Rime of the Ancient Mariner," *English Literary History*, 65, pp. 675–700.

Loomba, Ania and Kaul, Suvir (1994) "Location, culture, postcoloniality," *Oxford Literary Review*, 16, pp. 3–30.

——(1998) "Interview: Edward Said in Conversation with Neeladri Bhattacharya, Suvir Kaul and Ania Loomba," *Interventions*, 1: 1, pp. 82–96.

McClintock, Anne (1995) *Imperial Leather*, London: Routledge.

Machery, Pierre (1990) *The Object of Literature*, Cambridge: Cambridge University Press.

MacKenzie, John M. (1984) *Propaganda and Empire: The Manipulation of British Public Opinion 1880–1960*, Manchester: Manchester University Press.

——(1995) *Orientalism: History, Theory and the Arts*, Manchester: Manchester University Press.

Marez, Curtis (1997) "The other addict: reflections on colonialism and Oscar Wilde's opium smoke screen," *English Literary History*, 64, pp. 257–87.

Menchu, Rigoberta (1984) *I, Rigoberta Menchu: An Indian Woman in Guatemala*, ed. Elizabeth Burgos-Debre, London: Verso.

Meyer, Susan (1996) *Imperialism at Home: Victorian Women's Fiction*, Ithaca, NY: Cornell University Press.

Miyoshi, Masao (1993) "A borderless World? From colonialism to transnationalism and the decline of the nation state," *Critical Inquiry*, 19, pp. 726–5.

Mudimbe, Valentin (1988) *The Invention of Africa: Gnosis, Philosophy and the Order of Knowledge*, London, James Currey.

Norris, Christopher (1993) *The Truth About Postmodernism*, Oxford: Blackwell Publishers.

——(1994) *Truth and the Ethics of Criticism*, Manchester: Manchester University Press.

Parker, Kenneth (1995) "Very like a whale," *Social Identities*, 1: 1, pp. 55–74.

Parry, Benita (1994) "Resistance theory/theorizing resistance," in *Colonial Discourse/ Postcolonial Theory*, ed. Francis Barker, Peter Hulme, and Margaret Iversen, Manchester: Manchester University Press.

——(1994–5) "Signs of our times: a discussion of Homi Bhabha's *The Location of Culture*," *Third Text*, 28/9, pp. 5–24.

——(1998) "Liberation movements: memories of the future," *Interventions: The International Journal of Postcolonial Studies*, 1: 1, pp. 45–51.

Perera, Suvendrina (1991) *Reaches of Empire*, New York: Columbia University Press.

Pieterse, Jan Nederveen (1992) *White on Black: Images of Africa and Blacks in Western Popular Culture*, New Haven, CT: Yale University Press.

Plasa, Carl (1994) " 'Silent Revolt': slavery and the politics of metaphor in *Jane Eyre*," in *The Discourse of Slavery: Aphra Behn to Toni Morrison*, ed. Carl Plasa and Betty J. Ring, London: Routledge.

Prakash, Gyan (1993) "Postcolonial criticism and Indian historiography," *Social Text*, 31: 2, pp. 8–19.

——(1996) "Whose afraid of postcoloniality?" *Social Text*, 49: 14, 4, pp. 187–220.

Quayson, Ato (1997) *Strategic Transformations in Nigerian Writing*, Oxford: James Currey.

Richards, Thomas (1990) *The Commodity Culture of Victorian England: Advertising and Spectacle, 1851–1914*, London: Verso.

Said, Edward (1978) *Orientalism*, London: Routledge and Kegan Paul.

——(1993) *Culture and Imperialism*, London: Chatto and Windus.

San Juan, Epifanio (1988) "The resposibility to beauty: toward and aesthetic of national liberation," in *Rupturing Schisms, Interventions: Cultural Revolution in the Third World*, Manila: De La Salle University Press.

——(1998) *Beyond Postcolonial Theory*, New York: St Martin's Press.

Seth, Sanjay, Gandhi, Leela, and Dutton, Michael (1998) "Postcolonial Studies: A Beginning," *Postcolonial Studies: Culture, Politics, Economy*, 1: 1, pp. 7–11.

Sharpe, Jenny (1993) *Allegories of Empire*, Minneapolis: University of Minnesota Press.

Sivanandan, A. (1998) "Globalism and the left," *Race and Class*, 40, 2/3, pp. 5–19.

Smyth, Gerry (1997) "'The Crying Game': postcolonial or postmodern?" *Paragraph*, 20: 2, pp. 154–73.

Sparks, Colin (1996) "Stuart Hall, Cultural Studies and Marxism," in *Stuart Hall: Critical Dialogues in Cultural Studies*, ed. David Morley and Kuan-Hsing Chen, London: Routledge.

Spivak, Gayatri Chakravorty (1985) "Three women's texts and a critique of imperialism," *Critical Inquiry*, 12: 1, pp. 243–61.

——(1988) "Can the subaltern speak?" in *Marxism and the Interpretation of Culture*, ed. Cary Nelson and Lawrence Grossberg, London: Macmillan.

——(1990) *The Postcolonial Critic: Interviews, Strategies, Dialogues*, ed. Sarah Harasym, London: Routledge.

Stepan, Nancy (1990) "Race and gender: the role of analogy in science," in *Anatomy of Race*, ed. David Theo Goldberg, Minneapolis: University of Minnesota Press.

Suleri, Sara (1992) *The Rhetoric of English India*, Chicago: Chicago University Press.

Thomas, Nicholas (1991) *Entangled Objects*, Cambridge, MA: Harvard University Press.

Vaughan, Megan (1991) *Curing Their Ills: Colonial Power and African Illness*, Cambridge: Polity Press.

Von Sneidern, Maja-Lisa (1995) "*Wuthering Heights* and the Liverpool slave trade," *English Literary History*, 62, pp. 171–96.

Warwick, Alexander (1995) "Vampires and the empire: fears and fictions of the 1890s," in *Cultural Politics at the Fin de Siècle*, ed. Sally Ledger and Scott McCracken, Cambridge: Cambridge University Press.

Wood, Marcus (forthcoming) "The price of Fanny's improvement: Jane Austen, Adam Smith and the economics of empire" (manuscript on file with author).

Chapter 5

Racial Rule

David Theo Goldberg

On the periphery . . . people . . . learned quickly enough that Progress in the abstract meant domination in the concrete.

Tom Nairn, *The Break-up of Britain*

As much as the modern state has been about anything – about increasing bureaucratization and rationalization, about increasingly sophisticated forms of democratization and social control, about the rule of law and the control of capital – it has been about increasingly sophisticated forms and techniques of racial formation, power, and exclusion. Most commentators have presumed a singularity to racially configured states. Racial rule accordingly is taken to be legitimated in virtue of the assumption that non-Europeans are inherently inferior to Europeans, indeed, so inferior as to be incapable for the most part of self-governance. Thus Charles Mills is not untypical in insisting that "since its emergence as a major social category several hundred years ago, race has paradigmatically been thought of as a "natural," a biological fact about human beings, and the foundation of putatively ineluctable hierarchies of intelligence and moral character" (Mills 1998, p. xiii). This tradition, which I will call "naturalist," runs from Hobbes and Pufendorf through Rousseau and Kant to Hegel and Carlyle. Its contemporary representative is *The Bell Curve*.

There is, however, an equally powerful tradition, almost always overlooked, not least because in some ways revisionary. Here the claim is not that those not white are inherently inferior but developmentally immature, historically not yet capable of self-goverance and so requiring the guidance of European colonial benevolence. This is the expression of state racial con-figuration and racial rule running from Locke to Comte and Marx, John Stuart Mill and Lord Acton, Thomas Sowell and Shelby Steele. I call this tradition "historicist" or "evolutionary."

Naturalism and Historicism

The two traditions I have identified in conceiving and writing about racial states, while conceptually distinct and seemingly mutually exclusive, coexist historically. The naturalist conception dominated from the seventeenth well into the nineteenth century, the historicist or progressivist one displacing its dominance in the second half of the nineteenth century but far from eclipsing it. It is revealing that the rise of what I am calling the historicist conception, for those societies in which it actually attained prominence, is more evident in the administrative expression of colonial rule than in popular culture or even in prevailing intellectual commitments. Popular culture and intellectual fashion came to embrace racial historicism, if at all, more slowly, grudgingly, ambivalently. Indeed, one could say that each tradition has licensed various embodiments and expressions throughout the twentieth century – in fact, as I have hinted, continues to – and in that sense each is internally diverse. It is too easy to think that greater familiarity of those of European descent with those who are not would prompt the shift from naturalism to historicism, for such growing familiarity just as easily promoted contemptuous dismissive segregationist sentiments as progressivist sensibilities or egalitarian commitments.

These two traditions of racial conception are linked to two broader traditions of state formation, namely, to coercion- and capital-based states. Particular states have emerged and matured out of specific histories that emphasized capital accumulation or coercion as the principal basis of state creation, expansion and structure. As Tilly (1994, p. 8) argues, cities have tended to be containers of capital, states cells of coercive power like the military and later the police. By extension, I want to suggest that those states in Europe and their satellites that tended to emphasize coercion in their emergence, unification, and elaboration – Germany, for instance, and later South Africa – were likely to have been prone to a naturalist conception of racial formation, of racial superiority and inferiority. Here racial rule was considered imperative, if not the product of a Divine hand then the logic of Nature. The racially dominant were seen to set laws, impose order, maintain control because destined by their blood or genes to do so. Dilution of their blood or genes was considered at once transgression of nature, with dire consequences. It follows that colonial rule (imperial or self-determining), expansion, governmental imposition, and state control might be motivated as manifest destiny or natural law and effected principally at the crack of the whip, the point of the sword, or the barrel of the gun.

By contrast, those states growing out of financial centers and founded predominantly on capital formation and circulation – England, for example, or France – tended in the history of their development to have inscribed in their racial administration, implicitly or explicitly, a historicist or progressivist set of presumptions. Racial rule here was seen as the outcome of history, domination ordained by the hidden hand of historical development, the "fact" of historically produced superiority. Likewise, their colonial legacy would tend to be predicated on developmentalist assumptions, committed at least on the face of it through a long slow process of "progressive development and maturation" to colonial self-rule.

These links, it must be stressed, are a matter of emphasis and nuance. So I am not suggesting that there weren't those in coercive-based states committed to racial historicism, or those in capital-directed states rationalizing claims to superiority and practices of subjugation on naturalist grounds, just as there were resistant voices to both in either state form. But again there is no natural relation between the force or vehemence of resistance and forms of racial disposition. A naturalist might just as well dismiss intellectual contributions by those regarded racially inferior as "mimicry of the parrot"[1] and physical resistance as the "restlessness of the natives." And they might equally respond with vehement repression as with an attitudinal shift to historicism. The progressivist, in turn, might respond to resistance with further liberalizing reforms or with an inclination to naturalist rationalizations for more repressive subjugation, an ambivalence already reflected in the conceptual ambiguity of "progressivism."

In similar vein, those committed to naturalist principles on some issues or for some racially conceived groups might be found to express themselves in historicist terms on other issues or regarding different groups. So, for example, in 1857 Chief Justice Taney of the US Supreme Court declared in his majority opinion in *Dred Scott vs. Sanford* that "it has been found necessary, for their sake as well as our own, to regard [American Indians] as in a state of pupilage." Because he saw them effectively as members of foreign nations, he claimed American Indians could be naturalized as citizens of the United States. Black people, Taney argued by contrast,

> had for more than a century before been regarded as beings of an inferior order, and altogether unfit to associate with the white race, either in social or political relations; and so far inferior they had no rights which the white man was bound to respect; and that the negro might justly and lawfully be reduced to slavery for his benefit.

Taney concluded that black people were excluded intentionally from being considered citizens under the US Constitution, unprotected by constitutional rights, immunities, and privileges (*Dred Scott vs. Sanford* 1857, pp. 403–7; Bell 1992, pp. 20ff.). From the 1880s until at least the 1930s, not unrelatedly, American Indians were regarded in the US as assimilable, while people of African descent were considered segregable because the two groups were seen to occupy different rankings on prevailing racial hierarchies. The former were deemed open to evolutionary progress, of being whitened precisely in the way the latter prevailingly were not.

The distinction between naturalism and historicist progressivism likewise accounts, at least in part, for the vacillation regarding slavery and social integration by US politicians like Jefferson and Lincoln. Lincoln's is a case of espousing initially a naturalist commitment (inherent inferiority) and acting on (later expressing also) historicist assumptions precisely in the name of a racial political progressivism. So Lincoln's debate with Stephen Douglas in 1858 make clear his sense of "Negro" inferiority. But his commitment to expatriation of blacks to Liberia, in keeping with the prevailing migrationism of the day, at least implicitly acknowledged their capacity for self-governance.

Thus, in drawing the distinction between racist naturalism and historicism I am mapping dominant trends preparatory to delineating different forms of racial rule in the different styles of state formation. The naturalist tradition is most evident in the intellectual trajectory regarding racial studies running from pre-Adamism through polygenism to eugenicism and the likes of *The Bell Curve*. It informs state formation in the "cruelty" of Spanish colonial rule even as the Spanish Crown struggled in the sixteenth century with establishing laws recognizing the "equality" of colonial subjects (Merivale 1841/1928, pp. 3–4). "The great principle of the Spanish law respecting the Indians", writes Herman Merivale in his extraordinarily revealing lectures on colonization in the early 1840s, "was that of preserving them in a state of *perpetual minority*" (ibid, p. 6; emphasis in original). Similarly, Jefferson notoriously insisted that "the difference [between black and white] is *fixed in nature*," indeed, that

> the blacks . . . are inferior to the whites in the endowments both of body and mind. . . . The [Roman] slave, when made free, might mix with, without staining the blood of his master. But with us [Americans], [w]hen freed, [the black slave] is to be removed beyond the reach of mixture. (Jefferson 1781/1955, my emphasis)

What makes Jefferson's insistence more troubling than those of most contemporary or later racial scientists is precisely that he stood in a position to act on it politically. Jefferson could invoke the state apparatus at his disposal to effect his proto-segregationist imperative even though in fact he proved reluctant to do so (cf. Appiah, in Appiah and Gutmann 1996, pp. 42–7).

In terms of state expression, then, the naturalist tradition is exemplified in the vicious violence of Belgian colonization of the Congo (most notably under Leopold II), in Nazi apocalyptic megalomania, in slavery and the Jim Crow segregationist South, as well as in respect of apartheid South Africa. In a speech in 1932 Hitler, for one, foamed forth that the "economically privileged supremacy of the white race over the rest of the world" can be understood only on the basis of

> a political concept of supremacy which has been peculiar to the white race as a *natural phenomenon* for many centuries. . . . The settlement of the North American continent was . . . a consequence not of any higher claim in a democratic or international sense, but rather of a consciousness of what is right which had its sole roots in the conviction of superiority and thus the right of the white race. (Hitler 1990, p. 96; my emphasis)

In like fashion, a Southern white leader could claim more or less publicly unchallenged at the height of imposed segregationism that

> The Negro's skull is thicker, his brain is smaller than the white man's. . . . This accounts for the fact that while Negro children at school often compare favorably with whites, adults do not.

And a newspaper editorial in Maryland at the time insisted that black people develop

> a greater respect for toil – manual toil. . . . What the negro needs is to be taught and shown that labor is his salvation – not books. The state appropriation is intended to encourage that teaching. (Both quotes in Litwack 1998, pp. 102–3)

These were claims to be echoed a half-century later by H. F. Verwoerd, principal architect of explicit apartheid, who as Minister of Bantu Affairs in the South African government infamously asserted in 1952 that blacks should not expect to be educated for positions they would have no hope of occupying. We should note in these remarks the fear of black capability, in South Africa as in the American South, hidden just beneath the (imposed) surface presumption of inherent intellectual inferiority. Here we find an acknowledgment that collapses the productivity of discursive force with *ex post facto* ideological rationalization characteristic of racist naturalism.

The new historicism, by contrast in the liberalizing hands of John Locke and John Stuart Mill and the developmentalism of Comte and Marx, marks British rule in India and Egypt. The model, incipient in the claims of Bartolomeo de las Casas about the convertibility of indigenous Indians in the sixteenth century, fueled the commitments of British and French abolitionists in the late eighteenth and nineteenth centuries. But it also underlay French assumptions about assimilation or association in governing its colonies in Southeast Asia and Africa, the explicit "developmentalism" of British colonial policy from the 1940s on, as well as the ethno-immigrant model of race relations in the US associated above all with Gunnar Myrdal's *An American Dilemma* (cf. Omi and Winant 1986, pp. 16–24). And, it could be argued, though I won't here, that racial historicism similarly informs contemporary neo-conservative commitments to colorblindness, in the US, South Africa, Britain, and Europe.

It should not be thought, nevertheless, that I am claiming that the historicist is relatively more benign (because somehow more "progressive") than a naturalist mode of racial governance. Naturalist forms, it is true, tended to be more viscerally vicious and cruel, historicist ones more paternalistic. But by the same token the naturalist tended to be bald, bold, and direct concerning racist presumption and commitment, the historicist ambiguous, ambivalent, indeed, hypocritical. With the naturalist accordingly the battle lines could be more directly drawn, the historicist tending to politeness, coded significance (the very implications of "progress" tending to hide assumptions about inferiority), and tolerance as veils for continued invocation of racial power. But as with all tendencies, these are trends only rather than hard and fast rules.

Merivale's comprehensive lectures on colonialism were delivered between 1839 and 1841 at the University of Oxford, academic center for preparing candidates for British colonial administration. Contrasting his own brand of incipient racial progressivism with the naturalism of the Spanish, Merivale generalized one anonymous colonial observer's conclusion concerning "the case of Australian Aborigenes" to the effect that "native peoples" are as "apt and intelligent as any other race of men I am acquainted with: they are subject to like affections, passions and appetites as other men." As soon as they are declared British subjects, Merivale's observer continued, they should learn "that the British laws are to supersede their own" (Merivale 1841/1928, pp. 500–1). Such rules must apply, as Merivale insisted – citing the support also of Sir George Grey, colonial administrator in Australia and the Cape of Good Hope – both to

> violations of the eternal and universal laws of morality: such as cannibalism, human sacrifice and infanticide [but also] to customs less horrible, yet, from the greater frequency of their operation, perhaps still more injurious and incompatible with civilization: such as the violent abuse of the authority of husbands over wives, and barbarous ill-usage of the weaker sex in general, and some of the features of slavery among [the colonized themselves], if not the practice itself. (Ibid, p. 502)

Protect them from themselves, by making them other than what they currently are, by undoing their uncivilized conditions.

Amalgamation and Assimilation

That "natives' uncivilized conditions" can be undone entails that such conditions are not considered inherent but the product of custom, climate, and habit. "Native races," Merivale emphasized, "must in every instance either perish, or be *amalgamated* with the general population of their country. By amalgamation he intended "the union of natives with settlers in the same community, as master and servant, as fellow-laborers, as fellow-citizens, and, if possible, as connected by intermarriage." Every "native," he stressed, should potentially be regarded as a citizen at the earliest moment possible (ibid, pp. 510–11, my emphasis). Merivale later summarised the range of empirical documentation he assumed available at the time evidencing "improvement" of "the inferior races" – Africans, American Indians, South Sea natives, Australian Aborigines – once influenced by their European "superiors" (ibid, pp. 549–53).

Colonization, astonishingly in this historicizing view, was sought to provide the virtue of protecting colonized women from the savagery of colonized men. This twist is replete with Anglicized irony. Racist protection against sexual invasion usually has assumed the fashion of white men claiming to protect white women against the projection of voracious sexual appetites of black men. It has hidden behind this presumption the sexual proclivities of white men's desire satisfied by the rape of black women, real and fantasized. Merivale's enjoinder to racial upliftment effected by means of "amalgamation" was evidently to be pursued through white men marrying black women. Intermarriage, he apparently thought, would produce racial upliftment, biologically as much as spiritually and culturally, through generational enhancement. Far from being the "predestined murderers" of the colonized, he concluded that colonizing whites "are called to assume . . . [the latters'] preservers" (ibid, p. 549). Here the polite Victorian hope of racial improvement sprang eternal through the gendered domination of racial intermarriage and interracial offspring. Haym remarks, not unrelatedly, that sexual interaction was as important to the effective running and extension of empire as the more obvious concerns of government and commerce. "In the erotic field, as in administration and commerce, some degree of 'collaboration' from the indigenous communities was helpful to the maintenace of imperial systems" (Haym 1991, p. 2). The euphemism notwithstanding, sexual domination – homo- as much as heterosexual, as Haym reveals – has proved a central feature if not condition of racial rule.

Merivale added another liberalizing advantage of the intermarrying "mixture of blood," namely, a "considerable check on the prejudices of colour . . . for which there can be no substantial reason where slavery does not exist" (Merivale 1840/1928, p. 538). This is all the more curious in light of Merivale's ready admission of the destructive force of "our profligacy, our fraud, our extinction, our invasions, the terror and the hatred which Europeans excite at almost every point of the earth where they are brought into contact with unsubdued races of inferior civilization" (ibid, p. 561). It is useful to see Merivale, accordingly, as representing the bridging shift from naturalist to historicist presumptions, adding social and cultural influences of amalgamation to the biological, and without reducing the former to the determination of the latter.[2]

All this may seem a far cry perhaps from the deadly presumptions of Leopold's Congo or Hitler's Reich, of subjection in the segregationist South or apartheid South Africa. What is evident here, it must be stressed however, is not that the historicist assumptions are somehow more appealing than or morally superior to the naturalist's, more benign because less physically vicious. As the tone of Merivale's insistence suggests, historicists have been moved to make such a claim in the name of a variety of "racial realism." "Almagamation," as the later assimilationist experience of American Indians from the 1880s on revealed rather tellingly, could be as devastatingly destructive of a people, as violative of forms and conditions of social being, as any extremes of physical violence.

"Amalgamation, by some means or other, is the only possible Euthanasia of savage communities," concluded Merivale in an astounding turn of phrase.

"Amalgamate, or perish" is but one historical remove from "perish through amalgamation." And that step is all but explicit in the exhortation to euthanasia. The paranoias of degeneration had not quite fully taken hold so that intermarriage could yet be conceived as a mode of racial upliftment, as much physical as cultural, biological as civilizational, indeed, the one not so distant from the other. The year 1840, it seems, is not all that far in some respects from 1990.[3]

The policy of *assimilation* clearly rests on historicist grounds, and it rules by historicist design. Assimilation emerged in the 1880s to dominate French colonial policy and US "internal colonialism" regarding Native Americans and Canadian policy concerning First Peoples. French or Anglo "civilization," as the case may be, "represented the apex of development." Peoples "less fortunate" than Europeans should be provided the "universally applicable principles" of "colonial development and good government" (Lee 1967). "Everywhere," writes Roberts of French assimilationist policy, "political development was to be as far as possible Europeanization." And yet "[a] good law," Condorcet insisted, "is good for all men, just as a sound logical proposition is sound everywhere" (Roberts 1929, 100ff.). Colonial assimilationists were confident of their possession of universally just laws, building the policy on the assumption that natives should become civilized through their acquisition of the rule of law and the custom of the colonizers, by ceasing that is to be native. Education was the principal mode. The first act of French colonizers like Galleni once they had established themselves in a colony was to found a school, free to natives, conducted solely in French and emphasizing French culture, history, values, habits. Local elites were created and elevated, for the dual purpose of mediating French culture to the mass of the local population and assisting in the running of local government. The children of the elite were sent to university in France, in strict proportion to the number of jobs available to them in the colony, so as not to foment rebellion on the part of a local "literate class" with too much time on their hands (Crocker 1947, pp. 52–3). Indeed, it turned out to be just this literate class of largely European-educated middle-class elites that provided the intellectual inspiration for the nationalist anti-colonial movements at the middle of the twentieth century.

Similarly, US officials, most notably between the 1880s and 1930s, tore American Indian children from their rural reservation environments where they were likely to learn indigenous custom and rebellious habits, shipping them off over the plaintive and painful protests of their parents for adoption by white families and assimilation into white schools. Stripped of family and culture, in a sense deracialized, they could be recreated, racially reconfigured – as white. Out of indigenous context not only did they look white but they were "reinvented" as white in terms of custom, habit, culture, practice. In a sense, official American disposition towards "the racial question" from the later 1880s to the aftermath of World War II was a mix of naturalist assumptions concerning "negro" segregation and historicist commitments concerning Indian assimilation.

These examples suggest a distinction in colonial disposition also regarding governance of the racially different. The French were disposed to treat many of their colonies effectively as provinces or *départements* of France, worldly extensions of the body politic. The British saw their own colonial policy evolve to embrace developmentalism, a concern with the economically and educationally determined development of the colonized society to ultimate self-sufficiency and self-rule. Even the troubled, ambiguous and ambivalent history of US policy regarding indigenous populations can be read through the struggle over sovereignty.

This is not to deny or under-represent the force of local resistance in prompting the demise or shift in the scope or forms of racial rule. Such transformations in no way would have been initiated or have struck so deep in the absence of the racially subjugated and repressed striking back. Power is never ceded or shifted without resistance, in the limit case even where the resistance is internalized. I mean only to emphasize that all of the dominant and dominating political projects listed here are underpinned by or represent or reflect historicist assumptions, commitment to which was more or less explicit and conscious. Those modes of racially inscribed governance tied to naturalist commitments, by contrast, were moved to treat the societies considered racially inferior either as free space for the (profit-) taking – as space needing to be cleared of the supposedly inferior inhabitants, as sources simply of wealth provision directly as a consequence of raw material or mineral provision – or indirectly due to (artificially) depressed labor costs. As a result, rule was to be imposed directly just as the space of the racially distinct and differentiated was to be kept at a distance, to be maintained as lands apart.

The claim to universal principles as ideals to be pursued or emulated that underlay both progressivist racial historicism and naturalism hides from view the fact that, touched by Africa or Asia, South America or the South Pacific, Europe could never be the same again. This was especially so in the historicist case, though the internalization of naturalist-provoked violence had telling effects too. In seeking to assimilate Africans and Asians, indigenous Indios and Pacific islanders – economically and culturally, religiously and intellectually, socially and politically – Europeans would be forever transformed. Little did the English, French, or Dutch, in (former) colonies as in their metropolitan "homes," realize how profoundly Empire would alter them, what libidinal forces it would loosen and license, what consumptive desires it would liberate, what fashion – clothing and jewelry, art and body art, music and literature, food and drink – it would spawn, what habits of the heart as much as heartless darkness it would engender, what modes of spirituality, religiosity, and flights of fancy it would suggest. Seeking to impose values and practices upon the colonized from without, from social contexts and political arrangements radically different, European colonizers failed to understand how deeply altered they would be, whether at close hand or from the "safe" distance of European centers.

It follows that the naturalist and historicist traditions of racist commitment always contained the seeds, the incipient presumption, of each other. Only the historicist window would allow (for) such provocative developmentalist possibilities, but no sooner allowed, acknowledged, and embraced than the naturalist warnings echoed through European consciousness and culture. "Look, Mama, a Negro." Dare not touch. Fear of contamination, the terrordome of a "black/brown/red/yellow" world. And no sooner touched by the whip of naturalism than the plaintive dignity of slave songs and narratives, the pull of native wealth and tastes, tales and fictions, the lure of silks and spices, landscapes and spaces, in short, the irrepressibility of forbidden fantasies raised the teleological possibility of humanist historicity. Dance with the orangutan and an orangutan one degenerately just might become. So human hope for the orangutan, at least developmentally, progressively, there must be.

Naturalizing Order, Historicizing Governance

The differences between the naturalist and historicist traditions, however, are clearly revealed in their respective considerations regarding both miscegenation and access of those not completely of European descent to offices of governmental power. Racial naturalists almost always have been committed to anti-miscegenation laws. For the naturalist, miscegenation prompts the fear of degeneracy or cultural and physical pollution, the bringing down of the superior by socializing with the inferior. Rape of black women by white men, nevertheless, if not condoned, was more widely engaged than acknowledged. It obviously effected for white men release of sexual frustration, or the raw expression of libido or power, or in some cases sexual practice by young white men for their impending marriage to white women (cf. Haym 1991). Racial historicists, by contrast, might – Merivale's amalgamationism notwithstanding, one might think would – frown socially upon mixed-race partners and offspring though not necessarily preclude their possibility legally. Here, racial taboos on intermarriage or miscegenation mirrored inter-class taboos. As such, they were (to be) socially discouraged rather than legislatively precluded. The distinction is borne out by policy differences between pre-apartheid British rule in South Africa, where miscegenation was socially discouraged but not outlawed, and the apartheid regime that banned all sexual relations between whites and other racial groups between 1950 and 1988.[4]

Similarly, naturalists tended to deny access to offices of governance to those considered racially inferior. Historicists, by contrast, were likely to encourage such access within strictly delimited parameters and for more or less well-defined purposes: maintaining control, guaranteeing a steady supply of migrant labor at minimized costs, securing racial and social peace, hands-on preparation of the historically less developed for ultimate self-governance, and so on. Again, the apartheid regime maintained strict educational segregation at almost all levels, whereas the British in India or in their African colonies provided mixed schools not least for children of local elites. Many a European and US university has been advantaged by the likes of Achimota's legacy.[5]

Now the civilizing mission of colonial missionaries obviously must have presupposed, at least in principle, the presumption of racial (including cultural) progressivism. If it were to be possible to convert the colonized to Christianity, and in conversion to introduce the infidels to the virtues of civilization, to the habits and manners of righteousness, and to the promise of "the heavenly city," this must presuppose not only convertibility and comprehension on the part of the momentarily inferior. It must presume in addition the very *possibility* of progress, advancement, civilization. The civilizing mission, as John and Jean Comaroff have spelled out in fascinating detail regarding the Tswana of Southern Africa, involved "methodically" transforming the everyday life of the natives, their modes of "personhood and production, . . . habits and homes, . . . notions of value and virtue" (Comaroff and Comaroff, 1997, p. xvi). Ironically, as this civilizing project necessarily presupposed the possibility of historical development and cultural, social, and intellectual progress on the part of natives considered racially naive and immature, it presumed the claim to transcendental value at once economic and epistemological, legal and moral. Transcendental value was represented in the universal currencies of money and the word, productive labor and sanctified truth, industry and knowledge, rational legality and moral virtue. The assumption is ironically universalist, for these imposed aspirations to universal ideals were always no more than embodiments of European, Christian virtue and practice, morality and truth.

We can see at work here the twin sides of colonialism: historicist and universalist, educational and forceful, developmentalist and destructive, pious and power-mongering. If the naturalist version of colonial racial rule governed by unswerving principle, the historicist ruled through the pragmatics of political, moral, cultural (in short, racial) imposition, local in effects and global in reach. Historicists struggle always with the tension between "obvious" racial differentiation, heterogeneity, and heterodoxy and their seemingly necessary drive to the civilizing imperative of a created homogeneity, a structured sameness. If naturalist logic was differentialist and ultimately segregationist, the historicist's was assertively assimilating and in the end integrationist. Colonialism, it could be said, was always negotiating, if mostly all too unhappily, the space between required conformity and rebellious dissent, the latter a tradition found throughout the history of Christianity, as the Comaroffs are quick to comment regarding Protestantism (ibid, pp. 7–8). Indeed, colonial rule is stretched repeatedly between the rule of law and the rule of force, extravagant excess and modest self-sufficiency; between promoting and prompting conspicuous and "careful" consumption, radicalism and civility, consensual consort and violence. "A hand of iron beneath a glove of velvet," implored Arthur Girault of French colonial policy, "must always be the rule in our relations with the natives" (quoted in Roberts 1929). The impositions of developmentalism are not so far a cry from the terrors of destruction.

In their colonial applications, historicism or progressivism was to naturalism as the velvet glove was to the iron fist. The former was inclined to be soft and smooth, proceeding through the imposition of education and ideology, subtle coercion and calculating manipulation, but bristling to the critical touch. The latter tended to be vicious and vindictive, bald in design and ends, cruel and forcefully commanding in its means, sometimes driven to transgress genocidal limits, and tolerating no opposition.

In both colonial and postcolonial worlds dominated by racial conception, racist exclusion, and racially tinged resentments, the naturalist conception has been more prone to critical attack, to moral disapprobation, and ultimately to governmental and state distantiation. This was so precisely because of the extremities of violence and cruelty to which the naturalist conception "naturally" lent itself, both as discursive progenitor and as *ex post facto* rationalization. Dehumanize people in group terms – "racialize" them, precisely as Fanon (1968) would first use the term – and they are rendered more disposed to dehumanized abasement. Render *them* abject and there is little to prevent their dehumanized dismissal, their "moral eviction," to invoke Zygmunt Bauman's characterization of Nazi treatment of Jews, among others. Nothing indeed within the scope of naturalism *per se*. It turns out that naturalism is little disposed to auto-critique, to moral self-reflection. What critical objection it faced historically was likely to come as much from historicist quarters as dismissive outrage on the part of the subjugated, at least until well into the twentieth century.

The racist predispositions and presumptions of progressivism or historicism, as we have seen by contrast, are more nuanced and hidden, less self-assertive, more worried about appearing so. But the dominant effect of this trajectory has been not the dismissal of racist commitment and expression as such but the replacement – one might say displacement – of naturalism by racial historicism, of one form of racist articulation by another. The perpetuation of racial commitments and racist exclusions has been veiled behind this shift, preserved anew in the vocal dismissal of the bald and extreme in the name of the polite and subtle, of the presumptively unsustainable in wake of the enlightened. Enlightened racism is camouflaged beneath its liberal historicist enlightenment. This is a point that concerns the very meaning and legacy of colorblindness as underpinning more or less contemporary state policy.

Racial Subjection, Ambivalent Rule

It is possible to map out the different forms social subjection assumes under the two models. By subjection here I have in mind the sense both of the making of the social subject and the modes of racial domination, of racial rule. The naturalist and progressivist conceptions are alike in viewing as agents those defined as white and those occupying the position of colonizers. For the naturalist, whites and colonizers are considered agents of biological or inherent destiny; for the progressivist, they are agents of history. So both traditions assume or inscribe a teleology, the former reductively determinist, the latter the product of a logic of temporality. For the naturalist, Europeans are living out the superiority of their biology or inherent nature; for the historicist they are satisfying some teleological logic, the end(s) of history. They differ more deeply, the naturalist and progressivist, regarding the social subjectivity of those considered colonized, not white, and non-European.[6] The naturalist takes the colonized and those rendered racially inferior to have no (or little) agency. For the historicist, the agency of the colonized, those categorized non-white or non-European, is undeveloped. Such agency has to be promoted by developing their potential for self-determination, saving natives from their (pre-)historical selves, the effects of their undeveloped or uncivilized conditions.

I stress here accordingly the ways in which racially embedded presumptions about social subjectivity and racial rule mutually reinforce each other. Both the naturalist and progressivist presuppose a notion of universal subjectivity, a subjectivity closed off by the naturalist to those considered not white while potentially reachable for all in the historicist or progressivist view. The historicist thus claims to recognize, by presuming actually, an abstract, neutered, universal agency in the personhood of the colonized, a potential agency not yet actualized among the differentiations of their social specificity. That ambivalent tension identified above between the assumption of an embedded universalist nature hidden beneath historically undeveloped, particularistic ways of being is reasserted here in the historicist conception of social subjects. Peeling away the specificities of native ways of uncivilized existence through education was supposed to reveal the possibility of the universal subject, presumed in the example(s) of European high culture and modes of governance. Amalgamation, as Merivale would have it, was to help kill off the savage dispositions (or to help the colonized kill off the specificity of their own subjectivities) through the sanctity of intermarriage, the attendant mixed offspring, and the cultural upliftment supposed to follow.

This way of casting the issue reveals at once the deeply gendered character of racial subjection and the rule of racial subjects. Until well into the twentieth century white women were fashioned in racial terms as the media of national reproduction, in at least three ways. First, they were the bearers of future generations of citizens and citizen creators, providing care as nurses of military or administrative agents of the colonizing state. Middle- and upper-middle-class women served also ideologically to reproduce the body politic in ethnoracial and national terms, via their principal positions as governesses and teachers. Working-class women by contrast serviced the economy largely by working up the raw materials from the colonies into commodities for both domestic consumption and global circulation, while expected also to reproduce new generations of workers. Non-European women in the colonies served as

domestic labor for the colonizers as well as field hands, in many instances effectively nurturing young white children while all the time considered fair game
for satisfying the sexual proclivities of their masters. They were simultaneously
objects almost incessantly of a Malthusian discourse of population control
through family planning and more extremely sterilization (cf. Stoler 1995). As
slaves, African, Asian, and Indian women assumed added value on two related
counts: as commodities to be bought and sold at "fair value" on the market,
and as the reproductive bearers of additional profit, the generators of potential slaves or indentured servants. Black women especially were seen as
the means to surplus value in a triple sense then: as making commodities, as
making babies, and as themselves commodified objects for possible trade (Davis
1984; Anthias and Yuval-Davis 1989, pp. 6–11).

Colonizing, as Helen Callaway makes clear, was considered men's work, the
work of white men's regulative control, to be exact. The colonies, it was
emphasized repeatedly, "were no place for white women" (Callaway 1987, pp.
4–5). European women – "nice girls" as the characteristic infantalizing identification with African "boys" employed as servants and workers would have it
(ibid, pp. 6, 23) – were more or less excluded from British colonies in Africa
until the early twentieth century. Even in the dying decades of direct colonialism, white women were admitted to the colonies only grudgingly, whether
or not seeking to accompany their husbands serving as colonial agents. Indeed,
lower male ranks in the colonial service were required to sign a contract
restricting marriage in their first three years of foreign service, so as not to be
distracted from the duty of empire (ibid, p. 20).

The colonies thus were male clubs of a kind, at once the laboratory, factory,
and stable of white men's making, their fantasies forcibly serviced by the local
population, men and women of color alike. Colonization in effect was about
European men teaching their like to be men, to do men's work, to exercise
power and to serve country, king (no doubt preferably), and God (undoubtedly masculinized). Here the traditional tension between Kantian duty and
utilitarian instrumentality got resolved neatly in service of the imperial imperative, the sense of superiority and the civilizing mission tenuously and ambivalently combined as European men's prerogative. White women were seen as
getting in the way of completing the "rough" work colonization necessitated
and its vast profits required, too squeamish in the face of the necessary violence, too soft and tearful before health and hellish hazards, too sensitive even
for the hardships of difficult administrative decision-making. But – and this is
all too little stressed – white women were regarded as the bearers or symbols
of too much moral conscience, in the way then not only of white men expressing unmitigated power but of fulfilling their most extreme sexual fantasies.
They were, as one time governor of the Gold Coast, Sir Alan Burns, remarked
all too priggishly, "intruders into what had been essentially a bachelor's
paradise, where a man could dress as he pleased, drink as much as he liked,
and be easy in his morals without causing scandal" (quoted in Callaway 1987,
p. 19).

In those colonizing states where naturalism clearly gave way to historicism as the dominant colonial disposition towards the close of the nineteenth century (most notably among the British, French, and Dutch), increasing numbers of women began to appear in colonial service. It is illustrative of this point that European women were all but absent from Leopold's Belgium, for instance. Thus European women came to occupy positions in the colonies first as nurses and later as teachers, secretaries, doctors, welfare officers, and in the dying moments of colonial rule as junior level administrative officers, exceptions like Margery Perham and Flora Shaw (Lady Lugard) dramatically proving the rule (ibid, pp. 6–7).

In general, and perhaps prompted by their own experiences, white women showed greater sympathy than men for the plight of the colonized, a more charitable spirit to the local children and women with whom they were likely to have more contact, and stronger support for their educational advancement (ibid, p. 4). If colonial practice was predicated upon a mix of Kantian duty and utilitarian calculus, women's moderating influence, not to make too much of it, turns Kohlberg's masculinist model of moral developmentalism on its head. I do not mean to deny in this white women's privileged position regarding colonized women and men, the benefits white women accordingly enjoyed, the possibility of their class elevation as a result of relations between madams and maids. Nor for that matter to pass over in silence the "preexisting hierarchies of power," gendered precisely in their inscriptions of domination, that met European imperializing missions (McClintock 1995, pp. 5–7). Yet precisely because of these preexisting forms of gendered domination on both shores of the colonizing ocean, ambivalence surely marked colonial relations between women on each side of the racial divide more deeply than it did the dominant master – slave relation between white men and black people. European women, it is safe to say, engaged in a less totalizing, more tenuous embrace of whiteness than their male counterparts. Not unrelatedly, I have to think that the sexual desire of white men for black women, admittedly motivated by and reinforcing their own sense of power, sparked the sort of hesitation one finds toward slavery in the likes of Thomas Jefferson. What does it say after all about white men's sexual desire, whether or not rationalized (away) at the time as biological instinct or drive in the absence of European women, that it be satisfied by those recognized only as animals?

This ambivalence is deeply configured in racially cohering terms, gender differentiation notwithstanding. If ambivalence is a constitutive mark of the modern condition, as Zygmunt Bauman (1991) has argued forcefully, modern ambivalence is clearly revealed in relation to race. In governmental terms modernity has been about undertaking to impose order, to assert and manage with the view to guaranteeing the conditions that make order as much possible as invisible. Order is projected as the antithesis of nature. Nature, as Bauman remarks, "means . . . nothing but the silence of man" (ibid, p. 6). Conceived in naturalistic terms, those classified or considered not white are reduced to silence – both incapable of speech and in the end of being spoken about. In kantian terms they are merely phenomena, objects, lacking the capacity for rational autonomy that is the authorizing mark of noumenal beings. Silence and invisibility – neither heard nor seen – are mutually reinforcing. Being written into the official record as not white is at once to be whitened out, so to speak, to be made part of the natural landscape, the silent backdrop in relation to which life is lived, taken for granted or passed by while being ignored.

There is an inherent unsatisfactoriness attendant to the constitutive ambiguity at work here conceived precisely from the point of view of imposed order. In this arrangement, those not white are taken on one hand to inhabit a nature that places them as such beyond (the very possibility of) order. On the other hand, they are supposed to be ordered through nature, for they are (pre)-conceived as inhabitants of a natural order controllable by enacting the laws of nature. Nature is that about which – in the face of which – "man" is driven to silence as much as it is the metaphor for silence itself. Those conceived racially as nothing more than the products of nature accordingly inspire awe, in the way in which nature can. Nature in this formulation stands in stark contrast to, the dark or underside of, humanity. Thus nature is not just that about which man is driven to silence but about which there cannot be anything to say. It is beyond knowledge because beyond speech.

The "cannot" here itself is ambiguous, indicative of the ambivalence at work. It falls between the "cannot" of inherent inability or incapacity and the "cannot" of imperative impossibility, of commanded incapacity. The ambiguity embedded here, in other words, is a particular expression of the classic modernist tensions between fact and value, nature and norm, description and prescription. It is this ambiguous ambivalence that marks modernity, that fractures the world of the past half-millennium and that has been called into question so sharply of late. Race accordingly is not just part – an aspect – of that modern world but *emblematic* of it, as much the exemplary condition of the modern as one example of modern practices and conditions among others. As much synecdoche of the modern as an instance, an index as an outcome. Thus the "constructedness" of race, about which so much has been made in recent racial theorizing, is more complex than most contemporary analyses all too glibly make out. For modern racial order, as I have outlined its conditions of possibility here, is as much "discovered" as it is (re)produced; it is as deeply the "product" of some presumed laws of nature as the outcome of law's imperiousness.

The shift from naturalism to historicism or progressivism is the (re)admission of those deemed not white into a history not simply naturalistic. It represents the elevation of those who had been considered objects of nature to subjects of history, of being placed not before but in time, even if as inhabiting a time not yet modern. Here, in contrast to racial naturalism where those regarded as racially inferior are restricted to spaces before or frozen in time, the racially differentiated are defined in terms of inhabiting an earlier pre-modern time. In either case those not white are placed outside: outside time or outside the space(s) of modern time. Thus for modernity the space of race is that of *the outside* – the external, the distant. The trick of race in either case then was to turn imagined conditions, those conditions (re)created and (re)produced, into the presumed and discovered, the given because natural.

Classifying schemas, of course, have been central to modern modes of administration precisely because classification is all about imparting order to and imposing it upon the world. In some ways, modern modes of thinking became consumed with classifying mentalities. The modern condition as a consequence caught itself between worlds always more than any order(ing schema) can "capture," on one hand, and the incessant drive for – the imperative of – control, on the other. All those concerns with racial classification schemas marking modern social thought from the late seventeenth century onwards accordingly are about the insistence on epistemological order in the face of the unknown, of control in the face of the anarchic – in general, of order in the face of disorder. Thus modern states – the state of imposed order naturalized – are not simply consistent with racial classification schemas but perfectly conducive to – in a sense dependent upon – them. Modern states invoke the classifying of races as offering structure to worlds seen as if by nature (recall the state of nature). They order worlds otherwise altogether unstructured, unformed or deformed, indeed, worlds considered as incapable in their "natural" form of structure. Colonial order accordingly was as central to elaboration of racial classification schemas as such schemas were to the material order of the colonies.

Classification, as Bauman argues, is at basis about setting apart, about cutting things off from each other into discrete containers, about *segregation*. Classification thus involves those acts of inclusion and exclusion so central to the experience of racism (cf. Bauman 1991, pp. 1–2). In seeking through classification to impose order upon an otherwise unformed world – or one seen and experienced as lacking form – the social world becomes mapped onto the natural, the natural is filtered through, alchemically transformed into, the social. And in the process the modern order of nature ironically comes to offer a model for the social.

Race is the perfect medium for this collapsing of the social, the historical, into and upon the natural, of value into fact, of "seeing" – really conceiving – social conditions and relations, identities and subjectivities in natural terms. Racial naturalism, as such, emerges as the seemingly fitting ordering of the social in terms of the natural, the "natural" veil of the socializing of the natural. Racial historicism may be read in this light as trying to have it both ways, reading the historical against lingering naturalist assumptions. It follows that racial naturalism almost perfectly suits modernity's twin mandates of order and control. Almost but not quite, for racial naturalism refuses to take into account two ultimately undeniable and related considerations. First it refuses to acknowledge that the modes of objectifying imposition it presupposed and promoted rubs up against the abilities and capacities, needs and wants of those supposed in the naturalist classificatory schemas not to have any, or to have them but not in quite the forms they would actually manifest. And second, it flees from the unhinging phenomenon of the fantasies and desires of those for whom the classifying forms were supposed to guarantee order and control. Those distantiated in virtue of their racial distinction are at once rendered desirable in virtue of their difference; those fashioned as somehow fantastic are at once constituted, ambiguously and ambivalently, as the objects of fantasy, pursued as much as fabricated, desired as much as denied, in those terms.

Thus, modernity's ambivalence strikes at its very "foundations," its core. Modern consciousness increasingly comes to recognize the heterogeneity it was so deeply implicated in prompting. To this recognition it responds, however, with various epistemological and practical interventions in seeking to reimpose order. On the one hand, there is a recourse through repressive state assertion to insist on the implications of a naturalist order by materially imposing it through law and policy, through classificatory modes and material control. The long history of racially exclusionary immigration policies throughout "Western" societies is ample testament to the point. On the other hand, there is grudging revision of the categories in view of which the racial outsider could claim to be known. The revision prompts shifts from naturalist to historicist or progressivist or evolutionary terms, from the stasis of "Being" to the developmentalism of "Becoming," from objects of natural order to subjects (though not – at least not yet – as citizens) of the state, from racial subjection through technologies of the whip, sword, and gun to racial management via the funneling technologies of education, opportunities, and access.

Racial order, at the very heart of the modern state machine then, suffers the ambivalence of modernity multiply. Racial order imprisons modern subjects under the control of classifying schemas always delimiting of possibilities. It thus splits selves and subjects between the "can" and "ought," between possibility and impossibility, requirement and liberty. But in this, the tension between racial naturalism and historicism perfectly represents the ambivalence of broader modern tensions, exacerbated by the order of race: between determinism and freedom, structure and indeterminacy, form and formlessness, the before of history and its end. The ordering of the state accordingly by, in, and through race is at once representative of modernity more generally as race serves centrally to define and refine the modern condition.

For the racial naturalist the engagement with the racially subjugated is one of strict, unmediated exploitation. The racially inferior are seen as surplus value, both as usable labor and discardable detritus. In this, they are considered both laboring means to the production underpinning the possibility of profit and as objects themselves from which profit can be elicited by being traded as commodities themselves, bought and sold on the market, much as garbage has become both a bother and a commodity. For the racial historicist, the racially immature are inserted into historical development. They accordingly are promised progress, a promise at once undermined by racial imposition in being progressively postponed to a future never quite (to be) achieved. Historical progress is to come, as Homi Bhabha revealed so insightfully (Bhabha 1994, pp. 86–92), through mimicry of the European, a "colonial mimesis in which to be Anglicized is emphatically not to be English," where the colonized can be "almost the same, but not quite" – "not quite/not white." The colonized are inserted into global markets perpetually as laboring means, promised equality as economic players but perennially shortchanged as political and social equals. The effect is that those deemed racially undeveloped and immature are reproduced almost inevitably as unequal – as exploitable labor in the colonies, as discardable in the postcolony, and in both as abusable migrants employed to take on work no one else will – or apparently needs to.

So, behind the promise of racial progressivism, as Nairn hints at in the epigram, in the name of its proffered utilities, lies the rule of a racial domination. This is a racial domination no longer naturalized perhaps, but it is one deeply modernized and modernizing nevertheless. "All is race," as Benjamin Disraeli once would have it, because race and the exclusions it licenses are at the very heart of the modern project, central to its modes of governance – and by implication not so distant, as all too many seem to think, from ours.

Notes

1 This is David Hume's characterization of eighteenth-century "evidence" of "Negro" intellectual contribution.

2 Harriet Martineau's *Dawn Island*, written in 1845, provides a literary expression of this shift, in her terms from the racial extinction of some groups so "savage" they are incapable of being saved from themselves, to those groups whose racial salvation is the benevolent product of European civilization. See Brantlinger (1995), pp. 43–4.

3 The view that racism is reducible to the naturalist assumption, I have argued, has dominated the secondary literature on race and racism. Charles Mills represents a widespread assumption in this regard. It follows that it is unproductive to look to the secondary historical literature for evidence of the historicist expression, for the secondary literature tends to replicate and thereby reinforce the naturalist presupposition. It is at once blind to and blinds analysts from seeing the revisionary force of the historicist interpretation. For one example among many, see Bolt (1971).

4 In some cases miscegenation was seen as fuel for upliftment: "An accession to European blood in the urban and detribalized communities of Africa will do no harm" (Crocker 1947, p. 53). Crocker, it ought to be noted, served in the British Colonial Administration principally in West Africa in the 1930s and 1940s.

5 Achimota is the highly regarded British-founded school for Ghanaian elites that assumed significance in the wake of World War II.

6 Historically, Europeans and whites were considered synonymous, as much represented accordingly in formal state classifications as assumed informally in the culture. Thus prior to the 1960s, the official state designation for whites in South

Africa, for instance, was "European" and "Non-Europeans" for blacks – "Coloureds," Africans, and indeed Asians inclusively. In good part, in the face of the insistent pressure of Black Consciousness in the 1960s, the designation shifted to "Whites" and "Non-Whites," the insult of negation nevertheless remaining in place.

References

Anthias, Flora and Yuval Davis, Nira 1989 *Women – Nation – State*. London: Macmillan.

Appiah, K. Anthony and Gutmann, Amy (1996) *Color Conscious: The Political Morality of Race*. Princeton, NJ: Princeton University Press.

Bauman, Zygmunt 1991 *Modernity and Ambivalence*. Ithaca, NY: Cornell University Press.

Bell, Derrick 1992 *Race, Racism and American Law*, 3rd. edn. Boston: Little Brown.

Bhabha, Homi 1994 *The Location of Culture*. New York: Routledge.

Bolt, Christine 1971 *Victorian Attitudes Towards Race*. London: Routledge and Kegan Paul.

Brantlinger, Patrick 1995 "Dying Races": Rationalizing Genocide in the Nineteenth Century," pp. 43–56, in *The Decolonization of the Imagination: Culture, Knowledge and Power*, ed. Jan Nederveen Pieterse and Bhikhu Parekh. London: Zed Books.

Callaway, Helen 1987 *Gender, Culture and Empire: European Women in Colonial Nigeria*. London: Macmillan.

Comaroff, John L. and Comaroff, Jean 1997 *Of Revelation and Revolution: The Dialectics of Modernity on a South African Frontier*, Vol. 2. Chicago: University of Chicago Press.

Crocker, Walter 1947 *On Governing Colonies: Being an Outline of the Real Issues and a Comparison of the British, French and Belgian Approach to Them*. London: Allen and Unwin.

Davis, Angela Y. 1984 *Women, Race and Class*. New York: Vintage.

Dred Scott vs. Sanford 1857 60 US (19 How.).

Fanon, Frantz 1968 *Black Skin White Masks*, London: Paladin.

Haym, Ronald 1991 *Empire and Sexuality: The British Experience*. Manchester: Manchester University Press.

Hitler, Adolph 1990 *Hitler: Speeches and Proclamations, 1932–45*, vol. 1, ed. Max Domarus, Chicago: Bolchazy-Carducci.

Jefferson, Thomas 1781/1955 *Notes on the State of Virginia*, ed. W. Peden, Chapel Hill: University of North Carolina Press.

Lee, J. M. 1967 *Colonial Development and Good Government: A Study of the Ideas Expressed by the British Official Classes in Planning Decolonization 1939–1964*. Oxford: Clarendon Press.

Litwack, Leon 1998 "The White Man's Fear of the Educated Negro: How the Negro was Fitted for his Natural and Logical Calling," *Journal of Blacks in Higher Education* 20 (summer): 100–8.

McClintock, Anne 1995 *Imperial Leather: Race, Gender and Sexuality in the Colonial Contest*. New York: Routledge.

Merivale, Herman 1841/1928 *Lectures on Colonization and Colonies*. Oxford: Oxford University Press.

Mills, Charles 1998 *Blackness Visible: Essays on Philosophy and Race*. Ithaca, NY: Cornell University Press.

Nairn, Tom 1977 *The Break-up of Britain: Crisis and Neo-Nationalism*. London: New Left Books.

Omi, Michael and Winant, Howard 1986 *Racial Formation in the United States: From the 1960s to the 1980s*. New York: Routledge.

Roberts, Stephen 1929 *History of French Colonial Policy (1870–1925)*. London: P. S. King and Son.

Stoler, Ann Laura 1995 *Race and the Education of Desire: Foucault's History of Sexuality and the Colonial Order of Things*. Durham, NC: Duke University Press.

Tilly, Charles 1994 "The Time of States," *Social Research*, 61:269–95.

Chapter 6

Racist Visions for the Twenty-First Century: On the Cultural Politics of the French Radical Right

Ann Laura Stoler

In a world in which racist perceptions and practices permeate our global space and private spheres, scholarly accountability has lied in understanding the tenacious resilience of race as a social, political, and psychological category that continues to define people and confine their options, to exclude and embrace, to grant and withhold entitlements. But scholars of racism in France have been far less attuned to asking why racist visions have such appeal to people who in good faith hold that they are not interested in race but in defending their nation, have nothing against those of "x" origin but don't want those cultural priorities influencing "their" children in "their" schools, that crime is the issue and not race and that they are not – and have never been – racist at all.

This essay is an effort to address why the French extreme Right's policies are "easy to think" for a broad population who neither considered themselves xenophobic or racist, nor politically "extreme" in any sense.[1] In part, it is about how we write about the abhorrent, why we treat as aberrant, and whether it is a conceit to imagine that ethnographers and historians of race have something to say about the quotidian face of contemporary racial politics.

At least part of the task is to understand the politics of comparison in which scholars engage, what it means to argue for the similarities of racisms in different time and place, why some anti-racist scholars so adamantly claim the unchanging face of racisms on the one hand, while others argue in as principled a manner for a new cultural racism on the other. Such a discrepancy prompts a basic question: what are we willing to ask about what racisms look

like on the cusp of this twenty-first century? Are racist visions taking predictable form and with familiar actors? Are racisms changing or merely our
analyses of them? Are we equipped with the epistemic tools to understand
their regimes of (moral) truth? Are they what those who track racisms'
archived and buried traces expect them to be? I am concerned that they are
not.

Over the last fifteen years my research has focused on the history of French
and Dutch colonialisms, on the making and malleability of racial categories,
on the differently racialized regimes of colonial states.[2] But over the last two
years I began studying a very different racial landscape in southern France
where the racial politics that saturate Aix-en-Provence and its surroundings
has produced at once a chillingly familiar and unfamiliar social world; one in
which far-right politics and the racial discourse that goes along with it commanded enormous presence and one in which issues of race are continually
effaced – irrelevant – a space in which nothing "happens at all." While earlier
racisms resonate with these contemporary figurations, the contours of those
today take shape in new sites and through new technologies unavailable in
the nineteenth and through most of the twentieth century.

By one reading, 1998 was a year in which extreme-right platforms and
candidates moved from the menacing margins of French politics well into the
center. It was the first time in the last thirty years (since the National Front
was established in 1972) that a number of center–right candidates in regional
campaigns accepted FN [Front Nationale] backing, acknowledged they
needed them to win, and (invoking "Vichy") were labeled "collabo" for doing
so. It was the year in which France's President, Jacques Chirac, made an
unprecedented address on national television to say what many already knew:
that such compromises with the Front were endorsements of a "xenophobic"
and "racist" France. It was a year in which media personalities who had long
resisted interviewing Front leaders conceded that by refusing to give them air
time, they would not disappear. It was a year in which the progressive press
could print headlines sounding the alarm that the "Front was everywhere" but
just six months later otherwise sensible persons and public figures could
applaud the World Cup victory of France's rainbow-colored soccer team as a
sign of the real France and as an anti-racist victory.

But there was also this strange phenomenon of "nothing happening." As
the anthropologist John Pemberton writes about Suharto's recently ousted
regime in Indonesia, this is the way things sometimes work in cultures of fear
and terror.[3] While well-heeled southern France with its folkoric appeal is
neither obviously besieged by police nor silenced on issues of race, it is still a
place where talk of "racism" is not really for polite company (which, by
definition, excludes students and the press) – where acquaintances become
palpably uncomfortable if you bring up the "Front" – where "race" is almost
a dirty, four-letter word. While numerous university courses are offered on
issues related to migration and "immigration," there are none offered at the
universities in Aix or Marseille on the historical or contemporary face of racism

in France. After-dinner political discussions that turned to the FN's increasing presence in May 1998 could be met with coughs, impatient dismissal, awkward silences. Now that the FN is turning against itself and in decline in May 1999, there is smug satisfaction in its impending disappearance and no need to talk about it at all.

But this present–absence is disconcerting, for it is also a place where the victories of the National Front – founded by Le Pen, its once "charismatic" leader – can be daily front-page news, and demonstrations against it are run of the mill events. In Provence's towns and cities, Front-elected officials have closed down local cultural centers, censured theater performances, banned "inappropriate" children's books that illustrate parents of different hue, mixed-marriages, toddlers of color. Provence last year is where in Vitrolles (a small town equidistant from Marseille and Aix) Front-elected city administrators first allocated municipal funds to install their own beefed-up squad of civil guard outfitted with motorcycle boots, truncheons and black shirts, evoking memories of blackshirts of another era. While the outfits were soon replaced, as one woman put it, by "more respectable" and conventional blue uniforms, Vitrolles' city hall and central square are still well-wired with surveillance cameras aimed on its own inhabitants for their "security."

What was troubling in the aftermath of the World Cup this past summer, then, was not this euphoric explosion in a depressed economy but how sure people seemed to be that France's multicultural soccer team and the widespread support and adoration for it symbolized a defeat of the extreme Right. Similarly, this past fall and winter there has been a furor over the "implosion" of the FN as Le Pen and his former dauphin, Megret, are in public standoff. But in both cases the emphasis seems misplaced: How could the evidence of two decades of increasing support for National Front candidates (no French extreme-right party has ever survived as long) be annulled by a post-victory celebration of racial harmony? Why was one player's popularity – that of Zidane, the son of a "poor Algerian immigrant" (evinced in street chants, "Zidane for President") – interpreted as evidence of a meaningful multicultural romance rather than a one-night stand? How could the president of the French National Commission on the Rights of Man claim the World Cup "inflicted a defeat for racism" (August 12, 1998). In the streets and in the press, one could hear people say: "See we've got *them* now. The FN has been silenced by this outburst of racial goodwill. The Marseillaise belongs to us again." Even left-wing weeklies wrote of a "real national communion," a French anti-racist "dream," a "plebiscite" for nationalism without exclusions, what intellectuals of diverse leanings labeled a nationalism without chauvinism that was truly French.

Optimism is one thing, political delusion is another. My intent here is to analyze responses neither to the World Cup nor recent euphoria around the FN's "civil war." Rather, I take those responses as indices of a much deeper set of misconstruals about what makes up the force of the radical Right, what constitutes racism in France today, and what relevance the FN brand of racism has for its hard- and soft-line constituencies. That people *expected* the FN to be unsettled and irreparably damaged by the nationalist ecstasy around the World Cup derives in part from misidentifying what racialized discourses have looked like in the past and therefore what distinguishes them today. It derives from missing their polyvalent mobility, the discrepancies they can sustain. It derives from treating the celebration of multiculturalism as fundamentally subversive of racial regimes when much more historical evidence suggests how smoothly those cultural hybridities can be folded back within racialized societies and social formations. Most of this essay was completed in early fall 1998 just before the French Front Nationale, as the press so optimistically put it, "imploded" in an internecine battle between its longstanding leader Le Pen and his once right-hand man, Bruno Megret. Press coverage over the last few months has continued with sanguine predications, reveling at the Front's acceleration into a high gear of "self-destruct," its impending and much anticipated fall from grace. But such sensationalism is a curious sociological phenomenon in itself that may be argued to be symptomatic of a more general trend in analyses of French racial politics: namely, a reluctance to engage the fundamental issues which make racialized thinking both commonsense and so broadly relevant.

"An-Other Year in Provence"

The research that begun with the year I spent in Provence has not been "fieldwork" in the sustained sense that has defined ethnography. Instead, it has been what one might call "ethnography in the public sphere"; for what characterizes its context and "locale" are the movements of people and politics, discourses and differences that crisscross local and national contexts. It is ethnography that has tracked connections made through café conversations, televised soundbites, movies, radio, and cyberspace. The racialized landscape of Vitrolles is both tactile and intimate, but also national and European.

My movements followed those contours: I went to National Front demonstrations in Marseille as well as those against them, attended court hearings at the provincial magistrates in Aix where the family of a girl denied access to a high school was pitted against her Front assailants. I surfed the Front's websites, read newspapers heavily committed to the Front's program as avidly as those aggressively against it. I talked with women and men affiliated with the Front's parent–teacher organizations, followed Front candidates as they "worked" local markets in municipal elections, spoke with Front-elected city officials as well as city workers fired (because their first or family names were North African) when the Front moved in. I watched television interviews with National Front leaders, tracked the new wave of documentaries on Front-occupied towns, spoke with journalists writing on the Front in Toulon and Orange, spoke with lawyers defending those aggressed by the FN, visited the Front's national headquarters outside Paris and sought out FN cafés where I had been told there would be lots to hear. In the popular press, books on FN persons and politics were something of a cottage industry. I read most and collected all those I could get my hands on from the last ten years. This is a haphazard list that neither necessarily produces good history nor very good ethnography. I neither "infiltrated" the Front nor hung-out with its opponents, but instead tacked between trying to understand what place racialized politics had in people's lives while trying to figure out the scope and nature of the space it occupied in the public sphere.

Provence is the countryside made famous by Cezanne, Picasso and Van Gogh and more recently by Peter Mayle's bestselling bedside reader *A Year in Provence, de rigueur* for those with longings for loquacious rural souls who dish out fragrant soups and earthy breads. Mayle's book is so singularly unpopular in Aix I thought I might call this paper "An-Other Year in Provence," for the *département* in which Aix is located gives onto Shell refinery smells, less seemly visions and vistas. An hour and a half from Aix there are the four towns of Toulon, Marignane, Orange, and Vitrolles, the now infamous sites of National Front victories where as much as 45 percent of their populations have voted for platforms committed to "France for the French," "French first," expanded police forces, exclusion of welfare for "immigrants" (a misnomer in itself), and cash bonuses for couples producing "French" babies.

This area is the radical Right's epicenter and the small town of Vitrolles one of its prime "laboratories," as both the Front and its opponents agree. Vitrolles-en-Provence – as its FN officials have renamed it to emphasize its cultural attractions and tourist appeal – is a site where the FN's national programs have been rehearsed, where experiments in vigilantism, cultural censorship, barred entry to schools for those of the wrong shade, have been tried to gauge whether they get too much publicity or not enough, whether they scandalize too many people or are too tepid to mobilize more support for the Front's constituencies.

The story told in this way is dramatic but almost clichéd. The politics of the Front seem excessive, blatant, unreasoned, extreme. And one could – as many scholars and journalists have done so far – tell this predictable story of the Front's success. There is even comfort in such an account. We know its elements, we can imagine its actors – men of repressed violence, a region beset by a population of uprooted ex-colonials longing for a long-lost "French Algeria," people whose visions are narrow, whose employment opportunities are bleak, those desperate and too easily duped by the wrong answers to troubling questions.

But there is another side to the Front that is less easy to demonize, one less dissonant with mainstream public concerns. Its proponents speak in the language of democracy and liberty. They condemn violence. It is one harder to distinguish from other positions. It is one that those who assume they "know" the FN are less apt to hear.

For perhaps what is most striking about the platform of the Front, the persons who make up its constituency, the issues that it raises, is how

unexceptional and commonplace they are. Take, for instance, the FN's platform and practices around increased urban security. Virtually every effort to
outline the FN's political program has described its heavy-handed crackdown
on crime and juvenile delinquencey. In Vitrolles in spring 1998 people talked
in whispers about municipal funds swiped from cultural centers and reallo-
cated to pay for more police. Vitrolles' FN city officials spoke unabashedly
about the possible benefits of withholding state welfare payments to families
who could not control their youth. To their mind, a critical problem in Vitrolles and elsewhere in France is that the schools are too *laxiste* ("too lax"),
insufficiently "authoritarian": there are just too many families that do not
know how to parent, high schools with too many Left-leaning teachers cater-
ing to "problem kids" while those deserving attention and with real potential
are neglected and left on their own. The "problem" students and their "negli-
gent" families, not surprisingly, are those with Algerian and Moroccan family
names.

On the face of it, the position is a quintessentially FN and racist one: juvenile delinquency touches poor families and many poor families in urban France
are of North African origin. It is a policy, if implemented, with discriminatory
effects designed to target those most dependent on state resources, those living
in badly maintained state-subsidized tenements, either unemployed or with
low-paying jobs with dismal prospects and everything to lose. It reads as a
policy invested in buttressing a disciplinary, punitive exclusionary state, not a
nurturing inclusive and liberal one.

But that is both true and false. If one looks at reportage that has *not* been
on the FN over the last two years, it is clear that it is not only the Front
concerned with these issues. How different, in fact, is this position from the
parliamentary report on juvenile delinquencey, issued by the socialist government, that recommended prison punishments for parents who could not sufficiently monitor their young? (*Provence*, April 17, 1998). Or the proposal a
month later of the right-wing mayor of Aix-les-Bains – a non-FN town of
28,000 – to withhold state welfare from families with delinquent youths (*Le
Monde*, May 25, 1998)?

This overlap touches on a wider set of issues that reflect more than the
FN's stakes in juvenile delinquency alone. What is disconcerting here is
the slippage between FN rhetoric and that in the more general public sphere,
the chameleon-like form that FN positions assume, the fact that it is increasingly difficult to identify a purely FN position, in part because the Front has
been so effective at appropriating the rhetoric of the Right, the Left, the
extremes and everyone in between. The examples are too many and too
obvious. It is not only as the political theorist Pierre-Andre Taguieff pointed
out some ten years ago, that the radical Right has appropriated the language
of the French revolution and patriotic nationalism,[4] nor that it has played on
anxieties over national identity prompted by a future with a borderless Europe,
compounded by fears of what the substitution of the new Euro for the Franc
will bring.[5] It is not only that it has disabled more open discussions of immi-

gration because it has made raising the issue of problems associated with immi-grants synonymous with a racist discourse and appropriated it as its own. But keywords of the liberal state ring hollow when the language of "democracy," "individual liberty," and "the public good" appear as often in FN speeches as among those of its opponents.

Even accusations of racism – so long directed at the FN's leaders and their platforms – are no longer confined to anti-FN discourse alone. During 1998 the FN mounted a new discursive campaign, claiming that the problem in France today is not its racist tendencies – which it adamantly denies – but rather the anti-patriotic, "anti-French racism" of its "attackers" that more seri-ously threatens national heritage and identity and thus the very essence of France. One could dismiss this as merely a clever ruse, a distorting twist of the term "racism" into its very opposite. Rather than a relationship of power in which white Frenchmen come out on top, the FN's definition of "racism" crit-icizes the country's current leaders for being too swayed by a "cosmopolitan" intellectual Left more committed to globalization than to local French inter-ests – not unlike Pat Robertson's injunctions against a conspiratorial "New World Order" spearheaded by a deracinated intellectual Left.[6] In the FN scenario such "anti-French racism" victimizes longstanding French citizens made vulnerable to encroachments on their jobs, denigration of their cultural heritage, degeneration of their schools, and infringements on their most basic human rights.[7]

But the politics of appropriation has gone both ways: the FN may be talking with ease about their defense of liberty, but those fiercely opposed to FN xeno-phobias are finding themselves working from categories not dissimiliar to some of those of the FN. For example, public discussions are now unproblematically about a deluge of immigrants pouring into the country, despite the fact that immigration has not increased in France for the last twenty years.[8] Mainstream politicians unaligned with and opposed to the policies of the radical Right nevertheless now talk about the evils or virtues of supporting the FN's platform for a "national preference" – whether they agree or not with its basic tenets; namely, demand for strict quotas on immigration, for a "return" of immigrants to their countries of origin, for a war against a population that would deny access to medical benefits, social assistance, and other basic citizenry rights.

These are more than deft language games. They are part of a broader cul-tural repertoire of verbal and visual images that have widespread resonance and appeal. The point is that while the tactics of the Front can be character-ized as often excessive and unprincipled, its internal logic is powerful, it has ready answers to hard questions, what it conceives of as "problems" are identifiable, while those of its opponents are often not. What is impressive is not so much the rhetoric of Front leaders – on which Front-watchers have focused for years – but rather the discursive space it offers to its potential, non-committed sympathizers as well as its militants. Women and men with whom I talked in Vitrolles – some who avowed being supporters of the

Front – most who did not – expressed their fears and distastes in compelling terms. Almost everyone expressed their distrust of traditional politicians and politics.

The frontal attack on the Front's racist and xenophobic qualities that has characterized the profusion of books and newspaper articles appearing over the last few years has enabled some discourses and closed off others. Some might argue that it has created an engaged and active public sphere in which the immorality of racism can be openly argued and multiculturalism can be celebrated. But one could also argue the opposite; namely, that with so much attention focused on the evils of the Front, as well as its rise and fall, far less attention has been paid to the sympathies of a much broader French population that hold visions and political principles compatible with those of their more blatantly exclusionary FN counterparts. Probably one of the most frequently heard statements in France today among those who distance themselves from the FN and are decidedly not its supporters is one that begins: "I'm not a racist, but . . .", then filled in with injunctions about why too many immigrants is the real problem of contemporary France. In treating the FN as if it had a monopoly on racist visions and racist practices, there is little room to examine the broader terrain that nurtures it and on which it rests.

The FN's Common Sense: On Being Independent of Politics

In talking with people in Vitrolles, I posed a basic question: "What does it mean to be educated in France today? What sorts of knowledge and know-how should go into that equation?" To my question on education, most people responded that they were not interested in politics (although I rarely referred to politics *per se*). They were tired of teachers' organizations, local interest groups, regional leaders and national parties that were all *trop politicise* ("too politicized"). Women of the parent–student association (APPEVE) supported by the Front insisted that theirs was strictly an "independent" organization, unfettered by political party. Their concern was for their children's education and safety, but unlike those associations backed by the socialist and center conservative parties, not *politicise*. No one with whom I spoke in APPEVE acknowledged its affiliation with the Front. What concerned them was an educational system too subservient to politics, teachers who brought their politics to the classroom, not enough discipline in schools. "Laxity," "lack of discipline," "lack of limits" were the most frequent terms.

At one level it would not be inappropriate to say that "discipline" was their keyword. But easy answers are easy to get; for the issue of discipline is at once distinctly FN and not. "Mothers of the Front" spoke forcefully about discipline but so did those women whose affiliations were squarely elsewhere. What differed was what they all meant by discipline and who was deemed to lack it.

Beyond the Extremes of the Far Right:
Are There Reasoning Women and Men?

Pierre-Andre Taguieff was perspicacious when he first critiqued anti-racist organizations for pathologizing those on the extreme Right in ways evocative of the scapegoating of the Other so central to racist discourse itself. But one could go further. FN militants and constituents have been pathologized in specific ways: they are treated as those outside reason, persons unduly swayed, deluded by crises of identity, morally weakened by disempowerment. This image of FN supporters viscerally *other*, delusional, and duped has specific effects (as if one could almost smell their politics on their breath). Considered outside the humanist tradition, they are in *any* context and *all* instances labeled irrational and unreasonable men (*sic*). As such, their fear is taken as the FN's most powerful "common denominator."[9]

But one could start from another, less intuitive premise: not that the radical Right is full of fearful malcontents on the margins of French society, but of reasoning women as well as men. Not "monsters" but those who are "rather likable," or as one FN watcher put it, "faces that might occupy the ranks of any political formation."[10] What happens if one starts, not from the assumption that its platforms are based on ill-will, small-mindedness, and sinister imaginings (which they may be and often are) but, rather, that the force of the Front comes from more than its trafficking in carefully crafted slogans and deft manipulations of signs, but from its nuanced, even subtle cultural politics? What happens if racisms are not the excesses and anomalies of modern states, bureaucratic machines gone out of wack, but fundamental technologies of them, as Foucault suggested some twenty years ago to an unreceptive College de France audience?[11] These are unpopular premises, but they may offer a better starting point to understand the FN's appeal and the popularity of its claims.

One would not ordinarily use the word "subtlety" to describe the extreme Right in the US or in Canada, much less in Germany, England, or France. By definition, the term "extreme" or "radical" indicates a set of perceptions and practices beyond the pale, exaggerated, outside the norm. In many ways this accurately describes white supremacist groups like the Canadian Western Guard or the US Ku Klux Klan, as well as some members of the FN. But to begin and end there is to miss the registers in which the radical Right operates. "Subtlety" may not capture what typfies the FN's cultural know-how, but the metaphors of excess that invoke flat-footed, crass, uninspired powers of persuasion, attractive to few other than simple-minded thugs and skinheads, are not either.

The National Front's commitment to the trinity of *famille, travail, patrie* ("family, work, and fatherland") has cross-cultural relevance, cross-class and cross-national appeal. It commands a moral righteousness that touches not only those situated in the "deep US South," in North America's outback West, or in France *profonde*. These are images that have informed nineteenth-century racial regimes in colony and metropole, that have long appealed to women as much as men, that appear in a wide range of nationalistic tracts of different political persuasions. As exclusionary invocations they are powerfully posed as defenses of society against itself. They invoke the coziness of belonging, speak in the language of protection of the majority, promise to "weed out" the enemy within for the common good, the good of all. They are often not unsympathetic to the blight of impoverished *cité* families of Magrehbin origin – and are not unlike the comfortable politics of compassion that underwrote colonial social reforms.[12]

But the FN's nuanced cultural politics comes in other forms. The FN has its own small coterie of committed scholars that publish on the true "origins of France" and who are prominently advertised as professors at the Sorbonne.[13] Its publications are not cheap political tracts. They are printed with glossy covers on high-quality paper in paperback form. Its poster art is pop, catchy, and impressive. While some poster and postcard art is inspired by fascist populist imagery (bare-chested white young men with short-cropped hair, toned and taut, working tools in hand with eyes raised to the banner of France and the Front's eternal flame), others make subtler commentaries, such as the poster, hot off the press, I was proudly shown in the basement of the FN's national headquarters. It showed cartoon-like figures: one wasted, disheveled, drug-ridden student of left-wing vintage with the year 1968 written above his head; the other a well-groomed, bright-eyed youth with "1998" written above his head in bold type. Another poster stated in bright red "REBELLE-TOI! [REBEL!] JOIN THE FRONT." What could better invoke the fight against the status quo, an alignment with the Right revolution on the side of the Front and France's future leaders? As the retired schoolteacher from the South who sorted posters reminded me, "See, we have our own intellectuals too."

It is not just poster culture which is on the mark. The FN's cyberspace connections are informative, clear, and interactive for those who join. Its website is updated regularly with statistics on local and national elections, with new political tracts, with on-line copies of FN books and excerpts from the anti-FN popular press. In the tradition of the French Communist Party, whose annual festival combines family fun, cultural and political events, the FN too hosts an array of summer universities, institutes for "cultural action," scientific meetings, colloquia for journalists, and educational workshops, like one held last August in Toulon's Neptune Palace concert hall that took as its theme "Liberate the Republic." FN national rallies have been glitzy sound and light shows with singers of color blasting rap and reggae music. Radio Le Pen offers non-stop news.

Until the split this fall the FN press itself provided impressive daily and weekly analyses of national events, incisive commentaries on articles appearing in *Le Monde*, *Liberation*, and the foreign press. Attacks on the FN are reported by its journalists as a badge of honor and minutely tracked, buttressing its claim that it is FN supporters who are undemocratically harassed and violently aggressed. The *Canard Enchaine* (a satirical weekly that has committed itself for years to sustained FN goading) is mocked by the FN dailies. Nonetheless, those same dailies scrupulously mimic its black and red bold type and layout.[14] Is it significant that at a glance one cannot distinguish the format and font of the FN press from that of its opponents?

But this is only part of the problem. For while this may seem good evidence of a clear FN position and well-honed rhetoric, never has it been so difficult to isolate and specify what constitutes the discourse of the extreme Right in France. This may seem contradictory, but at a very fundamental level it is not.

Figuring the FN: Analyses of the Man, the Movement, the Nation

Problems in specifying what is specific to the FN are strongly reflected in changes in how journalists, scholars, and activists have profiled the extreme Right and what sort of emphasis they place on Le Pen, its founder and leader. Over the last five years there has been a virtual explosion in the literature about the "FN phenomenon" that displays a very distinct set of registers in which that phenomenon is identified and cast. While typologies never hold fast, one can identify several shifts in emphasis in the documentation about the FN that runs broadly from a focus on the leader Le Pen, to the FN as a fascist institution, to the radical Right as a reflection of French society itself.

The first register conforms to what one might call a "big man theory of history" or the "cult of the man." In such analyses the FN's power to persuade was framed as one solely based on its extraordinary leader, his debating skills and rhetorical flourish. Implicitly and often explicitly assumed in such accounts is the notion that radical Right politics is what explains the rise of the FN. On the contrary, the argument is that people are pulled to its extremisms almost inadvertently, accidentally because of the force of Le Pen as a leader. Ergo if the FN is Le Pen, then it is only a short-lived, conjunctural phenomenon that would reasonably weaken with his fall. (Thus titles such as *In the Shadow of Le Pen, The Le Pen Effect, Le Pen: the Words*, or *The Said and the Unstated of Le Pen*).[15] The recent rise of Bruno Megret does not undermine that model. Now the focus is on Megret's more youthful, up-to-date style and panache. The "big men" are changing but not the structure of the analysis itself.

Journalists have a penchant for flashy newsworthy personalities, but even they can no longer argue that the Front is only Le Pen. In fact the newest wave of books is precisely on the conflict in successionary rights – from Le Pen to Megret and the growing tension between them. Optimistic sorts who once imagined that the FN would dissolve with Le Pen's demise now predict the very opposite; namely, that the FN seems to be taking on new force as the offensive brashness of 'Le Pen is replaced by those of more respectable style: Cendrine Le Chevallier, mayoral candidate in Toulon, is hard to bill as a

populist candidate with her Hermes scarves and Chanel outfits. The oppositional press lingers over her sparkling jewels and gold bracelets that tinkle as
she brushes hands with would-be supporters in urban crowds. If being brash
and outspoken were hallmarks of the FN in earlier years, now it is just the
opposite. Megret and his cohort wear expensively cut banker suits and preach
alliances with the Right, not distance from it. If being outrageous and provocative was the strategy of an earlier moment, then confusing the camps, blurring the distinctions, tangling the terms of what is possible to discuss publicly
signals appeal to a different set of sensibilities today.

This second register of political and historical analysis gives less emphasis to
Le Pen *per se* than to the nature of the Front itself, its recruitment strategies,
its partisans and its institutional frame. Demographic analyses of regional and
national elections have made continual effort to identify the specific populations that have succumbed to the FN, with focus on their idiosyncrasies and
on the susceptibilities of those that might "fall" in the future. Starting nearly
two decades ago, with the first alarm at the FN's electoral success, the effort
was to isolate those vulnerable to it. This was a reasonable effort when the
FN's numbers were still small and scattered unevenly throughout the population. What is more telling is that as recently as 1996 the flagship journal of
Parisian intellectuals, *Nouvel Observateur*, could point to an FN constituency
made up of "special" groups: for example, of *pieds noirs* (repatriated Frenchmen born in Algeria), of first-wave European immigrants from Italy and
Portugal, or of dislocated, emasculated, unemployed young men.

This demographics of blame has had lots of targets: some studies optimistically asserted it was really only "the aged" who were attracted, hardline nos-
talgics for colonialism and/or those fearful of change. Others focused on the
particular attraction of the FN for young males, ignoring the numerous women
who have voted for it. Many studies have addressed the regional clustering of
FN support in the troubled working-class outskirts of Paris and of southern
France. In the latter case, the "cause" is found more specifically in a population known to have supported the Petain/Vichy government during the
wartime occupation, who then fled at the war's end to France's North African
colonies, only to be grudgingly forced back in the early 1960s with Algeria's
independence.

These studies certainly have something to say about the nature of FN
support, but perhaps more to say about what researchers expected to find:
namely, evidence that the FN is a decidely non-French phenomenon. Scholars shared this perspective with activists and the press. It is best captured
perhaps in the favored slogan "F is for fascist, N is for Nazi," so often plastered
across anti-FN posters, chanted in anti-FN rallies, and that is still popular today,
as though one had to look to the history of Italian and German political
extremisms for a set of sympathies that were born and bred in France.

But much as it is no longer possible to hold that the Vichy regime was a
foreign imposition on an unwilling French population, so too have analyses of
the FN in its third register turned away from this search for a foreign etymol-

ogy. No longer seeking the anomalous nature of the FN within an otherwise republican French society, some analyses have, as one recent title put it, sought other roots, that of an "FN MADE IN FRANCE."[16] Vaguely concurrent with the increasingly broad regional and class spread of the FN and its ever widening constituencies, emphasis here has been more on the FN as a product of French nationalism gone awry, as an accurate mirror of the ills of French society or alternately as a distorted mirror of its malaise.[17] Here commentaries have turned to the making of an endemically xenophobic movement – neither foreign nor imposed – but organically French.

Not surprisingly, these shifts in exposé style and scholarship are not dissimilar to the course of Holocaust studies over the last fifty years, which have also moved from studies of "the man" (Hitler/Le Pen), followed by those focused on the party (Front or Nazi) and those more attentive to economic depression, to the anonymity of urban sprawl, to the Nazi party/FN as a product of a technocratic state machine and a swollen and alienating bureaucracy.[18] But a glaring difference remains. In the German case, the relationship between racism and the (Nazi) state is fundamental to the analysis. Studies of the FN, on the contrary, systematically beg the statist question, in part because the starting premise is that the French republican state is the FN's nemesis and by definition opposed to it.

But what happens if Michel Foucault was right – that racism is not a part of certain state formations (be they fascist, capitalist, or socialist) and no others, but fundamental to the making of the modern state itself?[19] Perhaps we should be asking whether state racisms may take varied form, not only as firmly and explicitly entrenched in the state's central institutions, but in displaced sites as a shadow presence. What is the relationship between the history of the radical Right and the history of the French welfare state? What does the political presence of a vocal extreme Right allow or disallow the state to do? One obvious question is whether a new Europe without borders is calling for a more stringently defined set of interior frontiers.

But it may be that, as Wittengstein once argued, these are not the wrong answers but the wrong questions. For how do we know whether there really have been radical changes in the tactics of the Front rather than in scholarly analyses of it? Perhaps we need another starting place all together. In order to assess how powerful the FN is perhaps we should not be looking at its increased electoral successes, at its increasing media presence, or even at the FN itself. Perhaps we should be looking at the racialized field it has helped to landscape, to assess how much it governs a wide range of gestures, dictates the behaviors of those unsympathetic to it, shapes the rules rather than the particular strategies of the game. Perhaps we should be asking another (Foucauldian) question: not what is its aim, its strategy and its tactics, but what are its practical effects?

Take, for example, the "culture of fear" that is said to surround the FN. Is it produced by the FN or those who oppose it? Is it generated out of FN practices or the result of the discourse of its opposition? In developing this project over the last year, many colleagues and friends have discouraged me from continuing. I have been advised to order an unlisted phone, to get a post office box rather than use my home address, to refrain from talking to anyone at FN rallies, to avoid carrying a camera, not to attend anti-FN demonstrations, to watch my back, to keep my distance from the press. At one level these are not unreasonable precautions: the FN is "known" to harass its opponents, threaten their spokespersons, and retain beefy bodyguards to protect their leaders in potentially hostile crowds. When I told friends that on a visit to the FN head-quarters outside Paris I deposited my Michigan driver's license at the door, I was chided for reckless bravado. How do these figure as intimidations? Again, are these constraints produced solely by the FN or by an anti-FN caricature of it?

The answer is not obvious, in part because cultures of fear, like power itself, permeate social relations in a wide political field. If power is defined by the capacity to impose the categories of discourse and practice, then the FN is a strong player. The FN has both reproduced a culture of fear and ensured that it reproduces itself. This was strikingly evident in watching the effect of the FN victory in Vitrolles. With nearly half the population having voted for the FN in the last elections (and it did not seem to matter, as some people claimed, that many in Vitrolles had only registered a "protest vote" against the preced-ing spendthrift, socialist mayor), people repeatedly talked about an atmosphere in town that was tense, that people were uncomfortable even greeting their neighbors, that a newly heightened suspicion, distrust, and avoidance were oppressive and not unlike a new brand of terror.

But discourses are neither homogeneous nor shared. In returning to Vit-rolles this spring it was clear that "security" was a prevailing trope with a mul-tiple sense. Thus the city's monthly publication boasted that "Security in '98 was still better than '97!" with the introduction of more police dogs, eques-trian police, more surveillance cameras, and a new "rapid intervention police brigade." In contrast, young women in Vitrolles' state housing complexes saw the issue of security the other way around; they described something like a state of siege, of a police presence so intense that they and their friends were uncomfortable walking about at night – they only felt that the streets were safe and "secure" in the absence of police in the light of day.

The Family Front: On the Gender Politics of the Radical Right

The point of looking at scholarship on the FN is not to conclude that the analy-ses have all been wrong, but rather to question the assumptions that organize those frames. At one of the first Front demonstrations I attended in fall 1997 on the waterfront in Marseille, two angry and vocal elderly women stood in the midst of a large crowd, chiding "France" for not upholding its democratic principles. Assuming they were anti-FN demonstrators, I was impressed with their gutsy stance until realizing they were staunch Front supporters and that the day's slogan "we've had enough" (of liberalism, immigrants, anti-Front attacks) was on their lips too. There was nothing out of the ordinary about the event – only my assumptions about it.

As one looks to the issues that have been omitted from the current research agenda on the French radical Right, nothing is more striking than the singular effacement of its gender politics. Both academic and journalistic commentary and coverage have focused on the FN and men: on the male elite that formulates its policies, on the young male immigrants at which its policies are aimed, and on the insecure and unemployed male population to which it supposedly has most appeal. While men have made up the majority of the Front's voting public, the fact remains that as much as 25 percent of the voting population who have voted for the FN are women, a percentage that has been decisive for the narrow margin by which the FN has won local elections. Not examining the appeal of the Front for a large female constituency seems in part to be based on the unstated assumption that those women who vote for the Front are following their fathers, brothers, sons – their men.

What is more, in the last few years women unexpectedly have emerged in key positions of the FN's leadership, as both pawns and strong players in the Front's juggling of posts and persons in local politics. As FN figures such as Le Pen, Megret, and de Chevalier have been disqualified from elections, their wives have replaced them as candidates in mayoral and regional campaigns. Most recently, following the FN's split in the fall, Le Pen's youngest daughter "defected" to Megret's camp, highlighting a basic tension between loyalties to political kith vs. intimate kin, especially charged because the FN's central platform has been so closely tied to "family values." The gender dynamics reflected in the fact that Megret's wife, Catherine, could legitimately "stand in" for him as Vitrolles' mayor, despite her inexperience in politics or public life, pushed on the relationship between family and politics yet again, snidely signaled in the non-FN press by referring to her husband Bruno Megret as the "mayor consort."

Family, gender, and politics emerged again last summer with the surprise announcement by Le Pen that his wife, Janny, would stand in for him in the European parliamentary elections rather than Megret, an event that many would argue first publicly marked the severing of the FN into two camps.[20] The conflict (and Janny's unexpected and much publicized response to the press that she neither wanted to run nor knew anything about politics) brought the gender politics of substitutability to a new heightened level. At stake were not only the new divisions within the FN, but conflict over its very political credibility.

However, what makes the lack of attention to female voters most surprising – and contrasting with the coverage of the internal machinations of affinal substitutes in party politics – is the fact that many of the major themes played out in public discourse are about areas of life thought to be controlled by, and of special importance to, women: primary school education, daycare, child-rearing, family planning, and sexual morality. In the Front's favored slogan "family, work, and fatherland" it is "family" that is first. Emphasis on the male contours of the Front fails to address critical arenas in which the extreme Right has made its presence and power felt – all domains in which women have been actively called upon to police the boundaries between the moral and the immoral, between what is public or private, between what should be handled at school and what are affairs of parenting and the home.

While these are issues that feminist scholars working on the appeal of the conservative Right in the US have addressed for sometime, this is decidely not the case for French scholarship.[21] If the issue of gender politics is examined at all, it focuses on how extreme Right parties view women, rather than *how women view them.* In trying to learn something about the ways in which women of the Front process its programs and present its appeal, this spring our research focused more pointedly in that direction. Among others, we interviewed women who worked for Vitrolles' FN-run city government, mothers with school-age children, well-educated, well-heeled, and politically learned. Unlike those women in the teacher–student organizations backed by the FN who categorically refused any association or sympathy for its politics, these were women of the Front – young Megretistes, who characterized Le Pen as an out-dated model for the FN and who bet their futures on Megret.[22]

Schools are the problem, but they cast their net of concern wider, in an idiom that frequently invokes the problem of figurative and literal "thresholds." Here it is the FN that polices the dangerous borders between France and its outside (with immigration quotas), the FN that understands the need to police the entries to schools, the FN that is vigilant about what belongs in school and in the home. They are disconcerted by contemporary parenting styles and blame "some" parents for neglecting the moral rearing of their young, for not instilling a sense of "good taste," for abandoning jobs to teachers that they should be doing themselves. They blame teachers for not leaving their politics at home. When they tell us that mothers should have the opportunity to stay at home, we ask why they are at work. Madame C. sighs and says it is she who suffers, that she (and France) underwent a bit "too much feminism" when she was growing up, that work hours are not designed with women in mind. On the other hand, both she and her coworker adamantly oppose propositions for gender parity, what they refer to as an "aberration of the Left."

Future Directions/Old Connections

What is striking about the Front's interventions in public education, welfare, immigration policy, library acquisitions, theater openings, and in scholarship is the face of racial thinking it fashions for France and a wider European community for the twenty-first century. It is neither a new racism nor a replica of the old. France today harbors a racial discourse that is flexible and porous, malleable, modernizing, and imbued with cultural currency. Those who pose this as a new racism, as a cultural racism fundamentally distinct from racisms of the past, are missing how much colonial racisms spoke in a language of cultural competencies, "good taste," and discrepant parenting values.[23]

The cultural ambiguities that characterized racisms in the nineteenth-century Dutch East Indies or French Indochina should not serve as a point of historical contrast so much as suggestive of the sorts of questions one might pose. Tracking what designated "race" there and then should alert us to the fact that even those quintessential forms of racism honed in the colonies were never built on the surefooted classifications of science, but on a potent set of cultural and affective criteria whose malleability was a key to the sliding scale along which economic privilege was protected and social entitlements were assigned. In short, the porousness we assign to the contemporary concept of race is a fluidity inherent in the concept itself and not a hallmark of our postmodern critique – much less our postcolonial moment.

Still, what the face of racism looks like on the cusp of this twenty-first century cannot be derived from its eighteenth- and nineteenth-century templates alone. Nor can it be derived from the last three years of the FN's rapid ascension or its more recent succession of splits, failures, and weakening in mainstream politics. That more than two-thirds of France in the last summer's poll could avow that it was sympathetic to at least some of the National Front's platform should remind us that racisms never have (and do not today exist) in distilled form. They are as easily embraced by those eager for change as those who are not. Racial discourses can serve central state concerns as much as those opposed to them. They can herald utopian visions as much as nostalgic ones. Predicating an understanding of today's racism on a flattened, reductive history of what racism once looked like may be consoling but it is neither helpful nor redemptive. Genealogies of racisms must reckon with racisms' power to rupture with the past and selectively and strategically recuperate it at the same time. We need to take seriously the ways in which exclusionary politics have created and continue to produce a repertoire of responses, solutions that their adherents see neither as racist nor exclusionary, but as reasonable, measured, even compassionate and commonsense.

Notes

1   This essay is based on presentations delivered as the keynote address for the conference "Making History, Constructing Race," University of Victoria, and for the workshop "Europe and Algeria," held at the Johns Hopkins Center in Bologna in May, 1999. Funding for the project has been provided by the LSA faculty fund, the Office of the Vice President, and the Institute for Research on Gender at the University of Michigan. Initial research for this project was conducted in 1997 with the help of Chantal Fevrier, Annie Roquier, and Frederic Cotton. Research in 1999 has been carried out with Delphine Mauger, an undergraduate in Anthropology at the UM.

2   See, for example, *Race and the Education of Desire: Foucault's History of Sexuality and the Colonial Order of Things* (Durham, NC: Duke University Press, 1995), and "Racial

Histories and their Regimes of Truth," *Political Power and Social Theory*, vol. 13, fall 1997.

3   John Pemberton. *The Subject of "Java"* (Ithaca, NY: Cornell University Press, 1996).

4   See Taguieff's rich and subtle analysis of the multilayered mobilizing tactics of the Front in "The Doctrine of the National Front in France (1972–1989)," *New Political Science* 16–17 (fall/winter 1989): 29–70.

5   See Pierre-Andre Taguieff's *Les Fins de l'antiracisme* (Paris: Michalon, 1995).

6   The comparison between far Right political discourse in the US on the perils of immigrants and of globalization, as embodied in Pat Robertson's *The New World Order* (Dallas: Word Publishing, 1991) and that of the French National Front is yet to be made.

7   In a public colloquium on "Anti-French Racism" organized by the municipal library of the FN-run city of Marignane in June 1998, at least one prevailing definition targeted those who "spoke of" and "encouraged *metissage* (mixing)." "Compte Rendue d'un colloque public a Marignane sur le theme: 'Le racisme anti-francais'" (June 12, 1998).

8   The confused use of "immigrant" to include "jeune Francaise d'origine immigree" and "jeune immigres non français" is not fortuitous but part of the racial politics of this discourse. See Yannick LeFranc, "Comment le parti de l'exclusion traite un mouvement pour l'integration," *Mots* 58, March 1999, p. 60.

9   Michalina Vaughn, "The Extreme Right in France: 'Lepenisme' or the Politics of Fear" in *The Far Right in Western and Eastern Europe*, ed. Luciano Cheles, Ronnie Ferguson, and Michalina Vaughn (London: Longman, 1995), pp. 215–33.

10   As Mark Hunter puts it, "There are, in reality, monsters in the Front; I have met several of them. But one equally finds people rather likable, *attractice (sympathetique)* which raises another question: what are they doing here among these monsters?" (see *Un Americain au Front: Enquete au sein du FN* (Paris: Stock, 1997), p. 11; Jonathan Marcus, *The National Front and French Politics* (New York: University Press of New York, 1995), p. 2.

11   See chapter 3 of my *Race and the Education of Desire*, entitled "Toward a Genealogy of Racisms: The 1976 Lectures at the College de France," pp. 55–94.

12   On the distancing and differentiating politics that underwrite "empathy" see Julie Ellison's "A Short History of Liberal Guilt," *Critical Inquiry* (winter 1996).

13   Among some of these are *Les Origines de la France*, published "under the direction of Professor Jacques Robichez" among others, with the names of Bruno Megret and Jean-Marie Le Pen included as co-authors. This volume, published by the FN press, Editions Nationales, was a product of its "XIIth Colloque du Conseil Scientifique du Front National". *L'Immigration sans haine ni mepris: les chiffres que l'on vous cache* ("Immigration without hate or misapprehension: the numbers that are hidden from you") Pierre Milloz, 1997.

14   Since the split between Megret and Le Pen the FN articles have become noticeably innocuous with safe and familiar targets, like immigrants, but with no comment on the divisions that have sundered it apart.

15   Examples of these genres of analysis include Pascal Perrineau's *Le Symptome Le Pen: radiograhie des electeur du Front national* (Paris: Fayard, 1997); Maryse Souchard, Stephanie Wahnich, Isabelle Cuminal, Virginie Wathier, *Le Pen le mots: analyse d'un discours d'extreme-droite* (Paris: Le Monde editions, 1997); Lorrain de Saint Affrique and Jean-Gabriel Fredet, *Dans l'ombre de Le Pen* (Paris: Hachette, 1998), the latter a former press officer for Le Pen.

16   Hubert Huertas, *FN: Made in France* (Paris: Autres Temps, 1997).

17   Alain Bihr, *Le Spectre de l'extreme droits: les français dans le miroir du Front National* (Paris: Les Editions de l'atelier, 1998).

18   On the Holocaust as "deeply rooted in the nature of modern society and in the central categories of modern social thought" see Zygmunt Bauman, *Modernity and the Holocaust* (Ithaca, NY: Cornell University Press, 1989).

19   Again see Foucault's final set of lectures in 1976 on "the birth of modern racism," discussed in *Race and the Education of Desire* (1995) and now available in French under the title *"Il Faut Defendre la Societe": Cours au College de France*, 1976 (Paris: Seuil/Gallimard, 1997), pp. 213–35.

20   See, for example, the article "FN: L'Histoire interdite" in *L'Evenement*, April 8, 1999.

21   See, for example, *L'extreme droite et les femmes*, ed. Caludie Lesselier and Faimmetta Venner (Paris: Golias, 1997).

22   This was just a month before the court decision that the logo, name, and funds designated as those of the "FN" rightfully belonged to Le Pen and that Megret could not use them without severe penalty.

23   On the importance of a proper moral and culturally attuned education for European colonials see my "A Sentimental Education" in *Carnal Knowledge and Imperial Power* (forthcoming, University of California Press) and "Sexual Affronts and Racial Frontiers" in *Tensions of Empire: Colonial Cultures in a Bourgeois World*, ed. Frederick Cooper and Ann Laura Stoler (Berkeley: University of California Press, 1997).

Chapter 7

Breaking the Silence and a Break with the Past: African Oral Histories and the Transformations of the Atlantic Slave Trade in Southern Ghana

Anne Bailey

In Southern Ghana along the stretch of land off the Atlantic Ocean formerly known as the Old Slave Coast, there are only a few stories that are remembered about the Atlantic slave trade. Amongst the Anlo Ewes, residents of this area for hundreds of years, there is a loud silence on the question of slavery. But how could a period of almost 400 years be blotted out of historical memory? How could a period that had profound effects on a community become a faint memory?

Perhaps the regrets are too many to live with. Perhaps the deep wounds inflicted by the trade are not a part of a distant past but a continuing part of the present and future. Perhaps the community is still wrestling with the effects of the cruel trade – effects that bore deep into the crevices of institutions they held dear. Perhaps they understand the true meaning of the anchors in the sand and on the ocean bed along their shores. These anchors, left by European and American slave traders as they sailed away with their human cargo, to this day, obstruct the efforts of local fishermen. Encrusted with rust and immovable by human hands, they tear their nets and allow their bounty to go free. Like these anchors, the oral traditions of the Anlo on the period of the slave trade are half buried in the sand and encrusted with rust. As the rust peels, however, there is one story that sheds light on an era that many would rather forget.

It is the story of a group of drummers who were kidnapped by European traders on the shores of a town called Atokor. All over Eweland and wherever Ewe people of Ghana may now reside, this story is remembered almost universally. It connects the Ewe university professor to the Ewe farmer and is significant not only because it is one of the few stories remembered about the trade but also because it is a *metaphor* for the different phases of the Atlantic slave trade. The Atokor incident breaks the silence on the question of slavery while simultaneously representing a break with the past in terms of trading operations along the coast. It marks a critical shift from organized structures and mutual agreements of the eighteenth-century trade to disorder and chaos in the post-abolition period. Finally, this story as a metaphor and to some extent a cautionary tale is significant because it represents an *independent mode of historical representation*: a unique understanding and conception of history and the process of history-making consistent with important aspects of Ewe culture.

Questions of impact and agency in the Atlantic slave trade have been vigorously debated for years. Scholars have often looked to the numbers to find answers to the question of impact. Was the number of Africans taken from the shores of Africa 9.5 million or 15 million? To date, there has been little consensus on an exact figure. Though the numbers are important, it can be said that no number can quantify the depth of human suffering; no number can adequately reveal the devastating impact of the trade on African social and political institutions. Such was my assessment of the story of the Atokor incident and other oral accounts collected in 1992 and 1993, as well as colonial and trading records.

This essay is part of a larger study which not only looks at the social impact of the slave trade, but also the question of agency. Starting with the assertion that the two are interrelated, the impact of the trade is assessed in light of the various roles played by both African and European traders. Much attention is paid to the *transformations* of the slave trade throughout the centuries culminating in its last phase, 1850–90 (Lovejoy 1983; Manning 1990). This period is significant because it coincides with the revival of the trade precipitated by the tremendous demand of plantations in Cuba and Brazil. Secondly, 1850 marks the first serious attempt by the British to extend their rule over Anlo territory by the purchase of slave forts from the Danes. In 1890, after a period of resistance on the part of the Anlos, British efforts finally met with success. This last phase of the trade was characterized by an acute disruption in previous trading practices and operations.

In general, the issues of impact and agency as seen through Ewe oral histories intersect three important historiographical debates, including the effects of the slave trade on African society. Here the emphasis will be on issues of social impact as opposed to "the numbers game:" the question of how many Africans were transported across the Atlantic (Curtin 1969; Rodney 1972;

Inikori 1982; Law 1991; Miller 1988; Greene 1996). The issue of agency will
also be assessed. Recent studies have concluded that Africans played an active
if not controlling role in the area of slave supply. This essay attempts to reassess
these conclusions in terms of the complex reality of the African role and in
light of the larger context of agency in transatlantic operations of the slave
trade in Europe and the Americas. Finally, this essay is a contribution to the
ongoing debate on the utility of oral histories and the literature on memory
(Vansina 1985; Quayson 1997; Ranger 1983). How can African oral history
material be used in the production of African history? How should this material be assessed in conjunction with other records? How should it be viewed
on its own terms? These and other issues will be discussed, as well as the role
of human memory in the adaptation of oral traditions.

First, it will be helpful to describe briefly the historical and cultural context
for these accounts. It should be noted that in the following discussion the word
"traditional" with respect to various aspects of Ewe culture refers to institutions indigenous to the African continent as opposed to those introduced by
foreign traders, missionaries, and the like. Tradition here is also not intended
to represent a static or essentialist view, but rather refers to the ideals of the
society which must necessarily be contrasted with practice.

The Anlo Ewes comprise the groups Anlo, Some, Aflao, Klikor, Dzodze,
Wheta, Awe, and Whenyi and reside in towns and villages along the southeastern coast of Ghana. The most significant for this study are Keta (formerly
the site of a major slave market and the location of Fort Prinsenstein), Atokor
(formerly a major slave way station), Anloga (the capital of Anlo), and Woe
(the former base of key African and European slave traders). Several of these
towns and villages were once bustling centers of trade and commerce. This
past reality stands in stark contrast to the present state of most today. Their
narrow roads and lanes, instead of being overrun by the business of daily activity, are dusty and bare. Furthermore, even the sea has taken its toll. Everywhere along the southeastern coast there has been a gradual erosion which
began early in the century. This has only added to the pressures of daily life
in this area. It was in these venues that the few stories that are remembered
about the trade were recounted.

The absence of a pervasive and detailed remembrance of the slave trade is
significant because it is clear that the Anlo Ewes deeply revere their history.
Most members of these communities can tell the story of the migration of the
Ewes from Ketu, a Yoruba town in Benin, and again from Notsie. They left
Notsie in the mid-seventeenth century and moved to their present locations
along the Volta and Mona rivers in flight from a tyrant king called Agokoli
(Amenumey 1972, p. 1). Schoolchildren know this story as well as they know
their alphabet. The annual Hogbestosto festival was established to commemorate this early history of the community. Actors reenact scenes marking the
grand exodus of the people from Notsie to their present location. The dance
and drumming selection, *Misego*, which literally means "gird your loin tight,"
is played to recall this period (Fiagbedzi 1977, p. 56). The songs and stories

associated with their departure which are assiduously recalled at this event and throughout the year represent their commitment to safeguarding their history.

That such history is remembered in song and drumming styles is not incidental. Ewe music has traditionally functioned as much more than art and entertainment. Drumming and song styles are connected to every important life-cycle event as well as to all the major events in the community. Drummers in this context occupy a special place in society, as they are in effect historians, who through their talking drums record the history of the people and convey the values of the community (Chernoff 1979, pp. 35–6, 143).

Such values include what some speculate is a certain suspicion of highly centralized structures given their experience with the oppressive King Agokoli. Politically, since their last migration they have remained a group of loosely organized clans in villages and towns along the coast. In general, the chief was the constitutional head and his position was hereditary. His power, however, was not unchecked. He was obliged to consult with a body of elders about every important matter in the village. Such a structure was meant to ensure the responsiveness of the chiefs. They then led with the knowledge that they could be destooled if they took positions contrary to the will of the people. Consistent with this essentially democratic structure was the relative absence of a complex system of social stratification in Anlo society (Amenumey 1986, pp. 12, 27).

Above this structure of local chieftaincies was the hereditary position of paramount chief or *Awomefia*. As the highest political office in Anlo, he presided over internal and external matters that affected the state. Like the local chiefs, the awomefia was guided by various councils of elders. Furthermore, he also had the ultimate say in matters of law and order. Cases of very serious offenses were brought before him and his sentences included capital punishment. He oversaw, for example, the *Nyiko* system of law which involved arbitration of the chiefs leading to capital punishment for serious offenders (Bailey fieldnotes 1997).

The maintenance of law and order was second only in importance to the sacred in traditional Anlo culture. For the traditional believer, religion permeates all areas of life and there is a marked reverence for their ancestors and the hereafter. In fact, it is believed that life on earth is only a small part of a greater continuum which begins with the concept of *Se* (the pre-earthly soul) and migrates to *Gbogbo* (life or divine soul). Upon death, the gbogbo returns to *Mawu*, the Supreme God, and joins the society of ancestors in the hereafter. At this juncture, the same spirit reincarnates as another soul on earth (Gaba 1965, pp. 55, 327–8). From this brief outline, we can see that Anlo traditional culture views life and death along a continuum. Such elements of Anlo culture are highly suggestive of a long-term view of life in all its forms and manifestations.

In short, history is important here. How then can we explain the relative silence on the question of the slave trade? One reason for the silence is the perceived shame attached to the issue of slavery. Little distinction is made between transatlantic slaves and domestic slaves in this regard. They both share the same level of shame, though it can be said that domestic slavery is a more contentious issue because of the existence of people in the community who are descendants of slaves. As Ghanaian scholar Kofi Awoonor points out in his review of Ewe oral literature, "one of the most fearsome insults centers around slavery." Traditional griots such as Komi Ekpe used their awareness of this shame in performance of what is called *halo poetry*. Halo is the performance of poetry which includes insults of a particular person or group. Halo was often used as a means of diffusing real-life conflicts, since it was an opportunity to insult an offending party without resorting to violence. In fact, up until it was banned by British authorities in the early part of this century, halo was considered a useful social practice since it helped community members to express their grievances in a non-violent manner (Awoonor 1976, pp. 122–3).

Ekpe's poetry contains statements referring to opponents as the descendants of slaves. This was thought to be particularly offensive because before the intensified pursuits of the Atlantic slave trade, domestic slaves were usually criminals or debtors sold into slavery. Domestic slavery played the role of prisons in industrialized societies. The stigma remained long after many of those who became slaves were taken from the general populace and suffered their new status through no fault of their own. The oral accounts that I collected corroborated this view that the descendants of slaves do not take kindly to the mention of previous slave status in their families. Many resorted to changing their names to obscure their history. Moreover, slavery in general is recognized as one of the saddest moments in their history and a subject that people generally avoid (Bailey fieldnotes 1997).

The relative silence on the issue can also be attributed to the neglect of institutions. A contemporary review of the issue of slavery in Ghana found that "slavery as a general topic and the transatlantic Slave Trade in particular have not been treated as important themes in Ghanaian history. The study of colonialism and its impact on Ghana has been a dominant theme in Ghanaian history with one result being that the study of slavery in Ghana (both domestic and transatlantic) has been treated as a marginal topic." This point has been summarized by Van Dantzig, who wrote: "one of the most neglected subjects in the well documented history of Ghana is that of the slave trade. Very little is really known about how it was carried on" (Dillard 1992). The concentration on colonialism is perhaps as much a colonial legacy as the social and political structures that the British left behind. One result has been a certain institutional neglect which has obvious ramifications for what Ewes and other Ghanaians have learned in school.

The Incident at Atokor

It is in this context that one story – the incident at Atokor – has been retained and retold over the years. The rest of this essay is divided into four sections.

In the first section, I have attempted to relate a few important versions of this story as they were told to me, with minimum analysis and comment. Perhaps the most important of these was the version of Togbui Awusa III, Chief of Atokor, with whom I spoke on two different occasions (Bailey fieldnotes 1997). In the second section, I have placed the incident in the context of other historical accounts, including contemporary sources and travelers' records. Third, I attempt an analysis of the story in terms of the central issues under discussion: impact and agency with respect to the Atlantic slave trade. I also look at the metaphorical connotations of the story, as well as the ways in which these different versions, as memories of the past, may have been affected by events of the recent past and present. Finally, I attempt to situate this story in broader historical discussions about the utility of oral history.

Chief Awusa's Version

It was said that the chief's great grandfather, Togbui Awusa Ndorkutsu of Atokor, was the first to allow the Danes to ply their trade on the shores of Atokor. As the trade progressed, Atokor became a major way station for slaves. Its very name means "I will buy and I will go." The name comes from the Akan "meto meko" and was said to describe the experience of a royal visitor of Kumasi with mosquitoes along the coast (Yegbe 1966, p. 69). A system developed in which the chief's great grandfather, Ndorkutsu, had agents stationed near Anyako, Hatorgodo, and further inland. These agents collected slaves from the interior and brought them to Ndorkutsu's "big house" on the shore, where they awaited European and American ships. Most of these slaves, then, came from the interior; they were not from the coast. They were, however, in the main, Ewe-speaking people.

One day, a group of drummers – famous drummers from the area – were playing their drums on the shores of Atokor. The type of drum they were playing was called the *adekpetsi* drum. On this day, these drummers included in their number two of the Ndorkutsu's relatives, his grandson and his grandfather. As the drummers played, the Europeans came to collect the slaves. The captain of the ship, as he was preparing to go, invited these drummers to come aboard and play. He gave them barrels of drinks and offered the same to the crowd of people that had begun to assemble on the Atokor shore. There ensued an atmosphere of merriment and many became drunk. In the midst of this merriment, the ship set sail with the drummers on board. According to Chief Awusa, "They were tricked into going on the boats to play their drums." They, too, joined the newly captured Africans of the interior as slaves to be sold in the Americas (Bailey fieldnotes 1997).

The story goes that emotions ran so high about this incident that the neighboring towns of Atokor and Srogbe almost went to war. No one wanted to go to war, but it was a distinct possibility, since it was widely thought that this incident was prearranged. The captain of the drummers was said to have offended one of the wives of Chief Tamaklo from the neighboring town of Wuti. In response, Chief Tamaklo arranged with Ndorkutsu for the drummers to play on the Atokor shore. In any event, according to Chief Awusa, "This was the first time that people from this area were taken as slaves" (Bailey fieldnotes 1997). Slaves were always from the hinterland, not from the coast.

Other versions of the Atokor story

This story was told to me by several different sources, particularly elders in formal and informal settings. Many agreed with most of what Chief Awusa of Atokor recalled in his interviews. Others, such as Mama Dzagba, a female chief based in Anio-Ga, added a few other details to essentially a similar base. Some of these are worth mentioning here:

> [The Anlo] were stolen by white people; there was a higher ratio of men to women. The Europeans brought a sailing ship and anchored off the coast of Anlo. They started drumming, dancing, drinking and merrymaking in the ship. The people of Atokor were amazed and gathered on the beach to watch them. The Europeans then invited the people on the beach to join them in the drumming and merrymaking on the ship. The people entered their fishing boats and rowed over to the ship. [They used about four surfboats.] They then joined the whites in the ship and danced and drummed with them. At the end of the dance, the Europeans offered the people of Atokor some kind of large biscuits [believed to be German biscuits]. At the time of the incident there was a slight famine in the region. When they were given the biscuits, they were also given beef and rice and other gifts and then they left the ship and went back to their homes. They showed all the food and gifts they had received on the European ship to others at home [husbands to wives, wives to husbands.] They ate this food for about a month. The European ship then sailed away and then returned later with more gifts for the people of Atokor. They came a third time with food and gifts for the people and when the people entered the ship, they gave them a lot of alcohol to drink and lots of food to eat and whilst they were drumming and having a good time, the ship set sail and took them away. They were unaware of the time that the ship set sail. (Bailey fieldnotes 1997)

Mama Dzagba emphasizes something that was not raised in other accounts: that this was a planned effort on the part of European traders gradually to entice and solicit the trust of the Anlo people only to kidnap them at a later date. Food as well as drinks were offered, and as this was a time of famine, the people were vulnerable to this enticement.

The Paramount Chief, Togbui Adeladza, in his interview, concurred with Chief Awusa's account that there was some sort of collusion on the part of local inhabitants. He also claims that the cause of this incident was a dispute over a woman called *Enunato* – the wife of one of the senior drummers. This drummer, in seeking revenge, quickly arranged to sell the drummers, including his enemy, when the slave traders arrived. They were told that the white men wanted them to play. When they obliged, they were taken away. Some resisted by jumping into the sea, but most remained on board. In the end, the woman in question left for Ada and got married to an Ada man. They then made the decision to change their name to *Kanase* (Bailey fieldnotes 1997).

Still another perspective comes from Chief James Ocloo of Keta, whose family played a great role in the history of the Anlo coast. His version suggests that the cause of the conflict was not because of a woman but because the town of Atokor was in debt to the Europeans. "Chief Nditsi used to buy tobacco from the Europeans and send to others; he would come and leave goods for the chief to sell. Later on, he would come and collect the money. The town of Atokor became in debt to the Europeans. They saw some people drumming, so they want them to make the same drumming on the ship. . . ." (Bailey fieldnotes 1997).

Historical Confirmation of the Atokor Story

In spite of the fact that this story is pervasively told all over Eweland, it is literally a footnote in the European and American historical record. The most significant source of information comes from a Revd. Chas Thomas whose contemporary account, *Adventures and Observations on the West Coast of Africa and its Islands* (1860), provides detailed information about trade on the coast of Africa. In his narrative he records a journey which originated in America on a sloop called the *Jamestown*. The *Jamestown* was a flagship of the African Squadron, which was established by the American and British governments to suppress slave-trading activities on the high seas. The Squadron was established in 1843 as a result of the Treaty of Washington which gave the American and British navies the right to patrol the coast in their pursuit of slave ships.

The *Jamestown* sloop was commanded on this particular voyage by a Captain James Ward (African Squadron logbooks, M89). The sloop sailed from 1855–7, stopping at various ports in Africa and its islands. Revd. Thomas was chaplain of the sloop during this period. It is his chapter on the Old Slave Coast which situates and gives the closest approximate date of the Atokor incident. In a December 23, 1856 entry, Thomas says that the peoples of the old Slave Coast tell the story of

> a Yankee captain who visited this river lately. After paying the headmen, or traders, for five hundred lively darkeys, he invited them into his cabin to take a drink. He was profuse in his hospitality, made them all drunk, put them in irons, sank their canoes, pocketed their money and got under weigh. Two of the twenty-five thus taken jumped overboard shortly after, and were drowned; the remainder he sold in Cuba for four hundred dollars each. (Thomas 1860, p. 240)

This account is the closest written evidence we have for this story. We can deduce from Thomas's book that the incident must have taken place within the past year, 1856, because he says in his entry that they had crossed the Volta River twelve months before and there was no mention made of the incident. *Thus, the Atokor incident probably took place in 1856.*

Other information that we gain here is that the ship was an American ship, or at least it sailed under the American flag. This is highly possible given the immense amount of slave-trading activity carried out by Americans at this time. There exists an enormous amount of archival material on the use of the American flag in the continuation of the slave trade. The American flag was used in part because the Treaty of Washington protected the rights of Americans doing legitimate business off the coast of Africa. The English and the American vessels of the Squadron were not legally allowed arbitrarily to search American vessels, yet these vessels were principally involved in the slave trade.

It is possible, however, that the ship that kidnapped the drummers had a number of different European and American nationals on board. Ironically, the system that prevailed at the time was one in which the nations of Europe and America joined forces in much the same way that Anlo elders and chiefs refer to them in their oral history accounts. This system, called an "abuse of the American flag" by many US Navy officials, was one in which a vessel would be fitted in New York under the American flag for legitimate trade (African Squadron logbooks, M89). On board would be a Spanish crewmember. On the coast of Africa, this Spaniard would oversee the embarkment of equipment, cargo, and crew (more Spanish and Portuguese). This crew would then take charge of the vessel for the rest of the voyage (PRO: FO 313/27/34). Most of the trade in this period of the 1850s was thus being carried on as a "multinational" effort. Still, the lion's share of this effort was carried out by Americans in American-built ships. A British officer of the African Squadron stated that "at least one-half of the successful part of the Slave Trade is carried on under the American flag, since the number of the American cruisers in the station is so small in proportion to the immense extent of the slave dealing coast" (Lloyd 1968, p. 169). As such, it is highly probable that Thomas's account is accurate – that it was a Yankee captain involved in the Atokor incident.

Revd. Thomas's account also helps to confirm other parts of this story: the fact that those kidnapped included relatives of the chief ("After paying the headmen . . . he [the Captain] invited them into his cabin to take a drink etc."). This corresponds well to Chief Awusa's account and that of others where we learn that the Chief and his relatives were the chief traders or headmen. Finally, in terms of what we can establish as probable facts, we have the mention of Cuba as the destination of the drummers in Thomas's account. This also corresponds with some of the oral accounts which point to Cuba as the destination of the ship.

These are the facts of the incident according to Revd. Thomas. Ghanaian scholar Kofi Awoonor, in his own research, uncovered the story as told to him by residents along the Ewe coast:

In the little village of Vuti in Anlo-Ewe country, the story is told of how a group of drummers were persuaded to come aboard an English ship to drum for the Captain. Those on the shore saw the ship vanish over the horizon. The song "On which shores are they going to land" is still sung today. (Awoonor 1976, p. 12)

This account places the village of Vuti (Wuti), which is a neighbor to Atokor, at the center of the story. Though it does not say that the ship left from Wuti, it is possible that the reason the story is told in Wuti is that some of the drummers were residents of this town. This would be consistent with the oral accounts which indicate that the drummers hailed from a number of neighboring towns. Still, the major difference here is that the ship is said to be an English ship, not an American one. This may, however, be attributed to the fact that local people tended to use the terms "American" and "European" interchangeably. Finally, the existence of the song "On which shores are they going to land" fits with the practice of local people recording important aspects of their history in song texts and drumming styles. This song in its entirety goes as follows:

> Gokanua dze gee woyina
> Gokanu dze gee woyina
> Gokanu?
> Adose kpl' Afedima woe yina daa
> Adose kpl' Afedima woe yina daa
> Gokanu dze gee woyina

On which shores are we going to land; On which shores are we going to land; On which shore? There go Adose and Afedima far away; There go Adose and Afedima far away. (Bailey fieldnotes 1997)

These two accounts are among the only sources of written literature on the incident at Atokor. Though sketchy and incomplete, they confirm four basic facts about this incident: (1) it took place in or around 1856; (2) kidnapping of local residents did occur and those kidnapped included the chief's relatives or headmen; (3) the ship in question had a multinational crew that included English and/or American crewmembers; (4) Cuba was the likely destination of the ship. It is around these central facts that most of the following analysis hinges.

Significance of the Incident at Atokor

Notwithstanding a general comfort level with certain facts, issues of memory must be addressed. We have two major markers of the story – a contemporary account by Thomas writing in 1857 and today's accounts by elders and chiefs in Ewe villages along the coast. As already discussed, an extensive review of archives in Africa, America, and Europe did not reveal any other record of this story in the interim years. What is noteworthy, however, is that since that original record till now, there has been little change in these basic facts. The four pieces of the story that can be confirmed (the date, the ship, composition of those who were taken away, and the destination) have not been altered. Furthermore, the work of Kofi Awoonor in collecting versions of this account in the 1970s shows that in the seventeen years since I collected versions of the same account, there has been little change. The other elements of the story, however – the cause of the conflict, the exact names of people involved etc. – may have been altered over the years.

The many important events that have taken place between 1856 and the present in the history of Ghana and in Africa in general may indeed have had an effect on the telling of this story. These include the onset of the colonial era, Ghana's independence under Nkrumah in 1957, and the coming to power of Jerry Rawlings in 1981. Though we do not have concrete evidence of the changes in the story that may have occurred during these periods, we are able to speculate on how these periods affected present-day versions of the story. For example, one of the results of colonial rule was an intensified effort on the part of the Ewe people to be unified. The Ewe Unification Movement was a response to historical events of the latter part of the nineteenth century and the early years of the twentieth. By 1890 the British, after many years of resistance from the Ewes, were finally able to extend their rule over Ewe territory in what was then the Gold Coast. Around the same time the Germans also became important players on the coast and competed with the British for control of the land. This resulted in an agreement to split Ewe territory: the Gold Coast (Ghana) territory going to Britain and the Togo territory going to Germany. At the end of World War I Germany's territory was ceded to France, much to the consternation of local Ewe chiefs. Advocates of the Ewe Unification Movement since the 1920s till well after World War II concentrated their efforts on the unification of Ewe territory in both countries (Amenumey 1972, pp. 8–11; 1989).

We know from work done in this area by Sandra Greene that Ewe traditions of origin were slightly altered during this period to emphasize the unity of the Anlo with other Ewe-speaking peoples. With the exception of the Blu clan, all Anlo clans then claimed they participated in the great exodus of the Ewe from Notsie in the late seventeenth century. Furthermore, *The Ewe Newsletter*, launched by Daniel Chapman in 1947, was used to assist in forging an Ewe consciousness (Greene 1996, pp. 144–51). Notwithstanding these efforts, to this day the ultimate goal of unification has not been achieved.

In light of this colonial record it is possible, then, that certain elements of this story were adapted to the spirit of the age. From the standpoint of colonialism it would be important for Anlos to see themselves as unified in opposition to foreign forces; it would be important to emphasize the elements of the story that suggest that the Anlos were *tricked* by European traders. It would be important to point to the negative impact of dissension and division within the community.

In a similar way, the period of independence – before, during, and after – which is almost synonymous with Kwame Nkrumah, can be seen to have influenced this story as well. From his days in London prior to his return to the Gold Coast in 1947, Nkrumah considered himself an agitator for the freedom of black people not only on the African continent but all over the world. His eventual victory for Ghana in 1957 he saw as a victory for all those under the colonial yoke in Africa, the West Indies, and beyond (James 1977; Agyeman 1992). His Pan-African ideology had a profound effect on the population of Ghana, including residents on the Anlo coast. The desire for internal unity then, as well as the building of bridges with other Africans, African Americans, West Indians, and others, may very well have led elders and others to emphasize certain parts of the story.

Finally, Rawlings' assumption of power since 1981 may be said to have influenced adaptations of the story. First, Rawlings, on his maternal side, hails from this part of Ghana, although he himself was born in Accra in 1947. Secondly, in the last few years in particular, he has attempted to forge international ties with West Indians and others in the African diaspora (Shillington 1992, pp. 32–3). Domestically, he has encouraged the growth of heritage tourism and the preservation of historic sites such as Ghana's many slave forts and castles. In 1997, for example, he received Minister Louis Farrakhan on his visit to Ghana and also made a high-profile visit to Jamaica.

The fact of the matter is, however, that the four basic facts of the story that can be confirmed have not changed since 1857. Furthermore, what is striking about present-day accounts is a presence of balance. Even Mama Dzagba's account, which directly accuses Europeans of trickery in the slave trade and is perhaps the least balanced of the interviews, includes information on the role of African traders. At one point she explains that the Anlos did regular business in Dzogbe in the interior and other places exchanging slaves for salt.

> However, it is true that our ancestors went to Dzogbe (northern parts) to buy slaves. They used salt as a means of exchange and this sort of trade was not common. There was no salt water to make salt, so salt was of major importance. They introduced salt to the northerners who ate without salt before then. After they tasted the salt, they asked Anlos to bring them some more on the next trip. They were obliged to exchange the salt for something else, so the Dzogbe people offered slaves in exchange. One cup of salt was equivalent to one slave. So the more salt you carried the more people you bought. For example, if you could carry twenty cups of salt there, you could return with twenty slaves whom you sold expensively to others (the rich) along the coast. (Bailey fieldnotes 1997)

Chief Ndorkutsu, likewise, before describing the kidnapping incident, gives a detailed account of the fact that his ancestor had an established system of agents in the interior whose job it was to collect slaves. Both sides of the story are presented. There are thus few apologies given for African involvement in the supply side of the slave trade in these accounts. Furthermore, the presence of such balance suggests that if informants happened to hold strong Pan-African views and were particularly sensitive to African American sensibilities, such views appeared not to have played an important role in our discussions.

The Atokor incident as metaphor

Finally and most importantly, the Atokor incident, after issues of historical corroboration and memory have been assessed, is best read as a metaphor for issues of agency and impact of the Atlantic slave trade. First, it is a general metaphor for transformations that took place during the slave trade era. The story represents the different phases of the trade, in particular the change in European/American and African agency from a period of organized trading to disorganized and random activity. In this way, it is a cultural marker or watershed between periods of order and disorder.

In terms of European and American agency, it is additional evidence of piracy along the African coastline. It shows that as late as the 1850s European and American ships were still engaged in trade, or in this case kidnapping, along the coast fifty years after the official abolition of the trade in 1807. It questions the nature and extent of the abolition if some fifty-plus years after it was legally abolished, the slave trade enjoyed perhaps its greatest revival since its inception.

Numerous sources concur that the African Squadron commissioned by the Treaty of Washington in 1842 was ineffective in suppressing the trade. This incident is additional evidence of this fact. The ineffectiveness of the Squadron can be attributed to many factors. First, there was not a significant amount of ships deployed for the effort. This suggested an uneven commitment on the part of the British and American governments. For example, it was said that between 1,500 and 2,000 vessels disembarked at Havana annually in those years, yet in 1853 there were only 19 ships in the African Squadron; 15 in 1854 and 14 in 1856. These few ships were expected to police over 2,000 miles of coast. This was a feat that various Commadores later testified was impossible (Lloyd 1968, pp. 121, 167).

Secondly, the continued debate regarding the method of policing the shores was also an impediment to the Squadron's success. In general, there were two schools of thought: in-shore versus off-shore cruising. Off-shore cruising, for reasons that are unclear, became the *modus operandi*, much to the consternation of some of the Squadron Commodores. Lastly, US administrations stood in the way of the more aggressive searches of various ships along the coast and in the West Indies. The question of the Right to Search and the specific limitations of this right prevented Squadron Commodores from doing an adequate job.

As seen in a letter to Commodore Crabbe of the African Squadron from the Secretary of the US Navy, there was more of a concern in protecting the individual rights of Americans engaged in "legitimate" commerce than in the pursuit of human rights in Africa. "The rights of our citizens engaged in lawful commerce are under the protection of our flag and it is the chief purpose. . . . the chief duty of our Naval power, to see that these rights are not improperly abridged or invaded" (African Squadron logbooks, M89). As such, Crabbe is advised to use his "judgment and discretion" regarding ship searches. This view coming from the highest ranks of the Navy and, one may imagine, the President, suggests that their commitment was first to American traders, second to the abolition of the trade.

Finally, it is clear from these records that there were no real "teeth" to the law. No real attempt was made fully to enforce the laws of 1807 and 1820, which declared that any breach of the law would be punishable by death. In fact, there exists on record only a few cases in which the captains of slavers were captured and actually punished beyond the loss of their ship and cargo (Lloyd 1968, p. 168). The lack of true enforcement certainly did little to prevent and discourage individual traders from engaging in what at this time was one of the most lucrative business ventures in the world.

It is possible that traders themselves understood the limitations of this commitment to abolition, for there was not only insufficient policing of the African coast, but also insufficient enforcement. Officials stationed at Cuba asserted that the problem was that slave-trade treaties stopped short of declaring participation in the slave trade as piracy subject to Martial law:

> General Serrano has several times expressed to me his opinion that, an advisable means of putting down the Slave Trade is that of declaring it piracy and treating the masters, crews and all concerned as pirates, subject to Martial law. He has several times repeated to me his determination to propose and recommend the adoption of that measure to his government [i.e. Spain]. (PRO: FO 313/29/172)

Furthermore, if, as it is estimated, approximately 300,000 slaves were imported into America between 1806 and 1860, how were these slavers allowed to disembark their cargo in American ports if the trade was indeed illegal? How were the ports of New Orleans, Florida, and the Mississippi Delta policed? (Dubois 1969, pp. 110–12; Lloyd 1968, p. 168). What messages were being sent about the reality of the trade? Was it really illegal if few were prevented from pursuing it and those captured were not punished to the full extent of the law?

This incident is further significant because it suggests that during this period in the nineteenth century the trade was not always a trade – an exchange of goods and resources. It sometimes involved theft, trickery, and kidnapping. Brodie Cruickshank, a member of the Legislative Council at Cape Coast Castle during this period, recorded similar impressions of the Gold Coast in *Eighteen Years on the Gold Coast of Africa*:

> We see the white man, at one time, having recourse to the grossest dissimulation, enticing the unsuspecting African within his power and breaking his pledged

faith without compunction; at another, we behold him leagued with a friendly tribe, carrying fire and sword into defenceless hamlets and bearing off to his boats the shrieking natives.

Further along in his narrative Cruickshank talks about the sense of arbitrariness and constant state of fear and chaos that developed as the trade continued:

> During the continuance of the slave trade, which added tenfold to the general lawlessness of men, opportunities of disposing of such stray waifs as the solitary traveler, the hunter who had wandered too far from his home, the labourer in his plantation, and the water carrier returning form the distant pond, were so frequent and attended with so little chance of detection (where fear, for the most part, detained every one within the limits of a small circle of friendly intercourse), that it was certain slavery to venture beyond the short precincts without suffi- cient numbers to maintain their freedom. (Cruickshank 1966)

This incident and other sources strongly suggest that the trade did not always involve mutual exchange between more or less equal parties. This stands in contrast to one school of thought on the slave trade that posits that the slave trade was carried out by two mutual parties – European/American and African – both of whom were on fairly equal ground. In fact Africans, according to this view, had the upper hand because they developed a sophis- ticated system of slave supply upon which the white trader was dependent. Furthermore, large states such as Asante and Oyo imposed various turnpike fees and levied tribute obligations from coastal communities. Finally, it is said that through these and other methods Africans consistently restricted the movement of Europeans to the coastal shores. This view suggests a systemati- zation of the trade promulgated by Africans which purposely curtailed the activities of European and American traders (Thornton 1992, pp. 1–7). The significance of the Atokor incident is that it stands as one piece of compelling evidence that shows that at a critical moment in the development of the trade in the nineteenth century (a moment of intense and competitive revival), the trade came to involve a certain amount of arbitrariness and unsystematic actions on the part of European and African traders. In fact, the Ewe example shows that though there was indeed a period of almost a century (1730–1800) in which Chief Awusa and other individual traders enjoyed an organized system of trade with European traders, such an established code of operations was not representative of the entire slave trade era. The Atokor incident was a watershed incident that represented a break with the past in terms of oper- ations along the coast. In other words, this story makes a good case for close examination of the transformations of the slave trade in Ghana and in West Africa in general.

On this question of agency, there also has to be consideration of the broader context of the Atlantic slave trade. It is difficult to suggest that Africans played an equal role in slave-trade operations when they did not exert any control over trading operations on other continents. The trade involved, after all, several legs on different continents. These included the plantation system and its consistent demand for slave labor, investors and insurance companies whose interests were tied to the trade, the Middle Passage journey, the sale of slaves in the New World, and the manufacturing of slave by-products in Europe and America. In conjunction with the importance of periodization, this is the context in which the issue of agency must be assessed.

Questions of impact and the Atokor incident as cautionary tale

Another reality which we learn from this incident is that Anlo indigenous institutions were profoundly affected by the Atlantic slave trade. This is particularly evident in the discussion of the causes of the incident. Though the cause of the conflict is difficult to discern given present information, two causes stated by informants shed some light on the issue. One version suggests that the trade became a corrupting force in the society. Paramount Chief Togbui Adeladza, in his account, says that eventually the chiefs and other inhabitants began to use the slave trade as a means of disposing of people with whom they had a quarrel (Bailey fieldnotes 1997). In this case, there was a dispute between two residents of the area which was resolved in the "kidnapping" of the drummers. Instead of resorting to traditional legal means of redress, they turned to the slave trade. The Anlo custom of *Nyiko* which included a trial whose verdict had to be approved by the chiefs and the elders was summarily bypassed.

Another source says that the town of Atokor was in debt to white traders and thus arranged to pay this debt by the covert kidnapping of the drummers. If this indeed was the case and if such cases were widespread, then it augurs the future role of debt *vis-à-vis* the African continent and major industrialized nations. It prefigures what has now become a standard relationship with Europe and America: burgeoning debts paid for by the raw material and resources of the land. This notion of a town being in debt to traders, then, could possibly have started this disturbing spiral trend. Furthermore, if indeed the move towards becoming a debt-carrying nation began in the era of the slave trade, then it is possible to say that this is one extremely devastating effect of the Atlantic slave trade. These issues are suggestive of areas in which more research could be done in an attempt to answer the following: Did entire African towns become indebted to traders? Were towns encouraged to become indebted? Did they ever repay these debts or did such debts have the effect of prolonging slave-trade activities? Did the current process of globalization that includes the carrying of enormous debt for many developing nations begin with the operations of the Atlantic slave trade?

At the same time, this is at once a colorful story told by many people in a dramatic way. Though it is not an invented tradition given that basic facts of the story can be confirmed, certain elements of the story have been invented. These elements are reminiscent of the great tradition of West African folklore as cautionary tales. Among its most colorful aspects which are perhaps also fictionalized are the mention of crowds of people drinking and making merry on the shore as the drummers were taken away. Though this was described in almost every account, it is possible that both the mention of drummers and merrymaking were added by storytellers in part to add a sense of drama and suspense to the story. It often occasioned a laugh from informants at the thought of the local people drinking and making merry without any idea that respected members of the community were being kidnapped. The drinking and merrymaking seem to be the community's poetic way of saying that they were oblivious to what was happening in their midst. *It is a way to dramatize the fact that they did not expect such a thing to happen given the relationships that had been previously established with white traders.* After all, Ndorkutsu's "big house" where the slaves were housed as they waited for the arrival of European ships stood in the community as a constant reminder of the strength of this relationship.

The Atokor story shows that by the mid-nineteenth century almost anyone was vulnerable. Given the increasingly arbitrary nature of the trade, if some were not free, all were not free. This may be one reason that the story is remembered to this day: the fact that before this incident the coastal people felt a certain immunity from the vagaries of the trade. Perhaps members of the community felt confident that there was an established "system" of slave supply. "Other" Africans from the interior were taken and shipped abroad, not those along the coast and certainly not the most respected in their community – the drummers and the relatives of the chief. Certainly they would never be sold or kidnapped. Or so they thought. Hence their shock and disbelief when they discovered the contrary.

This part of the story may well be an acknowledgment to contemporary listeners that the people of that time did not understand the full ramifications of their involvement in the activities of the slave trade. They did not have control of the different legs of the slave trade, many of which were operational on other continents. They may have felt they exercised a certain control on the continent, but did not have any concrete influence over the flow of capital in Europe and America that drove the slave traffic, the demands of the plantation economy, and the interests of a growing industrial global complex. They were part of a much larger picture over which they exerted little influence. In this way this story, like many tales in the West African tradition, is almost an admonition to those who listen of the dangers of participation without full and extensive knowledge of the context and the ramifications of one's involvement.

The reference to drummers has additional significance because the drummers were traditionally the mouthpieces of the chiefs. By being taken out of the community, the drummers were in effect silenced. A silence that at least on the issue of slavery remains with the community today. Furthermore, there seems to be a subtle suggestion here that as their leaders were misled ("taken away"), so were the people. They, too, did not understand that their active involvement in the trade would eventually have a profound and negative impact on the land and its people. Here again, this says something not only about the reality of the Atlantic slave trade in the nineteenth century, but also seems to caution contemporary listeners about the present and the future. It is perhaps a subtle call for leaders and others to understand the essential interrelatedness of all sectors of society. Those who may profit in the short term at the expense of others less fortunate are encouraged to understand that short-sighted actions today affect all tomorrow. Leaders without a vision, in effect, jeopardize not only the lives of the people but their own lives as well.

This lack of vision, however, was not only attributed to the leaders, as is evidenced by another likely fictional element dramatically portrayed in the account of female chief Mama Dzagba. She goes to great lengths to dramatize the copious amounts of food and drink that were received from the traders over the course of three visits to the Atokor shore. According to her account, it was a time of famine. The people were, as a result, so content with these gifts that "they showed all the food and gifts that they had received on the European ship to others at home [husbands to wives, wives to husbands]. They ate this food for about a month" (Bailey fieldnotes 1997). Such references suggest that the people were tricked as much by their bellies as by the European traders. They drank, they ate, they were content, perhaps too content. They were metaphorically asleep and so were not alert to the impending danger of the final visit of the ship to their shores. They were drunk, not sober, while the drummers who represented the wealth of their community were being taken away. Though these were a people whose indigenous religions encouraged a long-term view of life and death, they were now living in the moment. They were concerned only with meeting their most immediate needs without the realization of what that would mean. Finally, we may also note here that they were enticed by what was new and what was foreign. Mama Dzagba refers to the biscuits received by the people as German biscuits. The fact that they were so happy with these new gifts may suggest that a disproportionate appreciation for what was foreign (versus what was homegrown) only served further to blur the vision of those who failed to grasp the full and devastating reality of their participation.

Oral History as a Method and as a Medium

Finally, these issues point to the multi-faceted nature and use of oral history material. They show that oral history material is not only useful as a historical source but can also be viewed as an *independent mode of historical representation*. Here I would like to suggest, as a precursor to future research on the subject, that African oral history (and perhaps oral history material of the Black Atlantic) represents the merging of Western models of history and literature. It may be that the many metaphors, symbols, and references to the supernatural contained in oral narratives need not be relegated to the genres of myth, fiction, and religion. The metaphorical elements of the story of the incident at Atokor, including the merrymaking, the drinking, and the drumming which symbolized the community's lack of vision regarding the true ramifications of their involvement in the slave trade, may help make a case for consideration of material in this light. Such fictional elements and the interpretations that may be made of them buttress the facts of the incident that can be historically confirmed – the most important being that in 1856, almost fifty years after the abolition of the slave trade, trade was intensely revived but not in a systematic way. Disorder not order, chaos not organization, characterized this last phase of the era.

At the same time, the fictional elements in these stories appear to contain lessons from the historical experience. They seem to leave gaps in the story that the listener is expected to fill. The invented traditions and the performative aspects of the story beg listeners to listen closely, not just to the established facts, but to the lessons of the past that can be helpful to present and future generations.

In this way oral histories are reminiscent of at least one biblical scholar's view of the Bible. Robert Alter in *The Art of Biblical Narrative* is of the view that though there is much history in the narratives of the Old Testament, "none of these involves a sense of being bound to documentable facts that characterizes history in its modem acceptation" (Alter 1981, p. 24). The Old Testament, he contends, is a kind of "historicized prose fiction" or "fictionalized history," in that while it records events and people to be found in the historical record, writers employed a certain poetic license in the creation of dialogue and the ascription of motives (ibid, pp. 25–36). At the same time, these twin elements in no way take away from the divine mission of these biblical writers or the sacred messages that were meant to be historical information, but suggest the use of some creative license. In some cases they border on myth. These myths, however, appear not to be myths in the sense of pure fiction, but more in the style of the early Greeks. Before Herodotus introduced the notion of chronology in his history of the Greeks in the fifth century BC, the early Greeks were much more accepting of myth as a way to understand their past and to provide continuity to the present. M. I. Finley, in his article "Myth, Memory and History," goes as far as to say that "the atmosphere in which the Fathers of History set out to work was saturated with myth. Without myth, indeed, they could never have begun their work" (Finley 1964, pp. 281–3). The timeless quality, the absence of coherent dating, the patchwork of concrete facts, as well as the creative element of oral histories, are all reminiscent of this ancient tradition.

Finally, this discussion also has implications for narratives of the Black Atlantic. Useful comparative work could also be done, for example, with respect to classic slave narratives. As pointed out by Henry Louis Gates, slave narratives also bridge categories of history and literature, as they contain metaphor and irony, as well as messages for readers and listeners. These narratives, too, prior to Emancipation, broke the silence of slave attitudes towards their own enslavement (Gates 1987, pp. x, xi, xv). Ewe oral traditions, in this case the story of the Atokor incident (ironically roughly contemporaneous with many of the great slave narratives), break the silence on the issue of slavery on the African continent. At the same time, they represent a break with the past: a shift from established relations with European and American traders in the eighteenth century to a post-abolition period of disorder which was not without its devastating effects on Anlo society and culture.

Note

I owe a great debt to many scholars and others who have assisted me in the development of this work. Though it is not possible to mention them all here, I would like to acknowledge the following: Dr. Mary Frances Berry, Dr. Lee Cassanelli, Dr. Sandra Greene, Dr. John W. Chambers III, Dr. Deborah Gray White, Dr. Mia Bay and the other scholars of the Black Atlantic project of the Rutgers Center for Historical Analysis, Dr. Ato Quayson, Dr. Michael West, Dr. Belinda Edmondson, Dr. G. K. Nukunya, Dr. D. E. K. Amenumey and all my informants in Southeastern Ghana.

References

Archival sources

Public Records Office, Kew Gardens CO 96. Dispatches from the Gold Coast Havana Mixed Court Commission FO 313/ 24–9, 1851–64.

National Archives, Washington DC. Letters received by the Secretary of the Navy from commanding officers of Squadrons, African Squadron, 1843–61, Rolls 105–9, M89, 1851–9. Reverend Charles Thomas's private papers.

Agyeman, Opoku. *Nkrumah's Ghana and East Africa: Pan-Africanism and African Interstate Relations.* London and Toronto: Associated University Presses, 1992.

Alter, Robert. *The Art of Biblical Narrative.* New York: Basic Books, 1981.

Amenumey, D. E. K. *The Ewe in Pre-Colonial Times: A Political History with Special Emphasis on the Anlo, Ge and Krepi,* 1986.

——"Geraldo de Lima: A Reappraisal," *Transactions of the Historical Society of Ghana,* vol. 19.

——*The Ewe Unification Movement.*

——"A Political History of the Ewe Unification Problem." Ph.D. dissertation, University of Manchester, 1972.

——The Ewe People and the Coming of European Rule, 1850–1914. MA thesis, London, 1964.

Awoonor, Kofi. *The Breast of the Earth: A Survey of the History, Culture and Literature of Africa South of the Sahara.* Garden City, NJ: Anchor Press/Doubleday, 1976.

Bailey, Anne. "The Impact of the Atlantic Slave Trade on the Anlo Ewe of Southeastern Ghana." Ph.D. thesis, University of Pennsylvania, 1997.

Chernoff, John. *African Rhythm and Sensibility.* Chicago: University of Chicago Press, 1979.

Cruikshank, Brodie. *Eighteen Years on the Gold Coast of Africa, Vol. 1.* London: Frank Cass., 1966.

Curtin, P. D. *The Atlantic Slave Trade: A Census.* Madison: University of Wisconsin Press, 1969.

Dillard, Mary. "The Legacy of the Transatlantic Slave Trade in Contemporary Ghana." Paper presented at the Institute of African Studies, Legon, Ghana, 1992.

DuBois, W. E. B. *The Suppression of the African Slave Trade 1638–1870.* Baton Rouge: Louisiana State University Press, 1969.

Fiagbedzi, Nissio. *"The Music of the Anlo: Its Historical Background, Cultural Matrix and Style."* Ph.D. dissertation, University of California, Los Angeles, 1977.

Finley, M. I. "Myth, Memory and History." *History and Theory,* no. 4, 1964: 281–3.

Gaba, Christian Robert. *"Anlo Traditional Religion: A Study of the Anlo Traditional Believer's Conception of and Communion with the 'Holy.'"* Ph.D. thesis, University of London, 1965.

Gates. Henry Louis, Jr., ed. *Classic Slave Narratives.* New York: Penguin, 1987.

Greene, Sandra. *Gender, Ethnicity and Social Change on the Upper Slave Coast: A History of the Anlo Ewe.* Portsmouth, NH: Heinemann, 1996.

Hobsbawm, Eric and Terence Ranger, eds. *The Invention of Tradition.* Cambridge: Cambridge University Press, 1983.

Inikori, Joseph. *Forced Migration: The Impact of the Export Slave Trade on African Societies.* London: Hutchinson University Library, 1982.

James, C. L. R. *Nkrumah and the Ghana Revolution.* London: Allison and Busby, 1977.

Law, Robin. *The Slave Coast of West Africa 1550–1750: The Impact of the Atlantic Slave Trade on an African Society.* Oxford: Clarendon Press, 1991.

Lloyd, Christopher. *The Navy and the Slave Trade: The Suppression of the African Slave Trade in the Nineteenth Century.* London: Cass., 1968.

Lovejoy, Paul. *Transformations in Slavery: A History of Slavery in Africa.* Cambridge: Cambridge University Press, 1983.

Manning, Patrick. *Slavery and African Life: Occidental, Oriental and African Slave Trades.* Cambridge: Cambridge University Press, 1990.

Miller, Joseph, ed. *Way of Death: Merchant Capitalism and the Angolan Slave Trade.* Wisconsin: Currey, 1988.

Quayson, Ato. *Strategic Transformations in Nigerian Writing: Oral History in the Work of Samuel Johnson, Wole Soyinke and Ben Okri.* Oxford: James Currey, 1997.

Rodney, Walter. *A History of the Upper Guinea Coast 1545–1800.* Oxford: Oxford University Press, 1970.

——*How Europe Underdeveloped Africa.* London, 1972.

Shillington, Kevin. *Ghana and the Rawlings Factor.* New York: St. Martin's Press, 1992.

Thomas, Chas, Revd. *Adventures and Observations on the West Coast of Africa and its Islands.* New York: Negroes University Press, 1969. Originally published in 1860.

Thornton, John. *Africa and Africans in the Making of the Atlantic World 1400–1680.* Cambridge: Cambridge University Press. 1992.

Vansina, Jan. *Oral Tradition as History.* London: James Currey, 1985.

Yegbe, Joseph. *"The Anlo and their Neighbors, 1850–90."* Thesis, University of Ghana, 1966.

Chapter 8

Forgotten Like a Bad Dream: Atlantic Slavery and the Ethics of Postcolonial Memory

Barnor Hesse

They forgot her like a bad dream. After they made up their tales, shaped and decorated them, those that saw her that day on the porch quickly and deliberately forgot her. It took longer for those who had spoken to her, lived with her, fallen in love with her, to forget until they realized they couldn't remember or repeat a single thing she said, and began to believe that, other than what they themselves were thinking, she hadn't said anything at all. So, in the end, they forgot her too. Remembering seemed unwise.

Toni Morrison[1]

Introduction

Remembering occurs most profoundly where it is intensely contested and inescapably traumatic, and where a compelling desire to forget confronts the impossibility of doing so. I have been reflecting on Stephen Spielberg's 1997 film *Amistad*. This, if you recall, portrays the historical events surrounding an 1839 slave rebellion aboard the ship of the same name. Whatever the merits or defects of the film, it manages to provoke a simply expressed but profoundly thoughtful question. How should "we" (in any sense of that collective pronoun) remember the plantation enslavement of Africans by Europeans in the Americas, during the sixteenth to nineteenth centuries? As we shall see it is also a difficult ethical question since it can entail "working through" and the "work of mourning" memories in the "fight for the acceptability of memories"

(Ricouer 1999, p. 7) which are deeply disturbing of Western culture. All this may even seem a daunting if not distracting prospect at the beginning of the twenty-first century. Yet we cannot doubt that racism endures in the political detritus of that modernizing period of Euro-America's racial commodification of African humanity, continuing to disturb, if not disrupt, ritual commemorations of Western democratic achievements. Any sense of value in remembering racial slavery since the dislocation of its institutional forms has been largely ejected from representative Western cultures of remembrance. Its history has been rendered less than peripheral to the postcolonial meaning of our contemporary political lives. In this essay I argue that it is precisely because the social development of Atlantic slavery was distinctly constitutive of "European modernity" (Habermas 1987) that it still seems prudent to ask, is *racial* slavery best forgotten or best remembered?

It should be noted of course that whatever our answer we are left with the profound difficulty of comprehending the continuing modern relation of American and European racism to Western liberal democracies. Understanding this is not something that can be done without careful negotiation through the contested relations between the politics and ethics of history and memory in relation to plantation slavery. So, why choose to begin this discussion with the film *Amistad*? Although slavery generally has been an intermittent topic for movies since the early days of cinema (Davis 2000), it is rare for mainstream Hollywood to depict *Atlantic* slavery as a historical and political process. It is rarer still for historically documented black anti-slavery rebellions to cast their shadow on the silver screen. Spielberg's *Amistad* somehow despite itself achieves both these rarities. This is all the more remarkable if we accept that the "nightmare of slavery" is usually avoided within the white cultural climate of Hollywood (Guerrero 1993). Indeed, where cinematic treatments do occur they are often "presented from a dominant, usually evasive, sentimentalized, or nostalgic perspective" (ibid, p. 42). Such a form of *cinematic repression* is no less extensive than *cinematic displacement* where slavery and the resistance to it are usually air-brushed out, becoming "sedimented into a range of contemporary film narratives and genres" (ibid, p. 43). Although, as I argue below, both these representational strategies are at work in *Amistad*, it still represents one of the most significant Hollywood interventions in remembering the historical contours of Atlantic slavery, if only due to the scarcity of such interventions. Yet, it scarcely remembers *racial* slavery at all.[2]

The *Amistad* Affair as Narrative

In trying to think about the historical significance of "one of the most remarkable of all slave rebellions in the [nineteenth] century" (Thomas 1997, p. 718) as a narration on the meaning of *racial* slavery, we are clearly asking *how* is it to be remembered? Or to put matters slightly differently, what ought to be the primary context of its memory? The difficulties arising from confronting a distinction between what *is* remembered and what *ought* to be remembered will be considered much later. At this point the distinction is instructive, since in any historical narrative accounting for the facts of history cannot be easily separated from the factors underlining the form that the historical account takes. This is what makes summarizing hazardous. It also raises the problem of the "ethics of memory" because it is "precisely through narratives that a certain education of memory has to start" (Ricouer 1999, pp. 8–9). This should be borne in mind as we consider some of the agreed forensic details that characterized the "*Amistad* affair" (cf. Cable 1977; Jones 1988; Sale 1997).

In 1839 a cargo of enslaved Africans was being transported along the north coast of Cuba in a ship called the *Amistad*. On board were 53 enslaved Africans, mostly Mendes, plus the captain, crew, and the owners, Pedro Mantes and Jose Ruiz. The ship was owned by a Spanish syndicate, which was sending the slaves to be "refreshed" prior to being sold on an island, somewhere near the coast of Honduras. It is unclear what sparked the rebellion, although there is some suggestion that the slaves anticipated they would be killed at the end of the voyage. Once the revolt, led by Joseph Cinqué, was underway, the captain and crew were killed and thrown overboard, while the Spanish/Cuban slave owners were ordered by the liberated Africans to sail the ship in the direction of Africa. However, the slave owners sailed the ship off course during the night and eventually with food and water supplies running low, the ship was forced to anchor off Long Island, New York. At this stage the vessel was seized by the US authorities, initially on charges of smuggling, and the enslaved Africans were imprisoned at New Haven. The Spanish government argued that the ship and the slaves be returned to Spain. Only after a number of US abolitionists became aware of the case did it develop into a *cause célèbre* and a lawsuit soon followed. The legal question was whether the enslavement of the Africans had been lawful. The abolitionists were able to enlist John Quincy Adams, an ex-president and leading (albeit cautious) abolitionist in the House of Representatives, to conduct the case before the US Supreme Court. Adams successfully argued that the Africans had not been enslaved lawfully. He also argued that the Africans under the law of nature had the right to rebel and organize their return to Africa. Once the verdict in favor of the illegally enslaved Africans had been entered, in 1841 they were released and allowed to travel to Sierra Leone in West Africa. The whole affair had taken three years to process.

How should we react to the *Amistad* affair, this side of the abolitionist movement? In the post-slavery era, what is the significance of the *Amistad* rebellion or indeed of the US Supreme Court's decision? Clearly, the events surrounding the *Amistad* have a certain historical or political cachet. Yet it is not entirely evident what historically makes this event so remarkable *today*. Nearly two centuries after the event, how ought it to be remembered? For example, we could reasonably construe it as a profound development in the history of anti-slavery abolitionism, if only because it has already been remembered in this way. Equally, it could be represented as a curious, but ultimately insignificant episode in the history of the Atlantic slave trade. Perhaps we ought to recall contextually that the *Amistad* decision did nothing to remove the idea that legal slaves were property, and that they had no rights under American law. Alternatively, it may be more important to acknowledge its place in the history of black anti-slavery resistances. The diversity of questions like these suggests that in any narrative tradition it is always possible to remember otherwise, although this can be studiously avoided.[3] As there is no alternative to remembering something, we are always implicated in considering what this something is, could be, or should be. This locates us within the terms, dilemmas, and possibilities of endeavor in the ethics of memory: the *oughtness* of remembering and the justness of its "drawing out the exemplary significance of past events" (Ricouer 1999, p. 9). Before proceeding to that, however, I want to consider what it has meant historically and symbolically for the *memory* of slavery to take the form of a narration.

Slave/Master Narratives

Between the eighteenth and nineteenth centuries, Western representations of plantation life in the Americas were inscribed in either pro-slavery or abolitionist discourses. Often the visual motifs and images of the former were used and subverted by the latter in an attempt to cultivate the sympathies of a popular literary culture (Wood 2000). This was a perversely "peculiar institution" in which both the master and the slave left records, the masters their memoirs and the slaves their "narratives." In effect, the struggle over the memory of slavery was being fought at the same time as its unrelenting privations on the plantations were being incurred by the slaves and its ostentatious profits indulged by the masters. The narrative indictment of slavery in the Americas, however, could only be undertaken by ex-slaves who had escaped to territories where the plantation had no stranglehold (cf. Gates 1987). Within the terms of abolitionism, the populist critique of slavery depended on the production and circulation of slave narratives consumed by a white constituency of readers. Slave narratives were packaged and sold to a mesmerized white audience as voyeuristic windows on bleak but distant, abject and horrific experiences. Although every slave narrative was personalized, their various expositions converged around the literary conventions that an expectant white audience both valorized and recognized. Consequently, the slave narrative was usually a co-production involving the escaped ex-slave *as author only*, with white abolitionists managing the whole enterprise from inception to dissemination. This included directing the framing of the genre, editing the emotional and political fabric of the material, producing the publication, and finally arranging for forewords to be written, which confirmed the eponymous slave in question really had written the narrative "himself" or "herself."

Like a film advertised as based on a true story, the slave narrative established its authenticity through the *memorable* staging of culture shock. This was
calculated to arise contemplatively in the testimonies, biographies, adventures,
and reflections from the exemplary enslaved lives of its narrators (Davis and
Gates 1985). Despite the important moral worthiness of the enterprise, the
mass production of conventionalized slave narratives tended to repress rather
than incarnate the "critical memory" (Baker 1995)[4] of slavery in order not to
alienate a sympathetic white audience (Morrison 1990). So how was slavery
actually being remembered? James Onley (1985) suggests that structurally
slave narratives were barred from anything but a "neutral memory." Although
slave narratives had the appearance of autobiography, they were denuded
of its structure because they were precluded from making use of symbolic
memory, where imagination and interpretation allow for a disquisition on the
products of memory. Slave narratives were designed, in spite of authorship, to
supply an exciting and racy story, a series of recognizable, emotionally challenging episodes. The producers and distributors of slave narratives were in
the business of moral suasion, not a political meditation on the meaning of
racial slavery in Western culture. Because the slave narrative was expected to
give an authentic account rather than a critical representation, *slavery as it really
was*, the discourse could not be seen to be emplotted. Neutral memory required
that it had to appear as a form of literary spontaneity, as if remembered in the
act of writing down or as told in one sitting to a stenographer. Strange as it
may seem, the slave narrative in the apparent extemporaneity of its remembering slavery, was more often than not a "non-memorial description fitted to
a pre-formed mold" (Onley 1987, p. 151). What might have been described as
the transatlantic odyssey of slavery and relayed in terms befitting the exposition of an Homerian epic, was all too often essayed and scripted into the format
of a political pot-boiler. A veritable *slave noir* was the "master plan for slave
narratives" (ibid, p. 153).

As a commemorative endeavor[5] the slave narrative was not free of its own
antinomies. The ex-slave in being vaunted for her/his redeemable humanity
escaped economic commodification only to be commodified politically. Given
the literary and performance culture surrounding the abolitionist production
of the slave narrative, there was a certain amount of celebrity if not glamor
attached to the social being of slave narrators, not least because these were *ex-
slaves*, *runaways*, *fugitives*. But there was also the ever present danger of recap-
ture, the continuing threat of the fugitive law[6] and the uncertain struggle with
white patrons over the public representation of the black ex-slave self on the
abolitionist circuit (Onley 1987; Wood 2000). Even Fredrick Douglas's[7] acclaim
as an abolitionist speaker, within two years of his escape from slavery in 1838,
was "marred by continual reminders that, as a black man, he was subject to
northern segregation laws, to mob violence, and to insulting condescension
at the hands of his white co-workers" (Sundquist 1994, p. 87). Within this
slave/ex-slave dialectic of racialized locations, whether commodified in the
North or South, the fugitive was wanted in effect by two different and opposed

formations of social mastery. In both cases for a crime she or he did not, and could not, have committed, *the theft of her- or himself*.

That the runaway or fugitive should be a prominently contested iconic commodity in pro- and anti-slavery discourses provided a highly creative if unstable ambiguity in the West's nineteenth-century dialogics of representation and counter-representation. In the United States the fugitive slave began to signify a morality struggle in national identity, between the plantation owners in the South, from where the slave was running, and the abolitionists in the North, to where the slave was running.[8] Placed in parenthesis, but only for excision, was the idea of political agency among the enslaved and ex-slaves themselves, the uncontrollable "self-liberation ethos of enslaved blacks" (Beckles 1991). What is most interesting about this nineteenth-century discursive formation is the longevity of its tenor/tenure in the post-abolitionist memory of slavery in popular culture. It is here that we can at last begin to understand the strange memorial horizon of Spielberg's *Amistad*.

The Return of the Fugitive

The image of the convicted but innocent *man or men* on the run from the law has become a highly memorable leitmotiv in twentieth-century American and European film culture, though its anti-slavery antecedents and precedent have failed to be acknowledged. Performed mostly in "white face" this image offers a paradoxical yet ultimately reassuring representation of an apparently questionable criminal justice system eventually vindicated by a self-correcting accountability to its liberal credentials. As soon as we encounter this leitmotiv, we seem to remember in advance that although there is a presumption of innocence prior to any indictment of guilt, it is always possible (and occasionally the case) for the innocent to be found guilty. But at the same time it is always possible (ultimately) for the innocent, though judged to be guilty, to prove their innocence. We are told repeatedly that in American culture, irrespective of background, *the truth will out*, unlike what might pass for justice culturally elsewhere.

The drama of Spielberg's *Amistad* develops around a commemorative repetition of the intricacies that flow from both the abolitionist tropes of the fugitive and its displaced televisual or cinematic equivalent. This is achieved in at least six discrete scenarios of the fugitive genre, which replay the abolitionist drama of the fugitive as the slave/ex-slave dialectic. During the first scenario there is the *conviction and imprisonment* following a frame-up: in *Amistad* this is signified through the capture and enslavement of the Africans. The second scenario details the *escape from custody*, the breakout: in the film it is the slave revolt. Third is the *re-capture* of the fugitive(s) and, in the light of new or contested evidence, the possibility of a retrial: here the dispute about the legality of slavery. Fourth is the attempt to convince the imprisoned to have faith in the court system again, through the *retrial*, plus the attempt to convince the best working or retired lawyer in the town or country to take on the case: here the involvement of the abolitionists and John Quincy Adams. Fifth is the trial, the difficulties of making the case, cross-examination of witnesses, the *dramatic closing speech*: here the ubiquitous and extended American courtroom scene. Sixth are the final scenes, the successful outcome, the *not-guilty verdict*, the freeing of the wrongly convicted, and the grateful free person: here the relief at the verdict expressed by the enslaved Africans when the sentence of slavery was quashed.

We have of course all seen this before, many times. This is why I question whether *Amistad* really is a film about slavery. It seems to remember something quite different. Almost like the abolitionist production of a conventionalized slave narrative, suitably revised for the post-slavery era, the film seems to be pedagogically in thrall to documenting the ideals of American justice, as an experiential inevitability. So clearly framed against the foreknowledge of abolition, the ultimately American *feel good* quality of this picture reinforces Western culture's proprietorial memory of slavery as *the memory of its abolition*. Using the trope of the slave as fugitive, seemingly displaced and sedimented in the cinematic convention of the fugitive as genre, *Amistad* becomes a master/slave narrative over which the ex-slave has lost control. The conflation of the ex-slave historically as fugitive and the fugitive cinematically as genre is complete where slavery, like a falsely prosecuted crime, is reduced to a miscarriage of justice that can be rectified by the courts. This of course says little about the role of the US courts in upholding slavery and legalizing racism (see Higginbotham 1978). Indeed the ubiquitous, unacknowledged *Zeitgeist* of racism is inexplicably exorcised in *Amistad*, its constitutive display of seemingly ineffable visual inequalities of racial categorization passed over in silence, leaving the profound if exoticized attempts to expose the unique traumas of slavery subordinated to the mass consumption of the fugitive story line. Ironic as it is perverse, the predatory violence of the capture, the voyeuristic stripping and chaining of the enslaved, the sadism of the middle passage where Africans are thrown into the sea, are used as *background*, not foreground, to the court case.

The main problem with this memorialization of slavery is its overwhelming erasure of any racialized sense of historical formation or degrading social process. Erased is the expansive, repetitive nature of enslavement, including the plantation work systems across the Americas and the centuries-long development of highly organized and systematic economic and racialized forms of governmentality. In the absence of these social encrustations being made explicit or explained, we are positioned to remember slavery as pathological ephemera, as if historically it was a minor crimogenic deviation from a progressive modernizing project. Remembering slavery through this cultural route becomes a reflexive excursion in the rehabilitation of the American dream, the restoration of reverence for the history that produced the Declaration of Independence, the Emancipation Proclamation, and civil rights legislation. A history, the normative memory of which remembers slavery, together with the constitutive and ensuing contexts of racism, as exceptions to the democratic longevity of civic rule within the Republic. In other words, the memory of slavery is established as the memory of its heroic and inevitable abolition.

Between the Masters' and the Slaves' Narratives

If the relation between history and cinema fosters a "replacement history" (Snead 1994), then in the West it can be argued that this proclaims a memory in which the makers of history are exclusively white Europeans. At the same time it insinuates that people of African descent "remain more or less the same, untouched by the passage of time" (ibid, p. 138). Under the normalizing regime of a whitewashed historical production, both off and on screen, black people are denied any "historical or material reference, except as former slaves" and are correspondingly depicted as "ahistorical" (ibid). In posing the question of "race" in these representational terms, within the cultural economy that produces the ex-slave and the ahistorical, we can begin to understand the figurative logic that inscribes a master/abolitionist memory of slavery. In other words, we can understand Spielberg's *Amistad* as writing over the history of the contemporary conjuncture a prescribed, honorific relation between "race" and American democracy. Because *Amistad* cannot ignore slavery, since this is the horizon of its dramatizations, it fixes its representations of this past in an ameliorative relation to the present. Henceforth, the legacy of slavery becomes the historical record of abolitionism, not the contemporary agenda of racism. It denies the failures to resolve past inequalities and violations by invoking the democratic largess of a shared, improved American condition. The problem with such a representational strategy, this figuration of "white amnesia" (Hesse 1997), is that it can only be achieved with reference to a politically muted if not absent black presence. In this way the political discourse of the film owes much of its liberal–colonial (Bhabha 1994) animations to its rerun of long-established racialized conventions in (white) American literature (Morrison 1992). In promoting the distinctiveness of the American "claim to freedom" (white) American literary and film cultures have variously concealed the political significance of the slaves, the ex-slaves, and black citizens with their pathologized traditions of dissent. Toni Morrison refers to this as "the presence of the unfree within the heart of the democratic experiment – the critical absence of democracy, its echo, shadow and silent force in the political and intellectual activity of some not-Americans" (Morrison 1992, p. 48).

Morrison also suggests that even on those infrequent occasions when some effort is made to address these contested discrepancies, the hegemonic orientation of these cultural forms invariably responds by deploying a "vocabulary designed to disguise the subject" (ibid, p. 50). *Amistad* sails straight into this American tradition. In creating a masters' narrative, while purporting to supply the slaves' narrative, it enforces a silence on the social significance and legacy of slavery, providing a ventriloquist's act, speaking for "Africans and their descendants or of them" (ibid). As Morrison points out, what could not and cannot be tolerated by the master narrative was/is "a response from the Africanist persona" (ibid). Hence its exclusion, the two could not coexist. This is evident where *Amistad* virtually ignores the US experience of black people in relation to slavery and racist exclusion, in order to comment on the humanity of white people in relation to abolition. Consequently it constructs "a history and a context for whites by positing history-lessness and context-lessness for blacks" (ibid, p. 53).

Because *Amistad* works as a "cover story" for the master narrative of white abolitionism, the "hypervisibility, very publicness [*sic*] of black people as a social fact, works to undermine the possibility of actually seeing black specificity" (Lubiano 1995, p. 187). For example, by isolating the *Amistad* incident from the US history of black rebellions in the early nineteenth century and in choosing the *Amistad* at all, the editorialized discourse of the film works in two mutually reinforcing ways. Firstly, it enables the issue of Atlantic slavery to be raised and condemned as an idea without condemning the practice of slavery in the US. It uses the ideals of the Declaration of Independence to indict slavery through the stress on inalienable liberty without using the issue of slavery to question the ideals of the Declaration, which were arguably based on racist exclusionary principles. Secondly, it separates the question of slavery from racism. In cultivating an ideal that all people are brothers and sisters under the skin, it neglects to consider why this ideal needs to be promoted and what continues to prevent it from becoming actualized. Not only does *Amistad* manage to elude any answer to the question "how was slavery related to racism?", it orchestrates the fiction that slavery no longer has a socially dehumanizing legacy. It implies, wrongly, that abolitionism was a direct confrontation with racism. Could *Amistad* be symptomatic of a larger problem concerning the un/remembering of slavery in Western culture? Is there anything we can learn from its reluctance and/or inability to acknowledge and engage with the contemporary political implications of the historical legacy of slavery, colonialism, and racism? Michel-Rolph Trouillot (1995) suggests the beginnings of an answer when he writes:

> That US slavery has both officially ended, yet continues in many complex forms – most notably institutionalized racism and the cultural denigration of blackness – makes its representation particularly burdensome in the United States. Slavery here is a ghost, both the past and a living presence; and the problem of historical representation is how to represent that ghost, something that is and yet is not. (Ibid, pp. 146–7)

While there remain alternative ways of remembering slavery, these may well require an ethical commitment to illuminating the contested politics of that history, something so far lacking in dominant or mainstream forms of Western popular and literary culture.

Freeing the Slave's Memory

W. E. B. Du Bois once remarked that in much discussion of the cultural, political, and economic labors mobilized in the nation-building of the United States
the "chief witness, [the] emancipated slave, [is] barred from court" (Du Bois
1935, p. 721). It matters therefore that we consider how the slaves/ex-slaves
themselves may have contextualized a memory of slavery irreducible to the
"white" jurisdiction of abolitionism, particularly where the challenge represented by these alternative recollections raises very different political implications. The experience of the Reverend James W. C. Pennington seems to
symbolize much of this. He was not only a fugitive slave, abolitionist, and
political activist at the time of the *Amistad* affair, but also the pastor at a local
Presbyterian church. He visited the imprisoned Africans on many occasions
from their initial incarceration in 1839 up until 1841 when they were
released.[9] He also helped to raise money to assist their eventual resettlement
in Sierra Leone (Bethel 1997). Pennington was one of a number of ex-slaves
who had produced an autobiographical narrative without the overbearing
involvement of white editors (Blassingame 1985, p. 83). However, what is
more important for our purposes is his earlier (1841) publication, *A Text Book
on the Origins and History of the Colored People*. It has been suggested it may have
been "the first effort by an African American to trace and record the history
of Africans and their descendants in North America." Whether Pennington was
"sensitized to the African issue" (Bethel 1997, p. 174) through his engagement
with the *Amistad* captives is certainly worth speculating about. What is clear is
that Pennington's invocation of a memory of African heritage and history,
together with his commitment to revitalizing the fading memory of slavery
for African Americans in the North, poses a much different context for the
remembering of the *Amistad*.[10]

It entitles us to ask whether the memory of its significance changes if we
locate it in the wake of other slave rebellions. What happens to the memory
of slavery if a different slave rebellion becomes our focus? As we have seen,
Amistad the film locates the memory of slavery outside any notional reference
to the stark tradition of black anti-slavery revolts against white American colonial authorities. To place the historical meaning of the *Amistad* rebellion in that
tradition requires that we recall not only the American Revolution of 1776
and the French Revolution of 1789 but also the anti-slavery Haitian Revolution of 1791. Only in terms of these revolutions taken together can we signify
the emergence of a modern political culture as centered on the rights-bearing
subject *and the contested racial difference of its representation* (cf. Geggus 1989;
Dayan 1998; Aravamudan 1999). For abolitionists, plantation owners,
and slaves in the South, the symbol of Haiti cast a long influential shadow at
the beginning of the nineteenth century (Robinson 1997; Sundquist 1994).
Although traditionally forgotten by the Western abolitionist memory of
slavery, the Haitian Revolution was inspirational to three highly planned but

ultimately unsuccessful slave revolts in the United States during the early part of the nineteenth century.

Prior to the *Amistad* rebellion of 1839 there was a political climate of black anti-slavery rebellions already in place. What is striking about the so-called slave plots organized by Gabriel Prosser in Richmond, Virginia (1800), Denmark Vesey in Charleston, South Carolina (1822), and Nat Turner in Southampton County, Virginia (1831) was the proactive and political nature of their collective planning. In each case, they were deeply threatening to the plantation regime they hoped to overturn. They were also characterized by the involvement of trusted slaves in the *conspiracy* to revolt. Combining ideological references to Haiti and biblical prophecy in their various mobilizations of slaves, these revolts intended to take over the local regions in which the plantations were located. In the case of Prosser and Vesey, they were caught and executed before they could carry out their plans, while Turner and his band of rebels were eventually put down and executed after four days of fighting (Mullin 1994; Robertson 1999; Sundquist 1994; Walvin 1993). The cumulative significance of these attempted revolts was that by the 1830s the fear of slave rebellions and resistances was as persistent among southern plantation owners as was the anticipation of challenges to slavery among the slaves themselves (Sundquist 1994; Walvin 1993). Although this contextual history is erased by *Amistad*'s mobilization of the abolitionist memory, it was not lost on the memory of the writer of one of the eloquent and insightful slave narratives of the century, Fredrick Douglas. In his 1857 address "West India Emancipation," Douglas cited the leaders of various nineteenth-century slave rebellions. These included Nat Turner, Joseph Cinqué, and Madison Washington. Douglas argued: "violent insurrectionary movements could act as a catalyst to abolition in the United States as they had in the British West Indies" (Sundquist 1994, p. 115). Although Douglas celebrated Cinqué's heroism during the *Amistad* rebellion and considered him a patriot, he did not consider him to embody the exemplary instance of a slave revolt. What is striking about Douglas's use of the slave narrative experience to interpret the rebellious experience of other slaves is the particular choice he makes of a slave rebel leader to represent what is symbolized by slave revolt. It is interesting because while he does not choose the *Amistad*, the circumstances of his choice are remarkably similar to it. This concerns the revolt led by Madison Washington on the *Creole*, an American slave ship.[11]

The slave revolt on the *Creole* took place in 1841, two years after the *Amistad*. The slaves revolted while the *Creole* was off the coast of Virginia en route to New Orleans. They managed to sail the US-owned ship to Nassau in the Bahamas where slavery was no longer established. What distinguishes the *Creole* from the *Amistad* is that the revolt was directed against *American* slave authorities. It was an indictment of slavery, not in the Caribbean under Spanish jurisdiction, but of slavery in the US under US jurisdiction. Arguments put on behalf of the rebels to the Supreme Court by abolitionists attempted to use the same law of nature arguments deployed by John Quincy Adams on behalf of the the *Amistad* slaves. Because the slaves had freed themselves, there was only one remaining issue, that of redress. This was eventually decided fourteen years later in 1855 by a claims commission that ruled the slaves had been property aboard the ship on a lawful voyage and thus remained subject to Virginia's fugitive slave laws. Thus, they were legally still slaves under American law. The fact that the US had outlawed the international slave trade but not its domestic trade in slaves was not considered a contradiction (see Sundquist 1994; Sale 1997).[12]

What Madison Washington represented for Douglas, on whom he based his novel *The Heroic Slave* (1853), was someone who had applied the same principles of 1776, liberty or death, to the institution of slavery. It was a successful slave revolt in the context of the United States, which owed nothing to the supervision of white abolitionists. In that sense, the *Creole* was no less remarkable than the *Amistad*. What is it that attaches a celebratory status to the *Amistad* in the post-slavery era when the opposing judicial decisions of the *Amistad* and *Creole* cases simply confirmed the continued institutional operation of racism in the American legal process (cf. Higginbotham 1978), since in both decisions the freedom won by the slaves was undermined by the fact that it conferred no right to rebel against legal slavery. The decisions did nothing to address the relation between slavery and racial hierarchy, since racial hierarchy was also perceived as guaranteed by natural law (Sundquist 1994, pp. 178–9). What the *Creole* signified, for those who like Fredrick Douglas cared to remember it, was a black political ethos and critique of *racial* democracy that denied and defied the paternalism of *white* abolitionism and the judicial partisanship of *white* Americanism. It pointed to a radically different *normative* memory of slavery, where memory itself was subject to the regulations of undecidability.[13] If the *Amistad* could be remembered without reference to the *Creole*, yet the *Creole* could not be remembered without reference to the *Amistad*, what did this mean about the social memory of slavery in each case? In addition, what was socially forgotten? If remembering slavery is deeply perspectival and unremittingly contested, then what does it mean to talk of the *memory* of slavery in the West at this point in the post-slavery era?[14]

Remembering/Forgetting Slavery in Western Memory

The problem of remembering Atlantic slavery in Western culture has been recently interrogated with pedagogic intensity in Marcus Wood's (2000) insightful study of its diverse visual representations. According to Wood, there "can be no archeology of the memory of slavery that corresponds to an identification with a lost reality" (ibid, p. 7). That said, the question remains as to how its production of representational materials is to be understood; in other words, what kind of remembering do they facilitate? Wood suggests visual interpretations of slavery in the West have largely been a speculative process, in the midst of a turning away from its blinding reality. This underwrites what he terms "blind memory" (never entirely explained), which seems to imply the intractability of a perceptual obstacle that interrupts "how the West can or cannot remember slavery" (ibid, p. 304). Although Wood does not put it in these terms, his study suggests that blind memory has given rise to two dominant, albeit inadequate, discursive forms of commemorating memories of slavery in the West. The first and earliest is our old friend, *abolitionist memory*. As we have seen in the symptomatic case of the *Amistad*, it focuses on the heroic consecration of white liberators, Wilberforce here, Lincoln there, as defining the cognitive limit on the political memory of slavery. Beginning in early nineteenth-century British historiography, this mnemonic spread quickly throughout Western colonial culture following the abolition of plantation and domestic slavery in the British Caribbean (1833), North America (1865), and Brazil (1888) (Wood 2000, p. 8).

The second and more recent (late twentieth century) mode of slavery's memory might be described as our new friend, *curatorial memory*.[15] This rearranges and recollects the objects, tools, weapons, exhibits, images, texts, scenes, and artefacts of African enslavement, displaying them "experientially," if not aesthetically, in a gallery or museum (or on the film screen) to the curiosity of any contemplative eye. Curatorial memory directs our attention to "the easy option of an unthinking moral outrage" (ibid, p. 296). Wood's analysis suggests this memorial discourse is itself constrained by two mutually reinforcing cultural reflexes. First, a "Western obsession with representing the memory of slave torture through objects" (ibid, p. 208). The curatorial dramatization of objects like chains, whips, and shackles reduces the memory of slavery to the banalities of its routine, ubiquitous violence. It caricatures the master/slave relation, eclipsing the contextual social and emotional violations that generationally defined the experience of day-to-day enslavement. Secondly, there is a Western desire to come to curatorial terms with the horror of slavery by constructing knowledge of what really happened as a form of accepting the past.

Because of its dramaturgical obsessions the curatorial memory of slavery offers a peculiar pathos of distance that replicates yet another way in which the generational, emotional, social, and political relations of the people who were enslaved are simply forgotten. At the same time, its epistemological desires culminate in a parochial bathos of historical proximity that disavows the genealogical relationship of contemporary, Western racialized societies to the political–cultural economy of slavery. When considered against such a background, Wood is undoubtedly right to argue "the West has been misremembering and disremembering slavery for more than three centuries" (ibid, p. 300). However, it needs to be said, acutely conceptual problems begin where he attempts to formulate an alternative approach to the remembering of slavery. So far the question of "race" and racism has been absent in our discussion of Wood's understanding of the cultural formation of slavery's memory. It does, however, make an astonishing entrance in his analysis, almost as a lengthy aside, where he ponders the curatorial problem of white empathy for the black victims of slavery's regime of violence:[16]

> For example, one major problem in the presentation of slave torture relates to the *omnipresence of racial codification*. If the slave body is black, then it is immediately separated from white experience through *racially encoded psychic reflex*. How can a white audience get beyond the acculturated sense that they are looking at a skin that appears different from their own, and *which consequently must be assumed to respond to pain differently? One solution consists of doing away with the skin completely and going for what lies beneath it.* (ibid, p. 281; emphasis added)

What can explain Wood's apparent, albeit indirect recourse to the explanans of biological racism? It seems to transmute an erstwhile liberal desire to get beyond "race" into its colonial double, to oversee the universal memory of slavery, through the *exclusion* of any reference to its racialized formations. The alternative possibilities of comprehending the relation between the enslavement of Africans and the constitution of European racism, in development of a white tradition of anti-racist political and epistemological formations, seem quite *naturally* out of the question. It appears Wood is specifically motivated by the aesthetic requirements of an undifferentiated white audience, as if the latter are exclusively *the* audience. Unfortunately, this provides little scope for thinking beyond the "race" of the white gaze, since it is the visual jurisdiction of the latter that accompanies his ventilation of the liberal ideal to "go beyond race" in the Western memory of slavery. It comes as no surprise, therefore, to witness Wood pondering the value of doing away with the black skin of the putative exhibit. He contemplates reducing the figure of the African slave to a skeletal presence, in order to communicate the slave's humanity, through the "universal similitude of human bones." However, the aesthetic rationale that "all skeletons are white and they all look the same" (ibid) ignores the profound irony in regurgitating the Western imperial desire to transform the alleged refractoriness of blackness into the acceptability of whiteness. Nevertheless, for Wood, because aesthetics has the capacity to go beyond "race," it has a central place in the memory of slavery, it "asserts the primacy of Art as the most effective tributary cultural response" (ibid, p. 305). Through the cognitive, emotional, and perceptual transformations of visual and literary art, "we" no longer attempt to come to terms with the past of slavery; rather "we" question how this could have happened at all. Unlike curatorial memory, which purports to represent the total slave experience, *aesthetic memory* understands that when "we try to look at the inheritance of Atlantic slavery what we are capable of seeing remains to be seen" (ibid, p. 307).[17]

Leaving aside, if only for the moment, Wood's inadvertent flirtation with the discourse of racism, it is still worth asking to what extent can the aestheticization of slavery's memory resolve the problem of its remembrance in Western culture. Wood is certainly right to insist on the enormity of the slavery experience, its resistance to total recall, and the impossibility of its adequate empirical representation. Nevertheless, his aesthetic alternative shares a *family resemblance* with the distorting sensibilities and racially exclusive sensitivities of both the abolitionist and curatorial memories from which he is supposedly distancing himself, although it promulgates the idea that the thematic challenge of aesthetic memory is to *remember through* the different ways art explores questions of guilt. We still need to ask for whose memory does the crack of the slave master's whip stimulate feelings of guilt? Does this not simply resume the moral tradition of the master/abolitionist narrative so scrupulously scripted in *Amistad*? Why would feelings of historical guilt be privileged over, say, contemporary feelings of disfranchisement, as might arise if we also remembered the ex-slaves' attempts to *enter democracy* (cf. Du Bois 1935)? Wood's aesthetically contextual (empirical) idea that Atlantic slavery can be understood analogously in relation to great human or environmental catastrophes is surely at odds with the thematic of exploring guilt. Earthquakes, cholera epidemics, or airplane crashes are hardly matters for aesthetic adjudication in terms of guilt, nor are they the barbaric practices of an organized Western culture across several generations. To say that aesthetic memory never generalizes "about what it is which separates the middle passage and plantation slavery from other cultural and global disasters" (Wood 2000, p. 306), is to generalize about what constitutes slavery as disaster. Is the general idea of disaster, however devastatingly that is construed, the most appropriate mode through which to remember slavery? Does this not merely seek to redeem Western guilt through the insistence that slavery was a historical aberration in an otherwise progressive modernity, returning us, seduced by the prospect of better days ahead, as if we had never left, to a curatorial memory of plantation slavery that forgets its connection with contemporary forms of racism in the West? It seems the memory of slavery is haunted by the specter of a *de/colonial fantasy*.[18]

Succumbing To De/Colonial Fantasy

What might be described as the liberal–democratic problem of remembering Atlantic slavery in Western culture has been expressed, perhaps indirectly, by David Brion Davis. During the era of the US civil rights struggles, Davis wrote:

> Americans have often been embarrassed *when reminded* that the Declaration of Independence was written by a slaveholder and that Negro slavery was a legal institution in all thirteen colonies at the beginning of the Revolution. (Davis 1988, p. 3; my emphasis)

For our purposes, it is important not to construe this exclusively in the liberal terms of indictment, or feelings of guilt or shame that can reasonably ensue. What is equally, if not more, significant are the unthematized antidemocratic corollaries associated with being reminded in this way. Firstly, it positions us as witnesses to at least two competing "American" memories of slavery, insofar as some memories need reminding about the United States' foundational juxtaposition between independence and slavery while "others" do not. Secondly, where reminders are necessary, clearly embarrassment only occurs because the discrepant juxtaposition, though routinely marginalized, is sufficient to warrant the questioning of a democratic ideal held not to be susceptible to contamination. Thirdly, the occasionality of these reminders highlights the hegemonic celebratory self-image of the democratic nation as transcending its blighted slavery history. Finally, the privileged idea of American citizenship or "natural" cultural affinity to the Western nation seems to be associated with those who have to be reminded of their capacity to forget the history of slavery. Here, revealed, is the prevailing Western context in which the memory of slavery and its forgetting are carefully phrased within a liberal–democratic disavowal (Hesse 2000a).

In resistance to this, we need to ask why the contemporary status of the memory of Atlantic slavery in Western (popular) culture is subject to liberal–democratic disavowal. Clearly the problem with the abolitionist, curatorial, and aesthetic memories discussed above is that they treat plantation slavery as a socially discrete, politically aberrant, albeit recognizably barbaric, *singular event*. Even if it is considered to be sublime, its memory formations assume the absence of historical consequences, they ignore the *racialized trajectories* of continuity and reconfiguration in contemporary social relationships, governance, and cultural representations. They obscure how and why the development of republicanism, liberalism, and democracy in the West emerged in *conjunction* with slavery, ethnocide, and racism (cf. Mignolo 2000). When Western history seems so unrelated to its shadowy imperial constitution – readily comprehensible only as a successful psychic investment in a European, American, democratic enterprise – we are experiencing an episode of *de/ colonial fantasy*.

The abolition of slavery, the dissolution of empire, and racial desegregation which occurred between the greater parts of the nineteenth and twentieth centuries are usually considered to be major events in the transatlantic experience of Western decolonization (Betts 1998; Chamberlain 1999). The idea of decolonization itself has tended to be understood as a transformative break or rupture with the colonial regime (e.g., the abolition of slavery); a discrete transition to a decolonized future, irrespective of the actual protracted qualities of the identifiable process itself. The orientation of this thinking is marked by the formative anti-colonial (or anti-slavery) context prior to formal decolonization (Scott 1999). It raises the question of how decolonization is to be understood, *now*, in the aftermath of its formal declarations, precarious institutions, and various derelictions, even if we accept, substantively, the classical Fanonian *anti-colonial* conception of decolonization as a complete calling into question of the colonial situation (Fanon 1963). Now another question exists: "how do (should) we understand this questioning in the formal postcolonial period?" (Scott 1999, p. 203). According to David Scott, since contemporary critical thought is formally located *after* colonialism, its questions cannot continue to be those of realizing the threshold of an anti-colonial national sovereignty. The "revised questions" we ought to be posing now "have rather to be those of unsettling the settled settlements of this very postcolonial sovereignty itself" (ibid, p. 204).

Despite the establishment of the United Nations in 1945 and its formal commitment to decolonization, the years since have not seen the dismantling of the international regime that legitimized colonialism and imperialism since 1492 (Otto 1999). At the same time the Western domination of the world economy continues under the nomenclature of globalization, despite decolonization, the emergence of the Third World, and the apparent political independence of previously colonized peoples (ibid, p. 154). Meanwhile, it still seems that without "significant exception the universalizing discourses of modern Europe and the United States assume the silence, willing or otherwise, of the non-European world" (Said 1993, p. 58). That this occurs both in relation to the former colonies and through the legacy of racism within Western nations themselves suggests that cultures of imperialism are still defining the social orientations of Western liberal democracies. It is as if decolonization never took place, that it remains interrupted and incomplete, and that its failure to materialize is constitutive of what we should now understand as the postcolonial condition (Hesse 2000a).

If decolonization is to be rethought and refought, as it must, it will need to work through and against the West's liberal–democratic culture of de/colonial fantasy. By this is meant those Western attitudes, practices, and discourses that *imagine against the evidence, against counter-interrogation*, the comprehensive undertaking and successful completion of decolonization, both within the metropolis and the former colonies or sites of racial segregation. At the same time, the notion of decolonization needs to be wrested from the provenance of a Western liberal–democratic tradition that disavows how it was bitterly fought and grudgingly conceded by formations in the West every step of the way. The interruption or blockading of decolonization is now part of the Western postcolonial settlement, as is the evolution of a constitutional liberalism that emerged within the horizon of imperialism (Mehta 1999). De/colonial *fantasy* is "an attempt to overcome, to conceal this inconsistency" (Žižek 1989, p. 124). It is preoccupied with a desire to close the gap of discrepancy between representations of the liberal–democratic ideal and the threatening idea of an unsettled postcoloniality. Within the Western nation the latter is symbolized by the questioning intrusions of unresolved social rituals of white European/American racism. We should be mindful that "symbolic and/or imaginary identification never results in the absence of any remainder, there is always a leftover which opens the space for desire" (ibid). It is precisely in relation to the social critiques posed by the legacy of racism, refusing to be pacified, unresolved, by incorporation into the democratic symbolism of the Western nation, that de/colonial fantasy intervenes. It accentuates a desire to view the Western nation as an elevated spectacle, as the realm of indiscriminate and undiminished freedom, *from (and compared to) its "others."* What remain, *left over from hegemonic symbolization*, and become the problematic status of decolonization in Western culture, are its incompleteness, interruptions, disavowals, and preclusions. De/colonial fantasy is stimulated by a compulsion to imagine the Western nation, or at least the one "we" live in, as having resolved or avoided any disruptive legacies of the failures to decolonize. It assumes in advance what it desires to deny; correspondingly, it conceals the relation of this liberal–democratic disavowal to the West's contemporary political formation. This is the terrain of postcolonialism.

Responsibilities of Postcolonialism

Gabriel Garcia Marquez has observed, "What matters in life is not what happens to you but what you remember and how you remember it."[19] There is a corollary to this: what and how you remember depends on what has been happening to you in life. In postcolonial discourse the personal becomes ethical. Because of liberal democracy's disavowal of its imperial continuities, the postcolonial remembering of slavery in the West has the potential to transform the agonistics of incomplete decolonization into the agonistics of incomplete democracy. It offers a continuing uncommemorated reminder and questioning of what passes and has passed for postcoloniality, in the context of limited, perverse, and racist forms of decolonization. When dwelling within metropolitan subaltern discourses, it remembers what is ritually forgotten in historicist eulogies of liberal democracy. These include numerous interdependencies that obtained between Christianity and slavery, liberalism and imperialism, democracy and racism, each of which was mutually constitutive of Atlantic capitalism's framing of modernity. Through insisting on the naming of these political formations we may "remember" something quite distinctive, yet traditionally unarticulated. How the slavery plantation complex's formative relations of exploitation, exoticism, racism, and violence produced the consumerist contours of Western culture, principally through customizing the transnational, cultural production and consumption of mundane staples of the Western lifestyle, such as coffee, sugar, cotton, and tobacco (Curtin 1990; Solow 1991; Blackburn 1997). We may "remember" that the commonest texture of the clothes we still wear, and the familiar ingredients of the beverages we continue to consume, remain intimately related with the history, blood, sweat, and tears of African enslaved labor. So what does it mean to "remember" these particular formations now? What does it mean to cast this relation between "history and memory" (Le Goff 1992; Hutton 1993) in a postcolonial idiom?

Ania Loomba has suggested that many postcolonial perspectives "remain curiously Eurocentric" (Loomba 1998, p. 256). However, while the lure of this conceptual ensnarement should not be underestimated, neither should it be overestimated. Much depends on how we understand Eurocentrism. Since the late twentieth century the idea of the West itself has been subject to incessant contestation in domains concerned with the meaning of national identity, cultural representativeness, and social equality.[20] The combined impact of dispersed patterns of inadequate decolonization myriad migratory sojourns, and uneven forms of globalization increasingly have to be borne in mind. These have recast the relationships between places, people, identities, and discourses in new and discontinuous ways, always bearing the imprint of an unsettling and unsettled multiculturalism (Hall 2000; Hesse 2000b). Clearly many of the contested socioeconomic inequalities of First World/Third World relationships remain deeply dislocating of any notional sense of a global community. However, they now inscribe not only anthropological scenarios on the margins of the West, but question the very idea of "society" in the West itself, whether through recurrent public exposures and denials of institutional racism; daily urban negotiations with ethnically diverse communities; campaigns against "non-white" immigration; movements emphasizing the rights of citizens of color; proliferations of racist attacks; generational disseminations of Islam; black music's dominance of popular culture; racially segmented and cross-cultural cities; or nationalist fundamentalisms of right-wing racists. Increasingly and protractedly, the West may be where it was but is no longer what it was. It can no longer signify, without elaborate qualification, a series of "racially" unified nationalist civil societies, democratized through an exclusive, in some instances unmarked, whiteness. Various configurations of Western societies now have to contend with unrelenting cultural and political practices framed by contested notions of globalization, transnationalism, and multiculturalism.

What we have traditionally understood as the West therefore refers not so much to a place but a project or formation (Glissant 1989; Hall 1992). It signifies a political–cultural economy in which formalized, racialized, creolized, and imbricated sets of relationships have developed between unevenly essentialized "European" and "Non-European" designations, where the former exerts hegemony over the latter. Eurocentrism has long been the representational discourse, which provided such a spectacle with its own version of natural and universal history, as well as legislative, worldly authority (cf. Amin 1989; Said 1993). It is this that is being culturally unsettled, discursively challenged, and politically interrogated, not only outside but also inside the West itself (Hall 2000). It is as if the West no longer has a non-"Other" and is increasingly becoming marked and questioned as *the* "Other." What might be described as the late modern or postcolonial history of a Eurocentrism can be understood as the "discourse that emerges in the context of the decentering of the West" (Sayyid 1997, p. 128). How we understand that context is crucial, since it marks the locus in which "the relationship between the Western enterprise and universalism is open to disarticulation and rearticulation." The reference here is to a primarily cultural decentering of the West. Eurocentrism has become increasingly distinguished as a particularism, subject to cultural, ecological, religious, and political questioning of its previous claims to universalism. At the same time Eurocentric institutions and discourse endeavor to resume the idea of universalism, repositing their hegemony of the West as the legislative center of world culture. Ironically, the endeavor now signifies "a project that is only possible when the West and the center are no longer considered to be synonymous" (ibid).

The temporalities implied in this analysis are significant. In order to grasp the value of its insights we need to embrace the idea that there are two modern histories of Eurocentrism in the constitution of the "West and the Rest" (Hall 1992). The first can be described as *imperialized Eurocentrism*, centering the world on the conventions, legislations, and aesthetics generated within the terms of the two European empires (Pagden 1995) between the sixteenth and early twentieth centuries. Without seeking consent it imposed the categories of "race," governmentalized them, and policed the economic idealizations of a colonizing European culture within the assumed remit of a universal mandate (cf. Amin 1989). What emerged as the West was a constellation of cross-cultural relations between dominant Europeanized formations and subordinated "non-European" exclusions (Glissant 1989; Pieterse 1994). Typified by the European decimation of Native Americans, enslavement of Africans in the Americas, European colonialism in India, Africa, and the Pacific, imperialized Eurocentrism assumed and maintained the metropolitan West uncompromisingly as the universal center of world civilization (Cesaire 1972; Fanon 1963). If anything the twentieth century, especially the middle to later period, saw this particular knowledge–power configuration subject to intense and incessant challenge, interrogation, and military and civil struggles. Since 1945 social movements motivated by anti-colonialism, civil rights, black power, feminism, anti-racism, anti-apartheid, Third World debt, environmentalism, Islamism, and reparations for slavery, to name but a few, have radically undermined and decentered the *naturalized* imperial claims of the West. While Eurocentrism has not disappeared, it has been markedly dislocated, albeit reconfigured. Since the late twentieth century what can be described as a *globalized Eurocentrism* (cf. Hall 1991) has been sold through commodity globalization in "an attempt to sustain the universality of the Western project, in conditions in which its universality can no longer be taken for granted" (Sayyid 1997). In this postcolonial sense Eurocentrism is "only possible when the relationship between universalism and the Western project has been problematized, that is, when the West cannot be subsumed within universality" (ibid, pp. 128–9). Consequently, the idea of postcolonialism as I intend that term to be understood emerges as the very form that this problematization takes; it is the articulatory space created mainly through the *epistemological decentering* of the West. It constitutively resists the global recentering of the West, facilitating an interrogation of global postcoloniality. Here lie the mnemonic responsibilities of postcolonialism.

The Ethics of Remembering Slavery

The specific idea of "postcolonial memory" has been suggested by Alessandro Triulzi to describe anti-statist contestations over the appropriation of memories in the "ex-colonial capitals of independent Africa" (Triulzi 1996, p. 79). In contrast to the formalized accounts or official memories of the "postcolonial years," Triulzi sees it as a "contestatory memory" in which "postcolonial events" and their various interpretations become subject to "rediscovered" historical memories "whose connection with the nationalist memory of independence has been severed" (ibid, p. 82). If we broaden and radicalize the idea of postcolonial memory to encompass various sites of the ostensibly decolonized, racially desegregated world we can begin to emphasize postcolonialism as the critical counter-point of incomplete forms of decolonization. For example, Homi Bhabha (1994) has suggested that "postcolonial criticism" "bears witness" to the unequal and uneven forces of cultural representation staked out in the struggle for political and social authority in the modern world. In particular, it stalks discourses of modernity, which attempt to normalize global uneven development and the different, dislocated histories of nations, "races," communities, and peoples. Because postcolonial criticism arises in the geopolitical sites of the formerly colonized *and* the former colonizers, it also highlights both "the crisis of the uncompleted struggle for decolonization and the crisis of the post-independence state" (Hall 1996, p. 244).

The profound excavatory work of postcolonial memory is symbolized by Stuart Hall's (1996) paradoxical question, "when was the postcolonial?" Since it is not possible to point to a discrete period of effective and thoroughgoing decolonization, it is not something that can be remembered as such. Paradoxically, what can and ought to be remembered are the failures of decolonization to materialize, the contexts in which these failures took place, and their contemporary social consequences. Within the changing global dynamics of the world after formal decolonization, it also necessitates a rereading or a re-remembering of the modern colonial experience. This would include a "retrospective rephrasing of Modernity within the framework of globalization in all its various ruptural forms and moments" (ibid, p. 250), from the slavery formation of the Americas to the current transnational marketizations of the globe. We need to refuse the formal decolonizing distinction between metropolises and former colonies, as well as that "between colonization as a system of rule, of power and exploitation, and colonization as a system of knowledge and representation" (ibid, p. 254). At the very least this requires that we rethink the politics of the postcolonial present in terms of how ethically we "re-member" the decolonized past.[21]

By the end of the twentieth century the sparse public commemorations of slavery in the West were articulated through either abolitionist, curatorial, or aesthetic invocations of memory. These, despite their differences, tended to shore-up the liberal rights traditions of political modernity, thereby valorizing the cosmopolitan sociality of contemporary Western societies. Yet, the style of remembering evoked, tied through historicism to a moral vindication of Western civilization, ironically supplies the point of departure for distinguishing a radical postcolonial form of remembering. It may be argued that conventional Western styles of remembering slavery exhibit an obsession with what Gilles Delueze (1994) describes (in a different context) as "empirical memory." Immersed in the idealization of direct experience, empirical memory "is addressed to those things which can and must be grasped: what is recalled must have been seen, heard, imagined or thought" (ibid, p. 140). Remembering slavery in this way is confined to a racialized form of a "possessive individualism" (Macpherson 1964), the self-ownership of a debilitating psychological legacy, ascribed racially. Through a historically positioned racialized embodiment, the black subject remembers slavery through trauma and the white subject remembers it through guilt. Empirical memory, however, is also entwined with an "empirical forgetting" (Delueze, 1994). What is forgotten by empirical memory is deemed to be beyond the experience of memory as such. It cannot be recalled, it is in effect lost to memory: "forgetting has effaced or separated us from the memory" (ibid, p. 140). We can think of the effacements effected by "forgetting" within the empirical memory of slavery in at least four related ways. Firstly, the constitutive relation between Atlantic slavery, "race," and racism is recurrently "forgotten." Secondly, the modern location of plantation slavery within the theater of distinct European imperial formations is conveniently effaced. Thirdly, the historical recurrence and impact of black anti-slavery movements, particularly symbolized by the Haitian Revolution, the only successful slave revolt in recorded history, is erased almost absolutely. Fourthly, the idea of the plantation complex as an early modern exemplar of globalizing capitalist barbarities is eclipsed by the narratives of nationalist horror stories and white abolitionist heroes. These all too easily obscure the diverse competitive European involvement and the diaspora of ethnically diverse Africans across the whole of the Americas.

While accepting that within the empirical memory of slavery the mobilization of the category of "experience" is clearly "productive of a certain kind of insight" (Wood 1999, p. 112), its limits, demarcations, and effacements suggest a cultural economy of remembering that cannot be reduced to "experience." Because empirical memory has established the traditions of remembering slavery in the West, it fails to ask, because it cannot conceive of doing so, "what does it mean to forget slavery in the here and now?" Or, to put this slightly differently, what are its conditions of possibility? Turning to Deleuze (1994) again, we may refer to this as the problem of "transcendental memory." Directed towards the forgetting in empirical memory, it signifies only that which can be recalled in the *first instance*; it is unrelated to direct experience, "it does not address memory without addressing the forgetting within memory" (ibid, p. 140). In this sense, a transcendental memory of slavery makes explicit the cultural economy of effacements established in empirical memory. Not only does it highlight what is "shaping the essence of our experience," of remembering slavery "rather than being experienced as such" (Hobson 1998, p. 28), it invites a questioning of the relation between what is forgotten and what is remembered.

What remains forgotten by the triumph of liberal democracy in the West, even in the act of its remembering slavery, is the colonial, foundational relation of slavery to the modern constitution of *racialized governmentalities*. By this I am referring to the political formations of "race" and racism (cf. Goldberg 1993) which inscribed the written and unwritten constitutions of social relations of governance and dominant forms of cultural representation in Western societies. This continues in the post-slavery and postcolonial eras to animate the administration of the state, the conduct of civil subjects, and their regulation of the conduct of "others" (Hesse 1997). It therefore raises a very different context for the memory of slavery than we have considered so far. Racism emphasizes the continuing "existence of past injustice and the continued memory of that injustice, raises the question of the rectification of injustices" (Connerton 1989, p. 9). It is here that we can begin to see how the transcendental dimension of memory is also its ethical dimension. The latter outlines the basis of what Paul Ricouer (1999) describes as a "duty to remember." Ricouer suggests the "ethical question of memory" resides in asking how "do we make the past visible, as if it were the present, while acknowledging our debt to the past as it actually happened" (ibid, p. 10). To ask in our current contemporaneity whether slavery is best forgotten or best remembered is now a question of the ethics of postcolonial memory. It means we have to address the "problem of evolving a culture of just memory" (ibid, p. 11).

What I call postcolonial memory takes the form of a critical excavation and inventory of the marginalized, discounted, unrealized objects of decolonization and the political consequences of their social legacies. When we survey the prevalence of one of these social legacies, racism in the West, remembering rather than forgetting its relationship to the meaning of Atlantic slavery cannot be addressed within the terms of abolitionist, curatorial, or aesthetic memories. The ethics of postcolonial memory concerns itself less with the historical "wrongs" of the colonial question than with interrupted and incomplete forms of decolonization and their relation to contemporary social constructions of injustice/justice. In this precise sense, postcolonial memory in the West is not concerned with the (colonial) past through an obsession with the past, but through an engagement with the (liberal–democratic) present. In the West to remember in a postcolonial idiom is to encounter or confront the (liberal–democratic) contemporaneity in terms of what has constituted its (imperial) history. It is triggered by an awareness of the discontinuities of decolonization and global justice and continuities of racism and global inequalities. Not all history can be remembered in this way. Nor does the remembering of the past depend on how long passed that past is or has become. In postcolonial memory it is the memory of present predicaments that recalls the dislocations of the past. In the ethics of postcolonial memory, remembering slavery can no more be experienced than generations of racism can be experienced. It is less a structure of feeling than a passionate intervention. The *oughtness* of Atlantic slavery's memory and the justness of its excavation reside in refusing to efface through forgetfulness the historical complicity and contemporary failures of Western liberal democracies. It is this which foregrounds the passage from ethics to politics, rather than the reverse.[22]

Acknowledgments

I would like to cite my appreciation for helpful comments and observations from Bobby Sayyid, Tania Mason, David Theo Goldberg, David Okuefuna, and Dionne Gravesande.

Notes

1 Although I do not address Toni Morrison's novel *Beloved* (1987, p. 274), the problematics of remembering slavery configured in that text do represent something of a point of departure for this essay.

2 The idea for filming the *Amistad* incident originated in 1984 when producer Debbie Allen optioned the screen rights to William Owen's 1953 book, *Black Mutiny* (a telling title!). Allen was reportedly outraged that the *Amistad* affair was not more generally known. After seeing Spielberg's *Schindler's List* she approached him with the idea to tell the story from the "Africans" point of view, centering on slave leader Sengbe Pieh, renamed "Cinque" by his captors' (Taylor 1999). Prior to its release, *Amistad* was the subject of an unsuccessful lawsuit for plagiarism by historical novelist Barbara Chase-Riboud. The film was released to American audiences in December 1997 (British audiences in February, 1998). Having been budgeted around $75 million, it was not a commercial success. It grossed only $31 million in five weeks, slightly less that its advertising costs (Taylor 1999). Leaving aside box office criteria, of broad concern to critics have been questions of historical inaccuracies (e.g., Davis 2000) and exoticism (e.g., Rogin 1998). Unfortunately, these important commentaries overlook the relation between slavery, "race," and racism ignored by the film and hence by the commentaries themselves. Also, while the film itself occasionally referred to the larger "Atlantic" dimension of slavery through the Spanish connection, evoked by the term "Amistad," both the film and commentaries associated with it tend to depict slavery as an exclusive US experience. In this essay I have variously used the term "racial slavery" to convey the sense in which slavery also instituted "race" as a category defining the polarized European (white) and "non-European" (black) proprietary positions in relations of governance. At the same time when I refer to "Atlantic slavery" I have in mind a globalizing formation, one which does *not* privilege the US experience, but renders the latter as part of competitive European exploitations in the context of a diaspora of African enslavement strewn across the whole of the Americas.

3 The idea that historically the *Amistad* decision had a significant impact on the eventual abolition of slavery in the US seems now to be an established part of a liberal memorial tradition. It is unclear how any of this can now be sustained. If left unexamined now the claims made for the *Amistad* decision can wander into the realms of the fantasy. Consider the following: "The *Amistad* decision constitutes an historic milestone in the long struggle against slavery and for the establishment of basic civil rights for everyone regardless of color" (Jones 1988, p. 219). There is no evidence for this, although it is clear it has become remembered in this way as part of a narrative tradition. Unlike the Somerset decision in 1772, issued by Lord Chief Justice Mansfield in England, which ruled that a slave absconding in England could not be compelled by his/her master to be sold abroad, the *Amistad* decision had no such

general application. The Somerset decision has subsequently been wrapped in the myth that absconding slaves ceased to be slaves in England, though it too hardly sounded the last rites of slavery as a lawful institution (see Walvin 1993). Nevertheless, it was something that could be used to the political advantage of runaway slaves. This is not something that can be shown for the *Amistad* decision.

4   Houston Baker, Jr. suggests *critical* memory "judges severely, censures righteously, renders hard ethical evaluations of the past that it never defines as well-passed." In addition he argues it has a political role in the "cumulative, collective maintenance of a record that draws into relationship significant instants of time past and the always uprooted homelessness of now" (Baker 1995, p. 7).

5   As well as selectively invoking the memories of the enslaved, the slave narrative could also be seen as a symbolic commodity, which commemorated the ethos of (white) abolitionism. As commodities for popular consumption slave narratives were not immune to the "abuses of ritualized commemorations" (Ricouer 1999, p. 9), since their very success provided an "excess" of commemoration, which all too readily inserted the memory of slavery in a "reverential relationship" (ibid) to the narrower range of remembering invoked by the traditions of (white) abolitionism.

6   Throughout the Americas the institution of slavery enacted laws and regulations against slaves running away, transgressions were punished severely, the harboring of runaway slaves was a criminal offense, while mobile slaves were required to carry passes (Walvin 1993). In the United States draconian fugitive slave acts were passed by Congress in 1793 and 1850 in efforts to regulate, police, and impede the movement of runaways (Conniff and Davis 1994; Robinson 1997).

7   Fredrick Douglas, the most acclaimed ex-slave and black abolitionist of the nineteenth century, probably exerted more control over the production of his slave narrative, particularly in its writing, than any other fugitive slave in the United States. He should not therefore be regarded as typical of the slave narrative experience (see Andrews 1996; Sundquist 1990).

8   It is important not to conceive the so-called "fugitive slave" in individualist or strictly masculine terms, or as an occasional event. This was a social movement of resistance to enslavement. Although younger men predominated, all ages, men and women, were involved individually as well as in groups. The context for this is also important. What was known as the "Underground Railroad" described a secret system of routes and safe houses between the southern and northern states negotiated by guides, which facilitated the escape of thousands of slaves. Between 1830 and 1860 about 40,000 slaves escaped this way. Harriet Tubman, a fugitive slave herself, the most famous black guide, made 19 journeys south and led over 300 slaves to freedom. She was a "wanted" woman: slaveholders offered $40,000 for her capture dead or alive (Everett 1996; Robinson 1997). Of course, in the rest of the Americas where the landscape and racial demography were different, runaways were more often able to establish their own independent communities. For example, these were known as "maroons" in Jamaica, "Palenques" in Mexico, and "Quilombos" in Brazil (see Robinson 1997, Campbell 1990; Segal 1995).

9   Maggie Montesinos Sale (1997) provides an impressive analysis of the political and discursive strategies framing the significance of the *Amistad* affair (and also the *Creole*: see below). Sale particularly draws attention to the newspaper and pamphlet frenzy that surrounded the whole episode. Part of what made the *Amistad* so significant was its extensive media coverage, especially in an age when news or information on black anti-slavery resistances was generally suppressed. What

perhaps galvanized the white media interest was an anthropological fascination with the exoticized Africans, the importation of enslaved Africans having been outlawed by Congress in 1808. Indeed, Sale reports that during the two years of incarceration the *Amistad* Africans became something of an exhibit. They were visited by over 4,000 US Americans. At the same time there was considerable interest among the non-citizen African Americans, both in their newspaper coverage and personally. As suggested by James W. C. Pennington's involvement, such an interest in the Africans brought together a political desire for justice and a cultural identification with African heritage and history.

10 It is worth pointing out something of the emergent political culture amongst African Americans in the North during the second third of the nineteenth century. The period 1830–65 has been described as the time of the most "militant and aggressive 'abolitionist crusade'" (Lowance 2000). There is a tendency, however, in popular mythology to view the abolitionist movement, particularly its literature, as springing from liberal white Americans. This ignores a cross-cultural formation, in which two sometimes distinct, sometimes complementary, sometimes divergent, groups were engaged. The first and generally fêted in historical memorializations were white abolitionists like William Lloyd Garrison, John Brown, Lydia Maria Child, and Harriet Beecher Stowe. The second, less celebrated group comprised African Americans like Fredrick Douglas, Sojourner Truth, Harriet Tubman, and David Walker (Lowance 2000). In relation to the latter, of early significance was the publication in 1829 of David Walker's *Appeal to the colored citizens of the world but in particular and very expressly, to those of the United States of America.* Walker's *Appeal* was an indictment of both slavery and racial oppression. It represented a powerful political call to arms among African American *men* and the circulation of the pamphlet was greatly feared among southern slaveholders. As the first authored, sustained challenge by an African American to slavery and white supremacy in the United states, it made Walker a wanted man (see Sale 1997, pp. 49–54). Its uncompromising yet insightful language berated any acquiescence of black people to a system that degraded them. It also extended to a critique of the hypocrisies of liberal–democratic culture in the US and a critical awareness of the Western imperial system. James Turner (1993, p. 14) has suggested a "well-organized movement for the abolition of slavery did not exist before Walker's publication." Walker's mysterious death, a year after the publication of the *Appeal,* has been attributed to a political murder (Turner 1993; Sale 1997).

11 What concerns me here is not so much the masculine, heroic representations of these revolts (see Sale 1997), but rather the political and discursive differences in their respective historical representations. Such factors underline why the *Amistad* is remembered and the *Creole* is forgotten.

12 For a more detailed analysis of the *Creole* revolt, see Sale (1997) and Sundquist (1994).

13 I want to suggest that to think of memory in Jacques Derrida's terms of "undecidability" is to break with the idea of memory as something always calculable, as if directed towards something waiting to be remembered, or its object as something immutable, always remembered, or always remembered in the same way. In the undecidable sense memory is not instinctive or repetitive, it is certainly not a tradition. It comprises the outcome of "decisions" taken in relation to conflicting, diverse, and uncertain claims for interpretations of the past in the *act* of

remembering. As the past is not always where it was or in the form that it was, the decision (e.g., cultural practices, political deliberations, personal reminiscences) to remember also determines the line between what is "remembered" and what is "forgotten." This is not a line that is given; it has to be constituted. On Derrida and "undecidability" see Laclau (1996).

14   Although this essay is partly concerned with the "Amistad"/*Amistad* as a histori-cal, literary, and cinematic trope in remembering slavery, it is perhaps worth emphasizing the importance of recognizing that Atlantic slavery was a globalizing complex of institutions. Consequently, racial slavery was as extensive in the trans-formation of societies in South America (e.g., Brazil) and the Caribbean, as it was in the US (cf. Trouillot 1995). The memory of slavery now needs to be as "global" as it is "local" (cf. Mignolo 2000).

15   As Wood (2000) has observed, part of the problem of exhibiting the memory of slavery in museums, as evidenced in Hull and Liverpool in the UK, is the merchandising and packaging of the "experience." As a link in wider relations of packaged "experiences" (cinema, amusement parks, shopping malls), remembering slavery now appears as just another option for things to do on vacation.

16   What concerns me here is the conceptual status and meaning of Wood's desire to "get beyond race." However laudable it may sound, it leaves what is left of the memory of slavery with no contemporary relation to the formative culture of racism in Western societies.

17   Wood seems to employ a Kantian notion of aesthetic judgment. Distinct from cog-nitive judgments, which aspire towards "objective" status, aesthetic judgments of taste are subjective, although like cognitive judgments they are expected to be universally valid. Aesthetic judgments concern either the beautiful or the sublime; the latter refers to catastrophic events or climatic phenomena that overwhelm the imagination, appearing unrepresentable (Lash 1999). Wood clearly sees the memory of slavery as part of the sublime. Such judgments, however, presuppose a *sensus communis*, a unified sense of interpretive community drawing upon uni-versal ideas of reason. However, such a community of "commonsense" has to be created, it cannot be done through the voluntaristic act of indivual imagination; paradoxically, it is constituted through a shared aesthetic judgment (Cascardi 1999). Wood's only indication of an interpretive community is one bound by feel-ings of guilt. Of course, this excludes from the notion of community the descen-dants of the enslaved Africans.

18   I introduce the concept of "de/colonial fantasy" to capture the sense in which impeded, distorted, and unrealized forms of decolonization inside and outside the West have been transformed (through "fantasy"; see Žižek 1989) into signifiers of its actualization.

19   The *Observer*, January 21, 2001, p. 19.

20   It may well be that we are currently experiencing through increasing globalization the expansion and proliferation of multicultural/global cities in the West, distinct from the nationalisms of Western nations.

21   The idea of re-membering or "re-memory" in Toni Morrison's (1987) *Beloved* sug-gests all the senses of being gripped, or ensnared, or haunted by the past in negotiating the present. See also Henderson (1991).

22   It has recently been suggested that the turn to ethical matters may constitute a rejection of politics (see Garber, Hanssen, and Walkowitz 2000). The argument pre-

sented here does not conform to the object of that critique. In beginning with the ethical it sees the passage from ethics to politics as analogous to the "move from responsibility to questioning" (Critchley 1992, p. 220).

References

Andrews, W. L. (1996) *Fredrick Douglas: Reader*. New York: Oxford University Press.

Amin, S. (1989) *Eurocentrism*, London: Zed Books.

Aravamudan, S. (1999) *Tropicopolitans: Colonialism and Agency 1688–1804*. Durham, NC: Duke University Press.

Baker, H. (1995) "Critical Memory and the Black Public Sphere" in the Black Public Sphere Collective, ed., *The Black Public Sphere*, Chicago: University of Chicago Press.

Beckles, H. (1991) "Caribbean Anti-Slavery: The Self Liberation Ethos of Enslaved Blacks" in Beckles, H. and Shepherd, V., eds., *Caribbean Slave Society and Economy*. London: James Currey.

Bethel, E. (1997) *The Roots of African-American Identity: Memory and History in Antebellum Free Communities*. New York: St. Martin's Press.

Betts, R. F. (1998) *Decolonization*. London: Routledge.

Bhabha, H. (1994) *The Location of Culture*. London: Routledge.

Blackburn, R. (1997) *The Making of New World Slavery: From the Baroque to the Modern, 1492–1800*. London: Verso.

Blassingame, J. W. (1985) "Using the Testimony of Ex-slaves: Approaches and Problems" in Davis, C. T. and Gates, H. L., eds., *The Slave's Narrative*. New York: Routledge.

Cable, M. (1977) *Black Odyssey: The Case of the Slave Ship Amistad*. London: Penguin Books.

Campbell, M. (1990) *The Maroons of Jamaica 1655–1796*. Totowa, NJ: Africa World Press.

Cascardi, A. J. (1999) *Consequences of Enlightenment*. Cambridge: Cambridge University Press.

Cesaire, A. (1972) *Discourse on Colonialism*. New York: Monthly Review Press.

Chamberlain, M. E. (1999) *Decolonization*. Oxford: Blackwell Publishers.

Connerton, P. (1989) *How Societies Remember*. Cambridge: Cambridge University Press.

Conniff, M. and Davis, T. (1994) *Africans in the Americas: A History of the Black Diaspora*. New York: St. Martin's Press.

Critchley, S. (1992) *The Ethics of Deconstruction: Derrida and Levinas*. Oxford: Blackwell Publishers.

Curtin, P. (1990) *The Rise and Fall of the Plantation Complex: Essays in Atlantic History*. New York: Cambridge University Press.

Davis, C. T. and Gates, H. L. eds. (1985) *The Slave's Narrative*. New York: Oxford University Press.

Davis, D. B. (1988) *The Problem of Slavery in Western Culture*. New York: Oxford University Press.

Davis, N. Z. (2000) *Slaves on the Screen: Film and Historical Vision*. Toronto: Vintage Canada.

Dayan, J. (1998) *Haiti, History and the Gods*. Berkeley: University of California Press.

Delueze, G. (1994) *Difference and Repetition*. London: Athlone Press.

Du Bois, W. E. B. (1935) [1995] *Black Reconstruction in America 1860–1880*. New York: Touchstone.

Everett, S. (1996) *History of Slavery*. London: Grange Books.

Fanon, F. (1963) *Wretched of the Earth*. London: Penguin Books.

Gates, H. L. ed. (1987) *The Classic Slave Narratives*. New York: Mentor Books.

Garber, M., Hanssen, B., and Walkowitz, R. L. eds. (2000) *The Turn to Ethics*. New York: Routledge.

Geggus, D. (1989) "The Haitian Revolution" in Knight, F. W. and Palmer, C. A., eds., *The Modern Caribbean*. Chapel Hill: University of North Carolina Press.

Glissant, E. (1989) *Caribbean Discourse*. Charlottesville: University of Virginia Press.

Goldberg, D. (1993) *Racist Culture: Philosophy and the Politics of Meaning*. Oxford: Blackwell Publishers.

Guerrero, E. (1993) *Framing Blackness: The African American Image in Film*. Philadelphia: Temple University Press.

Habermas, J. (1987) *The Philosophical Discourse Modernity*. Cambridge: Polity Press.

Hall, S. (1991) "The Local and the Global: Globalization and Ethnicity" in King, A. D., ed., *Culture, Globalization and the World System*. New York: Macmillan.

——(1992) "The West and the Rest: Discourse and Power" in Hall, S. and Gieben, B., eds., *Formations of Modernity*. Cambridge: Polity Press/Open University Press.

——(1996) "When was the post-colonial?" in Chambers, I. and Curti, L., eds., *The Post-Colonial Question*. London: Routledge.

——(2000) "The Multicultural Question" in Hesse, B., ed., *Un/settled Multiculturalisms: Diasporas, Entanglements, Transruptions*. London: Zed Books.

Henderson, M. G. (1991) "Toni Morrison's *Beloved*: Re-Membering the Body as Historical Text" in Spillers, H. J., ed., *Comparative Identities: Race, Sex and Nationality in the Modern Text*. New York: Routledge.

Hesse, B. (1997) "White Governmentality: Urbanism, Nationalism, Racism" in Westwood, S. and Williams, J., eds., *Imagining Cities: Signs, Scripts, Memory*. London: Routledge.

——(2000a) "Diasporicity: Black Britain's Postcolonial Formations" in Hesse, B., ed., *Un/settled Multiculturalisms: Diasporas, Entanglements, Transruptions*. London: Zed Books.

——(2000b) "Un/settled Multiculturalisms" in Hesse, B., ed., *Un/settled Multiculturalisms: Diasporas, Entanglements, Transruptions*. London: Zed Books.

Higginbotham, A. L. (1978) *"In the Matter of Color": Race and the American Legal Process in the Colonial Period*. New York: Oxford University Press.

Hobson, M. (1998) *Jacques Derrida: Opening Lines*. London: Routledge.

Hutton, P. (1993) *History as an Art of Memory*. Hanover: University of Vermont.

Jones, H. (1988) *Mutiny on the Amistad*. New York: Oxford University Press.

Laclau, E. (1996) "Deconstruction, Pragmatism, Hegemony" in Mouffe, C., ed., *Deconstruction and Pragmatism*. London: Routledge.

Lash, S. (1999) *Another Modernity, a Different Rationality*. Oxford: Blackwell Publishers.

Le Goff, J. (1992) *History and Memory*. New York: Columbia University Press.

Loomba, A. (1998) *Colonialism/Postcolonialism*. London: Routledge.

Lowance, M. ed. (2000) *Against Slavery: An Abolitionist Reader*. New York: Penguin Books.

Lubiano, W. (1995) "Don't Talk with Your Eyes Closed: Caught in the Hollywood Gun Sights" in Henderson, M., ed., *Borders, Boundaries and Frames: Cultural Criticism and Cultural Studies*. New York: Routledge.

Macpherson, C. B. (1964) *Possessive Individualism*. Oxford: Oxford University Press.

Mehta, U. S. (1999) *Liberalism and Empire: A Study in Nineteenth Century British Liberal Thought*. Chicago: University of Chicago Press.

Mignolo, W. D. (2000) *Coloniality, Subaltern Knowledges and Border Thinking*. Princeton, NJ: Princeton University Press.

Morrison, T. (1987) *Beloved*. London: Picador.

——(1990) "The Site of Memory" in Ferguson, R., Gever, M., Minh-ha, T. T., and West, C., eds., *Out There: Marginalization and Contemporary Cultures*. London: MIT Press.

——(1992) *Playing in the Dark: Whiteness and the Literary Imagination*. Cambridge, MA: Harvard University Press.

Mullin, M. (1994) *Africa in America: Slave Acculturation and Resistance in the American South and the British Caribbean, 1736–1831*. Chicago: University of Illinois Press.

Onley, J. (1985) "'I was born': Slave Narratives, their Status as Autobiography and as Literature" in Davis, C. T. and Gates, H. L., eds., *The Slave's Narrative*. New York: New York University Press.

Otto, D. (1999) "Subalternity and International Law: The Problems of Global Community and the Incommensurability of Difference" in Darian-Smith, E. and Fitzpatrick, P., eds., *Laws of the Postcolonial*. Ann Arbor: University of Michigan Press.

Pagden, A. (1995) *Lords of All the World: Ideologies in Spain, Britain and France c.1500–c.1800*. New Haven, CT: Yale University Press.

Pieterse, J. N. (1994) "Unpacking the West: How European is Europe" in Rattansi, A. and Westwood, S., eds., *Racism, Modernity and Identity*. Cambridge: Polity Press.

Ricouer, P. (1999) "Memory and Forgetting" in Kearney, R. and Dooley, M., eds., *Questioning Ethics: Contemporary Debates in Philosophy*. London: Routledge.

Robertson, D. (1999) *Denmark Vesey: The Buried History of America's Largest Slave Rebellion and the Man who Led It*. New York: Alfred A. Knopf.

Robinson, C. J. (1997) *Black Movements in America*. New York: Routledge.

Rogin, M. (1998) "Spielberg's List", *New Left Review*, no. 230, July/August.

Said, E. (1993) *Culture and Imperialism*. New York: Vintage Books.

Sale, M. (1997) *"The Slumbering Volcano": American Slave Ship Revolts and the Production of Rebellious Masculinity*. Durham, NC: Duke University Press.

Sayyid, B. (1997) *A Fundamental Fear: Eurocentrism and the Emergence of Islamism*. London: Zed Books.

Scott, D. (1999) *Refashioning Futures: Criticism After Postcoloniality*. Princeton, NJ: Princeton University Press.

Segal, R. (1995) *The Black Diaspora*. London: Faber and Faber.

Snead, J. (1994) *White Screens, Black Images: Hollywood from the Dark* Side. New York: Routledge.

Solow, B. ed. (1991) *Slavery and the Rise of the Atlantic Slavery*. Cambridge: Cambridge University Press.

Sundquist, E. J. (1990) *Fredrick Douglas: New Literary and Historical Essays*. Cambridge: Cambridge University Press.

——(1994) *To Wake the Nations: Race in the Making of American Literature*. Cambridge, MA: Harvard University Press.

Taylor, P. M. (1999) *Stephen Spielberg: The Man, his Movies and their Meaning*. London: B.T. Batsford.

Thomas, H. (1997) *The Slave Trade: The History of the Atlantic Slave Trade, 1440–1870*. London: Picador.

Triulzi, A. (1996) "African Cities, Historical Memory and Street Buzz" in Chambers, I. and Curti, L., eds., *The Post-colonial Question*. London: Routledge.

Trouillot, M.-R. (1995) *Silencing the Past: Power and the Production of History*. Boston: Beacon Press.

Turner, J. (1993) *David Walker's Appeal*. Baltimore, MD: Black Classic Press.

Walvin, J. (1993) *Black Ivory: A History of British Slavery*. London: Fontana Press.

Wood, D. (1999) "The Experience of the Ethical" in Kearney, R. and Dooley, M., eds., *Questioning Ethics: Contemporary Debates in Philosophy*. London: Routledge.

Wood, M. (2000) *Blind Memory: Visual Representations of Slavery in England and America 1780–1865*. New York: Routledge.

Žižek, S. (1989) *The Sublime Object of Ideology*. London: Verso.

Chapter 9

Connectivity and the Fate of the Unconnected

Olu Oguibe

As we cruise on the ether of staggeringly rapid advancements in science and technology, especially information technology, cultural practitioners are challenged in innumerable ways to articulate our moment in history, as well as define their own place and vision as creative individuals in relation to these developments. Today, information technology has become the backbone of social and cultural interaction on a global scale, spurning social codes as well as political, economic, and cultural imperatives beyond the farthest reaches of prior predictions. As a result, new forms of artistic and broad cultural expression are emerging, some of them built around new opportunities for the convergence of science and culture, on the one hand, and of diverse polities and cultures, on the other. Alongside these are other forms and strategies concerned with the mass media potentials of new information technology, and its abilities to traverse traditional confines and broach new and previously unimagined frontiers. In certain respects it could be said that humankind is headed for that "unified language for the multiverse of cultures" that Marshall McLuhan predicted for the information age (McLuhan 1953, pp. 117–27).

From its own intricate history of evolutions between the late 1960s and the present, a dominant strand of this technology has emerged in the form of the Internet, an amalgam of networked information systems that today connects several million users and producers of digitized information around the world. This elaborate global, electronic architecture, with its vast numbers of "content" providers and consumers, also offers real-time interactivity across vast geographical expanses, enabling individuals to engage in instantaneously reciprocal exchange on a level that is not replicable in other media. In his day, McLuhan had observed the endearing intimacy of the microphone and its unique ability to empower the individual pitched against the vast arena of mass communication networks. Such intimacy is amplified several times over for privileged participants in this new digital network or Net by their ability to reach incomparably more recipients and correspondents, but even more especially by their ability to engage in simultaneous, interactive conversation on a scale that was unimaginable two decades ago. The Internet has become the voice rediscovered; speech visualized and magnified for the electronic age.

When the digital network emerged from the confines of its origins in Cold War military counter-intelligence and paranoia and began to enter the public domain, the fervor of its elevation to a mass media was summarized in a very popular epithet by one of its earliest propagators, Nicholas Negroponte. The epithet was "simply connect." Intended or not, this little injunction and other like rhetoric nevertheless created the impression that all it took to become part of the new information age, and to partake in its possibilities for communication and exchange, was to up and connect. Just as quickly, a new rhetoric of advocacy whirled up, creating in its wake an exponentially growing body of literature that in the main affirmed, as indeed it continues to, the exhilarating potentials of the new medium. In time, however, we have come to acknowledge that the requisites of entry into this network involve a little more than simply connecting. Many now recognize that connectivity carries with it a string of conditionalities, and in order to connect, the average individual must meet these conditionalities, most of which many are ill-disposed to fulfill.[1]

Perhaps more important, we have also come to acknowledge that a gulf has emerged between those who belong within the network and are thus able to partake of its numerous advantages,[2] and those who are unable to fulfill the conditionalities of connectivity. It is increasingly evident that as we connect, we become part of a new ethnoscape,[3] what one might call a netscape or cyberscape, where information and individuals circulate and bond into a new community. And as this community broadens in spread and significance, we are effectively implicated in the relativization[4] of the rest who remain on the outside of its borders. Inconsequential as it might seem, this situation nevertheless has broad cultural implications, not only for individuals and groups already in the network, but even more so for those others who exist on the outside.

For one, populations on the outside are effectively excluded from the myriad conversations taking place in this enclave of power and privilege, some of which have significant bearings on or consequences for their condition or well being. As a result, the Network often breeds representation within itself, on behalf of such polities. By default, it readily locates or fabricates voices within who assume the authority to speak for the Other since, quite often, parties and individuals are not in short supply who would ride on the event to appoint and delegate themselves as representatives of the absent. Today such individuals and groups abound across the capillaries and nodes of the Net. They include lone campaigners and makeshift pressure groups, organizations of concerned friends and self-appointed revolutionaries, messianic figures coming to the rescue of the helpless, anarchists in search of preoccupation and activists left over from failed causes eager to find new ones that might assuage their passion to serve. Sometimes, there is a genuine purpose behind these acts of self-delegation. At other times the driving passion fails to rise above a self-righteous desire to attract attention or find prominence through such acts of supposed good intention. Often there is little or no contact, communication, consultation, or mechanism for reciprocal exchange between such delegate voices and the constituencies that they elect to speak for on the Net. Like free agents, they inhabit the nooks and crannies of the Net and engage in innumerable activities and negotiations on behalf of groups and cultures who are essentially unable to deny or withdraw the authority that such representatives appoint unto themselves. Whatever the intents or contexts are, humanitarian or otherwise, certain very crucial questions are raised, nevertheless, other than merely the ethics of representation.[5] Among them is the issue of the apparent vulnerability of the unconnected. Within the vast territories of the Net, populations on the outside obviously do not possess the privilege of agency because they can neither speak on their own behalf nor are they able to exercise control over the dynamics and dialectics of the Network. While they may and indeed do have agency within their own spaces and lives as a critical attribute of their existence, this agency is however impacted on when a new force such as the Net emerges with the ability to encroach upon that space.[6] With its enormous capabilities as an emergent global, social system, one is forced to ask: might the Network perhaps further disfranchise or incapacitate these populations already battling their way out from under the avalanche of progress and its debatable consequences, by moving the posts of modernity even as they struggle to grapple with it? Has the Network made it easier for entities and individuals privileged to possess its empowering devices, to displace such populations by appropriating their voices and purloining their identities in an arena from which they are effectively debarred? Given the relative ease with which participants in the Network can generate and disseminate information, sometimes on a bewilderingly vast scale, has this medium entrusted some of us with the power to fabricate and disseminate possibly fictive and potentially injurious constructs and narratives of the Other to the rest of the world, when such populations have no equally enabling devices to encounter, evaluate, critique, challenge, or seek to invalidate images and representations of their selves and their state of being? If the Net empowers us to possess the voice or invent the narrative of the absent, does it not by so doing also enable us to scar her body?

A recent case from outside cyberspace may indeed illustrate quite cogently the dangers that this power of self-delegation portends. In April 1996 a white South African artist and curator staged an exhibition at the South African National Gallery on the history and material culture of the Khoisan, one of the country's indigenous peoples. The largely ethnographic exhibition, which featured mostly archival images and documents on European colonial assault on and near extermination of the Khoisan, nevertheless involved strategies of construction and realization that caused offense to the group. After viewing the exhibition, a representative forum of the group, the Griqua National Conference, denounced the exhibition, describing it as a "questionable and active contribution to furthering the marginalization of the first nations of Southern Africa" (*Weekly Mail & Guardian*, April 19, 1996). While pointing out the curator's failure to consult the group, and the absence of Khoisan participation in what was an exposition of and about them, the forum condemned "non-indigenous people's persistence in hijacking and exposing our past for their own absolution". Another forum of the Khoisan, the Hurikamma Cultural Movement, equally condemned the exhibition as "yet another attempt to treat brown people as objects" (ibid).

A considerable body of literature already exists on the debacle related here (see Enwezor 1977). As a demonstration of the importance of agency on the part of the represented, the critical response and intervention of the Khoisan succinctly defined and positioned the event itself, as well as erased the authority to represent, which the curator arguably had involuntarily appropriated unto herself. This crucial intervention was possible only because the group was aware of the exhibition in question, had access to it, and therefore the opportunity to witness, engage, and evaluate it. Let us imagine a like situation where, contrary to these conditions, the discourse in question is staged on the Network, in a virtual gallery, for instance, or a net-forum, or worse still in any of the several thousand limited-access fora now operating on the Net. Further, let us imagine that the group whose bodies and history are paraded, is also unconnected. Let us imagine that they have no route to the information disseminated on and about them, supposedly on their behalf or in their perceived best interest. Not only would they have no opportunity to engage that information, worse still, they would have no way to register, as the Khoisan most forcefully did, their disapproval and disdain.

In effect the digital Network provides a new corridor of infringement and trespass which the infringed may not always be privileged to broach. Within this corridor, opportunities abound for misfeasance, even maleficence. With such rampant and unbridled possibilities at the disposal of the networked, is it the case, perhaps, that the unconnected are set up for digital violation?[7]

Today the Network is not only a powerful ethnoscape, it has also become a formidable knowledge system. Its repositories of information are complemented by the ready accessibility of content providers, experts, and quacks. Once ensconced in the intricate relays, addictions, and cushions of the Network, many increasingly rely upon it for information and knowledge of the world beyond their own door. Information gathered on the Net becomes our readiest access to other cultures and sections of society as it inveigles us in the lazy preoccupation of going through its own portals of voices and informants for our knowledge of the unconnected. More often than not, despite voiced skepticism, such information is taken by many at its face value. Indeed, the truth-value of information gathered from the Net is reinforced rather misleadingly by its essentially textual proclivity and in turn by the fact of the text's historical and scriptural association with truth, especially in the West.[8] Today many are quick to cite information from the Net as authoritative, but even more disturbing, they are quick to turn to it rather than look outdoors. With this in mind, one cannot but wonder, should the Network continue to displace other knowledge systems as it seems bound to, should its participant-citizens continue to tune in to it as their *a priori* source of information, especially on those who are considered otherwise remote and inaccessible because they are unconnected, might it not become a barrier instead of a bridge? Might it not preclude proper and meaningful contact and exchange, by encouraging the false notion that we know the Other and that that Other is in fact part of the new global community that we take for granted? Might it not impede rather than facilitate our reach for genuine interaction across social and cultural divides by creating simulacral rather than real contact and exchange? In the end, might the Net not come between us and the Other we do not know?[9]

Not to be ignored is the fact that the global information infrastructure has become perhaps the most significant mechanism for the ongoing process of globalization. If traditionally we understood this process to comprise principally the dissemination and imposition of Western culture and cultural products around the world, we must now also factor in a reverse flow in the form of the possession and uploading of goods from beyond the perimeters of the West. In other words, it is valid now to speak of a truly global circulation of cultures and cultural products. The Network in all its forms and manifestations is a formidable channel for this global traffic. It is estimated that US$327 billion worth of goods will be exchanged via the Internet alone by the year 2003.[10] With trade occurring through other global communication networks factored in, this statistic rises to an even more astronomical figure. Of the goods and services involved in this global trade, an increasingly substantial portion consists of cultural products, especially objects of material culture. This, too, has its implications for populations on the outside of the Network.

First, for as long as they are unable to gain entry into the Network, such populations are effectively debarred from exercising control over any significant aspects of this traffic, never mind that a sizeable portion of the goods circulating in this trade is obtained or purloined from within their territories. In the absence of any such participatory agency, not only are they relegated in the hierarchy of transactions, they are also increasingly precluded from any substantial part of the proceeds from their own material culture. Even more disturbing is the fact that as the accessibility of these products becomes more apparent, so does the desire grow to locate, acquire, and circulate them without significant involvement of those on the outside. So does the desire to obtain and own them without the traditional encumbrance of physical travel and transportation.

For instance, the number of Internet sites dedicated to the market in African art objects has exploded from single digits a few years ago to several hundred in the past year. Some of the objects traded on this network marketplace are of little historical value. Others are of immense cultural and historical import, and often these are obtained illicitly. It is tempting to think that the open platform on which a good deal of this exchange now occurs would improve the chances of monitoring illicit trade in cultural products. But this is not the case. On the contrary, through the numerous secret passages which the Net provides, dealers and collectors are even more able to trade in objects, exchange information, or hatch conspiracies aimed at further depleting the material cultures of Africa, which are then tunneled into private collections especially in the West.

On a philosophical level, we are faced with the advent of an exponential desire and readiness to locate and consume the Other in the form of material and visual symbols, without the moral or social responsibilities contingent on a physical encounter with that Other. Entire worlds, geographical and corporeal, are opened up for the privileged to explore and possibly purloin and ravage without once having to leave the comfort of their home–office or confront the possible ramifications of their adventures.

On purely social and material levels, this desire to locate and consume that is facilitated by the Network exposes such populations to the unscrupulous machinations of traders desperate to satiate a growing demand. In effect, unwitting peoples whose material cultures service this demand are made vulnerable to plunder, thanks to the driving machinery of a networked exchange system. Moreover, because of their exclusion from the system, they are left largely at the mercy of players in an intricate game outside their realms of comprehension or agency.

These are some of the realities which the Net constitutes for those who are unable simply to connect. Not only are they relegated to the outside of a powerful, global machinery, they are equally laid bare to the rapacious potentials of this machinery. A question then arises as to what can be done to correct or ameliorate this situation, and this is a question that must engage not only those who debate the merits and future of the Net, but those who propagate expansion of the Network society, also. We began this brief exploration by observing that the global digital network has become an inescapable part of the machine of progress at the millennium. It is the logical conclusion to a century of relentless assaults on the fort of knowledge and the frontiers of possibility. Whatever its demerits, it is nevertheless irreversible. We also observed ways in which cultural practitioners may put it to use, indicating that it may not be approached only as a system to loathe or condemn. Indeed, for those who are already situated within it, its myriad possibilities make it a most endearing facility for survival in a new age. To contend with the realities outlined above, therefore, we may look in only two directions.

The first is to encourage a different kind of activism within the Network itself, an activism which aims to engender a culture of sensitivity and responsibility within the Net. There is a nascent if inchoate morality already developing in the Network, and this could be extended to include awareness of and a conscionable relationship with those who are on the outside. This is an area where artists and other cultural practitioners could play a useful role corollary to their tradition in regular society. Nor do they need to inject a certain criticality into their own practice with regard to the place and fate of the unconnected; they could also help to raise the awareness advocated here across the platform of the Network.

Additionally, though the issue of regulations within the Net remains moot, even incendiary, it is valid to suggest that the Network, like any other community, be subject to a level of enforceable regulation to protect individual freedoms within and outside its constituencies. Such a social apparatus recommends itself most especially on the evidence that the ethics of individual self-regulation most favored by the Network community has not worked, and cannot possibly sustain so vast and variegated a human system. The idea of the Net as a sacred corridor of limitless freedom is not only ludicrous but dangerous, also, as its history amply and cogently demonstrates.[11] A combination of cultural and political work, and a negotiable modicum of statutory regulation, is needed in order to reverse the predatory proclivities of the Network.

The second, inevitable challenge is to engage those sociopolitical, cultural, and technological strategies that will bring a greater proportion of humanity into the new, global community of the networked. In the few years since a discourse began to develop around the implications and prospects of connectivity, especially as it relates to the unconnected, it has become customary for some to pose it against supposedly more pressing concerns such as global hunger, deprivation, and disease. However, this rhetoric of invented priorities is a mistake, insofar as it fails to acknowledge that these conditions are not implacable, but only testimonies to a global lack of will to address easily containable blotches on our claims of progress. It is beyond dispute that we already possess the means and technological know-how to provide food, literacy, and global network access to the majority of humanity without necessarily prioritizing one above the other. And we will need to apply that wherewithal to those tasks. As long as some remain outside the burgeoning new world which the Network has introduced, and as long as the balance of power is in favor of this new world, it is impossible to achieve that "unified global field of awareness" which McLuhan once called for (McLuhan 1963, pp. 41–4). Ultimately, we will have to contend with not simply the possibility or viability but the necessity of a more cohesive digital age whose fundamental technologies are at the service and disposal of the greater majority.

Acknowledgment

I would like to mention my indebtedness to Jordan Crandall, Gilane Tawadros, and Scan Cubitt who read this essay in the making and offered very useful advice, and to the staff and residents of the Rockefeller Study and Conference Center in Bellagio, Italy, where the essay was conceived and written.

Notes

1   In "Forsaken Geographies: Cyberspace and the New World 'Other'" I demonstrate that the social and material contexts of non-connectivity transcend traditional geopolitical delineation and may just as easily be found in the highly industrialized nations as in the so-called Third World. See Oguibe (1998).

2   What William Gibson calls "legitimate operators" in his 1984 sci-fi novel *Neuromancer*.

3   In his work on modernities, Arjun Appadurai makes a distinction between what he terms mediascapes or arenas for the circulation of information, and ethnoscapes or spheres where individuals circulate. However, the arena of the Network functions not simply as a platform for the circulation of information or signs but as a place for the circulation of individuals and the formation of new ethnicities also, hence my preference for the term "ethnoscape." See Appadurai (1996).

4   Malcolm Waters argues that in a globalized culture, different and disparate ethnicities and communities are forced to position and define themselves in relation to one another within a unified, global configuration. What differentiates this relationship from that which exists between the Network and the unconnected is that they are not unified into a singular, global configuration, and as the Network becomes a dominant force in global power-relations and exchange, and as individuals turn to it more and more for validation and a sense of belonging in the post-global age, the less visible, less powerful world of the unconnected is relegated and forced to define itself, or be defined, on the outside and beneath this dominant ethnoscape.

5   Quite interestingly, while cultural activists and advocates of the Net are quick to point to "successful" representations of less privileged communities on the Network, such as Commandant Marcos's use of the Net to globalize the cause of the indigenous people of Chiapas, Mexico, what is rarely broached is under what moral authority such representations are made, and what ethical questions are raised by salvage ventures such as the Chiapas campaign and Commandant Marcos's Guevarian messianism among the indigenous people. Some might want to draw a line between the Marcos Net campaign and the declaration of war against Iraq and China in July 1998 by an American hackers' group known as the Legion of the Underground (LoU). According to LoU, their plan to hack into and destroy the communications infrastructure of these two countries was in support of human rights and victims of human rights violations. It took the critical intervention of seven other hackers' groups to discourage LoU in its self-delegated mission by pointing out that this kind of cultural or political activism on the Net (now known as hacktivism), when taken to irresponsible extremes, could have unintended but devastating consequences on innocent victims. In the case of Iraq such an attack could have paralyzed what is left of the country's already beleaguered public health system, leading to the deaths of hundreds of women, men, and children. Yet the fundamental principle is not particularly different, namely, assumption of the right to represent or self-delegate on behalf of a group – in this case the supposedly oppressed masses of Iraq and China – without consultation or consent.

6 In "Desiring the Involuntary" Jonathan L. Beller writes about "involuntary forces" possessing the ability to "break the integrity of the subject," an expression that most aptly describes the potential impact of the Network on the inherent agency or subjectivity of individuals and communities who cannot connect. See Beller (1996).

7 Though we cannot possibly deal here with all the numerous other examples of this situation, one may point out quickly that such violations are perhaps most evident with one of the most powerful enterprises on the Network, pornography. A good deal of the pornographic material traded or exchanged on the Net belongs to a category known as "user posts," some of which comprise genuine images of unsuspecting individuals photographed in private or compromising circumstances and transmitted on the Net. Sometimes pooled under "voyeurism," many of these are obtained through discreet mini-cameras planted in such unlikely places as the floors of public elevators or in public conveniences to capture compromising images of unsuspecting victims. There is no gainsaying the gender bias in this pre-occupation. Often, too, the market for paedophilic images is serviced by such devices. Again, the unconnected are more vulnerable since they have no means whatsoever to detect such infringements on their person. The fundamental ethical problem of encroachment on individual privacy that these practices raise does not in any particulars differ from that raised by another practice which is equally enabled by the Network. Here I mean the invasive use of web-cams in new media art where artists photograph or video-record unsuspecting individuals on street corners, public transit terminals, even public conveniences, and transmit the images on the web. Though some may consider it moot, it is my contention nevertheless that such practices may not be excused on grounds of creative license.

8 For a brief investigation of the persistence of the literary or textual mindset in general approaches to hypertext and cyberspace, see Michel A. Moos's (1997) reading of Marshall McLuhan, "McLuhan's Language."

9 Of course, physical contact and exchange in themselves may not constitute guarantees against the violation of the Other, as history indicates. However, it seems to me particularly frightening that the very concreteness of such contact, its shortcomings and uncertainties notwithstanding, should be replaced by severance and withdrawal into the virtuality of symbols, of signs taken for wonders. One may also point out that in those historical instances when contact bred tragedy rather than understanding – slavery, colonialism, the conquest and decimation of first nations – there was little exchange in evidence, the same absence of exchange that increasingly characterizes the relationship of the networked to the unconnected.

10 This figure is credited to Oliver Smoot of the Information Technology Industry Council (ITI).

11 In "Imaginary Homes, Imagined Loyalties: A Brief Reflection on the Uncertainty of Geographies" (1996), I appear to question any breaches of freedom on the information superhighway (the Network). However, the specific object of my reservation in the essay is the transfer of traditional geophysical or national borders that breach the interzonal essence of the Net, or statutory interventions that infringe conventional freedoms. The idea of the Net as a free-for-all, no man's land is of course as unrealistic as it is repugnant.

References

Appadurai, A. (1996) *Modernity at Large: Cultural Dimensions of Globalization*. Minneapolis: University of Minnesota Press.

Beller, J. L. (1996) "Desiring the Involuntary" in R. Wilson and W. Dissanayake, eds., *Global/Local*. Durham, NC: Duke University Press.

Enwezor, E. (1977) "Reframing the Black Subject," *Third Text*, 40: 21–40.

McLuhan, M. (1953) "Culture without Literacy" in *Explorations: Studies in Culture and Communication 1*. Toronto: University of Toronto Press, pp. 117–27.

——(1963) "The Agent Bite of Outwit," *Location*, 1: 1, 41–4.

Moos, M. M. (1997) "McLuhan's Language" in M. M. Moos, ed., *Media Research: Technology, Art, Communication*. London: Gordon and Breach.

Oguibe, O. (1996) "Imaginary Homes, Imagined Loyalties: A Brief Reflection on the Uncertainty of Geographies" in O. Zaya and A. Michelsen, eds., *Interzones: A Work in Progress*. Regensburg: Taba Press.

——(1998) "Forsaken Geographies: Cyberspace and the New World 'Other'" in M. Keen, ed., *Frequencies: Investigations into Culture, History and Technology*. London: Institute for International Visual Arts.

Chapter 10

Towards (Re)Conciliation: The Postcolonial Economy of Giving

Pal Ahluwalia

Everyone knows that a place exists which is not economically or politically indebted to all the vileness and compromise. That is not obliged to reproduce the system. That is writing. If there is a somewhere else that can escape the infernal repetition, it lies in that direction, where it writes itself, where it dreams, where it invents new worlds.

Hélène Cixous

In his book *Africa in Chaos* George Ayittey writes how Keith Richburg, the African-American journalist, appalled by the Rwandan and other African crises, was tormented emotionally and moved to write *Out of America: A Black Man Confronts Africa.* Ayittey narrates the events at a book launch in Virginia, where Richburg

> concluded that he was glad to be an 'American' and the designation 'African-American' was meaningless – devoid of content. Perhaps the slave traders did him a favour by shipping his ancestors out of Africa in slave ships for America. (Ayittey 1998, p. xiii)

As one would expect, the audience which Ayittey reports was about 40 per cent black did not share Richburg's sentiments. Ayittey also notes his own disgust at the images of the Rwandan genocide:

> I could say that one television scene probably did more to smash my African dignity and pride than 200 years of colonialism, but *non-African* blacks would probably misinterpret that statement. (Ibid., p. xiv; my emphasis)

It is precisely the images of the Rwandan genocide by which I was also appalled. As an African whose parents migrated to North America, and as somebody who now lives in Australia, it was difficult to fathom how such inhumanity and cruelty could be inflicted by one group of people upon another. In order to understand this process, in 1995 I spent nearly six months in Rwanda and the former Zaire. It quickly became clear to me that it was not African but human dignity that was at stake. This was all the more so because of the commitment of the world community in the aftermath of the Jewish Holocaust that never again would there be another genocide. The roots of the Rwandan tragedy, I discovered, are located firmly in the continent's colonial past, as well as its postcolonial present (Ahluwalia 1997).

The stance adopted by both Richburg and Ayittey is part of the general rise of Afro-pessimism. It is hardly a new revelation that Africa is in crisis. The 'African crisis' has been recorded, reported, analysed and widely discussed for more than a decade (Leys 1994, 1996; Mamdani 1996b; Davidson 1992; Rush and Szeftel 1994; Chabal and Daloz 1999). Patrick Chabal provides a good summary capturing the extent of the crisis by categorizing it into four distinct but interrelated factors:

> an acute economic crisis, political instability, the so called 're-traditionalization' of African societies, and the marginalization of Africa on the international scene. (Chabal 1996, p. 29)

The African crisis feeds into the prevailing representations of both Africa and Africans as part of the 'dark continent' – primordial, tribal, violent, unable to feed itself and with a permanent begging bowl in hand. If the power of representation in earlier centuries led to the colonization of Africa by Europeans who embodied the civilizing mission, in the closing stages of the millennium there are echoing calls for the recolonization of the continent (Pfaff 1995; Mazrui 1994, 1997; Helman and Ratner 1992).

The ascendancy of Afro-pessimism, of which this type of thinking is representative, has a tendency to homogenize the 'African tragedy', concluding that Africa has neither the political will nor the capacity to deal with its problems. The African condition, it is claimed, is largely of Africa's own making and therefore there is little or no hope for improvement. Afro-pessimism resonates in metropolitan centres where both former colonial powers and the United States, in the aftermath of the Cold War, are seeking ways to disengage themselves from Africa. This is a convenient way for the West to wash its hands of a problem largely of its own making.

This does not mean that Africans and in particular their leadership can be absolved of the responsibility for the African crisis. Rather, it entails a recognition of the manner in which the cultures of both the colonizer and the colonized are deeply intertwined and implicated and that they are a product of colonialism and its continuing legacy. As Robert Young has observed, both have a responsibility:

The means of administration may have often moved from coercive regiments
to regimes supported by international aid and the banking system, the 'white
man's burden' may have been transformed by the wind of change into the
TV appeal for famine in Africa. But the burden of neocolonialism remains for
all those who suffer its effects; and responsibility cannot be ignored by those who
find themselves part of those societies which enforce it. (Young 1991,
p. 3)

The notion of shared responsibility is an important one, for it marks its
distance from a 'rhetoric of blame'. What is called for is a different mode of
analysis.

The Uncanny and Postcolonial Sites

It is in this context that three postcolonial sites, Australia, Palestine and
Rwanda, are examined here through the notion of the uncanny. This notion
is derived from Freud's 1919 essay entitled 'The Uncanny'. Homi Bhabha
points out that the notion of the uncanny double emerges in Freud's exposition of psychic ambivalence. As Bhabha explains:

For the uncanny lesson of the double, as a problem of intellectual uncertainty,
lies precisely in its double-inscription. The authority of culture, in the modern
episteme, requires at once incitation and identification. Culture is *heimlich*, with its
disciplinary generalizations, its mimetic narratives, its homologous empty time,
its seriality, its progress, its customs and coherence. But cultural authority is also
unheimlich, for to be distinctive, significatory, influential and identifiable, it has to
be translated, disseminated, differentiated, interdisciplinary, intertextual, international, inter-racial. (Bhabha 1993, pp. 136–7)

It is this double inscription which the uncanny portrays – the combination of
the familiar and the unfamiliar at the same time – that is extremely useful.
This notion is captivating precisely because it illustrates the manner in which
the differing identities within each nation-state appear familiar and strange at
the same time. In the case of Rwanda, for example, the uncanny can be seen
in the manner in which both the Hutu and Tutsi appear to be so familiar –
they speak the same language, share a common culture and religion – yet they
are so different in the way in which they construct their identities. The coexistence of the familiar and the unfamiliar is particularly pertinent to postcolonial situations where 'one remains within the structures of colonialism even
as one is somehow located beyond them or "after" them' (Gelder and Jacobs
1998, p. 24). It is important to examine different and diverse political sites such
as Australia, Palestine and Rwanda in order to understand the complexities,
divergences and differences across postcolonial locations and yet still to note
the uncanny similarity which characterizes all three postcolonial societies. It is
through such a reading of these diverse locations that it is possible to reflect

on the particular crisis in Africa and to learn from the shared experience of postcoloniality.

Australia

In 1992 Australia's highest judicial body overturned in a ruling the founding myth of *terra nullius* upon which the modern nation had been built. The decision was a response to the case mounted on behalf of a Torres Strait Islander group by Eddie Mabo who claimed that his native title had not been extinguished and that consequently the group he represented retained proprietary rights over their land. In deciding in favour of Mabo, the court went much further than most expected, ruling that Aboriginal Australians had, and as such, retained native title interests in the land. The High Court ruled that in those cases where the state had not explicitly extinguished native title, the indigenous population had, and retained, title as long as they maintained the traditional customs, beliefs and practices which allowed them to maintain their separate Aboriginal identity. The Mabo case triggered a process of recognition of the dispossession and marginalization of Aboriginal peoples. The then prime minister, Paul Keating, embarked upon reconstructing the nation around the imaginary of a shamed and redeemed nation by recognizing that Aboriginal people had been wronged. But as Elizabeth Povinelli has observed:

> The potential radical alterity of indigenous beliefs, practices, and social organiza-tion was not addressed. Instead the court decision and the public discourse sur-rounding it urged dominant society on a journey to its own redemption, leaning heavily on the unarguable rightness of striving for the Good and for a national reparation and reconciliation. (Povinelli 1998, p. 587)

If in the aftermath of the Mabo decision there was an appearance of progress, there was equally a backlash led by the National Farmers' Federation and the mining industry, who argued that their land and industry was under threat from Aboriginal claims. Furthermore, in a scare campaign, they suggested that even suburban Australia (which was clearly excluded in the decision) could be subjected to land claims and that everyone's back yard was insecure. At the very time that indigenous Australians were seen to be gaining some ground, it was those who had marginalized and dispossessed them the most – large-scale farming interests and the mining industry – who claimed that they were the victims. These debates were being played out when the Labor government lost the 1996 election and John Howard's Liberal Party took over the reins of power. The election of a conservative government unleashed a backlash not only against Aboriginal peoples but against the notion of a multicultural Australia which had been fostered by the Labor government.

It is important to question why such a backlash occurred at this time. Was it a mere response to the Keating government's stance on indigenous questions as well as Australia's position in the Asian region – one which envisioned an Australia whose future prosperity and security would be linked inextricably to the Asia-Pacific region? Clearly, Keating was reflecting the reality of a globalized world in which cultures are increasingly hybrid. However, it was this stance that notably was challenged by John Howard, who proclaimed that Australia was unquestionably European. The backlash manifested itself also in the political programme of Pauline Hanson, the Federal Member for Oxley, who subsequently formed her own political party, One Nation. Hanson claimed to be the spokesperson of a disaffected 'mainstream' Australia that was being rampaged by Aboriginals and multiculturalism. This reassertion of the mainstream evoked by Hanson had much in common with Howard and his views about culture. Jon Stratton points out that both Hanson and Howard

> believe that the official government policy of multiculturalism threatens the unity of Australian society by undermining the homogeneity of the Australian culture which provides the basis for that unity. (Stratton 1998, p. 14)

Pauline Hanson's use of emotive language, vitriolic exaggeration and spurious argument were strategic weapons designed to create an 'other' – Aboriginal and multicultural – against which mainstream Australia needed to defend itself. It is in this context that John Howard's position was untenable. His refusal to denounce Pauline Hanson unequivocally left little doubt that he sought a reassertion of the mainstream that he imagined had been eroded by the Keating government (Ahluwalia and McCarthy 1998).

These examples illustrate the uncanny. At the very time when Anglo-European Australia appeared to be shedding its racist past by dealing with the indigenous population, it was more interested in self-redemption and atoning for its sins. Although proclaiming the dawn of a new era characterized by the recognition of Aboriginal people, it sought simultaneously to draw the indigenous population within its own unmistakably Anglo-European liberal referents. All the indigenous people could do was once again react to a discourse defined by their protagonists, those who had pursued a policy of obliteration and assimilation. In order to retain the status they had legally gained, Aboriginal peoples had to do this within the confines of proving their authenticity, their very Aboriginality which once again was mired in conceptions of race and identity formation reminiscent of the nineteenth century. In an uncanny manner, the structures of colonialism reappeared at the very time that a post-colonial moment of reconciliation was being inaugurated.

Palestine

Over the last five decades relations between Israel and Palestine often have resulted in violent conflict. The major periods of conflict can be witnessed in the 1948 War of Independence, the Six Day War in 1967, the 1982 war in

Lebanon and the *Intifada* which erupted in 1987 (Gazit 1998; Beinin 1998; Lieberfeld 1999). In addition, both sides – for the want of a better term – have engaged in acts of 'terrorism'. Edward Said points out that the 'question' of Palestine is how to understand 'the contest between an affirmation and a denial', a contest that is well over a hundred years old. This entails shaping history 'so that this history now *appears* to confirm the validity of the Zionist claims to Palestine, thereby denigrating Palestinian claims' (Said 1980, p. 8).

The 1948 War of Independence that led to the displacement and dispossession of the Palestinian people can be traced to the recommendation of partition by a British Commission. The British played a key role in Palestine as part of the League of Nations mandatory system (United Nations 1988). In this sense, the processes leading to the formation of Israel have been equated to a process of colonization. However, this colonization was not simply a matter of establishing a settler class for whose benefit an indigenous population could be mobilized. Rather, it was a project which entailed displacing the Palestinians as well as creating a state which was the state of all Jewish people with a 'kind of sovereignty over land and peoples that no other state possessed or possesses' (Said 1980, p. 84).

Since that time, Palestinians have resorted to various campaigns, often violent, to exercise their right to self-determination. It was not until the *Intifada* began in December 1987, a movement that can be equated with some of the great acts of anti-colonial resistance, that public opinion shifted, as a result of the images aired on television screens in the West, of the Israeli soldiers killing Palestinians. The initiative seized by the *Intifada*, however, was lost, in part by the PLO's support for Iraq during the Gulf War. Nevertheless, Israel's vulnerability – demonstrated by the Iraqi scud attacks as well as by changed domestic conditions with a large proportion of the Israeli population advocating peace in the aftermath of the Gulf War – meant that Middle East peace was negotiated with a much-diminished role for the PLO in the actual negotiations (Beinin 1998). Within Israel, there were increasing pressures for the establishment of a successful European secular state without the twin pressures of Zionist traditionalism and Palestinian suppression. That process finally concluded with the accession to power of a Labour government that was able to reach agreement over limited Palestinian autonomy and the signing of a Declaration of Principles (DOP), commonly called the Oslo Peace Accord. This accord assumed ill-defined parameters relegating Palestinian demands for sovereignty and territory to final talks (Said 1994a). Joel Beinin has summarized the major forces that led to the DOP. It was a way of maintaining US hegemony in the region, regional Israeli dominance, the political and diplomatic isolation of the PLO in the wake of the Gulf War, as well as of allaying Arafat's fear of being marginalized in the occupied territories. In addition, the signing of the DOP was aided by Israel's failure to conclude a peace treaty with Syria over the Golan Heights, as well as by the Israeli elite's adoption of a neoliberal vision of a secular and capitalist market economy (Beinin 1998). The peace process, however, stalled because of the intransigence of Benjamin

Netanyahu's Likud Party that defeated the Labour party on the issue of Israel's security. Although Labour once again has regained power with a clear majority following last year's elections, it is too early to predict what this new government will achieve. Nevertheless, it is important to note that Prime Minister Barak committed himself to resuming the stalled peace process.

Palestine demonstrates a number of paradoxes that illustrate the notion of the uncanny. It is a postcolonial nation where the imperial power, Britain, was able only to recommend the very strategy that it deployed in India, namely, partition. In the process, the group of people who had been subjected to perhaps one of the greatest tragedies of the twentieth century came to occupy the mantle of power and reproduced the very practices of colonialism that sought to marginalize and dispossess the Palestinian people. In an uncanny manner, the victims become the perpetrators, thereby blocking the narratives of the Palestinian people. It is in this context that the Palestinian demand for the 'permission to narrate' has been undertaken increasingly by Israel and the US. While the Oslo Accord may have signalled a departure and fundamental shift in policy for some, including Yassir Arafat, there is for critics such as Said no atonement of past injustices, no remorse for the Palestinian losses or dispossession, but an indefinite relegation of the Palestinians to the occupied territories. There is no acknowledgement of the millions of Palestinians outside these areas who continue to remain in exile. Again, the uncanny can be witnessed in the manner in which the Palestinian leadership under Yassir Arafat, after a long and arduous process, simply accepts the colonial solution of separate states. In essence, it was the colonial solution of partition, albeit with considerably diminished conditions, that Arafat accepted. Here again we can see that, at the very dawn of the postcolonial moment, the structures of colonialism reappear uncannily.

Rwanda

Rwanda, in 1962, gained independence from Belgium, which had ruled the country since 1916 as a mandate of the League of Nations. The colonial administrations, German[1] and later Belgian, ruled through the existing order which can be delineated roughly in ethnic terms: with a Tutsi minority at the top with a *Mwami* or King, and a large Hutu majority at the bottom. In addition, there was a very small Twa population, stereotyped as 'pygmies', who were seen to be irrelevant to the dominant political order.

In Rwanda and Burundi, although the Tutsi dominated the Hutu, there was considerable evidence of peaceful coexistence. As Davidson points out:

> the manner of this nineteenth-century dominance was mild, and was regulated by 'lord and vassal' relationships . . . 'The rich man in his castle, the poor man at his gate' appear to have been the outward and visible forms of a mutually acceptable relationship between Tutsi and Hutu; at least in principle these forms represented an agreed sharing of rights and duties. (Davidson 1992, p. 249)

Clearly, there were certain commonalities which gave precolonial Rwandan society some coherence and basis for organization that allowed it to exist with some order. This order was altered fundamentally with colonization. The colonial powers, the Germans and the Belgians, disrupted the balance that existed. They compartmentalized the Tutsi and Hutu on explicitly racist assumptions whereby the Tutsi were considered to be more intelligent because they appeared to be 'more European'. By utilizing such racist assumptions, Rwanda was administered through the Tutsi monarchy and an elaborate system of chiefs. The Tutsi were privileged in every aspect of the colonial state. What the colonizers failed to recognize was that the differences between the two groups were not marked: they spoke the same language, practised the same religion and shared the same culture. The colonial policy of 'divide and rule', however, ossified and heightened differences that fundamentally altered the manner in which the two groups viewed each other. As Alain Destexhe has noted, the Belgians 'passed on the notion of ethnic difference to the Rwandans themselves' (Destexhe 1994, p. 6; see also Hunt 1990; Mamdani 1996a).

The decolonization project that aimed to devolve political power to the Rwandese was hampered by the death of the *Mwami* in 1959, which in turn sparked bloody Hutu uprisings against the Tutsi minority.[2] In the light of such violence, the pre-independence elections of 1961 resulted in the electoral victory of the Hutu Emancipation Movement, commonly known as the Parmehutu. In short, at independence, Rwanda's traditional political order was transformed with a Hutu-dominated government, led by Gregoire Kayibana as President.

The virtually identical ethnic mix prevalent within Rwanda and neighbouring Burundi has meant that the ethnic tensions and politics in the two countries are linked inextricably. There has been a pattern whereby violent events in one country are mirrored by reprisal killings in the other. The events have been described by a Burundi priest as 'double genocide' (Nursey-Bray and Ahluwalia 1994; Lemarchand 1994). In September 1990 Rwanda again faced confrontation between the Hutu and the Tutsi. This time, the violent confrontation was sparked by the invasion of Ugandan-based, mainly Tutsi exiles of the Rwanda Patriotic Front (RPF) (Mamdani 1996a). The RPF sought to topple the Habyarimana government, claiming that it operated a policy of discrimination against the Tutsi. The government's efforts to quell the outbreak of violence and suppress the RPF were not as effective as in the past when it had dealt successfully and brutally with opposition. Between 1990 and 1994 there were numerous attempts to end the war and to embark upon a project of democratization. On both counts, little progress was made due to Habyarimana's intransigence. The deaths of the presidents of Rwanda and Burundi, Juvenal Habyarimana and Cyprien Ntaryamira, in 1994 as a result of a rocket attack on the plane that was returning them from a peace summit in Tanzania provided the catalyst which sparked inter-communal violence that culminated in genocide. This genocide witnessed the killing of over a million people as well as the fleeing of over 2 million people into neighbouring countries.

The most pressing issue arising out of the Rwandan genocide is to bring those involved in the genocide to trial. Given the large numbers of people involved, this is no easy task. Currently, Rwandan prisons are overcrowded with more than 100,000 prisoners awaiting trial in prisons designed to accommodate less than 20,000 people. An elaborate classification system for crimes during the genocide has been devised (Zarembo 1997). And yet progress remains slow, as it does in the special UN international criminal tribunal for Rwanda located in Arusha, Tanzania. In both Rwanda and Arusha justice has been slowed not only by an ineffective bureaucratic system, but also by the enormous difficulty of securing testimony from witnesses. In addition, the war in the Democratic Republic of Congo and the reformulation of Hutu paramilitary organizations mean that not only is Rwanda in a particularly precarious position but the entire Great Lakes region has been destabilized. The RPF government that came to power in 1994 urged the refugees to return, advocated tolerance, coexistence and respect for human rights. It was a government that gained considerable international admiration for its stance. However, four years on, that admiration has been gradually eroded as many international observers and agencies realize that the new regime has come to resemble its predecessor. As Samantha Power has noted:

> the government has locked up tens of thousands of Hutu without explanation, harassed its political opponents, and expressed little public remorse about massacring civilians while ferreting Hutu rebels. (Power 1998, p. 16)

Despite the uneasiness of international human rights organizations, European and American governments have provided the Rwandan government with unprecedented aid and President Clinton paid a visit to Rwanda announcing further assistance.

In Rwanda we can again see the notion of the uncanny at work where the minority Tutsi and majority Hutu community, that coexisted prior to colonialism, have been rendered separate and incompatible by the processes of colonization. The end product of such a policy was that at independence the very modes and practices of governance were reversed with the triumph of the Hutu over the Tutsi aided by the colonial power. This was an uncanny process where the colonizer that had encouraged the dominance of the Tutsi simply reversed the prevailing order at the time of decolonization. More importantly, these identities were polarized into Hutu and Tutsi, identities which previously had been more fluid and which had allowed movement to occur from one to the other. In an uncanny manner, the very structures of colonialism continue to predominate within postcolonial Rwanda with the process of identity formation firmly locked into the representations and practices once ascribed by the colonial power. Hence, for a people inseparable in terms of culture, language and religion, it is the colonial identity card that above all becomes the signifier of difference. It is through this process that Rwanda's postcolonial history has oscillated like a pendulum between the oppressor and the oppressed.

Trauma

The effects of the uncanny can be highlighted through the suffering that people endure and the traumatic reaction that inevitably results. But traumatic recall is not merely a simple memory, for it is a process that cannot be subjected to conscious recall. The paradox of trauma is that it is an experience that is repeated after its forgetting and it is only through forgetting that it is experienced. In a sense, memory appears to repeat what it cannot understand. It is a process that Freud documented:

> [People] think the fact that the traumatic experience is forcing itself upon the patient is proof of the strength of the experience: the patient is, as one might say, fixated to his trauma . . . I am not aware, however, that patients suffering from traumatic neurosis are much occupied in their waking lives with memories of their accident. Perhaps they are more concerned with not thinking of it. (Freud 1920, p. 13)

Cathy Caruth has noted that the study and treatment of trauma is beleaguered by

> the problem of how to help relieve suffering, and how to understand the nature of the suffering, without eliminating the force and truth of reality trauma survivors face and quite often try to transmit. (Caruth 1995, p. vii)

The manner in which trauma is treated, by drugs or through the telling of stories, is one that Freud recognized as part of the cure, a mechanism through which the event can be eventually forgotten. To those who listen to the stories of the trauma, the task is to move beyond the 'truth' that is being told and to find a way to avoid the repetitions of traumatic suffering.

Although trauma is generally conceived as a phenomenon encountered by individuals, it is important to note that trauma has a social dimension and that it is possible to think of traumatized communities. Kai Erikson points out how trauma can become an important concept for social scientists:

> Sometimes the tissues of the community can be damaged in much the same way as the tissues of the mind and body . . . but even when that does not happen traumatic wounds inflicted on individuals can combine to create a mood, an ethos – a group culture, almost – that is different from (and more than) the sum of the private wounds that make it up. (Erikson 1995, p. 185)

It is this sense of shared trauma that galvanizes a community that serves as a source of commonality in which 'there is a spiritual kinship there, a sense of identity, even when feelings of affection are deadened and the ability to care numbed' (ibid., p. 186). In the context of events like the genocide in Rwanda, it is the community that has to act as the main locus for the sharing of pain, intimacy and tradition. Because the community itself is affected, it becomes possible to see that the community is damaged in a manner analogous to the individual damaged body. It is because of this sense of community damage that the healing has to take place at the level of the community. And it is through such cathartic undertakings as symbolic trials which deal with the genocide, which try to recollect the past, which provide a space for speaking and for the telling of stories, that the basis of a new 'imagined community' emanates from the abyss of the past. Nevertheless, it is important to move beyond recollecting the past, beyond the space of telling, and listening to different narratives. It is here that the notion of the gift is instructive.

The Gift

In his seminal study *The Gift*, Marcel Mauss examined the notion of gift-giving which, he argued, although seen to be a voluntary act, entails systems of repayment and obligation. His focus was on prestations which signified gifts given either freely or under obligation and could include not only material goods but also services, entertainment, courtesies, ritual, military assistance, women, children, dances and feasts (Mauss 1969, p. 3). This system of exchange between ethnic groups in which individuals and groups exchange everything was characterized by Mauss as total prestations and he called it 'potlatch'. He explained that

> Total prestation not only carries with it the obligation to repay gifts received, but it implies two others equally important: the obligation to give presents and the obligation to receive them. (Ibid., pp. 10–11)

The gift has clear implications in the 'primitive' societies he examined. It was meant to confer meaning and establish a complex system of exchange defining social, political, economic and cultural relations between different groups. It represented mechanisms through which a sense of stability and coexistence could be fostered. However, for Mauss, when reason is opposed to emotion, 'peoples succeed in substituting alliance, gift and commerce for war, isolation and stagnation' (ibid., p. 80). The squandering of fortunes during ritual was an important part of those societies because those who had excess wealth could not consume their wealth in private. In short, fortunes had to be 'wasted' but in the process it entailed the possibility of gaining status.

In his book *The Accursed Share* Georges Bataille, the theorist of expenditure as excess, is interested in examining aspects of human culture which cannot be reduced simply to the classical economic balance between production and consumption. Bataille seeks to illustrate the difficulties associated with viewing human existence in a mechanistic manner. He argues thus that the sun is an example of giving without receiving:

Solar energy is the source of life's exuberant development. The origin and essence of our wealth are given in the radiation of the sun, which dispenses energy – wealth – without any return. The sun gives without ever receiving. Men were conscious of this long before astro-physics measured that ceaseless prodigality; they saw it ripen the harvests and they associated its splendor with the act of someone who gives without receiving. (Bataille 1991, pp. 28–9)

By drawing on the analogy of the sun, Bataille examines the theory of the pot-latch, which Marcel Mauss had posited, arguing that the system of exchange did not necessarily entail reciprocity. For Bataille, the purpose of gift giving is not merely to receive gifts in return, but that through the act of giving there is an acquisition of power.

And this action that is brought to bear on others is precisely what constitutes the gift's power, which one acquires from the fact of losing. (Ibid., p. 70)

But the one who receives then feels obligated to return a gift, and in the process seeks to outdo the original gift-giver in order to obliterate the effect of obliga-tion. And yet, for Bataille, the ideal potlatch would be one that could not be repaid. It is this sense of spending and dissipation that determines and mea-sures wealth. He points out that the purpose of the potlatch is not simply reciprocity but the conferring of rank upon whomever has the last word. The potlatch thus should be seen as an example of the general economy where excess and luxury are the key defining aspects. The general economy is an economy without equilibrium, one characterized by loss and expenditure without return. In short, gift giving without the expectation of return within the principle of the general economy is a luxury – the excess that is necessary to keep the system in balance.

It is this notion of the gift that Hélène Cixous appropriates from Bataille. Much like the distinction which Bataille makes between the economy proper and the general economy, Cixous distinguishes between the Realm of the Proper and the Realm of the Gift, with the former equated to masculinity and the latter to femininity. For Cixous, then, there are two types of gift giving, the one masculine and the other feminine. The former is tied up in mecha-nisms of exchange with expectations of immediate return, whilst the latter is a form of giving without receiving. She points out:

Can one speak of another spending? Really, there is no 'free' gift. You never give something for nothing. But the difference lies in the way and how of the gift, in the values that the gesture of giving affirms, causes to circulate; in the type of profit the giver draws from the gift and the use to which he or she puts it. (Cixous and Clèment 1985, p. 87)

It is this differing conception of giving that Cixous argues is characteristic of an alternative feminine writing practice. It is a form of writing that breaks down binaries, rejects fixed categories, and recognizes the possibility of multiple identities and subjectivities that are plural and dynamic.

The Postcolonial Economy of Giving

The notion of the gift, I want to suggest, is one that is critical to the process of reconciliation within postcolonial societies. It is a notion that I seek to develop and understand through an elaboration of postcolonial theory. In other words, I wish to understand the manner in which postcolonial theory can be developed in order to facilitate reconciliation. Gift giving is a process that needs to be inculcated in order to break down the cycle of revenge which has come to characterize many postcolonial societies. It is a process of giving which does not entail a direct return, but rather one that can be manifested in postcolonial situations. It is in this context that I suggest that the gift be considered under the rubric of a postcolonial economy of giving. However, it is important to clarify what is meant here by the postcolonial and postcolonial theory.

In current debates, the 'post' in postcolonial no longer accepts the mere periodization of the 1970s debates that signalled a new era after decolonization. Rather, the postcolonial seeks to problematize the cultural interactions between both the colonized and the colonizers from the moment of colonization onwards. Such a reworking of the postcolonial means that the postcolonial condition is not universal, and cannot be generalized as a theory. As Bill Ashcroft notes:

> 'Postcolonial' does not mean 'after colonialism'. . . . It begins when the colonizers arrive and doesn't finish when they go home. In that sense, postcolonial analysis examines the full range of responses to colonialism. . . . All of these may exist in a single society, so the term 'postcolonial society' does not mean an historical left-over of colonialism, but a society continuously responding in all its myriad ways to the experience of colonial contact. (Ashcroft 1997)

A particularly important trope in postcolonial theory is the notion of binarism. If one looks at Western rationalism as a product of modernity and development as its social signifier, we begin to see how the notion of 'traditional' society is embedded deeply within imperial culture and the colonial imagination. Binarisms allow us to establish meaning by defining concepts in contradistinction to each other. Hence, when we look at reason or rationality, it can be juxtaposed to emotion or madness. What such binarisms suggest is that there are no positive terms in isolation, 'in language, there are only differences *without positive terms*' (De Saussure 1974, p. 120). Just as feminist theory has demonstrated that binarisms operate within Western patriarchal thought where reason is associated with masculinity and emotion and hysteria with femininity, there is a similar binarism that operates within developed and developing or First and Third World countries.

These binarisms are clearly in opposition, but more importantly they are unequal and hierarchical – replicating the master/slave relationship. This is precisely the kind of relationship Frantz Fanon captures in *The Wretched of the Earth*, where there are two opposed zones. First, there is the settler's town occupied by white people, which is a 'well-fed town, an easy-going town, its belly is always full of good things'. The other zone is the town of colonized people, 'a hungry town, starved of bread, of meat, of shoes, of coal, of light . . . a town of niggers and dirty arabs' (Fanon 1967, p. 30).

Fanon's example and the oppositions he deploys confirm the binary logic of imperialism which represents the way in which Western thought in general views the world. This is where postcolonial theory differs. It endeavours to break down the tyranny of imperial structures and binaries which seek to dominate the subject. In postcolonial formulations such dichotomies are no longer adequate. By seeking to disrupt imperial binarisms, postcolonial theory investigates the interstitial space arising out of the postcolonial condition that raises the possibility of an ambivalent and hybrid subjectivity. It is this that leads to the possibility of social transformation. This sense of agency makes the 'post' in postcolonial different from other post- formulations. An important dimension of such disruptions is that, while imperial binaries suggest a uni-linear movement of domination from colonizer to the colonized, postcolonialism opens up the possibility of movements in both directions.

Postcolonialism highlights this interaction between the colonizer and the colonized, and it is this interaction which underscores my analysis here. I deploy a postcolonial perspective in order to elucidate the complexities of the postcolonial condition. It is a process which recognizes that Africa has to deal with its past in order to understand its present and confront its future. This is where postcolonialism is instructive, as it does not degenerate into establishing binaries that ascribe a politics characterized by a 'rhetoric of blame'. How does one transcend this dividing line which so easily degenerates into a rhetoric of blame? It is through the evocation of a postcolonial economy of giving that such a question begins to be answered. The very idea of reconciliation can be found in the breaking down or examining of the etymological roots of the word. (Re)conciliation entails returning to a prior stage, a stage where there was conciliation. In each of the three postcolonial sites which we examined, this sense of conciliation was existent and it is because of this that it is possible to conceive of a postcolonial economy of giving which has the capacity of returning these societies to a new state of reconciliation. In each of the three sites, Australia, Palestine and Rwanda, it is colonialism which fundamentally alters the basis of society. It is colonialism that changed the very course of history. While some critics have questioned the efficacy of allowing colonialism such prominence within the very long histories marking these societies, it is important to recognize that colonialism fundamentally alters historical trajectories. More importantly, as postcolonialism has demonstrated, it is no longer possible to return to some essentialized precolonial conception, because the very act of colonization has a fundamentally rupturing effect. It is colonialism that breaks down conciliation and necessitates reconciliation. And it is here that postcolonialism is instructive, recognizing that it is possible to imagine both a reconciled present and future. It is in this act of reimagining that the gift occupies a key role. It is through the gift that the attendant cycle of revenge and counter-revenge can be broken. In the case of Africa, the phenomenon of founding fathers provides an important example of this process of gift giving.

Nelson Mandela and Jomo Kenyatta are two of a long list of founding fathers who the struggles against colonialism and the formation of nation states in Africa have produced (Ahluwalia 1996). In both instances, the narratives of nation and man elide to breathe life into the abstract social and political concept of nation. What founding fathers have been able to do is to bridge past and present, dignifying and affirming the postcolonial nation through their personification of the rightness of daring to struggle against colonial rule and the reality of self-determination.

These founding fathers come to represent the interpenetrating histories of the postcolonial struggles of the Sub-Saharan African nations. And here the relationship between the narratives of Kenyatta and Kenya and Mandela and South Africa are suggestive. They emerge from prison, not with a sense of revenge, but with the intention to break the cycle of revenge. In both cases, they are able to draw on all the decolonizations preceding them. They not only draw upon them but transform them. In each case, they come to symbolize the very space from which the nation can reimagine and reconstruct itself. It is this sense of transformation that becomes central to a postcolonial economy of giving. It is one recognizing that cultures are not static but dynamic and that they constantly appropriate from other cultures and, in the process, transform themselves. It is in this way that the postcolonial economy of giving seeks to break down the cycle of revenge. However, it cannot be limited to founding fathers, but it is one that has to be imbued within the organic intellectuals of societies and must be operationalized through a different conception of democratic citizenship.

The Role of Intellectuals, Citizenship and Subjectivity

In Edward Said's 1993 Reith Lectures, *Representations of the Intellectual*, the overarching theme is 'the public role of the intellectual as outsider, "amateur", and disturber of the status quo' (Said 1994b, p. x). Such a role necessitates that the intellectual tries to speak the truth to power. In identifying an intellectual, Said points out the distinction between traditional and organic intellectuals. It is with the latter that he identifies, claiming that

> organic intellectuals are actively involved in society, that is, they constantly struggle to change minds and expand markets . . . organic intellectuals are always on the move, on the make. (Ibid., p. 4)

Said's view of the intellectual can be discerned by an amalgamation of two diametrically opposed figures, Gramsci and Benda. He recognizes the realities of the existence of Gramsci's organic intellectuals in this postmodern, late imperial world but insists that such individuals cannot be submerged or rendered faceless as merely part of a particular class. Rather, the intellectual must be

> an individual endowed with a faculty for representing, embodying, articulating a message, a view, an attitude, philosophy or opinion to, as well as for, a public. (Ibid., p. 9)

There remains still the vexed question of nationality and nationalism, which is based on the creation of others. These representations are repeated to maintain a national identity. Said argues that the creation of the 'other' consolidates 'our' identity as 'beleaguered and at risk' (ibid., p. 24). The short answer for Said is 'never solidarity before criticism'. It is here that one has to be the outsider, the amateur and the disturber. The intellectual makes political choices to follow the difficult path. The modern organic intellectual's role, then, is to disrupt prevailing norms precisely because they are tied to nation which is always triumphalist, always in a position of authority, always exacting loyalty and subservience rather than intellectual investigation and re-examination (ibid., p. 27).

The intellectual, Said argues, is always faced with the problem of loyalty. There is no escape from this problem because all intellectuals belong to some community that has a particular identity. These questions of loyalty take us back to the kinds of political choices that intellectuals such as Fanon and Camus had to make in the Algerian War of Independence. It is because of such choices that Said is compelled to argue that 'an intellectual must speak out against that sort of gregariousness, and the personal cost be damned' (ibid., p. 33). In the essay 'Speaking Truth to Power' Said asks the basic questions for an intellectual: 'how does one speak truth? What truth? From whom and where?' (ibid., p. 65). Said wants the intellectual to push the boundaries, to reconcile his or her own identity with the reality of other identities, other peoples rather than dominating other cultures. It is this critical role organic intellectuals within postcolonial states must perform.

In his widely acclaimed book *Citizen and Subject* Mahmood Mamdani points out that the advent of colonization entailed differentiating between peoples in the colony. The movement of administrators and settlers to the colonies necessitated that these individuals were seen to be separate from the indigenous population. In this way, the former were accorded citizenship and certain rights while the latter were ascribed the status of subjecthood with none of the attendant rights enjoyed by citizens. It is a process, Mamdani claims, which has persisted after independence largely through the persistence of colonial administrative structures, particularly in the rural areas.

One might well begin by questioning what makes or who is a citizen and who is a subject? In Western political thought subjects are individuals who have consented to a sovereign's rule and who, by according that consent, have certain rights and obligations. It is on the basis of the relationship between the sovereign and the subject that a polity functions. The consent of the subject

> is thought to provide the sovereign with the *right* to govern, the attendant obligations of those subjects are supposed to provide the sovereign with the capacity to do so. (Hindess 1996, p. 13)

In response to the problematic of who comes after the subject, Etienne Balibar has responded forcefully: the citizen. The citizen, he notes, is that ' "nonsubject" who comes after the subject, and whose constitution and recognition put an end (in principle) to the subjection of the subject' (Balibar 1991, pp. 38–9). The claim that citizens succeed subjects is one that Balibar develops by questioning 'who is the subject of the prince? And who is the citizen who comes after the subject?' (ibid., p. 40). Citizenship in such a conceptualization is a kind of freedom rooted within certain rights and entitlements. Such a perspective shifts the debate that arises in questions of nationality and immigration based on querying 'Who are citizens?' to one fundamentally asking 'Who is *the* citizen?'

This distinction is far more useful than the binary between citizen and subject established by Mamdani. Within postcolonial sites – rent with violence, genocide and characterized by difference – notions of citizenship centred around questions of nationality and physical space alone are not enough. In the practice of everyday life for the majority of Africans, the notions of boundaries and borders have little meaning or relevance. Every day, people cross borders in many parts of Africa as part of their daily lives. These borders and boundaries can hardly be policed given their colonial artificiality and they hold little meaning for the millions of people in Africa who cross them without the trappings of passports, visas and immigration departments. Hence, it is not 'Who are citizens?' that becomes important, because most people are ascribed citizenship either by birth, by choice (as in the case of migration), or by being ascribed a particular citizenship out of necessity (as in the case of refugees). Similarly, one's citizenship can be taken away through dispossession and displacement. Hence, for citizenship to have any meaning, the question that needs to be asked is 'Who is the citizen?' It is this form of citizenship that has meaning beyond allegiance to a specific geographical space and becomes rooted in a sense of community. It is also a form of citizenship that has the potential to be tied to forms of democracy that recognize difference (Mouffe 1993, 1995). As Pamela Johnston Conover points out, citizen identities are the defining elements that shape the character of communities. Such identities can be socially cohesive. However, when they are found to be lacking, legitimacy itself becomes problematic. She points out that there are three key components to citizenship. The first is membership in a political community signified by some legal notion. Although in the modern world citizenship is embedded strongly in the nation-state, individuals are also members of other political communities and 'thus citizens experience multiple levels of citizenship nested within each other' (Conover 1995, p. 134). It is important to recognize that despite the association of nation-states with citizenship, it is at the local level and in the local contexts that people experience being and express themselves as citizens. In short, citizenship is not something that is simply ascribed and results in a fixed identity allocated by the state. Rather, postcolonial subjects have multiple identities which are shaped continually by the practice of everyday life in which they have the capacity to resist, to speak and to act as citizen/subjects. It is in this way that the role of organic intellectuals and an alternative form of citizenship, one that is not simply tied to a specific geographical space, is vital. It is through organic intellectuals and a form of democracy rooted within local communities that recognise difference, that a postcolonial economy of giving can operate effectively.

Conclusion

This essay has examined three different postcolonial sites where there is a need for reconciliation. The mode of analysis suggested here is based on the notion of postcolonialism. This is not a repudiation of the African past, but an engagement with the manner in which Africa has dealt with institutions and practices which it has inherited. It is a mode of analysis that shows the complexity of African politics and the manner in which postcolonial African subjects negotiate their lives. It is a process through which Achille Mbembe has noted that the

> postcolonial 'subject' mobilizes not just a single identity, but several fluid identities which, by their very nature, must be constantly 'revised' in order to achieve maximum instrumentality and efficacy as and when required. (Mbembe 1992, p. 5)

In short, postcolonialism forces one to think of the plurality and diversity of African identities and implores us to heed the ethical call of responsibility.

The three sites, Australia, Palestine and Rwanda, were examined through the lens of the notion of the uncanny. The effect on postcolonial subjects within these sites is one of trauma. The uncanny must be overcome if any genuine process of reconciliation is to take place. It is suggested that this can be accomplished through the gift. Here, it is advocated that a postcolonial economy of giving be considered in order to break down categories and identities that have been ascribed or constructed in order to maintain power structures. A postcolonial economy of giving is linked inextricably to organic intellectuals and a reconceptualized sense of citizenship is one that can further processes of (re)conciliation.

Notes

1 From 1889 Ruanda and Urundi were part of German East Africa, a portion of Germany's spoils from the 'scramble for Africa' of the 1880s which divided the continent between the leading European powers. Germany was divested of its empire as part of the Versailles treaty.
2 This uprising caused a large number of Tutsis to seek refuge in Uganda where there was already a steady flow of migrant Rwandan labour (see Ahluwalia 1995).

References

Ahluwalia, P. (1995) *Plantations and the Politics of Sugar in Uganda*, Kampala: Fountain Publishers.
—— (1996) *Post-Colonialism and the Politics of Kenya*, New York: Nova Science Publishers.
—— (1997) 'The Rwandan Genocide: Exile and Nationalism Reconsidered', *Social Identities*, 3 (3 October): 499–518.
Ahluwalia, P. and G. McCarthy (1998) 'Political Correctness: Pauline Hanson and the Construction of Australian Identity', *Australian Journal of Public Administration*, 57 (3): 79–85.
Ashcroft, B. (1997) 'Globalism, Post-Colonialism and African Studies', in P. Ahluwalia and P. Nursey-Bray (eds), *Post-Colonialism: Culture and Identity in Africa*, New York: Nova Science Publishers.
Ayittey, G. B. N. (1998) *Africa in Chaos*, New York: St Martin's Press.
Balibar, E. (1991) 'Citizen Subject', in E. Cadava, P. Connor and J.-L. Nancy (eds), *Who Comes After The Subject*, London: Routledge.
Bataille, G. (1991) *The Accursed Share: An Essay on General Economy, Vol. 1*, trans. R. Hurley, New York: Zone Books.
Beinin, J. (1998) 'Palestine and Israel: Perils of a Neoliberal, Repressive "Pax Americana"', *Social Justice*, 25 (4): 20–40.
Bhabha, H. (1993) *The Location of Culture*, London: Routledge.
Caruth, C. (1995) 'Introduction', in C. Caruth (ed.), *Trauma: Explorations in History*, Baltimore, MD: Johns Hopkins University Press.
Chabal, P. and J. P. Daloz (1999) *Africa Works: Disorder as Political Instrument*, London: James Currey.
Chabal, P. (1996) 'The African Crisis: Context and Interpretation', in R. Werbner and T. Ranger (eds), *Postcolonial Identities in Africa*, London-Zed Books.
Cixous, H. and C. Clèment (1985) *The Newly Born Woman*, Minneapolis: University of Minnesota Press.
Conover, P. J. (1995) 'Citizen Identities and Conceptions of the Self', *Journal of Political Philosophy*, 3 (2): 133–65.
Davidson, B. (1992) *The Black Man's Burden: Africa and the Curse of the Nation-State*, London: James Currey.
De Saussure, F. (1974) *Course in General Linguistics*, Glasgow: Fontana.
Destexhe, A. (1994) 'The Third Genocide', *Foreign Policy*, 97 (winter): 3–17.
Erikson, K. (1995) 'Notes on Trauma and Community', in C. Caruth (ed.), *Trauma: Explorations in History*, Baltimore, MD: Johns Hopkins University Press.

Fanon, F. (1967) *The Wretched of the Earth*, Harmondsworth: Penguin Books.

Freud, S. (1920) [1955] *The Standard Edition of the Complete Psychological Works of Sigmund Freud*, Vol. 18, translated under the editorship of J. Strachey in collaboration with A. Freud, assisted by A. Strachey and A. Tyson, London: Hogarth.

Gazit, S. (1998) 'Israel and Palestinians: Fifty Years of Wars and Turning Points', *The Annals of the American Academy of Political and Social Science*, 555.

Gelder, K. and J. Jacobs (1998) *Uncanny Australia: Sacredness and Identity in a Postcolonial Nation*, Melbourne: Melbourne University Press.

Helman G. B. and S. Ratner (1992) 'Saving Failed States', *Foreign Policy*, 89: 3–20.

Hindess, B. (1996) *Discourses of Power: From Hobbes to Foucault*, Oxford: Blackwell Publishers.

Hunt, N. (1990) 'Domesticity and Colonialism in Belgian Africa: Usumbura Foyer Social, 1949–1960', *Signs*, 15 (3): 447–74.

Lemarchand, R. (1994) *Burundi: Ethnocide as Discourse and Practice*, Cambridge: Cambridge University Press.

Leys, C. (1994) 'Confronting the African Tragedy', *New Left Review*, 204: 33–47.

——(1996) *The Rise and Fall of Development Theory*, London: James Currey.

Lieberfeld, D. (1999) 'Post-Handshake Politics: Israel/Palestine and South Africa Compared', *Middle East Policy*, 6 (3): 131–40.

Mamdani, M. (1996a) 'From Conquest to Consent as the Basis of State Formation: Reflections on Rwanda', *New Left Review*, 216: 3–37.

——(1996b) *Citizen and Subject: Contemporary Africa and the Legacy of Late Colonialism*, Princeton, NJ: Princeton University Press.

Mauss, M. (1969) *The Gift: Forms and Functions of Exchange in Archaic Societies*, trans. I. Cunnison, London: Cohen and West.

Mazrui, A. (1994) 'Development or Recolonization?' *New Perspectives Quarterly*, 11 (4, fall): 18–19.

——(1997) 'The Tutsi-Trigger: Redrawing Africa's Colonial Map', *New Perspectives Quarterly*, 14 (1): 48–9.

Mbembe, A. (1992) 'Provisional Notes on the Postcolony', *Africa*, 62 (1): 3–37.

Mouffe, C. (1993) 'Liberal Socialism and Pluralism: Which Citizenship?' in J. Squires (ed.), *Principled Positions: Postmodernism and the Rediscovery of Value*, London: Lawrence and Wishart.

——(1995) 'Feminism, Citizenship, and Radical Democratic Politics', in L. Nicholson and S. Seidman (eds), *Social Postmodernism: Beyond Identity Politics*, Cambridge: Cambridge University Press.

Nursey-Bray, P. and D. P. Ahluwalia (1994) 'Double Genocide: The Crisis in Central Africa', *Current Affairs Bulletin*, 70 (11): 26–7.

Pfaff, W. (1995) 'A New Colonialism: Europe Must Go Back into Africa', *Foreign Affairs*, 74 (1): 2–6.

Povinelli, E. A. (1998) 'The State of Shame: Australian Multiculturalism and the Crisis of Indigenous Citizenship', *Critical Inquiry*, 24 (winter): 575–610.

Power, S. (1998) 'Life After Death: Barriers to Reconciliation in Rwanda', *The New Republic*, 218 (14): 16–19.

Rush, R. and M. Szeftel (1994) 'States, Markets and Africa's Crisis', *Review of African Political Economy*, 21 (60): 147–56.

Said, E. (1980) *The Question of Palestine*, London: Vintage.

——(1994a) *The Politics of Dispossession*, London: Chatto and Windus.

——(1994b) *Representation of the Intellectual*, London: Vintage.

Slater, D. (1993) 'Political Meanings of Development – New Horizons', in F. Schuurman (ed.), *Beyond the Impasse: New Directions in Development Theory*, London: Zed Books.

Stratton, J. (1998) *Race Daze: Australia in Identity Crisis*, Annandale, NSW: Pluto Press.

United Nations (1988) *The Origins and Evolution of the Palestine Problem 1917–1980*, New York: United Nations.

Young, R. (1991) 'Neocolonial Times', *Oxford Literary Review*, 13 (2): 2–4.

Zarembo, A. (1997) 'Judgement Day', *Harpers*, 295 (April): 68–80.

Chapter 11

The Economy of Ideas: Colonial Gift and Postcolonial Product

Zane Ma-Rhea

Introduction

The starting point of this chapter is the problematic of postcoloniality: a collision/collusion of many discursive frames, ideas from all over the world formalized in academic theory, reproduced and disseminated in the university ideas-production systems and legitimated under numerous local conditions. As a cluster of ideas, 'postcoloniality' has value in the global ideas market and has been the stuff of complex exchange rituals bouncing between binary opposites, always shifting in meaning and application. This chapter seeks to explore some of the exchange machinery for such a concept as 'postcoloniality', exploring dimensions of its historical location and its economic function.

The phenomenon of 'postcoloniality', the lived experiences of diverse peoples previously colonized or colonizer, is in a process of translation within universities around the world. These translations do not solely tend towards theory but also raise questions about methodology and the epistemological justifications for the whole project. Neither are they static translations. They exist in conversations with other translators and the broader community about the accuracy, applicability or veracity of the translation.

In attempting to understand how university-generated translations of everyday life, called ideas, theory or 'knowledge', are actually transferred across cultures the irony of the intellectual domain's separation of 'postmodernism/sociology/the West' and 'postcoloniality/anthropology/the rest' becomes apparent. It is crucial to closely examine how and by whom university ideas are generated and exchanged, and such an examination gives a fascinating insight into the concept of 'postcoloniality'. Building on earlier work (Ma Rhea 1997a, 1997b), this chapter examines 'postcoloniality' through the lens of six universities in the former British Empire, now Commonwealth of Nations, tracing the dissemination of ideas generated within that system.

As with all discussions of translation, there is at the outset a need for some clarification of the choices of words used in this chapter. Firstly, and possibly most important, the word 'knowledge' is used here in a very specific way. A catchword in the global marketplace and within universities, I use it here only as an embodied state. Knowledge is held in the minds of humans as a composite of lived experience and received ideas. The stuff of the exchange between persons is not 'knowledge' but is the transfer of ideas across space and time. Nobody can ever know another's knowledge but we can communicate information and our ideas arising from and as a reflection of our knowledge, and we can exchange information. 'Information' is stuff that is passed on without being filtered through the communicator's own ideas.

I will also be examining the term 'postcoloniality' in two specific ways. The first looks at 'postcoloniality' as a grounded term with social, economic, political and historical specificity, such that there was a period of violent territorial colonization, a period of subjugation of the colonized, a 'liberation/loss of empire' period with a final colonial rupture. Postcoloniality in this sense translates the 'now', the time after colonization. It is another thing to employ the terms 'postcolonial' or 'postmodern' as theoretical constructs, as manoeuvres to unground people's lives from real structural constraints and to free their stories from the weight of history, to think beyond the appalling aftermath of colonization and capitalist supremacy, to reinsert a sense of agency where it was felt there was none. It proposes a break with past academic ways of categorizing the human activities in this world through linear historicity, 'high' politics, grand narratives and truth-seeking methodologies, asking the previously unaskable and thinking the previously unthinkable.

Inescapably, the pool of ideas which enabled the term 'postcoloniality' and its resonant, postmodernity, to come into existence is embedded in the cumulative *Weltanschauung* of the contemporary internationalized university (Scheler 1954). Early theorists of 'knowledge' (*sic*) (for example, Scheler 1963, 1980; Marx 1947) attempted to map the formation of ideas in their sociological and philosophical dimensions and to point out the function of the universities in the production, reproduction, dissemination and legitimization of such ideas. More recently, writers such as Gibbons et al. (1995), Hill and Turpin (1995) and McCarthy (1996) focus on the mechanisms of contemporary 'knowledge' production in universities, indicating a crisis of legitimation seen to be occurring (most strongly argued in Readings 1997) and attempting to see a way forward in the new global world of relativity. A closer examination of the economics of ideas production is still wanting in the recent literature.

The processes of the production, reproduction, dissemination and legitimization of academic ideas as a derivative of Western ontology and pedagogy cannot in the end begin to be understood by the fragmentary literary readings that are presently proposed. The complex social formation of the post-imperial Commonwealth university cannot be engaged with if there is no grounded understanding of the economics of the colonial period. The literature of postcoloniality is a commodified product of universities. The discourses of postcoloniality and postmodernity are also vulnerable to the very ontological formations they attempt to explicate. Can universities themselves be post-colonial or are they ontologically neocolonial or even anti-colonial in their attempts to apprehend dramatic global phenomena?

The creation of a globally connected university system during the colonial period and the subsequent dissemination of ideas in the time of British Empire and contemporary Commonwealth provides an interesting canvas for the exploration of postcoloniality in both the senses suggested above. As Springer (1988, p. 39) says:

> The Commonwealth family will continue to diversify. It therefore becomes of prime importance to promote a free trade in ideas, and of men who specialize in ideas, between Commonwealth countries. This is most easily done through universities.

Universities in their present form cannot simply be studied in the present. Their genealogical antecedents also need discussion: the period during the era of trading and missionary activities, higher education during the colonial period of militarily backed territorial occupation, and university education during the overlapping periods of decolonization, nationalism, republicanism, Commonwealth and independence.

In an historically grounded reading, a brief discussion of the University of Sydney, Australia, the University of Calcutta, India, the University of Cape Town, South Africa, the University of Ghana, Ghana, Universiti Malaya, Malaysia, and the University of the West Indies, Jamaica will be undertaken. In the second part of the chapter I will attempt to look at the economy of ideas as practised in such universities.

The Universities of Empire and the Commonwealth

The university has not been a fixed monolithic entity through time and in geographical location, although one of its most consistent claims has been that of the 'search for knowledge' and the discovery of scientific facts. This claim has coexisted alongside broader functional aims of universities within society. The evolution of the British antecedent, the German university of Von Humbolt, is in itself an intriguing study beyond the scope of this work. More important in the long historical view, there are scraps of information suggesting that there have been long-established centres of advanced teaching and learning all over the world that have arisen and fallen with the rise and fall of empires and civilizations.

Le Goff (1993) gives us a fascinating account of the birth of the intellectual and later the university. He records that in the twelfth century it was the Arab centres of learning in Byzantium, Damascus, Baghdad and Cordoba where people of Western Europe sought out books, first to translate and later to incorporate these ideas into their newly developing education system. Daniel of Morley says he hastened to Toledo where the Arabs were giving instruction available to all in the arts of the quadrivium (or sciences). Here, he attended the lectures of the most learned philosophers in the world. Oriental thought was brought to the West through centres in Chartres and Paris (Le Goff 1993).

A working definition of the now-prevalent Western university model is recorded in the Oxford English Dictionary (1993, p. 3493):

> ... a corporation of teachers and students formed for the purpose of giving and receiving instruction in a fixed range of subjects beyond that provided at a school. Later, an institution of higher education, offering courses and research facilities in mainly non-vocational subjects and having acknowledged powers and privileges, *especially that of conferring degrees* ... (my italics)

This neatness of definition hides the complexities by which a university comes to exist in the first place, its symbolic potential, its educative mission, the power derived from the production of ideas, its relationship to the state, and its variously configured gendered, class and ethnic assertions. The secular British university tradition developed, according to Ashby (1963; see also Harte 1986) from a concept of Von Humbolt's of scholarly training for the German aristocracy, in the early 1800s. It was a significant evolution of the Aristotelean Lyceum that had been maintained through the middle ages. The new British universities, such as the University of London, departed from the Oxbridge universities in their decision to be secular and undertook to train their students to cultivate intellectual skills, vocations being taught elsewhere. Like its German counterpart, the idea was to produce educated gentlemen rather than clerics, a new elite. With the increase in numbers of the middle class at home and colonists abroad, coupled with a revolution of ideas towards a scientific way of viewing the world, the role of the university quickly moved away from the Liberal Arts and the aristocracy.

What is fascinating in looking back at these developments is that the transplanted university found itself in such colonies as Australia and India in the middle of the nineteenth century, when the transition from aristocratic to bourgeois control of society was being felt most keenly in the universities in Britain, and the application of Darwinist sociobiological ideas was gathering momentum. Thus, to these new colonial universities were brought all the unresolved conflicts, along with the strongly stated civilizing mission. Some colonies like Australia established universities explicitly to serve the colonists and not the colonized inhabitants.

Some colonies, such as in South Africa, were denied full universities because there was not the political or economic will to establish them, and there were not substantial numbers of colonists. In most colonies, the colonized peoples were not seen as 'ready' to benefit from university education, although the people of India provided an effective argument to challenge this practice. The University of London developed a significant role with the peoples of such colonies as Ghana, Malaya and the West Indies, being given the power by the Crown to confer degrees to people who had attended colleges established in these colonies. It was not until after the First World War for the University of Cape Town, and after the Second World War, in the decline of the British Empire, that the universities of Ghana, Malaysia and the West Indies achieved independence from Britain (see, for example, Judd 1996). In all examples, the university in these ex-colonies has evolved through time and modification to meet the symbolic and structural administrative needs of the respective national governments, the panopoly of individual aspirations of citizens, and the labour demands of globalized capital.

The university in each geographical location serves a pivotal function in organizing locally relevant theoretical justifications for globalization, just as the political and economic importance of the control of the production of ideas was clearly understood by the architects of the British Empire, and their French and American counterparts. German universities had been 'the finishing school for both British and American scholars and scientists since the 1880s' (Ashby 1963, p. 18) and after the First World War Balfour, then the Foreign Secretary, saw the need for the universities of the United Kingdom

> not merely to fill the gap inevitably made by the exclusion of Germany from the place she had hitherto occupied in advanced teaching and in promotion of research, but also to strengthen the higher intellectual bonds which united Britain and her Allies. (Cited in Ashby 1963, p. 20)

He foresaw the increasing importance of the university as a way of facilitating a common mechanism of expression (ibid., p. 21), indelibly stamping the imperial network of universities with the task of creating a global academic culture with Britain as its creatrix. Ashby surmizes that of the four substantial assets of British colonization – Christianity, representative government, educational institutions and the English language – 'the most universally accepted, and the least changed by the indigenous cultural environment, are the educational institutions exported from Britain to her Commonwealth' (ibid., p. 92).

The establishing of universities was a contentious issue in British government circles. Two clusters of metaphors were common in discussions. The first clustered around the notion of the family, sometimes stratified by age, such that the British university was the parent and the colonial one the child, and sometimes by the more ethnically ascribed 'kith and kin', arguing for the maintenance of the superiority of the British stock through education. This metaphor became more and more problematic as the non-white, culturally diverse, colonised peoples demanded to be recognized as part of the family. Was it to be the blended family, the hybrid, and who were to be the legitimate and illegitimate heirs? The second cluster comprised agricultural metaphors such as the notion of the tilled and untilled soil. In the metaphoric sense, the civilized person was likened to tilled, fertile soil. In the British liberal tradition all people were seen as having the potential to be cultivated, but some were seen to be more ready than others. This was extended to access to universities. Time and time again, the 'readiness' of the colonized to be cultivated and civilized to the 'highest' levels was questioned, and the liberation struggles of the complicitly colonized often found a means of expression through making counter-assertions of their fitness to run their own universities.

Alongside these metaphors, many accepted the university as a symbol of intellectual capacity, as the head of the body in the emerging postcolonial nations. As such, the 'health' of the emerging nation has been judged by the health of its universities. As producers of new ideas, translators of this globalized world, and recipients of powerful metaphoric social meaning, contemporary universities respond to and configure postcoloniality.

What is it about the British university that made it such an important inclusion into the colonial project and maintains its place postcolonially? Ajayi et al. (1996, p. 199) suggest that 'the university is a key player in providing the nation with the power of knowledge' and it is around this insight that the universities of the selected nations will be discussed.

The University of Sydney and the University of Calcutta were established at a similar time. The colonists who occupied and established outposts of the British Empire demanded to be educated in the European fashion (CUY, various; Harte 1986; Ray and Gupta 1957; Turney, Bygolt and Chippendale 1991; Walker 1929). The University of Sydney, as something of an anomaly, sprang fully formed from its father's head in 1850 as an important 'civilizing agent'. It was never intended to be accessible to the colonized or the convicts.

It was assimilated into an Empire-wide exchange of academic ideas which academics drew on, while also contributing to the collective imperial information base. Significant investment was made in the early Australian universities and they were, and continue to be, ensured of access to the information and ideas that are the product of British universities. British academics were encouraged to bring their knowledge to Australia to assist with the development of the new universities. The historical and philosophical foundations of the University of Sydney saw it develop through a rapid maturation process in a short hundred years which spanned the establishment of the university as a civilizing agent in a far-flung colony to its legitimation as participant in the Colombo Plan, principally involved in the economic development of Asia.

The University of Calcutta, established in 1857, was initially a problematic idea for the British colonizers. Primarily concerned with trade and profits, most of the British policy in India was managed through the East India Company. The British employees of the company saw no need for the development of

Indian universities and, while finding it difficult to accept that Indian people had access to a thriving system of education and a high regard for it, also found it in their interests to support local education for their officers in Sanskrit, Persian and Arabic. When English replaced Persian as the official language in 1837 and when in 1844 those receiving English education were given preference in all government appointments, the role of the university was seen, in the words of Macaulay, to 'create a clan who would be interpreters between us and the millions whom we govern, a class of persons Indian in blood and colour, but English in tastes, in opinions, in morals and intellect', new consumers of British goods, and new recruits for the subordinate ranks of the East India Company's civil service and loyal to the Raj (from CUY, various; Ray and Gupta 1957, pp. 8–34).

The University of Calcutta was modelled on the University of London but was soon criticized for an over-dependence on examinations because of the large numbers of students. The demands of a university in India were ontologically and pedagogically distinct from the British experience and the role of the university in Indian society was, and is, a contested one. As the Indian nationalist movement gathered momentum, the colonial universities, such as Calcutta, continued to support the Raj while other universities developed to foster an Indian nationalist spirit. The University of Calcutta left the Association of Commonwealth Universities in 1996.

The University of Cape Town, South Africa (founded in 1829) was developed from a secondary school, South African College. The early colonizers had a more difficult time convincing various funding bodies that a university was necessary in South Africa. Indeed it was not until after the Boer War that the British government saw a need to commit more infrastructure funds to the colony, as it was more interested in exploiting the mineral wealth than educating the colonists. After the Second World War, when South Africa achieved foreign-policy and financial independence from Britain, the University Act (1916) was passed and the University of Cape Town came into being as an autonomous institution responsible for its own academic standards, including the conduct of its own examinations. Under apartheid black citizens were refused access to the university even though academics at UCT argued against the exclusion of non-white students. When, in 1985, the last restrictions were lifted, the University of Cape Town moved to become a non-racial institution and is now fully engaged in the education of all citizens in the changed political climate of South Africa. Although traditionally a 'Historically White University', UCT is now actively engaged in the new South Africa.

The University of Ghana (1948, 1961), Universiti Malaya (1949, 1962) and the University of the West Indies (1948, 1962), while geographically remote from one another, all shared a common 'special relationship' with the University of London. Under this scheme, used also to establish universities such as Calcutta and Cape Town, a university college was established that taught according to University of London programmes. The examinations were University of London examinations, as were the awarded degrees and diplomas.

All these special relationships were entered into at a time after the Second World War when many colonies was arguing for their independence, and the establishment of an independent university, a potent symbol, was often as a direct consequence of colonies regaining their territorial sovereignty with economic and political independence. In the case of Cape Town, Ghana, West Indies and Malaysia, the university was a place where nationalist ideas were developed and independence demanded. As sites of liberatory impulse, the universities were symbols of hope for a new postcolonial era, for the redefinition of ideas and the possibility of new social formations.

From all of the above it is possible to see some of the ideas by which the colonial universities were established. In the metaphor of the family, the British colonial powers designated the University of London as the model child by whose emulation legitimacy could be eventually gained. This situation was in contradiction to the function of the University of London at home of being, amongst others, a rebellious child breaking away from the Oxbridge tradition and not itself being seen as quite proper. The universities of the colonies that emulated it were also implicated in the structures of colonial control, by their training of the new local elites who would assist the British in maintaining and legitimating their colonial control. The cultivation of a new local elite was always a negotiation of power and while those in Britain saw British education as almost impervious to local adaptation, many educated colonized people became spokespersons for anti-colonial movements. In this era after territorial colonization, universities continue to exist. They continue to be responsible for the dissemination of ideas and information, and more particularly to produce and reproduce new technological and social ideas that have had a profound impact on the way people in this globalized world perceive themselves. Certainly, advances in information technology are important, but the people who work in universities still have impact on the potential range of human ideation.

All of the universities examined are independent now. All confer degrees and all except Calcutta are members of the Association of Commonwealth Universities. Their dual position as products of the colonial period and symbolic of postcolonial independence gives them a difficult location from which to become involved in thinking about the phenomenon of postcoloniality.

The Economics of Ideas

Is it then possible to look at the new production, reproduction, dissemination and legitimization of ideas in universities in economic terms? What of the idea of postcoloniality itself? It is important to consider these questions because the people in universities continue to be involved both in producing ideations that justify neocolonialism on a global scale and are also producing ideations that may allow us to think beyond the colonial *Weltanschauung*.

One way to look at these questions is to consider the economic conditions under which ideas have been and continue to be exchanged. As has been suggested by Davis (1997, p. 47),

> the notion of exchange is a composite classification, and the force which underpins it is not any kind of natural law, but the social force of morals, laws, governments and the human agents of divine authority.

Like Mauss, Davis tends to stress the moral aspects of exchange, but morals operate in an economy. Ideas, that we are now able to speak of as 'things' or 'stuff', have an economic aspect even when that aspect has been obscured by a larger conceptual framework. When looking at the production of ideas in universities, it is possible to recognize certain economic aspects in the production and dissemination of ideas that can form part of the extensive continuum that is human economic exchange behaviour.

The metaphors used by the colonizers give some insight into the nature of the exchange of ideas under colonization. Predominantly the behaviour was constructed as a gift within a moral/religious economy. The discursive frame relied on a relational exchange between colonizer and colonized because it was not seen to be sufficient that the ideas simply be transferred but that they be internalized. There was a parental aspect to the giving/receiving relationship, especially for the universities which had a special relationship with the University of London. While the act of establishing universities could be seen to be an act of generosity, there was also the fact that if the colonizers had not been there, then there would have been no need for a university. Under the logic of a moral economy, there was seen to be a need to have a balanced exchange, to extend and manage very difficult social relations. The British colonizers needed to be seen to have a civilizing role, a redeeming feature of conquest. Establishing universities fulfilled this need but the receivers, the colonized, were not always so enthusiastic in expressing their gratitude. During the time of decolonization the cry of 'ingrate' was common.

In the period after colonization the exchange of ideas can be seen in two allied but distinct economic discursive frames. In the first, the exchange of ideas between universities began to assume the characteristics of a commodity in a market exchange, with translators and idea makers beginning to speak about their ideas as 'property'. There was a distinctive shift away from an almost aristocratic ideal, the moral obligation to maintain the 'freedom' of ideas to move amongst the community of scholars, within the Commonwealth family, towards the necessity of being able to assert the 'ownership' of an idea, of being able to show status, power, wealth or position by that ownership. This also led to the demand for mutually recognized legal safeguards by which to protect ideas.

The ascendancy of legal powers over aristocratic powers is only now becoming manifest. Further, under these legal arrangements, an 'owner' of an idea has the right to dispose of that idea, that is to alienate the idea, and pass the intellectual property right to another. Are ideas ever alienable? In a very real sense, if I sell you an idea of mine, you now have it (whether you understand it or not is another matter), but I also still have it. By extension of developing legal powers, the owner of an 'idea' is now the one who can control the reproduction and dissemination of that idea, can legally control its adaptation and can claim financial recompense for its use.

The second, allied discursive frame is the exchange of ideas within the crude economy. The seemingly logical conclusion to the processes of globalization is that ideas are no longer simply commodified (functioning within a political economy) but are further demystified, now to be exchanged like any other product, packaged and sold with a fixed market value and the production of which now increasingly operates within the discursive frame of service provision. The shift of ideas to being 'products and services' completes the transfer away from the obligations of the moral economy, under which many ex-colonial academics laboured, freeing those academics but only as consumers, not as legitimate producers of ideas. Ownership still rests with the old and new grand narrativists and scientists, the globally mobile, intellectually propertied academic stars of the United States of America, the European Union and Japan.

The postcolonial world is a different configuration of economic behaviours but there are convincing arguments that the colonial dynamic has been reconfigured from a morally asserted, territorial economic control into a legalistically asserted, ideational, economic control, the basis of virtual reality. The ownership of ideas certainly seems to confer strikingly similar levels of power and control to that of the previous territorial colonizers. While the University of Sydney can now reconfigure itself under global capitalist metaphors, sometimes as a 'respectable' branch office of Britain, or at other times as a 'legitimate' world-class education vendor, universities such as Calcutta with an equally long period of establishment cannot. The academics at the universities of Ghana, the West Indies or Malaysia can offer their universities as education services providers in the global marketplace, but the principle of hierarchies is still in place.

Which academics make the largest profit out of the ideas of postcoloniality? Who can claim legal ownership of such ideas? Which academics have privileged speaking positions as the new postcolonial critics? What is the global language of debate?

Conclusion

The title of one of Ngugi's books, *Decolonizing the Mind*, presents a significant challenge to scholars of the postcolonial. In universities at least, it is premature to be arguing that ideas are postmodern/postcolonial. The consequences of the colonial period have not yet played themselves out. The power to produce and legitimate ideas in our global world still rests with the few, and it seems that the idea of 'postcoloniality' will itself in the end do nothing more than confirm an economic reconfiguration of the status quo of haves and have-nots. It also seems probable that the potential to think beyond the colonial will be only possible when an economy of ideas exists in a conceptually different frame from the present, when the possibility of owning an idea is unthinkable.

Acknowledgments

The author gratefully acknowledges the kind assistance of the Managers of the Smuts Visiting Fellowship in Commonwealth Studies, Cambridge, and staff at the Association of Commonwealth Universities, London, whose financial and material support made this research possible.

References

Ajayi, J. F., Ade, G., Lameck, K. H. and Johnson, G. A. (1996). *The African Experience with Higher Education*. London and Ohio: James Curry and Ohio University Press.

Ashby, E. (1963). *Community of Universities 1913–1963*. Cambridge: Cambridge University Press.

——(1964). *African Universities and Western Tradition*. The Godkin Lectures at Harvard University, 1964. Oxford: Oxford University Press.

Carr-Saunders, A. (1948). *Report of the Commission on University Education in Malaya*. Kuala Lumpur: Government Press.

Commonwealth Universities Yearbooks (1915, 1918–20, 1925, 1930, 1935, 1940, 1947, 1949–50, 1955, 1960, 1965, 1970, 1975, 1980, 1985, 1990, 1995, 1997–8). Selected entries. London: Association of Commonwealth Universities.

Davis, J. (1992). *Exchange*. Buckingham: Open University Press.

Dickson, K. B. (1973). 'The University of Ghana: aspects of the idea of an African university.' In T. M. Yesufu (ed.), *Creating the African University: Emerging Issues in the 1970s* (pp. 102–16). Ibadan: Oxford University Press.

Gibbons, M. et al. (1994). *The New Production of Knowledge*. London: Sage.

Graves, R. (1960). *The Greek Myths: Complete Edition*. London: Penguin Books.

Harte, N. (1986). *The University of London 1836–1986*. London: Athlone Press.

Hill, S. and Turpin, T. (1995). 'Cultures in collision.' In M. Strathern (ed.), *Shifting Contexts: Transformations in Anthropological Knowledge* (pp. 131–52). London: Routledge.

Judd, D. (1996). *Empire: The British Experience from 1765 to the Present*. London: Fontana.

Le Goff, J. (1993). *Intellectuals in the Middle Ages*, trans. T. L. Fagan. Oxford: Blackwell Publishers. (Original work published 1957)

Ma Rhea, Z. (1997a). 'University Knowledge Exchange: Gift, Commodity and Mutual Benefit.' *Californian Sociologist*, 17/18: 211–50.

Ma Rhea, Z. (1997b). 'Gift, Commodity and Mutual Benefit: Analysing the Transfer of University Knowledge between Thailand and Australia.' *Higher Education Policy: The Quarterly Journal of the International Association of Universities*, 10 (2): 111–20.

McCarthy, E. D. (1996). *Knowledge as Culture: The New Sociology of Knowledge*. London: Routledge.

Marx, K. (1947). 'Concerning the Production of Consciousness.' Reprinted in J. E. Curtis and J. W. Petras (eds) (1970) *The Sociology of Knowledge: A Reader* (pp. 97–108). London: Duckworth.

Ray, N. and Gupta, P. (eds) (1957). *Hundred Years of the University of Calcutta 1857–1956*. Calcutta: University of Calcutta.

Readings, W. (1996). *The University in Ruins*. Cambridge, MA: Harvard University Press.

Scheler, M. (1954). *Philosophische Weltanschauung* [Philosophical Worldview]. Bern: Franke Verlag.

——(1963). 'On the Positivistic Philosophy of the History of Knowledge and its Law of Three Stages.' Reprinted in J. E. Curtis and J. W. Petras (eds) (1970) *The Sociology of Knowledge: A Reader* (pp. 161–9). London: Duckworth.

——(1980). *Problems of a Sociology of Knowledge*, trans. M. S. Frings. London: Routledge and Kegan Paul. (Original work published 1924)

Sherlock, P. and Nettleford, R. (1990). *The University of the West Indies: A Caribbean Response to the Challenge of Change*. London: Macmillan Caribbean.

Springer, H. W. (1988). *The Commonwealth of Universities 1963–1988*. London: Association of Commonwealth Universities.

Turney, C., Bygolt, U. and Chippendale, P. (1991). *Australia's First: A History of the University of Sydney*, Vol. 1. Sydney: University of Sydney in association with Hale and Ironmonger.

Walker, E. A. (1929). *The South African College and the University of Cape Town 1829–1929*. Cape Town: Cape Times.

Chapter 12

Looking Awry: Tropes of Disability in Postcolonial Writing

Ato Quayson

Mr Jeremy Beadle, host of *You've Been Framed* and *It Could Be You*, parried criticism made against a televised practical joke he seems to have once made on a disabled person. The comic potential in any disconcerting scene was because the spectator always heaved a sigh of relief that it was not them at the receiving end of the confusion or discomfiture. And this, he continued, applied in any situation where someone was alone in being confused about something that to others around was plain to see. The fact that the person was disabled was not directly relevant to the comic potential of such scenes, he thought.[1]

It is obvious that Mr Beadle's definition of comedy ignores the fact that when it is at the expense of the disabled or of the weaker in society it achieves its effect partly because these weak ones cannot 'strike back', as it were. There is an implicit privileging of the strong versus the weak in any comedy that depends for its effect on putting the weak, or the disabled, or the racial minority for that matter, in a position of discomfort. Highlighting some of the obviously misguided media treatments of the disabled in opening an essay on tropes of disability in postcolonial writing, however, is not of interest in itself; rather its aim is to suggest that there is a curious affinity between what I am going to describe in greater detail as the primal scene of the literary encounter with the disabled and attitudes that pertain to disabled people in other contexts. To begin in this way is also to take a cue from Slavoj Žižek (1992), who, apart from providing the first part of the title of this essay, reroutes popular culture through the works of Jacques Lacan and shows how paradoxically 'looking awry' at an object (i.e. with a specific philosophical or ideological interest), allows it to come into focus and gain shape. Furthermore, Žižek demonstrates in his methodology the productiveness of juxtaposing the highest spiritual products of culture alongside the most common, prosaic and mundane. In doing this he suggests a fruitful way of understanding the tropes of disability that we are going to attend to in this essay. A looking awry at such tropes throws the subtle evasions of literary discourse into sharp relief.

I will be making three critical moves: the first will be to explore a Lacanian conceptual apparatus for theorizing what happens in the encounter with the disabled. This will be done through a strategic reading of two essays, namely, 'The mirror stage as formative of the function of the I' and 'Aggressivity in psychoanalysis', both in *Écrits* (Lacan 1948, 1949). The second will be to attend to the various discursive ways in which the disabled are figured in postcolonial writing, with particular reference to J. M. Coetzee's *Waiting for the Barbarians* (1980), Keri Hulme's *The Bone People* (1983) and Ben Okri's *The Famished Road* (1992). The third will be to conclude by arguing that these primal scenes may be useful for grasping traumatic postcolonial histories, especially when these are 'littered with disembodied pasts' as is the case in some African countries riven by present and past wars. What, in other words, does it mean for the reconstruction of civil imagining when history itself has to be seen through a trope of disability?

The Disabled, Lacan, and the Primal Scene[2]

Defining disability is fraught with problems. As Whyte and Ingstad (1995, p. 5) note, 'any attempt to universalize the category "disabled" runs into conceptual problems of the most fundamental sort'. Furthermore, they note that the category is often used to refer to a broad range of phenomena, covering manifest physical disability, less manifest forms, such as deafness, and insanity. More significantly, they join others in highlighting the need to see disability as a cultural as well as physical problem. However, it is in the seminal work of Erving Goffman, suggestively entitled *Stigma: Notes on the Management of Spoiled Identity* (1963), that the complex issue of the cultural dimension to disability is raised most fruitfully. In an illuminating account of the nature and sources of social stigma, Goffman points out that physical disability produces its own *gestalt* and that those confronting the disabled often have a whole range of attitudes based on stereotype (ibid., p. 6). More disturbingly, these stereotypes often work on the psyches of the disabled themselves, generating problems with their self-esteem, as Robert F. Murphy (1987, pp. 96–115) shows from personal experience. Physical disability, then, may be said to be constitutive of social and psychological relations in a very troubling way.

But how does this come to be as it is, and in what terms do we describe the primal scene of the encounter of the able-bodied with the disabled through a Lacanian reading? Without actually attempting to discuss Lacan in full (something which most commentators agree is easier said than done), I want to interleave my own ideas with his conceptions so as to indicate his line of thinking,

while at the same time distinguishing my own reasoning from his. To sum-
marize the argument in 'The mirror stage': when a child is between six and
eighteen months, they enter a curious phase in which they begin to recognize
themselves in a mirror and start a long-term process of subjectivity that
continues through life. The salient points of this mirror stage may be stated
schematically as (1) the baby learns to recognize its image and gestures in the
mirror; (2) the baby discovers that the image in the mirror has its own properties (pun intended) and, furthermore, that it is whole; (3) the baby develops an attachment to this specular image, which, though reflecting a unified
object back to it, is actually deluding the baby with a sense of wholeness. The
phase is attended by signs of triumphant jubilation and playful discovery. As
Malcolm Bowie puts it: 'At the mirror moment something glimmers in the
world for the first time. . . . The mirror image is a minimal paraphrase of the
nascent ego' (Bowie 1991, p. 22). But that the baby's sense of identification is
delusional is seen in the fact that even as it requires the support of parental
hands or of some artificial contraptions, it has begun to imagine itself whole
and powerful. For Lacan the ego is formed on the basis of an *imaginary* relationship of the subject with this specular image. Because this stage is actually
not a phase but a stadium (*stade*), the mirror stage rehearses a life-long process
by which the ego, as Maud Ellmann succinctly puts it, 'constantly identifies
itself with new personae in the effort to evade division, distance, difference,
deferral, death' (Ellmann 1994, p. 18). The result, she continues, is 'a wilder-
ness of mirrors in which self and object oscillate perpetually, each eclipsed
under the shadow of the other'. Ellmann's notion of perpetual oscillation is an
interesting one to which we will return later.

In translating Lacan's conceptions into a definiton of the primal scene of the
encounter with the disabled, it is crucial first of all to take away the mirror
while still keeping it in mind. One significant difference between the gaze of
Lacan's baby and that of the able-bodied as he or she gazes at the disabled is
that in the second case there is flow of affectivity. This affectivity relates to a
multiplicity of emotions, which include guilt, bewilderment and even fear.
Robert Murphy points out that the disabled serve as 'constant, visible
reminders to the able-bodied that the society they live in is shot through with
inequity and suffering, that they live in a counterfeit paradise, and that they
too are vulnerable (Murphy 1987, p. 100). But these often contradictory emotions arise precisely because the disabled are continually located within a
multiple frame of significance that is activated through the culturally regulated
gaze of the able-bodied. My use of the word 'frame' in this context is not idle.
It is useful to think of such a frame in the light of physical co-ordinates as if
thinking of a picture-frame. The frame within which the disabled are continually placed is one in which a variety of concepts of wholeness and
completion structure the disabled and place them at the centre of a peculiar
conjuncture of conceptions. At the same time, and quite paradoxically, this
frame always harbours behind it the earlier frame of the mirror phase of childhood. It is a conflation of the mirror phase of identification with a culturally

structured set of stereotypes about wholeness and personhood that gives this primal scene its particular intensities.

But how are we to attend to this contradiction? How does the new frame of wholeness and completion palimpsestically, as it were, overwrite the mirror stage of childhood? To clear this point, we have to turn to the second essay. In 'Aggressivity in psychoanalysis' Lacan notes the degree to which the analyst becomes an object of cathartic resolution for the aggressivity inherent in the analysand's self-imagining. But the aggressivity is often captured in what he describes as *imagos*, tropes, as literary critics might call them, some of which 'represent the elective vectors of aggressive intentions, which they provide with an efficacity that might be called magical' (Lacan 1948, p. 11). These *imagos* are the images of 'castration, mutilation, dismemberment, dislocation, evisceration, devouring, bursting open of the body, in short, the *imagos* that I have grouped together under the apparently structural term of *imagos of the fragmented body*' (ibid.). As he further points out, aggressivity is in the early stages inextricably linked to the images of the fragmented bodies:

> One only has to listen to children aged between two and five playing, alone or together, to know that the pulling off of the head and the ripping open of the belly are themes that occur spontaneously to their imagination, and that this is corroborated by the experience of the doll torn to pieces. (Ibid.)[3]

Crucially, however, Lacan also notes that 'in itself, dialogue seems to involve the renunciation of aggressivity'(ibid., p. 12). He has in mind the role of the analyst in establishing a dialogic context within which the analysand's repressions may be brought to the surface. But, unlike in the case of Freud, Lacan maintains that the analyst is never completely detached from the unfolding process of psychoanalysis but is inextricably involved in its very discursive composition. Transposing these insights into the primal scene of the encounter with the disabled, it may be argued that it is precisely the enframing within normative assumptions of personhood that disenables a liberated 'dialogue' or 'dialogic' encounter with the disabled. This represents the fact that the encounter is always overdetermined by stereotypes of wholeness. And, para-doxically, the notions and stereotypes of wholeness are grounded on the repressed *imagos* of the fragmented body. The primal scene of the encounter with the disabled may then be described as always being crossed by a prob-lematic aggressivity. The aggressivity, however, can rarely be expressed in its own terms, but is diverted in different directions and manifests itself as guilt, bewilderment, fear and, in a happy moment of sublimation, as charity.

If the mirror stage is taken as metaphorically extending throughout life, it is possible to argue that this phase represents for any growing subjectivity the figuring of wholeness as normative. For the disabled caught in the mirror stage, it is not only their own reflection that they see. As many commentators have noted, there is an endless internalization on their part of the images that define wholeness (see Goffman 1963; Murphy 1987; also Ablon 1984, pp. 23–30).[4]

The mirror is populated endlessly with the reflections of 'whole' people and a world in which things are made with such people in mind. At the primal scene, there is a series of double visions at play: the able-bodied sees a totality that is itself reflected back to them along with an anxious fantasy of dismemberment. For the disabled, the vision is of what is normative crossed with their own sense of fragmentation. Finally, and even more uncannily, they are both being made the objects of gaze of the frame of wholeness and completion whose repressed Other is all the figures of dismemberment that play across the mirror stage. The 'perpetual oscillation' in the making of the ego that Ellmann remarked in discussing the mirror stage may then be said to be hyper-inflected in the primal scene of the encounter with the disabled.

The Anxieties of Literary Discourse in the Encounter with the Disabled

It is now time to test these formulations against some postcolonial texts.[5] The first thing to note in the literary primal scene of the encounter with the disabled is that the narrative is often marked at such points by signs of what we might term 'discursive nervousness'. This is reflected in a variety of ways, either in a sudden effusion of violence and chaos accompanied by a change in the texture of the language, or by a general reversion to images of primary sensations, or even of a subliminal unease with questions of identity.[6] Coetzee's *Waiting for the Barbarians* (1980) is an interesting illustration of the last of these points. Coetzee's novel is about a character called the Magistrate through whose eyes the entire novel is narrated. At the opening of the novel he has been a dutiful functionary of the Empire for many years. Now, however, a propaganda frenzy has led to the arrest and torture of members of barbarian tribes who live at the edges of the Empire. One of these barbarian girls, blinded in torture and with broken ankles and sundry scars, is taken in by the Magistrate. His motives seem at first to be altruistic, but it doesn't take long for him to begin desiring her sexually. It is a relationship, however, which for a while is doomed to remain unconsummated, owing partly to the Magistrate's mental struggle to erase the scars from her body. At one point in the narrative, he is watching her eat while thinking about how much pain she must have suffered:

> I watch her eat. She eats like a blind person, gazing into the distance, working by touch. She has a good appetite, the appetite of a robust young country woman.
> 'I don't believe you can see,' I say.
> 'Yes, I can see. When I look straight there is nothing, there is –' (she rubs the air in front of her like someone cleaning a window).
> 'A blur,' I say.
> 'There is a blur. But I can see out of the sides of my eyes. The left eye is better than the right. How could I find my way if I didn't see?'

'Did they do this to you?'
'Yes.'
'What did they do?'

She shrugs and is silent. Her plate is empty. I dish up more of the bean stew she seems to like so much. She eats too fast, belches behind a cupped hand, smiles. 'Beans make you fart,' she says. The room is warm, her coat hangs in a corner with the boots below it, she wears only the white smock and drawers. *When she does not look at me I am a grey form moving about unpredictably on the periphery of her vision. When she looks at me I am a blur, a voice, a smell, a centre of energy that one day falls asleep washing her feet and the next day feeds her bean stew and the next day – she does not know.* (Ibid., p. 29; my emphases)

Because this novel is narrated entirely from the viewpoint of the Magistrate, the nervousness is as much his as that of the narrative in general. Particularly significant in this regard is the fact that, at the end of this extract, he shifts into a free indirect discourse that seems momentarily to conflate his own perceptions with those of the barbarian girl. In describing how he appears to her – like a grey form moving peripherally, or a blur, a voice and a smell – he seems to be uncannily 'seeing' himself through her eyes. This self-seeing, which folds into itself a self-unseeing, defines the precise space of an unnameable anxiety for the Magistrate. It is the anxiety of being effaced and disembodied in the partial gaze of the girl even as he thinks himself whole and in control of her immediate destiny. This is illustrative of the primal scene of enframing that we elaborated earlier, but with the added dimension that here the disabled girl is actively gazing back. The barbarian girl is a mirror that reflects back to the Magistrate his potential dissolution on its surface. Curiously enough, this uncanny moment of dissolution comes after the Magistrate's careful location of the girl in a stereotypical frame of reference. He notes matter-of-factly that 'she eats like a blind person, gazing into the distance, working by touch'. In addition, that 'she has a good appetite, the appetite of a robust young country woman'. What is this about blind people gazing at the distance while they eat, and what is it that sustains these broad generalizations? It is simply the fact that he feels himself empowered to enframe and name her, both as one who controls the tools of such procedures as well as one who regulates the movement of the narrative in the first place. It is therefore highly ironic that he finds himself later in the passage an object of effacement in the eyes of the girl.

Later on in the novel, the Magistrate makes an admission to himself that shows the extent to which the framing of the blind barbarian girl is a desperate attempt at stabilizing a sense of wholeness that would liberate his libidinal impulses:

No more than before does my heart leap or my blood pound at her touch. I am with her not for whatever raptures she may promise or yield but for other reasons, which remain as obscure to me as ever. Except that it has not escaped me that in bed in the dark the marks her torturers have left upon her, the twisted feet, the half-blind eyes, are easily forgotten. Is it then the case that it is the whole woman I want, that my pleasure in her is spoiled until these marks on her are erased and she is restored to herself; or is it the case (*I am not stupid, let me say these things*) that it is the marks on her which drew me to her but which, to my disappointment, I find, do not go deep enough? *Too much or too little: is it she I want or the traces of a history her body bears*? (Ibid., p. 64; my emphases)

The Magistrate seems to be in an odd position of psychological denial. On the one hand, he asserts that he is not with her for any possibility of rapture, but he cannot identify the real reason for his attraction to her. More important, however, is his admission that he simultaneously desires her without the marks of torture as well as seeming to be attracted to her because of them. The oscillation in his mind is nothing other than a figuring of the uneasy dialogical relationship he has attempted to establish with the disabled barbarian girl. He desires a dialogue with her as an equal and struggles to understand her historical position in the brutal narrative of empire. And yet, contradictorily, he finds himself frustrated from doing this not only because she is a barbarian (his view of her table manners reflects this sense) but also because her disability reflects to him all the negations of personhood which, as a liberal humanist, challenge unconscious assumptions he has held all his life. His problems are additionally compounded because he also recognizes that her body has been scarified by an imperial history to which he has somehow contributed. Her disability exceeds its frame of reference to envelop him in an embrace of complicity and guilt.

If the main features of the primal scene of the discursive encounter with the disabled may be seen in the bounded interaction of such scenes in Coetzee's novel, Keri Hulme's *The Bone People* (1983) illustrates a far more complex configuration of the primal scene in that the entire text rehearses the perpetual oscillation of the encounter. There are three main protagonists in the novel: Kerewin, an artist who lives by herself on a South Island beach in New Zealand; Simon, a dumb child; and Joe, his adoptive father. The first encounter with Simon is fruitful in the way in which it reproduces the contours of the primal scene:

She stands over by the window, hands fistplanted on her hips, and watches the gathering boil of the surf below. *She has a curious feeling as she stands there, as though something is out of place, a wrongness somewhere, an uneasiness, an overwatching.* She stares morosely at her feet (longer second toes still longer, you think they might one day grow less, you bloody werewolf you?) and the joyous relief that the morning's hunting gave ebbs away.

. . .

There is a gap between two tiers of bookshelves. Her chest of pounamu rests inbetween them, and above it, is a child. A thin shockheaded person, haloed in hair, shrouded in the dying light.

The eyes are invisible. It is silent, immobile.

Kerewin stares, shocked and gawping and speechless.

. . .

> *She doesn't like looking at the child. One of the maimed, the contaminating. . . .*
>   She looks at the smoke curling upward in a thin blue stream instead.
>   'Ah, you can't talk, is that it?' (Ibid., pp. 16–17; my emphases)

Keri Hulme's novel is marked by a highly poeticized mode of writing. Though it is essentially a third-person narrative, there is a constant integration of the thoughts and feelings of individual characters. From these extracts, however, two things are worthy of note in relation to our argument. The first is that Kerewin has a sense of a 'wrongness somewhere, an overwatching' when alone in her house whose source is not clearly formulated till a little later. Though this eerie feeling of being watched might be said to be a natural intuitive reaction to being the object of an undisclosed person's gaze, it is important to note that, later, the notion of a vague 'wrongness' is given a specific location when she thinks of the child as one of the 'maimed, the contaminating'. Significantly, though, she thinks of him in this way *before she fully discovers he is dumb.* Is this momentary foreknowledge attributable to Kerewin's heightened intuitions or does its significance lie elsewhere? At this point the issue is undecidable, but as the narrative progresses it is clear that Simon's proleptic framing as a maimed and contaminating factor in Kerewin's mind even before she discovers he is disabled resonates at a more complex level of the narrative's discourse.

As the novel progresses one senses a certain struggle to avoid a full disclosure of what it is that seems to be constantly disturbing Simon. Though, as I noted before, the novel frequently reflects the innermost thoughts of individual characters, what goes on in Simon's mind is rigorously withheld from us. All we get are his momentary sensations and reactions to events, not his thoughts on his own condition. In fact, for much of the time, the novel reads almost like a psychological mystery thriller in which we are constantly made to wonder at what possibly might have happened to Simon. We are shown signs of physical abuse, but led in a circuitous way to suspect various people other than Joe of harming the boy. When Kerewin arrives at a fair conviction that Joe is responsible for the boy's abused condition, her subliminal sensual attraction to Joe initially prevents her from dealing with him as ruthlessly as she would have wished and from reporting his actions to the Social Services. The moment of explicit disclosure of Joe's responsibility for Simon's abuse is a moment of great violence and bloodshed. It is also paradoxically the moment when Simon strikes back and we are allowed to grasp the intensity of his delayed response. In reaction to being beaten yet again by Joe for some misdemeanour, Simon launches wildly at Joe with a glass splinter, stabbing him in the stomach and almost killing him (ibid., pp. 306–9). It is only at this point that we are forced to reinterpret all the coded signals provided earlier in the text about the ambivalent looks that he often gave Joe, his strong attachment to Kerewin, his reluctance to go to his own home, and the tense behaviour that he often displayed in the presence of the two of them. Strangely enough, however, shortly after this explicit articulation of the boy's response to his abuse the three characters are separated and the text falls apart. Joe's confession to Kerewin and her subsequent reactions to the full disclosure are particularly relevant in this regard:

> 'You know what?' he asks again, on the last recital, and she shakes her head tiredly. She has become more and more sober as the night wore on. 'I think I was trying to beat him dead,' says Joe. 'I think I was trying to kill him then.'
>
> . . .
>
> He says something in passing that Kerewin wishes he had never revealed. A few words, but they make for horror.
> He says, 'I don't think I'm the only one that's hurt him. He had some bloody funny marks on him when he arrived.'
>
> . . .
>
> She stowed her backpack into a large suitcase, added a few clothes, all her remaining smokes, the last of the bottle of Drambuie, Simon's rosary and three books.
> One is the Book of the Soul, the one she normally keeps under lock and key.
> One is the Concise Oxford Dictionary.
> The last is peculiarly her own.
> It is entitled, in hand-lettered copper uncials, 'Book of Godhead', and the title page reads,
> BOG: for spiritual small-players to lose themselves in.
> It contains an eclectic range of religious writing.
>
> . . .
>
> It was a book she had designed to cater for all the drifts and vagaries of her mind. To provide her with information, rough maps and sketches of a way to God.
> *She had a feeling her need for the numinous will increase dramatically from now on.*
> (Ibid., pp. 328, 329; italics added)

We notice, first of all, that Kerewin refuses to pass judgement on Joe. This is especially odd, as she has been shown in the novel to be very strong-minded and forthright with her opinions. What is even more strange, however, is the fact that immediately after this confession, she decides to pack bag and baggage and leave her lovingly created spiral home. The books that she decides to take along are also significant in this respect: a dictionary and several spiritual books. But it is not for nothing that she senses an increasing 'need for the numinous'. The novel itself subsequently becomes highly religious and esoteric in tone, following Joe on a visit to a shaman in a quest for atonement for his cruelties and, sporadically, Kerewin, on a journey that seems not to have any clear direction. All this narrative 'falling apart', however, has to be understood in the light of the novel's special discursive location of Simon and the contradictions involved in his rebellion against oppression.

Simon is frequently described with an array of quasi-religious significations. His age is undecidable. He seems to be simultaneously five years and ten times that. His eyes are 'seagreen' (ibid., p. 22), and he is said by Joe to have come on shore as part of the jetsam of a shipwreck a few years earlier (ibid., pp. 51, 83–8). When she first sees him, Kerewin describes him as a 'thin shockheaded person, haloed in hair, shrouded in the dying light' (ibid., p. 17). He makes a gift to Kerewin of a magnificent rosary of semi-precious stones which seems to be some kind of heirloom. Looking at how his hair falls across his face, she is reminded of 'the skirts of dervishes as they spin to ecstasy' (ibid., p. 68). Later in the novel, when he is hospitalized following the brutal final encounter with Joe, his hands are said to be marked by a network of pink scars and his feet are described as being wrapped in bandages, covering 'what feels like holes' (ibid., p. 387). His hair is shown to be 'gone to a fine gold fuzz' (ibid., p. 389). And, to top it all, Simon claims with great conviction to be able to see people's auras in the dark (ibid., p. 93). What all these quasi-religious references suggest is that Simon is a sort of sacrificial figure and is made to carry, *pace* Shakespeare's Hamlet, the 'slings [stings] and arrows of an outrageous fortune'. The point, though, is that this outrageous fortune is not only the fact of being the adopted child of an abusive parent; it is also the fact of carrying a disability that makes him the butt of insults and the suspect of contamination, and, at a more complex discursive level, that operates so as to render him silent, spoken-for and misunderstood in the narrative. It is therefore significant to note that despite Kerewin's growing friendship with him, she consistently thinks of him in terms of negative epithets, repeatedly extending in different directions what she earlier defines intuitively as 'contaminating'. The novel rehearses the contours of the primal scene at several levels of its discourse. Much as in Coetzee's novel, the disabled in this text, though located within a particular frame, exceeds its regulative parameters and is seen to affect the boundaries of the entire narrative itself. It is almost as if the text is nervous about the disabled, its nervousness displaying itself in ways that undermine its narrative stability.

If Keri Hulme's novel can be said to produce a sense of discursive nervousness that spreads throughout its narrative, Ben Okri's *The Famished Road* (1992) is crucial for grasping the significance of surrendering the entire universe of discourse to a figure that is not only traditionally thought of as disabled, but, additionally, is believed to be liminal, existing between the interstices of this world and the next. Okri's novel is a bold experiment with narrative form in which the entire novel is narrated in the first person through the eyes of Azaro, an *abiku* child. The *abiku* is a child believed to be a 'born-to-die', one that has an umbilical connection to the otherworld, and, trapped in a restless cycle of rebirth, is born only to die again and be reborn to the same mother. Belief in the phenomenon is common in southern Nigeria and has figured prominently in Nigerian literature.[7] The key difference between Okri's use of the concept and its treatment by others is that, in his novel, there is a free interaction between the real world and that of spirits that disobeys all notions of boundaries or of a clear narrative teleology.

At various points in the novel, Azaro encounters disabled people who also seem to be lunatic:

There was a man standing near me. I noticed him because of his smell. He wore a dirty, tattered shirt. His hair was reddish. Flies were noisy around his ears. His private parts showed through his underpants. His legs were covered in sores. The flies around his face made him look as if he had four eyes. I stared at him out of curiosity. He made a violent motion, scattering the flies, and I noticed that his two eyes rolled around as if in an extraordinary effort to see themselves. (Ibid., p. 17)

He had on only a pair of sad-looking underpants. His hair was rough and covered in a red liquid and bits of rubbish. He had a big sore on his back and a small one on his ear. Flies swarmed around him and he kept twitching. Every now and then he broke into a titter.

. . . He had one eye higher than another. His mouth looked like a festering wound. He twitched, stamped, laughed, and suddenly ran into the bar. (Ibid., p. 84)

In the case of the first one, encountered early in the novel when Azaro is lost in a market and struggling to find his way home, the lunatic is strange in that the already bizarre nature of his eyes is further complicated by the flies that seem to multiply them. The second one, encountered much later when Azaro is tending Madame Koto's palm-wine shop, recalls the earlier lunatic, but with the crucial difference that this one is shown to be potentially more violent. But, because Azaro is constantly shifting between the real-world and that of spirits, he regularly meets characters who match these two lunatics in grotesqueness. It is as if to suggest that in the dispossession and destitution of the poor, whose conditions of existence are central to the novel, the anxiety-generating potential of the esoteric realm is equally at play in the real world. If it is remembered that the novel is being narrated by a figure thought of as liminal and disabled, we see how the entire universe is produced through a trope of disability.

A further complexity introduced by Okri's text is that the *abiku* child is also meant to stand for the fractious postcolonial history of his native Nigeria:

Things that are not ready, not willing to be born or to become, *things for which adequate preparations have not been made to sustain their momentous births*, things that are not resolved, things bound up with failure and with fear of being, they all keep recurring, keep coming back, and in themselves partake of the spirit-child's condition. They keep coming and going till their time is right. History itself demonstrates how things of the world partake of the condition of the spirit-child. (Ibid., p. 487; my emphases)

In this linking of a national history with the condition of the *abiku*, Okri echoes a suggestion made by Wole Soyinka in *A Dance of the Forests*, which was commissioned specifically to commemorate Independence in 1961. At a moment in Soyinka's play, the nation is figured as a half-bodied *abiku* child, challenging the substance of Independence. Reproducing the trope thirty years on, Okri destabilizes the relation between history and progress by centralizing the liminal *abiku* child and making it the (counter-)productive point of narrative unfolding. Unlike the previous examples we have looked at, in Okri's work the contours of the primal scene mark the potential dissolution of any certitudes that we might have had concerning the boundaries or hierarchized relationships between the able-bodied and the physically disabled. The perpetual oscillation in the primal scene of the encounter with the disabled is marked in this text by a restless oscillation between the real world and that of spirits, mediated through the liminal *abiku* figure of Azaro.

Conclusion: Postcolonial History through a Trope of Disability

The presence of disabled people in postcolonial writing marks more than just the recognition of their obvious presence in the real world of postcolonial existence and the fact that in most cases national economies woefully fail to take care of them. It means much more than that. It also marks the sense of a major problematic, which is nothing less than the difficult encounter with history itself. For colonialism may be said to have been a major force of disabling the colonized from taking their place in the flow of history other than in a position of stigmatized underprivilege. The devastating effect of colonialism on the psyches of the colonized has been written about by Frantz Fanon (1952, 1961) and need not detain us here. What it is important to note, however, is that the encounter with the disabled in postcolonial writing is as much a struggle to transcend the nightmare of history. But it is a nightmare which is also as much a product of warped postcolonial national identities as it is of the traumatic processes of colonialism. This is particularly the case in Africa, where wars and rumours of war succeed in proliferating disability on the streets daily. Angola, Mozambique, Liberia, Rwanda, Sierra Leone. In all these countries reckless wars have ensured that the disabled are a part of everyday life. In any attempt to create a civil imagining in these countries, the problem will always be how to confront a traumatic history of disability at the personal as well as social level. And though it is not wise to venture any answers we may yet add that there will be a perpetual oscillation between the painful past and the vital present that will make civil societies in such contexts liminal and riddled with emotional contradictions. A crucial step, perhaps, would be to recognize this for a fact and to account for it as a *process of becoming*, one that needs to be grasped in its full complexity before it can be overcome, requiring patience, fortitude, hope, and, above all, dialogue. A ceaseless dialogue.

Acknowledgments

I wish to say a special thanks to Jo Emeney, who, as a student of mine at Pembroke College, Cambridge in 1995/96 first drew my attention to the proliferation of disabled figures in postcolonial literature. Thanks are also due to Kate

Huntington and Bibi Jacob of Kings College, Cambridge, who in the Lent term of 1997 had to sit through what I think was an interminable supervision at which I struggled with great enthusiasm but little coherence to explore my ideas on Keri Hulme's *The Bone People*; also to Mark Wormald, my colleague at Pembroke, for reading and commenting on a first draft of this essay. Finally, I want to dedicate the essay to my father, a great storyteller who had one leg shorter than the other.

Notes

1   This was in a BBC television talk show called *Esther*, aired on 20 March 1997 and hosted by Esther Rantzen. The show was concerned with finding out what might be said to constitute comedy for a British audience.
2   Contrary to how the term is applied in Freudian usage, 'primal scene' is used here not to denote the child's witnessing of the sexual encounter between parents, but rather with the sense of being basic, primary and fundamental.
3   An example of this childhood fascination with dismemberment is reflected in Disney's *Toy Story* (1995). In this film about toys coming to life, fragmentation is continually represented in the figure of Mr Potato Head, a toy potato with detachable limbs and facial components. Not only does Mr Potato Head regularly detach parts of his body to stress his arguments or gain some advantage, at three different points in the film he suffers complete fragmentation on collision with fast-moving objects.
4   In a racial context, it is interesting to note the degree to which racial stereotypes often get internalized by racial minorities and constantly become the objects of struggle. Toni Morrison's *The Bluest Eye* (1970) offers a most interesting tragic account of this process.
5   Though I will be looking mainly at the three texts I have already mentioned, the general thesis may be tested and elaborated in relation to a variety of postcolonial texts in which the disabled appear either peripherally or centrally. A useful list of such works could include Ngugi wa' Thiongo's *Petals of Blood* (1977), Bapsi Sidhwa's *The Ice-Candy Man* (1989), J. M. Coetzee's *The Life and Times of Michael K* (1983) and even earlier works such as Wole Soyinka's *Madmen and Specialists* (1971) and Naguib Mahfouz's *Midaq Alley* (1947), among others.
6   An excellent illustration of these features is provided in Nayantara Saghal's *Rich Like Us* (1983) in an encounter with a cripple beggar who is a completely peripheral character to the main action. See especially the account of the attempt to seize the beggar for an enforced vasectomy on pp. 89–90.
7   Quayson (1997, pp. 123–39) explores this idea more fully.

References

Literary sources

Coetzee, J. M. (1980) *Waiting for the Barbarians*, London: Secker and Warburg.
—— (1983) *The Life and Times of Michael K*, London: Secker and Warburg.

Disney (1995) *Toy Story*.

Hulme, Keri (1983) *The Bone People*, London: Picador.

Mahfouz, Naguib (1947) *Midaq Alley*, London: Doubleday.

Morrison, Toni (1970) The Bluest Eye, London: Picador.

Ngugi wa' Thiongo (1977) *Petals of Blood*, London: Heinemann.

Okri, Ben (1992) *The Famished Road*, London: Cape.

Saghal, Nayantara (1983) *Rich Like Us*, London: Sceptre.

Sidhwa, Bapsi (1989) *The Ice-Candy Man*, London: Penguin Books.

Soyinka, Wole (1963) *A Dance of the Forests*, in *Collected Plays Vol. 1*, Oxford: Oxford University Press.

——(1971) *Madmen and Specialists*, in *Collected Plays Vol. 2*, Oxford: Oxford University Press.

Critical sources

Ablon, Joan (1984) *Little People in America: The Social Dimensions of Dwarfism*, New York: Praeger.

Bowie, Malcolm (1991) *Lacan*, Cambridge, MA: Harvard University Press.

Ellmann, Maud (1994) *Psychoanalytic Literary Criticism*, London: Longman.

Fanon, Frantz (1952) *Black Skin, White Masks*, trans. Charles Lam Markham, New York: Grove Press.

——(1961) *The Wretched of the Earth*, trans. Constance Farrington, Harmondsworth: Penguin Books.

Goffman, Erving (1963) *Stigma: Notes on the Management of Spoiled Identity*, Englewood Cliffs, NJ: Prentice-Hall.

Lacan, Jacques (1948) 'Aggressivity in psychoanalysis', in *Écrits*, trans. Alan Sheridan London: Routlédge, 1989.

——(1949) 'The mirror stage as formative of the function of the I as revealed in psychoanalytic experience', in *Écrits*, trans. Alan Sheridan, London: Routledge, 1989.

Murphy, Robert F. (1987) *The Body Silent*, London: J. M. Dent and Sons.

Quayson, Ato (1997) *Strategic Transformations in Nigerian Writing: Orality and History in Rev Samuel Johnson, Amos Tutuola, Wole Soyinka and Ben Okri*, Oxford and Bloomington: James Currey and Indiana University Press.

Whyte, Susan Reynolds and Benedicte Ingstad (1995) 'Disability and culture: an overview', in Susan Reynolds Whyte and Benedicte Ingstad, eds, *Disability and Culture*, Berkeley: University of California Press.

Žižek, Slavoj (1992) *Looking Awry: An Introduction to Jacques Lacan through Popular Culture*, Cambridge, MA: MIT Press.

Chapter 13

Theorizing Disability

Rosemarie Garland Thomson

Feminist Theory, the Body, and the Disabled Figure

The female body and the disabled body

Many parallels exist between the social meanings attributed to female bodies and those assigned to disabled bodies. Both the female and the disabled body are cast as deviant and inferior; both are excluded from full participation in public as well as economic life; both are defined in opposition to a norm that is assumed to possess natural physical superiority. Indeed, the discursive equation of femaleness with disability is common, sometimes to denigrate women and sometimes to defend them. Examples abound, from Freud's delineating femaleness in terms of castration, to late-nineteenth-century physicians' defining menstruation a disabling and restricting "eternal wound," to Thorstein Veblen's describing women in 1899 as literally disabled by feminine roles and costuming. Even feminists today invoke negative images of disability to describe the oppression of women; for example, Jane Flax asserts that women are "mutilated and deformed" by sexist ideology and practices.[1]

Perhaps the founding association of femaleness with disability occurs in the fourth book of *Generation of Animals*, Aristotle's discourse of the normal and the abnormal, in which he refines the Platonic concept of antinomies so that bodily variety translates into hierarchies of the typical and the aberrant. "[A]nyone who does not take after his parents," Aristotle asserts, "is really in a way a monstrosity, since in these cases Nature has in a way strayed from the generic type. The first beginning of this deviation is when a female is formed instead of a male." Here the philosopher, whom we might consider the founding father of Western taxonomy, idealizes bodies to produce a definitive, seemingly neutral "generic type" along with its antithesis, the "monstrosity," whose departure from such a "type" is a profound "deviation." Aristotle's spatial metaphor places a certain human figure, the "generic type," at the center of his system. On the outer margin is the "monstrosity," the physical consequence

of Nature's having "strayed" onto a path of deviance, the first stop along which
is the female body. Aristotle thus conjoins the "monstrosity" – whom we would
today term "congenitally disabled" – and the female outside the definitive
norm. In Book Two, Aristotle affirms this connection of disabled and female
bodies by stating that "the female is as it were a deformed male" or – as it
appears in other translations – "a mutilated male."[2]

More significant than Aristotle's simple conflation of disability and femaleness is his declaration that the source of all otherness is the concept of a norm,
a "generic type" against which all physical variation appears as different, derivative, inferior, and insufficient. Not only does this definition of the female as
a "mutilated male" inform later depictions of woman as diminished man, but
it also arranges somatic diversity into a hierarchy of value that assigns com-
pleteness to some bodies and deficiency to others. Furthermore, by defining
femaleness as deviant and maleness as essential, Aristotle initiates the discursive practice of marking what is deemed aberrant while concealing what is
privileged behind an assertion of normalcy. This is perhaps the original operation of the logic that has become so familiar in discussions of gender, race, or
disability: male, white, or able-bodied superiority appears natural, undisputed,
and unremarked, seemingly eclipsed by female, black, or disabled difference.
What this passage makes clearest, however, is that without the monstrous body
to demarcate the borders of the generic, without the female body to distinguish the shape of the male, and without the pathological to give form to the
normal, the taxonomies of bodily value that underlie political, social, and economic arrangements would collapse.[3]

This persistent intertwining of disability with femaleness in Western discourse provides a starting point for exploring the relationship of social identity to the body. As Aristotle's pronouncement suggests, the social category of
disability rests on the significance accorded bodily functioning and configuration, just as the social category of woman does. Therefore, feminist theory's
recent inquiries into gender as a category, the body's role in identity and selfhood, and the complexity of social power relations can readily transfer to an
analysis of disability. Moreover, applying feminist theory to disability analysis
infuses it with feminism's insistence on the relationship between the meanings attributed to bodies by cultural representations and the consequences of
those meanings in the world. As I bring feminism to disability studies, I will
also suggest how the category of disability might be inserted into feminist
theory so that the bodily configurations and functioning we call "disabled" will
be included in all feminist examinations of culture and representation. This
brief exploration aims then at beginning to alter the terms of both feminist and
disability discourses.

Feminist theory and disability discourse

Contemporary feminist theory has proved to be porous, diffuse, and – perhaps
most significant – self-critical. Thus, we speak now of "feminisms," "conflicts

in feminism," "hyphenated feminisms," and even "postfeminism."[4] Historically, academic feminism combines the highly political civil rights and accompanying identity politics impulses of the 1960s and 1970s with postructuralism's theoretical critique of the liberal humanist faith in knowledge, truth, and identity, often adding an insistence on materiality gleaned from Marxist thought. The focus of feminist conversation has shifted from early debates between liberal and radical feminisms, which focused on achieving equality, to later formulations of cultural and gynocentric feminisms, which highlighted and rehabilitated female differences. Most recently, the debate between those who would minimize differences to achieve equality and those who would elaborate differences to valorize the feminine has been complicated by an interrogation of gender construction itself and a recognition of multiple axes of identity, both of which profoundly challenge the very notion of "woman" as any kind of unified identity category.[5] Feminism's insistence that standpoint shapes politics; that identity, subjectivity, and the body are cultural constructs to be questioned; and that all representation is political comprise the theoretical milieu in which I want to examine disability.

The strands of feminist thought most applicable to disability studies are those that go beyond a narrow focus on gender alone to undertake a broad sociopolitical critique of systemic, inequitable power relations based on social categories grounded in the body. Feminism thus becomes a theoretical perspective and methodology examining gender as a discursive, ideological, and material category that interacts with but does not subordinate other social identities or the particularities of embodiment, history, and location that inform subjectivity. Briefly put, feminism's often conflicting and always complex aims of politicizing the materiality of bodies and rewriting the category of woman combine exactly the methods that should be used to examine disability.[6]

I want to extend in a fresh juxtaposition, then, the association of disability and femaleness with which I began this chapter. But rather than simply conflating the disabled body with the female body, I want to theorize disability in the ways that feminism has theorized gender. Both feminism and my analysis of disability challenge existing social relations; both resist interpretations of certain bodily configurations and functioning as deviant; both question the ways that differences are invested with meaning; both examine the enforcement of universalizing norms; both interrogate the politics of appearance; both explore the politics of naming; both forge positive identities. Nevertheless, feminism has formulated these terms and probed these concerns much more thoroughly than disability studies has.[7]

Eve Kosofsky Sedgwick's distinction, for example, between a "minoritizing" and a "universalizing" view of difference can be applied to disability discourse. According to Sedgwick's hybrid of feminist and queer theory, one minoritizes difference by imagining its significance and concerns as limited to a narrow, specific, relatively fixed population or area of inquiry. In contrast, a universalizing view sees issues surrounding a particular difference as having "continuing, determinative importance in the lives of people across the spectrum of [identities]."[8] Disability studies should become a universalizing discourse in the way that Sedgwick imagines gay studies and feminism to be. Disability (or gender or homosexuality) would then be recognized as structuring a wide range of thought, language, and perception that might not be explicitly articulated as "disability." I am proposing, then, a universalizing view of disability by showing how the concept of disability informs such national ideologies as American liberal individualism and sentimentalism, as well as African-American and lesbian identities. Such terms from feminist theory can be enlisted to challenge the persistent assumption that disability is a self-evident condition of physical inadequacy and private misfortune whose politics concern only a limited minority.

A universalized disability discourse that draws on feminism's confrontation with the gender system requires understanding the body as a cultural text that is interpreted, inscribed with meaning – indeed *made* – within social relations. Such a perspective advocates political equity by denaturalizing disability's assumed inferiority, by casting it as difference rather than lack. Although this constructionist perspective does the vital cultural work of destigmatizing the differences we call gender, race, or disability, the logic of constructionism threatens nevertheless to obscure the material and historical effects of those differences and to erase the very social categories we analyze and claim as significant. Thus, the poststructuralist logic that destabilizes identity can free marginalized people from the narrative of essential inadequacy, but at the same time it risks denying the particularity of their experiences.[9] The theoretical bind is that deconstructing oppressive categories can neutralize the effects of real differences.

A disability politics cannot at this moment, however, afford to banish the category of disability according to the poststructuralist critique of identity in the way that some feminists have argued for abandoning the concept of woman as hopelessly imprisoning and abstract.[10] The kind of access to public spaces and institutions that women gained in the nineteenth century and have expanded since the 1960s was only fully mandated for disabled people by the Americans with Disabilities Act of 1990, a broad civil rights law that is only beginning to be implemented. And while in the movement toward equality, race and gender are generally accepted as differences rather than deviances, disability is still most often seen as bodily inadequacy or catastrophe to be compensated for with pity or good will, rather than accommodated by systemic changes based on civil rights. On the one hand, then, it is important to use the constructionist argument to assert that disability is not bodily insufficiency, but instead arises from the interaction of physical differences with an environment. On the other hand, the particular, historical existence of the disabled body demands both accommodation and recognition. In other words, the physical differences of using a wheelchair or being deaf, for example, should be claimed, but not cast as lack.[11]

Both constructionism and essentialism, then, are theoretical strategies – framings of the body – invoked for specific ends, such as psychologically liberating people whose bodies have been defined as defective or facilitating imagined communities from which positive identities can emerge. Strategic constructionism destigmatizes the disabled body, makes difference relative, denaturalizes so-called normalcy, and challenges appearance hierarchies. Strategic essentialism, by contrast, validates individual experience and consciousness, imagines community, authorizes history, and facilitates self-naming. The identity "disabled" operates in this mode as a pragmatic narrative, what Susan Bordo calls "a life-enhancing fiction" that places the reality of individual bodies and perspectives within specific social and historical contexts.[12]

Imagining feminist disability discourse

But if the category "disabled" is a useful fiction, the disabled body set in a world structured for the privileged body is not. Disability, perhaps more than other differences, demands a reckoning with the messiness of bodily variety, with literal individuation run amok. Because disability is defined not as a set of observable, predictable traits – like racialized or gendered features – but rather as *any* departure from an unstated physical and fuctional norm, disability highlights individual differences. In other words, the concept of disability unites a highly marked, heterogeneous group whose only commonality is being considered abnormal. As the norm becomes neutral in an environment created to accommodate it, disability becomes intense, extravagant, and problematic. Disability is the unorthodox made flesh, refusing to be normalized, neutralized, or homogenized. More important, in an era governed by the abstract principle of universal equality, disability signals that the body cannot be universalized. Shaped by history, defined by particularity, and at odds with its environment, disability confounds any notion of a generalizable, stable physical subject. The cripple before the stairs, the blind person before the printed page, the deaf person before the radio, the amputee before the typewriter, and the dwarf before the counter are all proof that the myriad structures and practices of material, daily life enforce the cultural standard of a universal subject with a narrow range of corporeal variation.

Disability, as a formal identity category, can pressure feminist theory to acknowledge physical diversity more thoroughly. Perhaps feminism's most useful concept for disability studies is standpoint theory, which recognizes the immediacy and complexity of physical existence. Emphasizing the multiplicity of all women's identities, histories, and bodies, this theory asserts that individual situations structure the subjectivity from which particular women speak and perceive.[13] Incorporating postmodernism's challenge of the unsituated, objective Enlightenment viewpoint, feminist standpoint theory has reformulated gender identity as a complex, dynamic matrix of interrelated, often contradictory, experiences, strategies, styles, and attributions mediated by culture and individual history. This network cannot be separated meaningfully into discrete entities or ordered into a hierarchy. Acknowledging identity's particular, complex nature allows characteristics beyond race, class, and gender to emerge. Standpoint theory and the feminist practice of explicitly situating oneself when speaking thus allow for complicating inflections such as disability or, more broadly, body configuration – attributions such as fat, disfigured, abnormal, ugly, or deformed – to enter into our considerations of identity and subjectivity. Such a dismantling of the unitary category woman has enabled feminist theory to encompass – although not without contention – such feminist specializations as, for example, Patricia Hill Collins's "black feminist thought" or my own explorations of a "feminist disability studies."[14] So just as feminist theory can bring to disability theory strategies for analyzing the meanings of physical differences and identifying sites where those meanings influence other discourses, it can also help articulate the uniqueness and physicality of identity.

A feminist political praxis for women with disabilities needs, then, to focus at times on the singularity and perhaps the immutability of the flesh, and at the same time to interrogate the identity it supports. For example, in exploring the politics of self-naming, Nancy Mairs claims the appellation "cripple" because it demands that others acknowledge the particularity of her body. "People . . . wince at the word 'cripple'," Mairs contends. Even though she retains what has been a derogatory term, she insists on determining its significance herself: "Perhaps I want them to wince. I want them to see me as a tough customer, one to whom the fates/gods/viruses have not been kind, but who can face the brutal truth of her existence squarely. As a cripple, I swagger." Here Mairs is not simply celebrating the term of otherness or attempting to reverse its negative connotation; rather, she wants to call attention to the material reality of her crippledness, to her bodily difference and her experience of it. For Mairs, the social constructionist argument risks neutralizing the significance of her pain and her struggle with an environment built for other bodies.[15]

Disability, however, is left out of several mainstream feminist assumptions. For instance, while feminism quite legitimately decries the sexual objectification of woman, disabled women often encounter what Harlan Hahn has called "asexual objectification," the assumption that sexuality is inappropriate in disabled people. One woman who uses a wheelchair, for example, and is also quite beautiful reports that people often respond to her as if this combination of traits were a remarkable and lamentable contradiction. The judgment that the disabled woman's body is asexual and unfeminine creates what Michelle Fine and Adrienne Asch term "rolelessness," a social invisibility and cancellation of femininity that can prompt disabled women to claim the female identity that the culture denies them. For example, Cheryl Marie Wade insists upon a harmony between her disability and her womanly sexuality in a poem characterizing herself as "The Woman With Juice."[16] As Mairs's exploration of self-naming and Wade's assertion of sexuality suggest, a feminist disability politics would uphold the right for women to define their physical differences and their femininity for themselves rather than conforming to received interpretations of their bodies.

Wade's poem of self-definition echoes Mairs by maintaining firmly that she is "not one of the physically challenged." Rather, she claims, "I'm the Gimp/I'm the Cripple/I'm the Crazy Lady." Affirming her body as at once sexual and different, she asserts, "I'm a French kiss with cleft tongue." Resisting the cultural tendency not only to erase her sexuality but to depreciate and objectify her body, she characterizes herself as "a sock in the eye with gnarled fist." This image of the disabled body as a visual assault, a shocking spectacle to the normate eye, captures a defining aspect of disabled experience. Whereas feminists claim that women are objects of the evaluative male gaze, Wade's image of her body as "a sock in the eye" subtly reminds us that the disabled body is the object of the stare. If the male gaze makes the normative female a sexual spectacle, then the stare sculpts the disabled subject into a grotesque spectacle. The stare is the gaze intensified, framing her body as an icon of deviance. Indeed, as Wade's poem suggests, the stare is the gesture that creates disability as an oppressive social relationship. And as every person with a visible disability knows intimately, managing, deflecting, resisting, or renouncing that stare is part of the daily business of life.

In addition, disabled women must sometimes defend against the assessment of their bodies as unfit for motherhood or of themselves as infantilized objects who occasion other people's virtue. Whereas motherhood is often seen as compulsory for women, disabled women are often denied or discouraged from the reproductive role that some feminist thinkers find oppressive. The controversial feminist ethic of care has also been criticized by feminist disability scholars for undermining symmetrical, reciprocal relations among disabled and non-disabled women as well as for suggesting that care is the sole responsibility of women. Making disabled women the objects of care risks casting them as helpless in order to celebrate nurturing as virtuous feminine agency. Philosopher Anita Silvers explains that "far from vanquishing patriarchal systems, substituting the ethics of caring for the ethics of equality threatens an even more oppressive paternalism."[17]

Perhaps more problematic still, feminist abortion rationale seldom questions the prejudicial assumption that "defective" fetuses destined to become disabled people should be eliminated. The concerns of older women, who are often disabled, tend also to be ignored by younger feminists.[18] One of the most pervasive feminist assumptions that undermines some disabled women's struggle is the liberal ideology of autonomy and independence that fuels the broader impulse toward female empowerment. By tacitly incorporating the liberal premise that levels individual characteristics to posit an abstract, disembodied subject of democracy, feminist practice often leaves no space for the needs and accommodations that disabled women's bodies require.[19] Prominent disability rights activist Judy Heumann's angry and disappointed words reflect an alienation not unlike that between some black women and some white feminists: "When I come into a room full of feminists, all they see is a wheelchair."[20] These conflicts testify that feminists – like everyone else, including disabled people themselves – have absorbed cultural stereotypes.

Femininity and disability

Although I insist on disabled women's identity even while questioning its sources, I also want to suggest that a firm boundary between "disabled" and "non-disabled" women cannot be meaningfully drawn – just as any absolute distinction between sex and gender is problematic. Femininity and disability are inextricably entangled in patriarchal culture, as Aristotle's equation of women with disabled men illustrates. Not only has the female body been labeled deviant, but historically the practices of femininity have configured female bodies similarly to disability. Foot binding, scarification, clitoridectomy, and corseting were (and are) socially accepted, encouraged, even compulsory cultural forms of female disablement that, ironically, are socially enabling, increasing a woman's value and status at a given moment in a particular society. Similarly, such conditions as anorexia, hysteria, and agoraphobia are in a sense standard feminine roles enlarged to disabling conditions, blurring the line between "normal" feminine behavior and pathology.[21]

The disciplinary regimes of feminine beauty often obscure the seemingly self-evident categories of the "normal" and the "pathological." For example, the nineteenth-century Euroamerican prescription for upper-class feminine beauty – pale skin, emaciated body, wide eyes – precisely paralleled the symptoms of tuberculosis, just as the cult of thinness promoted by the fashion industry today mimics the appearance of disease.[22] In a similar example, the iconography and language describing contemporary cosmetic surgery in women's magazines persistently casts the unreconstructed female body as having "abnormalities" that can be "corrected" by surgical procedures that "improve" the appearance by producing "natural looking" noses, thighs, breasts, chins, and so on.[23] This discourse terms women's unmodified bodies as unnatural and abnormal, while casting surgically altered bodies as normal and natural. Although cosmetic surgery is in one sense a logical extension of beauty practices such as using makeup, perming or relaxing hair, lightening skin, and removing hair, it differs profoundly from these basically decorative forms of self-reconstruction: like clitoridectomies and scarification, it involves the mutilation and pain that accompany many disabilities.

All of these practices cannot, of course, be equated; however, each transforms an infinitely plastic body in ways similar to the effects of disability. Beautification changes are imagined to be choices that will sculpt the female body so it conforms to a feminine ideal. Disabilities, in contrast, are imagined to be random transformations that move the body away from ideal forms. In a society in which appearance is the primary index of value for women (and increasingly for men), beautification practices normalize the female body and disabilities abnormalize it. Feminization prompts the gaze; disability prompts the stare. Feminization increases a woman's cultural capital; disability reduces it.

But as Aristotle's equation of females with mutilated males suggests, even the ideal female body is abnormal compared to the universal standard of the male body. The normative female – the figure of the beautiful woman – is the narrowly prescribed opposite of the ideal male. If he is to be strong, active, large, hirsute, hard, then she must be weak, passive, small, hairless, soft. The normative female body, then, occupies a dual and paradoxical cultural role: it is the negative term opposing the male body, but it is also simultaneously the privileged term opposing the abnormalized female body.[24] For example, the nineteenth-century obsession with scientific quantification produced a detailed description of absolute beauty, laid out by Havelock Ellis, with a Darwinian ranking determined entirely by physical characteristics and ranging from the "beautiful" European woman to what was considered to be her grotesque opposite, the African woman.[25] Moreover, scientific discourse conceived this anatomical scale of beauty as simultaneously one of pathology. The further a female body departed from absolute beauty, the more "abnormal" it became. The markers of this indubitable pathology were traits like dark skin and physical disability, or behaviors like prostitution, that were often linked to body characteristics. Within this scheme, all women are seen as deviant, but some more so than others. So the simple dichotomy of objectified feminine body and masculine subject is complicated by other oppositions. Indeed, the unfeminine, unbeautiful body defines and is defined by the ideal feminine body. This aberrant figure of woman has been identified variously in history and discourse as black, fat, lesbian, sexually voracious, disabled, or ugly. What is important here is that this figure's deviance and subsequent devaluation are always attributed to some visible characteristic that operates as an emblem of her difference, just as beauty has always been located in the body of the feminine woman.

As one manifestation of the unbeautiful woman, then, the figure of the disabled woman, disrupts oppositional paradigms. This cultural figure of the disabled woman, not the actual woman with a disability, is the subject of this study. Because representation structures reality, the cultural figures that haunt us often must, like Virginia Woolf's Angel of the House, be wrestled to the floor before even modest self-definition, let alone political action, can occur. The figure of the disabled woman I focus on here is a product of a conceptual triangulation. She is a cultural third term, defined by the original pair of the masculine figure and the feminine figure. Seen as the opposite of the masculine figure, but also imagined as the antithesis of the normal woman, the figure of the disabled female is thus ambiguously positioned both inside and outside the category of woman.

Disabled women figures

My purpose here is to trace the complexities that arise from the presence of these ambiguous disabled women figures within cultural and literary texts in which, for the most part, they occupy marginal positions. In almost every case, the disabled woman figure functions as a symbol of otherness, either positive or negative. The presence of these often multiply marginalized figures complicates and unbalances seemingly stable narrative economies in the texts. In freak shows, for example, exhibitions of disabled women of color introduce race, gender, and ethnicity into freak discourse, which seems initially to turn upon the simple opposition between "normal" and "abnormal" bodies. Freaks always appeared not just as monsters, but as gendered and racialized monsters.

The complication provoked by the disabled woman figure is perhaps clearest, however, in the literary texts examined here. Shifting the analytical focus from main characters and central plots to the secondary, or even incidental, disabled women reveals complex alignments and otherwise buried tensions at work in the texts. For instance, the cluster of nineteenth-century sentimental fiction sets a feminine narrative voice and perspective against a masculine point of view. If, however, we recognize the triangle of the implicitly masculine cultural self, the feminine woman, and the disabled woman, fresh perspectives emerge. Examining the opposition that these social reform novels posit between the feminine woman and the disabled woman – between Elizabeth Stuart Phelps's heroine, Perley, and her deaf and mute anti-heroine, Catty, for instance – reveals the texts' otherwise obscured entanglement in liberal individualist ideology. Similarly, a primary discourse in twentieth-century African-American novels is one of race. Yet, as with the earlier group of texts, examining the disabled figures' rhetorical function complicates the primary opposition between black and white culture on which the novels turn. In Toni Morrison's *Tar Baby*, for example, the blind Therese's narrative empowerment must be contrasted with the beautiful Jadine's loss of power in order for the novel's social critique to be fully apprehended. Thus, the presence of the disabled woman figure challenges any simple textual reading that arranges dominant and marginal positions along a single axis of identity such as gender, race, or class.

Sociocultural Analyses of the Extraordinary Body

Erving Goffman's stigma theory

As I have suggested, the contemporary theory most suited to examining disability fuses identity politics with the poststructuralist interrogation of identity, truth, and knowledge, places its concerns in historical context, and forms a complex analysis of the relationship between society and the body. Although feminist theory's attention to the body and identity is useful in this regard, to satisfactorily formulate disability theory it is necessary to invoke several other theorists, though their main focus is neither gender nor disability. To clarify how representation attaches meaning to the physical differences we term disability, I discuss here the intersections of body and culture probed by Erving Goffman, Mary Douglas, and Michel Foucault, among others. Of these, only

Goffman's sociological stigma theory directly addresses disability; to utilize Douglas's, Foucault's, and others' work, I have extrapolated how disability could be included in their analyses. This brief survey highlights the aspects of these theorists' ideas that pertain to the ways the disabled body emerges from culture.

Erving Goffman's definitive 1963 analysis, *Stigma: Notes on the Management of Spoiled Identity*, lays out a theory of stigmatization as a social process that attempts to account for all forms of what Simone de Beauvoir's earlier study of women called "Otherness."[26] Despite its curiously insensitive title and disturbingly hostile tone toward its subjects – perhaps in the tradition of Freud – Goffman's work underpins the nascent field of disability studies in the social sciences. Like feminist theory, stigma theory provides a useful vocabulary for placing disability in social contexts. Whereas terms such as "otherness" or "alterity" dominate literary criticism, both are limited for explaining marginalized identities because they are nouns. In contrast, the term "stigma," taken by Goffman from the Greek practice of branding or marking slaves and criminals and from Christian notions about the wounds of saints, can take many grammatical forms to match the component strands of a complex social process. The transitive verb "stigmatize," for example, suggests a process with both a subject and an object. Such semantic flexibility can call to account a "stigmatizer," identify an institution that is "stigmatizing," isolate a "stigma" as only one aspect of a whole, complex individual, or describe people or traits as "stigmatized." Some social psychologists have extended Goffman's theory by using the term "mark" to name a potentially stigmatizable physical or behavioral trait. This subtle distinction stresses the separation between actual characteristics or behavior and the processes of devaluing them.[27] Individuals are "markable" because of particular traits, and "markers" are those who interpret certain traits as deviant. Stigma theory thus provides a means of precisely tracing the production of cultural "minorities" or "others." In short, "stigmatize" describes distinctions among people, their physical traits, what is done to them, who does it, and what it means.

In essence, stigmatization is an interactive social process in which particular human traits are deemed not only different, but deviant. It is a form of social comparison apparently found in all societies, though the specific characteristics singled out vary across cultures and history. Most important is that these social devaluations are collective, part of a communal acculturation process. Stigmatization creates a shared, socially maintained and determined conception of a normal individual, what I earlier termed a normate, sculpted by a social group attempting to define its own character and boundaries. Though any human trait can be stigmatized, the dominant group has the authority and means to determine which differences are inferior and to perpetuate those judgments.[28] Thus terms like "minority," "ethnicity," and "disability" suggest infusing certain differences with negative value. Stigmatization not only reflects the tastes and opinions of the dominant group, it reinforces

that group's idealized self-description as neutral, normal, legitimate, and identifiable by denigrating the characteristics of less powerful groups or those considered alien. The process of stigmatization thus legitimates the status quo,
naturalizes attributions of inherent inferiority and superiority, and obscures
the socially constructed quality of both categories.

Recent elaborations of stigma theory by social scientists probe the motivation for this apparently universal social process. A phenomenological account
suggests that stigmatization arises from the human impulse to categorize differences and impose some kind of meaningful order on experience. All people
apparently need to routinize their lives with interpretive schemata, or what
Alfred Schutz calls "recipes," that make their worlds seem knowable and predictable. But stigmatizing is more than organizing experience. In this complex
process, certain human traits become salient, such as the physiological characteristics we use to anchor "sex," "race," "ethnicity," and "disability." Goffman
identifies three types of physical and behavioral characteristics from which stigmata are usually constructed by a given social unit: first are physical disability, deformity, or anomaly; next are individual behaviors such as addiction,
dishonesty, unpredictability, lack of education or manners, or certain sexual
habits; finally are race, religion, ethnicity, or gender.[29] Complex hierarchies of
assigned social status are founded on such actions and characteristics.

Goffman further refines his analysis of social stigmatization by recognizing
that most people in this society possess some stigmatized trait to some degree,
making the group who meet the narrow criteria of the idealized norm a very
small minority. The prototypical figure whom Western society constructs as its
ideal and its norm is the remnant of humanity after all those bearing stigmatized traits have been peeled away. The normate figure Goffman acknowledges
– the "young, married, white, urban, northern, heterosexual, Protestant father
of college education, fully employed, of good complexion, weight and height,
and a recent record in sports" that I mentioned earlier – is an updated version
of the self-possessed individual delineated in nineteenth-century American
discourse. By pointing out how few real people conform to this description,
Goffman reveals the illusory, ideological nature of the normate subject position. It is an image that dominates without material substance, a phantom
"majority" opposed to an overwhelming and equally illusory "minority."[30]

The implicit question underlying stigma theory is why differences within
social groups are not simply perceived without assigned values. While poststructuralist theory posits that binary opposition is always hierarchical, social
scientists tend to ground explanations in data about social practices. An historicist approach, for example, asserts that parents, institutional practices, and
various forms of art and communications media inculcate stigmatization across
generations and geographies. On the individual level, motivational or psychological explanations suggest that projecting unacceptable feelings and impulses
onto members of less powerful groups establishes identity and enhances self-
worth. Regardless of the cause, such a widespread, if not universal, human
practice flies in the face of modernity's ideology of liberal democracy.

Stigma theory is useful, then, because it untangles the processes that construct both the normative as well as the deviant and because it reveals the parallels among all forms of cultural oppression while still allowing specific devalued identities to remain in view. It essentially resituates the "problem" of disability from the body of the disabled person to the social framing of that body. Finally, stigma theory reminds us that the problems we confront are not disability, ethnicity, race, class, homosexuality, or gender; they are instead the inequalities, negative attitudes, misrepresentations, and institutional practices that result from the process of stigmatization.

"Matter out of place": Mary Douglas's concept of dirt

Anthropologist Mary Douglas also points to cultural patterns that show how the disability category operates. In her classic study, *Purity and Danger: An Analysis of Concepts of Pollution and Taboo*, Douglas speculates about the relativity of dirt in ways that can be applied to the cultural meaning of disability. Dirt, she observes, is "matter out of place . . . the by-product of a systematic ordering and classification of matter, in so far as ordering involves rejecting inappropriate elements."[31] Hygiene and pathogenicity, Douglas points out, are relatively recent legitimations for the concept of dirt as a cultural contaminant. Dirt is an anomaly, a discordant element rejected from the schema that individuals and societies use in order to construct a stable, recognizable, and predictable world.[32] One might combine Douglas and Goffman to assert that human stigmata function as social dirt.

This cultural intolerance of anomaly is one of the most pervasive themes in Western thought. One example is Aristotle's *Poetics*, the founding document of Western literary criticism, in which the schemata we call "probability" and "rationality" delimit the tragic plot, determining which elements may be properly included and which do not fit. For the plot to be unified, which is Aristotle's essential requirement, anomalies must be excluded. Another particularly vivid instance of this antipathy toward difference occurs in Kant's aesthetic theory, "Critique of Judgment," in an exceedingly abstract discussion on beauty. Kant asserts that colors are beautiful only if they are "pure," only if they display a "uniformity [that] is troubled and interrupted by no foreign sensation." Consequently, Kant believes that simple colors are beautiful and composite colors are not. Such a definition of beauty parallels Douglas's conception of purity as the absence of dirt, the anomalous element. Such abstract value systems that structure elements into the pure and the corrupt, the legitimate and the illicit, might easily be transformed into the ideology of human racial purity that deems some people impure, unbeautiful, or unfit.[33]

Douglas's interpretation of dirt as anomaly, as the extra-ordinary, can be extended to the body we call "disabled" as well as to other forms of social marginalization. Like dirt, all disability is in some sense "matter out of place" in terms of the interpretive frameworks and physical expectations our culture shares. Visible physical disability lies outside the normative ordering system and can only be included and comprehended under Douglas's classifications of "aberrant" or "anomalous," categories that accommodate what does not fit into the space of the ordinary.[34] Douglas does not include disability in her theory, though she refers to the common infanticide of congenitally disabled new-borns as an example of the way cultures deal with anomaly. Nevertheless, her speculations suggest that disability is the systematic social interpretation of some bodies as abnormal, rather than any actual physical features. Douglas acknowledges that culture mediates all individual experience, imposing systems of perception that are not easily revised. She notes further that all societies must come to terms with the anomalies that their schemata produce. Because cultures do not tolerate such affronts to their communal narratives of order, what emerges from a given cultural context as irremediable anomaly translates not as neutral difference, but as pollution, taboo, contagion. Elaborating this process, Douglas discusses five ways that cultures cope with the extraordinary. These strategies correspond generally to the manner in which our culture frames and responds to disability.

First, social groups can reduce ambiguity by assigning the anomalous element to one absolute category or the other. Similar to other dualistic systems such as gender and race, the disabled/able-bodied dichotomy sorts people by interpreting physical traits that are in fact less easily categorized than the system admits. For example, although actual impairments usually affect particular body parts or physical functions, one specific difference classifies an entire person "disabled" even though the rest of the body and its functions remain "normal." According to this totalizing "master status," the deviant characteristic overwhelms all of a person's other, unmarked aspects.[35] Categories of cultural otherness thus reduce individuals to particular identifying traits, rendering a multifaceted individual a "black," a "gay," or one of the "disabled." Institutions such as legal systems have enforced such dichotomous classifications in the name of both justice and discrimination. Indeed, so powerful is the cultural imperative to structure experience with absolute categories that figures who seemingly defy classification – such as mulattos, freaks, transvestites, bisexuals, and others hybrids – elicit anxiety, hostility, or pity and are always rigorously policed.[36] The rigidity of social order testifies to the destabilizing threat of ambiguity as well as the artificial, constructed quality of all social identities.

Douglas identifies the second cultural solution to anomaly as elimination. She notes wryly that if the necks of night-crowing cocks are "promptly wrung, they do not live to contradict the definition of a cock as a bird that crows at dawn." This principle Douglas offers so casually becomes much more troubling when it is applied to people with disabilities. Both the modern eugenics movement, which arose from the mid-nineteenth-century scientific community, and its current counterpart, reproductive technology designed to predict and eliminate "defective" fetuses, reveal a determination to eradicate disabled people. While the rhetoric claims that such procedures are aimed at ending disability, the reality is often that people with disabilities are eliminated. Eugenics, "the

science of improving the stock," was a respected field that successfully promoted mandatory sterilization laws in the United States as well as the Immigration Restriction Act of 1924, both of which reflected fears that the "best"
people would be outnumbered by their physical or mental "inferiors." The
notion of improvement and its concomitant concept of degeneracy depend on
the values of autonomy and productivity included in liberal individualism, as
well as on the Platonic idealism that is our Western inheritance. Indeed, Ronald
Walters argues that eugenic thinking was a secular manifestation of the
nineteenth-century reform effort to perfect society. Eliminating disabled people
as discordant social elements is the logical extension of an ideology that
esteems national and individual progress toward self-reliance, self-manage-
ment, and self-sufficiency, a point to which I will return.[37]

A third cultural response Douglas recognizes is "avoiding anomalous
things." Historically, disabled people have for the most part been segregated
either as individuals or in groups. Much of Michel Foucault's analysis of the
modern subject reveals the way marginalized individuals – such as disabled
people – have been enclosed, excluded, and regulated. Societies encode their
collective prejudices in segregation legislation, such as the common US "ugly
laws" of the nineteenth and twentieth centuries that banned visibly disabled
people from appearing in public places.[38] Similarly, asylums and almshouses
that flourished in nineteenth-century America provided custodial segregation
as limited aid for disabled people. Perhaps the most enduring form of segregation has been economic: the history of begging is virtually synonymous with
the history of disability. Much of American disability legislation has attempted
to sort out this conflation, termed by Tom Compton the "vagrant/beggar/
cripple complex."[39] Today, disabled people, especially women, tend to be ghet-
toized by poverty and lack of education, those stigmatic situations that so
frequently coincide with and reinforce marginalization based on physical traits.

Segregation, despite its disadvantages, can forge the sense of community
from which politicized consciousness and nationalism emerges. Although a
fraught debate goes on regarding the merits and dangers of racial or gender
nationalism versus assimilation, the solidarity wrested from strategic sepa-
ratism often leads to political activism and challenges social attitudes. Because
disabled people tend to be scattered among the non-disabled, political unity
and consciousness-raising have emerged primarily as a result of traditional
segregation or the self-imposed segregation that often accompanies positive-
identity politics. The highly politicized deaf community, for example, arose
from segregated schools for the deaf. The independent living movement
also partly owes its existence to the practice of segregated education and
institutionalization.[40]

Douglas suggests that a fourth method social groups use to deal with
anomaly is to label it dangerous. Both segregation and elimination are social
and political practices based in part on the interpretation of physical disability
as not only anomalous but dangerous, indeed contaminating, like dirt. Douglas
points out that although an individual response to anomaly can be quite

complex, public beliefs tend to reduce dissonance among individual responses and promote a conformity that finds expression in larger social institutions. Consequently, anomaly often becomes synonymous with danger and evil. This is nowhere clearer than in the symbolic uses of disability in literature and film. That ubiquitous icon of physical anomaly, the monster, exemplifies culture's preoccupation with the threat of the different body.[41] Disabilities do not simply mark evil, but function as menace in such prototypical villains as Shakespeare's Richard III, Dickens's Quilp, Melville's Ahab, Poe's Hop Frog, and Stanley Kubrick's Dr. Strangelove. Like the monsters who are their fantastic cousins, disabled characters with power virtually always represent a dangerous force unleashed on the social order, as attested by Flannery O'Connor's one-armed villain Tom Shiftlet in "The Life You Save May Be Your Own," Carson McCuller's hunchbacked Cousin Lymon Willis from "The Ballad of the Sad Cafe," Nathanael West's crippled Peter Doyle of *Miss Lonelyhearts*, and Hawthorne's humpbacked Roger Chillingworth of *The Scarlet Letter*.[42] Because these characters operate as embodiments of an unnamed, profound peril, the narrative resolution is almost always to contain that threat by killing or disempowering the disabled character. The logic that governs this cultural narrative, then, is that eliminating the anomaly neutralizes the danger.

The interpretation of disability as a sign of evil or sin is explained in another way by Melvin Lerner's "just world" theory. According to Lerner, the human need for order and predictability gives rise to a belief that people get what they deserve or that the way things are is the way they should be. Such a theory accounts not only for the norms that establish justice, but also for the judgment of differences. It is the logic of theodicy: if something "bad" – like having a disability – happens to someone, then there must be some "good" reason – like divine or moral justice – for its occurrence. This troubling way of thinking gained much force and legitimacy from nineteenth-century social Darwinian pseudoscience, especially Herbert Spencer and his American disciples' application of Lamarckian evolution to social relations. Although this doctrine provides a psychological safeguard against the intolerable randomness of experience, it results in victim-blaming and scapegoating of those who are different. Because disability is such a contingent condition, it may inspire the kind of anxiety that a "just world" concept is most suited to relieve. Not only can anyone become disabled at any time, but the pain, bodily damage, or impairment sometimes associated with disability make it seem an uncontained threat to those who consider themselves normal. The belief that disabled people are simply the losers in some grand competitive scheme or the once-accepted conviction that masturbation caused blindness attest to the prevalence of just-world assumptions about disability.[43] Perhaps the most unfortunate current just-world assumption is the AIDS is a moral judgment on homosexuals and intravenous drug users.

Bodies that are disabled can also seem dangerous because they are perceived as out of control. Not only do they violate physical norms, but by looking and acting unpredictable they threaten to disrupt the ritualized behavior upon which social relations turn.[44] The uncontrolled body does not perform typically the quotidian functions required by the elaborately structured codes of acceptable social behavior. Blindness, deafness, or stuttering, for instance, disturb the complex web of subtle exchanges upon which communication rituals depend. Wheelchairs or paralysis require different ambulatory choreographies. Furthermore, the disabled body transgresses individualism's codes of work and autonomy by enacting patterns that differ from the norm, another point I will discuss more fully later.

The modern secular world's method of labeling disability dangerous is to term it pathological rather than evil or immoral. Freud's essay on "The Exceptions," for example, labels disabled people psychologically pathological. Conflating the inner and outer selves, Freud concludes that "deformities of character" are the results of physical disability. Indeed, disability has been almost entirely subsumed in twentieth-century America under a medical model that pathologizes disability. Although medical interpretation rescues disability from its earlier associations with evil, pathologized difference is fraught with assumptions of deviance, patronizing relationships, and issues of control.[45]

The fifth and final cultural treatment of anomaly Douglas observes is incorporating the anomalous elements into ritual "to enrich meaning or to call attention to other levels of existence."[46] Of Douglas's five solutions, this is culture's only potentially positive or transformative interpretation of the extraordinary. I will briefly mention here two of several theorists who expand Douglas's idea by exploring anomaly's potential to alter cultural patterns, though none specifically discusses disability. In *The Structure of Scientific Revolutions* Thomas S. Kuhn revises the narrative of incremental scientific discovery by tracing the role of anomaly in scientific understanding. What Kuhn calls "normal science" finds coherence and unanimity by excluding the extraordinary from its paradigms, by suppressing "fundamental novelties because they are necessarily subversive of its basic commitments."[47] Kuhn defines "novelties" as phenomena that cannot be aligned with scientific expectations, and argues that when such exceptional phenomena accumulate or become so compelling that they can no longer be dismissed, their presence forces a shift in scientific paradigms so that a new set of beliefs emerges.

Kuhn's view of the extraordinary's power to unsettle the ascendant order is echoed by Mikhail Bakhtin's notion that the grotesque body as carnivalesque disrupts the status quo and inverts social hierarchies. Whereas Kuhn sees anomaly as subverting scientific classification, Bakhtin posits the carnivalesque as a ritualistic use of the extraordinary body to disturb the social order. According to Bakhtin, the carnivalesque figure – perhaps his version of the disabled figure – represents "the right to be 'other' in this world, the right not to make common cause with any single one of the existing categories that life makes available; none of these categories quite suits them, they see the underside and falseness of every situation."[48] Bakhtin's concept of the disorderly body as a challenge to the existing order suggests the radical potential that the disabled body as sign for difference might possess within representation. The Bakhtinian carnivalesque figure frequently appears in critical analyses of the grotesque as a liminal aesthetic category that enables radical representations by straddling and transgressing categories.[49] Imagining anomaly and the grotesque as agents capable of reconstituting cultural discourses suggests the possibility of interpreting both dirt and disability not as discomforting abnormalities or intolerable ambiguities, but rather as the entitled bearers of a fresh view of reality. Moreover, because the disabled figure always represents the extraordinary, such interpretations open the way for us to imagine narratives of physical disability other than deviance and abnormality. Indeed, I argue that at specific sites of representation, the disabled figures operate in varying degrees as challenges to the cultural status quo, introducing issues and perspectives with the potential to refigure the social order.

Historicizing the disabled body: Michel Foucault's "docile bodies"

While Goffman and Douglas offer relational analyses that help us place disability in a social context, Michel Foucault's speculations on the constitution of the modern subject bring to disability the notion of historical change that both Goffman and Douglas omit. Foucault's conception of the ways that power embedded in everyday practices structures subjects suggests how cultural classification and stigmatization – which may indeed be universal, as sociologists assert – are nevertheless complicated by history. Whereas Goffman's stigma theory illuminates the modern context of disability, Foucault's theory of the eighteenth-century shift to a modern, Enlightenment, reason-based concept of the body supports other readings and treatments of the disabled body.

Arguing that the modern subject emerged in the Neoclassical age, as discourse and institutions solidified to reproduce new social relations of domination and subordination, Foucault asserts in *Discipline and Punish* that feudal society transformed into a "disciplinary regime" that systematically controlled the body as concern for its efficient operation and its ultimate utility increased. This concept of "docile bodies" yields the rigid taxonomies so fundamental to nineteenth- and twentieth-century Western science and medicine's project of distributing human characteristics in discrete and hierarchical relations to one another.[50] Architectural, pedagogical, and medical practices manipulated the body, both generating and enforcing the Cartesian image of an individual as a separate, isolated, efficient machine whose goal was self-mastery. Such a utilitarian concept of the body, incited by economic crisis, led in the seventeenth century to what Foucault calls in *Madness and Civilization* the "Great Confinement" of beggars, the poor, and the idle in hospitals. These hospitals were, however, not medical facilities but poorhouses, institutions established by the aristocracy and the bourgeoisie to segregate, assist, and punish a great "undifferentiated mass" of economically unproductive people, the ostensible failures at self-mastery. Concern with culling out the "sick poor" from economically useful mendicants gave rise in the eighteenth century to a dominant ideology of health and physical well-being as a civic duty and political objective. Medicine, then, as administered by doctors, enforced what Foucault terms in *Power/Knowledge* a "Politics of Health," rationalized by hygiene and bent not on aid but on containment through "curing."[51] This discourse, which classified the healthy body and the pathological body, focused on disciplining all bodies in the name of improvement. This instrumental view of the body as a productive, well-operating machine produced the idea of a norm, which Foucault calls a "new law of modern society" and a "principle of coercion," used to measure, classify, and regulate human bodies.[52]

Foucault's historical explanation of the norm as a uniquely modern concept brings us to the threshold of stigma theory, to oppressive hierarchies of physical appearance. Whereas Goffman's and Douglas's transhistorical and transcultural accounts naturalize the norm, Foucault aggressively presents the norm as both coercive and punitive by connecting it not merely to devaluing social attitudes, but to social institutions legitimated by historical conceptions of deviance. Foucault, however, never mentions disabled people specifically in his analysis. Although many paupers had physically disabilities, he never makes distinctions among them.[53] We can nevertheless extrapolate from Foucault's theory that the modern social identity of "disabled" emerged from the shifts he charts and that it arose in tandem with its opposite: the abstract, self-possessed, autonomous individual.

Foucault's suggestion that the modern individual is determined by its own particularity is the most useful insight for my purposes here. Whereas in premodern society individuating markers indicated power and privilege, in modern society an unmarked norm is the reference point. Those who most depart from the normative standard are most subordinated. Whiteness, for example, is concealed and neutral, while blackness carries the burden of "race." These differences are marked also in the costuming of pre- and post-Enlightenment aristocratic males. Before the nineteenth century, an array of ornate particulars – crowns, scepters, insignias, badges, wigs – distinguished the powerful individuals from the undifferentiated lowly masses. Today, however, male power is costumed in indistinguishable, undistinguished business suits and ties, while otherness is elaborately visible, whether marked by the prisoner's striped suit, the Star of David arm band, or the decorative woman's ornate gown and high heels. Foucault's theory thus predicts the position of power and privilege at the heart of Goffman's stigma theory: the unmarked, prototypical subject, the "unblemished" one, the normate.[54] In its complex social codification, power is veiled by a rhetoric of neutrality that creates the illusion of meritocracy. Yet power's visible non-particularity is its marker in the subtle economy of display that signals status in modernity.

Although disability has historically been seen as a disadvantage or a curse, in modern times markers of individuation like physical disability render one a "case" upon which power is exercised. But disability might have been more easily read in a premodern society as a distinguishing mark of power and prestige, whereas in the modern era, disempowerment is marked by visible stigmata. Indeed, Harlan Hahn offers archeological evidence suggesting that disabled people may have been held in high regard in earlier cultures. The saints' stigmatic wounds, Oedipus's and Socrates's lameness, Tiresias's and Homer's blindness, and Philoctetes's wound certainly seem to function as ennobling marks rather than signs of a diminishing abnormality like those of the modern "cripple."[55] Foucault's notion that the significance of particularity shifted in modernity, then, challenges the definition of disability as a corruption of the norm. Such speculations enable us to envision interpretations of the extraordinary human body other than deviance and inferiority.

Taken together, Goffman's analysis of disability as defined by social relations, Douglas's observations about cultural responses to anomaly, and Foucault's historical delineation of the modern norm as unmarked reveal the physically disabled figure as a culturally and historically specific social construction. Such a critical framework helps situate the disabled figure within the American ideologies of liberal individualism and the moral imperative of work, and illuminates how the disabled figure operates in literature.

The Disabled Figure and the Ideology of Liberal Individualism

Emerson's invalid and the doctrine of self-reliance

In anthropologist Robert Murphy's groundbreaking ethnography of his own disability, *The Body Silent*, he emphasizes that others' avoidance, discomfort, and devaluation of him amounted to a loss of status and a wound to his self-image as devastating as his recent paraplegia. Disability, Murphy observes, "is a social malady. . . . We are subverters of an American Ideal, just as the poor are betrayers of the American Dream."[56] Murphy goes beyond simply acknowledging the social dimensions of disability to examine the disabled figure's crucial role in establishing the boundaries of the normate American self. Like the poor, Murphy asserts, disabled people are made to signify what the rest of Americans fear they will become. Freighted with anxieties about loss of control and autonomy that the American ideal repudiates, "the disabled" become a threatening presence, seemingly compromised by the particularities and limitations of their own bodies. Shaped by a narrative of somatic inadequacy and represented as a spectacle of erratic singularity, the disabled figure delineates the corresponding abstract cultural figure of the self-governing, standardized individual emerging from a society informed by consumerism and mechanization. Cast as one of society's ultimate "not me" figures, the disabled other absorbs disavowed elements of this cultural self, becoming an icon of all human vulnerability and enabling the "American Ideal" to appear as master of both destiny and self. At once familiarly human but definitively other, the disabled figure in cultural discourse assures the rest of the citizenry of who they are not while arousing their suspicions about who they could become.[57]

Witness, for instance, a brief but exemplary invocation of the disabled figure in Ralph Waldo Emerson's rhetoric of "Self-Reliance." "And now we are men . . ." writes Emerson in the 1847 version, "not minors and invalids in a protected corner, not cowards fleeing before a revolution, but guides, redeemers, and benefactors, obeying the Almighty effort, and advancing on Chaos and the Dark." Using the disabled figure again in his later essay "Fate," Emerson disparages conservatives by characterizing them as "effeminated by nature, born halt and blind" and able "only, like invalids, [to] act on the defensive." Scholars have noted that Emerson's elaboration of liberal individualism as a neo-Platonic, disembodied form of masculinity depends upon his construction of and flight from a denigrated, oppositional femininity upon which he projects a fear not only of dependence and neediness, but also of what David Leverenz calls "the perils of the body."[58] What has gone unremarked, however, is Emerson's invocation of "invalids" as a related category of otherness that mutually constitutes his liberal self. Unlike the supposedly inviolable real "men," who act as "guides, redeemers, and benefactors" capable of "advancing," Emerson's disparaged and static "invalids" are banished "in a protected corner," along with "minors" and, presumably, women. The "blind," the "halt," and the "invalids" Emerson enlists to define the liberal individual by opposition are, above all else, icons of bodily vulnerability. The "invalid" body is impotence made manifest. By barring the disabled figure from his definition of the universal "man," Emerson reveals the implicit assumption of an exclusionary physical norm incorporated in the ideal of an autonomous individual self. With the specter of physical vulnerability exiled into "a protected corner" along with the feminine, Emerson's naturalized "man" emerges as Murphy's "American Ideal," unimpeded by the physical limitation that history and contingency impose upon actual lives.

Emerson's juxtaposition of an unrestricted cultural self with a muted other thwarted by physical limits exposes the problem of the body within the ideology of liberal individualism. The "American Ideal" posited by liberal individualism is structured by a four-part self-concept that is profoundly threatened by what Richard Selzer has called the "mortal lessons" that disability represents.[59] The four interrelated ideological principles that inform this normate self might be characterized as self-government, self-determination, autonomy, and progress. Such a self-image parallels the national ideal in an individualist egalitarian democracy that each citizen is a microcosm of the nation as a whole. A well-regulated self thus contributes to a well-regulated nation. However, these four principles depend upon a body that is a stable, neutral instrument of the individual will. It is this fantasy that the disabled figure troubles. For my purposes here, it is useful to disentangle these national and individual principles of self to examine how each relies on the disabled figure to absorb what it refuses.

Egalitarian democracy demands individual self-government to avoid anarchy. A system in which individuals make laws and choose leaders depends upon individuals governing their actions and their bodies just as they govern the social body. Consequently, the disabled figure is a unique and disturbing construct among the cultural others opposed to the ideal American self. It is perhaps easier to establish difference based on relatively stable, although highly policed, bodily markers like gender, ethnic, and racial characteristics than it is to distance disability. Disability's indisputably random and unpredictable character translates as appalling disorder and persistent menace in a social order predicated on self-government. Furthermore, physical instability is the bodily manifestation of political anarchy, of the antinomian impulse that is the threatening, but logical, extension of egalitarian democracy.[60] The disabled body stands for the self gone out of control, individualism run rampant: it mocks the notion of the body as compliant instrument of the limitless will and appears in the cultural imagination as ungovernable, recalcitrant, flaunting its difference as if to refute the fantasy of sameness implicit in the notion of equality. Even more trobling, disability suggests that the cultural other lies dormant within the cultural self, threatening abrupt or gradual transformations from "man" to "invalid." The disabled figure is the stranger in our midst, within the family and potentially within the self.

Just as the principle of self-government demands a regulated body, the principle of self-determination requires a compliant body to secure a place in the fiercely competitive and dynamic socioeconomic realm. The idea of self-determination places tremendous pressure on individuals to feel responsible for their own social stations, economic situations, and relations with others. Among the emerging middle classes of the nineteenth century, from whom traditional group affiliations had been shorn, the desire for identity produced conformity that was expressed in an intolerance of differences – precisely those distinctions that freedom encouraged. Because democracy precluded former class alliances and generational continuities, people had only one another after which to model themselves. By 1835 Tocqueville noted this tendency to conform, observing that "all of the minds of the Americans were formed upon one model, so accurately do they follow the same route."[61] Furthermore, the developing mass culture mandated by equality further encourages a uniformity that stabilizes threats of anarchy, enforcing conformity and punishing difference. Thus, democracy's paradox is that the principle of equality implies sameness of condition, while the promise of freedom suggests the potential for uniqueness. That potential amounted for many Americans to a mandate for distinctiveness – the kind of nonconformity that Emerson and Thoreau so vehemently extol in their efforts to formulate an individual self free from all restraint.

What often goes unstated is the body's crucial role in this paradoxical ideology of self-determination. For instance, nineteenth-century concern with health, especially the obsession with bodily functions such as elimination, cleanliness, and what G. J. Barker-Benfield calls "spermatic retentiveness" can be seen as a physical expression of pressures to control the corporeal self. Moreover, the rhetoric of nonconformity and anti-authority coexisted with the development of mass-produced goods and the standardization of appearance through reproducible images, encouraging the uniformity of lifestyle that serves modern consumer and mechanized culture.[62] The disabled figure speaks to this tension between uniqueness and uniformity. On the one hand, the disabled figure is a sign for the body that refuses to be governed and cannot carry out the will to self-determination. On the other hand, the extraordinary body is nonconformity incarnate. In a sense then, the disabled figure has the potential to inspire with its irreverent individuality and to threaten with its violation of equality. Indeed, I argue that a part of the fascination the freak show held for nineteenth-century Americans was this doubleness inherent in the extraordinary body.

Just as the dominant culture's ideal self requires the ideological figures of the woman to confirm its masculinity and of the black to assure its whiteness, so Emerson's atomized self demands an oppositional twin to secure its able-bodiedness. The freak, the cripple, the invalid, the disabled – like the quadroon and the homosexual – are representational, taxonomical products that naturalize a norm comprised of accepted bodily traits and behaviors registering social power and status. Thus translated, physical difference yields a cultural icon signifying violated wholeness, unbounded incompleteness, unregulated particularity, dependent subjugation, disordered intractability, and susceptibility to external forces. With the body's threat of betrayal thus compartmentalized, the mythical American self can unfold, unobstructed and unrestrained, according to its own manifest destiny.

Melville's Ahab: the whale-made man

This paradoxical, simultaneous demand for individuality and equality is perhaps what renders *Moby Dick*'s Captain Ahab – perhaps the quintessential disabled figure in American literature – so compelling a character. Although certainly not Emerson's impotent invalid, Herman Melville's Ahab nevertheless suggests the problem of the body in America's grand experiment of liberal individualism.[63] Both self-government and self-determination require individual autonomy, the hypothetical state of independence Emerson calls self-reliance. The disabled figure profoundly threatens this fantasy of autonomy, not so much because it is seen as helpless, but rather because it is imagined as having been altered by forces outside the self. After all, even though Ahab uses the crew to carry out his revenge, his indignation is personal: the whale impinged upon his body. Autonomy assumes immunity to external forces along with the capacity to maintain a stable, static state of being, like the "possessive individualism" described by C. P. MacPherson. According to such logic, physical alterations caused by time or the environment – the changes we call disability – are hostile incursions from the outside, the effects of cruel contingencies that an individual does not adequately resist.[64] Seen as a victim of alien forces, the disabled figure appears not as transformed, supple, or unique but as violated. In contrast, the autonomous individual is imagined as having inviolate boundaries that enable unfettered self-determination, creating a myth of wholeness.[65] Within such an ideological framework, the figure whose body is a neutral instrument of the self-governing will becomes a free agent in contractual relations. Conversely, the disabled figure represents the incomplete, unbounded, compromised, and subjected body susceptible to external forces: property badly managed, a fortress inadequately defended, a self helplessly violated. Ahab's outrage compensates for his vulnerability, rendering him both a sublime and a threatening version of the disabled figure.

Ahab is, perhaps above all else, different from other men. At once compelling and repelling, he represents both the prospective freedom of nonconformity and the terrible threat of antinomianism. The outer mark of his difference is his ivory leg, and the inner manifestation is his monomaniacal fury. Neither loss of function nor pain motivates Ahab's vengeful quest as much as his profound sense of violation by the whale, a force from outside.[66] Cast as an intractable external will, the whale has breached Ahab's individual boundaries, altered his very being, and determined his future. The whale's incursion and its power over Ahab's destiny mock the ideas of self-determination and autonomy. Ahab is not a self-made man, but a whale-made man; his disabled body testifies to the self's physical vulnerability, the ominous knowledge that the ideology of individualism suppresses. For such apostasy, Ahab's body is violently and definitively separated from the rest of the community on the *Pequod* as the whale pulls Ahab from the ship with the harpoon rope, controlling him in death just as in life.[67] Ahab's nobility, like his menace, arises from his physical difference, the symbol of bodily limitation and vulnerability that threatens the notion of the autonomous, inviolable self. Ahab, along with other disabled figures, poses the troubling question of whether any person is independent of physical limitations, immune to external forces, and without need of assistance and care from others.[68] The disabled body exposes the illusion of autonomy, self-government, and self-determination that underpins the fantasy of absolute able-bodiedness.

The life of a well-governed, self-determined man is imagined as a narrative of progress on which Protestant perfectionism, the doctrine of success, and the concept of self-improvement all depend. Democratic nations, Tocqueville notes, are particularly invested in the notion of human perfectibility and likely "to expand it beyond reason."[69] But the disabled figure flies in the face of this ideal, renouncing with its very existence the fiction of self-improvement and at the same time presenting the ultimate challenge to perfection and progress. Such diverse phenomena as faith healing, cosmetic surgery, medical separation of conjoined twins, and Jerry Lewis's Telethons testify not only to the cultural demand for body normalization, but to our intolerance of the disabled figure's reminder that perfection is a chimera. As a cultural emblem for the restricted self, the disabled body stubbornly resists the willed improvement so fundamental to the American notion of the self. Indeed, lurking behind the able-bodied figure is the denied, and perhaps intolerable, knowledge that life will eventually transform us into "disabled" selves. In the end, the body and history dominate the will, imposing limits on the myth of a physically stable self progressing unfettered toward some higher material state.[70]

The Disabled Figure and the Problem of Work

The proper pauper

As I have suggested, disabled people are often imagined as unable to be productive, direct their own lives, participate in the community, or establish meaningful personal relations – regardless of their actual capabilities or achievements. In fact, the limitations disabled people experience result more often from interaction with a social and physical environment designed to accommodate the normate body. In other words, people deemed disabled are barred from full citizenship because their bodies do not conform with architectural, attitudinal, educational, occupational, and legal conventions based on assumptions that bodies appear and perform in certain ways.

Nowhere is the disabled figure more troubling to American ideology and history than in relation to the concept of work: the system of production and distribution of economic resources in which the abstract principles of self-government, self-determination, autonomy, and progress are manifest most completely. Labor, the definitive creed of Puritan through contemporary America, transforms necessity into virtue and equates productive work with moral worth, idleness with depravity. The figure of the self-made American man has always held much cultural authority, especially in the nineteenth century, although poverty was widespread and industrialization was rapidly converting work into unrecognizable forms. The concepts of autonomy and independence essential to the work ethic became contorted as wage labor supplanted self-employment, the fragile economy surged up and down, and machines began to damage workers on a new scale. As modernization proceeded, the disabled figure shouldered in new ways society's anxiety about its inability to retain the status and old meanings of labor in the face of industrialization and increasing economic and social chaos.

American individualism is most clearly manifest in the conviction that economic autonomy results from hard work and virtue, while poverty stems from indolence and moral inferiority.[71] Paupers had to be held culpable for their socioeconomic situations in order to support the cherished belief that in a democratic society each individual was a self-determining free agent in a progress narrative of economic manifest destiny. However, a moral dilemma and contradiction emerges when this creed is applied to the "disabled," people whose bodies are different or transformed by life. What happens to the link between virtue and work when a person's body, through no one's volition, suddenly or gradually no longer fits the work environment? How, in short, can a culture founded upon and committed to the values of liberal individualism deal with physical disability?

In a world increasingly seen as free from divine determinism and subject to individual control, the disabled figure calls into question such concepts as will, ability, progress, responsibility, and free agency, notions around which people in a liberal society organize their identities. Moreover, secular thinking and a more accurate scientific understanding of physiology and disease prevented nineteenth-century Americans from interpreting disability as the divine punishment it had been labeled in earlier epochs. The problem of how to formulate disability as a social category arises from a conflict between the need to preserve a social hierarchy linked to individual economic condition and the need to recognize the freedom from divine intervention that makes individual achievement tenable. The disabled figure's existence mandates that society consider under what circumstances a person should be held responsible for "earning a living" and, conversely, when one should be released from that expectation because of circumstances beyond one's control. The social category "disabled" is a grudging admission of human vulnerability in a world no longer seen as divinely determined, a world where self-government and individual progress purportedly prevail. Such a classification elicits much ambivalence from a national consciousness committed to equating virtue with independent industry, especially during periods in which public policy toward those outside the labor force is being formulated.[72] That ambivalence expresses itself as social stigmatization and as rigorous, sometimes exclusionary supervision of people obliged to join the ranks of the "disabled."

The dawning industrial transformation of antebellum America forced the US legal system to address the issue of physical disability as contingency rather than divine punishment, as industrial accidents began to increase and stable communities and older forms of production began to dissolve. For example, as power was being transferred from male parents to male judges during the first half of the nineteenth century, a defining decision written by Lemuel Shaw in 1842 legally framed the disabled social category according to the precepts of contractarian economic individualism. Shaw reversed the common-law precedent that made masters liable for their servants' actions by formulating the fellow-servant rule that defined negligence in favor of employers, thus serving business interests at the expense of disabled workers by making it very difficult for injured workers to sue for compensation.[73] This ruling interpreted both employer and employee as autonomous agents entering freely into a contract in which the market wage compensated for the risk of injury. That this legal formulation did not follow the precedent, established early on, of compensating wounded soldiers may have represented an effort to free economic development, seemingly separating issues of private justice from state justice. Nevertheless, newly disabled workers had little recourse but charity or poor relief. As long as economic resources from the public sphere were not equitably available for injured workers, they not only lost their jobs but also dropped out of sight into a private sphere of charity where the marketplace and the state were no longer accountable for their economic situations. That a man might be a virtuous worker one day and an indolent pauper the next doubtless raised uneasy questions about an individual's capacity for unlimited self-determinism.[74]

Even though the legal and socioeconomic category of disabled admits to contingency, this classification must, nevertheless, be assiduously delineated and monitored, so great is its threat to Americans' belief in the link between "hard work" and economic and social success. If the myth of autonomy and self-determination is to remain intact, those whose situations question it must be split off into a discrete social category governed by different assumptions. Indeed, at least since the inception of English Poor Laws in 1388, the state and other institutions concerned with the common welfare have molded the political and cultural definition of what we now know as "physical disability" in an effort to distinguish between genuine "cripples" and malingerers, those deemed unable to work and those deemed unwilling to work.[75] Although "ability" and "will" are certainly complicated and questionable concepts in the social relation called "earning a living," it is clear that in distributing resources the state and the populace insist upon trying to draw a firm boundary between these two groups of people.[76]

From compensation to accommodation

While the social history of disabled people has generally remained consistently one of stigmatization and low status, the state's response to "disability" in America has widened and shifted from early and continuing reimbursement such as veterans' pensions for public service, to workmen's compensation for civilian workers in industrial America, to the mandate in the Americans with Disabilities Act of 1990 that accommodation rather than restitution is the appropriate response to disability. The notion of compensation that characterized disability policy before 1990 implies a norm, the departure from or loss of which requires restitution. Seen this way, disability is a loss to be compensated for, rather than difference to be accommodated. Disability then becomes a personal flaw, and disabled people are the "able-bodied" gone wrong. Difference thus translates into deviance. Moreover, the focus on war wounds and industrial accidents as definitive disabilities supports a narrow physical norm by limiting economic benefits to those who once qualified as "able-bodied workers," barring people with congenital disabilities and disabled women from economic "compensation" because they could not lose a hypothetical advantage they never had. According to the logic of compensation, then, "disabled" connotes not physiological variation, but the violation of a primary state of putative wholeness. The logic of accommodation, on the other hand, suggests that disability is simply one of many differences among people and that society should recognize this by adjusting its environment accordingly.

The twin myths of bodily wholeness and bodily lack that underpin a compensation model of disability structure the history of public policy toward the extraordinary body. The concept of able-bodiedness and its theoretical opposite, disability, were continually reshaped as the state attempted to qualitatively distinguish between people whose physical or mental conditions legitimately prevented them from obtaining wage labor and people who simply refused to work. As disability became increasingly medicalized with the rise of science and technology, methods for distinguishing between the "sick poor" who deserved aid and the "frauds" who merited punishment and discouragement became the state's guiding principles. Yet even as ideology demanded the separation of the "able-bodied" from the "disabled" to preserve the myths of autonomy and self-governance as keys to economic success, the conflicting impulses to comfort and castigate paupers often merged in public policy and social attitudes so that neither was accomplished effectively. The history of public and private distribution of resources to people termed the "disabled" has been tinged with the punitive and the paternalistic as well as the compassionate and the just.

Science and medicine promised mid-nineteenth and twentieth-century America the means for cordoning off the group of people it needed to class as unable to work so that supposed slackers could be rehabilitated. Medical technology such as the stethoscope and the X-ray finally provided what society believed was an objective and quantitative measure of a person's physical capability for work. In addition, a new understanding of specific disease-causing agents attributed disabling illnesses and impairments less to lack of personal responsibility and more to fate. Medical validation of physical incapacity solved the problem of malingering by circumventing the testimony of the individual. Under this confirmation scheme, the doctor sought direct communication with the body regarding its condition, eliminating the patient's ability for self-disclosure and, ultimately, for self-determination.[77] Rather than closing the gap between the work environment and the exceptional body, legal compensation further alienated disabled workers by separating their bodies from their conscious experiences of them. As a result, "disabled" became, in the twentieth-century welfare state, a medicalized category by which the state could administer economic relief in a seemingly objective and equitable manner.[78] Moreover, in constructing that legal social group, quite distinct conditions merge into a single administrative and social identity. Thus, a disabled figure whose bodily configuration was earlier read as divine retribution for some nameless sin was exonerated. Yet the new, clinically disabled category defined the person with a disability as a figure excluded from economic opportunities and therefore without free agency, self-determinis, and self-possession, the ennobling attributes of the liberal American individual.

To socially and legally construct a category of "proper paupers" whose extraordinary bodies exclude them from the burdens and privileges of work is to partially relieve anxieties about physical vulnerability by displacing them onto an identifiable group of corporeal others. Furthermore, granting exemption from work due to a "physical disability" is in one sense viewed as a proper act of mercy, if not moral generosity – the simultaneous recognition of human limitation and human obligation. Although the very young and the very old are released from official labor by similar logic, the disabled social category is harder to escape and far more stigmatizing than youth or age, which are seen more as stages in the lives of productive people than as immutable identities. On the other hand, to be officially or sympathetically relieved of the obligation of productive labor – cast out of the public economic realm into the private sphere of charity – is also to be excluded from the privilege of laboring in a society that affirms work as what Daniel Rodgers calls "the core of moral life."[79] Thus, the moral generosity that seeks to compensate for physical differences makes cultural outcasts of its recipients by assuming that individual bodies must conform to institutional standards, rather than restructuring the social environment to accommodate physical variety.

Notes

1   See Patricia Vertinsky, "Exercise, Physical Capability, and the Eternally Wounded Woman in Late Nineteenth-Century North America," *Journal of Sport History* 14 (1): 7; Thorstein Veblen, *The Theory of the Leisure Class* (1899; reprint, Boston: Houghton Mifflin, 1973); Jane Flax, *Thinking Fragments: Psychoanalysis, Feminism, and Postmodernism in the Contemporary West* (Berkeley: University of California Press, 1990), p. 136.

2   Aristotle, *Generation of Animals*, trans. A. L. Peck (Cambridge, MA: Harvard University Press, 1944), Book II, p. 175 and Book IV, p. 401. For discussions of Aristotle's conflation of femaleness with monstrosity and deformity, see Maryanne Cline Horowitz, "Aristotle and Women," *Journal of the History of Biology* 9 (1976): 183–213; Nancy Tuana, *The Less Noble Sex: Scientific, Religious, and Philosophical Conceptions of Woman's Nature* (Bloomington: Indiana University Press, 1993); and Marie-Hélène Huet, *Monstrous Imagination* (Cambridge, MA: Harvard University Press, 1993). Edwin Schur examines the assignment of deviance in *Labeling Women Deviant: Gender, Stigma, and Social Control* (Philadephia: Temple University Press, 1983).

3   For discussions of the notion of woman as an inferior version of man, see Thomas Laquer, *Making Sex*, and Nancy Tuana, *The Less Noble Sex*. For a discussion of whiteness, see David Roediger, *The Wages of Whiteness* (New York: Verso, 1991) and Richard Dyer, *The Matter of Images: Essays on Representation* (New York: Routledge, 1993). For a seminal discussion of the normal–pathological dichotomy, see Georges Canguilhem, *The Normal and the Pathological*, trans. Carolyn R. Fawcett with Robert S. Cohen (New York: Zone Books, 1989).

4   Examples are Diane Price Herndl and Robyn Warhol, *Feminisms* (New Brunswick, NJ: Rutgers University Press, 1991); Marianne Hirsch and Evelyn Fox Keller, eds., *Conflicts in Feminism* (New York: Routledge, 1990). "Hyphenated feminism" is used by Judith Grant, *Fundamental Feminism: Contesting the Core Concepts of Feminist Theory* (New York: Routledge, 1993), p. 3; Brigitta Boucht et al., *Postfeminism* (Esbo, Finland: Draken, 1991).

5   A good overview of the history of academic feminist theory is Elizabeth Weed, "Introduction: Terms of Reference," in Elizabeth Weed, ed., *Coming to Terms: Feminism, Theory, Politics* (New York: Routledge, 1989), pp. ix–xxxi. For discussion of these debates and bifurcations in feminism, see Linda Alcoff, "Cultural Feminism Versus Post-Structuralist Feminism: The Identity Crisis in Feminist Theory," *Signs* 13 (3): 405–36; Hester Eisenstein, *Contemporary Feminist Thought* (Boston: G. K. Hall, 1983); and Josephine Donovan, *Feminist Theory* (New York: Continuum, 1992). Early analyses of gender identity include Elizabeth V. Spelman, *Inessential Woman: Problems of Exclusion in Feminist Thought* (Boston: Beacon Press, 1988) and

Monique Witting, "The Straight Mind," *Feminist Issues* 1 (1): 101–10. Diana Fuss, *Essentially Speaking: Feminism, Nature, and Difference* (New York: Routledge, 1989) deconstructs the opposition of essentialism, often associated with cultural feminism, and constructionism, often associated with radical feminism. Judith Butler's *Gender Trouble: Feminism and the Subversion of Identity* (New York: Routledge, 1990) and *Bodies That Matter: On the Discursive Limits of "Sex"* (New York: Routledge, 1993) most fully articulates the constructionist approach to gender.

6	Feminist texts that announce themselves as postmodernist and materialist often take the positions I am outlining here; some examples are Susan Bordo, *Unbearable Weight: Feminism, Western Culture, and the Body* (Berkeley: University of California Press, 1993); Rosemary Hennessy, *Materialist Feminism and the Politics of Discourse* (New York: Routledge, 1993); Jennifer Wicke, "Celebrity Material: Materialist Feminism and the Culture of Celebrity," *South Atlantic Quarterly* 93 (4): 751–78; Judith Grant, *Fundamental Feminism*; Linda Nicholson, ed., *Feminism/Postmodernism* (New York: Routledge, 1990).

7	Most theorists of disability either naturalize it while protesting exclusion and oppression of disabled people, or adopt a strict social constructionist perspective to claim equality while asserting difference in order to establish identity. For an example of the former, see the collection of essays by Harold E. Yuker, ed., *Attitudes Toward Persons with Disabilities* (New York: Springer, 1988); an example of the latter can be found in Harlan Hahn, "Can Disability Be Beautiful?" *Social Policy* (fall 1988): 26–31.

8	Eve Kosofsky Sedgwick, *Epistemology of the Closet* (Berkeley: University of California Press, 1990), p. 1.

9	For discussions of this problem, see Susan Bordo, "Feminism, Postmodernism, and Gender Skepticism," in *Unbearable Weight*, pp. 215–43; Judith Butler, *Bodies That Matter*; and Betsy Erkkila, "Ethnicity, Literary Theory, and the Grounds of Resistance," *American Quarterly* 47 (4): 563–94.

10	For an example, see Monique Wittig, "The Straight Mind."

11	For histories of civil rights legislation for people with disabilities, see Joseph Shapiro, *No Pity*; Claire Liachowitz, *Disability as a Social Construct*; and Richard Scotch, *From Good Will to Civil Rights*. An anecdote illustrates that disabled people are only now gaining physical access: On September 6, 1995, the Modern Language Association headquarters in New York completed the building of a wheelchair ramp minutes before the arrival of a delegation of members who had been invited to discuss disability issues with the MLA's executive director. Although the MLA is a very progressive institution willing to recognize disability issues, apparently the fundamental problem of accessibility had never been addressed before. For more discussions of disability as a civil rights rather than as a pity issue, see Paul Longmore, "Conspicuous Contribution and American Cultural Dilemmas: Telethons, Virtue, and Community," forthcoming in David Mitchell and Sharon Snyder, eds., *Storylines and Lifelines: Narratives of Disability in the Humanities*. The problem of how to accommodate difference is addressed in many areas of feminist theory. Most often it appears as a critique of liberalism like the one later in this chapter. For a concise discussion of this problem, see the introduction and conclusion to Carole Pateman and Elizabeth Gross, eds., *Feminist Challenges: Social and Political Theory* (Boston: Northeastern University Press, 1986); also see, for example, Carole Pateman, *The Sexual Contract* (Stanford, CA: Stanford University Press, 1988); Jean Bethke Elsthain, *Public Man, Private Woman: Women in Social and Political*

Thought (Princeton, NJ: Princeton University Press, 1981); Iris Marion Young, *Justice and the Politics of Difference*; and Martha Minow, *Making All the Difference*.

12 Diana Fuss in *Essentially Speaking* examines this tension between constructionist and essentialist concepts of identity, concluding that to deconstruct identity is not to deny categories, but rather to expose their fictionality while using them to establish community. Benedict Anderson suggests the strategic aspect of such communities for political and psychological purposes in *Imagined Communities: Reflections on the Origin and Spread of Nationalism* (New York: Verso, 1991). I support here as well Judith Butler's subtle but significant point in *Bodies That Matter* that the social construction of the body does not simply overlay meaning on physical entities, but that culture actually creates bodies. Also see Susan Bordo, *Unbearable Weight*, quotation at p. 229.

13 This questioning of identity and focusing on difference has been analyzed using the feminist epistemological modes called perspectivism in Ellen Messer-Davidow, "The Philosophical Bases of Feminist Literary Criticism," *New Literary History: A Journal of Theory and Interpretation* 19 (1): 65–103; standpoint theory in Patricia Hill Collins, *Black Feminist Thought: Knowledge, Consciousness, and the Politics of Empowerment* (Boston: Unwin Hyman, 1990) and Bettina Aptheker, *Tapestries of Life: Women's Work, Women's Consciousness, and the Meaning of Daily Experience* (Amherst: University of Massachusetts Press, 1989); and positionality in Linda Alcoff, "Cultural Feminism Versus Post-Structuralist Feminism." However, standpoint theory has recently been criticized by Judith Grant in *Fundamental Feminism* as fragmenting the feminist communal project and risking a degeneration of feminism into individualism. Elizabeth Fox-Genovese also assails the tendency in recent feminist thought to sacrifice the benefits of community and shared culture for the sake of individuality in *Feminism Without Illusions* (Chapel Hill: University of North Carolina Press, 1991).

14 See Collins, *Black Feminist Thought*, and Rosemarie Garland Thomson, "Redrawing the Boundaries of Feminist Disability Studies," *Feminist Studies* 20 (fall 1994): 583–95.

15 Nancy Mairs, "On Being a Cripple," in *Plaintext: Essays* (Tucson: University of Arizona Press, 1986), quotation at p. 90. For a discussion of my own concerns about focusing on pain and dysfunction in disability discourse, see Thomson, "Redrawing the Boundaries of Feminist Disability Studies," in which I reflect on Mairs's elaboration of the critical subgenre she calls "The Literature of Catastrophe."

16 Hahn's comment is quoted from a personal conversation. The anecdote about the wheelchair user is from Fred Davis, "Deviance Disavowal," p. 124. Michelle Fine and Adrienne Asch, "Disabled Women: Sexism without the Pedestal," in Mary Jo Deegan and Nancy A. Brooks, eds., *Women and Disability: The Double Handicap* (New Brunswick, NJ: Transaction Books, 1985), pp. 6–22, quotation at p. 12. Cheryl Marie Wade, "I Am Not One of the," *MS.* 11 (3): 57.

17 Anita Silvers, "Reconciling Equality to Difference: Caring (f)or Justice for People with Disabilities," *Hypatia* 10 (1). For a critique of the feminization of caring for the disabled, see Barbara Hillyer, *Feminism and Disability* (Norman: University of Oklahoma Press, 1993); for discussions of the ethic of care, see Nel Noddings, *Caring: A Feminine Approach to Ethics and Moral Education* (Berkeley: University of California Press, 1984) and Eva Feder Kittay and Diana T. Meyers, *Women and Moral Theory* (Totowa, NJ: Rowman and Littlefield, 1987). Although cultural feminism

tends to view motherhood as less oppressive than do early liberal feminists such as Shulamith Firestone (*The Dialectic of Sex: The Case for Feminist Revolution* [New York: Morrow, 1970]), motherhood nevertheless is most often cast as a choice, but this choice is denied to some women on the basis of cultural prejudices; see Michelle Fine and Adrienne Asch, eds., *Women with Disabilities: Essays in Psychology, Culture, and Politics* (Philadelphia: Temple University Press, 1988), pp. 12–23.

18 Regarding the feminist position on "defective" fetuses, a recent example that supports my point is the new Maryland abortion legislation, hailed in the March 4, 1991, issue of *Time* magazine as a "feminist victory," in which unconditional abortion is permitted until fetal viability, but after that point, only if a woman's health is endangered or if the fetus is "deformed" (p. 53). I am not suggesting abortion restrictions here; rather, I am questioning the myth of "free choice" regarding bearing congenitally disabled infants in a society in which attitudes about the disabled tend to be negative, oppressive, and unexamined. Disabled people simply need advocates who will examine the cultural ideology inherent in these rationales and policies. For discussions of the issue of disability in relation to abortion and reproductive rights, see Ruth Hubbard, "Who Should and Should Not Inhabit the World," in Ruth Hubbard, ed., *The Politics of Women's Biology* (New Brunswick, NJ: Rutgers University Press, 1990); Marsha Saxton, "Born and Unborn: The Implications of Reproductive Technologies for People with Disabilities," in Rita Arditti, Renate Duell Klein, and Shelley Minden, eds., *Test-Tube Women: What Future for Motherhood?* (Boston: Pandora, 1984), pp. 298–312; and Anne Finger, "Claiming All of Our Bodies: Reproductive Rights and Disability," in Arditti et al., eds., *Test-Tube Women*, pp. 281–96; Fine and Asch, eds., *Women with Disabilities*, esp. chapters 12 and 13; and Deborah Kaplan, "Disability Rights Perspectives on Reproductive Technologies and Public Policy," in Sherrill Cohen and Nadine Taub, eds., *Reproductive Laws for the 1990s* (Totowa, NJ: Humana Press, 1989), pp. 241–7. For discussions of ageism in feminism, see Shulamit Reinharz, "Friends or Foes: Gerontological and Feminist Theory," *Women's Studies International Forum* 9 (5): 503–14; and Barbara McDonald and Cynthia Rich, *Look Me in the Eye: Old Women, Aging, and Ageism* (San Francisco: Spinsters, Ink., 1983).

19 Susan Bordo argues in a similar vein that the feminist search for equality has caused a flight from gender, and hence from the body, that often masquerades as "professionalism." Disabled women's inability to fit the standardized image of the "professional" often alienates them from feminists who enter the workplace on such terms. See Bordo, *Unbearable Weight*, pp. 229–33; for a discussion of this point, also see Fine and Asch, eds., *Women with Disabilities*, pp. 26–31.

20 Personal conversation, Society for Disability Studies Annual Meeting, June 1991, Denver, Colorado.

21 The philosopher Iris Marion Young argues for the construction of femininity as disability by asserting that cultural objectification inhibits women from using their bodies. "Women in a sexist society are physically handicapped," concludes Young in the essay "Throwing Like a Girl" (*Throwing Like a Girl and Other Essays in Feminist Philosophy and Social Theory* [Bloomington: Indiana University Press, 1990], p. 153). For discussions of foot binding, scarification, clitoridectomy, and corseting, see Mary Daly, *Gyn/ecology: The Metaethics of Radical Feminism* (Boston: Beacon Press, 1978) and Barbara Ehrenreich and Deirdre English, *For Her Own Good: 150 Years of the Experts' Advice to Women* (Garden City, NY: Anchor Books, 1979). For discussions of anorexia, hysteria, and agoraphobia, see Susan Bordo, *Unbearable Weight*; Kim

Chernin, *The Hungry Self: Women, Eating, and Identity* (New York: Times Books, 1985) and *The Obsession: Reflections on the Tyranny of Slenderness* (New York: Harper & Row, 1981); and Susie Orbach, *Fat Is a Feminist Issue: The Anti-Diet Guide to Permanent Weight Loss* (New York: Paddington Press, 1978) and *Hunger Strike: The Anorectic's Struggle as a Metaphor for Our Age* (New York: Norton, 1986).

22 Susan Sontag, *Illness as Metaphor* (New York: Farrar, Straus, and Giroux, 1977). For cultural critiques of beauty standards, see Lois W. Banner, *American Beauty* (New York: Knopf, 1983); Robin Tolmach Lakoff and Raquel L. Scherr, *Face Value: The Politics of Beauty* (Boston: Routledge, 1984); Naomi Wolf, *The Beauty Myth: How Images of Beauty Are Used Against Women* (New York: Morrow, 1991); Sharon Romm, *The Changing Face of Beauty* (St. Louis: Mosby-Year Book, 1992); Rita Jackaway Freedman, *Beauty Bound* (Lexington, MA: Lexington Books, 1986); Susan Bordo, *Unbearable Weight*, esp. Part II; and Susan Faludi, *Backlash: The Undeclared War Against American Women* (New York: Crown, 1991).

23 This language comes from advertising for cosmetic surgery in *Newsweek* magazine, although it can be found in almost any of the many ads or articles in women's magazines. One is reminded here of Foucault's "docile bodies" described in *Discipline and Punish: The Birth of the Prison*, trans. Alan Sheridan (New York: Vintage, 1979), pp. 135–69. For discussions of cosmetic surgery, see Kathryn Pauly Morgan, "Women and the Knife: Cosmetic Surgery and the Colonization of Women's Bodies," *Hypatia* 6 (3): 25–53; Anne Balsamo, "On the Cutting Edge: Cosmetic Surgery and the Technological Production of the Gendered Body," *Camera Obscura* 28 (Jan. 1992): 207–36; and Kathy Davis, *Reshaping the Female Body: The Dilemma of Cosmetic Surgery* (New York: Routledge: 1995).

24 Mary Russo's *The Female Grotesque: Risk, Excess, and Modernity* (New York: Routledge, 1994) observes what she calls "the normalization of feminism," which involves "strategies of reassurance" that encourage feminists to focus on standard forms of femininity and avoid what she calls "the grotesque," which I might term the "abnormal."

25 Gilman, *Difference and Pathology*, p. 90.

26 On reevaluating and expanding stigma theory, see Ainlay et al., eds., *The Dilemma of Difference*; Robert Bogdan and Steven Taylor, "Toward a Sociology of Acceptance: The Other Side of the Study of Deviance," *Social Policy* 18 (2): 34–9; also Adrienne Asch and Michelle Fine, eds., "Moving Beyond Stigma," *Journal of Social Issues*, 44 (1); Simone de Beauvoir, *The Second Sex*, trans. H. M. Parshley (1952; reprint, New York: Vintage, 1974), p. xix.

27 Edward E. Jones et al., *Social Stigma: The Psychology of Marked Relationships* (New York: Freeman, 1984), pp. 8–9.

28 See Ainlay et al., eds., *The Dilemma of Difference*, p. 212.

29 Schutz is quoted in Ainlay et al., eds., *The Dilemma of Difference*, p. 20; Goffman, *Stigma*, p. 4.

30 Goffman, *Stigma*, quotation at p. 128. Because perception rather than actual physical characteristics governs stigmatization and distribution of power, many people seek to normalize their social status, either by disavowing potentially stigmatizing conditions by "passing" or by compensating for them in some way. Nevertheless, the psychological costs of passing are often isolation and a self-loathing denial, as Audre Lorde shows in *Sister Outsider* (Trumansburg, NY: The Crossing Press, 1984). The familiar script of racial passing translates to disability; for example, Franklin Roosevelt escaped the marginalized status disability usually confers, because he

had the resources to minimize his disability in public and also because he possessed virtually every other normate characteristic. See Hugh Gallagher, *FDR's Splendid Deception* (New York: Dodd Mead, 1985).

31 Julia Kristeva's psychoanalytical theory of abjection is conceptually similar to stigma theory and to this concept of dirt, but where Goffman and Douglas deal with group dynamics and the construction of communal identity, Kristeva discusses the individual psyche. See Julia Kristeva, *Powers of Horror: An Essay on Abjection*, trans. Leon S. Roudiez (New York: Columbia University Press, 1982). Also see Ainlay et al., eds., *The Dilemma of Difference*, pp. 18–20, 101–3, and Jones, *Social Stigma*, p. 93; Douglas, *Purity and Danger: An Analysis of Concepts of Pollution and Taboo*, quotation at p. 35.

32 Whereas dirt is an anomaly, something that will not fit into established tax-onomies, treacle, for example, is an ambiguity, fitting into two categories. Neither liquid nor solid, yet both at once, treacle is "an aberrant fluid," according to Douglas, who muses over Sartre's essay on stickiness (p. 38).

33 Immanuel Kant, "Critique of Judgement," in Hazard Adams, ed., *Critical Theory Since Plato* (New York: Harcourt Brace Jovanovich, 1971), p. 358. For an example of how this principle of impurity operates in encounters among ethnic groups, see Leonard Cassuto's discussion of Mary Rowland's captivity narrative in *The Inhuman Race* (New York: Columbia University Press, 1996).

34 Douglas, *Purity and Danger*, p. 40. Also see Jones, *Social Stigma*, p. 89.

35 Jones, *Social Stigma*, p. 302.

36 For discussions of the roles of institutions in enforcing dichotomous identities, see Deborah Stone, *The Disabled State*, and Paula Giddings, *When and Where I Enter: The Impact of Black Women on Race and Sex in America* (New York: Bantam, 1984). For an incisive literary treatment of the hybrid figure, consider the mulatto Joe Christmas in William Faulkner's *Light in August*.

37 Douglas, *Purity and Danger*, quotation at p. 39. For a discussion of eugenics in the United States, see Hubbard, "Who Should and Should Not Inhabit the World," in *The Politics of Women's Biology*, p. 181. Ronald Walters's views on eugenics are drawn from *The Anti-Slavery Appeal: American Abolitionism After 1830* (Baltimore: Johns Hopkins University Press, 1976), pp. 85–6. Historians of science and medicine have recently shown that the Nazi "racial hygiene" program was not a historical excep-tion. Legitimated by eugenic ideology, the program to eliminate "lives not worth living" was approved and enacted by many highly regarded members of a scien-tific and intellectual community that extended well beyond the Nazi doctors and even German borders (see Robert Proctor, *Racial Hygiene: Medicine Under the Nazis* [Cambridge, MA: Harvard University Press, 1988], p. 177). Extensive forced sterilization of "undesirables" began in 1933, and in 1939 the government issued a secret plan for killing physically and mentally disabled children, beginning with registration and "selection" of congenitally disabled new-borns and the most "severely" or "incurably" disabled children and escalating to teenagers and non-disabled Jewish children by 1943, according to Proctor. The very gas cham-bers designed for killing disabled people were dismantled and shipped east to be used for the Jews and other ethnic groups in the notorious camps. For discussions of eugenics and racial hygiene, see also Hugh Gallagher, *By Trust Betrayed: Patients, Physicians, and the License to Kill in the Third Reich* (New York: Holt, 1989); Daniel J. Kevles, *In the Name of Eugenics: Genetics and the Uses of Human Heredity* (Berkeley:

University of California Press, 1985); and Mark H. Haller, *Eugenics: Hereditarian Attitudes in American Thought* (New Brunswick, NJ: Rutgers University Press, 1984).

38   Douglas, *Purity and Danger*, quotation at p. 39. For Foucault's discussion of marginalization, see *Madness and Civilization: A History of Insanity in the Age of Reason*, trans. Richard Howard (New York: Pantheon, 1965) and *The Birth of the Clinic: An Archeology of Medical Perception*, trans. A. M. Sheridan-Smith (New York: Pantheon, 1973). Regarding "ugly laws," see Burgdorf, "A History of Unequal Treatment," p. 863.

39   For discussion of asylums and almshouses, see Rothman, *Discovery of the Asylum*, and Tom Compton, "A Brief History of Disability" (Berkeley: unpublished manuscript, 1989), p. 42. For histories of disability legislation, see Scotch, *From Good Will to Civil Rights*; Shapiro, *No Pity*; Marvin Lazerson, "The Origins of Special Education," in J. G. Chambers and William T. Hartman, eds., *Special Education Politics: Their History, Implementation, and Finance* (Philadelphia: Temple University Press, 1983), pp. 15–47; Wolf Wolfensberger, *The Origin and Nature of Our Institutional Models* (Syracuse, NY: Human Policy Press, 1975); and Liachowitz, *Disability as a Social Construct*.

40   See Fine and Asch, eds., *Women with Disabilities*, pp. 9–12, for discussion of poverty and lack of education among the disabled. For accounts of deaf culture, see Harlan L. Lane, *When the Mind Hears: A History of the Deaf* (New York: Random House, 1984); Carol Paden and Tom Humphreys, *Deaf in America: Voices from a Culture*; and John Van Cleve and Barry Crouch, *A Place of Their Own: Creating the Deaf Community in America* (Washington, DC: Gallaudet University Press, 1989). For the effects of segregated education and institutionalization on the independent living movement, see Zola, *Missing Pieces*.

41   See the following discussions of disability in literature and film: Shari Thurer, "Disability and Monstrosity: A Look at Literary Distortions of Handicapping Conditions," *Rehabilitation Literature* 41 (1–2): 12–15; Douglas Biklin and Robert Bogdan, "Media Portrayals of Disabled People: A Study in Stereotypes," *Interracial Books for Children Bulletin* 8 (6) and (7): 4–9; Leonard Kriegel, "The Wolf in the Pit in the Zoo," *Social Policy* (fall 1982): 16–23; Paul Longmore, "Screening Stereotypes: Images of Disabled People," *Social Policy* 16 (summer 1985): 31–8; and Deborah Kent, "Disabled Women: Portraits in Fiction and Drama," in Alan Gartner and Tom Joe, eds., *Images of the Disabled, Disabling Images* (New York: Praeger, 1987); and Martin Norden, *The Cinema of Isolation*. For discussions of the monster in culture, see Jeffrey Cohen, ed., *Monster Theory: Reading Culture* (Minneapolis: University of Minnesota Press, 1996) and Marie Hélène Huet, *Monstrous Imagination*.

42   Nathaniel Hawthorne's story "The Birthmark" can be read as an exploration of culture's intolerance of anomaly and the danger that surrounds it. For discussions of Hawthorne's story in the context of bodily difference, see Diane Price Herndl, *Invalid Women: Figuring Feminine Illness in American Fiction and Culture, 1840–1940* (Chapel Hill: University of North Carolina Press, 1993) and Frances E. Mascia-Lees and Patricia Sharpe, "The Marked and the Un(re)marked: Tattoo and Gender in Theory and Narrative," in Frances E. Mascia-Lees and Patricia Sharpe, eds., *Tattoo, Torture, Mutilation, and Adornment* (Albany: SUNY Press, 1992), pp. 145–70.

43   For discussions of social Darwinism and Lamarckian thought, see Richard Hofstadter, *Social Darwinism in American Thought* (Boston: Beacon Press, 1944) and

Stephen Jay Gould, *The Mismeasure of Man* (New York: Norton, 1981). Regarding "just world" assumptions about disability, see Ainlay et al., eds., *The Dilemma of Difference*, pp. 33–4.

44   See Davis, "Deviance Disavowal," p. 124.

45   For Freud's delineation of "deformities of character," see "Some Character Types Met with in Psychoanalytic Work," in *Collected Papers*, vol. IV, trans. Joan Riviere (London: Hogarth, 1957), pp. 319–22. There are many studies about pathologizing difference, for example, Sander Gilman, *Difference and Pathology*. For a discussion of pathologizing disability, see Deborah Stone, *The Disabled State*.

46   Douglas, *Purity and Danger*, p. 40.

47   Thomas S. Kuhn, *The Structure of Scientific Revolutions* (Chicago: University of Chicago Press, 1992), p. 5.

48   Although M. M. Bakhtin does not explicitly associate the carnivalesque with disability in his privileging of the exceptional body (*The Dialogic Imagination*, trans. Caryl Emerson and Michael Holquist [Austin: Texas University Press, 1981], quotation at p. 159), it is worth noting that Bakhtin himself was disabled by a bone disease at the age of twenty-eight, leading to the amputation of his leg in 1938, at age forty-three, precisely when he was writing on Rabelais and the Middle Ages.

49   See, for example, Harpham, *On the Grotesque*; Peter Stallybrass and Allon White, *The Poetics and Politics of Transgression* (Ithaca, NY: Cornell University Press, 1986); Mary Russo, *The Female Grotesque*; and Leonard Cassuto, *The Inhuman Race*.

50   Michel Foucault, *Discipline and Punish: The Birth of the Prison*, trans. Alan Sheridan (New York: Vintage, 1979), pp. 193, 135.

51   Foucault, *Madness and Civilization*, pp. 38 and 48; Michel Foucault, *Power/Knowledge: Selected Interviews and Other Writings, 1972–1977*, ed. and trans. Colin Gordon (New York: Pantheon, 1980), p. 166. Echoing Foucault's analysis of Europe, both David Rothman in *The Discovery of the Asylum* and Deborah Stone in *The Disabled State* lay out this process in the history of the United States.

52   Foucault, *Discipline and Punish*, p. 184.

53   Both Foucault and his American counterpart, David Rothman (in *The Discovery of the Asylum*), occasionally imply that disability is a natural state justifying indolence and confinement. Only chroniclers of the disabled category, like Deborah Stone (*The Disabled State*) and Tom Compton ("A Brief History of Disability") question this.

54   Goffman, *Stigma*, p. 128. For a discussion of the costuming of power, see Richard Sennett, *The Fall of Public Man* (New York: Knopf, 1977), pp. 65–72 and 161–74.

55   Foucault supports this hypothesis by noting that the writing of lives in premodern regimes involved a "heroization" that delineated the "individuality of the memorable man," while the modern marked individual is objectified (*Discipline and Punish*, pp. 192–3). The phenomena of religious stigmata, an occurrence of functional disabilities and wounds like those of the crucified Christ, usually on the bodies of subsequently canonized saints, certainly testifies to a positive interpretation of bodily damage. St. Francis of Assisi displayed stigmatic wounds, which were always associated with ecstasy; and some Christians during the thirteenth century evidently actually maimed themselves in an effort to identify with Christ's sufferings, according to the *New Catholic Encyclopedia* (New York: McGraw-Hill, 1967, vol. 13, p. 711). Harlan Hahn draws from prehistorical archeological evidence through studies of the Middle Ages, concluding that in these premodern times, "the appearance of physical differences seemed to be associated with festiveness, sensuality,

and entertainment rather than loss, repugnance, or personal tragedy" ("Can Disability Be Beautiful?" p. 31).

56 Murphy, *The Body Silent*, pp. 4, 116–17.

57 My understanding of the ideology of individualism is informed by Yehoshua Arieli, *Individualism and Nationalism in American Ideology* (Cambridge, MA: Center for Study of History of Liberty in America, 1964); Robert N. Bellah et al., *Habits of the Heart: Individualism and Commitment in American Life* (Berkeley: University of California Press, 1985); Gillian Brown, *Domestic Individualism: Imagining Self in Nineteenth Century America* (Berkeley: University of California Press, 1990); Wai Chee Dimock, *Empire for Liberty: Melville and the Poetics of Individualism* (Princeton, NU: Princeton University Press, 1989); Jean Bethke Elsthain, *Public Man, Private Woman: Women in Social and Political Thought* (Princeton, NU: Princeton University Press, 1981); Myra Jehlen, *American Incarnation: The Individual, the Nation, and the Continent* (Cambridge, MA: Harvard University Press, 1986); C. B. MacPherson, *The Political Theory of Possessive Individualism: Hobbes to Locke* (Oxford: Clarendon Press, 1962); John W. Meyer, "Myths of Socialization and of Personality," in Thomas C. Heller et al., eds., *Reconstructing Individualism: Autonomy, Individuality, and Self in Western Thought* (Stanford, CA: Stanford University Press, 1986); and Marvin Meyers, *The Jacksonian Persuasion: Politics and Belief* (New York: Vintage Press, 1957).

58 Ralph Waldo Emerson, "Self-Reliance," and "Fate," in *The Works of Ralph Waldo Emerson* (1847; reprint, New York: Tudor, 1938), vol. 1, p. 32; vol. 3, p. 8; David Leverenz, "The Politics of Emerson's Man-Making Words," *PMLA* 101 (1): 49.

59 Richard Selzer, *Mortal Lessons: Notes on the Art of Surgery* (New York: Simon & Schuster, 1987).

60 For a discussion of antinominianism, see Amy Schrager Lang, *Prophetic Woman: Anne Hutchinson and the Problem of Dissent in the Literature of New England* (Berkeley: University of California Press, 1987).

61 For a discussion of conformity and intolerance, see G. J. Barker-Benfield, *The Horrors of the Half-Known Life: Male Attitudes Toward Women and Sexuality in Nineteenth-Century America* (New York: Harper & Row, 1976). Alexis de Tocqueville's remarks come from *Democracy in America*, vol. 1 (1840: reprint, New York: Vintage Books, 1990), p. 267.

62 Barker Benfield, *The Horrors of the Half-Known Life*, p. 178; Siegfried Kracauer, *The Mass Ornament: Weimar Essays*, trans. and ed. Thomas Y. Levin (Cambridge, MA: Harvard University Press, 1995).

63 It is interesting to note that one of Ahab's literary descendants, Captain Falcon of Charles Johnson's *Middle Passage* (New York: Macmillan, 1990) is also a disabled figure who invites interpretation. In Falcon, Ahab's missing leg is transformed into foreshortened legs that render this embodiment of evil a demasculinized dwarf.

64 See MacPherson, *The Political Theory of Possessive Individualism*. Susan Sontag's *Illness as Metaphor* examines this assignment of blame, analyzing cultural meanings attributed to tuberculosis and cancer in the nineteenth and twentieth centuries. The concept of "fighting" cancer or other diseases is just one example of our tendency to imagine ourselves as bounded, autonomous individuals.

65 Wai Chee Dimock explores the personification of the nation in this sense, showing Melville's commitment to "the institution of the discrete, a faith in the self-contained and the self-sufficient" (*Empire for Liberty*, quotation at p. 111; also see especially pp. 26–30).

66   The alternative, less dramatic, and less compelling response of simply leaving the whale alone is suggested by the English captain of the *Samuel Enderby*, who has lost his arm in an encounter with Moby Dick.

67   F. O. Matthiessen suggested as early as 1941 that Ahab stood for a critique of individualism, but he links Ahab's behavior, not his body, to his assessment (*The American Renaissance* [New York: Oxford, 1941], p. 459).

68   For a discussion of Emerson's denial of care and dependence, see Joyce W. Warren, *American Narcissus: Individualism and Women in Nineteenth-Century American Fiction* (New Brunswick, NJ: Rutgers University Press, 1984).

69   Tocqueville, *Democracy in America*, vol. 2, p. 34.

70   An interesting counternarrative of spiritual perfectibility in which the disabled figure is privileged appears in the case of Stowe's Eva and Dickens's Tiny Tim, where the physically vulnerable figure can attain spiritual perfection.

71   The problem of poverty in a society that equates work with virtue is explored by David Rothman in *The Discovery of the Asylum*, as well as by Frank Bowe in *Handicapping America: Barriers to Disabled People* (New York: Harper & Row, 1978), by Daniel Rodgers in *The Work Ethic in Industrial America, 1850–1920* (Chicago: University of Chicago Press, 1978), and by Deborah Stone in *The Disabled State*, all of which inform this discussion.

72   The concept of "disabled" was used as early as 1644 to designate soldiers compensated by law for war wounds. Legislation has always been clear about disabled soldiers, whose labor as warriors earned their compensation. The debate about who can legitimately be excused from the workforce still rages as questioning of the welfare system.

73   For discussions of the fellow-servant ruling see Lawrence M. Friedman and Jack Ladinsky, "Social Change and the Law of Industrial Accidents," *Columbia Law Review* 67, no. 1 (January 1967): 55–65, and Brook Thomas, *Cross-Examinations of Law and Literature: Cooper, Hawthorne, Stowe, and Melville* (Cambridge: Cambridge University Press, 1987), pp. 164–82. It is interesting to note that Lemuel Shaw was Melville's brother-in-law.

74   By the latter part of the century the fellow-servant rule was legally weakened as industrial accidents increased dramatically and society began to recognize that the precedent was untenable and inequitable. Between 1910 and 1920 workmen's compensation statutes were becoming the rule, though according to Friedman and Ladinsky ("Social Change," pp. 60–70), the last state to institute such a law was Mississippi in 1948.

75   The history of public policy toward disability and its development as a political category is found in Deborah Stone, *The Disabled State* (pp. 1–117); Claire Liachowitz, *Disability as a Social Construct*; Tom Compton, "A Brief History of Disability"; and Richard Scotch, *From Good Will to Civil Rights*. Stone's linking of the disability category to a need-based rather than a work-based system is essential to my analysis. However, I question the concepts of ability and will, analyze the place of the ideology of work, and accept disability more fully as a social construction.

76   The poor-law precedence, which basically advocated institutionalization rather than direct aid as a form of public relief, was brought to colonial America and was the guiding principle of public welfare until the emergence of the welfare state around the turn of the century. Although poor-law policy effectively incarcerated and punished both disabled and non-disabled poor, it prevailed throughout the nineteenth century because of apprehensions that direct economic public aid would

encourage idleness and compromise the motivation to work. The Jacksonian tendency to limit federal intervention and champion individual autonomy further discouraged revision of inherited poor-law policy. Only the glut of disabled Civil War veterans, the rise of private humanitarian efforts, and the movement into the Progressive Era finally rendered disability and other social problems issues appropriately addressed by the state rather than by families and locally. See J. Lenihan, "Disabled Americans: A History," *Performances* (Nov./Dec. 1976–Jan. 1977): 1–69, for an overview of American disability policy. For a discussion of the institutions that managed poverty, see David Rothman, *The Discovery of the Asylum*, and Michael B. Katz, *In the Shadow of the Poorhouse: A Social History of Welfare in America* (New York: Basic Books, 1986).

77 Stone, *The Disabled State*, pp. 91–9.

78 The modern welfare state's quantification of disability in order to administer economic aid uses formulas and charts to transform bodily conditions into percentages of ability that determine a person's eligibility for aid. These various public policy disability schedules locate disability exclusively in the body and presume an abstract notion of physical wholeness and ideal performance levels to which the "disabled" are compared. Certain physical states are then clinically evaluated as decreasing absolute able-bodiedness by a particular percentage. On one scale, for example, limb amputation translates as 70 percent reduction in ability to work, while amputation of the little finger at the distal joint reduces the capacity for labor by a single percentage point. What seems absurd here is the insistence that a precise mathematical relation can be posited between such complex, dynamic situations as bodily condition and ability to perform wage labor (see Stone, *The Disabled State*, pp. 107–17).

79 Rodgers, *The Work Ethic in Industrial America*, p. xi.

Chapter 14

Nature, History, and the Failure of Language: The Problem of the Human in Post-Apartheid South Africa

John K. Noyes

One of the most powerful and challenging messages emerging from Antje Krog's remarkable book on the South African Truth and Reconciliation Commission, *Country of My Skull* (1998), is the limitation of language when it is called upon to testify to the trauma that years of human rights violations have left on the consciousness of South African society, and when it is called upon to heal that trauma. The public imagination will long be scarred by the scenes of pain and the images of violence that accompanied the commission's public hearings, scenes and images whose compelling intensity and sheer human drama seem to want to escape linguistic formulation and repetition.

Krog observes that her task of reporting on the Truth Commission as a journalist left her and her colleagues "physically exhausted and mentally frayed. Because of language" (Krog 1998, p. 37). It is because of the limitations of language that the hearings are so powerful, and wherever language fails to do justice to the pain of the victims of apartheid it is overwhelmingly apparent that the concept of truth needs careful consideration.

The starting point of the human rights hearings was the indefinable wail that burst from Nomonde Calata's lips in East London. The starting point of the perpetrators' narrative is the uncontrollable muscle in Brian Mitchell's jaw. Mitchell is seeking amnesty for his part in the Trust Feed massacre in which eleven people died. When Judge Andrew Wilson asks him during his amnesty hearing: "Would you say you suffered a lot?" the only answer Mitchell can muster for the eight o'clock news is a frantically quivering jaw muscle. (Ibid, pp. 56–7)

In Krog's depiction, truth resides in the inarticulate cry of Nomonde Calata, whose husband Fort was one of the so-called Craddock Four murdered by a death squad in the Easter Cape region of South Africa in 1985. And, as Krog observes, it is the task of the commission to find "words for that cry of Nomonde Calata" (ibid, p. 43). But it must also find words for those responsible for the multiple murders and human rights violations: for the quivering jaw muscle of a murderer.

This, it seems, is how the problem of truth is destined to present itself in post-apartheid South Africa: as a painful discrepancy between the gestures of trauma and the language it is spoken in. The need to find words for the pain of the victims and the silence of the perpetrators presents a challenge to language which is of essentially the same order noted famously by Theodor Adorno when he asked if poetry was still possible after Auschwitz.

The question of poetry after Auschwitz, of language after the Truth Commission, is not a simple rejection of the cynicism, lies, and mythic aestheticism that the depoliticized language of the powerful uses to obscure its mechanisms. It is truly a question, in the best philosophical sense – an urgent and vital challenge for thought to consider the forms in which it expresses itself when dealing with suffering, and to interrogate the meaning of truth in relation to language.

The question Adorno felt so urgently in the aftermath of the Holocaust presents itself in South Africa today as the question of what happens to stories and narratives of violence, trauma, pain, and injustice when they find their way into the arenas commanded by those who are more versed in words than Nomonde Calata or Brian Mitchell. Thus the South African historian Premesh Lalu has asked "what occurs when these stories are subjected to the ritual contextualization by the TRC, and when they are appropriated by academics who will be expected to provide a synthesis out of what appears to be disparate episodes of national trauma?" (Lalu 1996, p. 32). It is worth noting that Lalu places the prime responsibility for the synthetic resolution of trauma with a certain (unspecified) field of academic disciplines. This certainly addresses those disciplines in the academy that interrogate the way language apprehends, sustains, and disavows trauma, and the way this process feeds into the constitution of politically stable identities. But it is important that we understand this concern as addressed also, perhaps even primarily, to a more general understanding of what happens in political processes.

It must be emphasized that Lalu's question is also addressed to the language in which the testimonies are embedded in the moment of their production – the legal, political, religious, and media discourses that collectively produce what I would call the political language of testimony. As Lalu implies, this language is not free of conflict, nor is it easily capable of negotiating an unproblematic post-apartheid South African identity that might be shared by victims, perpetrators, commissioners, lawyers, and journalists alike. What this shows is just how seriously we need an academic or critical discourse that can articulate the conflicting group identities that have to be negotiated if a democratic practice is to be possible in South Africa today.

But when we recognize that the problem of identity, truth, and representation is both a problem of political discourse and of academic discourse, we are forced to confront the close relationship between a sensitivity to violence and trauma on the one hand, and an analysis of their resistance to language on the other hand. Without this, we fall prey to the kind of skeptical rejection of language that Adorno warned against when he observed that naked anti-rhetoricism is allied to the barbarism in which bourgeois thought is destined to end (Adorno 1966, p. 66). Adorno realized in the wake of the Weimar Republic and its collapse into fascism that the failures of democratic politics need to be interrogated as a political failure, and that this failure is based upon the failure of discursive and rhetorical traditions to interrogate the way political, social, and economic power-struggles were built into the founding moves of these traditions. A philosophy – an encounter with the world of ideas – which fails to trace the processes that allow ideas to be treated as if they float free of the material world, will always threaten to slide into barbarism. Consequently, the task of any critical project is to interrogate the contradictions embedded in the entire set of conceptualizing moves out of which we construct our world. These are eminently political moves, for they are the moves that imagine a unity of agency in which subjectivity becomes ripe for political action – they are the moves that found the *demos*.

The conceptual constitution of a *demos* is about how any one democratic system negotiates the local and performative differences that resist the production of homogeneous group identity – the set of everyday practices and group loyalties that remain undiluted within a ritual contextualization that might produce a single normalized subjectivity. This is the prime challenge linking philosophy and politics in pursuit of a multicultural democracy. Adorno knew that fascism is what emerges when a normalized subjectivity is forcefully asserted and when its forms of representation are uncritically accepted. In a South Africa that is just emerging from decades of institutional and constitutional brutality, the threat of normalized subjectivity might not look like it did to Adorno in Germany in the wake of Nazism. But the threat remains just as acute. We simply need to give it a different name: the brand of identity politics whose ideal is the deracialized but ethnically targetable subject of consumption in a global economy. And "targetable" must be understood in both senses of the word – it is no chance fact that the global economy creates ethnically marked subjects of consumption in some places while seeking out ethnically marked victims of prejudice and cleansing in others. As I write, the conflict in Kosovo and its effective splitting of the Left shows how problematic the conceptualization of normalized and differentiated subjectivities remains.

We need to take Chantal Mouffe (1994) seriously when she pleads that intellectuals in the Western liberal democracies must challenge the brand of liberalism that believes it can overcome conflict simply by consensus:

overpowering or disavowing any non-standard forms of identity and group-belonging which challenge and deviate from the norm of a hegemonous class. In South Africa this situation was of course always complicated by the fact that the ruling class depended for its power base on a constitutionally grounded, racially coded white working class. In South Africa today, this situation is newly complicated, as Mahmood Mamdani (1996) has pointed out, by the emergence of a deracialized ruling elite alongside a constitutionally empowered yet impoverished majority that continues to rely on ethnically coded representations for access to privilege and property. As Mouffe observes, if we are to practice a politics of democracy, we need a critical theory that can unmask the sophist language of liberalism whenever it pretends that conflict is not at once a political and a representational issue, or that the goal of conflict resolution is the delimitization of identity according to the principles of maximized consumption.

The imperatives of political practice render an interrogation of the rhetorical foundation of the *polis* so necessary, and it is with these imperatives in mind that we must critically examine the conceptual basis for establishing a South African identity in the wake of apartheid. This is intimately related to the question of truth and language, of the ability of language to represent past trauma and transform it in a process of healing, leading to functional group identities for a new multicultural democracy.

When we listen to debates of reconciliation, of common identity, of nation building in South Africa today, they return us time and again to concepts of our shared humanity. And how could it be otherwise? What else is there to speak about when our goal is a future without violence? In much South African intellectual discourse of the 1980s and 1990s, the problem of language and violence is expressed as a struggle for an adequate conception of the human.

This is not only a feature of academic discourse. Indeed, the importance of ideas of shared humanity in everyday discourses of healing in South Africa today can scarcely be overestimated. One of the dominant rhetorical moments in the Truth and Reconciliation Commission has been Desmond Tutu's theological discourse of common humanity, which Antje Krog describes as an Africanized Western Christian humanism that states "you can only be human in a humane society" (Krog 1998, p. 110). Alan Boesak described a similar idea in 1984 when he observed that to be "truly human . . . means to be able to be, to live in accordance with one's God-given humanity. It means to be able to realize this essential humanity in the socio-historical world in which we have responsibility" (Boesak 1984, p. 112). And this discourse is replicated in the Truth Commission testimony of a number of the victims. Cynthia Ngewu, for example, the mother of Christopher Piet, one of the seven young men ambushed and murdered in Guguletu, Cape Town, in March 1986, put it like this:

> This thing called reconciliation . . . if I am understanding it correctly . . . if it means
> this perpetrator, this man who has killed Christopher Piet, if it means he becomes

human again, this man, so that I, so that all of us, get our humanity back . . .
then I agree, then I support it all. (Quoted in Krog 1998, p. 109)

The strength of comments such as these should serve to show the serious
challenge that the idea of the human presents for critical language in South
Africa today. In the face of poststructuralist and postcolonialist debates on
humanism, in the face of the urgency of human rights issues and their close
interlinking to issues of globalization, and in the face of persistent violence and
persistent apartheid structures of oppression in post-apartheid South Africa,
we need to interrogate carefully the function of the human in academic and
popular discourse.

The idea of common humanity is generally developed along two axes:
shared history and shared human nature. For this reason, if we are to take the
idea of the human seriously, we need to interrogate its founding conceptual
moments in nature and history. As a concept dependent on a grounding in
nature and history, the human becomes increasingly problematic when we
attempt to return it to the specificity of nature and history, to the space and
time of the body, and all that marks the body with signs of difference. There
is something about common humanity that constantly eludes the axes of
nature and history but still needs these axes. The idea of the human, itself
dependent on concepts of nature and history, can only be sustained in critical
language by consciously removing it from nature and history as totalizing
concepts.

To put the thesis of the human in these terms is to force an encounter with
a central problem in postcolonial theory: the widespread celebration of difference and heterogeneity in postcolonial theory requires a dialectic that can
account for the unifying and homogenizing moments: the negation of heterogeneity inherent in any act of theory and in conceptualization itself. Wherever this theoretical problem is not confronted, postcolonialism begins to look
like a simple confusion of two very different issues: the philosophical move
that opposes the hegemonic force of universalization on the one hand and, on
the other, a politics of difference aimed at empowering minorities (a point well
made by Varadharajan 1995). This is why, from Frantz Fanon through to
Edward Said, postcolonial theory has been able to sustain a strange combination of a politics of engagement with a theoretical humanism that borders on
the philosophically naive. And, in its worst moments, this humanism makes
it hard to distinguish the politics of difference from the rhetoric of global capitalism. Some of the most powerful criticism of postcolonial theory has come
from the theorists of globalization, who are quick to point out the ideological
moments in celebrations of diversity, hybridity, and difference in global capitalism (see, for example, the essays in Wilson and Dissanayake 1996; also Dirlik
1994). If the Coca-Cola corporation's motto is "Think global, act local", then
the challenge it poses to postcolonial theory is precisely this discrepancy
between thinking and acting, between the conceptualization of being and
a politics of beings, a philosophy and a politics of the human. Indeed, the

humanism that drives a certain tendency in Said's work (for example, Said 1996) would gain much by reflecting on the implications of Marx's distinction between what humanism means for thought and what it means for politics. After 1845 Marx rejected philosophical humanism while recognizing an ideology of humanism as a tool for enabling political action (see Althusser 1965).

The question of the human leads us directly to this particular problem within post-colonial theory simply because its post-apartheid interlocution is given by a reconceptualization of civil society along postcolonial lines together with an increasing integration into the global market. This is directly related to the problem in critical language I outlined above.

The question which the Truth and Reconciliation Commission poses for critical language is not a question of identity politics – of who is speaking for whom. Indeed, critical theory has to abandon the illusory quest for a perfect correspondence of the speaking subject and the spoken object. What must be retained is the difference embedded in *case*, the difference between the nominative, subjectifying case (who) and the accusative, objectifying case (whom). It is the question of how to speak against the hegemonic force of a universalizing theory while at the same time sustaining that theory in a way that enables not only a politics of reconciliation, but also of redistribution. This imperative forces us to bear in mind that redistribution – a political issue which is intimately tied to reconciliation – requires a sustained engagement with the differences introduced into universal subjectivity by the rhetoric and policies of apartheid. In this sense a politics of redistribution is profoundly opposed to the rhetoric of common humanity that drives the Truth Commission.

The question of "speaking for" – of representation – leads, in Spivak's observation, not only to "a critique of the subject as individual agent but a critique even of the subjectivity of a collective agency" (Spivak 1993, p. 72). Spivak's point is that representation contains a duality and discrepancy between language and action, between the linguistic practices that serve to constitute and sustain politically cohesive groups, and the structures of language that represent these groups as either historically or naturally constituted. For Spivak, the complicity and collusion between these two forms of representation, "their identity-in-difference as the place of practice . . . can only be appreciated if they are not conflated by a sleight of word" (ibid).

One of the most subtle and effective attempts to engage with this issue is Adorno's negative dialectic, which grew out of the problem of the dialectic of nature and history. Adorno's concern with natural history spans the period between fascism and the economic miracle in Germany, and confronts the persistence of a certain failure of critical language within totalizing philosophical systems. And I think the necessity that Adorno saw in his dialectic of natural history is present with equal force in South Africa today. The problem of critical language before and after apartheid places a similar imperative on intellectuals to confront the politics of our own critical thought.

When the testimony of the Truth and Reconciliation Commission evokes the image of our common humanity, it also evokes the image of that which is erroneous to the field of the human: the monstrous. What do we do with the monsters who persist – sometimes shamefacedly, sometimes in disguise, sometimes symptomatically, like a quivering jaw muscle – in brutalizing all that makes sense to us in terms of shared human values? What language can exorcise the acts of apartheid's henchmen, the past horrors, reenacted in the Truth Commission testimonies, of apartheid's undeniable inhumanity?

One of the persistent concerns surrounding the procedure of the Truth Commission is the difference between the way it deals with the victims and the perpetrators. The former seem to be able to access their own humanity only by a reliving of trauma; while the latter beg a similar question to that raised by redistribution: isn't it necessary to retain a certain political function of difference within the concept of the human? Doesn't the rehumanization of the monstrous rely on acts of reconciliation without justice? Is the simple act of forgiveness – for example in the words of Cynthia Ngewu, quoted above – enough to reintegrate the perpetrators of monstrous deeds into the field of humanity?

It is precisely in the drawing of a dividing line between the monstrous and the human that language becomes problematic. The image of the monster has always provided a symptomatics of the human failure to negotiate the gap between culture and nature. This failure expresses itself as a failure to reconcile appearance and thought, the nameable and the unnameable. The appearance of the monster displays the inherent resistance to cultural acts of regulation, description and classification residing within nature. Yet the failure of descriptive language to confine and control nature preserves in itself (at least this is Adorno's and Horkheimer's claim in *The Dialectic of Enlightenment*) a will to explanation that is, if not yet scientific or strictly causal, at least a reinstatement of language where it had failed in the face of the monstrous. It situates the human endeavor firmly between the failure of language and its reconstitution.

If the monstrous provides us with images that unsettle the difference between nature and culture, these images also unsettle the difference between the historical scheme and the contingent event. Temporality converts to history where the anecdotal gives way to the general discourse of history. As with theory, this is a necessary move for any discourse intended to function as a cultural stabilizing practice – and it applies to the Truth Commission. Explanatory language can sustain a general concept of the human if it succeeds in excluding the monstrous from history. But this is also a self-destructive move, because it threatens to erase difference, the essential experience of individuality and specificity that guarantees the human. There is something in the concept of the human that needs to canopy history. This is why the process of the Truth Commission is constantly threatened with failure. In compensation for the constant leaning of the human toward the monstrous, the discourse of the Truth Commission seems to want to set up memory as that which can take the place of history. But can it?

Language, in answering the demand that it must introduce significance into a world order constantly teetering on the brink of the monstrous, is itself in need of interpretation. For whenever explanatory language encounters the monstrous as that which lies outside of culture, that which problematizes history and nature alike, it responds by evoking myth to describe the limits of reason. Alternatively, language reinterprets natural phenomena within the paradigms of instrumental reason, in the same way Adorno and Horkheimer describe in the *Dialectic of Enlightenment*. In this way, the cultural uses of language indicate what it intends to do with the monsters it finds within its own core.

The relationship between the mythical and the instrumental forms of explanation needs careful specification, for the interrogation of a state of historical supplementarity (the "post" of postmodernity, postcolonialism, or post-apartheid) implies a language that moves toward its own self-realization. If myth is the linguistic rendition of a nature that still holds culture under its sway, then the language of history seems destined to work according to a demythologizing principle. But this is a gross simplification of what mythical and instrumental languages do with history. Here we should not forget Wittgenstein's critique of James Frazer's *Golden Bough* (1890) – that Frazer mistakes myth for insufficiently formulated scientific hypotheses. History does not follow a simple procession from the language of incomprehensible nature to that of nature rendered productive. If it did, it might be more successful in banishing its monsters.

This is why the question at stake here is how to conceive of the relationship between the appearances of nature, explanatory language, and the temporality of the entire process. It is the question of natural history.

If the dialectic of enlightenment that would banish myth in a language of explanation appears to lend itself to an easy association with historical time, what kind of temporality is required to make sense of the unsettling force of the monstrous within the regime of causal explanation? Perhaps it is the temporality inscribed by Manuel De Landa's (1991) robot historian, that intelligent, self-reflexive, philosophizing machine that, contemplating its own phylogenesis, is forced to confront humanity as a brief, not very successful and, we would have to add, mythical moment in its own history. The question is of course an impossible one, since it concerns the temporality of nature and of mythical beings; of monsters, machines, and historians – in short the temporality of the non-human, of what Adorno called the non-identical.

This leads to a second question: what then happens to causal explanation? In this case it would be the question of what remains after the monstrous has converted to the human – will our human timekeeper realize the continuing inherence of the monstrous in the very constitution of its own humanness. The idea of the monstrous shows that explanatory language fails because it requires the totality of nature in order to make sense of history, and the totality of history in order to make sense of nature. One of Adorno's chief objectives is to counter the dialectic that allows totality to issue in an unthought-about manner from the complementarity of nature and history. And "as long as it is not reflected on" such a view of nature and history "renders harmless the essentially historical process as a mere addition and an accessory in placing on the throne of being that which has not yet become" (Adorno 1966, p. 353). The key point here is the phrase "as long as it is not reflected on" (my translation of Adorno's *unreflektiert*).

The problem of natural history was of central importance to Adorno, from his address to the *Kantgesellschaft*, "The Idea of Natural History," in 1932, to his *Negative Dialektik* of 1966. This is because it allowed him to think about the role that philosophy has to play in articulating its own relationships with power. And this is why it remains such a vital discussion in South Africa today. The task of philosophy is to reveal the fault lines in the forms of appearance of both the material world and of history.

In the *Negative Dialektik*, quoting his earlier paper of 1932, Adorno declared his concern as follows:

> What would come to mind would be . . . to see all nature, and whatever might establish itself as such, as history and all history as nature, 'to grasp historical being in its external historical determination, there where it is most historical, as itself natural being, or to grasp nature, there where it apparently resides most profoundly within itself, as historical being. (Adorno 1966, p. 353)

There are two intimately interconnected issues here: temporality and language. When the human mediation of nature gives rise to a concept of nature without humans, it does so by imagining nature on the same temporal scale as the human. For how else can we imagine a realm of nature prior to the temporality of thought? If we think of it in terms of priority, we can only think of it as human nature, that is nature *thought*, *spoken*, or in Adorno's words, *reflected upon*. Adorno formulated the problem of natural history in the language of a self-reflexive anti-systematic philosophy, because the problem concerns the political consequences of our recognition that language fails at certain key moments in its apprehension of human history and human nature.

It is within the dialectic of natural history that language must seek the human. In the face of a dehumanizing representation of what humans have in common, such as presented on the post-apartheid stage of the Truth Commission, reflections on difference and the human make very pressing demands on critical language – and, by extension, on the postcolonial repertoire of political representations. Our problem as academics dealing with difference and the human in a postcolonial and post-apartheid world is that we are caught between two failures of language.

On the one hand, language fails in the same way we used to have to be silent when walking into a church – it fails as it recognizes the tautologies of its own interventions. This is the same endemic quietism that was found in the inability of many white liberal and even Leftist academics to speak publicly in the face of apartheid violence. This was only partially due to the efficacy of state repression. It was often only after the eruption of a specific event – Soweto 1976 or the murder of Steve Biko in 1977 – that this tautology could be broken. This problem of quietism is also a problem within post-colonial theory – what remains to be said once we say that the subaltern cannot speak? From the post-apartheid perspective, postcolonial theory seems to lack the events that provide a counter to the tautology of critical interventions. Where resistance to the monsters of the postcolonial era – Sani Abacha, Mobutu Sese Seko, Pol Pot, Augusto Pinochet, or the many others – solicits a language of collectivity and thereby undermines the performance of the individual voice, the remarkable achievement of the Truth Commission is to show how language can reveal events where there had only been "history." Writing this now, in April 1999, the findings of the Truth Commission have been published, but the Bosnian war-crimes tribunal in the Hague is still proceeding, and it is fair to assume that the war in Kosovo will produce its own testimonial forum for crimes against humanity. It appears that if critical language is to succeed in its political project, it will be through the production of events out of history. In a sense this has already happened over the war in Kosovo, which has given rise to a revival of critical language within the European Left – and could possibly even restore to it the critical sense of difference between a philosophy and a politics of humanism.

On the other hand, language fails in the same way that poetic language is a failed language – it fails as it recognizes that what can be said about another person's body cannot be divorced from the experience of one's own body. This realization constantly threatens to collapse the distinctions of case that separate the speaker from the spoken body. The question whether it is possible to act upon a monster to remove or reintegrate it into the fold of humanity at the same time invokes the question whether this action does not affect the humanity of the actor in the moment of action. This is the central issue that remains unresolved in the Leftist interpretation of the war in Kosovo – and it is telling in this respect that this event is the first in thirty years to split the European Left entirely, but also to give it back a sense of politics.

If this sense of politics is to blossom, it will have to do so via Adorno's plea to restore the "eventedness" of events within the leveling practices of conceptualization by forcing thought to think against itself. For, as Adorno observed in commenting on the possibility not only of poetry, but of thought and indeed of life itself after Auschwitz, the inhumanity that resides at the core of the human consists in "the ability to distance oneself and exalt oneself in the act of observation" (Adorno 1966, p. 356). When thought confronts the events of bodily experience, it requires a language that resists the contemplative distance that would negate these events. But language is also called upon to resist the barbaric politics that result from a refusal to consider the somatic grounding of thought that makes it possible to speak of the human in the first place.

In the age of global capitalism, this is where postcolonial theory should listen very carefully to Adorno's thoughts. For a celebration of diversity may not always be the best conceptual assemblage in the order of global capitalism. The moment when postcolonial theory recognizes its need for a unitary concept of the human is not a moment of failure, it is the moment when postcolonial theory confronts the full consequences of one of its central methodological tenets: to interrogate the idea of the human in the age of global capitalism requires a dialectic of nature and history, not only because these two concepts need to be deconstructed in the face of diversity, but because we need to imagine the totality of human nature and human history in order to speak of diversity.

The experiences surrounding the Truth Commission show that language doesn't fail because it somehow can't get at truth. Language fails because it has access to the historical imagination only via memory – a performance which presents itself as the historical at one remove. The totality of history is accessible only via a specificity which is memory – a personalized narrative that defines speech as an organic experience in the most literal sense, a somatic nagging that reminds the speaker of what language will never be able to say. This somatic force at the core of historical recollection is what marks an individual's position outside history. Discourses are always historically and institutionally determined, and their specificity always threatens to undo the narratives of truth within which they are "commissioned."

Acknowledgments

I wish to thank Jessica Dubow for helping me to engage with a number of the central problems dealt with in this essay. Her careful contributions were invaluable in shaping the direction of this essay. Thanks also to Ulrike Kistner for her acute and erudite comments on myths and monsters.

References

Adorno, Theodor W. (1932). "Die Idee der Naturgeschichte."
——(1966). *Negative Dialektik*. Frankfurt: Suhrkamp.
Althusser, Louis (1965). "Marxism and Humanism." In *For Marx*. London: New Left Books.
Boesak, Alan (1984). *Black and Reformed: Apartheid, Liberation and the Calvinist Tradition*. Braamfontein: Skotaville.
De Landa, Manuel (1991). *War in the Age of Intelligent Machines*. New York: Swerve.
Dirlik, Arif (1994). "The Postcolonial Aura: Third World Criticism in the Age of Global Capitalism." *Critical Inquiry* 20/2: 328–56.
Krog, Antje (1998). *Country of my Skull*. London: Random House.
Mamdani, Mahmood (1996). *Citizen and Subject: Contemporary Africa and the Legacy of Late Colonialism*. Princeton, NJ: Princeton University Press.
Mouffe, Chantal (1994). "For a Politics of Nomadic identity." In *Travellers' Tales: Narratives of Home and Displacement*, ed. George Robertson, Melinda Mash, Lisa Tucker, Jon Bird, Barry Curtis, and Tim Putnam. London: Routledge, pp. 105–13.

Said, Edward (1996). "Secular Interpretation, the Geographical Element, and the Methodology of Imperialism." In *After Colonialism: Imperial Histories and Postcolonial Displacements*, ed. Gyan Prakash. Princeton, NJ: Princeton University Press, pp. 21–39.

Spivak, Gayatri Chakravorty (1993). "Can the Subaltern Speak?" In *Colonial Discourse and Post-Colonial Theory: A Reader*, ed. Patrick Williams and Laura Chrisman. New York: Harvester, pp. 66–101.

Varadharajan, Asha (1995). *Exotic Parodies: Subjectivity in Adorno, Said and Spivak*. Minneapolis: University of Minnesota Press.

Chapter 15

Passing as Korean American

Wendy Ann Lee

Can it be that I cannibalize others' lives, the lives of others' words? Or am I simply going back to where I came from, not too long ago, to excuse whoever took my place when I was gone?

John Ashbery, "The Spacious Firmament"

A few years ago, I was in Los Angeles visiting relatives who, like me, are Korean American. One evening Grace, a friend of my 14-year-old cousin Janice, came over for dinner. She was Korean American and absolutely could not believe that I was too. Throughout the meal Grace sat across from me gawking and disbelieving: I didn't look like I was Korean, I didn't talk like I was Korean, I just did not seem – you know – *Korean*. Finally, I put down my fork and picked up a pair of chopsticks. Grace's eyes widened, her mouth dropped. "You know how to use chopsticks?" "Grace, of course I know how to use chopsticks." "Oh." She watched me for a minute until she was convinced, then she dropped it. *All right then, I guess she's Korean too.*

The anecdote suggests a performative aspect of race, but not in a simple sense of Korean drag. I was not entirely mimicking ethnicity, exposing Korean identity as the assumption of a particular posture. In this situation Korean-ness actually stood for more than "the way you look and the way you act."[1] Propping up my performance was kinship: Janice was Korean, I was Janice's cousin, therefore I was Korean. Not everyone wielding chopsticks would have "passed" in Grace's eyes. But for Grace the facts were more complicated: Korean is something you are, but it must also be corroborated by what you do. Or in performative terms, the "acting out" of cultural practices produces the "truth-effect" of ethnic identity. If you are Korean then obviously you'll act Korean, and if you act Korean then obviously you are Korean. Okay, I thought, I can play this game, too. But wasn't I already Korean? Didn't I identify with Grace, even though she did not identify with me? Before I picked up the chopsticks, where was my Korean-American identity located? In some place called Korean America?

Identity is site-specific. In Los Angeles, largely self-run cultural, commercial, and educational institutions shape a coherent Korean-American population. Teenagers listen to both K-ROC and imported Korean pop music, they eat Taco Bell with kimchi, they sport jackets like black rapsters and haircuts like Korean teen idols, they speak a hybrid language. None of these activities were familiar to me, but then cultural practice in LA differs considerably from that of other Korean-American communities in the country, especially the shipbuilding town in Eastern Virginia where I grew up. At dinner with Grace, I wasn't in fact "Korean too," I did not already identify with her, but I *wanted to.*

Last summer in Flushing, Queens, on a long tract of Main Street where well over 90 percent of the establishments are Korean, I tried shamelessly to pass. In a pink and white bakery a waitress asked me deferentially in Korean what I would like to order. Gleeful and mortified, I tried to deliver a Korean response, pronouncing coffee as "cup-ee" in dulcet tones while lowering my eyes dutifully. Sure enough, an uncontainable gruffness blew my cover and I ended up sputtering – *growling*, it seemed to me – "Uh, yeah, a cup of coffee. Milk no sugar." The waitress's angel-smile tightened into a grim, hard line, and in the most biting English she repeated, "One coffee. No problem," sealing my betrayal. To be embraced and then dismissed, taken unsuspectingly as an insider only to be exposed as an outsider (a traitor!) . . . how could I have let her down? She thought I was Korean. Yes, yes, I am Korean.

Race coordinates itself on the axes of identity and identification. The demographic givens of identity involve the less straightforward work of identification. Where identity might seem to be fixed or concrete, identification primarily expresses uncertainty. Freud writes: "Identification, in fact, is ambivalent from the very first; it can turn into an expression of tenderness as easily as into a wish for someone's removal."[2] At the dinner table in Los Angeles, my gesture towards identification overcame the instinct to recoil. At the Korean bakery, it didn't. If, as Freud describes, identification is an act of devouring the loved one or the loved one's remains, it is to do so for fear of being devoured oneself. Melancholy disguises the ambivalence in identification that betrays a disavowal in the articulation of desire. I want to be Grace (I am not Grace), I want to be Korean (I am not Korean). The wish covers up a lack, and the incorporation of the object carries on the task of impossible preservation. Identification gestures towards recovery as an act of love but also of resentment, worry (over a loss of love). But if loss motivates identification, what "Korea" did I ever lose and when did I "fall out" with Grace, needing then to "make it up to" her?

If identity is arrived at through the work of identification it is also always exceeded by those identifications that protest and spill over what Judith Butler has described as "the subject as a discrete and unitary kind of being."[3] Identity as such cannot properly exist, especially for the diasporic and the hybrid:

of course, I am not "Korean"; neither is Grace. But our shared desire to be so emerges from a specific history of diaspora, immigration, and generational conflict. Korean-American identity and its embedded nostalgia for "Korea" are admittedly borne out of late twentieth-century geopolitics: the Cold War, the enforced cleaving of Korea, US intervention and occupation, immigration and exclusion. I am not equipped to take apart and tackle this history, but I want to allow that the desire at the heart of identification is historical. "Identification names the entry of history and culture into the subject, a subject that must bear the traces of each and every encounter with the external world," writes Diana Fuss. "Identification is, from the beginning, a question of *relation*."[4] In Asian-American writing, the relation to the other that defines the self is articulated fundamentally as the relationship to nation. Book titles alone (*Typical American, China Boy, Accidental Asian, Native Speaker*) raise the issue.[5]

In "Mourning and Melancholia" Freud examines the practices of identification and incorporation that characterize the work of mourning and its pathologized form of melancholia. He writes: "Mourning is regularly the reaction to the loss of a loved person, or to the loss of some abstraction which has taken the place of one, such as one's country, liberty, an ideal, and so on."[6] Some months later into World War I, in a short essay entitled "On Transience," he observes: "We cannot be surprised that our libido, thus bereft of so many of its objects, has clung with all the greater intensity to what is left to us, that our love of our country, our affection for those nearest us and our pride in what is common to us have suddenly grown stronger."[7] Freud addresses the attachment to nation as a locus of loss and desire. His observation on the psychic conditions of war, when we are "bereft of so many of [our] objects," surely resonates with the experiences of political turmoil, separation, and exile woven into the Asian-American narrative or unconscious. The relationship to nation doubles or splits apart, and the phenomenon of assimilation runs counter-currently to the impulse towards an originality that is both phantasmatic and historical: phantasmatic because it represents the ruling fantasy of an absolute and authenticating Place of Birth, historical because it attests to the woes of displacement (an event that may even precede the subject, i.e., after the first generation). History then stages the fantasy, reiterating a psychic configuration of nostalgia and alienation in the secondary identity of Asian American. In this new identity that reaches beyond Korean-, Japanese-, or Chinese American, "the loss of some abstraction which has taken the place [of the loved one]" presents itself as abstraction as an entity which exceeds the reality of nation.[8] "Asia" exists only as what has been lost and loved by the "Asian American."

Grace and I are getting closer. Freud writes of girls who idolize the same celebrity, "Originally rivals, they have succeeded in identifying themselves with one another by means of a similar love for the same object."[9] For Grace and me, the object of our desire is the abstraction that stands in for our Beloved, a Never-Never-Land that recalls Judith Butler's interpretation of melancholy as the acting out of a foreclosure, in her particular critique, on the possibility of same-sex desire. Butler analyses the melancholic subject: "the straight man becomes (mimes, cites, appropriates, assumes the status of) the man he 'never' loved and 'never' grieved; the straight woman *becomes* the woman she 'never' loved and 'never' grieved."[10] Similarly, Asian-American melancholics express their "pervasive disavowal" of loss by becoming the Asian one never was. In becoming Korean Americans, Grace and I disavow the historically determined circumstance that we never knew, never loved, never left, and so never grieved for Korea in the first place. Our melancholic disposition deepens: if "Korean American" alleges the historical foreclosure on the possibility of a relationship to Korea, it also alleges the *racial* foreclosure on the possibility of a relationship to America. Twinkies or bananas that we are (yellow on the outside, white on the inside), we try to prove our true, albeit denied, color. Grace and I "originally rivals, have succeeded in identifying [our]selves with one another." However, the force that compels our rivalry is not Freud's sexual jealousy but racial privilege. Excluded from and greedy for a place in white and even black America, Grace and I inspect, denigrate, compete, identify, and refuse to identify with each other.

I take the license to read memoirs (including my own) alongside fiction in this study because it strikes me that the mode of autobiography is so often taken up and troubled by Asian-American writing. The politics of an Asian-American identity have something to do with autobiographical experience, but in writing, identification occurs as narrative practice in which the principle of identity undoes itself in the unrest of storytelling. The texts under consideration here are all first-person narratives in which the question of the narrator's cultural inheritance is posed by their identification with the dead: a father, mother, and sister, respectively. The psychoanalytic model of melancholy, which links identification to mourning, opens up these narratives dramatically, and its emphasis on failed identification correlates meaningfully with what I want to suggest is an irresolution demanded by the cultural phenomenon of Asian America.

In his recent memoirs, Eric Liu lists "some of the ways you could say [he is] 'white'". He begins, "I have few close friends 'of color'. I married a white woman. . . . I vacation in charming bed-and-breakfasts, I have never once been the victim of blatant discrimination. I am a member of several exclusive institutions. I have been in the inner sanctums of political power. I speak flawless, unaccented English."[11] Lucky Eric. But I'm not sure that I buy his aggressive demonstration of how fluency, access, and even a white wife can be wielded as symbolic capital, like an honorary badge into the country club of the power elite. Upper middle class and Yale educated, Liu exercises class showmanship under the banner of a colorblind meritocracy and represses the issue of Asian-American identity.

What interests me about Liu's book in addition to his persistent disavowal of a minority status, is an aspect of mourning that opens his memoirs by way of a preoccupation with his deceased father. *Accidental Asian* begins with a chapter entitled "Song for My Father," an elegy that memorializes the figure of "Baba" or "Dad." Liu is quick to distinguish Baba from the rank-and-file Chinaman. "Dad" was educated, progressive, an EBM manager. Liu portrays his father as having assimilated in the right ways (social graces, liberal politics, upward mobility), while refusing to assimilate in the wrong ways. For example, Liu takes pride in the fact that "unlike some of his Chinese immigrant peers, my father never took an 'American' first name like Charlie or Chet." The Chineseness of Baba's name, like Lacan's Name-of-the-Father, provides transcultural comfort as the signifier of incorruptible identity. It is the site and stamp of continuity and authenticity. The "selective kind of assimilation" that Liu lays claim to by mythologizing his father creates a personalized ethnicity for Liu, who acknowledges his own difference (from white Americans) by insisting that his difference differs still from other "ABCs," American Born Chinese.

Liu's fetishization of the passer does not altogether suffice for his narrative purposes. He writes partly to console himself for that which a white spouse, perfect English, and political access cannot compensate. His confidence is dispersed with lamentation. The narrator who proudly declares "I have assumed a sense of expectation, of access and *belonging*" (ibid., p. 53) is the same who denigrates, admits,

> so much of my inheritance today seems depthless and desultory. Where my father disdained cheap emotions, I deal in nostalgia and sugary sentimentality. Where my father knew how to salvage dignity from great dreams that had been eaten away, I have mainly a talent for mythmaking. Where my father seemed to have an endless reserve of inner strength and self-knowledge, I have but an echoing well. To fill the hollow, I look sometimes to my Chineseness. (ibid., p. 30)

Mourning precipitates into identity crisis with the figure of Liu's dead father raising the question of his "Chineseness." Liu's elegy bemoans a disinheritance. His self-portrayal as an overachiever deteriorates into an image of fraud and soullessness, recalling Freud's characterization of the melancholic whose pathologized mourning employs the mechanism of identification. Refusing to grieve the loss of a loved one, the melancholic introjects the dead, enacts an identification, and wages war with his own ego. In Liu's elegy we take note of melancholy's primary symptom of self-denigration, of which Freud remarks: "The melancholic displays something else besides which is lacking in mourning – an extraordinary diminution in his self-regard, an impoverishment of his ego on a grand scale."[12] Liu's inability to "salvage" becomes the focal point of his failure and the source of his "depthlessness." The work of preservation, understood as the privileged practice of his father, is feebly inherited as a "talent for mythmaking," an ersatz activity.

Allegories of mourning initiate a discourse on identity; through death we enter history. We keep records in the form of life-stories, writing to account for the dead and their survivors, writing to bear witness. In Asian-American narratives mourning is bound up with cultural identity. Personal implies ancestral death: what remains or else recedes irrevocably. Through death the loved one becomes invested with another kind of alterity that deepens the separation and also demands understanding. The Asian-American subject is thus compelled and doomed to salvage what becomes represented by the loved one, the idea of nation as true home. Liu is not only an "accidental" but also a theoretical Asian, just like every other Asian American.

But the failure to identify and to know does not result in unsuccessful memorialization. Rather, it might testify to a "true" history of the dead, which is in fact one of rupture and separation. Derrida writes in his *Memoires for Paul de Man*:

> What is an impossible mourning? What does it tell us, this impossible mourning, about an essence of memory? And as concerns the other in us, . . . where is the most unjust betrayal? Is the most distressing, or even the most deadly infidelity that of a possible mourning which would interiorize within us the idol, or ideal, of the other who is dead and lives only in us? Or is it that of the impossible mourning, which, leaving the other his alterity, respecting thus his infinite remove, either refuses to take or is incapable of taking the other within oneself, as in the tomb or the vault of some narcissism?[13]

The refusal to take or the incapability of "taking the other within oneself" corresponds to the event of disidentification. Its expression as failed mourning realizes and resists a breach with the other. Liu's realization that he is not his father, that he is not Chinese, is of critical moment. It enacts a lamentation that demands precisely those berated modes of sentimentality, nostalgia, and mythmaking in order to call attention to a rift in personal history that comes itself to constitute a new kind of person. Asian-American melancholy does not simply attest to imperialism but rather narrates the experiences of relocation and assimilation that are perpetually incomplete and fraught with the desire for home, return, pre-history.

Derrida asks, "What does it tell us, this impossible mourning, about an essence of memory?" The Asian American who mourns for a nation never experienced and therefore never lost carries then an impossible memory, a blind spot in individual history that multiplied becomes the basis of a collective identity. Experienced as a memory loss, the absence occasions anxiety and, further, fear in its irremediability: I cannot recover what I don't remember. Panic ushers in obsessive mourning, the devotion to remembrance and elegy, the songs for one's father and songs for one's mother that are the *topoi* of Asian-American literature. (I cannot think of one novel where this is not in some way the case.)[14] The struggle to remember raises further problems of access and intelligibility: I cannot hear the voices of the dead because I do not understand them. I do not speak their language.

Still, the unsuccessful mourner denies those barriers to identification and attempts the suture, wary – even paranoid – that they are lying or "mythmaking" because they do not know and therefore will not be able to recognize or reproduce what it is they want to preserve. This, to the melancholic, constitutes betrayal, yet fidelity resides exactly in this vigilance over the stories of the other, a paranoia that cannot counter but is supremely aware of the

ethics of narration. The Asian American's failed identification and failed narration unknowingly call history into question. The fidelity to a story that
cannot quite be told underlies the inquiry into difference. If Liu *could* be just
like his Dad, what history would have to be erased, kept quiet?

In her study of trauma and narrative, Cathy Caruth describes trauma as
"the enigma of the otherness of a human voice that cries out from a wound,
a voice that witnesses a truth that cannot be fully known."[15] What separates
immigrants from their children are the truths witnessed by one and made inaccessible to the other. Diana Fuss writes: "Trauma is another name for identification, the name we might give to the irrecoverable loss of the sense of
human relatedness."[16] In Asian-American writing the project of recovery and
the desire to make the other speak describe a preoccupation with trauma.
Insofar as mourning is the mechanism of identification, the way we deal with
loss and trauma, collective mourning becomes the mechanism of identity. As
we have learned from survivors of genocide, trauma is not just what happens
to you but what has happened to your loved ones. And because, as Dori Laub
observes, "massive trauma precludes its registration," it is only through narrative that trauma comes to light.[17] The practice of mythmaking that rests so
uneasily in Liu's conscience as a betrayal of the dead comes paradoxically to
constitute the work of true mourning.

Nora Okja Keller's recent novel *Comfort Woman* takes the form of a dialogue
with the dead, in which the survivor grapples with the question of how to
mourn her mother's loss. First-person narratives of mother and daughter,
interspersed as discrete chapters, confront each other with their respective
themes of trauma and mourning. The "comfort woman" names Aikiko, a
former prisoner of Japanese military camps during the occupation of Korea.
Aikiko revisits the scenes of her history: systematic torture and rape by the
Japanese during her internment and its aftershocks of numbed disorientation.
Beccah, her daughter, disrupts Aikiko's narrative with an account of the
present: a record of Aikiko's psychosis and finally of her death. Keller keeps
the narratives separate so that mother and daughter seem to speak to each
other but unknowingly. It is the reader who performs the work of integrating
the two stories, acknowledging the past in the present.

After Akiko's death, Beccah reflects on stories from childhood that her
mother told her. She digresses, "Now I wonder if I had been remembering the
wrong story, if every time my mother said, 'Remember the toad,' she meant,
'Remember the frog.' And I wonder if that changes anything. I find myself
second-guessing my interpretation of her stories, and wonder, now that she is
dead, how I should remember her life."[18] In contrast to Liu's guilty conscience
about mythologizing his father, Keller's narrator poses the problem of remembrance and mourning as an open question. Beccah's ostensible distrust of
memory and narrative ("I find myself second-guessing my interpretation")
explicitly acknowledges the status of remembrance as interpretation. Melancholic anxiety as to whether one is remembering correctly, whether the stories
of the dead can even be recovered, gives way to a meditation on uncertainty

that moves beyond the gestures of self-denigration. Beccah considers for a moment whether the fictions of memory are not only inescapable but also insignificant: "I wonder if that changes anything." Desire supersedes accuracy and precipitates into the recognition that it is precisely what cannot be known, the strangeness of the dead, that insists upon the inquiry into their lives, Beccah's attention to storytelling itself answers the question of how to mourn and how to remember.

In an attempt to resurrect her mother's voice, to listen without speaking, Beccah locates an audio-taped recording once made for her by her mother.

> Wanting to hear her voice once more, I unpacked the "Beccah" tape – my mother's last message, last gift to me . . . I listened, but only when I stopped concentrating did I realize my mother was singing words, calling out names, telling a story. I turned the volume knob on the stereo until my mother's voice shivered up the walls, as if the louder the words, the easier I would be able to understand the story. (ibid, p. 191)

The equation of Aikiko's "last message" with her "last gift' suggests an offering made not to the dead but by the dead. The reversal opens up the storytelling relation in mourning to reflect on the self who survives, a self constituted by the very event of loss. Beccah takes on the gift of her mother's story in a painful ceremony of dictation, blasting the tape on the stereo and writing her mother's words first on paper and then, "need[ing] a bigger canvas," on her bedsheets. Through amanuensis (writ lifesize) one might override interpretation and close the space between speech and writing, event and history, self and other. The facts of Aikiko's past appear to restrict Beccah's license as storyteller; atrocity demands memorials, it denies interpretation.

Keller is considering the problematic nature of traumatic language, how we speak about the unspeakable and who can possibly listen. In her taped narrative, Aikiko addresses Beccah across time, enumerating the names of the comfort women and announcing her own grief. But the injunction to remember the dead and their instant memorialization in the process of recording are tied to language that remains elusive and allegorical, that in a sense refuses representation. Aikiko sings the names of the comfort women: *"Induk. Miyoko. Hanako. Aikiko. Soon Hi. Soon Mi. Soon Ja. Soon Hyo. So many true names unknown, dead in the heart. So many bodies left unprepared, lost in the river"* (ibid, p. 192). Aikiko engages in the instant work of name-calling, of speaking the name that evokes the person. Her roll-call conjures up a line of ghosts, of those who recognize and will answer to their "true names." But the truth of these named selves slides into murkier waters of "names unknown," "bodies . . . lost." The material of memory and memorialization eviscerates in the abyss of human atrocity, in the unspeakable hell of name – and numberless bodies, unknown, unprepared, lost in the river of what cries for remembrance and is refused recognition.

But trauma defined as an experience of narrative, of "listening to another's wound" as Caruth writes, suggests an encounter more mutual and dynamic than the one-sided acknowledgment of another's alterity. Aikiko's account of the comfort women or *Chongshindae* (she speaks it in Korean and never translates) insists on the limits of Beccah's comprehension, but her message to Beccah disavows separation: "I have tried to release you, but in the end I cannot do it and tie you to me" (ibid, p. 197). In the final scene, Beccah sprinkles her mother's ashes into the river and prays, "Omoni, please drink. Share this meal with me, a sip to know how much I love you. . . . Your body in mine . . . so you will always be with me, even when your spirit finds its way home. To Korea" (ibid, p. 212). Incorporation is fantasized as a kind of eucharist in which the remains of the loved one are transubstantiated into food and drink that bind the dead to and inside of the living: "Your body in mine." Beccah brings the water mixed with her mother's ashes to her own lips and then bids Aikiko to partake of the meal, the ingestion of which will confer knowledge of an indissoluble love, "a sip to know how much I love you." The gesture of melancholic identification, in which the mourning subject incorporates the lost being, repudiates separation by overcoming it, overwhelming it with affection.

Beccah articulates melancholy on a register of national and cultural disidentification. Her rite of incorporation overcomes death and nation: "you will always be with me, even when your spirit finds its way home. To Korea." Beccah pronounces and overrides an essential difference about Aikiko's origin: "even when" you are there, you are still here "with me," on the inside, "your body in mine." The act of incorporation acknowledges, prevails upon, but also preserves difference by keeping it intact on the inside. Melancholics swallow their loved ones, but they swallow them whole. In this case, the place or space of Korea is taken in as a meaningfully empty sign, what is not my home but was my mother's. "Korea" functions similarly to Freud's uncanny or *Unheimlich* ("unhomelike"), with its contradictory force of denying recognition while demanding remembrance. Beccah's "Korea" does not depict the psychologically repressed and revisited uncanny object, but the historically repressed and removed home. Insofar as Aikiko embodies Korea, Beccah's incorporation brings both entities or identities inside.

In her latest novel, *The Hundred Secret Senses,* Amy Tan tells the story of half-Chinese, half-Caucasian Olivia and her troubled but primary relationship to her full-Chinese, half-sister Kwan. Like *Comfort Woman, The Hundred Secret Senses* unfolds in alternating narratives by the two women. Kwan resembles Aikiko in her foreignness. She invokes a history that claims but remains inscrutable to her American loved one. The novel unifies the two narratives after Kwan's death when Olivia can tell Kwan's story within her own narrative, having realized that Kwan's protracted, elliptical tale was always the story of her own (past) life. As with Beccah in Keller's novel, Olivia makes the identification through narrative, by fitting the other's stories into her own mouth.

Tan accounts for loss and preservation in the particular terms of cultural identity or "Chineseness." In a familiar gesture, Tan plays with the question of Olivia's identity in the trajectory of her name. Olivia considers:

> As I think more about my name, I realize I've never had any sort of identity that
> suited me, not since I was five at least, when my mother changed our last name
> to Laguni. . . . Olivia Yee. I say the name aloud several times. It sounds alien, as
> though I'd become totally Chinese, just like Kwan. That bothers me a little. Being
> forced to grow up with Kwan was probably one of the reasons I never knew who
> I was or wanted to become. She was a role model for multiple personalities. (ibid)

"Yee," the Chinese name of her Chinese father, would seem to confer cultural
continuity, signifying some un-American, non-homogenized remnant of identity. Tan, however, sharply undercuts this fantasy of a return to ethnic integrity
by delegitimizing the name of the father. Kwan debunks Olivia's myth of their
father by revealing his "true identity" as an imposter, a petty thief of someone
else's immigration papers and passport that happened to bear the name "Yee."
Olivia's qualms about turning "totally Chinese, just like Kwan" if she reverts
to a Chinese surname are later overturned by whole-hearted identification.
After Kwan's disappearance, Olivia appropriates Kwan's surname Li and passes
it on to her new child, whom she understands to be "a gift from Kwan, a baby
girl with dimples in her fat cheeks" (ibid, p. 320). The gesture affirms matri-
linearity with its new line of female descendants and the debunking of "Yee"
and "Bishop" (her husband's name) in favor of "Li" (Olivia had earlier observed
of Kwan's surname, "it was a Chinese tradition for girls to keep their mother's
last name"). During her name change, Olivia argues, "Why not? What's a
family name if not a claim to being connected in the future to someone from
the past?" (ibid, p. 320) The act of naming establishes lineage and generates a
family of one's own choosing. Olivia's license to perform this trick less undermines the notion of a fixed identity than endorses the liberty to choose which
one you're going to live with, or as. Matrilineal appropriation ousts patriarchal inheritance by offering a more meaningful and responsible relation to
the past.

My problem with Tan's novel lies in her representation of Kwan as an easy-
to-swallow other in the devouring scope of Olivia's search for a suitable identity. Kwan is quirky, benign, and selfless. Olivia is normal, neurotic, and greedy,
The framed story of their past lives as Ms Banner, a white missionary, and
Nunumu, her trusty Chinese servant and savior, gives way the lie in their relationship. The postcolonial characters, Olivia and Kwan, actually replay their
old colonial egos, Ms Banner and Nunumu. Kwan again plays the freak ethnic
other who sets in play the subject's drama of identification. Kwan, the bizarre
stranger who initiates Olivia's identity crisis, assumes a formal role in a plot
driving (hard) towards resolution. Even the history doled out to Kwan, her
upbringing in the village of Changmian, is usurped by Olivia, whose identity
quest takes her there on a life-changing journey.

In contrast, *Comfort Woman* unravels a relationship that is fraught with
impossible sympathies and identifications. Where Kwan is benign and accom-
modating, Aikiko is terrifying and inscrutable. Moreover, Aikiko's history
stands mournfully apart from Beccah's, outside the possibilities of her experience. Aikiko cannot be easily consumed, only painfully reconstructed, whereas

Kwan is ingested like candy or medicine. Tan's conclusion that love is all sounds hollow against Keller's insistence that love, wretchedly and imprecisely, answers the call of the dead. Keller's concern with the alterity of the other, expressed through the portrayal of trauma, successfully avoids a narcissistic economy of desires that always loop back into a discrete sense of self. Whereas by any other name, Amy Tan's Olivia is still just the same.

Even Eric Liu, who disowns Asian-American identity without scrutinizing his own white boy alter-ego, sensitively discusses his father's indecipherability as a Chinese man. Liu's acknowledgment of a certain disinheritance reinforced by assimilation and social mobility offers a more cogent vision of Chinese-American melancholy than Tan's patchwork of friendly ghosts. Liu actually reproaches Tan for her narrative shtick of sending the protagonist on a life-changing trip to the motherland (a plot that made its first appearance in her immensely successful *Joy Luck Club*). He writes, "In America, where people are always seeking mystical bonds to an imagined past, returning to the land of one's ancestors is usually a more syrupy affair. . . . Certain novelists have made it a stock device to send the assimilated second-generation protagonist to China on a melodramatic search for her soul."[19] In Liu's more compelling view of assimilation as a historical process that radically changes identity and the possibilities for identification, a simple change of name or a journey "back" to China achieves more wish-fulfillment than identification. Acculturation is neither reversible nor harmless.

Perhaps this bad news accounts for a popular disposition towards easily digestible tales of ethnicity. For example, Chang Rae Lee's *Native Speaker*, a novel that emphasizes the complexity and plurality of Korean-American experiences, gets hailed for its representation of *"the* immigrant experience" *(Vanity Fair)* or *"the* Asian immigrant in America" *(Vogue)* (my italics). Even Henry Louis Gates, Jr. makes the same reduction in praise of Eric Liu's *Accidental Asian*. Liu "renders the Asian American experience with a depth and a passion . . ." Gates's comment and the publisher's decision to print it on the inside of the book jacket strike me as particularly misinformed, since Liu's self-portrait is precisely that of the *Accidental* Asian, the Asian unlike most other Asians. (Does he not list the reasons why we could say he is white?)

But the misguided notion of a single monolithic Asian-American experience, which retroacts an original and authenticating "Asia," cannot be attributed solely to inept book reviewers or Henry Louis Gates, Jr. Didn't I buy into it myself? Why else would I have wanted so much to identify with Grace, the girl at my cousin's dinner table, and show her that I was Korean too, Korean just like her? Wasn't it already my belief and desire for "A Real Thing" that later convinced me of my own inauthenticity? The model of melancholia tells us that loss fuels desire and desire provokes identification. The allegory of the Asian American transposes the loss of the loved one into the loss of "Asia." To recover that place of integrity, which neither I nor anyone else has ever actually experienced, I am compelled to mime the appropriate gestures, to wield my chopsticks just like Grace, whom I have imagined as somehow closer to

"Korea" than I am. This is not to deny that some real experience of a real country and culture has been lost to me. The histories of my parents, which can only ever come to me as stories translated, are a constant reminder of disconnection. Origins will always exert themselves as lost loves, not as North Korea or the Republic of South Korea (nostalgia written into this divide), but as a home that was and yet was never my own. The myth of the Asian-American lies not in these particular and historical traumas, but in the marshaling of so many distinctive experiences and complex identifications into one totalizing and transhistorical group identity. A plurality of citizens, along with their unique problems and demands, are consolidated, but not in the form or sense of a coalition. In one fell swoop, even the melancholic gets consumed.

Notes

1 Walter Bem Nechaels, "The No Drop Rule," in *Identities*, ed. Kwame Anthony Appiah and Henry Louis Gates, Jr. (Chicago: University of Chicago Press, 1995), p. 411.

2 Sigmund Freud, *Group Psychology and the Analysis of the Ego*, in *The Standard Edition of the Complete Psychological Works of Sigmund Freud*, trans. and ed. James Strachey, 24 vols. (London: Hogarth Press, 1953–74), vol. 18, p. 105.

3 Judith Butler, "Collected and Fractured," in *Identities*, p. 446.

4 Diana Fuss, *Identification Papers* (New York: Routledge, 1995), p. 3.

5 By Gish, Jen, Gus Lee, Eric Liu, and Chang-Rae Lee, respectively.

6 Freud, "Mourning and Melancholia," *Standard Edition*, vol. 14, p. 243.

7 'Freud, "On Transience," *Standard Edition*, vol. 14, p. 305.

8 For the purposes of this essay, I refer only to East Asian countries, though certainly "Asian American" can denote a much wider ethnic constituency.

9 Freud, "Group Psychology and the Analysis of the Ego," *Standard Edition*, vol. 18, p. 120.

10 Judith Butler, *The Psychic Life of Power: Theories in Subjection* (Stanford, CA: Stanford University Press, 1997), p. 147.

11 Eric Liu, *The Accidental Asian: Notes of a Native Speaker* (New York: Random House, 1998), pp. 33–4.

12 "Mourning and Melancholia," p. 246.

13 Jacques Derrida, *Memoires for Paul de Man* (New York: Columbia University Press, 1986), p. 6.

14 Consider a few examples as heterogeneous as Lan Cao's *Monkey Bridge*, Gus Lee's *China Boy*, and Gish Jen's *Mona in the Promised Land*.

15 Cathy Caruth, *Unclaimed Experience: Trauma, Narrative, and History* (Baltimore, MD: John Hopkins University Press, 1996), p. 3.

16 Fuss, *Identification Papers*, p. 40.

17 Shoshana Felxnan and Dori Laub, MD, *Testimony: Crises of Witnessing in Literature, Psychoanalysis, and History* (New York: Routledge, 1992), pp. 57, 12.

18 Nora Okja Keller, *Comfort Woman* (New York: Penguin Books, 1997), p. 171.

19 Liu, *Accidental Asian*, p. 131.

Chapter 16

Myths of East and West: Intellectual Property Law in Postcolonial Hong Kong

Eve Darian-Smith

The identity of Europe was constructed out of a sense of spiritual superiority in the disavowal of its very own origin in the Orient.

Delanty 1995, pp. 26–7

Introduction

This essay is concerned with the endurance of myths of "East" and "West" and the role national and international law plays in affirming and legitimizing these myths.[1] Despite the current rhetoric of legal and cultural globalization used by many politicians, economists, and academics that promotes a sense of harmony, homogeneity, open communication, and equal power relations between people and places, I suggest that much of the rhetoric of globalization is still based on stereotypical images of East and West that perpetuate colonial hierarchies and asymmetric power relations. My argument is that at stake in this enduring mythology is the emergence of new forms of imperialism and new forms of colonialization as transnational corporations – legitimized and endorsed through so-called global legal practices – seek cheap labor pools, technological resources, and new commercial markets in a global political economy.

The rule of law plays a central role in perpetuating and endorsing myths of East and West. I suggest that by recovering the historical, political, and economic dimensions of law itself we can begin to understand the ways in which polarized images of East and West continue to distort and limit our understanding of legal globalization in postcolonial contexts (see Darian-Smith and

Fitzpatrick 1999). I use the case of intellectual property law in Hong Kong to show how literature on legal globalization persists in oversimplifying what law is, how it operates, and the degree to which different cultures understand the concept in the same way. My underlying concern is that when we as scholars idealize processes of legal globalization we depoliticize sociolegal practices in a late-capitalist world. By discussing legal globalization as a process separate from neocolonialism, for example when we speak triumphantly of the spread of the Western concept of "civilized" human rights, we perpetuate a dichotomy that implies oriental legal barbarism and authoritarianism on the one hand, and occidental progress and democracy on the other (see Mahmud 1999). While there never have been clearly defined borders containing East or West legal categories, ideologies, and philosophies, nonetheless the power of believing in the moral superiority of one perspective over the other essentializes legal understandings and makes it impossible to envision and analyze counter-hegemonic legal impulses issuing from the rearticulation of legal systems across international and transnational terrains.

My point of departure is an emerging body of literature analyzing the phenomena of global legal processes, or what is more commonly called the "globalization of law." What is exciting about the best of this sociolegal scholarship in disciplines such as sociology, anthropology, and political science is its attempt to examine the intersections between law, economics, and new forms of localized cultural politics in conjunction with heightened global interdependence (see Maurer 1997; Buchanan 1995; Merry 1992; Bosniak 1996; Coombe 1998; Nader 1999). That being said, what I find limiting about this genre of intellectual endeavor is a general inability among many of its theorists to move beyond Western legal concepts and categories that prevent its authors from fully analyzing the very processes of legal globalization, and their implications of power, that are the subject of their investigation (see Gessner 1995; Garth and Dezalay 1996; Santos 1995 and Darian-Smith 1998a). Moreover, many scholars examining this elitist, top-down perspective too readily privilege the relationship between law and economics as the only form of legal interaction that really matters between so-called "legal cultures."[2]

With this economic focus at the forefront, it is not surprising that much of the literature on the globalization of law assumes as given a neoliberal concept of "personhood" that operates – across a myriad of different jurisdictions, legal systems, cultures, and nations – as an independent and sovereign unit in the same way as an individual citizen supposedly does in Western liberal democracies (see Collier, Maurer, and Suarez Navaz 1995). One result is that this universalizing tendency continues to perpetuate – as it did in nineteenth-century modes of national imperialism – myths of East and West legal systems as being either "barbaric" or "civilized" based on respective legal constructions of the individual self. And the political and legal language of intellectual property law, which as discussed below relies upon the idea of an autonomous individual with rights to personal as well as real property, epitomizes this neoliberal assumption of a particular form of legal subjectivity.

By analyzing the historical contexts of the eighteenth and nineteenth centuries in which the myths of modern Western law developed against an exoticized and objectified East, fascinating parallels emerge between this earlier historical period, with its rise of modern nation-states, and today, with the much discussed dismantling of state authority (see Hannerz 1996, pp. 81–90). Western imaginings of the East, historically oscillating between admiration and repulsion, continue to play out in current academic, political, and popular characterizations of Asia. And I would argue that these contradictions and tensions are indicative of our own insecurities about the enduring stability of the rule of law and the integrity of modern state centers and national boundaries. So similar to the turbulent period corresponding to the rise of the modern nation-state in the eighteenth century, today's processes of globalization and a decentering of the nation-state causes Western scholars once again to project onto an "East" alternating positive and negative images that in different ways serve to bolster our own increasingly vulnerable image of a distinct and discrete West.

Historical Continuities

The idea of China, and more generally Asia, as symbol of the East has always evoked strong emotions of either fascination or repulsion amongst Europeans. In the late seventeenth and eighteenth centuries European political and social upheaval fostered a climate of intellectual curiosity and led philosophers such as Hobbes, Locke, Leibniz, and Voltaire to explore and consult non-Western legal models in the process of codifying the law of their own respective nation-states and empires (Locke 1988; Leibniz 1994). This intellectual curiosity about non-Western peoples paralleled the serious yet superficial self-analysis emerging amongst educated Europeans reflecting upon their own distinct cultural differences, physical traits, tastes, and loyalties (Baudet 1965, p. 55; Lach 1965; Lach and Foss 1990; Mannsaker 1990). In particular, Europeans were preoccupied with the Chinese system of law as a marker of China's most "civilized" government. It was widely recognized that China possessed, "even earlier in its history than in the case of the West, many of the characteristics of a state: a centralized professional army, a trained bureaucracy charged with administrating the state and collecting taxes, and a body of political theory justifying the centralized authority of its governing institutions" (Wood 1995, p. 134). However, throughout the eighteenth century there was a gradual reversal of this positive image of the East. By the height of English industrialization in the nineteenth century, the East had come to represent the ills of premodernity including indolence, barbarism, stagnation, and tyranny.

In China's fall from grace in the eyes of the West, the idea of Europe and its imperial nation-states gained strength and solidity, as did the ideals of objective science, autonomous personhood, and a national citizenry. The notion of progress was key to the consolidation of Europe and a Western identity *vis-à-vis* the East. Industrialization, capitalism, modernization, rationalism – these were terms that were seen to have limited application in European discussions of China. By the early 1800s sincere intellectual curiosity in China among Western philosophers had virtually disappeared. Philosophers were now more interested in differentiating between the new nationalist states of Europe than searching for what the Orient could possibly offer other than an exotic and erotic orientalism (Schwab 1984; Said 1978; Goody 1996).[3] Significantly, this largely derogatory recreation of the Orient occurred at precisely the same historical moment that Europeans were consolidating themselves politically, culturally, and institutionally, as legally defined citizens of modern nation-states. In this historical moment, law, at least the symbolic value of a rationalized law, became a marker and pivot on which cultural difference was then ranked.

Today, China is again a subject of fascination for Western scholars, economists, and politicians. Over the past two decades, first Japan and now China have emerged as the big world players contesting the economic superiority of the United States and Western Europe. Despite faltering stock markets throughout 1997–8, there remains general fascination in the extraordinary financial successes of the "Asian tiger" economies of Taiwan, Korea, and Singapore and the achievements of so-called Chinese capitalism and alternative paradigms of modernity (Redding 1990; Tricker 1990).

The current allure that China holds in the West highlights a curious historical parallel. In the seventeenth century, when China first caught the widespread attention of Europeans, it was a time of intense anxiety and bloodshed in Europe with the overthrowing of the Catholic church and the struggles to establish stable legal and political institutions and overseas empires (Delanty 1995). Today, with new legal, political, and economic forces destabilizing the West as the "natural" center of the world, China has resurfaced as a space on which to map our anxieties and fears. China is represented as an economic model and opportunity by economists keen to emulate what has been identified as "Chinese capitalism," as well as a scapegoat for the shortcomings of rampant Western consumption. Today, as was the case in the seventeenth and eighteenth centuries, positive and negative images of China are prominent in our imaginings of the East (see Greenhalgh 1994). So while we are keen to represent China as somehow static, lost in an ancient world of custom and spirituality and exotic habits and so "naturally" inferior, at the same time, the current rhetoric of globalization and the successes of Pacific Asia sustain our desire to see "them" as modern as "us."

Of course neither these positive nor negative images accurately reflect what is happening in Hong Kong and China today (Abbas 1997, pp. 6–8; Kang 1999). That being said, an East/West binary representing an offensive structural division remnant of nineteenth-century imperialism should not be ignored (see Kang 1999, n. 1). Despite the ending of the Cold War and the increasing prevalence of North/South imagery, an East and West dichotomy remains politically, economically, socially, and legally important as a term of reference in the unfolding of international and transnational relations. Not only are East and West still widely used as a form of global spatial referencing, but also, I suggest, an image of East – whatever it may be – continues to be a necessary element in the defining of what constitutes the West and contemporary European and North American cultures. This new form of occidentalism raises a critical and very uncomfortable question: How are sociolegal scholars using images of Asian law that naturalize Western legal superiority and thereby perpetuate forms of neocolonialism? Or, to ask the question in a different way: To what extent is China challenging the hegemony of global capitalism and providing alternatives to both an understanding of globalization itself, and an understanding of Western law by which capitalist globalization is legitimized and promulgated?

Intellectual Property Rights and the Legal Subject

The Western legal concept of intellectual property embodies the liberal conceptions of legal personhood, authorship, and private property. These liberal concepts, and their accompanying ideology of "possessive individualism," explicitly conflict with a competing Chinese legal culture and its alternative views of collective property rights and the relationship of the individual to society. This conflict highlights the extent to which today's rhetoric of the globalization of legal processes both actively ignores the significance of local/regional cultural practices that give meaning to abstract legal concepts, and downplays the struggles for economic and cultural power that underlie a capitalist ideology of globalization. In particular, international struggles over intellectual property rights highlight the need by Europeans and Americans to perpetuate their own myths of an "inferior" Eastern law versus a "superior" Western law, and by implication a less evolved concept of self in Asian countries.

Stated very briefly, European-based intellectual property law refers to the laws governing patents, trademarks, and copyright. In all three areas the basic goal is to provide legal protection against the illegal reproduction of a work treated as belonging exclusively to a creator for a specific number of years. Creators are deemed to have a monopoly in the use of their work and so have power to authorize access, reproduction, and dissemination rights. Intellectual property rights and the creation of the "author" is a distinctly modern legal feature that developed in conjunction with capitalism's consolidation of the idea of ownership in real property and in the person (Foucault 1984; Coombe 1991; Bettig 1996). C. B. Macpherson, in his discussion of the writings of John Locke, highlighted this proprietary quality and called it "possessive individualism," which refers to the capacity to own "property in the person" as well as real property. This meant that individuals could own their own capacities and skills and so hire their "labor power" on the market, alongside their rights of ownership in land. According to Macpherson:

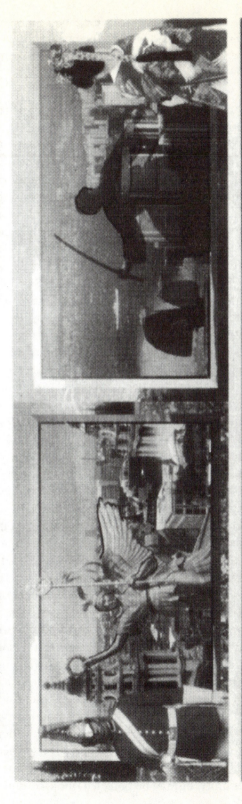

Figure 16.1 This advertisement for a capital investment fund plays on stereotypes of Western and Eastern culture: the front-facing, militaristic, male, and Christian world of Britain is contrasted with the backward-facing, shadowy, feminized, exotic, and traditional world of a rather threatening Orient. Note that images from Japan, China, and Hong Kong are conflated into one essentialized concept of the "Far East."

> Political society is a human contrivance for the protection of an individual's prop-
> erty in his person and goods, and (therefore) for the maintenance of orderly rela-
> tions of exchange between individuals regarded as proprietors of themselves.
> (Macpherson 1988, p. 264).

"Personality," "originality," and "genius" were translated into an individual author's capacity to hold legal rights protecting his/her creative works against illegal copying (see Woodmansee 1984; Boyle 1996; Sherman 1997).

Since the reproduction of texts did not have any significant economic impact until the invention of the printing press, the history of intellectual property law is bound up with the rise of print capitalism and the commodification of literature in the seventeenth and eighteenth centuries. England was the most technologically advanced in this area, and its burgeoning print capitalism prompted the first copyright statute to be enacted in 1710. As Mark Rose notes, at this time the "question of literary property" was essentially a commercial struggle between booksellers (Rose 1993, pp. 1–8).

Intellectual property law blossomed very quickly in the nineteenth century, dovetailing with the increasing attention given to the general rights of legal subjects as citizens of Europe's sovereign nation-states (see Aoki 1996). While rights were held by individuals, state governments were keen to protect intellectual property, which in a sense formed the resources and technological advantages of the nation. The desire to guard monopolies over industrial and scientific discoveries fueled the need for the international treaties such as the 1883 Paris Convention for the Protection of Industrial Property and the 1886 Berne Convention for the Protection of Literary and Artistic Works. While these conventions did not create a tightly integrated system of legal conformity (Endeshaw 1996a, p. 2; 1996b), they nonetheless promoted intellectual property law as a marker of Western modernity and as a symbol of its ideals of civilization, nationalism, equity, and justice.

Sociolegal scholars should be aware that this proprietary concept of self, and all of the corollary legal categories dependent on the concept of a sovereign individual, necessarily embody Western cultural ideals that are not harmlessly exported or imposed (see Coombe 1998, pp. 208–47). The Western conception of the self as property is a historically particular legal construction that developed with the rise of the modern nation-state in Western Europe. It upholds the protection of one's land, and by extension the reproduction of one's own original idea as a natural right existing prior to the social order.[4] Property is conceptualized as an object, or a relationship between people and objects, thus presupposing that it exists in some way as external to the individual. Yet anthropological literature on property suggests that not all societies make this distinction, and that sometimes objects constitute an extension of a person or equate with a person (Carrithers et al. 1985; Strathern 1988; Harris 1989; Appadurai 1986). In a similar vein, property is not necessarily considered the exclusive possession of one individual but, rather, may belong to the wider collective community, or may be parceled out according to use at certain times or under specific conditions (Malinowski 1985; Gluckman 1943; Hann 1993; Cronon 1983; Coombe 1998).

In contrast to the nineteenth-century growth of intellectual property law in European and American contexts, China did not have an equivalent legal code of civil protection. This does not mean that the Chinese government was indifferent to unauthorized reproduction of texts and scriptures (Alford 1995, pp. 12–29; Carter 1996). However, in reviewing prepublication materials, the state was primarily concerned with protecting imperial power and state stability through the control of publicly circulating ideas, and not with individuals maintaining their private property interests. Thus the horizon of copyright and trademark protection extended to materials deemed to be solely administered and controlled by the emperor as the representative of the state. Since particular printers were entrusted with the reproduction of these materials, the state at times would intervene on their behalf and protect the integrity of their trade names and chop marks (block signatures).

One result of these different cultural and legal understandings of ownership over creative ideas was, as discussed above, a shift in European attitudes to Chinese law from one of fascination and admiration to that of open disgust and blatant racism. By the height of the industrial revolution in the nineteenth century, China was depicted as a vast land of political backwardness and economic stagnation, filled with "swarming hordes" of poor pathetic people suppressed by an authoritarian and despotic emperor. Karl Marx was convinced China's isolation made it like "a mummy carefully preserved in a hermetically sealed coffin" (Marx cited in Mackerras 1989, p. 113). Writing to Engels in 1853, Marx stressed that what stamped the Asiatic mode of production and the East in general was "the absence of private property in land." Propertyless and so classless, "oriental despotism restrained the human mind within the smallest possible compass, making it the unresisting tool of superstition, enslaving it beneath traditional rules, depriving it of all grandeur and historical energies" (Marx cited in Mackerras 1989, p. 112). In short, it was (and in many cases still is) firmly believed by many Western scholars that the Chinese system of governance made no allowance for even the potentiality of individual choice, agency, and freedom.

However, William Alford, a well-known Chinese legal historian, argues that the view held by many Western scholars that individualism does not exist in China is misleading and false (Alford 1995). There is a distinct construction of the individual, but it is based on different criteria and values than those which inform the concept in a liberal legal regime. Historically, in Chinese society there was no such thing as a social contract existing between people and the state as there was in Judeo-Christian legal systems. In contrast to liberal ideologies, the state was not seen as the guarantor of people's inalienable rights, nor as an overriding power that could randomly encroach upon a person's privacy necessitating an intermediary bureaucracy. Rather, according to the rhetoric of those in power in China, the state was viewed as the patriarchal "father" of the land and so owed a fiduciary duty to those over whom it exercised power.

Chinese government officials were able to maintain tight control because, Alford points out, the failure of the state to carry out its fatherly obligation "represented a moral deficiency of the first order that might well lead those in power to lose their elevated position" (Alford 1986, p. 951). Confucian classics provided the moral justification or source for legal and governmental procedures that were deeply entrenched in family and economic matters (Alford 1995, p. 11). The classic literature granted the magistrate extensive powers in the administration of justice, and in turn expected him to act with impartiality, dignity, and honor as a trustee of the community's ethics. Chinese people were also expected to exercise their civic rights and duties to the wider community, as well as their immediate family (Yu-wei 1968, pp. 274–7). So while the idea of personhood exists within law derived from Confucian ethics, it centers upon an individual's duties subsisting within the notion of property in terms of its community and symbolic values. In this way, official law was used to buttress a particular social code promulgated through an individual's relationship to society, and as a result, the idea of personhood carried a very different legal status in China than it did in Western countries (Vandermeersch 1985, p. 3; Bodde and Morris 1967; Lau and Kuan 1988, pp. 131–5; Alford 1995, pp. 9–29; Butterton 1996).

Today, people's relationship to official law in China still highlights the greater emphasis placed upon family, patronage, and regional connections (*quanxi* relations), and a lesser significance in "possessive individualism" central to the concept of rights in private property (Kipnis 1997; Yang 1994; Jones 1994; Chen 1999, pp. 105–7; Appelbaum 1998).[5] Anthropologist Mayfair Yang, who has written extensively on *quanxi*, notes that this form of relationship between people is based implicitly on "mutual interest and benefit." The creation of *quanxi* establishes an expectation of reciprocity and the "expectation that the debt incurred will be repaid" (Yang 1994, p. 1). According to Yang:

> What has emerged is a dense structure of individual connectedness as opposed to atomism, in which reciprocity is a form of social solidarity and social investment. . . . This endless series of dyadic contracts as a mode of exchange is very different from market-dominated Western societies in which people are created as independent agents with formally equal access to goods and services, checked only by the size of their individual monetary incomes. . . . Therefore we can speculate that the postsocialist forms of capitalism developing in China today will assume a different form from the individual-based capitalism of the West. (Ibid, p. 172)

This brief discussion of different cultural conceptualizations of legal subjectivity and legal standing emphasizes that scholars of the globalization of law need to be sensitive to historically informed and culturally specific meanings embodied in different legal systems, particularly as they relate to the legal idea of personhood. Moreover, scholars should keep in mind that modern Western law developed within a system of colonial expansion, and was expressly used as a technology of power to mark off Europeans as "progressive," "civilized," and "rational" (Cohn and Dirks 1988; Fitzpatrick 1992). The qualities embodied in bourgeois law were used to justify domination and exploitation, especially when contrasted with so-called customary, irrational, and barbaric rituals of the "savage," the "negro," or "chinaman."

Legal mythologies of European superiority were endorsed by the great social theorists of the nineteenth century. To varying degrees, Marx, Durkheim, and Maine presented an historical and evolutionary continuum whereby mankind would emerge out of the constraining, "mechanical" kinship relations of small-scale societies to adopt the rational and orderly social relations promulgated through a predictive legal code (Kelly 1990, pp. 252–75; Unger 1976; Alford 1986; Mackerras 1989, pp. 110–25). The significance of this narrative of Western progress, what John Strawson calls "legal orientalism," should not be underplayed (Strawson 1995; cf. Springbord 1992). In tandem with the rise of science in the nineteenth century, legal knowledge provided a regulatory frame through which the nation-state and its citizens, as well as the peripheral colonial world, could be universalized, categorized, classified, systematized, and ultimately managed (Santos 1995, p. 56; Serres and Latour 1995, pp. 56, 62). The concept of the legal subject was naturalized as part of modernity's overriding common sense and a justification for colonialism.[6] Unfortunately, and this is my central point, among both academics and a wider population, the tendency to portray Western legal systems as evolutionarily more advanced than Eastern–primitive systems is not limited to an historical past and continues to play out in today's legal understandings and practices (Unger 1976; see critique by Alford 1986).

The Case of Intellectual Property Law in Hong Kong

Since the colony of Hong Kong was founded on a desolate island in 1841 it has performed the strategic function of articulating Asian and European business, legal, and military interests. As such, Hong Kong has been the quintessential historical and symbolic site through which competing "East" and "West" legal concepts and legal cultures were mediated. Of course, despite Europeans anxious to see Hong Kong as an enclave of Western law in China, there are no, and never have been, clearly defined borders containing East or West legal categories, ideologies, and philosophies (see Ruskola 2000, citing Berman). Hong Kong has never functioned as an isolated Western outpost of the British empire unaffected by locally imported Chinese values.[7]

With the resumption of control over Hong Kong by the People's Republic of China (PRC) on June 30, 1997, Hong Kong now more than ever represents the overlapping and merging of two different legal cultures. As noted by Vittorio Olgiati:

> The fact is that Hong Kong's reunification to mainland China cannot be compared to any other historical postcolonial experience. The decolonization policy

that took place during the 1960s in Asia and Africa concerned countries that were actually economically and technologically "underprivileged" as compared to Western countries. Hence the same policy did not challenge radically the hegemonic international role of Western-styled institutional arrangements, the technological–scientific supremacy of Western culture and the self-referential power-of-command of Western economy. . . . By contrast, Hong Kong's decolonization makes clear that a radical, symbolic and structural turn occurred for both East and West. (Olgiati 1999, p. 586)

Highlighting the overlapping and merging of two different legal cultures, Hong Kong now has its own Basic Law which is a legal system that seeks to maintain the "laws previously in force in Hong Kong," including the British common law, while at the same time functioning under the overall authority of the PRC. Under Article 8 of the New Basic Law, China has agreed to designate Hong Kong a Special Administrative Region and honor its British common law principles for the next 50 years. This pledge includes preserving Hong Kong's pre-1997 intellectual property regime whose common law principles ostensibly adhere to international organizations and trade agreements governed through the World Intellectual Property Committee. In acknowledging the endurance of Western legal ideologies in Hong Kong, China's "one country, two systems" policy supposedly guarantees the capitalist enclave a degree of future autonomy (see note 9).

Historically, Hong Kong's common law intellectual property system contrasts dramatically with intellectual property rights on the Chinese mainland, reflecting their different legal institutions, values, and cultures (see Brahm 1988). Before 1991 China maintained its own official legal culture by resisting international pressure to standardize its intellectual property practices. However, with increasing demands by the United States and the European Union, in 1992 the PRC signed the Memorandum of Understanding on Intellectual Property and in 1995 the Agreement on Chinese Enforcement of intellectual property rights. While violation of property rights continues to be a major problem, nonetheless there now exists in China an intellectual property regime that is recognizable as a "Western-style Rule of Law" (see Butterton 1996, p. 1083). No wonder that today many Anglo/European legal scholars and practitioners are welcoming the apparent legal "progress" in China.[8] This stance endorses a disquieting social evolutionary model, or at the least a Eurocentric diffusionist model, that suggests that Chinese progress has only started up again with Europeans bringing in new ideas (Blaut 1993, p. 115). For instance, the back cover of a recent book entitled *China's Legal Reforms* reads, "since the early 1980s the PRC has been building legal institutions where no meaningful ones had existed before" (Lubman 1996).

Many Europeans and North Americans are reassured by the presence of more lawyers and more legislation in China, which suggests a greater understanding of the centrality of law in governing modern social institutions and international legal arrangements. But as Brahm and Alford both caution, this does not necessarily mean that the Chinese are now endorsing the liberal legal ideologies embedded within a Western legal regime. According to Bhahm, "the right to monopolize an idea . . . an invention, or a form of artistic expression – of all which, in theory, should benefit and belong to the society as a whole – is not easily rationalized in China" (Brahm 1988, p. vii). Alford goes on:

> Because contemporary Chinese legal developments may seem less exotic and distant to us than those aspects of imperial Chinese law . . . by reason of the language within which the new developments are cast, the modern setting within which they occur, and our growing personal interaction with Chinese colleagues – we must be doubly vigilant in examining these developments. We must guard against the tendency, that even the most cautious among us may share, to see the Chinese as now finally realizing – or at least saying they realize – the need to organize their legal and economic life the way we believe that we have chosen to do, and so validating the grand theories and other constructs through which we in the West seek to order our existence. . . . We must take seriously both this unfamiliar language and the historical and contemporary cultural, political, and economic settings from which these legal pronouncements have emerged, for each qualifies and imparts meaning to the words of due process and other familiar language. If we do so, we shall see that just as the Chinese selectively adapted to domestic circumstances and so transformed the original message of Buddhism, Christianity, and Marxism (to the extent they adopted each other), they are now doing the same with the law of the modern liberal state. (Alford 1986, p. 955)

In recent years the People's Republic of China has made extreme efforts to alter its reputation as a violator of international intellectual property laws and has enacted legislation accordingly. For instance, the first live broadcast of court proceedings on Chinese national television in July 1998 involved a case brought by three Chinese film studios against companies who had copied films onto compact disks and sold them without copyright permission. Significantly, the judge found in favor of the film studios. At first glance, this event upholds the idea of China's legal reform and the disavowal of accusations of its secret legal operations behind closed doors. The national broadcast affirms that not only does copyright law exist in the PRC but also that China's legal system is willingly enforcing it. Similarly, Hong Kong's Basic Law dramatically illustrates the PRC's willingness to appear to accommodate Western legal ideologies, and not coincidentally to encourage non-Chinese trading investors. China, in short, is keen to represent itself as capable of participating in international legal standards and appropriating a liberal legal discourse. However, despite these legislative efforts China is not actively enforcing intellectual property laws, and infringements are rampant on the Chinese mainland as well as in Hong Kong. Accompanying the apparent "lawlessness" is a dramatic shift in the legal profession of Hong Kong, which is being permeated by the presence of mainland Chinese officials who, with the resumption of Chinese control in 1997, now hold two thirds of Hong Kong's 60-seat Legislative Council.[9]

This lack of enforcement is causing immense friction between China, the United States, and other international trading partners anxious to control access to and investment in knowledge and technology. Trade sanctions have been repeatedly threatened by the United States in an attempt to protect its competitive advantage deriving from technological innovation and so ensure continuing economic profits from exports into China. And to support their position, at times the US government has intimated that Chinese people are "primitive," "sly," and not to be trusted – characteristics that echo nineteenth-century descriptions of the Chinese by Europeans angry at their expulsion from Chinese trading markets in the wake of the Opium Wars (Endeshaw 1996a, pp. 145, 163). Yet it could be argued that no matter how sincere and determined the PRC is to follow international law, it cannot force its people to conform to a foreign system of values that reflect cultural and institutional differences in the idea of legal authorship and subjectivity. New technology makes copying music and videos part of a huge blackmarket venture in China and Hong Kong, and one that many people do not consider so much as "illegal" as sensible business practice and the necessary price a performer or artist has to pay.

Against this backdrop of a very different popular legal consciousness, the Chinese government is dealing with competing demands and needs. According to Endeshaw:

> The reality of the situation is that, after a decade or so of imitation of everything the government thought would be appreciated by the West, China has come up against conflicting demands of domestic economic and technological forces, on the one hand, and foreign, particularly US, interests to which China has made various commitments, on the other. The growing internal demands for more social, economic and technological information than is available within China compel not just a "failure of enforcement" but also a reversal of those commitments wherever possible. (Ibid, p. 14)

Moreover, a basic purpose behind the control of intellectual property rights is being lost in these accusations by the United States of China's violation and deception:

> The US is unrelenting in exerting pressures on China to make it adopt all conceivable measures and standards in blatant disregard of the essential characteristic of intellectual property, that it is supposed to protect primarily national interests, that is Chinese ones. Certainly, from the US standpoint, it is pursuing its own interests by compelling China to abide by agreements, which benefit US businesses above all. However, where international interests (it may be proper in this instance to say US interests) come into a country and seek to obtain more protection than the locals are likely to demand or require, then that betrays not only a departure from the common understanding of what intellectual property is all about, but an inclination to deploy economic power to cover up such a flaw. (Ibid, p. 16)

With respect to Hong Kong and its new function as a Special Administrative Region of the PRC, while some liberal conceptions of personhood do operate, Western countries cannot expect this new region to remain autonomous and so guarantee common law principles when its ultimate authority, and competing legal ideology, emanate from mainland China. As has always been the case under British colonial rule of Hong Kong, there may well remain a minority legal elite that abides by common law principles, but these practitioners should not be assumed as representing Hong Kong's legal culture on the ground. Given that the vast majority of people who make up Hong Kong's working class are immigrants from the Chinese mainland, it is likely that the local population will continue to maintain an unofficial sociolegal culture that is not recognized or accommodated by the formal principles of modern Western law.

What is indicated by these arguments about intellectual property, and the extent to which China can or cannot prevent infringement, is that there exists a failure on behalf of many European and North American sociolegal scholars to appreciate how and why China's different domestic legal and cultural values and decentralized local court system must resist global legal processes in order to retain a sense of stability. Moreover, these arguments, which rely upon the extent to which non-Western legal norms conform or not to those in the West, necessarily fail to take into account the possibility that European laws may themselves be changing and adapting to alternative legal cultures and norms. As the legal scholar Teemu Ruskola suggests in a compelling article on corporate law from a Chinese perspective:

> One may argue that today both Chinese *and* American law are in a dynamic process of convergence, from opposite directions. At least for now, it seems that Chinese and American corporate law are converging, not only on the level of legal rules but even on the deeper level of conceptualization: increasingly, American corporate law academics alienated by contractarian models are turning to communitarian solutions, and calls for strengthening the fiduciary aspects of the corporation are proliferating. (Ruskola 2000)

It is crucial that we do not think about law as an ahistorical and apolitical abstraction. It is only this high degree of abstraction, and the concomitant disconnection from political power, which allows scholars to talk about a "hybrid legal system" (Garth and Dezalay 1996), or a "third legal culture" (Gessner 1996) existing among a very small legal elite employed in major corporate law firms. However, in our enthusiasm to identify these important, but limited, new arenas of elite legal exchange, we should not overlook the extent to which these particular legal cultures are not local phenomena, but rather rooted in leading American and European law schools, and dependent upon what has been called "relational capital," referring to the "personal ties and social connections lawyers can draw on as a result of their legal education or social background" (Chen 1999, p. 113)

Identifying legal homogeneity in the international merchant community –
the *lex mercatoria* – may in fact indicate very little about how law operates on
the ground at the local civil and criminal level, be it that of a region, state, or
city. For whom, in short, is the third legal culture a reality and who profits
from it? This question is important because "global" and "local" fields of legal
action cannot be so neatly defined and distinguished from each other (Smith
1984, p. 136; Darian-Smith 1996). Despite scholarly claims that the *lex mercatoria* operates autonomously in some cases, law merchants are not devoid of
cultural bias, nor do they operate in a relational vacuum. It is highly problematic to isolate institutional practices from cultural values emanating both
from within the legal culture of elite lawyers, company executives, judges, and
investors who actually function in the so-called global legal world, and from
more ordinary people who indirectly sustain and legitimate wider value
systems, general attitudes, and forms of behavior through which any given
legal culture operates.

Neocolonialism and Neoliberalism

The argument outlined above suggests that in the case of Hong Kong the
impact of a globalization of law must also be understood historically, as the
latest episode in a long history of colonial and postcolonial imperialism by both
British and Chinese governments. Despite the PRC's "one country, two
systems" policy, Hong Kong will not be able to maintain its autonomy from
Chinese state intervention in the future, any more than in the past it was able
to function as a Western outpost of the British empire unaffected by local
Chinese values. Nonetheless, East/West legal imagery continues to be
strategically used in transnational and international political and economic
relations. Hence we need to be aware of the larger ideological issues at stake
as certain political economies continue to carve up the world map along
redefined "moral geographies" (cf. Passavant 1996; Bhabha 1994; Gregory
1994). By this I mean that the imperialist civilized/uncivilized divide of the
nineteenth century has been replaced with a more seductive freedom/oppres-
sion moral crusade in which modern democratic law plays a substantial role.
With the fall of the Berlin Wall and the failure of communism, the idea of
Western democracy is emerging triumphant and is promulgating a "resurgent
liberalism that has stepped onto the stage to claim for itself a victory, a claim
in fact that it constitutes our only possible future" (Scott 1996, p. 12; see also
Ruskola 2000).

In a manner analogous to the way Marx and other nineteenth-century
thinkers believed the West would provide the source of change to static and
isolated China, similar rhetoric is playing out in the United States' foreign economic policy. In a news conference in February 1997 President Clinton
announced that liberty is bound to increase in China over time "just as eventually the Berlin Wall fell. I just think it is inevitable" (*LA Times*, February 12,

EYES ON THE PRIZE

Figure 16.2 Tony Auth (1997) *The Philadelphia Inquiry.* Reprinted with gratis permission of Universal Press Syndicate. All rights reserved.

p. 5). Dubbed Clinton's "Berlin Wall" theory, it represents a shift in attitudes by the US towards China. No longer do threats of Chinese communism hover so darkly on the horizon.

In the Western media what can be seen are oscillating positive and negative images of Chinese government, law, and people according to the economic agenda of the US and European trading powers. At times, the PRC is characterized as "backward," "sly," and "shifty" when not complying with the enforcement of intellectual property law and international legal standards. This sort of lurid rhetoric prevailed in the media coverage surrounding the alleged scandal of Chinese spying on American nuclear secrets in early 1999. Mr. Lee, a Taiwan-born nuclear physicist and US citizen, was charged with violating security regulations and passing secrets out of the Los Alamos laboratory to China. Chinese-American rights organizations responded by declaring that Mr. Lee was unfairly targeted. According to the former chief of counter-intelligence at the Los Alamos National Laboratory, Robert Vrooman, there was no evidence that the information came from his lab and the data could have been leaked from documents distributed to hundreds of locations within the US government. In targeting a Taiwan-born physicist, Vrooman noted that "Mr. Lee's ethnicity was a major factor" (*International Herald Tribune*, August 18, 1999, p. 5).

The release of the Cox report in May 1999 that investigated the apparent charge of Chinese espionage concluded, despite there being no solid evidence, that China had stolen information about American warhead designs. Over 900 pages in length, the Cox report contains numerous mistakes and misinformation.

> And, most irresponsibly, the Cox report suggests that every Chinese visitor to this country, every Chinese scholar, every Chinese student, every Chinese permanent resident, and even every Chinese-American citizen is a spy, potential spy, or "sleeper agent," merely waiting for the signal to rise up and perform some unimaginable act of treachery. (Nelson 1999, p. 6)

A great deal more could be said about the Cox report and its official reception and role in the wider US political and electoral process. What I want to stress here is that the scandal and emotional reaction that the report helped to generate, and its allegation that as many as 3,000 Chinese state-owned firms operating in the United States may be engaging in covert and illegal activities, resonates and sustains wider popular ideas about Chinese people as untrustworthy and deceitful. In Silicon Valley, where the "best and brightest of China have streamed to the US by the thousands" in search of technological and engineering advances, company managers are having to review their employees on the basis of ethnicity and nationality (*Los Angeles Times*, October 18, 1999, p. 19). According to Richard Xu, a representative of a Chinese trading firm which owned a lucrative US subsidiary company but sold it in fear the US government would force him out of business on the basis of security concerns,

"Chinese who are working in high-technology worry that maybe someday the FBI will investigate their background. People psychologically feel that way, they feel that shadow" (*Los Angeles Times*, October 17, 1999, p. 22).

In contrast to this image of Chinese people as being conniving and insidious, when the US wants to take advantage of the opening up of Chinese markets, the PRC is portrayed as benevolent despite its well-documented record of civil and political human rights transgressions (for a discussion on human rights in China see Davis 1995). For instance, Clinton's diplomatic trip to China in late June 1998 epitomized this new attitude toward a country previously denounced for its human rights violations and anti-democratic regime. Clinton's trip achieved what it set out to do, which was not to change China's values and politics through highly symbolic but ultimately ineffectual denouncements of the Tiananmen Square massacre on Chinese media. Rather, the trip was specifically designed to change "American perceptions and politics, to get the American public at large to accept the anodyne, uncritical view of China now firmly entrenched in the ranks of American business leaders and academic specialists" (*Guardian Weekly*, June 28, 1998, p. 14). When China suspended official dialogue with the United States on human rights in 1999 the issue was effectively silenced, and, one imagines, embraced with relief on the part of leaders of US international business/political interests.

The presidential attempt to modify US views toward China culminated in October 1999 with successful negotiations for China's entry into the World Trade Organization (WTO). While separate agreements have yet to be conducted by China with Canada and the European Union, the accord with the United States represents a breakthrough after 13 years of often unstable trade talks. Chinese leaders agreed to certain concessions in order to win US support, including access to China's 1.2 billion consumers which are projected to boost Western exports to $21 billion annually. In the words of President Clinton, the agreement is "good for the US, good for China, and good for the world economy." It makes, noted one political commentator, the world safe for American-style global free enterprise (*Guardian Weekly*, November 18, 1999, p. 14). And importantly, it forces China to abide by international legal standards governing intellectual property. The WTO, in effect, underpins, internationalizes, and protects the US intellectual property regime and so massively increases royalty payments to northern transnational companies, at the same time making poorer countries even less likely to enter and afford the technologies necessary for their entry into a global economy and trading system.[10]

Of course, the political consequences resulting from the WTO meetings in Seattle in early December 1999 may well disrupt the emerging trade accord between the US, China, and the other WTO members. Congressional approval of a permanent normal trading status for China may prove to be very difficult in the light of opposition from labor organizations, as well as environmental and human rights activists objecting to PRC violations. Precisely because of these political and economic instabilities and realignments, what I want to stress is that oscillating positive and negative images of China and Chinese people continue to play out in domestic and international relations and have serious political, economic, and social repercussions. The difficulty in anticipating what will happen is compounded by the peculiar alliances occurring between Democrat and Republican interests, with conservative presidential candidate Steve Forbes siding on particular issues with progressive liberals in his denouncement of Clinton's negotiations with China and his recourse to characteristically clichéd "West/East," "us/them" rhetoric:

> No more shutting our ears to the cries of Christians, Buddhists and others suffering religious persecution in Chinese gulags. No more turning a blind eye to Chinese spies in our nuclear labs. No more leaving our children and allies vulnerable to Chinese nuclear missiles. And no more sweetheart trade deals. (*Los Angeles Times*, November 13, 1999, p. 10)

Conclusion

Rather than analyzing the extent to which China is an authoritarian violator of human rights, or a progressive frontier of democratic and capitalist expansion, my point is that underlying both of these images, and the many variants that exist between these two extremes, is an assumption that the American/European legal system, including the concept of a sovereign individual, is the natural and desirable model for social change. It is our unquestioned narcissism that leads many theorists of legal globalization to simply assume that some level of Western, and specifically a United States, intervention is necessary to lead the world to a democratic rule of law.

Charting some of the problems surrounding intellectual property law in postcolonial Hong Kong highlights the degree to which the imposition of the "West" on the "East" of supposedly innocent legal categories including private property, intellectual property, and human rights cannot occur without a significant impact on local cultures (Aoki 1996). This imposition requires a competing concept of individualism that is unavoidably destructive, or at least disruptive, to the fabric of Chinese culture. While many Western scholars remain steadfastly unaware of the political and social implications of their own sociolegal paradigms, many non-Western scholars are acutely aware of the ongoing epistemic violence and its effects at the local level. For example, Sin Wai Man and Chu Yiu Wai call this process an "occidentalization strategy of the rule of law," which is endorsed at many levels by Hong Kong's government, legal profession, and general public to form a grand narrative of dominance and control (Man and Wai 1998, p. 151). What should be appreciated is that this legal occidentalization also represents an attack on China's legal bureaucracy and Chinese and Hong Kong cultural values.

In order to reduce the degree to which we as sociolegal scholars are implicated in the process of legal and cultural domination, we must refrain from relying on formulations that present specific legal ideologies and cultures as natural, and so apolitical and ahistorical, abstractions. We need to rethink our own categorical assumptions about personhood and property ownership and take seriously the power implications of our utopian rhetoric. A more modest and cautious approach to the impact of legal globalization may not only promote more successful communications across cultural divides and socioeconomic classes, and among law and society scholars from China, postcolonial Hong Kong and elsewhere, but it may also enable us to present more sophisticated and socially penetrating analyses of sociolegal processes that take into account a range of changes and appropriations and reconceptualizations of legal meaning amongst ourselves.

Notes

1   Special thanks to Philip McCarty and Melody Knutson for their comments on earlier drafts, as well as the American Philosophical Society and the Institute for Social, Behavioral and Economic Research, University of California, Santa Barbara for research support.

2   Legal culture is difficult to define and so compare (see Nelken 1997, and for a review Darian-Smith 1998b). One of the biggest limitations in comparative work of various legal cultures is the prevailing presumption that legal culture is necessarily a subset of particular political and cultural units and social structures (i.e., nation-states). A more creative and dynamic notion of legal culture is to examine the various strategies and images about law employed by people in the ongoing practices of daily life. This forces us to rethink and re-explore how legal difference emerges through cultural interaction and accompanying reconfigurations of power. Such an approach resonates with contemporary studies in anthropology, where the study of law is one approach by which to examine the wider contexts of power governing racial and gender politics, constructions of identity, and the ongoing historical processes of cultural differentiation in a particular field or setting. Importantly, these settings are not limited to comparative analysis of national arenas, but can be such things as a town, a border region, or a transnational political entity such as the European Union (Just 1992; Gupta and Ferguson 1997; Maurer 1997; Darian-Smith 1999; Gibson and Caldeira 1996, p. 57).

3   Notwithstanding *Orientalism's* immense theoretical impact raised by its then radical critique of the production of a Eurocentric positioning *vis-à-vis* a developing Third World, in recent years criticisms have rightly been leveled at Said for his polarizing of the world according to "two unequal halves, Orient and Occident" (Said 1978, p. 12; e.g., Breckenridge and van der Veer 1993, pp. 5–6; Sprinker 1992). As Colin Perrin has argued, this in turn raises "an equivocation in the ontological status of the Orient itself" (Perrin 1995, p. 58). Said's adoption of a constructivist methodology whereby the Orient is both cause and consequence of Orientalism leaves him "equivocal, therefore, regarding an Orient which comes before or after discourse – as something distorted or misrepresented by it or, alternatively, as something produced by it" (Perrin 1995, p. 58). Said's one-way analysis effectively circumscribes the East and West's mutual dependency by his claiming that the Orient's capacities to resist and appropriate power from the West is always negotiated through the discourses of a superior Occident (Said 1978, p. 8).

4   Of course, intellectual property law in and of itself does not always defend personal liberties. As Rosemary Coombe has convincingly argued, intellectual property law can also be used for effectively suppressing and censoring ideas (Coombe 1991, p. 1855).

5   There is a popular rhetoric prevalent in the media that *quanxi* equals corruption, while in contrast events such as the debacle in the late 1990s over Chinese money being used to support the Clinton administration in return for certain commercial favors is exempt from moral criticism. The popular view of Chinese corruption also tends to overlook the United States' "old boy's network" operating through such institutions as Harvard and Yale law schools and MBA programs. Such educational ties create related channels of personal connection, family obligation, and, to use a phrase of Bourdieu's, "cultural capital" in similar ways to China's *quanxi* system or Mexico's enduring arrangements of patronage.

6   The irony however, as pointed out by Peter Fitzpatrick, is that Western moral superiority, and the idea of the autonomous legal subject on which it is based, is promoted precisely because it has never existed:

The subject recognized in law is the universal, autonomous individual – the given and ultimate being, "posited by nature". . . . The legal subject – the individual who is able to take action checking on legality, who is able to enter into and enforce legal relations – is constituted negatively, like the general subject of which it is a form. Being a child, a woman, a slave, being colonized or mentally incompetent, have all operated to mark what fully-fledged legal subjectivity is not (cf. Foucault 1979, p. 16). The abstract legal subject is free and equal with all other legal subjects, liberated from all substantive ties and immune from all determinations not of itself. It could only be operatively constituted in terms of what it is not. (Fitzpatrick 1992, p. 136).

7   In a fascinating discussion of Hong Kong's colonial relationship with Britain and mainland China, anthropologist Allen Chun notes: "As a colonial society, the British administered Hong Kong in accordance with their own judicial conventions, as a colony. Yet in spite of its colonial status, there was no question as to the cultural identity of its ethnically Chinese inhabitants. Before 1950, most people just called themselves Chinese, there was no notion of Hong Kongers, and there was little to differentiate Hong Kong from foreign enclaves in other treaty ports. . . . Thus, the autonomy of an emergent Hong Kong society in the succeeding decades was in effect an illusion that took shape initially with its marginalization from the Chinese mainstream" (Chun 2000, pp. 298–9).

8   Throughout the 1980s China instigated widespread legal reform. The revival of a formalized rule of law, marked by its new constitution of 1982, led to a flurry of interest in economic and administrative legislation, practices of mediation and arbitration, legal education, and a codification of the General Principles of Civil Law (1986) (Brugger and Reglar 1994, pp. 219–21). This interest in legal reform helped raise the status of lawyers in China from being merely employees of the emperor. Thus in the early 1980s there were only 3,000 lawyers in China, but by 1991 this figure had increased to 50,000 (still allowing, however, for only one lawyer per 20,000 inhabitants) (ibid, p. 217).

9   For instance, the trial in 1998 of Cheung, Hong Kong's most notorious gangland criminal, in a court on the Chinese mainland has raised fears among Hong Kong's legal profession of their authority being usurped by increasing PRC intervention into the Basic Law system and Hong Kong's supposed legal autonomy. This is

despite growing pro-democracy populist movements in Hong Kong, and the Democrats securing 13 seats in the 60-seat legislature in Hong Kong's May 1998 elections. More recently, in early 1999, Hong Kong's government appealed to Beijing to "interpret" a decision made by the Hong Kong Court of Final Appeal that allowed children on the mainland with one Hong Kong parent to claim a right to reside in Hong Kong. In effect, this "interpretation" amounted to the overturning of the decision reached by the Hong Kong judges and signals increasing surveillance and control of local decision-making by Beijing.

10 Political analyst William Greider observes that globalization degrades law: "business interests do not talk about escaping from the law. . . . Instead, they promote the goal of greater efficiency – a 'harmonization' of national law that will remove barriers and thus encourage greater trade. Harmonization cuts in different directions. In one area after another the harmonization of regulatory standards usually pulls the law downward in a search for the lowest common denominator. The most alarming aspect of how globalization degrades law is in the conditions of work." Greider concludes that "Global business and finance seem to be astride a giant contradiction: while they campaign to dismantle legal restraints in one part of the world, the wealthiest societies, they are simultaneously urging poorer nations to adopt mainly ones that will protect private property from political interferences" (Greider 1997, p. 34) (see Nader 1999, pp. 94–5).

References

Abbas, A. (1997) *Hong Kong: Culture and the Politics of Disappearance*. Minneapolis: University of Minnesota Press.

Alford, W. P. (1986) "The Inscrutable Occidental? Implications of Roberto Unger's Uses and Abuses of the Chinese Past." *Texas Law Review* 64: 915.

——(1995) *To Steal a Book is an Elegant Offence: Intellectual Property Law in Chinese Civilization*. Stanford, CA: Stanford University Press.

Aoki, K. (1996) "(Intellectual) Property and Sovereignty: Notes Toward a Cultural Geography of Authorship." *Stanford Law Review* 48 (5): 1293–355.

Appadurai, A. (1986) *The Social Life of Things: Commodities in Cultural Perspective*. Cambridge: Cambridge University Press.

Appelbaum, R. P. (1998) "The Future of Law in a Global Political Economy." *Social and Legal Studies* 7 (2): 171–92.

Baudet, H. (1965) *Paradise on Earth: Some Thoughts on European Images of Non-European Man*. New Haven, CT: Yale University Press.

Bettig, R. V. (1996) *Copyrighting Culture: The Political Economy of Intellectual Property*. Boulder, CO: Westview Press.

Bhabha, H. (1994) *The Location of Culture*. London: Routledge.

Blaut, J. M. (1993) *The Colonizer's Model of the World: Geographical Diffusionism and Eurocentric History*. New York: Guildford Press.

Bodde, D. and C. Morris (1967) *Law in Imperial China: Exemplified by 190 Ch'ing Dynasty Cases*. Philadelphia: University of Pennsylvania Press.

Bosniak, L. S. (1996) "Opposing Prop. 187: Undocumented Immigrants and the National Imagination." *Connecticut Law Review* 28.

Boyle, J. (1996) *Shamans, Software and Spleens: Law and the Construction of the Information Society*. Cambridge, MA: Harvard University Press.

Brahm, L. J. (1988) *Intellectual Property and Technology Transfer in China*. Hong Kong: Longman.

Breckenridge, C. A. and P. van der Veer (1993) "Orientalism and the Postcolonial Predicament." In C. A. Breckenridge and P. van der Veer (eds.), *Orientalism and the Postcolonial Predicament: Perspectives on South Asia*. Philadelphia: University of Pennsylvania Press. Pp. 1–22.

Brugger, B. and S. Reglar (1994) *Politics, Economy and Society in Contemporary China*. Stanford, CA: Stanford University Press.

Buchanan, R. (1995) "Border Crossings: NAFTA, Regulatory Restructuring, and the Politics of Place." *Indiana Journal of Global Legal Studies* 2 (2): 371–94.

Butterton, G. R. (1996) "Pirates, Dragons and the US Intellectual Property Rights in China: Problems and Prospects of Chinese Enforcement." *Arizona Law Review* 38 (4): 1081–123.

Carrithers, M. et al. (1985) *The Category of the Person: Anthropology, Philosophy, History*. Cambridge: Cambridge University Press.

Carter, C. (1996) *Fighting Fakes in China: The Legal Protection of Trade Marks and Brands in the People's Republic of China*. London: Intellectual Property Institute.

Chen, A. H. Y. (1999) "Rational Law, Economic Development and the Case of China." *Social and Legal Studies* 8: 97–120.

Chun, A. (2000) *Unstructuring Chinese Society: The Fictions of Colonial Practice and the Changing Realities of "Land" in the New Territories of Hong Kong*. Netherlands: Harwood Academic Publishers.

Cohn, B. S. and N. B. Dirks (1988) "Beyond the Fringe: The Nation-State, Colonialism, and the Technologies of Power." *Journal of Historical Sociology* 1 (2): 224–9.

Collier, J., B. Maurer, and L. Suarez Navaz (1995) "Sanctioned Identities: Legal Constructions of Modern Personhood." *Identities* 2 (1–2): 1–28.

Coombe, R. (1991) "Objects of Property and Subjects of Politics: Intellectual Property Laws and Democratic Dialogue." *Texas Law Review* 69 (7): 1853–80.

——(1998) *The Cultural Life of Intellectual Properties: Authorship, Appropriation and the Law*. Durham, NC: Duke University Press.

Cronon, W. (1983) *Changes in the Land: Indians, Colonists, and the Ecology of New England*. New York: Hill and Wang.

Darian-Smith, E. (1996) Introduction. In E. Darian-Smith and P. Fitzpatrick (eds.), Special Issue on Law and Postcolonialism. *Social and Legal Studies* 5 (3): 291–9.

——(1998a) Review essay of Boaventura de Sousa Santos (1995) "Toward a New Common Sense: Law, Science and Politics in the Paradigmatic Transition." *Law and Social Inquiry* 23 (1): 81–120 (my essay is followed by a response from Santos).

——(1998b) Review of David Nelken (ed.) (1997) *Comparing Legal Cultures*. Aldershot: Dartmouth. *Social and Legal Studies* (in press).

——(1999) *Bridging Divides: The Channel Tunnel and English Legal Identity in the New Europe*. Berkeley: University of California Press.

Darian-Smith, E. and P. Fitzpatrick (eds.) (1999) *Laws of the Postcolonial*. Ann Arbor: University of Michigan Press.

Davis, M. C. (ed.) (1995) *Human Rights and Chinese Values: Legal, Philosophical, and Political Perspectives*. Hong Kong: Oxford University Press.

Delanty, G. (1995) *Inventing Europe: Idea, Identity, Reality*. New York: St. Martin's Press.

Endeshaw, A. (1996a) *Intellectual Property Law in China: The Roots of the Problem of Enforcement*. Singapore: Acumen.

——(1996b) *Intellectual Property Policy for Non-Industrial Countries. Aldershot: Dartmouth.*

Fitzpatrick, P. (1992) *The Mythology of Modern Law.* London: Routledge.

Ford, R. T. (1994) "The Boundaries of Race: Political Geography in Legal Analysis." *Harvard Law Review*: 1841–1921.

Foucault, M. (1979) "My Body, The Paper, This Fire." *Oxford Literary Review* 4 (1): 9–28.

Foucault, M. (1984) "What is an Author?" In *The Foucault Reader*, ed. P. Rabinow. New York: Pantheon. Pp. 101–20.

Garth, B. and Dezalay, Y. (1996) *Dealing in Virtue: International Commercial Arbitration and the Construction of a Transnational Legal Order.* Ch. 12, "Law at the Frontier: Hong Kong and Transitions from One Imperialism to Another." Chicago: University of Chicago Press.

Gessner, V. (1995) "Global Approaches in the Sociology of Law: Problems and Challenges." *Journal of Law and Society* 22 (1): 85–96.

——(1996) "Globalization and Legal Certainty." Paper prepared for the Onati Workshop on *The Infrastructure of Cross-Border Legal Interaction.*

Gibson, J. L. and G. A. Caldeira (1996) "The Legal Cultures of Europe." *Law and Society Review* 30 (1): 55–86.

Gluckman, M. (1943) *Essays on Lozi Land and Royal Property.* Livingstone: Rhodes Livingstone Institute.

Goody, J. (1996) *The East in the West.* Cambridge: Cambridge University Press.

Greenhalgh, S. (1994) "De-Orientalizing the Chinese Family Firm." *American Ethnologist* 21 (4): 746–75.

Gregory, D. (1994) *Geographical Imaginations.* Oxford: Blackwell Publishers.

Greider, W. (1997) *One World, Ready or Not: The Manic Logic of Global Capitalism.* New York: Simon and Schuster.

Gupta, A. and J. Ferguson (eds.) (1997) *Anthropological Locations: Boundaries and Grounds of a Field Science.* Berkeley: University of California Press.

Hann, C. (1993) "From Production to Property: Decollectivization and the Family–Land Relationship in Contemporary Hungary." *Man* 28: 299–320.

Hannerz, U. (1996) *Transnational Connections: Culture, People, Places.* London and New York: Routledge.

Harris, G. (1989) "Concepts of Individual, Self and Person in Description and Analysis." *American Anthropologist* 91: 599–612.

Jones, C. (1994) "Capitalism, Globalization and Rule of Law: An Alternative Trajectory of Legal Change in China." *Social and Legal Studies* 3 (2): 195–221.

Just, P. (1992) "History, Power, Ideology, and Culture: Current Directions in the Anthropology of Law." *Law and Society Review* 26: 373–412.

Kang, Liu (1999) "Is there an Alternative to (Capitalist) Globalization? The Debate about Modernity in China." In F. Jameson and M. Miyoshi (eds.), *The Cultures of Globalization.* Durham, NC: Duke University Press. Pp. 164–90.

Kelly, D. K. (1990) "From Civil Science to the Human Sciences." In *The Human Measure: Social Thought in the Western Legal Tradition.* Cambridge, MA: Harvard University Press.

Kipnis, A. B. (1997) *Producing Guanxi: Sentiment, Self, and Subculture in a North China Village.* Durham, NC: Duke University Press.

Lach, D. F. (1965) *China in the Eyes of Europe.* Chicago: University of Chicago Press.

Lach, D. F. and T. N. Foss (1990) "Images of Asia and Asians in European Fiction, 1500–1800." In R. W. Winks and J. R. Rush (eds.), *Asia in Western Fiction.* Honolulu: University of Hawaii Press.

Lau, S.-K. and H.-C. Kuan (1988) *The Ethos of the Hong Kong Chinese*. Hong Kong: Chinese University Press.

Leibniz, W. (1994) *Writings on China*, trans. with introduction by D. J. Cook and H. R. Rosemont. Chicago: Open Court.

Locke, J. (1988) [1690] *Two Treatises of Government*. Cambridge: Cambridge University Press.

Lubman, S. B. (ed.) (1996) *China's Legal Reforms*. Oxford: Clarendon Press.

MacCormack, G. (1996) *The Spirit of Traditional Chinese Law*. Athens, GA: University of Georgia Press.

Mackerras, C. (1989) *Western Images of China*. Hong Kong: Oxford University Press.

Macpherson, C. B. (1988) [ca. 1962] *The Political Theory of Possessive Individualism: Hobbes to Locke*. Oxford: Oxford University Press.

Mahmud, T. (1999) "Colonialism and Modern Constructions of Race: A Preliminary Inquiry." *University of Miami Law Review* 53 (4): 1219–46.

Malinowski, B. (1985) [1926] *Crime and Punishment in Savage Society*. New Jersey: Littlefield, Adams.

Man, S. W. and C. Y. Wai (1998) "Whose Rule of Law? Rethinking (Post-)Colonial Legal Culture in Hong Kong." *Social and Legal Studies* 7 (2): 147–70.

Mannsaker, F. (1990) "Elegancy and Wildness: Reflections of the East in the Eighteenth-Century Imagination." In G. S. Rousseau and R. Porter (eds.), *Exoticism in the Enlightenment*. Manchester: Manchester University Press. Pp. 175–96.

Maurer, B. (1997) *Recharting the Caribbean: Land, Law, and Citizenship in the British Virgin Islands*. Michigan: University of Michigan Press.

Merry, S. E. (1992) "Anthropology, Law, and Transnational Processes." *Annual Review of Anthropology* 21: 357–79.

Nader, L. (1999) "The Influence of Dispute Resolution on Globalization: The Political Economy of Legal Models." In *Globalization and Legal Cultures*. Onati Papers 7: 87–99, Publication of the International Institute for the Sociology of Law.

Nelken, D. (ed.) (1997) *Comparing Legal Cultures*. Aldershot: Dartmouth.

Nelson, L.-E. (1999) "Washington: The Yellow Peril." *The New York Review of Books*. July 15: 6–10.

Olgiati, V. (1999) " 'Butterfly Effect': Hong Kong's Transition to China and Europe's Shift from (Western-Centered) Modernity." In *60 Mal Recht en 1 Maal Wijn: Sociology of Law, Social Problems and Legal Policy*. Leuven: Amersfoort. Pp. 583–94.

Passavant, P. (1996) "A Moral Geography of Liberty: John Stuart Mill and American Free Speech Discourse." In E. Darian-Smith and P. Fitzpatrick (eds.), Law and Postcolonialism. *Social and Legal Studies* (special issue) 5 (3): 301–20.

Perrin, C. (1995) "Approaching Anxiety: The Insistence of the Postcolonial in the Declaration of Human Rights of Indigenous Peoples." *Law and Critique* 6 (1): 55–74.

Redding, S. G. (1990) *The Spirit of Chinese Capitalism*. Berlin: Walter de Gruyter.

Reichwein, A. (1925) *China and Europe: Intellectual and Artistic Contacts in the Eighteenth Century*. New York: Alfred A. Knopf.

Rose, M. (1993) *Authors and Owners: The Invention of Copyright*. Cambridge, MA: Harvard University Press.

Ruskola, T. (2000) "Stories About Corporations and Families: A Look at Corporation Law Jurisprudence from a Chinese Perspective." *Stanford Law Review* (in press).

Said, E. (1978) *Orientalism*. New York: Vintage.

Santos, Boaventura de Sousa (1995) *Toward a New Common Sense: Law, Science and Politics in the Paradigmatic Transition*. New York: Routledge.

Schwab, R. (1984) [1959] *The Oriental Renaissance: Europe's Rediscovery of India and the East, 1680–1880*. New York: Colombia University Press.

Scott, D. (1996) "The Aftermaths of Sovereignty: Postcolonial Criticism and the Claims of Political Modernity." *Social Text* 48 (14): 1–26.

Serres, M. and B. Latour (1995) *Conversations on Science, Culture, and Time*. Ann Arbor: University of Michigan Press.

Sherman, B. (1997) "Remembering and Forgetting: The Birth of Modern Copyright Law." In D. Nelken (ed.), *Comparing Legal Cultures*. Aldershot: Dartmouth. Pp. 237–66.

Smith, N. (1984) *Uneven Development: Nature, Capital and the Production of Space*. Oxford: Blackwell Publishers.

Springbord, P. (1992) *Western Republicanism and the Oriental Prince*. Austin: University of Texas Press.

Sprinker, M. (ed.) (1992) *Edward Said: A Critical Reader*. Oxford: Blackwell Publishers.

Strathern, M. (1988) *The Gender of the Gift*. Berkeley: University of California Press.

Strawson, J. (1995) "Islamic Law and English Texts." *Law and Critique* 6 (1): 21–38.

Tricker, R. I. (1990) "Corporate Governance: A Ripple on the Cultural Reflections." In S. R. Clegg and S. G. Redding (eds.), *Capitalism in Contrasting Cultures*. Berlin: Walter de Gruyter. Pp. 187–214.

Unger, R. M. (1976) *Law in Modern Society: Toward a Criticism of Social Theory*. New York: Free Press.

Vandermeersch, L. (1985) "An Enquiry into the Chinese Conception of the Law." In S. R. Schram (ed.), *The Scope of State Power in China*. London: SOAS, University of London; Hong Kong: Chinese University Press.

Wood, A. T. (1995) "Statecraft and Natural Law in the West and China." In *Limits to Autocracy: From Sung Neo-Confucianism to a Doctrine of Political Rights*. Honolulu: University of Hawaii Press. Pp. 132–47.

Woodmansee, M. (1984) "The Genius and the Copyright: Economic and Legal Conditions of the Emergence of the Author." *Eighteenth-Century Studies* 17 (4): 425–48.

Yan, Y. (1996) *The Flow of Gifts: Reciprocity and Social Networks in a Chinese Village*. Stanford, CA: Stanford University Press.

Yang, M. M. (1994) *Gifts, Favors, and Banquets: The Art of Social Relationships in China*. Ithaca, NY: Cornell University Press.

Yu-wei, H. (1968) "The Status of the Individual in Chinese Ethics." In C. A. Moore (ed.), *The Status of the Individual in the East and West*. Honolulu: University of Hawaii Press.

Chapter 17

A Flexible Foundation: Constructing a Postcolonial Dialogue

Dawn Duncan

Even as Postcolonial Studies is gaining ground in the academy, the critical dialogue is threatened by an identity crisis. On the one hand, a rigidity, a vying for territorial critical rights, traps the dialogue in old constructional notions of race and political governance. Scholars argue about who has legitimate right to a voice in the dialogue, bordering such rights with the use of continental or color arguments and indicating a continued colonial structure mindset with such terms as "First World" and "Third World." Giving into these notions is paramount to allowing those participating in the postcolonial dialogue to have their terms defined externally, forcing the internal reality to match borders mapped by old ideologies that have ceased to represent reality (if indeed they ever did). The threat of such rigidity has become all too apparent to many within the dialogue. On the other hand, members of the academic community who do not participate in the dialogue but criticize what they observe accuse the postcolonial dialogue of being simultaneously about everything and nothing. Without coherence, and according to these critics without clarity in the writing of postcolonial scholarship, the dialogue has become a babbling brook, eroding any definition and, thus, meaningless. In an effort to address both these threats to the postcolonial dialogue, I have attempted to build a flexible foundation in my approach to postcolonialism. Bart Moore-Gilbert (1997, p. 188) also calls for "as broad and flexible a conception of the cultures of (neo-)colonialism as is possible." Moore-Gilbert recognizes that "there has been increasingly heated, even bitter, contestation of the legitimacy of seeing certain regions, periods, sociopolitical formations and cultural practices as 'genuinely' postcolonial" (ibid, p. 11). Yet he prefers to examine the conflict between postcolonial theory and criticism. As a postcolonial critic who is attempting to create a theoretical base for the work I do, I appreciate

Moore-Gilbert's analysis of the situation and encouragement of a dialogue that includes the voices of theoreticians and critics alike, as well as those of us who attempt to mediate that space. In order to practice criticism from a theoretical base that provides some integrity, I would like to create a foundation that is not so rigid that it will crack under the pressure of global realities, nor so fluid that it cannot provide a basis for the participants who share in the dialogue. Like the houses built on the sands of Galveston Bay, the fault lines of the San Andreas, or the clay of the Red River Valley, the dialogue we construct requires a floating slab. To build under these conditions, pylons are driven more deeply into such ground, then the floating slab provides a base that is flexible enough to adjust to the shifting conditions yet sustain the integrity of the structure. However, before turning our attention to constructing such a flexible foundation, we must address the pitfalls that have called for this reconstruction. We must also keep in mind the many parties involved in the building of the dialogue, for dialogue takes place between the stories, between the critics, and between the critics and the stories. As I address the pitfalls, I turn my attention to the dialogue between the critics, because it is the critics who have framed the space into which they fit the stories, and it is this framing that stands now on shaky ground. When I move to the flexible foundation that I propose, I will be speaking of the dialogue between stories and how the suggested basis makes room for more inclusion; the critics belong here, too, by implication, such a space becoming the place where all parties rejoin the dialogue.

Critical Pitfalls of Rigidity: Race and Place

I first referred to this threat to narrow and possess the dialogic space in an essay I published on the work of Brian Friel, Irish playwright, as clearly postcolonial. In that essay (Duncan 1994) I termed the tendencies *continentalization* and *colorization*, referring to the prevalent definition of postcolonial as writing that emerges from non-European cultures once colonized by white Europeans. While certainly the particular form of postcolonial cultures so indicated may represent the majority postcolonial condition, the definition fails to give voice to cultures that do not squarely fit the continental and color parameters. Unfortunately, rather than shaping a responsive and respectful transformation of those parameters, the dialogue has, if anything, heated into a debate which may well determine the vibrancy and validity of postcolonial studies. In the interest of opening the dialogue to include all people, regardless of place or skin color, who have lived under colonial constructs and who emerge from a postcolonial condition, we must rethink the danger embedded in the constricting racial definition that has been too easily accepted or assumed by postcolonial scholars.

For many critics, race functions as one of the border elements currently defining the postcolonial realm. Indeed, the race issue lies at the heart of a question that led to a heated debate on the postcolonial list serve moderated through the University of Virginia. In February 1997 Lynnette Kissoon of the University of Toronto asked "do Irish writers count as postcolonial writers? And if so, does that change the way we perceive postcoloniality?" Eugene O'Brien of the University of Limerick replied:

> This is a cogent question, and one which has been the subject of some debate. If by postcolonial one means writing from a place that was colonized by another government, then yes it must be. Ireland is an unusual case in that it is a first world country (some might question aspects of this) and white in racial composition. As such, it does not fit comfortably in the paradigm of the third world/racial other dimension of the postcolonial. One need only observe the paucity of references to Ireland in *The Empire Writes Back* where the issue of Ireland can be seen to destabilize the whole theoretical dimension of the book. I think that the case of Ireland, as a colonized country which fought a war of independence to free itself from British rule, is obviously broadly similar to other postcolonial cultures, but I reckon a lot depends on the definition of the postcolonial that is used. (postcolonial listserv 2/4/97)

Certainly within Irish studies a number of scholars quite reasonably assume that Ireland should take its place in the postcolonial dialogue. In his introduction to *Nationalism, Colonialism, and Literature*, Seamus Deane describes Ireland as "the only Western European country that has both an early and late colonial experience" (Deane 1990, p. 4), referring to pre-independence for the Republic and the ongoing situation in Northern Ireland. One of the founders of Field Day, the effort in the 1980s of Irish artists and scholars to respond to the "nature and genesis of the present impasse," Deane emphatically states, "Field Day's analysis of the situation derives from the conviction that it is, above all, a colonial crisis" (ibid, p. 6). Even before the foundation of Field Day, linguists dedicated to the revival of Irish located the root of the problem in the colonial effort of England to kill the native language. The work of sociolinguists such as Hilary Tovey, Damian Hannan, and Hal Abramson in *Why Irish? Irish Identity and the Irish Language* and Reg Hindley in *The Death of the Irish Language: A Qualified Obituary* contributes greatly to an understanding of the complexity of the language issue. Other Irish scholars have followed on the heels of Deane and his colleagues to illuminate more fully the Irish postcolonial condition beyond the language issue. David Lloyd focuses on the obsession with the question of identity, a theme which he says "saturates the discursive field, drowning out other social and cultural possibilities" (Lloyd 1993, p. 3). Lloyd points out the danger of attempting to define an Irish identity when he argues "one principal and consistent dynamic of identity formation has been the negation of recalcitrant or inassimilable elements in Irish society" (ibid, p. 5). While Lloyd is quite right in calling into question any essentialist definition of national/cultural identity, his critique should not move us away from an examination of how identity is formed, of the multitude of postcolonial pressures brought to bear on the individuals who are heirs to the postcolonial condition, and the resulting difficulty of identity formation. Lecturing at the 1993 Yeats Summer School in Sligo, the same year as the publication of Lloyd's study, Declan Kiberd declared, "Ireland is, for me, a supreme postcolonial instance." Kiberd has continued to provide one of the most clear and thorough analyses of Ireland's postcolonial condition with the publication of *Inventing Ireland: The Literature of the Modern Nation*. While Kiberd's overview and close analysis of Irish literature and culture provides the kind of breadth and depth to which all scholars should aspire, he still seems to identify the starting point of postcolonial Irish writing as following decolonization of most of the island in the 1920s. His analysis of "the expected wrong-turning" that the Irish made on the heels of decolonization is brilliant, and his comparison of Daniel Corkery's view of independent Ireland with Ngugi's commentary on Kenya illustrates Ireland's deep connectedness to the postcolonial dialogue. However, we need that same kind of attention to brilliantly illuminate the postcolonial situation of the Irish from the point of colonization forward.

As I consider my own work as a postcolonial critic, I attempt to address three gaps in the current dialogue. First, while Irish postcolonial scholars are speaking out strongly, these voices are most often heard chiefly within Irish studies rather than in the wider postcolonial dialogue, a situation I wish to rectify. Second, while sociolinguists recognize the evolutionary nature of language use, Irish postcolonial critics have not taken into account the evolutionary nature of oppositional writing from the point of colonization and thus too narrowly define the authors and texts considered postcolonial. In my own work, I am increasing my investigation of oppositional strategies, to date reading back as far as the 1800 Act of Union. Finally, rather than continuing to privilege the novel as the literary location of the postcolonial voice, I particularly turn attention to Irish drama and its ability to more fully engage public perceptions of identity and responses to postcolonial struggles.

From O'Brien's response and the work of Irish scholars, it is clear that a group of us believe the way in which we define postcolonialism must provide room for the Irish; yet the Irish do not readily fit the racial and geographic borders assumed by a great many postcolonial scholars. The definition of postcolonial that still seems to hold sway was voiced by Helen Tiffin in a 1988 essay. Tiffin, notably, is one of the authors of *The Empire Writes Back*. Tiffin's summary definition reads: "writing and reading practices grounded in some form of colonial experience occurring outside Europe but as a consequence of European expansion into and exploitation of 'the other' worlds" (Tiffin 1988, p. 170). If we continue to operate under the definition of postcolonialism established by Helen Tiffin over a decade ago, then we remain blind to our own cooperation in racial bigotry.

A critic who has done much to address notions of racial bigotry and whose own work speaks of pitfalls, my mirror here acknowledging my admiration of her work, is Anne McClintock. McClintock has written cogently about how during the nineteenth century the "imperial race" used the concept of race to define "groups as 'natural' and 'biological' rather than social." Those in power were interested in establishing what McClintock refers to as "'contagious' classes," in which the Irish were included, to indicate the superiority of those in power over inferior groups of people supposedly delineated by biology and given genetically to degeneration (McClintock 1988, p. 158). While McClintock includes the Irish among the "contagious" groups in the hierarchy that she describes as established by the imperial mindset, the Irish are still included among the white race, though at the low end, "with the (Irish) working-class female in the lower depths of the white race" (ibid, p. 163). Perhaps McClintock is unaware that a popular representation of the Irish by those in power clearly placed the Irish among the black race. A December 9, 1876 illustration in *Harper's Weekly: Journal of Civilization* shows the likeness of the Irish to the Negro. The caption explains that Africans "came to Ireland, and mixed with the natives of the South and West, who themselves are supposed to have been of low type and descendants of savages of the Stone Age." Even if a bit shortsighted, McClintock is right in pointing out how imperialists use the race card. However, it is time that we remove race as a way to line up our enemy in our sights. By now, we should comprehend that biology has long since proven such racial theories to be ridiculous, to lack a basis, and to reveal bias. When San Juan (1998, p. 119) declares, "Race is the mask of class, in the ultimate analysis," he draws attention to the fictional construct of race (mask) and how it functions to purposely create an underclass. San Juan's understanding of race as "a property of dominance relations between groups" (ibid, p. 129) rather than anything to do with biology can accurately move us away from committing the error of colorization and toward the clear need to illuminate and refute the way in which those in power use race as a tool to undermine the other.

The real issue is not race but how the one in power superscribes an image for the oppressed. Edward Said certainly recognizes that the issues of race and place are imaginative creations of those in power. Though Said has been accused of setting up binary oppositions between East and West, this is an oversimplification of his view unless one imagines that Ireland has been geographically relocated in the East. Or perhaps that is exactly what Said imagines when he places Ireland outside of Britain and even Europe, designating it as one of the "distant or peripheral worlds, conceived of as desirable but subordinate" to the imperialist mindset of British culture (Said 1993, pp. 52, 106). If we are to legitimately include the Irish as postcolonial people, then we must either imagine them to be black and in the East or scrap Tiffin's definition. As Eugene O'Brien notes, those who have adopted the notion of colonizers as always white Europeans and the colonized as always non-white races "run into the danger of perpetuating, in an inverted form, the racialist essentialisms that they sought to overcome and displace" (postcolonial listserv 2/4/97). Racialist essentialism led to apartheid in South Africa. But I do not think that most postcolonial theorists would want to be guilty of exercising apartheid of any sort. Jacques Derrida writes: "Racism always betrays the perversion of a man. . . . It institutes, declares, writes, inscribes, prescribes. A system of marks, it outlines space in order to assign forced residence or to close off borders. It does not discern, it discriminates" (Derrida 1985, p. 290). As we attempt to describe the postcolonial space, we should be more discerning and less discriminating. What ever borders we reconstruct should be flexible enough to support all peoples who have suffered colonization and emerged into a postcolonial condition. If race is no longer used as a determining factor in who can have a voice in a postcolonial dialogue, then we will finally have a symphonic blend of voices that includes the Irish, Koreans, Native Americans, and a multitude of others whose skin color, geographic location, or same-race connection to their colonizers has left them standing outside the borders. Because of his concentration on real life struggles with "inequality of power and control over resources" (San Juan 1998, p. 13), San Juan is able to escape the false constructs of continentalization and colorization, including in his citation of those "being subjected to unconscionable treatment such as systematic brutalization and genocide" the people of Northern Ireland and Hawaii (ibid). In fact, San Juan suggests "a 'Third World' domain of subjects-in-process that is not so much geographical as political and social" (ibid, p. 16). Under San Juan's definition, "Third World" ceases to be a physical concept and becomes instead what he refers to as "a trope as well as the site of dissent and insurgency . . . that anticipates change and renewal" (ibid, p. 17).

Critical Pitfalls of Rigidity: Time and Governance

Scholars continue to argue about what the *post* in postcolonial means. For many, the overly rigid interpretation of *post* as after the departure of the colonizers still holds sway. Certainly *post* contains the notion of *after*. However, would many of us be willing to argue that the identity crisis, the resistance to a prescribed identity coming from the empire, the need to reformulate and voice an identity which is now partly shaped because of the entrance of empire, only comes after the departure of the colonizer? The *after* reference for *postcolonial* more fittingly applies to after the onset of colonization, when the identity conflicts originate and shape the contributing cultural identities for years to come. Texts that emerge after the point of colonization and up to a stabilizing in the construction of identity can contribute much to the voicing of and understanding of the postcolonial condition. It is actually rather amazing that scholars who trace the origins of postcolonial theory to Frantz Fanon and Edward Said would see *post* in any other light. When *The Wretched of the Earth* was published in 1967, to use only one glaring African example, South Africa still lay under the colonial construct of apartheid regardless of the legal independence from the former empire. Palestine continues to struggle with colonization, and Said writes freely about subjection of any culture, including his own, as well as others such as the Irish, for whom the time construct needs negotiation.

Regardless of these realities some scholars have mounted an argument against the notion of *post* with which I hold, but it is time to reevaluate such arguments. McClintock takes issue with associating the *post* with "everything that has happened from the very *beginning* of colonialism" (McClintock 1994, p. 293). She calls to mind what seems to be an unsettling image for her, Henry James and Charles Brockden Brown in conversation with "more regular members" Ngugi wa Thiong'o and Salman Rushdie. McClintock makes a surprising mistake here that seems at odds with her concern that postcolonial scholars too often fail "to denote *multiplicity* . . . [and] run the risk of telescoping crucial geopolitical distinctions into invisibility" (ibid). McClintock avoids oversimplifying the roles of place and governance but falls into the time trap even while struggling, which she admits in her introduction to her essay, to avoid that linear construct as well. The postcolonial dialogue does not and should not sound like a monologue, not with regard to place, nor power structures, nor time. While McClintock's conversational comparison may be unsettling for many good reasons, time should not be one of these. If we are going to take up McClintock's challenge to see the multiple perspectives, hear the multiple voices in the postcolonial dialogue, then we must recognize that the postcolonial voices who are speaking from close to the point of colonization will necessarily sound a different note than those speaking after independence; yet all of these are concerned with a similar problem – how to achieve an identity that is not prescribed by the colonizer. Do we really want, as McClintock suggests, to leave the Northern Irish, the Palestinians, the Native Americans out of the postcolonial dialogue because they are still within the colonial experience? Do they have nothing to contribute, no share in the voicing of the identity struggles that have emerged since the point of colonization? For one who has struggled mightily to get us to recognize that postcolonialism has much more to do with power constructs than linear time, McClintock ironically supports the linear time trap herself.

San Juan rightly recognizes "the failure of national liberation struggles to achieve a complete radical break with the past of shame and invisibility" (San Juan 1998, p. 3), and so does not fall into the linear time trap. Yet he does commit another kind of governance flaw. His commitment to address injustice and inequalities suffered by those under the colonizing efforts of international capitalism is admirable, particularly in his specificity, his attention to the details of places, people, and events. However, what might happen if San Juan would as carefully focus on Marxist states involved in colonization? It seems to me that his commitment to upholding self-determination "for all communities and peoples tyrannized by capital and other irrational forces" (ibid, p. 17) would gain credence if it did not bracket away Marxist regimes. Secondly, there indeed may be grounds for San Juan's criticism of postcolonial discourse as a product of capitalism arising out of "First World" academies, but to insist that academicians working in such institutions must necessarily be suspect seems overly essentialist and somewhat disingenuous when we recall that San Juan earned both of his upper graduate degrees at Harvard and has taught in numerous such academies, as have many historical materialists who challenge the ability of postcolonial critics to work within power structures while calling into question the legacy of empires. If we are to turn our theory into praxis and our critics into agents for social change, then we must cease turning on one another and present a more unified front, create within our field a real solidarity.

Critical Pitfall of Vagueness: Dealing with Critics of Postcolonial Criticism

Russell Jacoby accuses postcolonial theorists of providing "few political insights or conclusions" (Jacoby 1995, p. 36). While I am not willing to reach hard-drawn conclusions that would essentialize the postcolonial condition and postcolonial writing, there are some conclusions I am willing to draw about the nature of our dialogue.

Most postcolonial scholars seem to understand power as the ability to wield control over an other. Even the part of the debate about postcolonialism that defines the *post* as after colonization has begun or after independence gained from the colonizer has to do with who is in power when. For my part, since I believe the postcolonial story is rooted in an identity conflict that begins from the time of colonization, I conclude that the *post* must mean after colonization has begun. Defining *post* in this way broadens the dialogue but in no way weakens it. There is, however, a more important debate raging with regard to power. Some postcolonial theorists see the native in the postcolonial condition as powerless, always being done unto, always being spoken for and never able to speak. Gayatri Spivak has created quite a flurry with her insistence that the subaltern cannot speak. A correlate to this position is the idea that the one who speaks for the subaltern can never speak truthfully. Certainly this concept of power as external and repressive owes much to Michel Foucault. However, if there is more than one kind of power, if power can be an internal state of being, then the postcolonial person may maintain power even under oppression. It is the internal power of being which has helped many an oppressed individual to survive, even to create under such conditions. Kyle Pasewark (1993) provides illumination of this very kind of power. The perceptive postcolonial scholar should recognize that both kinds of power, the external use of power over an other and the internal power of being, are revealed in the postcolonial condition.

In his criticism of postcolonial scholars Jacoby declares "most postcolonial theorists cannot write a sentence" (Jacoby 1995, p. 36). Unfortunately, this piece of criticism is too often warranted. Yes, there are many reasons the postcolonial critic might choose to write in a manner less than clearly understandable. Postcolonial story writers certainly employ such a strategy as part of their subversion of the colonizing language. Coded language indicates that the speaker wants only a select few, those as counted inside the group, to understand what is being said. If there is danger to the speaker, this practice is a commonsense survival technique. However, what danger lurks for the postcolonial critic? Does the critic fear that clarity will open his or her argument up to attack? Jacoby notes that postcolonial scholars particularly like to play the one-upmanship game, and he seems to believe that we are more prone to this than other academics. Perhaps Jacoby needs to join us as we look in the mirror, for academia itself has trained us to the one-up game. For my part, I think academia in general and postcolonial scholarship in particular would benefit from a less aggressive debate style. However, if we are to risk an open dialogue, then we must risk making ourselves understood. If we want our message to reach beyond the select few with whom we group ourselves, then we must remove the code. Clarity does not equate with simplicity; complexity does not equate with obfuscation. And it is at this juncture that I now attempt a clear articulation of what I see as a basis for postcolonial study.

A Flexible Foundation

The flexible foundation I suggest may best be conceived as a shape able to shift but maintaining certain points of intersection. The first point of intersection takes the form of a series of open-ended questions. These questions reveal how the postcolonial condition cuts across boundaries. The three central questions all deal with identity: Who am I? How did I come to be who I am? To whom am I connected? Now these questions are not unique to the postcolonial condition, so while they are the basis of concern they cannot alone set apart postcolonial writing. It is true that many a non-postcolonial text might well deal with such identity issues. However, explorations of these questions permeate postcolonial literature with a ferocity of need and complexity of depth.

The second point of intersection in the postcolonial dialogue is the sociopolitical domination of a native people by an encroaching alien power. This is the level of the postcolonial realm – the context. The postcolonial person who asks the initial identity questions is emerging from a struggle that has established conflicting identities. On the one hand, the historical identity of this individual is linked to the native land and a familial identity; on the other, like it or not, to a state-imposed identity. Eventually those who descend from the colonizers and those who descend from the natives both may consider themselves "native" to the contested space. Note that this two-part historical conflict in identity works to explain the struggle of those who emerge from the native colonized and those who emerge from the buffer colonials (i.e., the two Northern Ireland communities). Certainly Mishra and Hodge (1994) moved toward such a constructional notion with their description of the oppositional and the complicit postcolonial. However, their suggestion that the native is always oppositional and the settler always complicit remains problematic. Within many a postcolonial story we may find the complicit native or the settler who has become so immersed in the native culture that he or she becomes oppositional to the imperial power. The struggle for the individual is to achieve an identity that is his or her story rather than merely history.

The third point of intersection is, of course, the storytelling. This is the portion that rises out of the postcolonial context and depends on the identity questions that are deeply rooted in the contextual land and history. While non-postcolonial scholars may not recognize fully the postcolonial context in which the identity questions are rooted, even these readers will note the form of the storytelling. And here I simply put in my own words what many of my colleagues have already said in other ways. Because of the struggle that always has at least three sides – the native history, the state construct, and the individual – we will hear a story that is layered, made of fragments attempting a whole. The language will often cut in two or more directions, distancing one group and reaching out to another or interrogating all groups in favor of the individual story. To see more clearly, the author will place history under a lens, studying the mutations in earlier tellings. And the new telling will be less about the questionable facts and more about the image experienced. Irony and metaphor, as language that doubles, will be the tools of speaking the conflict itself to a new level of understanding that accommodates the disparate parts.

Testing the Construct

If we recognize that the onset of the postcolonial condition begins after the point of colonization and does not necessarily adhere to constraints of place or race, continent or color, then we are called to look again at the work of some writers we have too easily dismissed. I will test the foundation I have suggested by briefly surveying the struggle with identity as illustrated by four Irish dramatists (a broadening of the usual privileging of the novel) over four generations. For the illustration, I choose 1800, which marked the Act of Union between Ireland and Great Britain, as the point of departure. In 1812 Alicia LeFanu, sister of more widely known Richard Brinsley Sheridan, wrote *Sons of Erin; or, Modern Sentiment*. At this point in the postcolonial experience the Irish were under thorough domination, asked to assimilate to the dominant identity construct yet continually treated as inferiors. LeFanu must move cautiously, raise her voice gently to make her point of equal value. Accordingly, she writes a play in which her Irish protagonist goes to England (reverse invasion of a sort), passes himself off as the most intelligent and worthy man ever encountered by the English nobility with whom he acquaints himself and who wrongly supposes he is English, then reveals his Irishness, stripping the English of their ignorance and prejudice. The conflict is easy to see – an Irishman who can be more English than the English yet is thoroughly and proudly Irish, forced to play the game in order to win realization of his worth. This comedy of manners could easily be overlooked if one does not note the context in

which the text is written as postcolonial, or likewise if one does not understand the necessity of the strategy, masking the message under the guise of
romantic comedy.

I think also of the Irish melodramas of Dion Boucicault written in the 1860s
and 1870s, works scorned by Yeats and other members of the Celtic Revival
as making a mockery of the Irish for the sake of pandering to the English.
However, Boucicault was working on the heels of the famine and various
unsuccessful uprisings, an inflammatory time to say the least. Using the
popular melodrama form, he could deal with murder based on ethnic identity
but turn the tale to his advantage, as he did in his 1860 *The Colleen Bawn*. Dra-
matizing a widely known murder case that had already been fictionalized in
Gerald Griffin's 1829 novel *The Collegians*, Boucicault changes the ending,
allowing the heroine to escape with her life and teach the complicit Anglo-
Irish gentry (and perhaps his English audiences, which included Queen Victoria on four occasions for this play alone) a lesson in identity. Eily, the heroine,
is secretly married to Hardress, the Anglo-Irish gentleman who keeps the marriage secret because of his shame of Eily's thoroughly Irish nature and way of
speaking (both Irish phrases and Irish-english pronunciations). Unbeknownst
to him, his servant-henchman sets out to rid his master of this burden, seemingly killing Eily (who actually survives a drowning). At the end, when all is
revealed and Eily's nobility of spirit is well-established above and beyond any
nobility of birth, her husband's mother and his Anglo-Irish intended fiancée
declare that from now on everyone will speak with Eily's noble tongue. The
irony is apparent in that actually the identity embraced, the Irish ethnicity, is
still being told in the dominant English, but now quite an Irish-english. The
English audiences delighted in the romantic turn to the melodrama, never
noting the message to the Irish audiences, many of whom had immigrated to
England and sat in the same theater. The Irish of Boucicault's time could hardly
fail to note the message, however, especially when he began handing out his
tract, *The Fireside History of Ireland*, prior to performances. Certainly Boucicault
was not engaged in the same project as the Celtic Revivalists, leaping back to
a point in history that precedes English colonization in order to reaffirm Irish
identity, but in his own way he was indeed resisting English control of the
Irish identity.

For those like W. B. Yeats and his colleagues in the Celtic Revival who were
writing in a crucible that contained the end of colonization and the seeds
of independence, rediscovering what Stuart Hall calls "cultural identity" by
looking back to a common history that preceded colonization was a natural
move. Thus, Yeats would write his nation's story in his dramatic recreation of
the life and death of Cuchulain. The character of Cuchulain as dramatized can
be seen to personify the postcolonial moments through which Yeats lived: the
dangerous forming of tribal allegiances and how to yoke might with wisdom
in the battle for Irish unity (1904, pre-independence, *On Baile Strand*), questioning if the hero is dead and if not what sacrifice must be made to bring
Ireland's heroic self back to life (1919, post-failed Easter Uprising and pre-

independence, *The Only Jealousy of Emer*), and seeing the dream of total unity dying (1939, post-independence minus Northern Ireland, *The Death of Cuchulain*). While Yeats and the other Celtic Revival writers revived ancient Irish images to construct their national identity, they were still working with masks, though of a different making from earlier generations.

In the current postcolonial dialogue, when empire-building is no longer glorified but villified, writers are free to take off the masks and practice, again as Hall notes, "the *production* of identity" through "the *retelling* of the past" (Hall 1994, p. 393). In this retelling the writers refuse to give into a nostalgia, matching Spivak's test of how postcolonialists must deal with the archives. Certainly we can see such critical reconstruction in Brian Friel's 1980 *Translations*. Looking back to the British ordnance survey that remapped Ireland, translating Irish place names to anglicized versions, and to the emergence of the national schools in the 1830s that finally allowed for Irish Catholics to be educated but at the price of their language and religion, Friel does not glorify old Irish ways nor totally villify the English soldiers involved in the survey. Instead he shows the impact of this crossroads on the Irish and on at least one of the English soldiers. We recognize the damage done, the difficulty of blending unlike ways of life, and we recognize the irony of voices silenced for too long now given voice in Friel's reconstruction.

At different moments in the struggle for identity among those who have emerged from colonialism, different ways of speaking are necessitated by the power structures and cultural context of their times. Hall rightly recognizes that

> we cannot speak for very long, with any exactness, about "one experience, one identity." . . . Cultural identity . . . is a matter of "becoming" to as well as of "to being." It belongs to the future as much as to the past. It is not something which already exists, transcending place, time, history and culture. Cultural identities come from somewhere, have histories. But, like everything which is historical, they undergo constant transformation. (Hall 1994, p. 394)

Because of the work of J. A. Laponce (1987) I've become increasingly aware of the need to recognize the postcolonial condition as an evolutionary one. While Laponce is a linguist who deals with the strategies of cultural groups whose primary language becomes dominated by another language, the native tongue giving ground to the colonizer's tongue, her recognition that strategies must change from the onset, to completion of domination, to attempted revitalization of the native tongue, should make postcolonialists sit up and take notice. After all, the linguistic shifts in identity with which she is dealing are integrally linked to colonialism and postcolonialism. If the linguistic strategies evolve, then literature that treats the identity shift should reflect a similar evolution. It is this evolution in Irish writing that lies at the heart of my study *Language and Identity in Post-1800 Irish Drama*. I am indebted to Laponce for helping me comprehend that the postcolonial dialogue is of greater range and depth than many of us have been willing to recognize, even while it is engaged in an ongoing thematic struggle.

An Epilogue?

Just as there are some who might prefer a rigidly structured postcolonial space, there may be some who are looking for an answer to what kind of story is emerging from the postcolonial condition, what does the identity look and sound like toward which the postcolonial author speaks. Is there a positive outcome on the other side of postcolonialism? However, just as my notion of the postcolonial dialogue begins with a series of questions, I am more comfortable with a dialogue that "ends" with more open-ended questions than narrowly construed answers. The cure to the conflicted identity probably cannot be a shared one, or we are back to that which is a reflex to empire – entrenched tribalism in the form of nationalism. For the postcolonial to achieve identity that is genuinely new, old tools must not be used for the shaping. So while I cannot guess what shape any given identity will take, I confess that I optimistically hope the direction will be a post-national identity, and then we will be called upon once again to rethink basic structures.

References

Boucicault, Dion. (1987). "The Colleen Bawn." In Andrew Parking (ed.), *The Selected Plays of Dion Boucicault*. Washington, DC: Catholic University of America Press.

Deane, Seamus. (1990) *"Introduction." Nationalism, Colonialism, and Literature*, pp. 3–19. Minneapolis: University of Minnesota Press.

Derrida, Jacques. (1985). *Racism's Last Word*, trans. Peggy Kamuf. *Critical Inquiry*, 12: 290–9.

Duncan, Dawn. (1994). *"Pushing the Post-Colonial Boundaries: Freeing the Irish Voice in Brian Friel's Translations." Working Papers in Irish Studies*, 3: 1–10.

Friel, Brian. (1981). *Translations*. London: Faber.

Hall, Stuart. (1994). *"Cultural Identity and Diaspora."* In Patrick Williams and Laura Chrisman (eds.), *Colonial Discourse and Post-Colonial Theory: A Reader*, pp. 392–403. New York: Columbia University Press.

Jacoby, Russell. (1995). *"Marginal Returns: The Trouble with Post-Colonial Theory." Lingua Franca*, Sept.–Oct.: 30–7.

Kiberd, Declan. (1993). *Multiculturalism: Some Irish and Indian Comparisons*. The Thirty-fourth Yeats International Summer School, Sligo, Ireland.

——(1995). *Inventing Ireland: The Literature of the Modern Nation*. London: Jonathan Cape.

Kissoon, Lynnette M. E-mail to postcolonial@jefferson.village.Virginia.EDU. February 4, 1997.

Laponce, J. A. (1987). *Languages and Their Territories*, trans. Anthony Martin-Sperry. Toronto: University of Toronto Press.

LeFanu, Alicia. (1812). *The Sons of Erin; or, Modern Sentiment*. London: J. Ridgway.

Lloyd, David. (1993). *Anomalous States: Irish Writing and the Post-Colonial Moment*. Durham, NC: Duke University Press.

McClintock, Anne. (1988). *"Maidens, Maps, and Mines: The Reinvention of Patriarchy in Colonial South Africa." South Atlantic Quarterly*, 87: 147–92.

——(1994). *"The Angel of Progress: Pitfalls of the Term 'Post-colonialism'."* In Patrick Williams and Laura Chrisman (eds.), *Colonial Discourse and Post-Colonial Theory: A Reader*, pp. 291–304. New York: Columbia University Press.

Mishra, Vijay and Bob Hodge. (1994). *"What is Post(-)colonialism?"* In Patrick Williams and Laura Chrisman (eds.), *Colonial Discourse and Post-Colonial Theory*, pp. 276–290. New York: Columbia University Press.

Moore-Gilbert, Bart. (1997). *Postcolonial Theory: Contexts, Practices, Politics*. London: Verso.

O'Brien, Eugene. E-mail to postcolonial@jefferson.village.Virginia.EDU. February 4, 1997.

Pasewark, Kyle A. (1993). *A Theology of Power: Being Beyond Domination*. Minneapolis: Fortress Press.

Said, Edward. (1993). *Culture and Imperialism*. New York: Vintage.

San Juan, Jr., E. (1998). *Beyond Postcolonial Theory*. New York: St. Martin's Press.

Tiffin, Helen. (1988). *"Post-Colonialism, Post-Modernism and the Rehabilitation of Post-Colonial History." Journal of Commonwealth Literature*, 23: 169–81.

Yeats, W. B. (1973). *The Collected Plays of W. B. Yeats*. New York: MacMillan.

Chapter 18

Linguistics and Postcolonial Literature: Englishes in the Classroom

Laura Wright and Jonathan Hope

The core of this chapter is a method for addressing the language of post-colonial texts in seminars. We have used this technique with students with no linguistic training, and have found that it not only facilitates discussion of linguistic issues, but encourages and supports students who are otherwise shy in seminars, and positively advantages students from non-standard backgrounds because of the emphasis it places on linguistic experience. In illustrating how this technique works via a sample lesson plan, the chapter also discusses the place of language within postcolonial studies, with specific reference to Indian English.

The politicization of language within postcolonial literature has made language a central issue for many writers and critics – but this debate has tended to focus on political/power issues rather than linguistic ones, treating languages as discrete entities (for example, 'English' versus 'Yoruba') and often assuming that languages which are used to transmit cultures also somehow endorse and embody the values of the culture(s) they transmit (so 'English' is seen as inherently colonialist).[1] Linguists, however, would reject each of these notions: a term such as 'English' is a very vague label which is used to cover a large number of spoken and written dialects, not all of which are mutually intelligible. Speakers and writers of these dialects naturally mix and switch between dialects of English and any dialects of other languages they know. Linguists such as Braj Kachru have developed the notion of 'Englishes' as a way of acknowledging that 'languages' (which we like to pretend are concrete objects which can be fixed and defined in dictionaries and grammars) are in fact behavioural continua, continually merging in and out of each other.[2]

Linguists would also reject the notion that languages either determine, or inevitably reproduce, the values of the cultures which use them. This is not to

deny that languages carry and disseminate cultural values, but it is a basic
principle of modern linguistics that despite their apparently great differences,
all languages share the same basic linguistic structure and operate on the
same set of fundamental rules – and that, potentially at least, any language
can be used to do any linguistic job.[3] The association of many modern
European languages with colonialism is a historical accident: there is
nothing about the linguistic structure of those languages that predisposed
Europeans to exploit and oppress other peoples, just as today there is nothing
inherently democratic, or liberal, in the structure of English, despite Edward
Said's bafflement when he found Iranian students learning English in 'a
seething cauldron of Islamic revivalism'.[4] The connotations and associations,
and usefulness, of English (or any language) are not predetermined but can
be changed by its users, as the Asian Women Writers' Collective in London
point out:

> Given the wider interpretation of Asianness with its attendant rise in the number
> of linguistic backgrounds, and the increasing number of monolingual women in
> the group, English assumed a centrality in our proceedings, which further mili-
> tated against our attempts to work in the mother tongues. English may have been
> the colonizer's language and a mark of privilege and class in our home countries
> but here it also enabled us to break out of our regional identities and make
> common cause with other black communities and, for that matter, the different
> cultures that inhabited the term 'Asian'. (Rukhsana Ahmad and Rahila Gupta,
> eds, *Flaming Spirit: stories from the Asian Women Writers' Collective*, p. xiii (London:
> Virago, 1994)

Moving away from the notion of languages as discrete objects and accepting
the linguistic model of the *dialect continuum* allows us to be more sensitive to
the stylistic choices made by authors when they produce texts. Multilingual or
multi-dialectal postcolonial writers have several grammars available to them
(corresponding to different dialects, registers, and substrate languages) and
from these they make choices. These choices can be seen as movements up
and down a linguistic continuum characterizing the extent of mingling of languages and dialects.

Standard English can be defined as English which is not geographically localizable. For historical reasons there is a tendency to identify Standard English
with Britain (or in some areas, the USA), but linguists today would characterize Standard English as a common core of syntactic and lexical features
which are shared by all formal varieties of English around the world. In any
of the centres of English the local standard will show some lexical and/or
orthographic peculiarities, and a very few syntactic ones,[5] so Standard English
can be distinguished from Standard American English, and Standard Indian
English – these are all examples of *World Englishes*. Borrowing occurs when
words from one language appear in a text otherwise written in another language. The donor language is termed the *substrate*. Borrowing may involve just
a few words in a whole novel or short story: as the number of substrate words

increases, borrowing merges into *codeswitching*. Full codeswitching involves alternate passages of two or more languages, but borrowing and codeswitching cannot be precisely separated. Borrowing and codeswitching involve the use of the substrate language in discrete, easily recognizable units; however, it is also common for writers to employ *substrate influence* where, for example, the words of the text might come from English, but they are arranged according to grammatical rules which show the influence of the substrate language or dialect.

Borrowing, codeswitching, and substrate influence allow writers a considerable degree of choice in constructing texts, and in the way they present their characters and narrators. Once students have some basic information about linguistic context and possible features, the analysis of the language can produce some highly sophisticated close readings of texts. Thus a Ghanaian author may choose to write in, say, Ewe, or Standard English, or in a kind of English that is accepted as normal in Accra, but not in the UK or USA, or in a mixed form, with Ewe words sprinkled throughout the English or in an English modelled on some aspect of Ewe, such as its grammatical system or its pragmatic constraints on story-telling, or, conversely, in Ewe with interference from English. Or, more likely, in a mixture of some or all of the above. For this reason, it is useful to be able to distinguish positions on the dialect continuum (though of course the very point about representing this linguistic behaviour as a continuum is that the positions are not discrete).

Figure 18.1   The linguistic continuum

Demonstration of the Linguistic Approach to Postcolonial Literary Analysis

To demonstrate our linguistic approach to teaching postcolonial literature, we present a lesson as we would present it to students. We take as our theme Indian English and Indian English literature. The teaching point is to introduce some facts and figures about Indian English (how it is a continuum rather than a single entity, how it is used in India) and to demonstrate some linguistic characteristics of Indian English. As with any multilingual society it is important to stress the everyday normality of codeswitching between languages. We then present two texts, both written by Indian authors in English. The students are asked to apply what they have learnt about Indian English, and to draw any literary conclusions.

The structure of teaching sessions

Each teaching session follows this pattern:

- The students are divided into groups of four, with each student having a copy of the texts for analysis (sometimes it is useful to restrict this to one text between two students to encourage discussion); each group nominates a spokesperson.
- The seminar leader reads the passages.
- The seminar leader covers any technical material, and poses some specific questions for discussion (sections 1 and 2 below).
- The seminar leader leaves the room for about 25 minutes.
- The students analyse and discuss the passages in groups: the absence of the seminar leader means that students cannot ask questions, and must work things out for themselves by discussion – this puts students from non-standard linguistic backgrounds at an advantage, since they will tend to have more experience on which to draw; it also means that student discussion is not inhibited by the thought that the seminar leader is over-hearing and being silently critical – this encourages reticent students to contribute, since the use of a spokesperson means that they do not have to speak in front of the whole group if they do not wish to. We have also found that repeating this format over a number of weeks encourages less-confident students to take part, as it provides them with a familiar and reas-suring structure in the classroom.
- The seminar leader returns, and each spokesperson summarizes. The seminar leader notes points for discussion (interesting insights, incorrect statements), and after the final discussion, ends with a summary.

Although this structure may seem prescriptive to some, we have found that it provides students with a reassuringly familiar context, and produces some very good work. The technique works better the more varied the linguistic backgrounds of the students are.

1 Linguistic features of Indian English[6]

India is a multilingual country: nearly 800 million people speak over 1,652 mother tongues,[7] 67 of which are designated media of education, and 15 of which are provided for in the Indian constitution. Codeswitching between two or more languages is a normal part of daily verbal intercourse. The official language in India is Hindi, spoken by over a third of the population, but it is not spoken over the entirety of the country; that is, many Indians have to learn it as a second language.[8] English is designated the 'associate official language' of India, and has been spoken in India as part of the colonial legacy for hundreds of years. The non-Hindi-speaking parts of India (especially the South) use

English in preference to Hindi, because use of Hindi puts them at a disadvantage, whereas use of English puts everyone on an equal footing as everyone has to learn it. English is the main language of administration, higher education, commerce and the law, and so its use carries prestige and power. It has been estimated that less than 3 per cent of the entire population (over 23 million) speak English at varying levels of proficiency. However, these speakers represent the most powerful section of Indian society, so speaking English is a class issue in India.

Standard Indian English can be defined as the sort of English spoken by educated Indians, as these are the speakers who disseminate the dialect through the various media: journalism, education, technology, literature, and of course in everyday speech. English-language newspapers and magazines are published in all of the Indian states, unlike Hindi journalism, which is limited to the Hindi-reading areas. Nonetheless, there is little consciousness on a personal level that what Indians are speaking is a New English caged as Indian English, as this, they feel, would imply that they are speaking 'incorrect' English (although there is evidence that this attitude may be changing). From a linguist's point of view Indian English is an interesting group of varieties in its own right, with unique and identifiable features not found in either English or the substrate languages. A few of these characteristics occur in the texts given below, and are contrasted with Standard English:

1   The distinction between the present continuous (you may know it as the present progressive) and the simple present tense is often not made. In the sentence "You see how they are setting fire to football stadium in Calcutta every year?" British and American Standard English would use a simple present tense, 'they set (fire)'. Standard English uses the simple aspect for universal statements, which are not bound by time (this is known as the 'habitual' present); the implication is that they set fire to the stadium last year, this year, and will do so next year *ad infinitum*.

2   Similarly, Indian English uses the continuous present where Standard English uses the simple present tense for 'stative' verbs. This means that verbs which convey states (like the verb *to be*) or states of mind (like the verbs *to remember, to want, to think*) do not take the continuous present in Standard English. An example from Indian English is 'when they are speaking English no one is understanding', where the verb to understand is stative.

3   The distinction between the definite and indefinite article is not always made, nor is any article necessarily present where it would be required in Standard English. The sentence given in (1) if spoken in Standard English would require an article, '*the* football stadium', to designate the specific, single stadium in Calcutta. Similarly with the indefinite article, 'a'. In the sentence 'All I am wanting is good Madrasi tenant' Standard English requires an article, 'a good Madrasi tenant', to designate any, non-specific tenant (who happens to be good and from Madras).

4   In forming Wh-questions (which? where? when? why? who? how?) Indian English does not invert the subject and the auxiliary verb, and does

not always use an auxiliary verb at all. Thus to turn the statement 'it matters' into a question, Standard English uses the auxiliary verb *do*: 'Does it matter?', where the subject *it* follows the finite verb *does* ('finite' means 'marked for person, number and tense: contrast *I do, it does, we did*'). But in the Indian English sentence 'How it matters what English they are speaking?' *do* is not used, and the subject precedes the verb, as in statements (compare the Shakespearean form, 'how matters it?', where sixteenth-century English did invert the subject and verb, but, like Indian English, did not use an auxiliary).

5   Lack of copula: this merely means that Indian English is apt to lack the 'linking' verb *to be* where it is found in Standard English. In the Indian English sentence 'Bengali boys, nice as long as their temper not disturbed', Standard English would probably insert *are* before *nice* and would certainly insert *is* before *not*.

6   Prepositions: Indian English does not use prepositions in quite the same way as Standard English (all dialects of English show variation with regard to prepositions, including, to a limited extent, Standard English itself). In the Indian English sentence 'The electricity went off and the conversation petered off,' a Standard English speaker would be more inclined to use the phrasal verb 'petered out'.

7   Specifically Indian English coinages: in the Indian English sentence 'In every school and college Madrasi topping', the present participle 'topping' means 'top of the class'. There is no corresponding usage like this in Standard English.

8   Mixed registers: Standard English has a set of words that are used in one circumstance, and another set used in another – think of the words a doctor would use to describe an illness, the words you might use to another adult, and the words you might use to a child. Parents do not say, 'your abdominal region hurts because you have an inflamed intestine' but 'you have a tummy-ache'. Indian English is more apt to mix registers, so the Indian English sentences 'We Punjabis are not taking nonsense from anybody, Srivastavaji. And that is proving great problem for landlords' are unlikely to be heard in Standard English. The verb phrase '(not) to take any nonsense (from someone)' has a 'schoolmistressy' tone about it, whereas the context is the adult domain of paying rent.

2 Task: linguistic and literary analysis of texts

Here follow extracts from the work of two Indian writers, Kamala Markandaya and Anjana Appachana, Text (1) is the opening passage from Appachana's short story 'When Anklets Tinkle'. It depicts some North Indian men discussing the supposed qualities of men from Madras – or, as the glossary makes clear, men who come from nowhere near Madras but are nevertheless labelled 'Madrasis' by the Northerners. Text (2) is the opening passage, set in a drinks party in Madras, of Markandaya's novel *Possession*. The narrator, we can infer, is an Indian woman – this is borne out by reading the rest of the novel. She meets, talks to, and reflects upon an aristocratic Englishwoman. Both texts deal with issues of race, Text (1) by means of male characters, Text (2) by means of female characters. Text (2) is explicit about issues of class, in Text (1) the subject of class is rather more implicit. Can you identify any features of Indian English in either text? If so, why do you think the author chose to include them? If not, why do you think the author chose to ignore Indian English – what is gained by this choice? You may find it interesting to contrast the types of language used by the narrators and characters in the passages.

Text (1) Anjana Appachana, 'When Anklets Tinkle', from *Incantations and Other Stories*, London: Virago, 1991, pp. 65–7; previously published in *Namaste* and *The Webster Review*.

Mr Aggarwal chuckled. 'Madrasis, they are speaking such badly pronouncing English.'

'Yes,' Mr Singh guffawed. 'These Yannas, they are saying yex for x, yam for am . . . when they are speaking English, no one is understanding.' 'How it matters what English they are speaking?' Mr Srivastava groaned. 'All I am wanting is good Madrasi tenant for my barsati and only tenants I am getting are from north.'

The three men were relaxing in the Srivastavas' house on a hot summer day, drinking nimbupani and commiserating over the fact that the Srivastavas' barsati was still unoccupied, three months after he had bought the house. South Indian tenants seemed to have vanished, sucked into the summer loo. The Srivastavas had specially advertised their barsati on the weekend, specifying that it was available for a nice, simple, decent Madrasi boy. But no South Indians were forthcoming. Instead, Punjabi boys, UP boys, boys from MP, Bihar and Bengal arrived at his doorstep and were turned away.

'It is the irony of fate,' Mr Srivastava moaned. 'Punjabi tenant is never vacating any house, is always demanding and fighting and not agreeing to rent being raised.'

Mr Singh nodded sympathetically. 'I myself being Punjabi am seeing this. We Punjabis are not taking nonsense from anybody, Srivastavaji. And that is proving great problem for landlords.'

'As for Biharis,' Mr Srivastava sighed, 'they are lazy buggers. Not even having energy to write out cheque for rent.'

'And Banias,' roared Mr Aggarwal slapping his thigh, 'they are always being stingy.'

'What about Bengali?' Mr Singh asked. 'Bengali boys very nice, very quiet.'

Mr Srivastava shuddered and folded his hands. 'Bengali boys, nice as long as their temper not disturbed. Once these Bengalis get angry, they are setting fire to first thing they see. Always they carry matches for such times. I am not wanting to get on wrong side of Bengali. You see how they are setting fire to football stadium in Calcutta every year? That is why stadium is made of wood. One year one side loses and setting fire to it, and next year other side loses and setting fire to it. Thank you, Singhji, no Bengali tenant.'

'Bengalis having culture,' Mr Singh said wistfully.

'I am not wanting culture,' Mr Srivastava said firmly. 'I am wanting down to earth, simple, decent man who pays rent every month and goes when I say go.'

'Madrasi.'

'Yes, Madrasi.'

Mr Aggarwal began to chuckle again. 'Oh these Madrasis are speaking such comical English. Murdering English language. Still, they are most decent tenants. If you raise rent, they are paying; if you are telling them go, they go. Good people, Madrasis.'

'Very intelligent,' Mr Singh added. 'In every school and college Madrasi topping.'

'Very sharp,' agreed Mr Aggarwal. 'Though they are speaking comical English, they are writing top quality English. Now we, we are speaking good English but writing is not so good.'

The electricity went off and the conversation petered off. Soon Mr Aggarwal and Mr Singh took leave of Mr Srivastava, assuring him that they would do all they could to find him a Madrasi tenant.

In the kitchen, Mrs Srivastava sighed, tied her jooda into a tighter knot, dug the hairpin in and felt the sweat trickle down her back and neck as she stirred the kadhi. God knew how long the power cut would last. She had listened to every word of the conversation between her husband and his friends. All talk, she thought. All these men could do was talk. Three months and still no tenant. Her husband had retired a year ago and they had bought this house with their precious savings and a huge loan. Where were they to get the money to pay off the loan without a tenant? And all he did was talk . . . expound on South Indians and Bengalis and God knows who else. When did she get to retire? Was there ever any retirement from cooking and cleaning?

Glossary

Madrasi: a condescending and misguided term for all South Indians, used by most North Indians. *Yannas:* a derogatory term used for South Indians by many North Indians. *barsati:* a one- or two-roomed apartment at the top of the main house. *nimhupani:* a sweetened lime drink. *UP:* the state of Uttar Pradesh. *MP:* the state of Madhya Pradesh. *loo:* this word is not mentioned in the glossary; it means a sweltering, debilitating kind of summer heat in Gujarati and Urdu. *-ji:* a term of respect. *jooda:* hair tied in a bun. *kadhi:* a dish made of curd.

Text (2) Kamala Markandaya, *Possession*, Bombay: Jaico Publishing House, 1967, pp. 1–3.

I first met Caroline Bell at a party in Madras given by an old friend of mine, an ex-ruler of one of the smaller states of India who now cheerfully eked out his existence on parties and a pension of seventy-five thousand rupees a year.

She was the first person I saw as I entered the room, partly because she was magnolia-white and stood out in a company that was divided between brown and brick-red, partly because of the attention she was already attracting with her English good looks which, a rarity in India, passed here for a transcendent love-liness. But perhaps she was beautiful in her own right as well.

She was one of the few women in evening dress: a full-skirted gown of some sort of cloudy material in a dark grey that was almost the colour of her eyes, against which her skin was a dazzling white; and spun-silk hair, between silver and pale gold, hung down to her bare shoulders. In one hand she held a fruit-cocktail, from which now and then she selected, with great care like a child, the bits she liked best to pop into her mouth – daring behaviour which delighted the crowd by which, needless to say, she was surrounded.

I wondered who she was, feeling that I would quite like to meet her, though without any great urgency, in the vague way one woman feels about another, and thinking that probably I wouldn't because of the crush about her. A little later, however, I saw her looking at me, and then, even more to my surprise, she slid off the bar-stool on which she had been elegantly perched, brushed off her admirers with great competence, crossed the floor – hardly noticing the dancing couples in her way – and came straight up to me.

"I hear you've written a book about a village," she said. "I'd like you to take me there sometime."

She spoke directly, with that clear forthrightness just this side of insolence which the English upper middle-class use in speaking to anyone who is not English upper middle-class, and which would be insolence but for their serene unconsciousness of it. It is not always endearing.

"Surely it isn't necessary," I said, "for me to take you. Anyone can go. It is merely a question of buying a ticket and getting on a train."

She stared at me in pure puzzlement, as hard to offend as (in all fairness) to realize she was offending.

"But of course," she said. "Of course you could do that. But you'd never get to know the right people that way would you?"

It took my breath away. Who on earth were the 'right' people in a peasant village whom one ought to get to know, and what could this English milady's interest in them possibly be?

"An Indian village isn't like an English one," I said carefully. "I've no idea who the right people might be."

"I'm sure you have," she interrupted me. "The people who make arak. It is made in the villages isn't it? Or is that another piece of wrong information?"

I understood now. Madras was dry, held fast in the puritan grip of Prohibition. But the grip could be relaxed: the law was not barbarous, it took heed of foreign essentials for living and made due provision. Perhaps she didn't know, although this was usually the first point on which Europeans sought enlightenment.

"Your information is quite correct," I said. "But there is no need to brave an Indian village. You can get your liquor easily enough here in town, after a few formalities."

"Oh that farce, yes," she said impatiently. "I know all about that. I'm not interested. I can get all the liquor I want any day. It's the arak that's unique."

Just then our host bustled up, beaming, thoroughly and rather endearingly enjoying his own party although god knows there must have been thousands like it before, with a spate of saucy, witty small talk, and belated introductions.

Lady Caroline Bell. So that was who it was. I had heard about her a dozen times in the week I had been in Madras. She was rich, divorced, wellborn, said fashionable Indian society, concentrating upon essentials: really rich, in the English way, with landed estates and money in sterling; really well-born, descended from a long line of men who had ruled India in the days of the British Raj, not loosely linked to a little-known lord by marriage to an umpteenth cousin – which was the more usual cause for awe in India; and very boldly and publicly

divorced, with headlines in the papers. She had also been reputed to be beautiful, though no great stress had been laid upon this as far as I could recall, probably because even her astonishing good looks lost impact compared to her other
spectacular qualities.

And this darling of the gods, blessed by fairy god-mothers, wanted of all things
arak. Well, I suppose if you've got most of the things anyone could possibly want,
you've got to roam farther and farther, like an animal in search of the salt-lick
that gives savour to living.

But to me arak wasn't exotic. It was a cheap, crude liquor, made without any
refinements whatever by the poor for consumption by the poor, and I had seen
it bring so much wretchedness to human beings that I had come to think of it as
evil in itself, which of course it was not. I certainly was not going to encourage
its manufacture. I was about to say as much when I realized that we weren't
alone: our host was still there, bubbling genially away. I shut my mouth and
waited, and then Caroline said in that clear, high voice of hers:

"Jumbo, be an angel and run away will you? There's something we want to
discuss."

Discussion

The following discussion covers some of the points we have noticed about
these texts, and illustrates the kind of insights students can be expected to have
when approaching texts from a linguistic point of view. We have chosen to
focus on narratorial voice here.

There is clearly a linguistic difference between the ways in which our two
authors have chosen to present the themes of race and class. Appachana uses
Indian English, while Markandaya uses Standard English. Appachana's text is,
from the first line, funny – the humour arises out of the mismatch between
the racist opinions of the men and the strongly marked Indian English in which
they deliver them Mr Aggarwal's 'Madrasis, they are speaking only such badly
pronouncing English', and 'Oh these Madrasis are speaking such comical
English. Murdering English language' demonstrate his obliviousness to the distinction made in Standard English between the simple and continuous present
tense. By contrast, Markandaya not only uses Standard English (with only the
words 'rupees' and 'arak' from Indian Languages), but what strikes us as a
highly formal, literary register of Standard English. Both writers, however, use
the dialect continuum offered by English to differentiate between their characters and their narrators, and to make points about race and class – which
we will now investigate in more detail.

Appachana uses an omniscient narrator, whose English is clearly further
along the continuum towards Standard English than that of the men in the
passage. The narratorial voice still shows some elements of Indian English
though: borrowing vocabulary items like 'nimbupani', 'barsati' and 'loo', and
abbreviations such as 'UP' and 'MP', which seem to assume a familiarity with
Indian English on the part of the reader. Compared to the speech of the men,

the narrator's voice shows little substrate syntactic influence from Indian English, though it might be argued that for some users of Standard English the phrases 'on the weekend' (for 'at the weekend') and 'petered off (for 'petered out') illustrate an unexpected use of prepositions.

There seems to us to be a correlation in the passage between degree of standardization of voice and implied approval of views. The racist opinions of the men as to which type of person speaks or writes the 'best' English, ironically expressed in strongly marked Indian English, are distanced from the voice of the narrator:

'Though they are speaking comical English, they are writing top quality English. Now we, we are speaking good English but writing is not so good.' The electricity went off and the conversation petered off. Soon Mr Aggarwal and Mr Singh took leave of Mr Srivastava, assuring him that they would do all they could to find him a Madrasi tenant.

The point of view of Mrs Srivastava, significantly expressed not through direct speech but in free indirect style via the voice of the narrator, is presented in highly standardized English (again with only lexical evidence of Indian languages: 'jooda' and 'kadhi'):

In the kitchen, Mrs Srivastava sighed, tied her jooda into a tighter knot, dug the hairpin in and felt the sweat trickle down her back and neck as she stirred the kadhi. God knew how long the power cut would last. She had listened to every word of the conversation between her husband and his friends. All talk, she thought. All these men could do was talk. Three months and still no tenant. Her husband had retired a year ago and they had bought this house with their precious savings and a huge loan. Where were they to get the money to pay off the loan without a tenant? And all he did was talk . . . expound on South Indians and Bengalis and God knows who else. When did she get to retire? Was there ever any retirement from cooking and cleaning?

Appachana here uses the resources of the Indian English dialect continuum to influence the degree of identification between the reader and her characters, and to imply approval or disapproval of them. We are all strongly conditioned to value more standardized speech and writing over less standardized language, and Appachana makes use of this: the naratorial voice is given authority by its relatively high degree of standardization, and Mrs Srivastava's voice is associated with it.

An important point to stress here is that 'Standard English' is English which is not geographically localizable. As we said above, Standard English is a common core of syntactic and lexical features which are shared by all formal varieties of English around the world. It would be simplistic, and Anglocentric, to assume that increased standardization in Appachana's narrator implied a shift towards the cultural norms associated with England – all developed national Englishes show a continuum of styles which writers and speakers can exploit.

Markandaya's use of the continuum of English, and narratorial voice, is perhaps even more subtle. On first reading, it might have seemed perverse of us to have chosen this text in a piece ostensibly 'about' Indian English, since the text contains only one unfamiliar word: 'arak' (as well as the more familiar 'rupees'). This, however, is to make the mistake of assuming that standardized versions of English cannot be the 'authentic' voice of postcolonial writers. As we have stated, the linguistic definition of standard languages is that they are not restricted to one geographical location or cultural context. Standard English is an artificial dialect of English, only found in the written form, and equally the property of anyone who learns it, whatever their cultural background. Markandaya's text illustrates this apparent paradox: her narrator is an Indian woman who demonstrates a facility with the highly subordinated sentence patterns of formal, literary, standard English. The subject of the passage, Lady Caroline Bell, ostensibly the representative of the prestige 'English' culture, and with whom we might be tempted to identify 'Standard English', is in fact presented as the speaker of a restricted and communicatively dysfunctional dialect. The narrator's paragraphs develop elegantly, with introductory simple clauses steadily developed by subordination:

> I first met Caroline Bell at a party in Madras given by an old friend of mine, an ex-ruler of one of the smaller states of India who now cheerfully eked out his existence on parties and a pension of seventy-five thousand rupees a year.

Here, the simple opening clause ('I first met Caroline Bell at a party in Madras') is expanded, first by a subordinate non-finite relative clause giving more information about the party ('given by an old friend of mine'), then by two structures giving more information about the 'old friend' – a noun phrase in apposition ('an ex-ruler of one of the smaller states of India') and a finite relative clause ('who now cheerfully eked out his existence on parties and a pension of seventy-five thousand rupees a year'). The effect is one of controlled formality – we subconsciously recognize multiple subordinate structures like this as a feature of highly literate English.[9]

This impressive formality contrasts with the abrupt voice of Lady Caroline:

> "I hear you've written a book about a village," she said. "I'd like you to take me there sometime . . .
>   "But of course," she said. "Of course you could do that. But you'd never get to know the right people that way would you?" . . .
>   "I'm sure you have," she interrupted me. "The people who make arak. It is made in the villages isn't it? Or is that another piece of wrong information?"

Lady Caroline doubtless knows the rules of Standard English grammar, but it is clear that she has a very different set of discourse strategies from those assumed by the narrator to belong to the reader:

> She spoke directly, with that clear forthrightness just this side of insolence which the English upper middle-class use in speaking to anyone who is not English

upper middle-class, and which would be insolence but for their serene unconsciousness of it. It is not always endearing.

Lady Caroline's use of blunt statements and questions, without any of the
politeness markers most English speakers use (for example: 'If it wouldn't be
too much trouble I wonder if it would be possible for you to take me
there sometime . . .'), clashes with the narrator's syntax, as well as her expectations. Markandaya thus manages to make Lady Caroline into an exotic
'other' via language, much as her opening paragraph does via colour ('She was
the first person I saw as I entered the room, partly because she was magnolia-white and stood out in a company that was divided between brown
and brick-red'). By using the linguistic continuum, and occupying the space
of Standard English, Markandaya marks off upper middle-class English as
a restricted sociolect (that is, the dialect spoken by a single class), and establishes an identification between her narrator and her reader in opposition to
Lady Caroline, irrespective of the racial, linguistic or social affiliations of the
reader.

Conclusion and Summary

Language has been a focus for study in postcolonial criticism for some
time. In this chapter we have argued for an approach to language informed
by linguistic descriptions of the languages of the postcolonial territories. In
tandem with this we have set out, in some practical detail, a linguistics-based
method for dealing with postcolonial texts in the classroom, As we stated
above, there are pedagogic reasons for adopting this method: focusing on the
linguistic detail of postcolonial texts ensures active participation in seminars
from the beginning of a course, provides a reassuring structure for less confident students, and positively advantages students from non-standard backgrounds, as they tend to have a more varied linguistic experience on which to
draw.

The major theoretical claim we make here is that previous work has often
made too close an association between Standard English and the colonizing
'centre'. In *The Empire Writes Back* Ashcroft, Griffiths and Tiffin try to set up a
distinction between what they term the 'English' of 'the centre' (=Standard
English) and the 'englishes' of 'the peripheries' (=varieties of World Englishes).
As we have tried to show, such a binary characterization of language does not
conform to the linguistic facts: it explicitly denies Standard English to 'the
peripheries' and implicitly ignores the variation which occurs in English at 'the
centre'. It ignores the grammatical, lexical, pragmatic and semantic relationship between the substrate languages and English at 'the peripheries', and presents English at 'the centre' as though it were spoken in isolation. It is not:
London's 850,000 schoolchildren currently speak 307 different languages from
Abe to Zulu, with more than a third of children speaking a language other

than English as their first.[10] In this chapter we seek to avoid the problems of such a binary model of language, firstly by stressing the lack of any necessary geographical identification for Standard English, and secondly by characterizing the relationship of Standard English with other Englishes, and indeed other languages, as a continuous, rather than an antagonistic one.

Notes

1   The classic texts in this postcolonial approach to language are Ngugi Wa Thiong'o (1986), *Decolonising the Mind: The Politics of Language in African Literature* (James Currey/Heinemann) and Chinua Achebe, 'The African writer and the English language' (1975), in *Morning Yet on Creation Day* (Doubleday). Ngugi's rejection of English (a political stance, rather than a piece of linguistic analysis) has since been tempered by the realization that postcolonial writers can use World Englishes to subvert colonialist discourse – and there is a growing literature which foregrounds a linguistic approach to language in postcolonial writing (for example: Chantal Zabus (1991), *The African Palimpsest: The Indigenization of Language in the West African Europhone Novel*, Amsterdam: Rodopi). But the deterministic view of the colonial languages, which metaphors them into handy monsters, is too attractive to be completely abandoned: it lurks in the background, a return of the repressor, in Homi Bhabha's (1984) analysis of the foreignness of language, *The Location of Culture* (Routledge), pages 164–9).

2   See, for example, Braj B. Kachru (1996), 'Teaching World Englishes' in Braj B. Kachru (ed.), *The Other Tongue: English Across Cultures* (University of Illinois Press), pp. 355–65, and Braj B. Kachru (1992), 'The second diaspora of English' in Tim W. McMahon and Charles T. Scott (eds), *English in its Social Contexts* (Oxford University Press).

3   This is still a highly controversial area in terms of its detail, but few, if any, linguists today accept the extreme forms of linguistic determinism associated with popular conceptions of the 'Sapir–Whorf hypothesis', which are, nonetheless, often implicit or explicit in literary-theoretical accounts of language. Larry Trask gives an accessible introduction to the field in *Language: The Basics* (Routledge, 1995), pages 60–7. More technical are: Jane I-Ell (1988), 'Language, culture, and world-view', in Frederick J. Newmeyer (ed.), *Linguistics: The Cambridge Survey, Volume IV: Language: The Socio-cultural Context* (Cambridge), pages 14–36; Penny Lee (1994), 'New work on the linguistic relativity question', *Historiographia Linguistica*, 20/1; Penny Lee (1996), ne Whorf neory Complex: a critical reconstruction (John Benjamins). The title essay in Geoffey K. Pullum (1991), *The Great Eskimo Vocabulary Hoax and Other Irreverent Essays on the Study of Language* (Chicago University Press), is also relevant.

4   Said recounts the following in *Culture and Imperialism* (Chatto and Windus, 1993): 'Asked in 1985 by a national university in one of the Persian Gulf States to visit there for a week, I found that my mission was to evaluate its English programme . . . I learned two facts that interested me as a secular intellectual and critic. The reason for the large numbers of students taking English was given frankly by a somewhat disaffected instructor: many of the students proposed to end up working for airlines, or banks, in which English was the worldwide *lingua franca*. . . . The

other thing I discovered, to my alarm, was that English such as it was existed in what seemed to be a seething cauldron of Islamic revivalism. . . . Thus using the very same English of people who aspire to literary accomplishments of a very high order, who allow a critical use of the language to permit a decolonizing of the mind, as Ngugi Wa Thiong'o puts it, coexists with very new communities in a less appealing new configuration' (pp. 368–70). Said objects to the learning of English for 'merely, instrumental purposes (to use in a well-paid job, for example) because, he implies, proper learning of English would also involve the learning of cultural values which would challenge those of Islamic revivalism. Aijaz Ahmad makes a similar point in greater detail in *In Theory* (Verso: 1992), pages 211–15: we were not aware of Ahmad's work until after this chapter had been completed.

5   In fact, English varies syntactically far more within the British Isles than it does globally.

6   The information about Indian English given here is taken from René Appel and Pieter Muysken (1987), *Language Contact and Bilingualism* (Arnold), p. 46; Thiru Kandiah (1991), 'South Asia', in Jenny Cheshire (ed.), *English Around the Word: Sociolinguistic Perspectives* (Cambridge University Press), pp. 271–87; David Crystal (1995), *The Cambridge Encyclopaedia of the English Language* (Cambridge University Press), p. 360; Stephan Gramley and Kurt-Michael Patzold (1992), *A Survey of Modern English* (Routledge), chapter 15, 'English in Asia', pp. 438–40; R. B. Le Page and André Tabouret-Keller (1985), *Acts of Identity: Creole-based Approaches to Language and Ethnicity* (Cambridge University Press), p. 239; Anju Sahgal (1991), 'Patterns of language use in a bilingual setting in India', in Jenny Cheshire (ed.), *English Around the Word: Sociolinguistic Perspectives* (Cambridge University Press), pp. 299–307; R. N. Srivastava and V. P. Sharma (1995), 'Indian English today', in R. S. Gupta and Kapil Kapoor (eds), *English in India: Issues and Problems* (Delhi: Academic Foundation), pp. 189–206. Aijaz Ahmad covers the Indian linguistic and literary context in chapter 7 of *In Theory* (Verso, 1992).

7   This figure comes from Srivastava and Sharma, 'Indian English today', p. 189; Appel and Muysken, *Language Contact*, p. 46, give the conservative figure of 'at least 800', but they explain that 'it would be much higher if many dialects are considered not as varieties of the same language, but as separate languages.'

8   Nor is Hindi the same all over India; see Le Page and Tabouret-Keller, *Acts of Identity*, (p. 239) for references to the Punjabi ex-population of Pakistan who fled to India on partition, and then referred to their language as 'Punjabi' if they were Sikh, and 'Hindi' if they were Hindu, even though they were referring to the same language. These Hindus settled in Delhi, and the concept of Delhi Hindi has been expanded to encompass the new variety.

9   For demonstrations and definitions of the terms used here see Laura Wright and Jonathan Hope (1996), *Stylistics: A Practical Coursebook* (Routledge); alternatively, any grammar of English will explain phrases and clauses.

10 Bill Ashcroft, Gareth Griffiths and Helen Tiffin (1989), *The Empire Writes Back: Theory and Practice in Post-colonial Literatures* (Routledge), pp. 7–8, 38–77. Our figures for the linguistic context in London's schools come from Philip Baker and John Eversley (2000), *Multilingual Capital: The Languages of London's Schoolchildren and their Relevance to Economic, Social and Educational Policies* (Battlebridge Publications).

Chapter 19

Post-Scriptum

Françoise Vergès

In 1998, during the 150th anniversary of the abolition of slavery in the French colonies, governmental authorities with the support of Creole intellectuals and local institutions organized a series of events to commemorate the event. The Socialist-led government declared that it wished to celebrate the "diversity of Creole society, their vitality and the project of republican integration." It hired an advertisement company which designed a billboard showing a row of beautiful smiling teens, female and male, of different ethnicities, with the slogan *Tous nés en 1848* (We were all born in 1848).[1] Our common date of birth was traced to the "beautiful revolution" of 1848, which in April abolished slavery and, in November, declared Algeria, where colonial troops were massacring civilian populations, to be a French *département*. Condemnation of slavery went uncontested; reconciliation was the theme.

The abolition of slavery was every one's favorite story. The French Republic could congratulate itself for a generous gesture, one which could, certainly not erase, but definitely atone for the French participation in the slave trade. France was true to its revolutionary promise, which had been betrayed by a tyrant.[2] Creole intellectuals could insist on the resilience of the slaves and their contribution to the world's cultures. Writers and artists of the former slave societies were invited to share with the French public the expressions of Creole artistic vitality: a festival with Creole artists was organized in a small French village whose ancestors had been among the very few who, in their petition to the Revolutionary Assembly in 1789, included among their demands the abolition of slavery; the writer and critic Edouard Glissant received the Medal of Paris from Jean Tibéri, the conservative mayor of the capital; a street was named after Delgrès, the slave leader of the troops which had heroically fought against the army sent by Napoleon to reestablish slavery in Guadeloupe.[3] Yet what was there to celebrate? What had happened in the colonies after the abolition of slavery? What was the cultural, economic, and political legacy of slavery? What process had transformed the former slave societies, which had become in 1946 French *départements*, into tropical *banlieues*? High rates of unemployment, high rates of families on welfare, high rates of criminality, high rates of suicide, of domestic violence, economies entirely supported by the former colonial metropole: what had led to it? The paradox was that its populations thought that they were wealthier than their neighbors because they were better, whereas it was the price they paid for their dependency. They were French citizens, and as such could travel to the European Community and work without immigration papers; their annual income was much greater than that of surrounding populations. In fact, poor immigrants, often illegal, came to a "promised land" where they worked for meager salaries in jobs no Antilleans or Réunionnais would do (Haitian and other islanders to the Antilles; Malagasy and Comorians to Réunion Island). One could find the latest European goods in local supermarkets and similar signs of wealth – cell phones, fancy cars – following the latest trends. *French Banlieues sous les tropiques*. Could this constitute reasons to celebrate? What had happened? Had we finally become the characters mocked by Frantz Fanon in *Black Skin, White Masks*, neurotic mimics, lusting for revenge, prisoners of our past?

And yet the situation was perhaps more complex. There might be something beyond celebration or despair, abstract optimism or cynicism, something to learn from the experience of peoples thrown together by the yoke of history on small territories. Descendants of slaves from India, Africa, Madagascar, Malaysia, of indentured workers from India, Africa, Madagascar, Malaysia, China, of European immigrants, had constructed a society under slavery, colonialism, and political assimilation. They had created a language, reinvented traditions and customs, creolized religious beliefs and rituals, ideas about health and disease, contributed to the anti-colonial struggle, and to the democratization of France.

Creole populations and cultures are the product of a continuous process of mixing and of a reconfiguration of identities. What was it then? Were Creole societies the model of a world to come? Glissant had claimed that the "entire world is experiencing the process of creolization" (*Le monde entier se créolise*).[4] Or did they embody, in their specificity, the complex, and far from attractive, legacy of dependency, with its culture of resentment, victimization, and hatred?[5] What was missing perhaps in both representations was the materiality of life and one of its by-products, a salutary effect of demystification. In other words, looking at everyday life, the thickness of daily expressions – of survival, suffering, passion, envy, jealousy, love, goodness, malice – and setting them side by side with discourses – political, legal, medical, artistic – would throw a different light on everyday practices *and* discourses. The goal could be thus: not to find systematically, in everyday life, the grounds for subversion and disruption, the "truth" – this would be another form of romanticization – but to remain humble and cautious in our statements. This attitude does not constitute an obstacle to political action; it is a reminder of our own limited power (or a reminder that our desire for omnipotence – theoretical or physical – will always encounter limits). It is the connection of this salutary effect of demystification with a commitment to political responsibility and action that

I have tried to illustrate in the following vignettes. My remarks on 1848–1998 introduce the vignettes. They are illustrations about notions that have become part of the postcolonial vocabulary: memory, trauma, reparation, reconciliation, race thinking, hybridity, creolization, diaspora, (post)colonialism, and crime against humanity. The paragraphs are organized neither in hierarchical order (from the most important to the less, or vice versa) nor in order of preference. It is a random organization that obeys more the laws of serendipity than the laws of categorization.

(Post)colonial

I do not wish to review the literature that deals with the "post" in "postcolonial" and to question its political agenda. I do not think that I will add anything of substance to the debate. What interests me here is to ask if the colonial impulse has entirely disappeared with the collapse of European empires. In other words, I am not considering the lingering traces of colonialism, its reconfiguration into "neocolonialism," "cultural imperialism," or "globalization." Rather, I wonder if the *model* of colonization, i.e., occupying a territory, controlling its resources and justifying it, is not alive and well. The colonial project is still legitimized: in the name of historical anteriority (our ancestors were there first), of technical superiority (the natives do not know what to do with these resources), or of altruistic interests (we are doing it in order to protect humanity's patrimony because natives do not understand it, or are irresponsible, or lack expertise). Am I saying that colonization is a human impulse like, for instance, the sexual impulse? Am I implying that there is not much that can be done about it? If it is inevitable, why fight against it? If history is an endless repetition of events, not necessarily as farce or tragedy, but as an inescapable fact, why bother? Let us consider an example of colonization today. On the African continent and in Madagascar, NGO or multinational companies have bought land on which threatened animal species and flora live. The threatened species "belong to humanity," they argue, and local authorities have been unable, or unwilling, to protect them. Outside intervention is thus legitimate and urgent. "We" have the responsibility to preserve and protect the species for following generations and the future of the planet. Experts are brought in; programs even train natives as help, educate them in the field of environment protection, instil in them the sense of "global responsibility," and learn from them about the healing qualities of plants and the behavior of animals. Is it that bad? Don't we all wish to preserve and protect the biodiversity of the planet? Don't we all agree that the scientific discoveries will benefit all of humanity? But what about the redistribution of benefits? Do institutions that will enforce it exist? Are they reliable? Is it fair that indigenous knowledges are translated into profits for multinational companies that will market products, organize visits to "untouched land and its beauty," and become the "owners" of scientific discoveries made from these knowledges? Is it not a form of colonization? Have we finished with the *model of the colony*? Let us remember that before being connected with violence, erasure, and racism, the term "colony" was, in Europe, connected with politically radical utopia. Mettray,[6] the post-abolition plantation, the factory, the asylum, were conceived as utopian spaces in which new techniques of discipline and reform would be developed. The plantation was seen as the perfect form of colonial organization, once it was cleansed of slavery: its architecture, its social and economic structure served as a model for the penal colony, the factory.

The colonial model in which experts, settlers, workers, and peasants would work in harmony for the greater common good has survived, I argue, as a model of social organization. The postcolonial colony is a space organized along the model of the colony, but with tools, technologies, and expertise that demand the reconfiguration of representations and discourses. If colonialism is about settling in a territory to capitalize on its resources, to train and educate the natives so that they can become active members in the global project of "progress," are we not witnessing a new era of colonization? This is not to say that European colonialism – nineteenth century to mid-twentieth century – was not specific. It gave birth to peculiar forms of art, literature, and scientific, legal, and political discourses. Rather, I wish to argue that we need to examine new forms of colonization and their order of knowledge.

In his *Dictionnaire des idées reçues*, Flaubert wrote: "Colonie: S'attrister quand on en parle."[7] Being sad? Well perhaps, but pursuing the process of decolonization, definitely yes.

Memory and Trauma

Memory and trauma have emerged as powerful notions in current debates. In 1998, during the commemoration of the abolition of slavery in the French colonies, the *devoir de mémoire* was invoked more than once.[8] Who had this duty? How would it be enacted? What was the purpose of the duty? Ghislaine Mithra, a cultural activist on Réunion Island and a member of the association *Espace Afrique*,[9] declared that as long as people had not performed the duty of memory, they would lack their roots, and the lack of roots explained their distress, their suffering. Memory was connected with a therapeutic act, with social and political consequences. To be sure, the role of France in the slave trade and slavery has barely been acknowledged in class textbooks; it is not part of the curriculum, and it is far from being a subject that has mobilized intellectuals and scholars. When the role of race thinking in the elaboration of French identity, French nation, and French republicanism is studied, it is in relation to the empire, practically never in its relation with slavery. Slavery stands as an empty space in the French collective imagination. It is occupied by two figures, which have themselves been emptied of their materiality. They are not individuals of flesh and bone and psyche, but two stereotypical figures, one embodying the corruption of metropolitan values (the master), the other embodying the victimized body soon to be saved by the Republican abolition-ist. Empty figures standing on an empty space: is it not the perfect setting for the deployment of fantasies of origins and origins of fantasies to be at work? Projections rather than critical analyses? Melancholia for a loss that is never symbolized? Memory acts as a reading grid of the present, but what happens when the past returns as hallucinations, ghosts? The date of "birth" of Creole and French populations is not 1848. For the Creoles, it is related to a cata-strophe: being sold, being deported, being stripped of one's name, one's filiation, being colonized. The catastrophe needs to be integrated in collective public memory. In the case of French slavery, we witness a disjunction between the time of the catastrophe (two centuries of slavery, a century of colonialism) and the time of its commemoration (1998). The past as catastrophe remains prisoner of a past that does not act as a structure of memory and critique but as a ghost. Its commemoration resonates as an injunction: to live in *a present* that has no patience with, no place for, the past. Or rather, the past is celebrated as a source of artistic creativity (adding to the multiculturalism of France), but not as a source of political and philosophical reflection. When people in former slave societies were asked what they knew about slavery, they often answered with wide generalities, framed in a moralistic rhetoric. There was no recognized discourse about slavery. The memory of slavery is inscribed in oral tradition, geography (mountains named after famous maroons), and music, and if people refer to those traces they know that they have not received the same recognition as in a legitimized discourse, sup-ported by the educational system. Slavery is a *memorable* event but without a *memory*.

The discourse of cultural memory, Mieke Bal has written, mediates and modifies difficult or tabooed moments of the past.[10] "Narrative memories" are memorable because they are surrounded by an "emotional aura." In French (post)-colonies, many secrets inhabit the narrative memories of slavery. One secret is the complicity of ancestors of slaves in the slave trade.[11] Another is the complicity with the slave trade and slavery of the institution that freed one's ancestors (the French state). The Second Republic offered financial com-pensation to the owners of slaves. Their "loss" was recognized and legitimized by the state, which through its gesture acknowledged its complicity with slavery. Slaves were given a *colonized citizenship* and were forced to enter into a contract of indentured labor before the date of emancipation. They were freed by the state, reincorporated by the same state into a system of forced indentured labor, and bestowed with a citizenship that denied their equality. Finally, there is the secret of social death that slavery produced.[12] Slavery put its mark on the body of society, yet there has not been a work of anamnesis. The repression of the memory of slavery imposes a narrative of victimization *and* resistance. Two human attitudes thus delimit the entire field of human behavior: one is either victimized or resisting. Acts of resistance should not be underestimated, whether they were small, "insignificant" acts of resistance which were not recorded, or acts that scared the colonial society and were recorded in the police and court archives. Victimization was real, but its vocabulary and rhetoric are often a prison. We are summoned to come up with a narrative of loss and lack that perpetuates our status as victims, and therefore as people *in need*.

How can we speak of the *authority of suffering* and therefore of the body without falling into an ecstasy of the wounded flesh? Slavery was about dehumanization, exploitation, and a limitless ecstasy of punishing the flesh of the slave. The translation of slavery into cultural memory demands a vocabulary that does not sentimentalize the suffering but reintroduces it in its authoritative presence. "Speaking the unspeakable" is the injunction of our times. No longer a paradox but a conventional formula, it has become a central preoccupation. The truth has a public, a collective value. One *ought* to speak, for it will serve the common good. It is a duty. One cannot keep the truth, it would be an anti-social act. One speaks for humanity; one bears witness. "The Truth shall make you free." As Wole Soyinka has remarked, the adoption of a Christian theological precept as a universal precept is not without problems. It conflates the individual with the collective experience. The latter demands to find a legal, public, political expression. A distinction must be made between public memories – monuments, books, names, debates – and private memories, that made public may serve a *devoir de mémoire*, but cannot become a site of identifications for the collective. Slavery was global *and* peculiar, specific in its local configurations. What we can still learn from it cannot be accomplished through identification and lamenting. "No amount of empathy can make one a witness to events at which one was not present."[13]

In 1998 there were debates around what monument should be built to commemorate slavery and its abolition. The consensus was that there should be monuments rather than a monument, and that the choice of monuments should be left to local decision. On Réunion Island the city council of Saint-Denis, the administrative capital, picked up a proposal by a local artist: a stone upon which the names of slaves were carved parallel to the names they were given in 1848. The monument was defaced: names were erased on a night following the dedication of the monument. Journalists went into the (poor) neighborhood bordering the monument trying to find the reasons for the destruction of the monument. Was not the inscription in stone of the names of slaves (deprived of last names by slavery) a form of symbolic reparation? Those who were willing to talk said: "Why should we be reminded of an inglorious past? Why should *our present* be associated with their past of slavery?" The gesture was part self-destruction, part protest.

French abolitionism instituted an historical rupture between slavery and post-slavery. Yesterday, slaves, now citizens of the state. Post-slavery identities were not constructed with reference to the past, or rather the past was a source of shame, a past to erase. "Through remembrance, individuals and groups are linked with others: a person is represented as part and parcel of a chain of generations and a web of kinship relations which include the ancestors," Alcinda Honwana has remarked.[14] The sense of self and being is reestablished through rituals that acknowledge the web of connections from which the individual derives its sense of self, of being. In French slave societies, according to the republican metanarrative, the 1848 Republic gave birth to us. What identification with society was then possible? What could happen to those who "did suffer traumatic experience of the kind that results from environmental let-down, and who must carry with them all their lives the memories (or material for memories) of the state they were in at moments of disaster"?[15]

The paradoxical nature of the citizenship – citizens and colonized, racialized citizens – belied the myth of historical rupture. The connection with ancestors was kept alive in private rituals. Yet the privatization of the memorable event of slavery was an obstacle to mourning. Wrongs and suffering were not "transmuted into a totally different stage of sensibility from which one can derive a sense of peace, a space of Truth that overawes all else and chastens the human moral dimension."[16] Severance from the past has yet to be achieved for mourning to be achieved.

Reparation, Reconciliation, Crime against Humanity

At a recent presentation, Ato Quayson quoted an African novel whose character reflected on the fact that he loved the idea of humanity but did not like its materiality.[17] I thought that the quote expressed very well a common experience. We love the idea of humanity (and the idea that we belong to that species), but when it comes to human beings, we are disappointed, angry, we cannot believe that we belong to the same species.

In 1998 the question was how could we integrate the history of Creole creativity with the history of despair and self-destruction? Reparation was needed, some said, to operate the integration, reparation for the wrongs and damages of slavery. But how would reparation be expressed? Materialized? Did it mean that France should pay financial reparations? Or did it mean that France should recognize its guilt for committing a crime against humanity, as representatives of the former slave societies argued at the National Assembly? The year 1848 had instituted, I wrote in 1998, a *citoyenneté paradoxale* in the post-slavery societies: the slaves became citizens *but* remained colonized.[18] The institution of a colonized citizenship revealed, I argued, the project of French abolitionism: the construction of a Republican colonialism. It was the triumph of a hierarchical fraternity in which the white metropolitan French "brother" was entitled to the legacy of his fathers. It announced a politics of sentimentalism, masking the conflictual nature of colonial rule and constructing the figure of the benevolent abolitionist as the *good colonial*. Finally, it framed a psychic space in which the two poles of "never quite . . . not yet . . ." delimited the life of the colonized. Never quite a citizen, not quite French. In 1998 the representatives of former slave societies asked the French parliament to recognize slave trade and slavery as crimes against humanity. It was an attempt to connect the history and culture of Creole peoples with the history and culture of the French

Republic. The proposal was adopted by the Assembly, but not debated by the Senate.[19] No decision was made to include the role of France in the slave trade and slavery in the school curriculum.

What does it mean for the history of origins to be the history of a trauma? In interviews made in 1998 in former slave societies among high school students, young people often declared that they wanted to go forward, to look at slavery as something of the past, a buried past.[20] Echoing Frantz Fanon's conclusion to *Black Skin, White Masks*, they did not want slavery to be a burden, to be the slaves of slavery. To them, reparation meant to be able to be members of the European Community, to have a professional career, to have access to the Internet, and to participate in the process of globalization. Reparation was about access to knowledge and to the world, unencumbered by the past. The answers changed if poor urban youth were interviewed. They expressed anger, resentment, and rage. They declared that they "had nothing to lose, because there was nothing for them in this society." They were "Kaf" (Blacks in Creole) and therefore, relegated to the bottom of society. "Oté Sarda, ou la roul anou," they sang.[21] Slavery and race were operative "memories" in their lives.

Diaspora, Hybridity, Creolization

I use these terms in reference to their processes. Though distinctions have been made between them, their consequences can be compared: the process of displacement and flexible identities, the position of "in-betweenness" and impurity, and the experience of transnationalism and of cosmopolitanism. I look at these processes as expressions of lived experience as well as their dynamics, their complicity with metanarratives, and their resistance to hegemonic representations. These expressions have found a new life against the narrow and vicious discourse of purity.

However, I tend to be wary of any notion which, once translated into discourse, soon carries a redemptive dimension. There was a pastoral of decolonization in which the countryside was constructed as the true locus of anticolonial resistance. Peasants, "unpolluted" by the mixing and perversions of the city, were said to have kept alive customs and traditions of the "People," of the Nation to come. There is now a pastoral of postcolonialism in which the city is the locus of transnational politics. Mixed, hybrid, creolized cultures and identities embody the transnational world. In a recent issue of the magazine *Vibes*, the 18th *arrondissement* of Paris was presented as the most vibrant, lively "ghetto" of the city, where the visitor could find the best *couscous* and *yassas*, and look at "*Beur* Princesses," "African Queens," and native "homeboys." The mixing of the diasporas – North African and African – with French natives was celebrated. No class or historical analysis of the neighborhood.

Cities are now sold on the marketing of hybridities. They compete for the title of the "Best postmodern, postcolonial hybrid city." One cannot spend a week in Paris without being reminded of the high value of hybridity and *métis-*

sage (cultural miscegenation). The message does not obey the Benetton logic: ethnically defined individuals side by side. Rather, it aspires to go beyond that logic, offering a representation of a global world in which demarcations – of race, nation, class – are no longer divisive. Youth, urban culture, fusion, characterize the marketed hybrid. Now this is without doubt better than the paranoid and racist declarations of the far Right. Yet is it not fair to ask which hybridities are marketed and which are not? Why have the notions of hybridity and *métissage* been so rapidly incorporated into the market? How can we keep their subversive dimension alive?

The marketing of hybrid subjects and cities has accelerated with increased globalization and urbanization. Specific transformations have occurred, among which are the mixing and hybridization of genres, artistic expressions, cuisine, music, and fashion. The discourse of hybridity and creolization wants to reflect on these transformations and propose a new ethic. Capitalism has always showed its propensity to commodify new representations and notions. The *société du spectacle*, analyzed years ago by the French Situationist Guy Debord, has a cannibalizing capacity. Does it mean that we should surrender to its power, or that we should constantly rework the radicality of hybridity and *métissage*?

The inflated discourse about these terms often contrasts with the reality of daily life, that either deflates the omnipotence underlying a lot of academic discourse or demystifies its aggrandizing aspects. They might work as a "horizon," as utopian notions that keep us fighting and thinking. Creolization is a process, with a dynamics of consolidation and reification of identities. The world might be in the process of creolization; Creole identities remain "identities," that is, the processes of identification to which they adhere cannot be foreseen. Hybrid positions are certainly extremely gratifying narcissistically. A "good" humanity could perhaps be imagined *métisse*, hybrid, and diasporic. The idea of humanity is more appealing than the actual "disappointing" human beings. I prefer "disappointing" human beings and their demystifying acts.

Notes

1 The government of the Second Republic issued a decree on April 27, 1848 abolishing slavery on all French colonies: Martinique, Guadeloupe, La Réunion, Guyana, Saint-Louis of Senegal. Around 250,000 slaves were affected by the decree.

2 Slavery, which had been abolished in 1794, was reestablished in 1804 by Napoleon I.

3 It was not a major street of Paris.

4 Edouard Glissant, *Une Poétique de la relation* (Paris: Gallimard).

5 Glissant had powerfully described the ambivalent culture of dependency in *Caribbean Discourse*.

6 Mettray was created in France as a reform colony for male adolescents who had been orphaned, abandoned, or condemned. It became a model for reformers and

abolitionists who saw, in its organization and architecture, a perfected form of social organization. Mettray is discussed by Michel Foucault and appears in Jean Genet's writings.

7 "Colony: Being sad when hearing about it."

8 On that aspect, see my "I Am Not the Slave of Slavery: The Politics of Reparation in French Post-slavery Communities," in Anthony C. Alessandrini, ed., *Frantz Fanon: Critical Perspectives* (New Brunswick, NJ: Rutgers University Press, 1999), pp. 258–71.

9 The association promotes African roots and culture in Réunion Island. In 1998 the association asked that slavery be recognized as a crime against humanity "Because justice was never applied and because a crime without Justice negates the Law, negates Man. . . . The *droit à la mémoire* means that all Nations must acknowledge that three centuries of dehumanization constitute a crime against humanity."

10 Mieke Bal, "Introduction," in Mieke Bal, Jonathan Crewe, and Leo Spitzer, eds., *Acts of Memory: Cultural Recall in the Present* (Hanover, NH: University Press of New England, 1999), pp. vii–xvii.

11 This is particularly true for the Indian Ocean. Malagasy were very active in the slave trade and Madagascar was the native country of the majority of slaves sold to the plantations of Mauritius, Seychelles, and Réunion.

12 "Social death" is the expression borrowed from Claude Meillassoux by Orlando Patterson in his seminal work.

13 Michael A. Berstein, "Unspeakable No More: Nazi Genocide and Its Self-Appointed 'Witnesses by Adoption'," *Times Literary Supplement*, March 3, 2000, pp. 7–8.

14 See her remarkable study of child soldiers in Mozambique and Angola: Alcinda Honwana, "Negotiating Post-War Identities: Child Soldiers in Mozambique and Angola," *CODESRIA Bulletin*, 1999.

15 Donald Winnicott, *Home Is Where We Start From* (New York: Norton), p. 31.

16 Wole Soyinka, *The Burden of Memory, The Muse of Forgiveness* (New York: Oxford University Press, 1999), p. 68.

17 Ato Quayson, "Thunder in the Index: Nationalism and Disassembled Identities in African Literature and Culture," Center for African Studies, University of California, Berkeley, February 22, 2000. The text in question is Dambudzo Marechera's "House of Hunger": *The House of Hunger* (London: Heinemann, 1978).

18 Françoise Vergès, "Une citoyenneté paradoxale. Affranchis, Citoyens, Colonisés," Introduction to *L'Abolition de l'esclavage. Un combat pour les droits de l'homme* (Brussels: Éditions Complexe, 1998), pp. 17–47.

19 As the measure has not been debated by the Senate, it has not been adopted as an official declaration of the French state.

20 See *Le Monde, Libération, France-Antilles, Journal de l'Ile de la Réunion, Le Quotidien de La Réunion, Témoignages.*

21 From a song by Ziskakan (Until When): "Sarda, you has tricked us." Sarda Garriga was the envoy of the Second Republic, sent to Réunion Island to oversee the application of the decree of abolition, institute contract labor and new regulations whose goal was to preserve the colonial order and transform slaves into agricultural workers.

Index